MW00714552

ORDER, LAW, AND CRIME
An Introduction to Criminology

ORDER, LAW, AND CRIME
An Introduction to Criminology

Raymond J. Michalowski
University of North Carolina, Charlotte

McGraw-Hill, Inc.
New York St. Louis San Francisco Auckland Bogotá
Caracas Lisbon London Madrid Mexico Milan
Montreal New Delhi Paris San Juan Singapore
Sydney Tokyo Toronto

ORDER, LAW, AND CRIME
AN INRODUCTION TO CRIMINOLOGY

First Edition

5 6 7 8 9 DOR DOR 9 9 8 7 6 5 4 3 2

Copyright © 1985 by McGraw-Hill, Inc. All rights reserved. Typeset in the United States of America. Except as permitted under the United States Copyright Act of 1976, no part of this publication may be reproduced or distributed in any form or by any means, or stored in a data base or retrieval system, without the prior written permission of the publisher.

Library of Congress Cataloging in Publication Data

Michalowski, Raymond J.
  Order, law, and crime.

  Includes index.
  1. Crime and criminals—United States. 2. Criminal justice, Administration of—United States. I. Title.
HV6789.M49   1984   364'.973   84–11736
ISBN 0-07-554450-4

PHOTO CREDITS:

Page 43, Histroical Pictures Service; page 135, Charles Gupton/Stock, Boston; page 257, Barbara Alper/Stock, Boston.

Manufactured in Mexico.

Printed and bound by Impresora Donneco Internacional S. A. de C. V. a division of R. R. Donnelley & Sons, Inc.

To my parents,
Raymond and Angela Michalowski

Preface

This book was born in irony. Ten years ago while completing my doctoral studies, I began to sense that I had learned considerably more about crime and criminals than about the relationship between crime and *society*. The irony was that I was completing formal education in the central traditions of *sociological* criminology. Part of this irony is reflected in the fact that both then and now the majority of sociologically oriented books in criminology take as unproblematic the proposition that crime creates the need for law, and law in turn creates order. Questions regarding the interrelationships between social organization, the perception of social harm, and the dynamics of social control are often unexplored or given brief treatment. This creates the impression that the only relevant issues in criminology are what causes people to become common criminals and how they can be controlled.

Order, Law, and Crime: An Introduction to Criminology takes a different approach, reflecting a decade of research, teaching, and writing aimed at creating a sociological framework for the study of crime and justice. Its purpose is to introduce the student of criminology or criminal justice to the sociological questions regarding the relationship between social organization and the social control of harmful behaviors in America. To do this it begins with the proposition that the underlying elements of social organization—particularly the production and distribution of economic, political, and cultural resources—largely shape the perception of what constitutes unacceptable social injury. It is this social construction of harm which gives form and character to the processes of law and justice. That is, the nature of the social order in any society lies at the roots of both the concept of trouble and the options available for its control. My aim is to bring to the forefront for students of crime and society questions that until relatively recently have been submerged beneath a relatively unsociological sociology of crime. The roots of this un-sociology of crime are found in the peculiar history of sociology as discipline.

Nearly a century and a half ago the social philosopher August Comte held that, because of its ability to synthesize the knowledge of more narrowly focused academic pursuits into an overall understanding of human society, sociology would emerge as the "queen of the sciences." Not only has this grandiose promise remained unfulfilled, but in America particularly sociology moved in precisely the opposite direction, toward narrowness and specialization. Struggling to carve out a distinct and independent academic niche in the middle years of the twentieth century, American sociology came to rely heavily on concepts of voluntaristic action and the tools of opinion survey. In its attempt to achieve independent validation American *sociology* ironically came to be dominated by the theories and methods of aggregate *psychology*. There was relatively little integration of macrosocial processes in history, economy, and politics into the overall theory and methods of the discipline. Such topics were overlooked or examined only in terms of the specific social problems they generated, such as poverty and crime.

Nowhere has this trend been more obvious than in the sociological study of crime. Until the 1960s, and the rise of government funding for criminal justice research and criminal justice education, the study of crime in America was largely conducted as a subdiscipline of sociology. Within this subdiscipline the primary endeavors were to explain why certain *individuals* commit common crimes against persons or property, and to identify the most effective methods to control and/or rehabilitate them. Much less attention was given to fundamentally sociological questions regarding the relationships between social organization, social control, and criminal activity.

In order to integrate these topics into the study of crime I have followed a path somewhat different than that found in more traditional criminological writings. Considerably more attention is given to historic, economic, and political forces than is normally the case, and crimes of the powerful, such as corporate and political wrongdoing, are treated as topics equal in importance to those everyday offenses that constitute the popular image of the "crime problem." Correspondingly less attention is given to traditional, individualistically oriented theories of crime causation. Anyone familiar with criminology texts will notice the absence of a chapter devoted specifically to "theories of crime." There is both a theoretical and a pedagogical reason for this. First, since most theories of crime deal with the behavioral etiology of common crime, they are more appropriately considered theories of *criminality* rather than theories about crime as a sociologically constructed phenomenon. To devote an early chapter to theories of individual criminality creates the misapprehension that the sociological study of crime should be understood primarily in terms of the social-psychology of criminals—contradictory to the approach taken in this volume. Pedagogically, since most criminological theories seek to explain the behavioral causes of *common crimes* rather than crime in general, it is more appropriate to address them in chapters devoted to common crime rather than to isolate them in a "theories" chapter. This is particularly important here since common crime is treated not as the totality of crime, but rather as only *one* of the sub-sets of lawbreaking.

If the study of society tells us anything, it is that individuals accomplish very little "on their own." This book, like most social endeavors, has been shaped by the contributions and help of far more people than could ever be individually acknowledged. There are, however, some to whom my debt deserves more than an anonymous and general nod. My sincere gratitude is extended to Simon Dinitz and Paul Friday for pointing out the road; to Tony Platt, Paul Takagi, Richard Quinney, and William Chambliss whose own works, and criticisms of mine, served as important guideposts on the journey; to Walter Kossman, the first editor to believe; to Stephen Pfohl, Kenneth Robertsen, and Ronald Kramer for critiques, support, and friendship; to my colleague Michael Pearson for friendship, dialogue at many critical moments, and open access to his library; to Jill Dubisch, the anthropologist in my life who taught me so much, suffered through the entire process, and never failed to be the gentle sun on my back as I followed my way; and finally to Sam, my son, who was understanding of a father who was often busier than he should have been.

Raymond J. Michalowski

Contents

PART I

A Sociological Basis for the Study of Crime

EAUTY FOUND stifies he never

OAT SLASHED ceived payoffs

Weiner
Staff Writer

ner Lt. Henry Pecic
former Ph...

JUMPS TO THE TIME

Cops bust up numbers ring

By RANDY DIAMOND and RUTH LANDA

A multimillion-dollar interstate numbers ring that operated mostly in the Hispanic communi- of Union City and West New York, N.J. smashed with the arrests of 26 per enforcement officials announced yesterd

Officers seized $100,000 in cash, two c cocaine, drug paraphernalia and eight ha including three that had been reported when they made the arrests Monday in 24 lo in northern New Jersey.

Hudson County Prosecutor Harold Ruvold the $100,000 was believed to represent or receipts, and that based on that figure th ion was suspected of pulling in millions o year.

Prosecutors said the ring's operation ... on 57th and 58th Sts. in We ... conducted bi ... ity.

EX-CON RAPIST CHARGE COED'S MURDE

rily sur-
uestioning
sterday.
rce said he
three years
te prison for
sodomy, but
ncerning that

bury, police said.
He was charged with murder late yesterday afternoon after a full day of questioning. In-vestigators refused to believe his alibi that he was with ...hen

County Deputy Police Inspector Vincent Galanti.
"He's been talking, talking and said any-he hasn't said any-thing," Galanti said. "He has not confessed. ...ing he has noth-

He was working for a Great Neck firm, The Administrator for The Profession, at 560 North-ern Blvd. Bass was arrested after detectives learned that his white motorcy-cle had been at the crime scene. ... victim's

SIX COPS ments begun NAMED IN 's drug trial BURGLAR ROUNDUP

Gerald Scotti, a cement Age... g the trial gents on at he wa for the ...led S ...an" who was f resign from the DEA to av cution for leaking infor another case to a defens ...ld ...rial of a Sept. DEA su
15
☆

"Nowhere does it say that the first deal is for free."
Re told the jury the only deal De-...an had wanted to make was a ...ean investment deal.
...ean was frightened ...om he was ...ing to

Ex-Police Inspec Extortion in Ph

By WILLIAM ROBBIN
Special to The New York Times

PHILADELPHIA, Aug. 1 A for- lings and mer chief inspector of the Philadelphia of comman Police Department denied today that he had tions, they leading role in an extortion ring that was pressu prosecutors contend reached from "pa- of operations trolmen on the street" to the top com- Witnesses mand level of the department. from vice o The former officer, Joseph DePer. say to... was asked by his attorney, District Court ...

guilty in sex case

ction of mental dis-
and battery on his
whom were in their

damages because Mann "had suf-fered enough in loss of reputation and stress."

THE JURY
"Hopefull...

testified that Mann
n and ordered them
ual activities ...

Student Jyll Johnstone said "... we had more mone ... gotten ...

CHAPTER 1

Crime, Criminology, and the Crime Problem: An Introduction

CRIME AND CRIMINOLOGY

We are about to begin an intellectual journey into the field of criminology—a journey that I hope will lead us to a sociological understanding of crime. Our starting point is the question, "What is criminology?"

The simplest and most common answer to this question is that *criminology is the scientific study of crime.* Since it is a simple answer, however, this statement tells us very little about the actual content and conduct of criminology. While it is often said that criminology is the study of crime, in actuality criminology has tradionally focused more on the *crime problem* than on crime in general. Thus our first question leads us to another: "What is the difference between "crime" and the "crime problem"?

The Crime Problem versus the Problem of Crime

Crime is most often defined as any behavior *designated as criminal by law,* or as criminologist Paul Tappan wrote some years ago:

> Crime is an intentional act or omission in violation of criminal law . . . committed without defense or justification, and sanctioned by the state as a felony or misdemeanor.[1]

This definition encompasses a wide variety of behaviors. Many of these behaviors are not what either criminologists or people in general mean when they talk about "crime." That is, many things that fit the general definition of crime are not included within the "crime problem." Consider the following examples:

> In May 1978, David Berkowitz pleaded guilty to the murder of six women in New York City, bringing to an end the "Son of Sam" killings that had terrorized that city for nearly a year. Berkowitz was given a sentence of twenty-five years to life in prison.[2]

> On April 27, 1978, fifty-one workers were killed in Willow Island, West Virginia, when the generating plant cooling tower on which they were working collapsed. Subsequent investigation by the Occupational Safety and Health Administration

3

(OHSA) revealed that "the disaster was the direct result of illegal corner-cutting on the part of Research-Cottrel Inc., a New Jersey firm that was building the tower." OHSA proposed fining the company $10,000 for each of the ten willful violations of Federal safety rules.[3]

On April 6, 1979, a lone gunman entered a branch bank in Charlotte, North Carolina, approached a teller, demanded that she fill a bag with cash, and escaped with an undisclosed amount of money.[4]

In May, 1978, a Federal grand jury indicted Rep. Charles Diggs of Michigan on charges of diverting $110,000 in government funds for his own personal use. The thirty-five-count indictment alleged that Diggs had given salary increases to associates with the understanding that they would return the money to him, presumably to pay off mounting personal debts.[5]

In 1978 the National Highway Traffic Safety Administration (NHTSA) began an investigation into the growing number of consumer complaints about the failure of Firestone Radial 500 tires. Early in 1979 NHTSA reported that for three years after Firestone first became aware of the tire's defect, it had continued to produce this brand of tires, which were subsequently responsible for forty-one deaths and at least seventy injuries.[6]

The president of an Oklahoma meat firm was fined $2,000 and placed on six months probation in April, 1978, after being convicted of adding soy-protein extender to 40,000 pounds of meat labeled "ground beef."[7]

Each of these examples describes a behavior that is prohibited by law and potentially punishable by fines, imprisonment, or both. That is, each one fits the definition of crime. Yet for most Americans the term "crime" is largely limited to images of rapists hiding in shadowy places, masked burglars sneaking into homes under the cover of night, muggers lurking in apartment lobbies, and similar traditional threats to the security of our person and property. Many other criminal acts—like the examples of consumer fraud, violation of worker safety regulations, political corruption, and sale of known hazardous products described above—figure much less prominently in the everyday conception of crime. This is true despite the fact that (1) such acts fit the standard definition of crime and (2) the death, injury, and monetary loss caused by corporate and political crimes *substantially exceeds* that caused by more commonly acknowledged criminal offenses.[8]

Generally when people talk about crime they are really talking about the *crime problem*. That is, they are talking about *a social phenomenon about which they share a common concern and about which they feel action should be taken.* Some time ago the sociologist Herbert Blumer noted that social phenomena become social problems only when individuals take collective action to do something about them.[9] It is in this sense, *and this sense alone,* that the ordinary crimes of murder, rape, robbery, burglary, and theft constitute a greater crime problem than do deadly and costly acts of corporate and political crime. Because something is generally recognized as a social problem does not necessarily mean that it is more serious for individual and social well-being than something that is less clearly a part of everyday concern—only that it is more recognized.

It is important that a sociology of crime include an understanding of how some forms of injury come to be part of the common perceptions about crime while others, often equally grave in their consequences, remain outside our conception of crime. This book focuses on the *problem of crime,* not just the "crime problem." That is, we will examine closely the process by which societies choose to regard some forms of harm as criminal while leaving many others effectively beyond the reach of the law.

Criminology and the Crime Problem

Like the general public, criminologists have tended to define the problem of crime primarily in terms of traditional offenses against persons and property. In 1959 criminologist Albert Cohen observed that the question most commonly asked by criminologists was "How do people become the kinds of individuals who commit [common] criminal acts?"[10] While this question has dominated criminological inquiry for most of its history, there have been several changes in recent years.

One key change was an increasing concern with studying the criminal justice system. This development was fueled in no small part by a growing Federal role in the control of crime and the subsequent availability of support for research into the justice system. In 1967 the National Institute of Law Enforcement and Administration of Justice, the research arm of the newly created Law Enforcement Assistance Administration (LEAA), began dispersing millions of dollars to finance criminological research. The Institute, however, was more interested in funding studies of "what to do about the 'crime problem' than in financing studies about why there was a crime 'problem.'"[11] As a result the field of criminology became

". . . more and more concerned with increasing the efficiency of the punative legal apparatus and less and less concerned with trying to discover the processes generating the criminals to be punished and the laws and personnel doing the punishing.[12]

This focus on common crimes and the criminal justice system is clearly reflected in the contemporary content of criminological writings. Between 1979 and 1981, for example, three major criminology journals—*Criminology* (the official journal of the American Society of Criminology), *Crime and Delinquency* (the journal of the National Council on Crime and Delinquency), and the *Journal of Criminal Law and Criminology* (one of the oldest journals in the field)—published a total of 288 articles. Of these, 29 percent were devoted to the patterns or causes of common crime and 49 percent were devoted to how various components of the justice system handle common crimes. Thus 78 percent—228 of the 292 articles published—focused on the behavior and/ or control of common offenders. Less than 5 percent of the articles were concerned with white-collar or corporate offenses.[13]

What then is criminology? Criminology for the most part is a patchwork quilt of theory and research from a variety of academic disciplines (e.g., sociology, political science, economics, history, psychology, etc.) focused primarily on the causes and control of the "crime problem." Its guiding questions have been predominately "What are the characteristics of the common criminal?" and "How can the crime problem be alleviated through advances or improvements in the areas of crime control and rehabilitation?" Questions about the relationship of law to economic and political elements of social organization and investigations of the crimes and social injuries committed by the more powerful members of society have figured much less prominently in the history of criminological inquiry. At times these latter questions have been addressed with considerable vigor, but those who have done so have always been a minority. This has been true despite the fact that "a compelling case can be made that the discovery of answers to questions such as these ought to be the first order of business."[14]

Our own examination of criminology will not be limited to the "crime problem" as defined by everyday discussions about crime. Instead, basic questions about the nature of social organization, the relationship of social organization to state power and state law, and the relationship of state law to the definition and conception of crime will be examined as the "first order of business." We will then turn to an examination of specific patterns of crime and social injury in America.

CRIMINALIZATION AND THE VARIETIES OF CRIMINOLOGY

Criminalization is the process by which behaviors and individuals are transformed into crime and criminals. From a sociological standpoint this process has three components. The first and most basic component involves the processes by which *social order* is created. These include (1) the fundamental ordering of social relations so that those things necessary for social survival can be produced and distributed in some predictable fashion and (2) the development of values, beliefs, and ideas related to the concrete tasks of production and distribution. These can be called respectively *socioeconomic processes* and *ideological processes.* These processes determine what kind of behaviors will be considered "trouble" by a society, thereby providing the raw material out of which the legal definition of crime will be constructed.

The second component of the criminalization process involves the *legal order.* The term "legal order" refers to (1) the process by which power becomes centralized within the institutions of the political state, (2) the character and content of these institutions, and (3) the process by which specific political entities such as legislatures and judges come to define certain behaviors as crimes, that is, targets for state control.

The final component of the criminalization process is the actual outputs of the legal order. These are the individuals who have been defined as criminal and processed through one or more of the institutions of the justice system.

Criminology can be divided into three general branches, or "paradigms." These are (1) positivist criminology/criminal justice, (2) interactionist criminology, and (3) critical criminology. As indicated in Figure 1.1 each of these paradigms tends to focus on only certain components of the criminalization process.

The Positivist Paradigm

From an historical point of view the term "positivism" refers to the rise of science and the decline of religion as a basis for understanding the world. It represents the substitution of "natural" explanations of why events occur for "supernatural" ones.[15] While the rise of positivism began with the scientific study of the physical world, it was eventually extended to the study of human behavior. In 1859 Charles Darwin published *On the Origin of Species*, which provided scientific evidence of a process—"natural selection"—that substantiated the theory of evolution.[16] The consequent development of a theory of *human* evolution removed humans from the realm of the angels and placed them squarely in the world of animals governed by natural rather than theological laws. Moreover, if humans were governed by "natural" laws, then the same scientific method used to understand the physical world could also be used to explain human behavior. Thus, rather than being a matter of moral choice or lack of "grace," perhaps criminality had a more "natural" basis and could be understood through applying the techniques of the natural sciences.

As it was applied to the study of crime, the positivist approach developed several distinct characteristics. One was a focus on the *individual deviant* as the object of study. The other was a preeminent concern with research that would have *practical applications* for the control of crime. These two elements are not necessarily inherent in a positivist approach to social science. Their prominence within criminology is the result of social rather than scientific factors.

During the eighteenth century the dominant philosophical perspective on human nature placed a heavy emphasis on "individual" liberties, "individual" rights, and the individual as the key agent of social events.[17] This shift was closely related to the decline of feudalism and the rise of capitalism.[18] By the last half of the nineteenth century, when the scientific study of crime began to emerge, this philosophy of individualism had become so entrenched that when it came to studying crime the *individual* criminal appeared to be the only logical focus of study.

In addition to this philosophical perspective, several important political factors influenced the direction in which criminology developed. First, by the late nineteenth century, as a result of industrialization, the social order in England, Europe, and America was faced with a rising tide of social problems such as poverty, vagrancy, unemployment, and riots. Not the least of these problems was a sense that crime and violence were on the rise. This fear of crime produced strong sentiments, particularly in the middle and upper classes, that something must be done to stabilize the social order. Second, those who by virtue of their control over the sources of economic and political power were in a position to "do something" about crime found it difficult to imagine that *they* were the source of the problem. These factors tended to promote the development of a justice system designed primarily to control

Figure 1.1 The Process of Criminalization and Its Relationship to Criminological Orientations

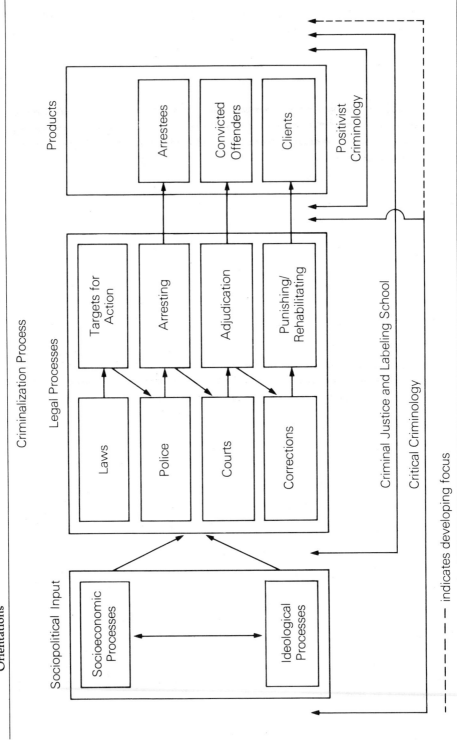

the "dangerous classes," that is, the poorer classes. This in turn fostered acceptance of developments in criminology that (1) focused on lower-class criminality, (2) tended to treat criminals as *individual* defectives rather than products of a faulty social order, and (3) sought strategies for the control of crime that would not disturb the status quo patterns of economic and political power. Thus positivist criminology became correctional in focus. It concentrated mostly on attempting to identify those factors that presumably made criminals different from other people, factors that would be amenable to some type of control strategy applied on an individual rather than class-wide or society-wide basis. The bulk of criminological inquiry has been guided by this principle.

Perhaps the first positivist criminologist was Cesare Lombroso, an Italian physician. Lombroso, influenced by Darwin's theory of natural selection, "discovered" in 1870 that criminals were indeed born, not made. His conclusion, based on extensive physical measurements of over 6,000 Italian convicts, was that by virtue of being less evolved than the average some individuals reproduce "the ferocious instincts of primitive humanity and the inferior animals."[19] Thus criminal behavior resulted from a "natural" error, not a moral one. Since then criminologists have attempted to locate the "natural" error leading to criminality in a number of ways.

The positivist search for the causes of criminal behavior developed along several lines: the biological, the psychiatric, the social-psychological, and the sociological. Following the general approach of Lombroso, biological positivism, has sought to identify biological anomalies or abnormalities that could explain criminal behavior independent of other factors. These have included studies of such things has heredity, body type, hormonal imbalances, lead poisoning, retardation, and central nervous system disorders.[20] Psychiatric positivism could also be called sociobiological criminology since it is primarily concerned with uncovering how the relationship between physiological abnormalities and the social environment can produce criminal behavior. The most common research of this kind focuses on studies of the "criminal personality," including "psychopathic" and "sociopathic" offenders—individuals apparently prone to unpredictable and often violent behavior.[21] Social-psychological positivism encompasses a broad range of theory and research on the role of interpersonal relationships in developing delinquent and criminal patterns of behavior. For instance, the family disorganization and "control" theories focus on how early experiences with parents and other significant people in our lives create positive or negative attachments to social rules and psychological orientations toward conformist or deviant behaviors.[22] A particularly influential variant of social-psychological positivism in criminology has been Edwin Sutherland's theory of differential association, which focused on the social processes by which individuals learned through association with others both the motivations and techniques of delinquent and criminal behavior.[23]

Sociological positivism is concerned with how various forms of social organization, rather than immediate interpersonal experiences, create greater or lesser pressures for crime and delinquency. Two key themes in sociological positivism have been theories of "social disorganization" and theories emphasizing "structural blockage." Social disorganization theories, first proposed by what came to be known as the Chicago school of criminology, concentrated on how "disorganized" communities (i.e., "lower-class" communities) lacked sufficient social integration to restrain the development of deviant patterns of behavior.[24] Theories of structural blockage refer to explanations for deviance and crime that are concerned with how different social systems, by "blocking" individuals from legitimate routes to achieving their goals, create the conditions and motivations for individuals to develop deviant and criminal routes to these goals.[25]

With the possible exception of sociological positivism, positivist criminology is primarily concerned with understanding the *behavior* of *individual* criminal offenders. (This characteristic of positivist criminology is indicated in Figure 1.1) For this reason it is limited largely to studying the outputs of the criminalization process—that is, those individuals who have been arrested, prosecuted, and/or placed under the custody of some correctional program. For the most part, it is only these lawbreakers who are available to be studied.

Because political states in Europe, England, and America have tended to criminalize and prosecute most vigorously the types of harms more likely to be committed by the poor and powerless rather than those committed by the wealthy and powerful, the outputs of the criminalization process in these states have generally represented the least fortunate segments of society. Thus positivist criminology introduced a type of systematic bias into the perception of crime and criminals. For positivists, crime is largely a matter of the offenses against persons and property committed by members of the lowest socioeconomic strata of society. The social injuries produced by the exploitation of labor, the plundering of the environment, the oppression of women and nonwhites, and various forms of corporate illegality have generally fallen outside the scope of positivist criminology.

Criminal Justice

An academic interest in the institutions of justice has existed for quite some time, although until recently it encompassed only a relatively small core of researchers and writers. In the 1960s there was a tremendous growth in academic and research concern with the criminal justice system. As previously mentioned, this growth was stimulated by substantial sums of Federal money made available for upgrading the justice system in response to the "law and order" concerns of the 1960s. While much of the money made available through LEAA was spent on police hardware, expanding police forces, and supporting expansion of prison systems, a proportion went to increasing college-level educational opportunities for police and other justice system workers and promoting research into questions concerning the operations of the justice system.[26] These latter expenditures were reflected in the growth of criminal justice as a distinct academic discipline, and the emergence of separate criminal justice degree programs in numerous universities.

As a field criminal justice has been less specifically focused on the causes of criminal behavior than has positivist criminology. However, criminal justice and positivist criminology are linked by both their common definition of the crime problem as essentially the kinds of crimes against persons and property most often associated with the poor and powerless segments of the society and their mutual limited concern with the political-economic forces underlying the definition of both crime and justice. Criminal justice for the most part is focused on the operations of police, court, and correctional institutions with a view toward understanding their operations and making them more effective and efficient.

Interactionist Criminology

At the time that criminal justice was emerging as a distinct area of study, a number of criminologists began examining the justice process from a somewhat different perspective. These criminologists, whose training was most often in sociology or social psychology, were concerned with explaining how certain behaviors come to be labeled criminal and certain individuals criminals, and the effect of such labeling on those individuals. Their focus was primarily upon the patterns of interaction between agents of the criminal justice system (e.g., police, court personnel, correctional staff) and the individuals handled by them. Unlike those more directly concerned with the criminal justice system, interactionist criminologists were more concerned with how that system selected and affected its clients than with the organizational details of how that system worked.[27]

While not specifically concerned with the political-economic basis for law and the institutions of justice, the interactionist criminologists—sometimes referred to as the *labeling school* of criminology—did raise questions about the process by which some behaviors and not others came to be defined as crimes. For the most part, however, these questions were limited to already "gray" areas of criminal law rather than its more central components. Influential interactionist writings such as Howard Becker's *The Outsiders* and Edwin Schur's *Crimes Without Victims* focused on offenses such as illegal drug use, prostitution, gambling, homosexuality, and abortion.[28] Such inquiries did not examine the political-economic basis for definition of personal and property rights, which were reflected in other more broadly supported criminal laws. They did, however, contribute to the eventual emergence—or perhaps more correctly reemergence—of a critical perspective within Western criminology.

Critical Criminology

In the late 1800s, when the writings of Charles Darwin were stimulating inquiry into the biological basis of criminal behavior, the ideas of Karl Marx and Friedrich Engels were giving birth to another, quite different perspective on crime. Emphasizing the impact of economic organization on all other aspects of social life, Marx and Engels identified the political state and its laws as (1) a reflection of the kinds of social relations and imperatives generated by the economic organization of society,[29] (2) a mechanism through which economically dominant classes sought to protect their interests and control subordinate classes,[30] and (3) an institutional representation of the dominant ideology of social relations.[31] Early applications of this perspective to the problem of crime and justice directly contradicted two of the basic assumptions of the emerging biological positivism. One was that law was the natural response of the social body *as a whole* to those within it who were defective or dangerous. Instead, as the Socialist Achille Loria wrote in 1899:

> The law is really derived from economic conditions, and it is only in the light of the latter that we are able to understand the genesis of legal sanctions, the history of law, the real structure of its various institutions; the law is also a monopoly of wealth . . .[32]

Socialists such as Loria also challenged the view that biological abnormalities among criminals, which many turn-of-the-century positivists sought to identify as the cause of crime, were simply problems of individual defects. Instead, they argued that the physical anomalies among the poor—who seemed to contribute the most to crime—were the result of such things as hard labor by pregnant women, unhealthy living conditions, poor nutrition, and all the other burdens placed upon the poor by an exploitative economic system.[33]

Because it was less congenial to the interests of those who dominated the economy and politics of England, Europe, and America at the time and also because it diverged from the dominant cultural understanding of the nature of social relations, the Marxist view of law and crime was not as readily incorporated into the dominant thinking about crime and criminals as was positivism. While there have always been criminologists who have concerned themselves with the relationship between political economy and the definitions of crime and justice promulgated by the state, the primary legacy of early Marxists to criminology during the first half of the twentieth century was a concern for the relationship between poverty and crime. This concern, which has figured centrally in criminology, has for the most part failed to consider the structural basis of poverty. That is, primary attention has been given to the effect of poverty upon the poor rather than on why this poverty exists in the first place.

This has been particularly true of American criminology. From 1870 to 1920, when the industrial and political leadership of America sought to and succeeded in breaking the radical labor movement that was threatening their power, the terms "Marxist," "socialist," and "anarchist" came to be ideologically associated with all that was evil and dangerous. One result was to all but eliminate any tradition of Marxist or neo-Marxist scholarship from American academia. Marxist and socialist perspectives were further repressed during the post–World War II era of McCarthyism, "red-baiting," and the Cold War.[34] Thus there were relatively few echoes in American criminology of Loria's suggestion that to understand crime we must also examine the political economy and the history of the legal institutions that define and handle the "crime problem."

In the 1960s there emerged a more critical perspective within criminology than had previously existed in American academia. This emergence was in part stimulated by the cultural and political conflicts of that time, particularly the civil rights movement, the anti–Vietnam War movement and the women's movement.[35] These conflicts stimulated greater interest among some criminologists in the role of political and economic structures in deciding what and who will be criminalized. This critical perspective consisted of two branches. One, characterized by works such as Austin Turk's *Criminality and Legal Order*, and Chambliss and Seidman's *Law, Order, and Power*, derive from a "conflict theory" orientation to the study of crime.[36] The conflict orientation is concerned primarily with the impact of unequal distributions of political power on what will be called crime and who will become criminals. This orientation is not specifically derived from Marxist or socialist thought and tends to focus somewhat more on the political rather than the economic aspect of the political economy. The other orientation has been variously called "radical criminology," "Marxist criminology," and "socialist criminology." This school of thought descends more directly from European and English Marxist and neo-Marxist scholarship and tends to emphasize the importance of understanding both the complex interplay between law and the cultural and ideological forces in society and the relationship between law and more basic economic arrangments.[37] This particular brand of scholarship has again come under attack in America. In recent years various influential business leaders have begun demanding that foundations and other granting agencies fund only "procapitalist educational programs" and "procapitalist" professors in an effort to stifle this growth of academic perspectives threatening to both their interests and their view of the world.[38]

The conflict and socialist branches of critical criminology reflect certain important theoretical differences. However, as indicated in Figure 1, they share a focus on the sociopolitical underpinnings of crime and justice and the institutions of social control that arise from them. In contrast to positivist and interactionist approaches to crime, critical criminology has been less concerned with the behavior of "criminals" *as individuals* than with why patterns of criminalization tend more often to identify as criminals wrongdoers from subordinate classes than wrongdoers from more dominant ones. Critical criminology has tended to devote more attention to questions like "Why do working class thieves and burglars appear in the ranks of the officially criminalized more often than owners, managers, and financiers who steal other people's property through legal or illegal manipulations?" than to those like "How do particular members of the working class come to be thieves and burglars?"

Orientation of this Book

This book is based on the view that questions concerning the nature of social order and its relationship to state power, state law, and the subsequent definition of crime ought to be the first order of business in any attempt to understand the phenomenon of crime. It takes, in effect, a *critical perspective*.

The word "critical" has several meanings. One is "inclined to criticize severely and unfavorably." Another is "exercising or involving careful judgment or judicious evaluation." It is this second definition, rather than the first, that characterizes the term as it is used here. The aim of a critical perspective is not to criticize simply for the sake of doing so. Its aim is instead to carefully and completely examine the phenomenon under study, judiciously evaluating its character and consequences. With respect to the study of crime a critical perspective demands that we examine not only what the law says is crime but also *why* the law says it is so. To do this we must dig beneath the everyday assumptions and unquestioned "truths" about crime and examine the social, economic, political, and historical roots of both crime and the ideas about it that are taken for granted. Doing so, however, means turning a critical eye upon often deeply held and comforting beliefs about crime.

Like any perspective, the critical perspective taken here must have a starting point. As in any inquiry, what we find will in large part be determined by the kinds of questions we ask. The kinds of questions asked will in turn arise from the initial postulates about the nature of the phenomenon. However, by making the postulates explicit at the outset of our inquiry they become available for critical scrutiny by others as part of the ongoing process of developing a critical understanding of crime.

The critical perspective taken here encompasses four postulates about the nature of crime and its relationship to social order.

Postulate #1.   Social order precedes and shapes the nature of law and the definition of crime. This assumption is somewhat different from traditional and popular views of the relationship between social order, law, and crime. The bulk of both traditional and popular writings about crime either implicitly or explicitly takes the view that crime creates the need for law, and that the enforcement of law then creates social order. Assumption #1 inverts this relationship. Specifically this and following chapters will attempt to show how *the form of social organization a society takes—not the mere existence of troublesome or harmful behaviors—determines the possibility for law, the need for law, and the definition of crime.*

Corallary A.   Social order has existed and can exist without the power of political states to define and enforce law. That is, the kinds of conflicts and contradictions that exist in modern societies, and which many people from the era of classical jurisprudence on down have taken as evidence that law is the only thing which stands between us and a "war of each against all," arise from certain elements of the ways in which those societies are organized, not from some innate inability of humans to live in relatively peaceful coexistence without some external political force governing their behaviors. Political states with the power to make and enforce laws arise in the context of certain, although not inevitable, forms of human social organization. Specifically, they arise in connection with an attempt to control the conflicts arising from forms of social organization that enable some individuals to acquire and centralize power over others.

Corollary B.   There is no such thing as an inherently criminal act. The meaning of any behavior is *socially* defined. All societies have rules governing property relations and interpersonal behavior, and the violation of these rules is deemed wrong by some or all members of the society. This does not mean, however, that there exists some universally consistent definition of theft and violence as criminal acts. In our own society, for example, taking a car away from an owner who cannot meet loan payments is not defined as an act of theft, while "borrowing" a stranger's car to drive across town is. Similarly, a police officer who shoots at a fleeing suspected bank robber is not committing a crime, while the bank robber is if he or she should shoot back.

The laws that make it a crime to take someone else's car to get across town or to shoot at a police officer who has fired at you do not reflect some quality of wrongfulness inherent in those acts themselves. Rather, the definition of those acts as crimes is intimately related to the nature of property and personal rights as they emerge in the context of a given social order. These are socially, not "naturally," determined rights. To understand why property and personal rights take the form that they do in this society, or any other, we must first examine the basic elements of the social order that gives shape to these rights.

Postulate # 2.   Economic organization shapes and interacts with other elements of social life in fundamental ways. No human society, however advanced or primitive, can be free of the need to extract from the environment the material requirements for maintaining and recreating life. In addition, a society must determine how these material requirements will be distributed or redistributed among its members, and the way in which it is organized to do so plays an important role in shaping the nature and form of other elements of social life, such as kinship patterns, religion, education, and art. Thus economic organization plays an important role in shaping how people will understand their world; that is, it will shape their *consciousness* of that world and their personal place in it.

This assumption differs from the more common one about the role of "values" and "beliefs" in American society, which is that we have the kind of society we do because we "value" freedom, private property, and material consumption. While it is true that these values play an important role in making contemporary American society a free-enterprise, materialistic, liberal democracy, their emergence as part of the dominant consciousness in America is related to important transformations in the economic organization of England and Europe as capitalism began slowly to replace feudalism over 500 years ago. This change in economic organization wrought fundamental changes in other elements of society such as where people lived and with whom, how they made their living, the role of religion in the everyday affairs of both people and the state, and the ways in which the wealth of society would be proportioned among its members. Slowly and with considerable social conflict these changes in basic patterns of life brought about changes in how people understood the meaning and purpose of their lives. Many of the beliefs and values we find around us and take for granted today emerged as a result of these basic changes in economic and social life.

While heavily shaped by economic organization, social institutions and individual consciousness are not simply passive products of that organization. Social institutions (e.g., religion, family structure, education, and so forth) and consciousness (i.e., the way people understand the world) exist in constant interaction with underlying elements of economic organization. At times they play an important role in maintaining the basic pattern of economic relations. They also have the potential for altering it in small—and sometimes large—ways.

To understand crime as a social phenomenon we cannot simply say that this thing or that is a crime because people believe it to be wrong or that it contradicts their values. To understand why these values are what they are, we must among other things examine how they are related to underlying patterns of economic organization.

Corollary A.   Patterns of economic organization shape patterns of political organization. How a society is organized to produce and redistribute the requirements for survival and satisfaction will largely determine (1) the possibility of the emergence of political power in that society, (2) who will hold that power, and (3) through what mechanisms or institutions it will be wielded. Power is based largely upon the ability of some individuals to control or alter the life chances of others. In primitive hunting and gathering societies there is little possibility that some can control the life chances of others with respect to acquiring wild game or foods. Hence there is little basis for political power as we know it to emerge in those societies. As the methods for producing survival change in ways that make it possible for some to control the access of others to survival goods—that is, production based upon things that can be "owned" such as land or livestock—political power becomes possible. This power will largely be shaped by how the society's economic organization proportions its material wealth among members. The more some individuals control the access of others to the means of survival, the greater will be their ability to influence the shape and character of political organizations.

Since it is the political state through its legal institutions that determines what will and will not be crime and in what ways those things that are crimes will be handled, it is important to understand the history and nature of the political state when attempting to understand crime in any particular nation. This in turn requires understanding the relationship between the evolution of the society's form of economic organization and the evolution of its political structure.

Postulate #3.   The study of crime should not be limited solely to those acts defined as crime by law but should incorporate an analysis and comparison of officially designated crimes with other forms of socially harmful behavior not designated as crime. In attempting to understand the relationship between how a society is organized and how it will define "crime," it is useful to compare official crime with other socially harmful acts. This contrast better illuminates the relationship between social structure and social control than an inquiry focusing only on those things that are politically designated as crimes.

Postulate #4. Criminal and other socially harmful behaviors emerge for the most part as individuals attempt to create meaningful lives as defined by their view of the world and the real and perceived alternatives for action that exist in a given economic, political, and social context. The essence of this postulate is that crime is not *caused* in the way— for example, we say a particular virus "causes" a cold—but rather evolves as individuals attempt to adapt to the experiences and influences that shape their lives. In negotiating and to some extent creating these experiences, individuals bring with them specific forms of consciousness that tell them how to interpret and respond to what they experience. This consciousness is constantly evolving and is comprised of such a multiplicity of experiences that it is difficult to abstract any particular element from it and say that this is what "caused" the person to commit a criminal or socially harmful act.

It has often been said, for example, that "Poverty is the Mother of crime."[39] However, throughout history many people have experienced the economic, social, emotional, and political deprivations of poverty and yet have created lives, some meaningful and some tragic, without recourse to crime. Furthermore, when seeking the "causes" of white-collar crime or crime by affluent political officials we would have to look to some cause other than poverty. We know that the experience of poverty and oppression increases the likelihood that some people will find recourse to common crime a meaningful form of behavior. To ask whether or not poverty "caused" their criminality, however, is asking the wrong question. It is much like asking whether or not an illness that occurred when a physically weakened individual was exposed to a virus was "caused" by the virus or the weakened state of the person's resistance. Crime is not a disease that someone catches, but as when someone with low resistance contracts a virus, criminal and other socially harmful behaviors emerge from an interaction of factors, none of which can be specifically indicated as causal.

The following chapters will examine what leads to certain forms of social harm being defined as crime in American society and also what elements of social life increase the likelihood that some individuals will resort to socially harmful actions as they seek to construct their lives. Thus this is not an inquiry into the "causes" of crime in the traditional sense. It is rather an examination of how a given social order defines crime and how crime and other socially harmful acts emerge as individuals attempt to fit their lives within the social experiences created by that order.

NOTES

1. Paul Tappan, *Crime, Justice and Correction* (New York: McGraw-Hill, 1960), 10.
2. *Newsweek*, 22 May 1978, 28.
3. *Newsweek*, 19 June 1978, 59.
4. *Charlotte Observer*, 7 April 1979, 1.

5. *New York Times,* 24 March 1978, 1.
6. *New York Times,* 11 January 1979, 5; 28 March 1978, 63.
7. *U.S. News and World Report,* 21 August 1978, 38.
8. Chamber of Commerce of the United States, *A Handbook on White Collar Crime* (Washington, D.C.: Government Printing Office, 1974), 6.
9. Herbert Blumer, "Social Problems as Collective Behavior," *Social Problems* 18 (Winter 1971): 298–306.
10. Albert K. Cohen, "The Study of Social Disorganization and Deviant Behavior," in Robert K. Merton, Leonard Broom, and Leonard S. Cottrell, Jr., eds., *Sociology Today* (New York: Basic Books, 1959), 462.
11. Donald D. Cressey, "Criminological Theory, Social Science and the Repression of Crime," in *Criminology,* 16, no. 2 (August 1978): 171.
12. Ibid., 174.
13. *Criminology* 16, no. 4; 17; 18; 19, nos. 1, 2, 3. *Crime and Delinquency* 25; 26; 27, nos. 1, 2, 3, 4. *Journal of Criminal Law and Criminology* 70; 71; 72, nos. 1, 2, 3.
14. Don C. Gibbons, *The Criminological Enterprise* (Englewood Cliffs, N.J.: Prentice-Hall, 1979), 7.
15. Auguste Compte, *Course of Positive Philosophy* (Paris, 1864). For discussion, see Robert Merton, *Social Theory and Social Structure* (New York: Free Press, 1968), 33–34.
16. Charles Darwin, *On the Origin of Species* (1859; reprint, New York: Random House, 1936); see also Loren Eiseley, *Darwin's Century: Evolution and the Men Who Discovered It* (Garden City, N.Y.: Doubleday, 1961).
17. Isaac Balbus, "Commodity Form and Legal Form." *Law and Society Review* 11 (1977): 571–588.
18. Karl Marx and Friedrich Engles, *The German Ideology* (London: Lawrence and Wishart, 1970).
19. Cesare Lombroso, introduction to Gina Lombroso Ferrero, *Criminal Man According to the Classification of Cesare Lombroso* (New York: Putnam, 1911), xv.
20. See for example J. B. Cortes and F. M. Gatti, *Delinquency and Crime: A Biopsychosocial Approach* (New York: Seminar Press, 1971); S. A. Mednick and Karl O. Christiansen (eds.), *Biosocial Bases of Criminal Behavior* (New York: Gardiner Press, 1977); George Vold and Thomas Bernard, *Theoretical Criminology* (New York: Oxford University Press, 1980); chapters 4, 5, and 6 provide a good overview of biological positivism in criminology.
21. See in general H. Cleckley, *The Mask of Sanity* (St. Louis: C. V. Mosby, 1976); Robert Hare, *Psychopathy: Theory and Research* (New York: Wiley, 1970); William McCord and Joan McCord, *The Psychopath: An Essay on the Criminal Mind* (Princeton, N.J.: Van Nostrand and Co., 1964); Richard W. Nice (ed.), *Criminal Psychology* (New York: Philosophical Library, 1962); the classic work in psychiatric criminology is probably Hans J. Eysenck, *Crime and Personality* (Boston: Houghton Mifflin, 1964); Gordon P. Waldo and Simon Dinitz, "Personality Attributes of the Criminal: An Analysis of Research Studies, 1950–1960," *Journal of Research in Crime and Delinquency* 4 (July 1967): 185–202 provides a good review of the early development of psychiatric positivism in criminology.
22. For an excellent brief review of development of the social-psychological model of criminal and deviant behavior see David Matza, *Becoming Deviant* (Englewood Cliffs, N.J.: Prentice Hall, 1969); see also Travis Hirschi, *The Causes of Delinquency* (Berkeley: University of California Press, 1969); Sheldon Glueck and Eleanor Glueck, *Unraveling Juvenile Delinquency* (New York: Commonwealth Fund, 1950) is an early example of the incorporation of social-psychological factors into quan-

titative research in deliquency; Walter Reckless, Simon Dinitz, and Barbara Kay, "The Self Component in Potential Delinquency and Potential Nondelinquency," *American Sociological Review* 22 (October 1957): 566–567, and Walter Reckless and Simon Dinitz, "Pioneering and Self-concept as a Vulnerability Factor in Delinquency," *Journal of Criminal Law, Criminology and Police Science* 58 (December, 1967): 515–523 provide a good assessment of the development of "self-concept" as a key social-psychological variable in the study of delinquency and crime.

23. The basics of Sutherland's theory of "differential association" were first presented in Edwin H. Sutherland, *Principles of Criminology*, 3rd ed. (Philadelphia: J. B. Lippincott, 1939), and with some modifications have appeared in each subsequent edition including the most recent, Edwin Sutherland and Donald Cressey, *Principles of Criminology*, 11th ed. (Philadelphia: J. B. Lippincott, 1982).

24. See for example Clifford R. Shaw and Henry D. McKay, "Social Factors in Juvenile Delinquency," *Report on the Causes of Crime* 2, no. 13 of the Report of the National Commission on Law Observance and Law Enforcement (Washington, D.C.: U. S. Government Printing Office, 1931): 192–198; Clifford Shaw, Harvey Zorbaugh, and Leonard Cottrell, *Delinquency in Urban Areas* (Chicago: University of Chicago Press, 1929); Louis Wirth, "Ideological aspects of social disorganization," *American Sociological Review*, 5 (August, 1940): 472–482; Ernest W. Burgess, "The Growth of the City," in Robert E. Park and Ernest W. Burgess (eds.), *The City* (Chicago: University of Chicago Press, 1925); Clifford Shaw, *The Jackroller: A Delinquent Boy's Own Story* (Chicago: University of Chicago Press, 1930); Edwin Sutherland, *Principles of Criminology*, 3rd ed. (Philadelphia: J. B. Lippincott, 1939).

25. Robert K. Merton, "Social structure and anomie," *American Sociological Review* 3 (October 1938): 672–682; Albert K. Cohen, *Delinquent Boys: The Culture of the Gang* (New York: Free Press, 1955); Richard A. Cloward, "Illegitimate means, anomie and deviant behavior," *American Sociological Review* 24 (April 1959): 164–176; Richard A. Cloward and Lloyd E. Ohlin, *Delinquency and Opportunity* (New York: Free Press, 1960); Thorsten Sellin, *Research Memorandum on Crime in the Depression*, Social Science Research Council Bulletin No. 27 (New York: Social Science Research Council, 1937).

26. U.S. Department of Justice, *Fifth Annual Report of LEAA, Fiscal Year 1973.* (Washington, D.C.: Government Printing Office, 1974).

27. See Howard S. Becker, "Labeling Theory Reconsidered," in *The Outsiders*, 2d ed. (New York: Macmillan, 1973), 177–212, for a synopsis of the interactionist approach to the study of crime.

28. Howard S. Becker, *The Outsiders*, (New York: Free Press, 1963); Edwin Schur, *Crimes Without Victims* Englewood Cliffs, N.J.: Prentice-Hall, 1965).

29. See in particular Karl Marx, *Capital*, vol. 1, chap. 2 (Moscow: Progress Publishers, 1978), 88–96.

30. See in particular Karl Marx, *Capital*, vol. 1 chap. 28, 686–693; also the writings of Karl Marx and Freidrich Engles on law and crime reprinted in David F. Greenber, ed., *Crime and Capitalism* (Palo Alto, Calif.: Mayfield, 1981), 37–56.

31. See Colin Sumner, *Reading Ideologies: An Investigation into the Marxist Theory of Ideology and Law* (New York: Academic Press, 1979), 246–285 for a discussion of law and ideology within Marxism.

32. Achille Loria, *The Economic Foundations of Society* (New York: Scribners, 1899), 114.

33. Ysabel Rennie, *The Search for Criminal Man* (Boston: D.C. Heath, 1978).

34. David Caute, *The Great Fear* (New York: Simon and Schuster, 1978), 403–455.

35. Charles E. Reasons, "The Politicising of Crime, the Criminal and the Criminol-

ogist," *The Journal of Criminology and Criminal Law,* no. 64 (December 1973): 471–477.

36. Austin Turk, *Criminality and Legal Order* (Chicago: Rand-McNally, 1969); William Chambliss and Robert Seidman, *Law, Order and Power* (Reading, Penn.: Addison-Wesley, 1971).

37. See for example, Antonio Gramsci, *Prison Notebooks* (London: Lawrence and Wishart, 1971); Alan Hunt, "Law, State and Class Struggle,", *Marxism Today* 20, no. 6 (1976): 178–187; David Hay et al., *Albion's Fatal Tree* (New York: Penguin, 1977).

38. Leonard Silk and Mark Silk, *The American Establishment* (New York: Avon Books, 1980), p. 134.

CHAPTER 2

A Critical Model for the Study of Crime

A MODEL FOR THE STUDY OF CRIME

Purpose of a Model

The purpose of conceptual models such as the one presented in this chapter is to organize in a useful way the significant factors related to a particular phenomenon or problem. This organization then serves as a guide to our thinking about the issue at hand. We must remember, however, that *conceptual models are not exact depictions of reality.* They are ways of representing a certain thing, not the thing itself. Thus the diagram of an atom, with its neutrons, protons, and orbiting electrons, is only a way of representing the various components believed to constitute an atom. It is not an exact picture of an atom; indeed, physicists are not in total agreement about the actual nature of atoms.[1] However, we can say that atoms behave *as if* they were constructed according to this model, and to this degree the model is a useful tool for thinking about atoms.

Models can be similarly useful when studying social life. Human social life is a continuous web of interactions and interrelations. However, it is difficult to think about a world where everything is connected to everything else. To facilitate our thinking about the social world we often draw lines on the undifferentiated fabric of life as guideposts to our thinking. This is the purpose of the model presented here: to provide a framework within which to think about the complex social phenomenon that we call crime.

The model presented here (see Figure 2.1) is divided into four segments labeled mode of production, state law, individual characteristics, and individual behavior. Each of these segments represents specific levels of inquiry with respect to the study of crime.

Mode of Production: The Basis for Social Order

Social order is a set of patterned and predictable social relations between people. The nature of these relations is shaped by the interaction of a variety of factors (see Figure 2.2) that together can be called the mode of production. Understanding the nature of a society's mode of production is fundamental

Figure 2.1   General Model for the Study of Crime

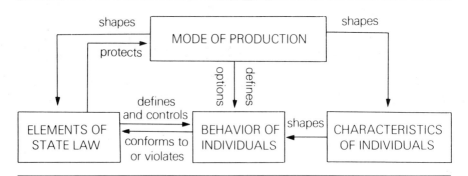

to understanding its definition of crime and its problems of crime control. This is true for several reasons.

First, it is the mode of production that will determine the nature and definition of property, and it is property that has always been the basic focus of law. While a body of material goods and resources exist in every society, "it is society and not the individual which creates the circumstances that make property out of it.[2] Second, the relations of production characteristic of any mode of production are *social relations.* That is, they are not merely abstract patterns of economic exchange but rather forms of social interaction that encompass a variety of patterned rules governing how people treat one another and how they feel toward one another. Third, the way people relate to one another with respect to the concept of property will fundamentally influence ideas about social life; that is, what is right and what is wrong.

The relations of property and the ideas about them vary with the economic organization of society. Among the traditional Eskimo, for example, hunting equipment not currently in use can be freely used by others. This pattern reflects the economic imperatives faced by nomadic hunters in a harsh environment where "it is necessary to keep all instruments of production in use as much of the time as possible." This externally imposed need for collective production also generates the cultural belief that "no man may own more capital goods than he himself can utilize."[3] This free exchange of the tools of production among the Eskimo and their beliefs about it differs radically from the kinds of relationships Americans have with one another concerning tools of production and items of value. In a capitalist society where nearly all things of material value are defined as the "property" of individuals, the acquisition or usage of someone else's property involves more complex relationships of exchange such as buying, selling, renting, leasing, and so forth. Thus the nature of possible conflict over property will be substantially different in these two societies.

A primary function of law is the maintenance of the mode of production in state societies. If the mode of production is feudal, for example, law is concerned primarily with issues of land tenure and inheritance. If it is cap-

Figure 2.2   Components of the Mode of Production

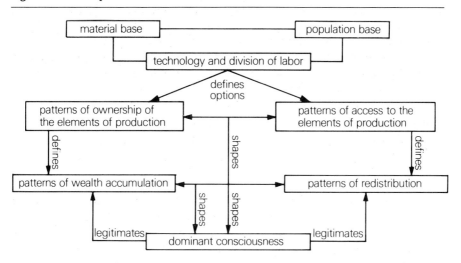

italist, the bulk of law will emphasize the protection of private property in a more generalized sense. If the mode of production is socialist, law devotes considerably more attention to maintaining the desired relationships between individuals and the state as the organizer of productive activities. To understand the functions of law and the nature of crime necessitates an understanding of its mode of production.

Components of the Mode of Production.   The mode of production in any society consists of three basic components: the elements of production, the relations of production, and the dominant consciousness. The elements of production and the relations of production each can be further subdivided.

Elements of Production.   The *elements of production* consist of a society's material base, its population base, its technology, and its division of labor. Together these four elements determine the society's range of possibilities for producing the material required for social survival.

Material Base.   A society's material base is determined by the geographical area it encompasses and the resources for survival and economic development it contains. How a society responds to its material base depends upon a number of factors: population size, technology, division of labor, and so forth. The resources available to a society are of fundamental importance, for they limit the range of productive activities and the level of economic development possible without drawing on the resources of some other society.

Population Base.   The population base of a society is determined by the size, distribution, and heterogeneity of the group that inhabits a given material base. Population size has some influence on the possibilities of technological advancement and material growth. Even if the natural resources are available, societies with relatively small populations cannot develop large-scale, diversified industrial economies unless they can expand the size of their labor force through increased birthrates, immigration, or conquest. For example, the rapid growth of the American industrial system from 1865 to 1928 was largely dependent upon successive waves of immigrants to meet the increasing need for factory and construction workers. As the political scientist and newspaper columnist Frederick J. Haskin wrote in 1913:

> The "new immigrant", with his willingness to work in the dirt and the filth and the danger that are a concomitant, has made possible much of America's splendid industrial development. . . .[4]

Technology and Division of Labor.   Technology and the division of labor are closely related. Technology encompasses all those skills, methods, and tools by which a society produces its material existence. The level of technology determines the level of material development in a society. Simple technologies can generally only produce a limited amount of material goods from a given resource base; advanced technologies, by contrast, yield enormous amounts of such goods.

The level of technology in a society also shapes the distribution of work tasks, that is, the *division of labor*. The entire material production of a society with a simple technology may result from just a few different work tasks such as simple horticulture, gathering wild edibles, and making baskets or pottery, and each of these tasks are usually performed by large segments of the population. As technology becomes more advanced the production of material goods is broken down into an ever-increasing number of work tasks requiring highly specialized but often limited knowledge—limited, that is, in contrast to the total amount of knowledge in the society. Each individual experiences and often understands only a small part of how the society as a whole makes its living.

Relations of Production.   While the resources and technology of a society constitute the basic elements of production, they are not sufficient for actual production. Human beings produce by working together and exchanging the products of this work. There has never been a human society where all individuals worked strictly by themselves for themselves, not sharing the fruits of their labor with others, even if only immediate kin. Production is a social act and requires that people enter into specific association with one another with respect to the elements or means of production (resources, tools, skills, etc.). These associations are what Karl Marx termed the relations of production.[5] The relations of production are shaped by the patterns of ownership of the means of production and the access to the means of production characteristic of a society.

Patterns of ownership and control regarding the elements of production are the most significant factors in determining the nature of productive relations within a given mode of production. Control over the elements of production means exclusive or near-exclusive right to determine *patterns of access,* that is, the right to use these things. In contemporary America, for example, managers of factories or other places of employment determine how many people and often which people will have access to the organization's resources in the form of jobs. By determining people's access to the elements of production, those in ownership and controlling positions play a large part in determining the *patterns of redistribution,* that is, who will get what share of the total amount of goods and services produced in the society. The greater the control some groups or individuals have over the access of others to the means of production, the larger will be the proportion of the total production received by those controlling access.[6]

Beyond a certain point, accumulated wealth can become the basis for acquiring additional shares of the redistributed production in societies with market economies, that is, societies where wealth can be bought, sold, or traded. In the United States, for instance, individuals with sufficient wealth to invest in stocks, securities, expansion of their businesses, or other income-producing activities can claim a proportion of the value produced through that investment independent of any other productive work. This can create a cycle of wealth accumulation and concentration that, as will be discussed in Chapter 10, can have an important bearing on the likelihood that certain kinds of crimes and social injuries will be committed by the powerful within society.

Patterns of ownership and control over productive resources, tools, and technologies are the fundamental shapers of a society's mode of production. These patterns define who will have access to the elements of production, how they achieve this access, the methods and rules of redistribution, and how and to whom the wealth of the society will accrue.

The mode of production in any society will be shaped to some extent by the society's level of technology and its subsequent ability to utilize available resources. As technology becomes more complex both the resources and tools of production are transformed from freely available or easily produced commodities into ones that *potentially* can be claimed as the private property of certain individuals.

Ownership of property means the exclusive right to control the use and distribution of that property. Where the primary productive resources are such things as fish, game, wild edibles, and so forth, claims of individual ownership are meaningless since no individual can actually control these items. However, when productive resources become such things as land, minerals, domesticated animals, and the like, ownership claims become *possible.* Similarly, when basic productive tools are transformed from things that can be easily made by anyone (spears, arrows, fishnets, etc.) into items that are more complex and less readily made by any single individual (e.g., machines, factories, ships, etc.), it becomes possible for some individuals to claim ownership of these and to control the access of others to them.

Based on differences in patterns of ownership, access to the means of production, and redistribution of what is produced, we can identify five modes of production. These are egalitarian, slave, feudal, capitalist, and socialist modes of production.

Under an egalitarian mode of production, found only in the simplest human societies, individuals have nearly equal access to both the elements of production and the redistribution of the things produced. Under slave and feudal modes of production, both of which are based upon primarily agrarian technologies and the associated possibility of the ownership of land as a productive resource, the access of nonowners to both the means of production and the goods produced is determined by the owning class in very direct ways. Beyond its earliest phases, a capitalist mode of production is characterized by the industrial production of commodities and the division of society into a capitalist class consisting of those who own and/or manage the means of production on the one hand and a working class consisting of those seeking access to the means of production in the form of hourly-wage or salaried jobs on the other. Within this broad definition of capitalist and working class there exists a number of subgroups or class fragments: industrial wage workers and salaried public employees in the working class and small businessmen, financiers, and high-level corporate managers in the capitalist class.[7] Patterns of redistribution in capitalist economies arise from a combination of wealth accumulation through investment within the capitalist class and a complex wage hierarchy encompassing the working class.

A socialist mode of production defines the resources and tools of production as the collective property of all members of the society, and there is a greater emphasis upon equality of redistribution of production than in slave, feudal, or capitalist modes of production. However, because these societies tend to also be industrial, individuals do not have the same free access to the means of production found in egalitarian societies. Socialist societies generally subscribe to the view that all individuals have a right to work, and some, such as the Soviet Union, include the right to a job as a basic constitutional right.[8] In practice, though, this access is managed through various bureaucratic structures, and some (e.g., Jews in Russia, government critics in Czechoslovakia, union organizers in Poland) may find their access curtailed.

Consciousness.   Human beings do more than engage in actions and enter into relationships. They *think about* what they do. This does not mean that we are always critically assessing our actions but rather that we have ideas and concepts that explain the meaning of our actions and those of others. When we go to the store and exchange paper for goods we say that we are "buying" something. When we "buy" something, we mentally recognize that it "belongs" to us. When we watch TV, play golf, go sailing, and so forth, we say we are "relaxing," and when we perform actions for which other people give us money we say we are "working." Each of these words imply a set of taken-for-granted social relationships. This taken-for-granted way of thinking about ourselves and the world around us is what is meant by the term "consciousness."

Societies are characterized by the existence of a *dominant consciousness*, that is, ways of thinking about the world that are taken for granted by most people in the society.[9] These accepted ways of thinking about the world provide people with explanations and justifications for their behavior and the behavior of others.

Consciousness is a product of experience; the kinds of relations people enter into will shape the way in which they think about the world. Hence, since the basic character of social relations in a society is largely determined by its mode of production, the dominant consciousness will reflect the mode of production. The meaning of the term "work" in American society, for example, is shaped by the fact that most Americans, to earn their subsistence, enter into relationships with others who own the means of production and who will return to workers, in the form of wages, a portion of the value workers produce by their labor. Because this is the way in which work is organized, the idea that one works for wages rather than an equal share of the value produced becomes part of the taken-for-granted way of understanding the nature of work.

The dominant consciousness of any society includes a number of abstract ideas concerning the nature of human relations. Regardless of how abstract, however, these ideas have their roots in the actual organization of the society. For example, ideas about human nature and human worth emerge from the actual nature of social relations in a society. If social organization is based upon competitive social relations, competitiveness will be viewed as a basic element of human nature, not because humans are in fact *inherently* competitive, but because competitive relations are predominant in the society. Similarly, in a society where *individuals* enter into competitive social relations with one another, the concept of human rights will be understood as one of *individual* rights, since individuals rather than groups are seen as the basic unit of action. Social organization shapes social behavior, and in doing so provides the raw material of experience from which abstract concepts about human nature and society are constructed.

The development of human consciousness is a process of applying meaning to events, experiences, and objects in our lives.[10] That is, humans *interpret* what they experience and try to fit those interpretations into a general framework for understanding the world around them and their place in it. To the extent that a given group or class of people derive special benefit from a particular mode of production they will have an interest in creating and maintaining interpretations of the existing mode of production that will contribute to its continuation. That is, they will have an interest in the creation of an *ideology* that explains why the existing social order is natural, appropriate, or inevitable. To the extent that they can establish this ideology as the dominant way of thinking among *all segments* of the society they reduce the likelihood of collective movements that seek to alter the social order from which they derive the maximum benefit. During the era of American slavery, for example, proslavery forces relied heavily upon ideas about the natural superiority of the white race and the God-ordained mission to civilize and

Christianize black Africans through the mechanism of slavery to create an ideology that would minimize opposition to slavery among both nonslave owners and slaves.[11] Similarly, the history of capitalism is characterized by the development of ideologies that stress the "God-given" right of *individuals* to own the elements of production, the "naturalness" of human competition to acquire material advantage over others, and the appropriateness of broad disparities in wealth as long as the wealthy achieved their position according to the rules of "fair play" as established by liberal, democratic institutions of government. As part of the dominant consciousness in a society, such ideologies serve both to legitimize and explain patterns of redistribution and patterns of wealth accumulation and to insulate those patterns from popular challenges.

The goal of dominant classes in any society is to achieve a position of *ideological hegemony*, that is, to so dominate the everyday consciousness in the society as to make unlikely the emergence of ways of interpreting everyday experiences that would threaten their dominance.[12] While this hegemony is seldom ever total—there are always individuals or groups who question the dominant way of thinking—it is often sufficient to blunt or slow effective challenges. As Karl Marx observed:

> The ideas of the ruling class are, in every age, the ruling ideas: i.e., the class which is the dominant *material* force in society is at the same time the dominant *intellectual* force. The class which has the means of material production at its disposal, has control at the same time over the means of mental production. . . . The dominant ideas are nothing more than the ideal expression of dominant material relationships, the dominant material relationships grasped as ideas. . . .[13]

Individuals who achieve positions of dominance within a particular mode of production tend to do so by adhering to the beliefs as well as the behaviors associated with that mode of production. In modern, capitalist societies, for example, the primary route to economic and political power is through participation in and adherence to the beliefs and behaviors appropriate to capitalist relations of production. As a result, the majority of economically and/ or politically powerful individuals tend to believe in the appropriateness, and often the inevitability, of competition, wealth accumulation, and *limited* forms of political democracy. While such individuals may disagree over the appropriate strategies to preserve and expand capitalism, they generally adhere to a belief in the appropriateness of its preservation. Because of their advantageous position within the economic order they are better able to present their world view to the rest of the society as the appropriate world view. This hegemony is achieved largely through financial inputs into major institutions of socialization such as education, the media, and religion. In the 1970s, for instance, the Business Roundtable—a group representing corporate interests—initiated a multimillion dollar "image-advertising" campaign to diffuse growing public opposition to such things as hazardous waste and low levels of corporate taxation. At the same time a number of American businesses pooled funds to establish 35 Chairs of Free Enterprise in universities, organize 150 Students in Free Enterprise Clubs, and launch an attack on media which carried "anti-business" news stories.[14] Proponents of ideologies—that is, ways of explaining the existing social order—that contradict the ideology of the economically and politically dominant classes generally lack equal money and opportunities to disseminate their world view to the population at large.

Law represents the institutionalization of abstract ideas about the appropriate form of human relations characteristic of the dominant consciousness in a state society. These abstract ideas generally reflect the ideology of the dominant class, whether this class consists of the owners and managers of the economy, as in America, or the bureaucratic elite in the USSR. When studying crime in America, it is important to identify the relationships that exist between abstract ideas expressed in the law (e.g., due process, legal equality, property rights, etc.) and the material and historical conditions that gave rise to the particular form of consciousness these concepts represent.

Institutions of Legal Order

The second component of the model consists of the political institutions of state law. Specifically, these are the institutions for making laws, the laws themselves, the institutions for enforcing laws and punishing offenders, and the institutions or mechanisms for resolving disputes and maintaining order. (See Figure 2.3.)

Law-Making Institutions. Legal order can be divided into several components, the first and most basic of which consists of institutions for making laws. These institutions constitute what we normally think of as the government of a society, though in its entirety government involves much more than the making of laws.

Law-making institutions can take a number of different, specific forms (e.g., a dictator and his counselors; a parliament, congress, or supreme soviet; etc.). However, they all share a common characteristic: They are based on the political power to make and enforce rules of conduct that are binding on other members of the society. This political power rests ultimately on force. It is the existence of and reliance upon centralized force in the form of political power that distinguishes state law from other forms of social control.

The existence of a political state—that is, a centralization of political power—depends upon the existence of one or more groups in the society possessing the power to dominate others. All state societies are class societies. While law-making institutions are based upon political power and the force it implies, in any particular state society the structure of political power, who wields it, who has access to it, and for what ends it will be used will be shaped by (1) basic characteristics of the society's mode of production and (2) limitations on state actions arising from beliefs inherent in the dominant consciousness (e.g., freedom of speech, equality under the law, due process, etc.) and embodied in the political organization of the state. These latter

Figure 2.3   Components of State Law

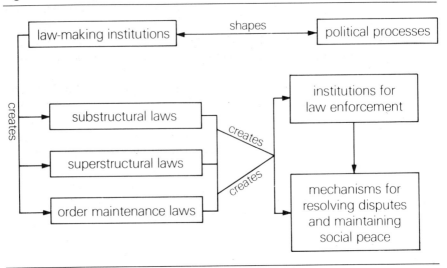

establish broad guidelines the violation of which can weaken or threaten state legitimacy.

The fundamental purpose of law is to protect social order. For this reason the law-making institutions of the United States, or any other nation, cannot be studied as abstract political processes. In an advanced capitalist society like America, the institutions of law making largely reflect the ideology and exigencies of modern capitalist society just as the law-making institutions of socialist states reflect the ideology and exigencies of socialist society. Laws and the institutions that make them must always be viewed in reference to the kind of social order they are designed to protect.

Legal Rules for Behavior.   State law consists of a body of legal rules for behavior backed by the political power of the state. This body of laws may consist of little more than the proclamation of a king or war lord, or it may encompass seemingly endless volumes of legislated law, judicial decisions, and governmental regulations. In general, the greater the number of competitive relations in a society, the greater will be its need for an extensive body of legal rules.[15] Competitive relations increase the potential for conflict and therefore increase the need for legal rules that define the rights and obligations of individuals so as to minimize this potential. In simple agrarian societies, for example, there is little need for an extensive body of laws to govern trade relationships since trade is relatively limited and usually takes place between individuals who have other ties such as kinship or community. However, as trade increases, so does the need for rules to govern trade relationships, for these relationships have considerable potential for misunderstanding and conflict.

State law defines the boundaries of acceptable behavior and also serves to predict how and when the state will respond to unacceptable behaviors or noncriminal disputes between citizens. Laws that specify what individual citizens can and cannot do are termed *substantive laws*. Laws whose purpose it is to define how and when the state will respond to violations of substantive law, or how and when the state's legal system can be used for the resolution of disputes between citizens, are termed *procedural laws*. Both substantive and procedural laws are important topics in the study of crime. While substantive laws define what behaviors constitute crimes, procedural laws in large part define the process whereby specific individuals are officially identified as criminals and specific disputes resolved.

As discussed in the preceding section, a primary function of law is to protect the basic social relations characteristic of society's mode of production. However, not all laws are specifically or directly concerned with this task. Instead, laws can be divided into three groups: substructural laws, superstructural laws, and public order laws. *Substructural laws* are those that serve to institutionalize, protect, or facilitate the basic relations of production in the society. For example, laws defining property rights and the rules for the exchange of property are substructural in focus. By defining what constitutes property and the rights of ownership (e.g., land law, patent law, laws governing water or mineral rights), legitimate patterns of redistribution (e.g., purchase vs. theft, "fair play" vs. fraud), legitimate forms of wealth accumulation (e.g., laws specifying the rights of investors and financiers), public versus private property (e.g., tax laws, laws of eminent domain) and the rights and obligations of individuals involved in specific economic relations (e.g., contract law, labor law), substructural law institutionalize and protect a society's mode of production.

Superstructural laws are those that define and protect public and private institutional arrangements not directly involved in basic productive activities. They may involve such things as religion, politics, education, communication, charitable organizations, marriage, or any of the other patterned forms of activity found in a state society. The institutions governed by superstructural laws are not necessarily unrelated to basic relations of production. However, they are a secondary rather than a primary level of activity with respect to production. For example, in industrialized societies educational institutions play a central role in producing a labor force adequately trained to operate and expand the productive system. However, to the extent that schools and colleges are not operating factories, marketing commodities, or providing investment capital as a primary activity, they are institutionally one step removed from basic productive activities. Similarly, in the United States, Federal, state, and local governments are not primary investors, owners, or managers of actual productive facilities. Thus most of the laws defining the nature of governments are superstructural in character. This would not be the case, however, in countries where production is socialized and government managers become directly involved in production. In these states many of the laws concerning government and politics would be substructural.

Laws of public order are those that govern the behavior of individuals outside of the spheres of productive or institutionally arranged activities. These laws are primarily aimed at controlling behaviors that either tend to disrupt social peace (laws against assault or other forms of interpersonal violence, noise control laws, public nuisance laws) or that violate specific cultural values of the public in general or some segment of it (e.g., vice laws, laws against nude bathing, antiabortion laws, etc.). Like superstructural laws, laws of public order are not always unrelated to more basic relations of production. For example, it has been argued that laws in America prohibiting recreational drug use reflect an attempt to protect the values of hard work and rationality central to capitalist production in the United States. Yet while such laws may facilitate certain aspects of productive relations as characterized by (in this case) a capitalist mode of production, primary proponents of these laws are often substantially removed from the direct benefits such laws might generate within the relations of production. Debates surrounding substructural laws such as tax laws, patent laws, and water rights laws are quite different, for here the various partisans are often specifically conscious of the economic benefits or liabilities that these laws will create.

Institutions of Law Enforcement.   The maintenance of legal order requires institutions that can enforce the legal rules created by the state. Only in the simplest state societies is law enforced by the same individuals who actually make the law. Beyond the level of tribal chiefdoms and small feudal societies, the task of law enforcement is carried out by specialized law workers using authority *delegated to them* by the law makers. In the United States these law workers are dispersed through a number of different institutions: police, courts, correctional agencies, tax collection agencies, numerous specialized regulatory agencies, and in some cases the military.

Law enforcement involves two interrelated tasks: securing compliance with the law and punishing those who violate it. The tasks of securing compliance and punishing criminals in the United States are performed by a variety of institutions. When considering conventional crime, the most visible law enforcement institutions are the police, courts, and correctional agencies, along with their auxiliary personnel, which would include prosecutors and defense attorneys. Each of these institutions rests upon that portion of state power delegated to it by law-making institutions in the form of substantive and procedural laws. Because law enforcement agencies have been delegated specialized functions (e.g., identifying and capturing suspected lawbreakers, assessing innocence or guilt and if guilty determining appropriate penalties, detaining convicted offenders, etc.), they tend to develop specialized concerns and ways of understanding the law enforcement process. This specialization of concern can at times bring various law enforcement institutions into conflict. Police, for example, are delegated the authority to bring suspected offenders to justice. Courts, on the other hand, must assess not only whether the accused are guilty but also whether they were brought to justice in accordance with procedural law. Thus a court may refuse to prosecute a case based on what it defines as an illegal search, bringing it into direct conflict with the police, who view such "technicalities" as a serious impediment to the performance of their delegated function. Specialization increases conflict within law enforcement as well as in the society at large.

Dispute Resolution. Disputes between individuals occur in every society. These may result from conflicting claims over property, insults, love triangles, unpaid debts, or any of the other ways in which human relations can go awry. In nonstate societies these disputes are usually resolved through face-to-face negotiation, negotiation through some chosen third party, and in extreme cases through self-help (e.g., simply taking what you think is owed to you) or resort to witchcraft. As societies grow in size and complexity important organizational relationships in the society become tied less to the bonds of kinship and community and more to comparatively impersonal market relations. Consequently, the possibilities for interpersonal disputes, particularly over property and money, increase while possibilities for face-to-face resolution decline.

An important function of the legal order in state society is to provide opportunities for the peaceful resolution of disputes between individuals. While some disputes are defined as crimes against the state and are prosecuted and punished by the state, others are not. However, many of these noncriminal disputes are seen as appropriate for resolution *within* the framework of the legal order. Such disputes may be submitted to a king or other leader for a resolution, or as in many modern, industrial states, argued in and resolved by a court of law.

In the United States the function of dispute resolution through law is performed primarily within civil courts. These courts adjudicate torts (noncriminal but legally recognized forms of harm), contract disputes, divorces, bankruptcy, patent claims, and a multiplicity of other cases, the bulk of which arise from disputes over property in some form.

Crime: Individual Characteristics

The third and fourth components of our model are focused on the individual characteristics that shape human behavior, and the behaviors themselves. It is the interaction between these two components which culminate in legal or illegal forms of behavior.

Where individual characteristics are concerned the model divides people into five separate components: biology, constitutionality, cognitive and emotional processes, acquired skills, and objective relations (see Figure 2.4). Yet human beings are not really mechanical assemblages of components. They are integrated organisms that perform a number of different functions such as growing, thinking, feeling, acting, and dying. None of the functions performed by the human organism is wholly disconnected from the others. What people think and believe influences what they will do, and what they do will have a bearing upon what they think and believe. Similarly, emotional

Figure 2.4   Individual Characteristics and Individual Behaviors

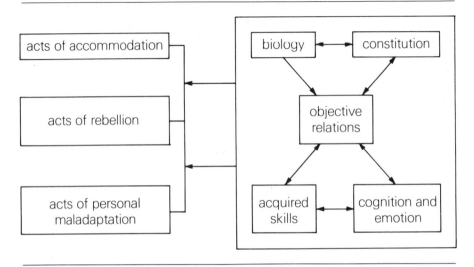

and physical well-being cannot be seen as wholly distinct processes, for each can influence the other.

As with the previous two elements of the model (the mode of production and state law), the division of people into separate components is done for the sake of discussion and study. It must be remembered, however, that while these divisions provide a way *of talking about* human beings, what we are considering is actually a unified organism.

Biology.   Human beings are biological organisms that have evolved through several million years of interaction with their physical environment and their own cultural creations. In recent years increased attention has been given to evolutionary biology and human genetics as a means of understanding human behavior. This increased attention is reflected in the writings of some criminologists, who see in human genetics possible explanations for criminality.[16]

This development has both positive and negative aspects. On the positive side, a more accurate understanding of the evolutionary processes by which humans achieved their present form can contribute to our overall understanding of the human organism. On the negative side in western science there is a longstanding history of overextending and misinterpreting the findings of evolutionary and genetic research in ways that are consistent with and supportive of the political and economic ideology of capitalist society.[17] In addition, some see in genetic theories of human behavior the attractive possibility of being able to identify and control *potential* as well as actual deviants.[18] At their worst, genetic theories of criminality and other forms of human behavior can advance politically expedient interpretations of crime under the authoritative banner of science.[19]

The study of crime should incorporate an appreciation of the fact that humans are biological organisms whose potentials for behavior are genetically determined. However, this appreciation must be tempered by the awareness that the process by which some of these potentials emerge as actual behavior is essentially social in nature. Furthermore, the *meaning* given these actual behaviors will be determined by fundamental economic, political, and social arrangements, not by a person's genetic makeup.

Constitutionality. The term "constitutionality" is used here to mean all those physical characteristics and conditions not strictly determined by a person's genetic makeup. Constitutionality includes such things as overall health, perceptual or motor defects, retardation (other than those forms caused by genetic abnormalities), and specific conditions caused by such things as dietary deficiencies and environmentally borne poisons.

The study of crime should not ignore or exclude the role of a person's constitutionality in the production of those behaviors defined as criminal. Like genetic makeup, however, constitutionality factors should not be thought of as *cause* of crime. For instance, lead poisoning in children is linked to high levels of aggressive behavior.[20] However, to say that this biological abnormality is the *cause* of aggressiveness is incorrect. Lead poisoning occurs most often among children of the poor who live in old, deteriorated housing where as toddlers they were exposed to flaking lead-based paints (in newer dwellings lead paints have not been used). Thus the *socially* derived system of inequality, which leads to some people living in deteriorating and inadequate housing, is as much a part of the aggressiveness in question as the lead poisoning itself.

Thus it is appropriate to include physical conditions as part of the study of crime. However, it is not appropriate to do so without examining the material, political, and social factors that influence the likelihood of those conditions and the definitions that will be applied to the behaviors to which they contribute.

Cognitive and Emotional Processes. The sociological and psychological study of crime has devoted considerable attention to the role of cognitive and emotional processes in the production of criminal behavior. People's attitudes, values, self-esteem, sense of alienation, feelings of powerlessness, need for social approval, and so forth have frequently been treated as key variables in the study of criminal behavior. Inquiries into beliefs, values, and emotional response patterns can be informative when trying to understand why some people engage more frequently in certain so-called criminal acts than others. However, when incorporating the study of cognitive and emotional processes into the study of crime, several cautions must be taken.

First, thoughts and feelings can only be inferred from what people say or do; they can never be directly observed. Thus, when criminologists study (for example) the relationship between self-concept and the willingness to participate in deviant or criminal activity, they must construct devices such as interview schedules or questionnaires that will serve as indicators of self-concept because the hypothesized operation of self-concept as an internal mental process cannot be directly observed.

Second, the relationship between thoughts and feelings on the one hand and behavior on the other is interactive. What people do will effect what they think and feel. Therefore, the kinds of thoughts and feelings expressed by people after they have committed crimes may not be the same as their thoughts and feelings before they ever broke the law. As a result, when criminological researchers find that lawbreakers respond to interview schedules, questionnaires, and other measures of hypothesized mental processes differently from noncriminals, it cannot be assumed that these differences are necessarily a cause of criminal behavior. They may be the result of having behaved criminally.

Third, what people think and feel is not the product of purely individual mental processes. Ways of thinking and feeling develop through experience with the very real social relations and other components of the external world. Criminologist Walter Miller, for example, identified "fate"—a belief in luck—as one of the focal concerns supporting participation in deviant activity among lower-class youth.[21] However, we cannot treat an emphasis upon fate as the independent psychological invention of lower-class Americans. Individuals who as the result of poverty, oppression, and exploitation have little realistic opportunity to control their own life outcomes and who observe others around them meeting with failure more often than success are not likely to develop a strong sense that they are in charge of their own lives. Lacking the political awareness and the class consciousness to recognize the sociopolitical nature of their experiences, these individuals develop a generalized belief in fate as a means of adapting to the experiences of being a "lower-class" American.

Cognitive and emotional processes are part of the equation culminating in behaviors defined as crime by the state. However, they must be situated in their actual material, social, and political contexts and not treated as an abstract psychological creation.

Acquired Skills.   The term "acquired skills" refers to learned abilities to perform specific behaviors. Nearly all human behaviors are learned through interaction with others. Our ability to speak, read, write, and perform life maintenance tasks (e.g., shopping, cooking, cleaning, etc.), work tasks (e.g., welding, accounting, carpentry, etc.), and all the other specific tasks that fill our days are learned through social interaction.

Learned behavioral skills define in part the boundaries of an individual's life chances. In industrial society, for example, individuals who are deficient in skill areas such as reading, writing, or mathematics will be unable to participate in certain kinds of occupations such as teaching, engineering, or management. Where there is a substantial difference in the income levels associated with various jobs, as in the United States, individuals deficient in these skills will find themselves limited to the lower-paying and less prestigious occupations. For some of these individuals, the reward from crime may seem a tempting alternative to the low reward from legitimate work.[22]

An individual's level of acquired occupational skills also determine his or her *options* for criminal behavior. Those who have acquired skills that qualify them for higher-paying and higher prestige jobs have options to participate in white-collar and corporate crimes unavailable to those in lower-paying jobs. Thus skill level influences a person's access both to legitimate and illegitimate sources of income.

Objective Relations. Every member of society is located within a set of specific material and social relations. These relations define the range of experiences various individuals are likely to have at any given time. In doing so they provide the raw material of experience to which each individual must respond, and for this reason they are an important part of understanding the production of specific human behaviors.

Many variables that criminologists have included in the study of crimes—poverty, social class membership, race, ethnicity, and education, for instance—are not static conditions or states. They are the manifestations of specific social and material relations. For instance, being black in America is not simply the condition of having darker skin. It is a set of social and material relations between black Americans and white Americans that extends back to the time the first black slaves were brought to the American colonies from Africa.

Being black in America means generally being less socially acceptable, and having on average less access to material and political resources *in comparison with whites.* Thus the meaning of being black in America is based on the material and social relations *between blacks and whites,* not on the quality of being black or being socialized into black culture.

Similarly, being poor means existing within and adapting to a set of material and social relations that provide others with greater access to wealth than oneself. Poverty in America is not simply a characteristic of the poor; it is the outcome of the particular material and social relations that characterize American capitalism.

Objective relations determine in large part the kinds of experiences to which an individual will have to adapt while at the same time contributing to the formation of the human self. To understand the "criminality" of any particular individual or group of individuals requires examining this process of experience, adaptation, and self-formation as it occurs within the context of specific material and social *relations,* rather than seeing individuals as being composed of some static set of qualities and characteristics such as age, race, sex, income, social class, or educational level.

Crime: One Variety of Human Behavior

Our model assumes three options for human behavior: behaviors that reflect conformist adaptations to the existing social order, behaviors that constitute acts of rebellion against the existing order, and acts of personal or interpersonal maladaptation, which while they may disrupt social harmony are not direct threats to more basic elements of the social order.

Acts of adaptation include all the varieties of everyday behavior that are commonly accepted as "normal," nondeviant, and law-abiding. They are termed acts of adaptation because they represent the various ways people conform to the requirements for getting along day by day. In America both getting a job and applying for welfare are conformist ways of adapting to the need to acquire some type of income. Not all acts of adaptation are, however, positive or neutral with respect to how they affect social life. Depending upon the dominant consciousness and the legal order arising in connection with a given mode of production, some very damaging behaviors can become legitimated as acceptable ways of adapting to everyday life. At one time in America, for example, owning slaves was an acceptable adaptation to the need to acquire income, just as at a later time employing child labor or exploiting workers in other extreme ways was also within the range of acceptable behavior. Thus the range of conformist adaptations is in a constant state of change as societies shift the line between acceptable and unacceptble forms of action and make, remake, or unmake laws.

Acts of rebellion are those varieties of nonconformist behavior that threaten the underlying bases for social order. In a capitalist society, for example, acquiring property in what is defined as an illegitimate manner such as theft or fraud would represent an act of rebellion. This does not mean that the individual engaging in such an act is necessarily undertaking some conscious or deliberate strategy to remake the social order. It means simply that the individual is rejecting the established, conformist routes for adapting to the demands of everyday life. The individual who decides to steal instead of, or in addition to, working for a living is rebelling against the constraints placed upon the acquisition of property as established by the society. Although most acts of rebellion are not undertaken with a view toward social change, genuine acts of revolution would also fall into this category.

Acts of personal or interpersonal maladaptation refer to those types of behaviors that have been defined by either law or popular belief as deviant but that do not threaten basic elements of social order. In America behaviors defined as insanity, drug abuse, illegal forms of domestic violence or other acts that disrupt social peace in illegal or deviant ways would fall into the category of acts of maladaptation. Acts of maladaptation are most often misdirected attempts to deal with the problems and pressures of everyday life without recognizing their underlying sources. The person caught in a traffic jam who winds up in a fight with the driver who cut in front of him, for instance, is responding to the overall system of traffic flow by striking out at the nearest, but also most insignificant, source of his problem. Similarly, husbands who physically abuse their wives or parents who abuse their children are frequently using their victims as means of releasing frustrations generated by more complicated and distant forces affecting their lives and their level of frustration.

It is the political economy of a society in connection with its cultural history that determines the definition of what acts are adaptive, rebellious, or maladaptive in a society. In modern state societies it is the institutions of state law that have the additional task of controlling rebellious and maladaptive forms of behavior.

Figure 2.5 Order, Law, and Crime: The Overall Picture

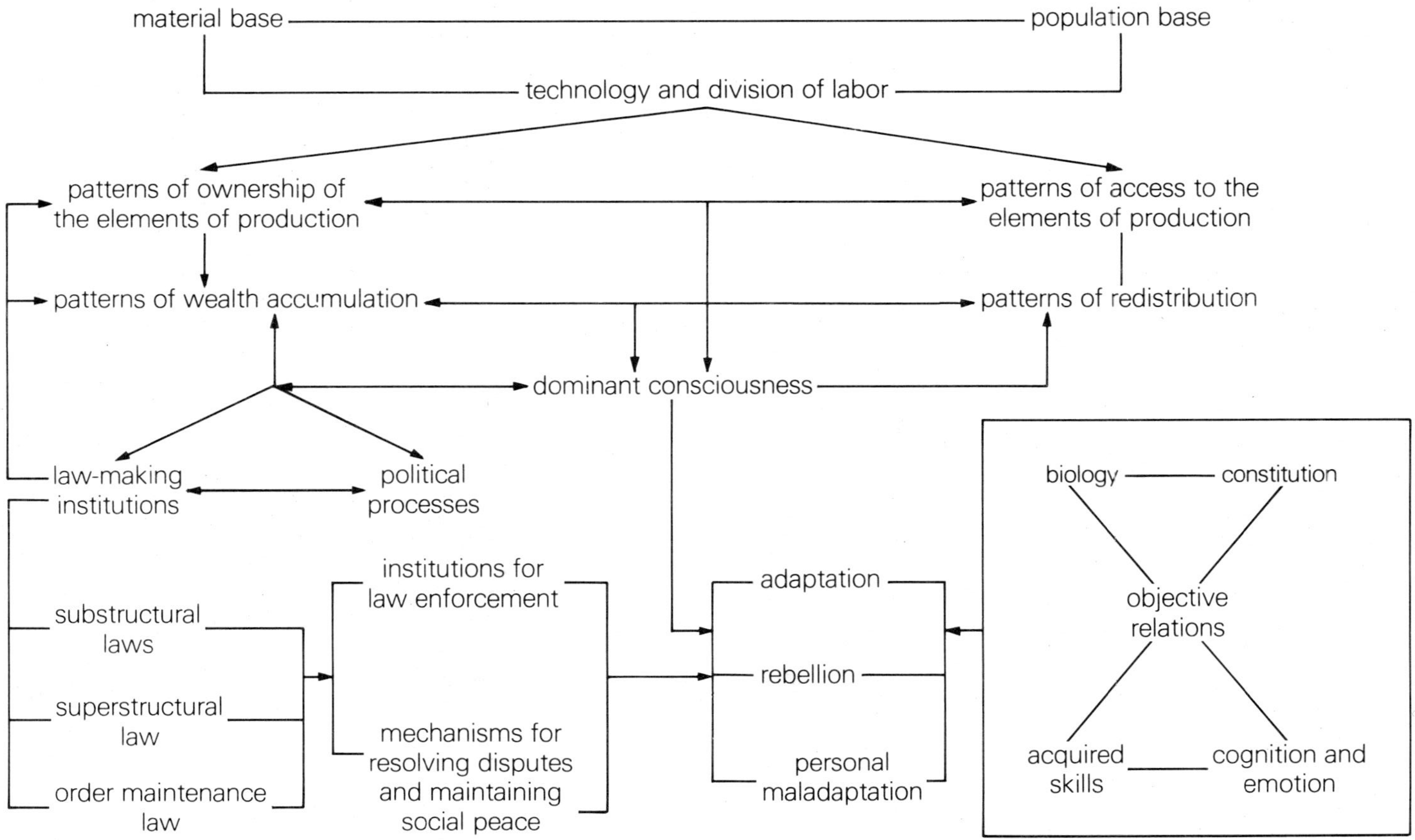

APPLICATION OF THE MODEL

Figure 2.5 brings together the basic elements that determine the varieties and definition of crime in state societies. The following chapters will be organized in accordance with the relationships expressed in this overall model. First, we will examine the relationship between underlying elements of social order and the possibilities for both trouble and its control in human societies. In doing this we will contrast the ways in which state and nonstate societies deal with disruptions of social order. Next we will examine the evolution of legal order, including legislation, police, courts, and correctional agencies within the context of the American political economy. Last, we will examine the patterns of crime and social injury characteristic of modern American society with a view toward understanding how and why they occur.

NOTES

1. Gary Zukav, *The Dancing Wu Li Masters: Overview of the New Physics* (New York: William Morrow, 1979).
2. E. Adamson Hoebel, *The Law of Primitive Man* (New York: Atheneum, 1973), 58.
3. Ibid., 69.
4. Fredrick J. Haskins, *The Immigrant: An Asset and a Liability* (New York: Fleming H. Revell Co., 1913), 34.
5. Karl Marx, *Capital,* vol. 1 (Moscow: Progress Publishers, 1978), 80–81.
6. See Barry Indess and Paul Q. Hirst, *Pre-Capitalist Modes of Production* (London: Routledge and Kegan Paul, 1975).
7. This definition of capitalist class is similar to that utilized by Michael Useem, "The Inner Group of the American Capitalist Class," *Social Problems* 25 (February 1978): 225–240.
8. "Basic Principles of Civil Legislation in the USSR and Union Republics," cited in Chaldize, *Criminal Russia,* 189.
9. See Trent Schroyer, *The Critique of Domination* (Boston: Beacon Press, 1973), for a discussion of the role of consciousness in everyday life. Peter L. Berger and Thomas Luckman, *The Social Construction of Reality* (Garden City, N.Y.: Doubleday, 1966) also provide an excellent discussion of consciousness as "common-sense knowledge" from a non-Marxist perspective.
10. Herbert Blumer, *Symbolic Interactionism* (Englewood Cliffs, N.J.: Prentice-Hall, 1969), 2–3.
11. John Higham, "Toward Racism: The History of an Idea," in Norman R. Yetman and C. Hoy Steele, eds., *Majority and Minority* (Boston: Allyn and Bacon, 1975), 207–221.
12. Antonio Gramsci, *Prison Notebooks* (London: Lawrence and Wishart, 1971). See also Colin Sumner, *Reading Ideologies* (New York: Academic Press, 1979) for a detailed discussion of the various theories concerning the relationships between ideology, hegemony, and the law.
13. Karl Marx and Frederick Engles, "The German Ideology," in Marx and Engels, *Collected Works* (London, Lawrence and Wishart), vol. 5, 82–83.
14. Harry C. Boyte, *The Backyard Revolution* (Philadelphia: Temple University Press,

1980) 16; see also Liston Pope, *Millhands and Preachers* (New Haven, Conn.: Yale University Press, 1942) for a description of how education and religion can shape working-class consciousness in ways consistent with the interests of elites.

15. Some, such as Harold Pepinsky, *Crime and Conflict* (New York: Academic Press, 1976), argue that while increasing specificity in law is presumed to reduce potentialities for conflict, it actually leads to increases by creating ever more detailed points of contention.

16. See for example S. Mednick and K. D. Christiansen, *Biosocial Bases of Criminal Behavior* (New York: Gardener, 1977).

17. See Stephen Jay Gould, *The Mismeasure of Man* (New York: W. W. Norton, 1981) for a review of the ways in which scientific analysis has been misused and misinterpreted to support dominant ideologies about genetic and racial differences.

18. C. Ray Jeffery, "Criminology as an Interdisciplinary Behavioral Science," *Criminology* 16, no. 2 (August 1978): 149–169.

19. See Ysabel Rennie, "Science and the Dangerous Offender," part II of *The Search for Criminal Man* (Boston: D.C. Heath, 1978), 57–96 for a description of "science" as a basis for politically advantageous definitions of who is the criminal.

20. J. Julian Chisholm, Jr., "Lead Poisoning," *Scientific American* 224 (February 1971), 3–11.

21. Walter Miller, "Lower Class Culture as a Generating Milieu of Gang Delinquency," *Journal of Social Issues* 14 (1958): 5–19.

22. Daryl A. Hellman, *The Economics of Crime* (New York: St. Martins Press, 1980), 38–42.

PART II

Creating Social Order and Coping with Trouble

CHAPTER 3

Order and Trouble in Simple Societies

Introduction

The preceding chapters examined the basic elements of social organization in human societies and the ways in which these elements are related to both the potential for trouble and the kinds of mechanisms that will be established to deal with it. In this chapter we will examine the particular relationships between social organization and social control as they developed in primitive forms of human society. The pattern of social organization and social control found in primitive human communities may seem far removed from everyday problems of crime in America, but they in fact reveal important relationships between these factors in general that have a direct bearing on the kinds of problems experienced by modern societies. By offering us a contrast to the way in which we normally view creating conformity and restraining wrong-doers, primitive societies can give us a broader perspective on our own society.

In modern complex societies law is often viewed as the primary tool for establishing and maintaining social order. For many Americans, *law* and *order* are inseparable, and there is a tendency to assume that societies without any formal legal system are probably characterized by violence, brutality, chaos, and theft. However, long before the emergence of political states with the power to establish and enforce laws—indeed, long before the emergence of societies with identifiable rulers—fully developed human beings lived in or-dered and generally peaceful communities. How they accomplished this offers some important clues to understanding both the problems and the possibilities for creating social order in modern societies.

Human societies can be broken down into two broad categories: nonstate, or acephelous, societies and state societies. State societies can be further subdivided into chiefdoms, or proto-states, and civilizations, a distinction that will be examined further on. This chapter, however, will examine the basis for order in the acephelous society.

WHAT ARE ACEPHELOUS SOCIETIES?

The term "acephelous" means "without a head." Acephelous societies are those that lack any indentifiable ruler with the power to direct or command other members of the society. This form of organization represents the earliest type of human community and the one that to date can be called the most basic and stable form thereof. Acephelous societies were the only type of human community for 30,000 of the 40,000 years since the evolution of modern humans (homo sapiens sapiens).[1] It is also highly probable that archaic humans (homo sapiens) had been living in acephelous social arrangements for the preceding 200,000 years.[2]

Acephelous societies are small, economically cooperative and relatively egalitarian societies with simple technology and divisions of labor based mainly upon age and sex. Stratification in terms of differential access to material goods and political power does not exist. While these societies lack rulers or governments with the power to command, direct, and correct the behavior of others, acephelous societies are generally characterized more by order and cooperation than by chaos and competition.

This does not mean that there are no variations in individual behaviors or personalities in acephelous societies or that there is no deviance. As Robert Edgerton details in *Deviance: A Cross-Cultural Perspective*, "troublemaking" occurs in all societies, and nearly all ethnographic accounts of primitive peoples include some descriptions of deviant behaviors. Indeed, the descriptions of perfectly "tranquil, contented people living a life of almost ideal social integration and individual adjustment" reported by early ethnographers such as Robert Redfield and Ruth Benedict may reflect the fact that

> Often when anthropologists wrote about the life of non-Western people, they generalized to such a degree that individual variability was lost in the search for patterns, regularities or typical behaviors.[3]

On the other hand, the existence of some deviance and social conflict in all societies does not mean that all societies are equally troubled, a conclusion sometimes drawn by observers of social behavior.[4] The fact that anthropologists have described many simple societies as well integrated and peaceful while at the same time reporting instances of deviant behavior is not a contradiction. The instances of deviance and social conflict observed by anthropologists may very well be relatively insignificant in comparison with the turmoil and class conflict that characterizes the Western civilizations from which these anthropologists come.

The significant question is not whether acephelous societies are free of all deviant behavior and social conflict—for they are not. Rather, it is how did primitive peoples, *without some central authority* to define right and wrong behavior and to punish deviants, establish sufficient predictability to enable many societies to function in an orderly and peaceful fashion for thousands of years? This question is even more significant in light of the fact that modern state societies have never achieved this kind of stability.

A Note on Evolution and Human Community

Before examining the patterns of conformity and trouble in primitive societies, it is important to address some popularly held misconceptions about the emergence of human communities in the prehistoric age. Early social contract philosophers imagined a prehistoric age when humans lived in some "natural" state, with each person a "law unto himself."[5] This idea, and the assumptions about human nature it embodies, have influenced modern-day thinking about crime and are often reflected in the writings of contemporary observers of the crime problem. For example, James Campbell, writing for the National Commission on the Causes and Prevention of violence, states:

> Since man *first moved into communities* and attempted to cope with the exigencies of life through joint and collective effort, he has been faced with the fact that not all members can be relied on to follow the rules of the community.[6] (emphasis added)

Similarly, in a speech made to the American Bar Association, in 1981, Chief Justice of the Supreme Court Warren Berger said:

> When our distant ancestors *came out of caves and rude tree dwellings* thousands of years ago to form bands and tribes and later towns, villages and cities, they did so to satisfy certain fundamental human needs: mutual protection, human companionship, and later for trade and commerce.[7] (emphasis added)

This type of imagery tends to obscure the fact that instead of "moving into" communities sometime after the emergence of humans on the planet, humans *evolved* as communal creatures. For over a million years before the evolution of biologically modern humans some 40,000 to 50,000 years ago, ancient hominids (ancestors of modern humans) were living in small, economically cooperative groups.[8] As anthropologist David Hunter noted:

> "The outstanding achievement at this state of evolution was the development of patterns of *cooperation*—patterns that are fundamental to the development of human culture.[9] (emphasis in original)

It was the capacity for cooperative action in food gathering, food sharing, and defense that enabled early hominids to develop the kinds of cultures based on a system of shared symbols that most social scientists recognize as the distinction between humans and animals.

Humans evolved not as individual, egoistic creatures but as members of cooperative social groups. There was never a point in human prehistory when these individualistic primitives whose lives were, as Thomas Hobbes surmised, "nasty, brutish and short," came together to form human communities as a means of fostering their own *individualistic* ends. That is,

> There is no such thing as human nature independent of culture. Men without culture would not be the clever savages of Golding's *Lord of the Flies* thrown back upon the cruel wisdom of their animal instincts; nor would they be . . . intrinsically talented apes who somehow failed to find themselves. They would be unworkable monstrosities with very few useful instincts, fewer recognizable sentiments, and no intellect: mental basket cases.[10]

The evolution of humans as conscious animals, capable of remembering a past and imagining and planning for a future, occurred *because* they were already members of cooperative social groups. It was through social interaction that the biological potential for symbolic communication characteristic of early hominids evolved into a recognizable human self.

The significance for the study of crime of recognizing the communal basis of human evolution is this: If we assume, as did social contract theorists, that human communities emerged as uneasy associations of individuals seeking to maximize their own egoistic gains, we will tend to believe that the problem of crime arises from the inherent or inevitable desire of humans to use others, in whatever ways possible, as means to their own selfish ends. As one contemporary sociobiologist put it,

> Where it is in his own interest, every organism may reasonably be expected to aid his fellows. Where he has no alternative, he submits to the yoke of communal servitude. Yet given a full chance to act in his own interest, nothing but expediency will restrain him from brutalizing, from maiming, from murdering— his brother, his mate, his parent or his child. Scratch an "altruist" and watch a "hypocrite" bleed.[11]

According to this view of human nature, the primary (and perhaps only) method available for reducing crime is to *restrain* the inherently bestial instincts that lie just below the thin surface layer of socialization. If on the other hand we recognize that collective organization and cooperative action were of elemental importance in human evolution, other alternatives begin to appear. Specifically, we can begin to ask not how do we restrain wrongdoers, but how can we create societies which foster social and cooperative rather than self-seeking and competitive forms of behavior.

Evolution, "Human Nature," and Capitalist Ideology. The philosophical conclusions about the egoistic character of "natural man" found in the writings of eighteenth-century social contract theorists were not derived from observations of humans in nonstate societies. They were philosophical conclusions drawn from observations of human social relations during the troubled birth of capitalism in England and Europe.

Capitalist societies are based upon competitive social relations. In such societies the view that individuals are essentially self-seeking and acquisitive is consistent with people's experiences since observable behaviors are more often competitive than altruistic. The problem is that when we generalize from immediate observable behavior in one form of society to all humans, we in effect *create nature in the image of our social system.*[12] This social construction of "nature" provides in turn a strong ideological justification for capitalism. If humans are inherently self-seeking, then competitive social relations are inevitable because they are *natural* rather than the alterable cultural creations of human beings. Thus nature, and not humans, is perceived as being responsible for whatever social ills and human misery might arise in such societies. Moreover, if individuals perceive competitive relations as inevitable, they are more likely to behave competitively themselves, thus helping recreate and reconfirm the existing order of competitive relations.

Humans emerged as cooperative beings. The evolution of modern humans was based upon over a *million years* of essentially cooperative relations among early hominids and was followed by 100,000 to 200,000 years of similarly cooperative social arrangements among archaic humans. This does not mean that humans are *instinctively* cooperative, but it does mean that there is little evidence that humans are self-seeking and competitive *by nature* or that they have an instinctive drive to acquire more material possessions than other people around them. In the words of anthropologist Sally Binford,

> Most of the hunting and gathering peoples of the world do not share our desire for possessions. . . . Two or three million years elapsed between the time humans began to live as hunters and gatherers and the development of the capitalistic system. If we are instinctively programmed for capitalism and if it is the basically satisfying human economic arrangement, why was it not developed sooner and why is it not the most common form of human economy?[13]

Acephelous societies were a natural outcome of an evolutionary pattern that favored cooperative social and economic relations. They were not based upon some powerful restraining force holding in check the savage self-interest of primitive humans. They were instead small bands of humans for whom self-awareness, as well as survival, was intimately linked to the interests and needs of the group.

SOURCES OF CONFORMITY IN ACEPHELOUS SOCIETIES

The simple technology and low levels of material production common to acephelous societies (1) require that nearly all members of the society engage in food production and (2) make it difficult for any individual to acquire material advantage over members of the society. Among foragers and hunters the source of food (wild edibles or game) can never be controlled, and the simple tools needed for acquiring this food can be produced by any adult. Under these conditions no individual is capable of gaining a significantly greater access to the means of survival than others, and thus no individual can use control over the means of production as a basis of power over others.

Simple agriculturalists and herders have a more stable and more controllable food supply than hunters and gatherers, yet many such groups retained cooperative patterns of production, remaining essentially acephelous in character despite the potential for the emergence of "private" productive property. Agriculturalists such as the Tiv in West Africa and herders such as the Nuer of the southern Sudan, for example, hold their productive property in common. While individuals own personal items (e.g., blankets, mats, knives, spears, etc.), the means of production (e.g., land among the Tiv or cattle herds among the Nuer) are held as the corporate property of the extended kin-group. While this productive property may be tended by individuals, it is in no sense "owned" by them and can only be disposed in accordance with the wishes of the entire group.[14] As a result of these patterns acephelous societies tend to be economically and politically egalitarian:

Everybody works at food production tasks; no one is systematically denied access to natural resources vital for survival; people tend to consume more or less the same quantities and qualities of valuables; and no individuals accumulate valuables produced by the labor of others.[15]

In acephelous societies there is no structural basis for some individuals to gain political power over others. Certain individuals may acquire more *status* than others because of greater prowess in some valued skill, membership in a clan believed to have special powers, or qualities attributed to age or gender. However, this status is qualitatively different from power in Weber's sense of being able to realize one's own interests regardless of the wishes of others.[16] Eskimo groups, for example, generally recognize one of their members as a "headman." However, unlike a political leader,

> The headman possesses no fixed authority; neither does he enter into formal office. He is not elected, nor is he chosen by any formal process. When other men accept his judgement and opinions, he is a headman. When they ignore him, he is not.[17]

Peter Freuchen tells us that the respect and difference shown an Eskimo headman is based upon his demonstrated superior skill as a hunter. Because of this skill he is allowed to make the arrangements for hunting expeditions, and "lesser men respect his wisdom and intuition" in these matters. Such leaders have no power to compel or force others against their will, however, and others will defer to the leader's wisdom only as long as such deference is vindicated by his continued skillful performance as a hunter.[18]

The "leopard-skin chief" of the Nuer, like the Eskimo headman, possesses significant influence but lacks the power to command. In fact, as E. E. Evans-Pritchard notes, the term "chief" is a misnomer, since the leopard-skin chief has no formal authority. Unlike the status of an Eskimo headman, the position of a leopard-skin chief is not based upon superlative skill but upon membership in one of the lineages believed to be endowed with hereditary ritual powers, powers especially appropriate to the settlement of disputes.[19]

Persons of importance in acephelous societies, whether Eskimo headman, Nuer leopard-skin chiefs, Luhya village leaders, Dinka "masters of the fishing spear," or Anuak headmen, may have the ability to influence others in some situations, but they normally lack any formal power to command.[20] This distinction is an important one. Where there is no formal power, there is no state. Because the concept of crime implies the existence of a centralized power that will punish wrongdoing, where there is no state there can be no crime. There are only private disputes between individuals that must be resolved without reliance upon some centralized authority.

Lacking any formal authority to define right and wrong and to punish wrongdoing, acephelous societies must rely on other means to create the conformity necessary for social order. While it is true that in acephelous societies cooperative action is necessary for survival, it would be a mistake to assume that conformity in these societies is simply a matter of the individual's being *forced* to conform because he or she recognizes that the group is the key to individual survival. In the area of productive arrangements, for example, every society develops a set of shared beliefs that support these arrangements. Individuals in acephelous societies conform to the rules of cooperative food production and food distribution not because they recognize these arrangements as necessary for survival but because they recognize them as the *correct way* of assuring survival and satisfaction.

The Pygmies, for example, view it as seriously wrong for one member to set his hunting nets in front of others, thereby assuring himself a greater share of the game. While this act may be seen from a competitive world view as an enterprising maneuver in the search for food, to the Pygmie it is an outrageous violation of the rules of hunting.[21] Pygmie culture does not include an elaborate analysis of why the material conditions of their society require cooperative hunting techniques. It simply contains the belief that seeking to acquire more game by reducing someone else's access to this game is wrong.

Acephelous societies enjoy certain advantages with respect to creating social order not found in more complex and competitively organized societies. These are (1) diffuse role structures, (2) kin-based social organization, and (3) belief systems emphasizing the collective nature of success, failure, and responsibility.

Before examining the ways in which these things contribute to the maintenance of social order in acephelous societies, a conceptual distinction must be made between their function as *sources of willing conformity* and their function as *controls on deviant behavior*.

The dominant consciousness that arises out of structured social relations tends to create patterns of willing conformity by socializing individuals into an understanding of why the established ways of doing things are also the *right* ways of doing them. Where this process is not sufficient to keep the individual from violating community norms, negative mechanisms that threaten, restrain, or punish deviant behavior will be activated. The distinction between creating conformity and restraining deviance is a subtle one, and often the two processes are closely related. For example, the punishment of some can serve as a lesson for others, showing them not only the dangers of deviating from the accepted patterns of behavior but also dramatizing the *rightness* of those patterns. However, the failure to make the distinction between the creation of willing conformity and the restraint of deviant behavior can lead to the error of viewing the role of "customs" in primitive societies as essentially one of restraining deviant behavior. Sue Titus Reid, for example, speaks of "submission to custom" and R. L. Trivers of "submission to the yoke of communal servitude," and William Seagle tells us that the "savage recognizes the binding character of his customs."[22] In each of these statements there is the implication that social order is primarily a matter of holding in check the contrary motives and tendencies of the individual members of society. To take this view, however, is to risk overlooking the powerful forces fostering willful conformity in such societies. In primitive societies diffuse roles, kin-based social organization, and concepts of collective responsibility help create commitment to the customary ways of society and also serve to restrain deviance.

Diffuse Roles and Conformity

Because of their small size and simple technology, acephelous societies require great versatility among their members. Because a complex division of labor is lacking, each individual must fulfill a number of roles: food producer, educator, arbitrator, warrior (in those societies that engage in warfare), friend, toolmaker, and so forth. This diffuseness of roles serves to create social conformity by emphasizing the individual's values to the group. Each adult is called upon to perform a number of different activities, all of which are important for the survival and success of the group. There are no unnecessary or unimportant individuals in an acephelous society because there is no pool of surplus labor. Nearly every individual experiences himself or herself as a contributing and valuable member of the group and correspondingly has few reasons to develop a set of goals separate from those of the group. In addition, diffuse roles tie individuals to one another in *multiple* ways and therefore provide the individual with numerous opportunities to receive positive feedback from the community. Individuals develop a strong sense of belonging, which is an important means of enforcing conformity to the beliefs and values of the group.

Kinship and Conformity

All human societies recognize boundaries that distinguish them from other groups and provide a sense of identity. In modern societies these boundaries are political; they refer to the geographical limits of a centralized authority's power to rule and can be altered through annexation, purchase, liberation, revolution, or the fortunes of war irrespective of the networks of social relations within these boundaries. Thus, for example, through purchase the American government was able to extend its power to rule over all of the native Americans living in the Louisiana Territory despite the fact that there existed no significant social relationships between these peoples and the American state.

Acephelous societies recognize no central political authority and in the case of nomadic peoples also no specific geographical boundaries. As a result the patterns of social relations within these societies constitute the *sole basis* of identity. It is the kinship system—a set of ties based upon loyalty, responsibility, obligation, and privilege among people who consider themselves to be related—that defines the patterns of social relations and thus the identity of acephelous societies. Kinship systems can take many different forms and often include not only individuals who are blood relations but also those who are related through marriage, adoption, or some other rite signifying entrance into the kin-groups. Kin-groups may also consist of individuals who perceive themselves to be related through common descent from some mythological ancestor. What is significant in kin-based societies is that there are no "unrelated" individuals. The boundaries of the society and the significant social relations between individuals are synonymous. A relatively high degree of social order is attainable without a centralized authority or a formal legal system in kin-based societies precisely because *relatedness and obligations to others are not abstract principles* but rather basic elements of all social interactions. In some acephelous societies kinship is so essential to defining the appropriate conduct of social relations that there is no ability to interact with strangers until they have been assigned some role in the kinship system.

Formal legal codes in state societies reflect an attempt to create a sense of relatedness and obligation among the members of the society. However, this relatedness is not based upon the strength of personal ties but upon the political power of the state to define the appropriate forms of relations between individuals, using abstract concepts of rights, duties, and obligations as both a basis and a justification for these rules.

Because of their size and complexity modern state societies must attempt to establish a sense of relatedness and obligation among people who often bear little personal significance to one another if any degree of social order is to be maintained. Consider, for example, the relationship between landlord and tenant. In American cities legal codes attempt to relate landlords and tenants through a set of obligations requiring, among other things, that the landlord provide adequate shelter, plumbing, and safety measures and that the tenant pay his or her rent and not destroy the property of the landlord. Apart from these legal requirements, however, there is no personal significance to the landlord–tenant relationship. Except in small, privately owned rental properties, landlords and tenants seldom know one another, and in many large cities landlords often do not, and never have, lived in the same neighborhood as their tenants. In many instances "landlords" are not even individuals but instead large management corporations. The basis for predictable social relations between landlords and tenants are the legal rules backed by threat of punishment and abstract principles such as respect for private property. While these do serve to establish a degree of obligation, they lack the more compelling force of personal relationships. Where a sense of personal relatedness is absent, conformity to social rules is highly dependent upon either the ability or willingness of the political state to enforce its rules or the individual's personal commitment to abstract principles.

The difficulty of establishing a sense of relatedness and obligation becomes increasingly difficult as the social structure and ideology of a society increasingly emphasize competitive and individualistic social relations. Individuals are required by law, and urged by abstract principles, to feel and to fulfill obligations to all other members of the society, while in both reality and perception these others are also threatening competitors in the struggle for personal gain. This contradiction between relatedness and competitiveness is much less acute in kin-based, cooperative societies and does not require the force of formal law to moderate social and material relations.

Collective Responsibility and Conformity

Because of the sense of relatedness resulting from kin-based social organization, acephelous societies often develop a concept of collective responsibility. That is, individual actions, whether successful, unsuccessful, normative, or deviant, are felt to involve the individual's entire kin-group or lineage. If an individual commits a deviant act or violates a taboo, the shame for this act is felt to fall not just upon the individual but upon the entire lineage. The group thus feels responsible for the behavior of its members, just as contemporary American parents often feel responsible for the behavior of their children.

The concept of collective responsibility places a significant burden upon the individual and hence is a powerful force for conformity in acephelous societies. Each individual learns to view his or her actions in relation to their effect upon the entire lineage. When individuals perceive that their behavior can affect the well-being of everyone comprising their network of important social relations, they have a more compelling reason to consider the needs of this group when selecting a course of action than when behavior is viewed as basically involving no one except one's self.

RESTRAINING DEVIANCE IN ACEPHELOUS SOCIETIES

All societies experience instances of troublemaking based upon self-interest, although their frequency differs from one society to another. The diffuse role structure, kin-based social organization, and concept of collective responsibility found in acephelous societies serve as powerful forces that bind the individual to the group and thus reduce the likelihood of egoistic interests arising. This in turn minimizes the potential for trouble. In addition to producing willing conformity to group values and interests, however, these factors can also place significant restraints upon individuals who may still be inclined to deviate.

A diffuse role structure and a kin-based social system are particularly important sources of restraint because they deny the individual any sense of anonymity. In such communities one can seldom escape the watchful eyes of someone who knows you. More importantly, any offending act will jeopardize the individual's relationships with other community members in a general and diffuse way. Social life in modern societies by comparison is highly compartmentalized. For example, a modern store manager running an appliance outlet in a low-income neighborhood may cheat his customers or lure them into exploitive installment contracts and yet remain in good standing with church, country club, neighbors, friends, and family in the suburb where he lives. Most of his social contacts away from work may in fact know very little about his daily activities. Protected by social distance from his victims, he retains an "illusion of innocence" and "remains erect, smiling and unscathed" by the consequences of his wrongdoing.[23] In acephelous societies life is not so compartmentalized, and wrongdoing in one arena can reverberate through the individual's entire network of social relations. This provides a substantial restraining force on deviance, since individuals must face the possibility of disrupting their entire support system should they engage in some violation of custom. This force acquires added impetus in economically cooperative societies where disrupting one's social standing in the community can seriously jeopardize one's access to participation in the collective economic life.

Concepts of collective responsibility also provide an important source of external pressure for the restraint of deviance. Among many tribal peoples of East Africa, for example, marriage always occurs between members of different lineages and requires the payment of "bride wealth" (often in the form of cattle) to the lineage of the prospective bride. Should the new wife begin to falter in her expected wifely duties, she will experience significant social pressure from members of her lineage to reform her ways, for her inappropriate behavior could have consequences for that entire lineage. That is, should the marriage fail, the bride's lineage will be required to return the bride wealth, a significant loss for the collective economy of the lineage.[24] Similarly, where violations of taboos or other social rules are thought to result in unpleasant consequences for the entire community, each individual has an important stake in insuring that other members refrain from such violations. Among the Semai of Malaya, for instance, thundersqualls are greatly feared, for they are usually accompanied by forty- to fifty-mile-an-hour winds that can damage or destroy their bamboo houses. The Semai also believe that thundersqualls occur as collective punishment when someone in the community is guilty of wrongdoing such as "breaking the incest taboo, eating mixtures of certain types of foods or being cruel to something defenseless." For this reason every Semai takes an interest in the behavior of community members and particularly that of children, reminding them that their behavior could bring supernatural displeasure and hence disaster upon the whole community.[25] This differs significantly from patterns of social control in America, where punishment is individualized and the right to interfere directly in the behavior of others is limited to people in specified positions of authority such as parent, police officer, or judge.

RESOLVING TROUBLE IN ACEPHELOUS SOCIETIES

When trouble does occur in acephelous societies it must be resolved without the help of a formal legal system. The first step toward resolving trouble in acephelous societies, as in more complex ones, is to define the problem and evaluate its seriousness. As Edgerton observed,

> It is apparent that no society has ever held all of its members as strictly accountable for all of their actions so that each and every breach of a rule carried with it an inevitable or identical punishment . . . rules are often very fuzzy around the edges—they are relative to the situation, the actor and the audience, and they leave substantial room for disagreement and negotiation about what is or is not just and proper.[26]

The evaluation of trouble in acephelous societies is highly contextual given the absence of formal laws and institutionalized enforcement. Colin

Turnbull, for example, reports that in the Pygmie community he studied, theft of food was considered an especially reprehensible offense. However, in this particular group lived an individual known to be a food thief who was relatively tolerated because he was valued as a storyteller and because he was a bachelor with no woman to prepare food for him. In addition, he tended to steal from individuals who were in temporary disfavor with the rest of the community. Occasionally, if he happened to steal too much or stole from someone not in temporary disfavor, he would be whipped and banished from the community to spend the night alone in the forest.[27]

This particular case highlights an important characteristic of the evaluation of trouble and the response to it. The seriousness of trouble is influenced by (1) the perceived value of the troublemaker and (2) the perceived value of the troublemaker's victims. This pattern is no less common in modern America than it is among the Pygmies. Crimes by racial minorities against whites are often seen as far more serious than crimes by whites against minority group members.[28] The major difference between acephelous and complex societies with respect to the selective evaluation of trouble is that while *individuals* in acephelous societies may for a time be in disfavor with the community, the structure of these societies does not produce the relatively permanent devaluing of entire *classes* of people. In America, by contrast, large groups of people such as the poor and minority group members exist in structured positions of disfavor.

Once trouble is identified and evaluated, it must be resolved in some manner, particularly if there are specific victims. The victims of trouble generally desire some form of satisfaction for the discomfort or loss they have suffered. This desire for "justice"—a balancing of the harm through some subsequent act done either for the victim or to the offender—appears to be felt by the victims of trouble in all societies, whether primitive or complex. However, every society develops its own concept of justice. Even among acephelous societies there are substantial differences in what is felt to constitute justice. In the case of homicide, for example, depending upon the society "justice" may require the death of the offender or one of his kinsmen, the payment of some objects of value, the promise of payment, or simply the opportunity to publicly accuse and condemn the offender.[29]

Given such variability, we cannot assume that humans have any universal understanding of what specifically constitutes justice. We can only conclude that there appears to be a desire for some form of satisfaction, *variously construed,* that is felt to restore the balance that was disrupted by the offender's troublemaking.

A nonstate society does not have a formal justice system to declare when trouble is resolved. Once trouble has occurred the community will remain in a state of unrest until the victim is satisfied, at least to some degree. Trouble is not over until the victim says it is. The greater the interdependence between the victim's and the troublemaker's kinship groupings, the greater the pressures for resolution. Since the concept of collective responsibility can place entire lineages in conflict with one another, the normal course of daily life cannot be resumed until the trouble is resolved. The more these groups have important economic and social ties, the greater will be the effort brought to bear in forging a resolution. This resolution is usually achieved through one of four mechanisms: (1) blood revenge, (2) retribution, (3) ritual satisfaction, or (4) restitution.

Blood revenge normally applies only in cases of homicide and in principle permits the victim's kinsmen to kill the murderer or one of his kinsmen. Blood revenge is intimately linked to concepts of collective responsibility, so much so that as a response to homicide it can usually only operate *between* kin-groups or lineages. Should a murder occur *within* a lineage, that unit is collectively both the victim and the offender. In this case blood revenge cannot be carried out since there is no distinct victim group to extract the punishment.

Blood revenge places the victim's kin-group and the offender's kin-group in a state of feud. The offender's kin-group may grudgingly accept the blood revenge as legitimate, and the matter is essentially ended when the offender or one of his kinsmen is killed. However, should the offender's kin-group view the alleged murder as justified or for some other reason not warranting blood revenge, they may view any act of retaliation by the victim's kin-group as itself a murderous act calling for blood revenge, thus initiating a cycle of revenge killings. Because it has this potential for causing more trouble than it resolves, blood revenge is seldom utilized as the basic response to murder in acephelous societies. The desire to avoid actual blood revenge is particularly strong in societies with large, mutually interdependent kin-groups. In these societies blood feuds could disrupt entire communities, as the various kin-groups within the community align themselves with either the victim's or the offender's lineage.

Within traditional Eskimo villages killing (generally over wife-stealing), while not continual, was not uncommon. Because these villages tended to be loosely knit, anarchical collections of small families, these killings did not constitute a community problem but were instead viewed as a dispute between the individual families. Murders would sometimes result in blood revenge, with the offender being killed by a member of the victim's family. This blood revenge was viewed by the Eskimo as a legitimate and often expected response. Under the worst circumstances blood revenge could escalate into a continuing feud, as each set of kin sought to avenge the previous death. This revenge cycle, however, appears to have been relatively rare, and when it did occur, most often it involved families from different villages.[30]

Normally, a killing has little impact upon an Eskimo village as a whole, and consequently there is little need for a *community* response. One factor that limits the impact of murder upon the community is that the victim's immediate responsibilities are discharged by the murderer.

> Murder is followed quite regularly by the murderer taking over the widow and children of the victim. In many instances the desire to acquire the woman is the cause of the murder, but where this is not the motive, a social principle requiring provisions for the bereaved family places the responsibility directly upon the murderer.[31]

Eskimo communities, having an established mechanism for insuring that the victim's wife and children will not become a community problem, experience no need for any additional response. Only when an individual appears to be a continual threat to the community by virtue of having committed several murders do the Eskimo engage in any collective response. As F. Adamson Hoebel says of the homicidal recidivist,

> He becomes a social menace liable at any time to strike down another victim. As a general menace, he becomes a public enemy. As a public enemy, he becomes the object of public action. . . . *Repeated* murder becomes public crime punishable by death at the hands of an agent of the community.[32] (emphasis added)

Retribution requires returning to the offender a harm that is in some way seen as equivalent to the harm caused the victim. It differs from revenge only in that it does not require that an *identical* harm be suffered by the offender. While blood revenge follows the specific calculus of a life for a life, retribution is a more abstract concept involving the exchange of one harm for another. The modern practice of assigning prison sentences in accordance with the "seriousness" of the crime is guided in part by this concept of equivalent retaliation, that is, "let the punishment fit the crime." The previously discussed whipping and nighttime ostracism of the Pygmie thief is an example of retribution within an acephelous society.

Wrongful injuries not as serious as a killing may also result in a retaliatory attack by the victim's kinsmen against those of the offender. The aim of such attacks is to make the offender's kin suffer for the harm done in some comparable but not necessarily identical way, as is the case with blood revenge. Like blood revenge, such attacks can create a situation of continual hostility between groups. The Yanomamo, for example, have developed the practice of retribution into a fine art, and as a result some villages live in a state of almost continual hostility with other villages.[33]

Both blood revenge and retribution have serious drawbacks as mechanisms for resolving trouble in communities that are highly interdependent and economically cooperative. Fortunately, for many small, essentially anarchic acephelous communities, serious trouble is relatively rare, with groups such as the Eskimo and the Yanomamo appearing to be more the exception than the rule. In more highly organized communities, "justice" is more frequently accomplished through ritual satisfaction and restitution. These mechanisms serve to (1) restore normalcy to the daily life of the community while (2) causing a minimum amount of social disruption in the process.

Small, interdependent and economically cooperative communities cannot afford to kill, expel, or in some other way render unproductive those who occasionally cause trouble. Furthermore, any response to trouble that does not result in killing the offender requires that the community find some way to continue living with that person in relative harmony. That is, the offender must be absorbed back into the community as a normal member fairly quickly. Frequent execution and incarceration are luxuries of more materially advanced state societies. Thus ritual satisfaction and restitution become the favored mechanisms for resolving trouble in all but the most anarchical societies. Even the Eskimo utilize mechanisms less potentially disruptive than revenge and retribution for most harms other than homicide.

Ritual satisfaction requires that the offender submit to some symbolic demonstration of his or her guilt, to suffer public ridicule or a token harm, or both. An excellent example of ritual satisfaction is provided by the Tiwi of North Australia. The social organization of Tiwi society is such that older men head large polygymous households comprised of mostly younger wives-in-residence. Infant daughters are usually bestowed upon older men as future wives. The result is that among the Tiwi there are no unattached females, and the young man has no legitimate access to heterosexual relationships. As described by C. W. M. Hart and Arnold Pilling,

> No Tiwi father, except in the most unusual cases, ever thought of bestowing an infant daughter upon any male below the age of twenty-five. . . . This meant that a youth of twenty-five had his first wife betrothed to him at that age but had to wait another fourteen years or so before she was old enough to leave her father's household and take up residence and marriage duties with him.[34]

This arrangement did not necessarily lead to chastity among all men until the age of forty or thereabouts. It led to numerous charges by the older husbands against the younger men of seduction of married or betrothed women. These charges apparently had some basis in fact since "most young wives continued to become pregnant with monotonous regularity, no matter how ancient and senile their husbands," although pregnancy was not the basis for seduction charges since the Tiwi do not recognize the relationship between sex and pregnancy.[35]

For the Tiwi, seduction constitutes serious trouble. However, the punishment for such troublemaking is more ritual than real. Surrounded by village residents the elder and the young offender face each other in a "deadly" duel. The elder arrives armed with hunting spears while the younger man by custom is usually either unarmed or carries only throwing sticks, a relatively insignificant weapon under the circumstances. After a period of publicly humiliating the accused, the elder commences to throw his spears at the offender, who is expected not to retaliate. However, he is permitted to dodge the oncoming spears, and because he is "much younger and hence almost invariably in much better shape than the older man," the offender can "dodge the old man's spears indefinitely if he wanted to."[36] However, rather than exacerbate the problem by publicly humiliating the older man, the young seducer:

> ". . . having for five or ten minutes demonstrated his physical ability to avoid being hit, then showed a proper moral attitude by allowing himself to be hit. . . . A fairly deep cut on the arm or thigh that bled a lot but healed quickly was the most desirable wound to help the old man inflict, and when the blood gushed from such a wound the crowd yelled approval and the duel was over. The young man had behaved admirably, the old man had vindicated his honor, the sanctity of marriage and the Tiwi constitution had been upheld, and everybody went home satisfied and full of moral rectitude. Seduction did not pay.[37]

The importance of this kind of resolution to trouble is that it allows a degree of honor to both offender and victim, and both parties can once again resume normal daily activities without continued strife disrupting village life and without the offender now being relegated to second-class membership because of his "crime."

Another example of ritual satisfaction is the Eskimo "song duel." From the Eskimo of the Bering Strait to those of Greenland, all manner of trouble, in some cases even murder, are resolved by singing contests. Through their skill and finesse in singing conventional Eskimo songs and in some cases also special compositions appropriate to the dispute, the two disputants attempt to please the audience of village members and win from them enthusiastic applause. The winner is the singer who receives the most hearty applause. Where special compositions are used their purpose is to "ridicule the opponent and capitalize on his vulnerable foibles and frailties."[38] The winner of the song duel receives no restitution or reward other than the prestige of emerging the victorious singer. Once the song duel is completed, however, the trouble is felt to be ended and both troublemaker and victim resume their normal roles in the community.

Like the ritual duel among the Tiwi, the Eskimo song duel serves to resolve trouble without creating long-term difficulties for the community and, more importantly, permits the troublemaker to return as a normal member of the community.

Restitution determined through negotiations culminating in some payment made to the victim or his kin-group in return for the harm done is another important mechanism for resolving trouble in many acephelous societies. In societies where it is the most common means of resolving disputes, restitution serves to exemplify the relationship between a society's organization and its attempts to handle trouble.

Restitution best functions as a *basic* mechanism for resolving trouble in societies that (1) are arranged into kinship networks holding property in common, (2) have an elaborated concept of property that allows for the development of a common medium of exchange, and (3) have a material base that allows the production of some surplus.

Kinship networks are essential for restitution because the underlying pressure to arrive at a negotiated settlement is the implicit threat of a feud between kin-groups should negotiations fail. Where property is held in common, kinsmen are more likely to feel sufficiently bonded to one another to offer this kind of unquestioning support. A common medium of exchange is necessary since restitution cannot be calculated unless the disputing parties share an understanding of the practical and/or symbolic value of the items to be offered in return for the harms done. Finally, only in societies with the ability to produce some degree of surplus are there sufficient goods to offer in restitution for a harm without destroying the offending kin-group's chances for survival. Consequently, restitution as a basic mechanism for resolving trouble tends to be more commonly found among agricultural and pastoral peoples than among nomadic hunters and gatherers. The greater geographic stability of food growers and herders aids in the emergence of societies composed of multiple kin-groups inhabiting neighboring areas for long periods of time. Their more stable economic base allows some degree of material accumulation and also the development of a rudimentary exchange system based upon cattle, goats, tools, or some other items of value. The Ifugao and the Nuer are good examples of the relationship between social organization and the use of restitution as a primary means of resolving trouble.

The Ifugao of North Luzon are an agricultural people whose survival is based upon growing rice in small irrigated fields. They are divided into kinship groups consisting, from an individual's point of view, all of the blood relations of one's parents. This network includes grandparents and their siblings (great-aunts and uncles), parents and their siblings (aunts and uncles), the children of one's parents (brothers and sisters), the children of parents' siblings (cousins), and all the children of this last group (sons, daughters, nieces, nephews). The Ifugao, however, do not distinguish between the members within these different generations so that cousins and brothers or parents and uncles are all identified by the same term. Each kin-group holds a portion of rice-growing land in common, which, while it may be divided into separate parcels to be tended by individuals, is never "owned" by these individuals. It is merely administered and tended on behalf of the kin-group.[39]

The Ifugao social system has no centralization of power or delegation of authority, and there is no basis for the "exercise of compulsive sanction." Thus among the Ifugao there can be no "criminal" acts. On the other hand, there is sufficient opportunity for trouble to arise. Nearly all harms among the Ifugao are treated similar to civil litigation under the Anglo-American system of law, that is, as disputes between an aggrieved party and an alleged perpetrator of the grievance. With the exception of certain cases of homicide calling for direct blood revenge, trouble is normally resolved through negotiated restitution.

A social system based upon irrigation agriculture, as is that of the Ifugao, tends to require a more legalistic mechanism for dispute settlement than that of foraging societies because "the control of water rights and the maintenance of the elaborate real-estate system that it entails demand effective mechanisms of ajudication and protection."[40] It might also be added that societies with these more elaborate notions of property rights also have greater opportunity for disputes over property.

When a dispute of any type arises among the Ifuago, the aggrieved party must initiate action by selecting a go-between who will relay demands and counterdemands between the disputing parties and also attempt to maneuver them into a settlement. Of course, the possibility for direct action by the aggrieved and his kinsmen exists, for as R. F. Barton tells us "the lance is in back of every demand of importance."[41] Plaintiffs and their kin, however, are not overly eager to attack the defendant and his kin. "The kin of each party are anxious for a peaceable settlement, if such can honorably be brought about. . . . Neighbors and co-villagers do not want to see their neighborhood torn apart by internal dissension. . . ."[42] Instead of feuding, claims and counterclaims are relayed by the *monkalun* (the go-between) until a settlement is achieved.[43] This procedure of entering into an established pattern of negotiation as an alternative to open conflict can be seen as a rudimentary example of a pluralistic model of social organization. While groups with competing interests exist among the Ifugao, there is general social support for a negotiated settlement process rather than a reliance upon direct self-help through violent confrontation.

The settlement of trouble through restitution represents an important step toward the development of law since it usually involves both clear procedural rules for the conduct of negotiation and often third-party negotiators performing quasi-legal functions. For example, among the Ifugao, once a *monkalun* has been selected, the procedural rules require that neither group can directly attack the other, and much like our modern "contempt of court" disrespect for this rule will be severely punished by the *monkalun* and his kinsmen.[44] The *monkalun,* however, is not a *legal* official, for he does not represent the delegated authority of any centralized power. Nor does he hold this position in any permanent sense, for a *monkalun* is a *monkalun* only when he is arranging a particular settlement. Yet while in that role a *monkalun* is also more than just another member of the community tending to his own personal interests. Rather, as Hoebel tells us:

> He explicitly expresses the general societal interest in the clearing up of tensions, the punishment of wrongs and the reestablishment of social equilibrium when the normal balance has been disturbed by an alleged illegitimate act. . . . He is not a judge; for he makes no judgment. He is not an arbitrator; for he hands down no decrees. He is merely a forceful go-between—an admonishing mediator of limited authority but of usually persuasive effectiveness.[45]

Because the Ifugao are a settled agricultural people they have a relatively stable food supply and also do not have to contend with the transportation problems of nomadic peoples. These factors permit the limited accumulation of surplus material goods that can be offered in settlement of some dispute. Items such as iron implements, kettles of various value, and ceremonial blankets are used as means of restitution among the Ifugao.[46] While such offerings may indeed be a loss for the defendant and his kinsmen, life among the Ifugao is not so tenuous that such payments directly threaten their survival.

Among acephelous societies restitution is one of the most basic mechanisms for resolving trouble. Like ritual satisfaction, it provides a means for bringing trouble to a close and enabling disputing parties to resume normal relations. Since the parties to restitution negotiations in these societies each retain some degree of control over the outcome, a compromise solution that allows each party to be relatively satisfied is possible. This is quite unlike our own criminal prosecutions, which are winner-take-all contests between the political state and an alleged offender.

The aggrieved party in an American criminal prosecution plays no role in resolving the trouble other than providing testimony that may enable the state to win its case and acquire the right to punish the now-convicted offender. The victim seldom receives any satisfaction other than the abstract knowledge that the offender was punished. At the personal level, punishment becomes increasingly important when it is the only mechanism for adjusting trouble. Punishment, as we normally use the term, is far less frequently practiced in acephelous societies than is restitution. The focus is not upon what is done *to the offender* but upon what is done *for the victim*.

While all human societies seek mechanisms for resolving trouble, the desire for revenge—that is, to do something to the offender–is not characteristic of some "perennial and universal sense of justice," as some observers have suggested.[47] It is easy to assume that punishment is the most universal way of responding to those who cause harm if we limit our investigation to state societies that for many reasons have difficulty employing other ways of resolving trouble. However, if we expand our analysis to include other forms of human society, we find many instances where restoring the victim and/or his kin takes precedence over doing something to the offender. While restitution does take something away from the offender, it is qualitatively different in its purposes and its consequences from punishment in the form of revenge or retribution.

Compromise between disputing parties is an essential component of restitution. As William Chambliss and Robert Seidman have noted, the principle of compromise is a far more appropriate mechanism of resolving trouble in those situations where "a continued relationship between the disputants is anticipated."[48] Under these conditions winner-take-all solutions do not contribute to the likelihood of future harmony, while compromise solutions do. Because acephelous societies tend to be relatively small, lack anonymity, and bind all individuals together into a complex network of social interaction, restitution is a far more adequate tool for resolving trouble than is some form of imposed punishment.

The importance of compromise for people who feel they must live together in some continuing relationship is exemplified by certain aspects of restitution among the cattle-herding people Nuer of the southern Sudan. Numbering some 300,000 in the late 1930s the Nuer were composed of numerous tribes with populations of normally 5,000 or more, and in some cases numbering as many as 45,000.[49] Within each tribe are a number of lineages. These lineages are bound together into a complex network of social relations and mutual obligations. The smallest lineage segments (minimal lineages) are part of larger lineages (maximal lineages), and several maximal lineages together form a segment of the tribe. Evans-Pritchard likens this kinship system to a set of small bowls nesting in larger bowls nesting in still larger bowls.[50] Villages are often comprised of several lineages, although usually from the same "segment" of the tribe. When disputes occur between members of different lineage groups but within a single tribe, the Nuer theoretically have mechanisms that allow for the payment of cattle in restitution for the harm done. Like the Ifugao, payment of restitution occurs in lieu of a feud between the disputing lineages, which is a far more dangerous and disruptive way of resolving trouble. In cases of minor harm the mechanism for restitution may be simply the seizure of some cattle belonging to the offender's lineage by kinsmen from the offended lineage. Evans-Pritchard reports,

> It is possible to obtain from Nuer a list of compensations for injuries to the person: e.g., ten cattle for a broken leg or skull, ten cattle for the loss of an eye, two cattle for a girl's broken teeth, etc.[51]

In some cases self-help to secure compensation is calculated to bring forth from the offender's lineage an offering of the *appropriate* compensation by virtue of the offended lineage's seizure of *more cattle* than normally would be their due.[52] If an offense is serious, such as a homicide, or the victim's lineage is unable to resort to self-help in collecting compensation, negotiations are carried out through the leopard-skin chief. Like the *monkalun* of the Ifugao, the leopard-skin chief is not a legal official but rather an influential mediator who guides the parties toward settlement rather than imposing any decision.

The important principle is that the more closely related are the lineages in terms of geography and structural relations, the more likely is the dispute, whether as serious as homicide or as minor as impregnating an unmarried girl, to be settled through compensation by the offender's lineage.

> In theory one can obtain redress from any member of one's tribe, but, in fact, there is little chance of doing so when he is not a member of one's district and a kinsmen.* The wider the area which contains the parties to a dispute, the weaker the feeling of obligation to settle it and the more difficult the task of enforcing settlement. . . . Within a village differences between persons are discussed by the elders of the village and agreement is generally and easily reached and compensation paid, or promised, for all are related by kinship and common interests. Disputes between members of nearby villages, between which there are many social contacts and ties can also be settled by agreement, but less easily. . . . The nearer we get to the [level of] tribe the less the chances of settlement.[53]

The more important and immediate the interactions between groups, the more important is maintaining continued peaceful relationships. Restitution becomes a more attractive mechanism for resolving trouble than does attempting to extract punishment through feud as groups become more socially and economically interdependent.

SUMMARY

Acephelous society constitutes the oldest form of human social organization and the only one that defines and responds to troublesome behavior without the participation of some form of centralized political power. Few such societies exist today. Where they do, they are within the political boundaries of some larger state society, although many such remaining acephelous groups often resist strongly efforts to force them to adopt a more "modern" way of life.[54] Despite their waning number acephelous societies can still help us

---

*A member of a common larger lineage group of which the disputing smaller lineages are both members.

understand the basic processes of creating social order and why the control of crime has always been a difficult and never more than a partially accomplished task of state societies.

It is ironic that modern state societies, with their elaborate institutions for law enforcement (often supported by an array of high-technology crime control devices such as cars, two-way radios, computers, etc.), cannot achieve the degree of social order and long-term stability characteristic of simpler societies that have none of these tools. The reason for this seeming irony is that *the degree of social peace a society enjoys depends upon the nature of its social organization,* not upon its ability to capture and punish those defined as deviant.

The social organization of acephelous societies contains a number of characteristics that contribute to order without government. First, acephelous societies are generally egalitarian, at least in comparison with state societies. This means that most individuals have roughly the same access to both material consumption and opportunities to develop a sense of personal worth. In a society where individuals perceive that all others as having the same amount of material goods as themselves there is little *basis* for the development of unsatisfied material desires of the kind that can lead to theft and other types of property crimes in societies characterized by material inequality. The evidence provided by acephelous societies suggests that the desire to acquire greater amounts of material goods than others is learned through the observation of inequality. It is not an inherent human trait. Also, in acephelous societies every person is important for the life of the community. There are no devalued, disgraced, isolated, or outcast *groups* in these societies, and disgrace for individuals is usually temporary, should it occur. This means that the majority of individuals in acephelous societies see themselves as valued and worthwhile members of their community. This type of self-affirmation provides a strong motivation to support the community and its rules and to avoid behaviors that would threaten this sense of value and belonging.

Second, acephelous societies tend to be small and the role structure very diffuse. All relationships and interactions are personal ones occurring between individuals who have bonds to one another that extend beyond their immediate interaction. This reduces both the possibilities and the desire to behave in deviant ways.

Third, in most acephelous societies responsibility for deviant behavior is viewed as collective. Deviance is not dismissed as simply the failure of an individual to behave appropriately; it is defined as both a community problem and a community failure. This provides a motivation for all individuals to take an interest in the behavior of other community members and a basis for collective responses to problems such as kin-based restitution.

Fourth, because acephelous societies lack centralized authority to enforce rules, their means of resolving trouble usually involves active participation of both the offender and the victim. This means that potential troublemakers must recognize that at some point they will have to confront, not some abstract system of justice, but those whom they have directly harmed. This may be a greater restraint on deviant behavior than any abstract legal threat.

Fifth, the frequent utilization of mechanisms such as ritual satisfaction and restitution enable all parties involved in a dispute to return to normal functioning fairly quickly. Offenders are thus permitted to retain their personal dignity and membership in the community instead of being relegated to a class of permanently disgraced outsiders, as they are in many modern societies when they are labeled "criminal."

It is unlikely that modern state societies will be replaced by acephelous forms of social organization at any time in the near future. The sheer size and density of the human population, as well as the advanced technology and complex divisions of labor that have become commonplace, militate against any such change. However, this does not mean that we can safely forget that the level of social peace in a society depends upon its form of social organization. The key to social peace is not in better *control* of the criminal. It is the creation of societies where people have little reason and little opportunity to behave criminally.

The following chapter will examine the ways in which the emergence of state forms of social organization increase the likelihood of troublesome behaviors while reducing the effective options for its prevention and resolution in comparison to acephelous societies.

NOTES

1. David Hunter and Philip Whitten, *The Study of Anthropology* (New York: Harper & Row, 1976), 62.
2. Marvin Harris, *Culture, People, Nature* (New York: Thomas Crowell, 1975), 89.
3. Robert B. Edgerton, *Deviance: A Cross Cultural Perspective* (Menlo Park, Calif.: Cummings Publishing Co., 1976), 12–16.
4. Biologically and psychologically oriented researchers concerned with identifying basic and stable characteristics of "human nature" are most prone to this type of reductionism.
5. See George Vold, *Theoretical Criminology* (New York: Oxford University Press, 1979) for a discussion of the impact of social contract theorists on criminological theory.
6. James Campbell et al., *Law and Order Reconsidered*: A Staff Report to the National Commission on the Causes and Prevention of Violence (New York: Bantam Books, 1970), 2.
7. Warren Berger, Chief Justice of the Supreme Court, address to the American Bar Association, Houston, Texas, 8 February 1981. Reprinted in *Crime and Social Justice* 15 (1981): 43.
8. M. Kay Martin in Hunter and Whitten, *Study of Anthropology,* 77.
9. Ibid., 51.
10. Clifford Geertz, "The Impact of the Concept of Culture on the Concept of Man," in *New Visions of the Nature of Man,* John R. Platt, ed. (Chicago: University of Chicago Press, 1966), 49.
11. R. L. Trivers, "The Evolution of Reciprocal Altruism," *Quarterly Review of Biology* 46, no. 1 (March 1971): 35–51.
12. Marshall Sahlins, *The Uses and Abuses of Biology* (Ann Arbor: University of Michigan Press, 1976), xv.

13. Sally Binford, "Apes and Original Sin," in *Annual Editions: Readings in Anthropology 75/76* (Guilford, Conn.: The Duskin Publishing Group, 1976), 21.

14. Laura Bohannan, "Political Aspects of Tiv Social Organization," in *Tribes Without Rulers,* John Middleton and David Tait, eds. (London: Routledge and Kegan Paul, 1967), 34; E. E. Evans-Pritchard, *The Nuer* (London: Oxford University Press, 1940), 16.

15. Harris, *Culture, People, Nature,* 282.

16. See Anthony Giddens, *Capitalism and Modern Social Theory* (New York: Oxford University Press, 1971) 154–163, for a concise discussion of the Weberian conception of power.

17. E. Adamson Hoebel, *The Law of Primitive Man* (New York: Atheneum Press, 1973), 82.

18. Peter Freuchen, *Arctic Adventure* (New York: 1935), 138.

19. E. E. Evans-Pritchard, "The Neur of the Southern Sudan," in M. Fortes and E. E. Evans-Pritchard, eds., *African Political Systems* (New York: Oxford University Press, 1961), 291.

20. For a more detailed discussion of these various types of informal leaders see *Primitive Government* by Lucy Mair (Middlesex, England: Penguin Books, 1970), 61–77.

21. Colin Turnbull, *The Forest People* (New York: Simon and Schuster, 1961), 109.

22. See Sue Titus Reid, *Crime and Criminology* (Hinsdale, Ill.: Dryden, 1976), 27; Trivers, "Reciprocal Altruism," 37; William Seagle, *The Quest for Law* (New York: Knopf, 1941), 33.

23. Edward A. Ross, "The Criminaloid," *The Atlantic Monthly* 99 (January 1907). Reprinted in Gilbert Geis and Robert F. Meir, eds., *White Collar Crime* (New York: Free Press, 1977), 29, 33.

24. Harris, *Culture, People, Nature.* 312.

25. Robert Knox Dentan, *The Semai: A Non-Violent People of Malaya* (New York: Holt, Rinehart and Winston, 1968), 22.

26. Edgerton, *Deviance,* 68.

27. Colin Turnbull, *African Pygmies* (Garden City, N.Y.: National History Press, 1965), 214.

28. Marvin E. Wolfgang and Marc Riedel, "Race, Judicial Discretion and the Death Penalty," *The Annals of the American Academy of Political and Social Science* 407 (May 1973): 119–133.

29. For many Eskimo blood revenge is the basic mechanism for resolving a murder. However, among those of East Greenland a kinsman of the victim may seek satisfaction through a song duel if he chooses; see Hoebel, *The Law of Primitive Man,* 93. While the Nuer require substantial restitution for homicide it appears that when a killing occurs between close lineages, simply the promise of restitution (which is seldom actually paid in these cases) is sufficient to resolve the matter. See Evans-Pritchard, "The Neur of the Southern Sudan," 156.

30. Hoebel, *The Law of Primitive Man,* 83.

31. Ibid., 87.

32. Ibid., 88.

33. Napoleon Chagnon, *The Yanomano: The Fierce People,* 2d. ed., (New York: Holt, Rinehart and Winston, 1977), 118–137.

34. C. W. M. Hart and Arnold R. Pilling, *The Tiwi of North Australia* (New York: Holt, Rinehart and Winston, 1962), 16.

35. Ibid., 79.

36. Ibid., 81.
37. Ibid., 82.
38. Hoebel, *The Law of Primitive Man*, 93.
39. R. F. Barton, *Ifugao Law*, University of California Publications in American Archaeology and Ethnology, vol. 15 (Los Angeles, 1919), 39.
40. Hoebel, *The Law of Primitive Man*, 101.
41. Barton, *Ifugao Law*, 94.
42. Ibid.
43. Ibid., 95–101.
44. Hoebel, *The Law of Primitive Man*, 121.
45. Ibid., 114.
46. Barton, *Ifugao Law*, 62.
47. Gwynn Nettler, *Explaining Crime* (New York: McGraw-Hill, 1974), 34.
48. William Chambliss and Robert Seidman, *Law, Order, and Power* (Reading, Mass.: Addison-Wesley, 1971), 29.
49. Evans-Pritchard, "The Neur of Southern Sudan," 278.
50. Ibid., 284–288.
51. Evans-Pritchard, *The Neur*, 167.
52. Ibid., 167.
53. Ibid., 169.
54. For a discussion of primitive peoples' resistance to modern ways of life, see James H. Bodley, *Victims of Progress* (Menlo Park, Calif.: Cummings Publishing Co., 1975).

CHAPTER 4

Creating State Law: The Case of England

Introduction

The previous chapter examined how societies that have neither leaders with power over others nor a formal legal system define and cope with trouble. This chapter examines how the process of defining and dealing with trouble alters with the emergence of centralized forms of political power. Most contemporary literature about crime in America begins by taking the existence of political power and state law for granted. Often these things are simply treated as inevitable facts of life, and little information about how political power and state law develop is presented. Overlooking these things does not mean that we have simply avoided being overburdened with unimportant historical facts. It means we have seriously limited our ability to understand how changes in the basic elements of social order in a society will produce changes in how it defines and deals with disruptions of that order.

In this chapter we will briefly examine the general patterns of change that characterize the transition to state law and will then see how this process occurred in England as it moved from a loose accumulation of quasi-tribal communities in the eighth and ninth centuries to a full-fledged political state with a formal legal system by the the end of the twelfth century. Attention will also be given to how the changes in the feudal mode of production that occurred between the thirteenth and eighteenth centuries, eventually culminating in the replacement of feudalism with capitalism, led to significant alterations in English law. This process of legal change has particular bearing upon law and crime in America today, for it was during that time that many of the legal concepts and principles that dominate contemporary American justice were established.

THE NATURE OF STATE SOCIETY

State societies are characterized by the centralization of power under some ruler or government with the authority to issue directives and commands binding upon all other members of the society. This authority usually includes determining or directing the settlement of most serious forms of dispute or conflict between members of the society. State societies can be divided into two types: proto-states and civilizations.

Proto-States

Proto-states are an advanced form of tribal organization with a recognized ruler or chief with the authority to issue commands and the power to enforce them. Proto-states are sometimes also referred to as chiefdoms.

Aside from the existence of some recognized ruler, proto-states tend to be similar to acephelous societies in many ways. They are generally characterized by relatively simple technology and simple divisions of labor, some form of communal control over productive property, social organization along kinship lines, and only limited material inequality.

While the rulers in proto-states exercise a degree of power over others, this power is substantially limited by certain conditions characteristic of these societies. First, because these societies are typified by low levels of technology and widespread distribution of the means of production among various kingroups, a ruler's potential for acquiring sufficient surplus to support a nonproducing class of administrators and warriors to enforce his will is limited. Since kinship units in proto-states, like those in nonstate societies, have access to the elements of production (e.g., land, cattle, fish, etc.) the ruler in a proto-state cannot exploit the labor of others by making them work for him, as would be the case in a society where the ruler or a ruling class could claim all the productive wealth as their own. Without the ability to support a class of rule-enforcers, the leadership in a proto-state has little chance of creating or enforcing rules of taxation. Unlike their counterparts in full-fledged states, rulers in proto-states normally cannot expand their law-enforcement capabilities by using the surplus acquired through taxation to hire more full-time specialists, such as police and judges, to enforce their will.

The commands of rulers in proto-states are administered and enforced through their own kin-group. This means, first of all, that the body of law-enforcers is limited by the size of the ruler's kin-group. Additionally, since there is not sufficient surplus to allow these individuals to engage in such activity full time, the ruler's kinsmen must spend a good portion of their time tending to their own livelihoods. This of course limits the amount of time that can be devoted to enforcing or expanding political power.

Furthermore, rulers in proto-states are often bound by custom concerning the types of decisions they might render or the rules they will make. The less developed the power of the ruler, the more closely he is bound by custom. In some tribal societies the ruler is little more than a closely watched interpreter of custom subject to disapproval and control by the community should he begin to depart from custom in his decisions. At first glance this might seem to be similar to the position of rulers in modern states who are subject to disapproval and control either through revolutions, coups, or elections. However, there are significant differences. Under normal circumstances rulers in modern states have sufficient *power* at their disposal to make and enforce rules contrary to the customs, values, or interests of whole classes of people in the society. For example, large groups of Americans find themselves subject to laws, such as those prohibiting the possession and sale of marijuana, permitting abortion-on-demand, requiring registration for the draft, or prohibiting prayer in schools, that they feel are a violation of their interests or values. Because they are not divided into social classes and other significant subgroups, the populations of proto-states generally share a more common set of customs and values, which by virtue of their mass support significantly limit the prerogatives of the rulers in these societies.

The following instance provides a good example of the uneasy relationship that often exists between custom and power in tribal chiefdoms:

> The king was supposed to maintain customary law. Zulu have illustrated this to me by quoting a case in which Mpande [the king] had to decide against one of his favorites and then sent men to wipe out the successful litigant's family so as to make it impossible for the decision to be carried out. But he could not decide against the law [i.e., the custom], for his favorite. Nevertheless, the king could in deciding a case create a new law for what he and his council considered good reason.[1]

This case also highlights an important difference between the way trouble is handled in societies with rulers, as compared with those without. The resolution of trouble in state societies occurs through the intervention of a third party (the ruler or government) with an active interest in the outcome and the power to direct that outcome in accordance with the interests of the ruling individual or group. Dispute resolution is no longer a matter between offender and victim; it becomes a matter of state concern and is directed by the state.

As a centralized ruler emerges and begins to take an increasingly active role in the resolution of trouble, the needs of the victim, as Stephen Schafer notes, are progressively replaced by the interests of the state as the basis for settling disputes.[2] Among the Zulu, for example, the people were said to belong to the king. As a result, restitution in cases of homicide or assault was not paid to the victim or his kinsmen but to the king. That is, instead of there being true restitution, the king collected a fine from the offender for having harmed one of *his* people.[3] The declining role of victim and their kinsmen in the settlement of disputes that occurs with the emergence of a state form of society signifies an important change in the nature of social control. As individuals are increasingly required to submit their disputes or problems to some form of central leadership for resolution, the locus of obligation and allegiance shifts from the kin-group to the state. Responsibility becomes increasingly individualized rather than collective, and the obligation to conform to social rules becomes more abstract. As historian Henry Maine observed, with the coming of state power "the individual is steadily substituted for the family as the unit of which civil laws take account."[4] As kinship and community are supplanted by state law as the basis of social control, the potential for trouble and conflict increase. Individuals become less "beautifully tied into a web of social relations," where "an unexpected move results in a magnitude of subtle counter-moves" and where "deviant behavior is not necessarily seen as deviance or called deviance, but is kept under control through daily interaction with a number of other persons who are of great importance. . . ."[5] While interpersonal social relations still play an important role in the control and shaping of individual behavior, their power is significantly weakened with the coming of state law.

The shift in the primary locus of control from kinship and community to central authority also creates new opportunities for a gradual weakening of custom. It is sometimes said that law is merely the formal institutionalization of custom. However, where a society is in fact ruled by custom—as are acephelous ones—there is no need for law. Laws in proto-states most often emerge as the leadership, seeks some way of sidestepping the limitations custom places upon their own interests, as in the case of the Zulu king. As anthropologist Stanley Diamond comments:

> We learn by studying intermediate societies [chiefdoms] that the laws so typical of them are *unprecedented*. . . . They arise in opposition to the customary order of the antecedent kin or kin-quivalent groups; they represent a new set of social goals pursued by a new and unanticipated power in society.[6]

In sum, chiefdoms can be seen as intermediate forms of social organization combining aspects of both acephelous societies and civilizations. While they lack the complex divisions of labor, material surplus, and entrenched social classes characteristic of civilizations, chiefdoms nonetheless possess that centralization of power that enables rulers to decide how disputes between individuals will be settled. Chiefdoms are generally characterized by constant attempts on the part of the ruler or ruling clan to consolidate and expand their power over the customary kin-groups that previously formed the basis of social organization, allegiance, and dispute resolution. While sovereign power in chiefdoms is not complete, rulers in these societies strive to achieve "that monopoly of force which characterizes the mature state."[7]

Civilizations

Civilizations represent the most complex and also the newest form of human social organization. The earliest known civilizations came into existence no more than 10,000 years ago, which is recent when compared with the amount of time humans have inhabited this planet. Though their specific forms differ substantially, civilization—whether Incan or American, ancient Rome or modern Sweden, have certain basic characteristics in common. These are (1) a technology capable of producing surplus, (2) a complex division of labor, (3) a politicized economy, and (4) social stratification.

The relationship between technological development and the emergence of civilizations is unclear. It is apparent that civilizations could not have emerged until the development of agriculture and the domestication of animals. Not until humans were capable of producing (rather than gathering)

their own food did the *possibility* of substantial material surplus emerge. However, not all human societies capable of producing surplus did so. In some
horticultural societies it has been noted that "the accumulation and exchange
of wealth are simply not culturally valued."[8] This raises some doubts about
the validity of the notion presented by some popular writers such as Robert
Ardry (*The Territorial Imperative*) that the desire to accumulate and defend property is an instinctive human trait.[9] As John Bodley points out in *Victims of
Progress*, many nonaccumulative peoples that have come in contact with more
developed societies preferred their own cultures to the materially more re-
warding but socially more competitive "advanced" societies.[10]

While all horticultural societies began with subsistence farming, at a later
point in time some shifted to a *deliberate* strategy of overproduction (i.e., the
deliberate production of more than can be consumed by the producers and
their immediate dependents).[11] The availability of economic surplus was essential for the rise of civilizations. Without surplus food there is no basis for
taxation, and without taxation there would have been no ability to amass
food supplies sufficient to support the kind of specialized, non–food producing labor that is the hallmark of civilizations.

There are two ways to explain the relationship between power and the
production of surplus. One is to postulate that surplus developed as a natural
outcome of increasingly efficient methods of horticulture and herding and
that competition over this surplus was the origin of power.[12] The other is to
hold that the limited power found in a proto-state was used to enforce taxation
and the conscription of labor, thereby forcing overproduction and enabling
the ruler to begin supporting specialists.[13]

It is difficult to know which of these two approaches is most accurate.
In all likelihood the development of centralized power involved a subtle
process of interaction between the ability to produce surplus and the ability
to coerce this production. What is clear, however, is that once some coercive
power existed, its use to coerce surplus production was essential to the development of civilizations.

Civilizations are based upon politicized economies, that is, upon the
existence of a centralized power base with the capability of compelling or
enticing surplus production from the work force. The shift from relatively
egalitarian economies to politicized economies is aptly described by Marvin
Harris:

> Economic organization fell increasingly under the control of state administered
> institutions that set production quotas and carried out lopsided redistributions
> based upon labor conscription, taxation and control over price-market exchanges.
> These administered systems involved a high level of *compulsion*. They obliged
> people to increase their work input not merely by promising prestige but by
> threatening them with socially imposed material sanctions. . . .[14] (emphasis added)

Without powerful centralized administrative units for extracting and redis-
tributing surplus production, civilizations would not have emerged. The de-

velopment of irrigation systems; the building of roads, fortresses, and cities; the maintenance of large standing armies and naval forces; and the further development of technology all required increased control over production and distribution of food supplies.

The benefits of civilization come with a cost. As Harris notes, surplus production is

> . . . not in any sense a superfluous quantity from the producers' standpoint. The producers can very well use the full amount of their output to raise their own standard of living. If they surrender their produce, it is because they lack the power to withhold it.[15]

All civilizations have been built to a significant degree upon the ability of the more powerful to extract surplus from the less powerful. Whatever the particular political form of organization, in civilizations the great mass of the labor force does not have control over raw materials, technology, work schedules, place and mode of productive activity, or disposition of the products of labor.[16] Control over these aspects of economic life becomes centralized within subgroups representing a relatively small proportion of the total society.

This centralization gives rise to civilization's most distinct characteristic—stratification. Stratification is structured inequality between *classes* of individuals. Unlike the simple inequality between individuals or kin-groups sometimes found in proto-states, structured inequality is *integral* to the organization of civilizations. The extraction and redistribution of surplus *requires* that some have greater control over the productive system than others. Consequently, there emerges a relatively permanent set of social relations wherein some category of individuals exerts significant control over the life chances of others. These relations are class relations.

In civilizations there usually exists at a minimum a class that enjoys primary decision-making authority over the productive system, a class of specialists (e.g., warriors, record keepers, technologists, etc.) brought into existence by the class of key decision makers, and the general labor force. The primary class is always the smallest in number but receives the largest per capita share of both economic and political resources. By virtue of its importance to the primary class, the specialist class enjoys on a per capita basis a larger share of redistributed surplus and political power than those in the general labor force. It is the general labor force that normally has the least effect on decision making. Only when they coalesce into a unified mass threatening or actually withholding their labor can they significantly affect the decision-making process. In democratic societies the labor force also has some effect through their voting power. However, since governments in these societies serve primarily to organize and administer the state rather than to exercise direct control over the production and distribution system, their influence seldom has a direct impact on the terms by which they labor.

The material and political inequities that are the basis of social class divisions in civilizations have been a continual source of trouble for these societies. Over the centuries civilizations have been jolted by revolutions, peasant and slave uprisings, labor strife, and common crimes as groups or individuals seek to effect either a personal or more general redistribution of wealth and power. The potential for such trouble is endemic to the organization of civilizations as class-based societies. The division of society into social classes and subclasses also requires the creation of a formal system of law.

CIVILIZATIONS AND THE EMERGENCE OF FORMAL LAW

Formal law consists of rules of conduct that are (1) enforced by the power of a political state, (2) administered by full-time law workers representing the state, and (3) usually represented in written codes or recorded court rulings. The emergence of formal law was brought about primarily by the need to administer and control property relations in civilizations. It has been said that the history of the concept of individual property and the history of law are inseparable.[17] Or as Jeremy Bentham commented, "Property and law are born together and die together."[18]

The advanced technologies and competition for material advantage that accompanied the development of civilizations brought with them three changes relevant to the emergence of formal law:

1. Increasingly differentiated work tasks
2. Centralized control over material surplus
3. The need for bureaucratic systems of administering property relations

While some of these factors are also present in intermediate states, that is, chiefdoms, they do not reach a sufficient level to require the development of formal legal systems.

Differentiated Work

Emile Durkheim categorized human societies into two ideal types: those characterized by "mechanical solidarity" and those characterized by "organic solidarity."[19] In a society marked by mechanical solidarity all individuals perform a number of different work tasks and are capable of meeting nearly all of their own needs on an individual basis. Both acephelous societies and chiefdoms approximate this ideal type. In these societies individual work tasks are varied and each small kin unit is capable of producing most of what it needs.

Societies marked by "organic solidarity" require that individuals perform specialized work tasks. Each person produces a smaller proportion of his or her own survival needs in comparison with people in simpler societies and therefore is highly dependent on the production of others. The modern industrial state, wherein very few individuals could survive by eating the products of their labor, is an approximation of Durkheim's concept of "organic solidarity."

Civilizations are based upon technologies that require the specialization of labor to produce surplus. As a result trade relations become an essential part of economic life, for individuals must offer their specialized outputs in return for daily necessities. In market relations it is the exchange of value and not the personal ties between individuals that is most important. Consider the difference in the way we reckon the value of an exchange of gifts between loved ones and the way we view the purchase of material items. Only in the market exchange is receiving equal value of primary importance.

Because of the importance of equal value in market relations, there is substantial room for conflict over value given and value received. As a result civilizations must have standard measures for reckoning value and formal mechanisms for resolving market conflicts.

The need to provide stable market relations is one of the key motivations in the creation of formal law. The creation of standard weights and measures and the coining of money become essential to complex market relations. This becomes particularly true as the network of trade becomes more extensive. The informal ties that bind individuals and create conformity and fair treatment in simple societies do not necessarily exist in trade relations among relative strangers.

The establishment of a politically based mechanism to resolve property disputes is an essential component of the emergence of state law. The political state, however, does not emerge as a simple spontaneous embodiment of the social will. The institutions and actions of political states tend to develop not in accordance with custom but with the views regarding right and wrong, desirable and undesirable that are held by those with the greatest opportunity to influence political decisions.[20] And those with this opportunity are generally those who wield the greatest economic power.

Law and the Control of Surplus

The rise of civilizations is characterized by the emergence of some group with the ability to command the extraction and redistribution of surplus. Law in its various forms (edicts, proclamations, court decisions, etc.) emerges along with civilizations as a mechanism whereby the will and visions of this dominant class can be represented to and, if necessary, forced on the general population.

The exact relationship between control of surplus and state power varies from one type of society to another. In many early imperial civilizations such as the Roman, Egyptian, Incan, and Mayan civilizations and the pre-Enlightenment states in Europe and England, the rights of economic ownership and law making were one and the same, and productive wealth was thus controlled directly through the state. State control of productive wealth is also characteristic of modern socialist states like the USSR and Cuba, although the concept of "ownership" of this wealth differs radically from other forms of economic organization. In capitalist states wealth is not controlled directly by the state but is owned by private individuals who may or may not be direct participants in state decision making. This is not to say the relationship between control of economic surplus and political power has been severed in capitalist societies. The will and vision of the ruling class remain the predominate influence shaping the state, although the political apparatus of democracy gives the state a quasi-independence that tends to obscure the multiple linkages between wealth and political power that remain central to the life of the state.

Whatever the particular relationship between economic power and political organization, as civilizations develop those with primary control over the productive wealth of the society seek mechanisms that will ensure a stable environment for the utilization of this wealth. Whatever these mechanisms are, they are instituted through the key tool of states to order social life: the law.

The Need for Bureaucracy

Civilizations represent the extension of centralized control over extensive geographical areas and large populations. To represent this centralized authority to many different people in many different places and circumstances civilizations require bureaucratic systems of delegated authority. The emergence of formal law is occasioned in part by the need to ensure consistency in the operation of these bureaucracies. The development of "common law" through a system of king's courts in early England exemplifies this need to provide consistency in the bureaucratic delegation of political authority. The essence of *common* law was not that it reflected the customs of the "common" people but that all people in the realm were *in common* governed by the same laws, as we shall see in the following section.

Another consequence of the need for the bureaucratic delegation of authority in civilizations is the creation of full-time law workers. The bureaucratic delegation of authority requires a stable work force trained in the operations of law and relatively committed to its purposes and the power it represents. Only in civilizations do we find the specialized functions of law enforcement, dispute judgment, and punishment being performed by designated individuals as their primary work activity. In nonstate societies and simple chiefdoms, individuals may serve these functions on an ad hoc basis but seldom as full-time law workers.

FROM TRIBALISM TO CIVILIZATION: THE FOUNDATIONS OF ENGLISH COMMON LAW

The transition from tribalism to civilization involves basic changes in almost all areas of social, economic, and political relations. One of the most fundamental is the shift from rule by custom to rule by formal law administered through a bureaucratic system of law enforcement. The basic characteristics of this change are exemplified by the emergence of the English monarchy and its system of common law. Though there presently exist important differences between the legal systems of England and the United States, it was during the period between the Norman Conquest of England and the settlement of the American colonies that many of the basic principles that eventually became part of the American system of justice were established. To understand why we define and deal with crime the way we do in America today we must first examine the legal and political roots of our justice system.

English common law emerged as an integral part of the transformation of England from a loose collection of what were essentially tribal chiefdoms or proto-states to a centrally governed civilization. By 500 A.D. the land that was to become England had been settled by diverse cultural groups migrating from the European continent and the Scandinavian peninsula. For these various tribal groups order was based not on law but on custom. Rules of conduct were not made, but as historian Helen Cam wrote, were "found" in the established customs. These customs were not the creation of some centralized authority, but rather were

> The possession of the people, preserved in the memory of men . . . declared by them in their local assemblies where they did justice to one another, finding the custom that applied to the case and adjusting it at need.[21]

The customary mechanisms for dispute settlement prior to the Norman Conquest of England in 1066 were similar to those found in many other tribal societies. As the legal historian Julius Goebel observed,

> In general the Anglo-Saxon system of dealing with wrongdoing corresponds with that of the continental folklaws, that is to say, it is based upon emendation substituting for feud . . . specific amends tarrif for personal injuries, value compensation for theft, bargain procedure and a sparing use of afflictive penalty.[22]

The emphasis in preconquest, Anglo-Saxon society was upon restoring social equilibrium when it was disrupted by trouble and compensating the victim of trouble rather than punishing the troublemaker. Disputes were treated as essentially personal matters to be settled through negotiation and restitution.

Over a 400-year period, from the eighth to the eleventh centuries, this system of compensatory justice became increasingly formalized as the hierarchical organization of feudalism began to slowly replace the more collective and egalitarian organization of the early tribal peoples in England. Wars between various tribal groups brought growing political consolidation and increasing individual ownership of land by powerful lords. As the once collectively owned tribal lands came under the private ownership and control of feudal lords, the responsibility of an individual to his kinsmen was replaced by the responsibility of a person to his lord. Where the collective responsibility of kin-groups had once served as the basis of dispute settlement, it now became the responsibility and the *prerogative* of feudal lords to see that justice was done to and for those under their control.

During the early feudal era compensation remained the primary mechanism for dispute resolution. However, it was no longer negotiated between kin-groups. As a means of consolidating power, emerging feudal lords began requiring that disputes be submitted to a local "court" for settlement. Compensation ceased to be an option as individuals were increasingly required to submit their troubles to their lord rather than their kin.

By the time of the Norman Conquest in 1066, England was organized into approximately eight large kingdoms, which were at best loosely knit collections of relatively independent feudal landholdings. The basic units of social and political organization were the counties and "hundreds." The hundreds were subdivisions of counties, somewhat obscure in their origin but often privately owned and independently governed. It is estimated that at the time of the Norman Conquest approximately half of all the hundreds were privately owned either by individual lords or by abbeys.[23] The large number of hundreds owned and governed by abbeys is an indication of what a powerful economic and political force the Catholic Church was in preconquest England, a situation that would bring it into direct conflict with a growing secular government in later years.[24]

Disputes arising among residents of the hundreds were required by lords, abbots, or abbeses to be submitted to the hundred courts. These "courts," however, should not be confused with modern-day law courts. The hundred courts were essentially meetings of important hundred residents at which all manner of local problems were discussed, among them the resolution of local disputes.

The right to hold court *and to profit from it* was the essential hallmark of a feudal ruler:

> The lord of a hundred is the person who has the hundredal soke; the right, that is, to exact attendance at the hundred court and *the right to take some if not all of the profits of justice arising there.*[25] (emphasis added)

The profits arising from court resulted from the transformation of dispute resolution from kin-based compensation to politically administered justice. Early feudal rulers required not only that disputes be submitted to them for resolution, but that compensatory damages be paid, not to the offended party but to the lord of the hundred. These compensatory damages were paid usually through the forfeiture of the individual's landholdings or other property to the lord of the hundred. In some cases, a portion of this forfeited property was then given to the victim as compensation, but in nearly all cases, a portion, and often all, of the forfeited property was retained by the lord. This right of a lord to collect the profits resulting from the administration of justice was to eventually become an essential force in the development of common law after the conquest.

In addition to the hundred courts, feudal justice was also administered in the county courts held by the overlords of counties. These overlords could command attendance at their courts by "the great men of the county (lords of the hundreds) and representatives of the lesser."[26] These early county courts prefigured the later bicameral (two-house) legislatures of England (House of Lords and House of Commons) and the United States (Senate and House of Representatives). The relationship between county and hundred courts also established a precedent for the latter relationship between lower and higher courts in both England and the United States. Because overlords of counties were in most cases more powerful both politically and economically than lords of hundreds, it was possible for county courts to review and even overrule decisions rendered by lords in hundred courts, much the same way as higher courts in the United States and England can review lower court decisions today.

At the time of the Norman Conquest feudal organization in England was not fully developed. By the eleventh century, the power of tribal organization had not yet been completely eliminated as a force for keeping order and resolving disputes; it had "not yet been fully displaced by the growing artificial bond of vassalage."[27] While county and hundred lords enjoyed some latitude in deciding disputes, they were not wholly free to do so as they saw fit because in many cases "custom decided what should be done, and generally who should do it."[28] By 1066 England was halfway between tribalism and feudalism, between rule by local custom and rule by state law.

The Norman Conquest

The importance of the Norman Conquest of England in 1066 for the development of English common law cannot be underestimated. By virtue of having "conquered" England, William the First was able to proclaim that all land, and all land-based rights, including those of keeping court, were now vested in the king. Individuals, William claimed, could now enjoy usage of the land and the court-keeping rights associated with lordship only through either franchise or direct grant from the king. This of course was more easily proclaimed than accomplished, and for the next 150 years the kings of England sought to consolidate their power and increase their treasury by transforming the once relatively independent and often custom-bound courts of counties and hundreds into bureaucratic arms of the crown.

William the Conqueror brought with him a large number of Norman noblemen who were given substantial grants of formerly Anglo-Saxon land in return for their support. William and his supporters also brought a far more centralized concept of government than had existed in preconquest England. Through this redistribution of the land with Norman nobles in positions of greatest power and the consolidation of all rights and relationships associated with land tenure under the crown, local courts eventually came under the administration of Norman rule.

Court-keeping rights were still granted in connection with land tenure. However, with these franchises came obligation of conducting courts in accordance with the king's interests, particularly his monetary interests. "Government in the upper tier was largely a matter of accounting for what had become due to the king from the lower."[29] Private landholders who, prior to the Norman Conquest were often real sources of judicial decisions, were slowly transformed into the functionaries of an increasingly bureaucratic system of justice.[30]

The king's interest in assuring a proper flow of justice-profits into the royal treasury brought about the institution of the *eyre*. Developed in the twelfth century as a powerful force for centralizing control over local courts, the eyre provided the structural basis for the development of a common law for England. The eyre consisted of itinerant judges representing the king who would periodically examine the activities of the county and hundred courts. "The coming of the justices in eyre was the coming of royal power," and it was apparently the cause of some anxiety at the local level. The first and most significant task of the eyre was the "pleas of the crown," which consisted essentially of a "list of questions, the articles of the eyre, about all matters of possible profit to the king."[31]

Of particular interest to the eyre was an accounting of cases involving acts of sufficient gravity to warrant forfeiture of the offender's property. The concept of forfeiture stemmed from the feudal doctrine that a man's right to hold property was based upon a relationship of good faith between that man and his lord. The term "felony" originally meant an offense "so fundamental as to break the relationship between them [a man and his lord] and to cause the holding to be forfeited to the lord."[32] Under Norman kings the concept of a violation of the king's peace was grafted onto this earlier doctrine of forfeiture. This enabled the king to claim the right to forfeit property for a broad miscellany of offenses that were not violations of the feudal contract in the original sense but were either affronts to the king or simple violations of order. It was through this doctrine of the king's peace that many forms of personal dispute came under the jurisdiction of state law. Acts of trespass and any harms done through force (*vi et armis*) were now defined as a violation of the feudal contract between the king and his subjects. It was the duty of the judges in eyre to insure that the king received his portion of forfeited property resulting from any such offenses occurring in the various county and hundred jurisdictions.

The doctrine of the "king's peace" was not created to insure public order or the punishment of offenders. This was handled at the level of the local community, particularly since the judges in eyre would usually arrive long after the offense had been committed and the offender punished. Its sole purpose was to provide a broader base of justice-profits for the king. Enforcement of the king's peace was profitable. As the English historian S. Francis Milsom noted, "Law and order on the national scale were first expressed in terms of revenue."[33]

The eyre began as primarily a review of prosecutions for crimes that had taken place in the county as a means of insuring that the king was paid his due. However, there soon evolved the notion that not only should the lords of the county report those offenses that had been prosecuted but that they were *obliged* to prosecute all possible offenses.

By the end of the 12th century the crown had placed upon local jurisdictions the obligation of charging suspects and ultimately bringing them before royal judges. The accuracy and diligence with which this was discharged was checked by the justices in eyre. Thus, the crown had managed to command that local citizenry through the county courts help insure that the proceeds from criminal prosecution were duly paid to the king, and that no potentially lucrative offenses went unpunished.[34]

This was the true beginning of a centralized legal order in England. No longer were communities able to resolve disputes in accordance with local custom. They were now bound to prosecute all acts deemed offensive *by the crown.* The lords of the counties and hundreds became bureaucrats in the royal machinery for manufacturing justice profits. Common disputes between in- dividuals became matters of state concern and state control, a legal doctrine that is the foundation of modern-day crime control by the state.

A secondary concern of the eyre was the hearing of common pleas. These were cases of ordinary litigation between ordinary citizens that could be presented to the eyre rather than the county or hundred court if the litigant chose to do so. This function of the eyre was not originally intended by the crown but arose through requests by citizens, most often Normans, that the eyre hear their cases.

After the conquest Norman settlers received not only land rights in England but the right to Norman rules of procedure in legal disputes. This produced a vested interest on the part of Norman settlers to have litigation heard in the king's courts rather than the traditional county or hundred courts.[35] The king's courts (of which the eyre was one) represented Norman concepts of law and justice, and it was advantageous and comforting for Normans to litigate disputes in these courts rather than local county and hundred courts, which in some cases were influenced by customs that were both unfamiliar and unacceptable to the Norman settlers.

It was the decisions made by the judges in eyre concerning the common pleas brought before them that produced the body of legal precedent that became known as the *common law,* that is, the rules of dispute settlement common to all England. As the itinerant judges in eyre settled common-plea cases they established precedents to be followed in similar cases. Because common law was built on a case-by-case basis the terms "common law" and "case law" are sometimes used synonymously. However, many of the specific precedents originally established through case law decisions in early England were later incorporated into legislated (i.e., statutory) law in both England and the United States.

Common law grew as judges in eyre were called upon to resolve an increasing number of disputes. However, the development of common law was an originally unintended by-product of the initial concern for producing a constant flow of justice-profits for the crown.

The development of English common law was not merely the institu- tionalization of traditional English customs. The rules of law established by the king's courts were often *unprecedented.* That is, they frequently differed from the local customs that, if followed, would not have served the crown's interest. The common law of England was "the by-product of an administrative triumph: the way in which the government of England came to be centralized and specialized during the centuries after the conquest."[36]

The establishment of common law in England did not begin with a commitment to some abstract concept of justice; it was rather a political response to a particular set of historical conditions, namely, the desire to unify England under centralized Norman rule. However, by seeking to eliminate variations in settlements arising from differences in local custom, the establishment of common law gave rise to a concept of justice that emphasized the *uniform* application of *standardized* laws and procedures. This concept was embodied in the doctrine of *stare decisis,* which emphasized the importance of legal consistency across time and place by requiring courts to adhere to the legal precedents established in previously settled cases. That is, once the courts had rendered a decision concerning a particular set of facts, it had to resolve future cases based on similar facts in approximately the same way. This particular concept of justice became a basic principle of Anglo-American law.

English common law emerged during the feudal era, a time when the only form of wealth and the only type of income-producing property was land. Consequently, the majority of the disputes submitted to the king's courts, and the precedents created by these courts, were concerned with defining property rights as they related to landownership. Common law was primarily oriented not toward protecting individuals from ordinary threats to person and property but toward maintaining social peace by regulating the economic arrangements characteristic of feudal land tenure and consolidating royal power under this system. Other than the requirement that they be submitted to king's magistrates for ajudication and review, no other innovations in the control of ordinary offenses such as larceny, trespass, murder, and assault occurred during the first 400 years of English common law. For the vast body of serfs, descendants of formerly free tribesmen now bound to the land under a feudal economy, the development of common law did little to improve either the security or the quality of their lives. If anything, its effects were negative. The common law of feudalism strengthened the bonds of their servitude and weakened the autonomy of the communities in which they lived to resolve disputes according to local custom.

The efforts of the Norman kings to consolidate their rule over all of England were only partially successful. In 1215, faced with the opposition of powerful landholders to the increasing authority of the crown, the king was forced to agree to the conditions of the Magna Carta. While this document is often hailed as a milestone in the development of individual liberty, its primary purpose was the resolution of a political dispute between two categories of elites—the landowning nobility and the crown. The masses derived no immediate benefit from this division of political power, which essentially curtailed the development of an absolute monarchy in favor of an oligarchy that was to control the life and law of England until the emergence of a new elite—the mercantilists. However, from a cultural point of view the signing of the Magna Carta was a significant event. It enshrined in law the basic principles of democratic government even if it failed to provide the structural conditions needed to fulfill these principles.

English Law and the Emergence of Capital

From the thirteenth to the sixteenth centuries, England, along with much of Europe, underwent fundamental changes in its economic system. This period of change was eventually to culminate in an economic order characterized by the division of society into a mass of propertyless wage laborers and a small group of wealthy employers. This development was not inevitable; it was the consequence of specific historical conditions. As Karl Marx wrote,

> Nature does not produce on the one side owners of money and commodities, and on the other men possessing nothing but their own labor-power. This relation has no natural basis, nor is its social basis one that is common to all historical periods. It is clearly the result of a past historical development, the product of many economic revolutions, of the extinction of a whole series of older forms of social production.[37]

The first step in the transition from feudalism to capitalism began with the emergence of trade as a significant source of wealth. Beginning in the late twelfth century with the trading of hides, cloth, and the products of guild craftsmen, there developed a class of merchants—individuals who dealt in *convertible* property.

Under feudalism land had been the primary form of wealth. However, it was not a form of wealth that could be bought or sold. Under laws of inheritance noble families held their lands in perpetuity. There were few ways to increase one's store of income-producing property other than advantageous marriage and outright military conquest. The economic order of feudalism also produced a particular form of social life, one that was characterized by little geographic mobility, integrated communities, and a set of mutual obligations between landowners and serfs. Outside of the small medieval towns, the population was tied to the land—nobles by the doctrine that the only legitimate access to landownership was through inheritance and serfs by the doctrine that serfs were part of a landowner's inheritance. Bound to the land, serfs were not free to sell their labor to the highest bidder, but neither could they be displaced from the land.

With the development of trade, wealth became fluid. Goods could be traded for money that could be used to purchase more goods that could in turn be sold for more money in an ever-increasing cycle of profit. With the development of mercantilism, wealth and power were no longer preordained by birth. Most importantly, this emergence of convertible property made possible the *accumulation of wealth* and the eventual emergence of capital.

Throughout the thirteenth and fourteenth centuries merchants in Europe and England began to amass fantastic fortunes while the land-based nobility found themselves increasingly burdened with the costs of maintaining armies and waging either defensive or offensive wars. Merchants, who had once been treated as social outcasts, increasingly found themselves in the advantageous position of being able to bankroll the military escapades of the landed nobility. Hereditary lands were mortgaged to members of the emerging mercantile class in return for the money to wage war. "Every war meant that the land of one of the parties in the conflict would fall to the merchant making the loan, and not to the winner of the battle."[38] Thus incrementally the wealth of England and Europe fell into the hands of the mercantile class. For this class land was not an historic birthright but merely another form of convertible property to be bought and sold in the search for profit. Land began to be separated from inheritance and thus from the obligations of inheritance, and the historic bonds between landowners and serfs began to disintegrate. As land passed into the hands of merchants, serfs were freed from their feudal ties to the land, becoming "free" labor. This meant that they were free to sell their labor, but it also meant that they had no right to a place on the land. Landholders under the emerging order were equally free not to buy the labor of these new freedmen.

This process was further accelerated by the willingness of many noblemen to sell serfs their freedom as another means of acquiring the needed revenues for military adventures and the desire of many serfs to migrate to the emerging industrial towns, which promised greater personal freedom and a higher standard of living. Life as "free" labor, however, offered mixed blessings:

> The historical movement which changes the producers into wage-workers, appears, on the one hand, as their emancipation from serfdom and from the fetters of the guilds. . . . But, on the other hand, these new freedmen became sellers of themselves only after they had been robbed . . . of all the guarantees of existence afforded by the old feudal arrangements.[39]

By capturing a greater share of the wealth of England, the growing mercantile class also captured a greater influence over the law of England. A common law designed primarily to protect the rights of feudal landownership was wholly inadequate to the needs of a class whose goal was the accumulation of profit through trade rather than the protection of hereditary lands. What was needed were laws that would protect capital and the rights to its accumulation, insure a steady flow of profitable trade goods, and control the problems posed by a growing class of mobile, urbanized laborers and artisans, no longer bound to the land, whose livelihoods were dependent upon the vagaries of both national and international trade. By the middle of the fifteenth century the English nobility, and even the crown, was firmly in debt to the mercantile class, and laws that would meet the needs of the powerful mercantile class began to emerge.

Protecting Capital

In feudal England larceny was intimately related to the crime of trespass, that is, taking something from someone who is in actual physical possession of it. During this period farm products, furniture, and cattle comprised nearly the sum total of movable property. The crime of larceny required trespass, or that the property be taken by force. All other forms of property disputes that did not involve trespass or force were treated under common law as civil matters—disputes that could be litigated in court but that were not actively prosecuted by the state.

The emergence of mercantilism created new possibilities for property disputes, and the state was called upon to decide the legal status of a new form of property: capital. A turning point in the concept of property crime occurred in 1473 with the resolution of the *Carrier's* case, which had been in dispute for some time. The facts of this case, as detailed by Jerome Hall in *Theft, Law and Society,* were that

> The defendant was hired to carry certain bales to Southhampton. Instead of fulfilling his obligation, he carried the goods to another place, broke open the bales and took the contents. He was apprehended and charged with felony.[40]

The problem posed by this case was that (1) the carrier had not committed trespass because he had lawfully acquired the bales from the merchant, i.e., he was in legal possession of the bales at the time he converted them for his own purposes and (2) the act was not committed *vi et armis.* Thus, while the carrier was charged with felony, there was in fact no basis in common law for charging him with a *criminal* offense. At this time, the only recourse found in common law for this act would have been a *civil* suit by the merchant against the carrier for a violation of contract. The courts of Star Chamber and then Exchequer were asked to decide whether the carrier's actions constituted a civil or a criminal wrong. That is, they were asked to decide whether the state should become the *active* protector of private individuals in their attempts to accumulate capital by declaring criminal those who interferred with such attempts.

While we may take the present laws of theft and fraud for granted, at the time of the *Carrier's* case, it was not at all clear whether the carrier had committed a *crime* or simply violated the terms of a contract. Justice Brian, reputed to be one of "the soundest of English judges," argued that because the carrier had physical possession of the bales he could not have committed a crime, and Brian's opinion was soundly supported by the weight of common law. Those judges representing the crown, however, argued that this case should be determined, *not by common law,* but by the "law of nature."[41] That is, they argued that the law of England and the procedural concept of *stare decisis* should be bypassed. Why they argued in this fashion can only be understood by placing the *Carrier's* case in the political and economic climate of the time.

The *Carrier's* case occurred only two years after Edward IV had recaptured the English throne, with the aid of the merchants of the Hanseatic League.

> It was on Hanseatic boats and under Hanseatic escort that Edward sailed to England, there to resume the war and emerge victorious on the battlefield of Barnet. For these services he promised to satisfy the Hanseatic complaints and demands. . . ."[42]

Edward was engaged in some capital accumulation of his own, having acquired merchant ships that he employed in trading through foreign agents.[43] Furthermore, Edward was well aware that his reign required the continued support of traders and merchants and that Richard III (whom he had defeated in the battle for the throne) had substantially weakened his own position by having alienated the mercantilists. Therefore, Edward "cultivated the business interests assiduously."[44]

The merchant involved in the *Carrier's* case was not a Hanseatic merchant but apparently an Italian. However, the principle of the case was of interest to all merchants operating in England; the opportunity to have the power of the state used to protect their interests in successfully transporting goods for trade would be a great help in the accumulation of capital. As Hall comments,

> It was to be expected that a king who was so definitely and so greatly indebted to mercantile interests, both native and foreign, would be sympathetic to these interests. . . .[45]

The evidence clearly indicates that at the time of the *Carrier's* case the judiciary was subservient to the will of the crown. Therefore, they ruled, not in favor of the English common law, but in favor of the merchant, as Edward wished.[46]

The actual ruling in the *Carrier's* case was based upon a clever legal fiction. It was decided that the carrier had possession of the bales but not their contents, that there is some intrinsic difference between a bundle of goods and the goods themselves. Because the carrier had broken open the bales, it was reasoned that he was guilty of trespass and could be punished as a criminal rather than merely sued for a civil wrong based on his failure to fulfill a contract. "By this refinement," Hall notes, "the door was open to admit into the law of larceny a whole series of acts which had up to that time been purely civil wrongs."[47]

Prior to the Carrier's decision, the English common law did not recognize as criminal any individual who legally acquired the physical possession of another's property and then at a later time converted it to his own use. The protection of such transferred property rested with its original owner, who it was assumed was responsible for selecting trustworthy persons to handle his property.[48] Had this view continued it would have evolved into the dictum of *caveat merchant,* that is, let those who seek to accumulate wealth through business transactions be solely responsible for the consequences of those transactions. However, the decision in the *Carrier's* case established that it was appropriate for the state to use its *criminal law* apparatus to help insure a stable and predictable environment for the accumulation of profit.

This development represented a significant change in the legal status of profit making. During the earlier feudal era profit making through mercantilism was held in such low social and moral esteem that merchants were often banned from medieval towns, and profit making through lending money was so despised an activity that in much of medieval England and Europe it was illegal for anyone except Jews—who at this time were considered social outcasts anyway—to lend money for profit. With the shift from feudalism to mercantilism the accumulation of capital rather than the husbandry of hereditary lands became the central productive process in the society. As capital became more central it increasingly enjoyed state protection in the form of criminal laws designed to punish those who interfered with what had come to be acceptable forms of capital accumulation.

Statutory Law and Labor

From the Norman conquest until the mid–fourteenth century nearly all of England was divided into feudal holdings with a considerable serf population bound to these holdings. Geographic mobility was strictly limited, and generation after generation of serfs were born and died on the fiefdom to which they were bound. During the later stages of feudalism, however, the landed aristocracy of England began experiencing increasing difficulty in finding sufficient supplies of cheap labor. The combination of the Black Death, which reached England in 1348 and eventually killed an estimated 50 percent of the island's entire population, and the emergence of mercantilism, which required free labor to produce trade goods, brought to an end the easy availability of people to work the land.[49] Many fiefdoms were forced to hire into their service persons who were not part of their hereditary serf population. At the same time, towns that were controlled primarily by mercantile and craft interests would offer asylum to any bound serf who reached them since such immigrants would provide a source of labor for the production of trade goods.

During this period of rapid social change the law was called upon by both the landed aristocracy and the mercantilists to provide a measure of social and economic stability. Because it is built incrementally, on a case-by-case basis, common law changes slowly, and hence significant alterations may take generations to develop. Common law was therefore ill suited for responding to rapid social change unless, of course, the courts departed radically from precedent, as they did in the *Carrier's* case.

Statutory law, on the other hand, consists of written rules enacted by some legislative body such as a parliament or congress, proclaimed by some central authority such as a king or emperor, or specified in a constitution. By a single act a legislature or a ruler can create an entirely new law or significantly modify an older one, making statutory law a far better tool for responding to social change than common law. Statutory law therefore played an increasingly important role in defining social order during the transition from feudalism to capitalism in England. Of particular importance during this time was insuring a supply of cheap labor for both agrarian and mercantile tasks and controlling the social dangers posed by a new category of people—the urbanized unemployed. These needs were met by the enactment and modification of a number of statutory laws that were to play an important role in shaping Anglo-American legal tradition.

Controlling Productive Labor.   In the early stages of the competition between landed interests and mercantile interests, the law of England was brought into service on the side of the aristocracy. The 1349–1351 Statute of Labourers required that all able-bodied persons, currently unemployed, be *required* to accept any employment offered.

> . . . if he in convenient service [his estate considered] be required to serve, shall be bounded to serve him which shall require. . . . And if any refuse, he shall on conviction by two true men . . . be committed to goal till he find surety to serve.[50]

The Statute of Laborers also fixed wages at the pre–Black Death level and prohibited either offering or accepting higher wages.[51] That the purpose of the statute was to guarantee the landed elite a supply of cheap labor by insuring that workers could not use the scarcity of labor to demand higher wages is clear from the introduction to the law:

> Because great part of the people, and especially of workmen and servants, late died in pestilence; *many seeing the necessity of masters, and the great scarcity of servants, will not serve without excessive wages* . . . it is ordained that every man and woman, of what condition he be, free or bond, able in body and within the age of threescore years, not living in merchandise . . . be required to serve. . . .[52] (emphasis added)

The provision for fixed wages was particularly important to the landed elite because it defined as "excessive" the higher wages that laborers could command by working in those trades and crafts that supplied the mercantile interests. Despite this, the position of the aristocracy continued to deteriorate, and in 1388 the law was further modified to help shore up their weakening ability to compete for labor by prohibiting those who worked on the land from entering the trades.

> . . . he or she which use to labour at the plough and cart, or other labour and service of husbandry, till they be of the age of 12 years, from thenceforth shall abide at the same labour without being put to any mistery or handicraft: and any covenant of apprenticeship to the contrary shall be void.[53]

The Statute of Laborers, as noted by sociologist William Chambliss in "A Sociological Analysis of the Law of Vagrancy," was clearly designed to protect the interests of what was at that time the most powerful economic elite—the landed aristocracy—by *criminalizing* individuals who would not serve those interests by working for artificially low wages.[54] The importance of this for both the English and the American legal tradition cannot be underestimated. It clearly established the precedent that it was appropriate for the state to use *criminal sanctions* to help insure that the laboring class did not disrupt the economic order or interfere with the prerogatives of the economic elite by attempting to control the conditions of their employment.

Controlling Surplus Labor. By the middle of the fifteenth century the balance of power had shifted to the mercantilists, and as already indicated, their interests began to take precedent over those of the landed aristocracy with the accession of Edward III. Of primary importance to mercantilists was a supply of *free labor,* that is, a body of laborers not bound to the land and therefore "free" to enter into trades and crafts and "free" to sell their products to merchants at the market price for these goods. This economic theory of "freedom," however, also meant that each individual was responsible for his own survival. If an individual could sell his labor or his goods in the free marketplace he had a right to whatever, but only whatever, his income could buy. If he was unable to find a buyer for his labor or goods, he had little legitimate claim on the necessities of survival and certainly none on the objects of material luxury. By defining all economic relations as "free," this view obscured the gross imbalance in bargaining power between those with the capital to buy labor as part of their search for *profit* and those who had to sell their labor in order to survive.

To the extent that the labor market at any one time could not absorb all of the available wage laborers seeking work there emerged a body of "free" but surplus labor. The size of the surplus labor force increased in bad economic times and shrank during good ones. In particular, it increased with the increase in size of the "free" labor force at the onset of the enclosure movement. Under feudalism serfs held a customary right to use certain parcels of "common" land to grow crops for their own subsistence. As a means of making available more pasture land for sheep and cattle, whose wool and hides were the basis of mercantile trade in wool and leather, these common lands were redefined by law as "private" property no longer available to serfs. Deprived of a means to produce their own subsistence, thousands upon thousands of former serfs were forced to leave the rural communities of their ancestry and seek a living through wage labor.

The existence of this body of surplus labor was advantageous to the developing capitalist economy. This "army of unemployed" served as a means of holding wages to the bare minimum by providing a ready pool of replacements for any of those employed who were not satisfied with their lot and as a continual reminder to workers that they were fortunate to have any job at all. At the same time, however, this body of surplus labor was clearly a threat to the social order of fifteenth- and sixteenth-century England. It was well recognized by statesmen of the time that wage labor produced a class of people "of worse condition to be governed quietly than the husbandman," particularly when the fortunes of the economy caused them to be unemployed and to "assemble in companies and murmur for lack of living."[55] Furthermore, a once settled agrarian population was now becoming an increasingly transient laboring class. As Walensky and Lebaux wrote,

> Should the workings of an impersonal market cast him [the laborer] in the role of unemployed, he had to hunt out another job (if there was one) which often meant another neighborhood or community.[56]

This produced a constantly moving body of "strangers," often impoverished and desperate, who threatened the security of travel and the transportation of goods. Additionally, if they could not find work in the places to which they traveled, these unemployed laborers became a burden upon the local relief measures, church-based organizations designed to handle only the worthy poor of the city or town and in no way prepared to serve outsiders. To cope with the growing threat posed by the body of surplus labor, legal remedies such as the laws of vagrancy and the Statute of Artificers were brought to bear.

As William Chambliss details, by the beginning of the sixteenth century the laws of vagrancy had begun to treat with increasing harshness those who were unemployed, wandered in search of work, or turned to "divers and subtil crafty and unlawful games and plays" as a source of income.[57]

Because the developing economic theory of capitalism emphasized the "free" nature of market relations, it was easily assumed that those without employment, had in some way "freely" chosen that condition through lack of industry, moral failing, deviant tendencies, or plain laziness. With these beliefs as a background it was easy to define such persons as criminals and threats to social order who should find no sympathy in the law. By the mid–sixteenth century the mere condition of being unemployed had become a criminal offense:

> Whoever man or woman, being not lame, impotent or so aged or diseased that he or she cannot work, not having whereon to live, shall be lurking in any house, or loitering or idle wandering by the highway side, or in streets, cities, towns, or villages, not applying themselves to some honest labour, and so continuing for three days; *or running away from their work;* every such person shall be taken for a vagabond. And upon conviction of two witnesses . . . the same loiterer [shall] be marked with a hot iron in the breast with the letter V, and adjudged him to the person bringing him, to be his slave for two years.[58] (emphasis added)

This particular statute served a number of purposes. By making unemployment a crime, and particularly by defining those who left employment as criminal, it placed employers in an exceedingly advantageous bargaining position. Laborers were compelled to accept the wages and whatever working conditions were offered or risk being declared vagabond. Incidentally, the law also provided an additional source of cheap labor in the form of those convicted of vagabondage and turned over to their accusers as slaves for two years. Most importantly, however, it reflected the growing tendency to control the surplus labor force through the use of criminal sanctions. That is, the law was used to define the victims of the social upheavals associated with the emergence of capitalism as criminally responsible for the negative consequences these changes brought to their lives.

Like the laws of vagrancy, the Law of Artificers of 1563 was designed to regulate labor in the trades and crafts, and like the modifications to the laws of vagrancy, it was aimed at combating the problems posed by a growing urbanized and mobile work force that suffered periods of high unemployment.

> The growth of industry, the uncertainties of the market, unemployment and idleness, discontent and vagabondage, violence and rebellion—this was the fatal sequence which must be prevented. Nearly all the steps in it were attacked by some one or more sections of the compendious statute enacted in 1563.[59]

The Law of Artificers is often viewed as the product of a proagrarian movement because it sought to limit the growth of industry by (1) prohibiting the apprenticeship of anyone already engaged in husbandry, (2) requiring that apprenticeships be of seven years' duration, thus limiting the rate at which tradesmen could enter the "free" labor market, and (3) restricting the right of laborers and craftsmen to move freely from one town to another seeking employment. However, both generally and specifically this law was also of considerable benefit to the growing capitalist class. While the mercantile capitalists desired a pool of "free" labor that could be moved in and out of the market as desired, an overlarge pool of discontented labor could foment, as it almost did in the insurrection of 1549, a rebellion that would destroy the social order enabling the capitalists to amass impressive fortunes amidst great general poverty.[60] By limiting the entrance of laborers into the trades and crafts, the pool of "free" labor—and consequently the pool of surplus labor—was kept at a *manageable* level. The requirement of seven years' apprenticeships insured a supply of cheap labor and provided existing craftsmen with a near-monopoly situation. Limits on the geographic mobility of laborers served to further weaken their ability to compete successfully in the "free market" for better wages.

SUMMARY: ENGLISH LAW AND AMERICAN CULTURE

The transition from tribalism to state law in England is characteristic of the process by which civilizations emerge. The development of some form of centralized power makes possible taxation and control over formerly customary forms of dispute resolution. In England these things were closely linked. The establishment of Norman rule led to the growth of state-mandated control over court procedures, initially as a means of generating revenue for the crown. This, however, required the creation of bureaucratic mechanisms for the enforcement of crown interests, the eyre being the first of these. As a result of the eyre and the eventual development of common law the right of individual kin-groups and communities to resolve disputes through informal and customary means was eliminated. At this point England had reached full maturity as a civilization governed by state law rather than popular justice.

The historical development of English law also demonstrates the interconnectedness of economic and political processes. As the mode of production in England shifted from feudalism to capitalism, so the basic structure and concerns of the law shifted, in this case away from protecting hereditary land rights and toward protecting privately owned capital. The one thing that did not change was the pattern of who was most able to shape the law. In both eras the law was fundamentally shaped by those who owned the productive wealth of the society. Under feudalism this group consisted of the landed aristocracy. Under emerging mercantile capitalism it was the merchant owners of private capital. While the emergence of capitalism led to a formal separation of government and wealth—the wealthiest were no longer necessarily the actual law makers—this did not mean that the wealthholders lost their ability to channel the law in directions that best served their interests.

English legal traditions and English law have had a substantial impact upon American legal thought. The Magna Carta and the development of the English Parliament predisposed the English colonies and later the fledgling American nation to establish constitutional governments and systems of legislative law making. Our definitions of many ordinary crimes against person or property, such as murder, rape, robbery, larceny, assault, and arson, are derived directly from English common law.

The practice of relying heavily on precedents established in common law to interpret statutes enacted by legislative bodies is also derived from the English common law system. While state legislatures or Congress may enact laws, it remains the province of the courts to interpret those laws and determine their constitutionality through examination and application of precedents established in common law. Likewise, the American practice of creating legislative bodies consisting of two separate units (e.g., a Senate and a House of Representatives) can be traced back to the early English county courts when "the great men of the county and representatives of the lesser" gathered to conduct county business and settle disputes. In short, "the principles developed in the common law became the basic law of all of the United States."[61] In addition to specific legal principles, several general themes that first emerged in postfeudal English law were reflected in the development of law in America.

Overall, during the 300 years preceding the establishment of English colonies in North America three important innovations were introduced into English law and English legal thought. First, law became an important ally of those seeking to maximize profit through capitalist market relations by defining many acts that disrupted the predictability of market relations as crimes, that is, as harms against the state, rather than as civil violations of contracts between individuals. Second, criminal law came to be seen as an appropriate tool for insuring an adequate supply of cheap labor, first for the agrarian economy and later for the developing industrial-mercantile economy of early capitalist England. Third, and perhaps most importantly for contemporary criminal law, members of the laboring class who turned to theft, violence, idleness, or other forms of deviance as an adaptation to the brutal conditions of their lives were defined as criminals. In doing so, the English state absolved the emerging capitalists, who profited greatly from the brutal conditions of working class life, of all responsibility for the consequences of these conditions. These innovations were to have an important impact upon the development of American legal thought and practice in the following centuries.

Law is not easily separated from the body of cultural beliefs about how society *ought* to function. Law plays an important role in shaping cultural beliefs in state societies as well as being shaped by them. As succeeding generations live under a particular social system sanctioned and protected by state law, there tends to develop a set of broadly shared cultural beliefs that explain why this particular system is both right and natural.

The force of law is a powerful source for building habit, and the habit of behaving a certain way, particularly if carried on through several generations, easily leads to belief about that behavior. For example, if a state passes a law that says "it is criminally wrong to marry your cousin" and is *capable* of enforcing that law, there will be a decrease in cousin marrying. After several generations of persons have grown up knowing that cousin marrying is criminally punishable, there will be a tendency to think "we don't marry cousins in this society." That is, what was at one time wrong primarily because it was punished tends to become wrong in the minds of individuals simply because it is not done, or done infrequently. It is in this way that revolutions, which are often supported only by a minority of a society, can over time result in a society the majority of which adhere to tenets of the revolution. When a revolution captures the law of a state society, it captures a tool that can and most often is used to alter the consciousness of the people in that society. Changing consciousness through changing law is a long-term process far more complex than simply passing a law and enforcing it for several years. However, it is through this process that changes in the consciousness in state societies are often brought about.

The shift from an agrarian to a mercantile economy in England was a situation characterized by tremendous social upheaval and cultural ambiguity. The laws developed at this time benefited both from a lack of organized cultural opposition and the fact that their enforcement was strongly supported by the most powerful members of the society. The various legal themes discussed above were born in social change and conflict, but they came eventually to reflect a degree of social consensus, a social consensus they served to create. This often unrecognized fact has led to considerable debate between those supporting a consensus model of law and those supporting a conflict model of law. Consensus theorists support their view by pointing to the popular agreement that appears to exist concerning the basic criminal laws of American society while conflict theorists find support in the historical records that demonstrate the importance of power and social conflict in determining the character and enforcement of these laws. Both these assertions are empirically correct but theoretically inadequate, for they fail to examine the dynamic relationship between culture and law. It is this relationship that over several centuries can transform laws clearly made to support powerful minority interests into broadly supported embodiments of cultural belief.

The legal trends that developed in mercantile England served to support the interests of the mercantile class and to control the threats posed by an impoverished and restless laboring class. However, by the time the colonies were established they had become incorporated as basic themes within English culture. This is not to say that they were supported unanimously, for in complex society almost nothing receives unanimous support from all sectors. Yet these themes were sufficiently accepted to provide a cultural basis for the development of law in the American colonies and later the independent American state, as we shall see in the next chapter.

NOTES

1. Max Gluckman, "The Kingdom of the Zulu of South Africa," in M. Fortes and Evans-Prichard, eds., *African Political Systems* (New York: Oxford University Press, 1961), 33.
2. Stephen Schafer, *The Victim and His Criminal* (New York: Random House, 1968), 21–33.
3. Gluckman, "The Kingdom of the Zulu," p. 35.
4. Henry Maine, *Ancient Law* (London: J. Murray, 1905), 140.
5. Nils Christie, "Youth as a Crime Generating Phenomenon," in Barry Krisber and James Austin, eds., *Children of Ishmael* (Palo Alto, Calif.: Mayfield Publishing Co., 1978), 226.
6. Stanley Diamond, "The Rule of Law vs. The Order of Custom," in Richard Quinney, ed., *Criminal Justice in America* (Boston: Little Brown Co., 1974), 37.
7. Ibid., 41.
8. David Hunter and Philip Whitten, *The Study of Anthropology* (New York: Harper & Row, 1976), 84.
9. Robert Ardrey, *The Territorial Imperative* (New York: Atheneum, 1966).
10. John H. Bodley, *Victims of Progress* (Menlo Park, Calif.: Cummings Publishing Co., 1975), 45–59.
11. Hunter and Whitten, *The Study of Anthropology*, 85.
12. Ibid., 86; see also Karl Marx, "So-called Primitive Accumulation," in *Capital*, vol. 1 (Moscow: Progress Publishers, 1978), 669.
13. Marvin Harris, *Culture, People, Nature* (New York: Thomas Crowell, 1975), 373–380.
14. Ibid., 297.
15. Ibid., 299.
16. Ibid., 298.
17. Maine, *Ancient Law*.
18. Quoted in Diamond, "The Rule of Law," 33.
19. Emile Durkheim, *The Division of Labor in Society*, trans. George Simpson (New York: Free Press, 1964).
20. Alexander B. Smith and Hariet Pollack, *Crime and Justice in Mass Society* (New York: Rinehard Press, 1972), 65.
21. Helen Cam, *Law Finders and Law Makers in Medieval England* (New York: Barnes and Noble, 1963), 12.
22. Julius Goebel, *Felony and Misdemeanor: A Study in the History of Criminal Law* (Philadelphia: University of Pennsylvania Press, 1976), 341.
23. S. Francis Milsom, *The Historical Foundations of the Common Law* (London: Butterworths, 1969), 5.
24. Ibid., 2.
25. Cam, *Law Finders and Law Makers*, 60.
26. Milsom, *Historical Foundations of Common Law*, 4.
27. Goebel, *Felony and Misdemeanor*, 341.
28. Milsom, *Historical Foundations of Common Law*, 2.
29. Ibid., 15.
30. Cam, *Law Finders and Law Makers*, 43.
31. Milsom, *Historical Foundations of Common Law*, 17.
32. Ibid., 355.
33. Ibid., 13.

34. Ibid., 357.
35. Goebel, *Felony and Misdemeanor*, 384.
36. Milsom, *Historical Foundations of Common Law*, 1.
37. Karl Marx, "Capital," in *Karl Marx: Selected Writings*, trans. T. B. Bottomore (New York: McGraw-Hill, 1956), 131.
38. Mark C. Kennedy, "Beyond Incumination: Some Neglected Facets of the Theory of Punishment," *Catalyst*, no. 5 (Summer 1970): 13.
39. Marx, "Capital," 135.
40. Jerome Hall, *Theft, Law, and Society* (Indianapolis: Bobbs-Merrill, 1952), 4.
41. Ibid., 5.
42. M. M. Posten, *Studies in English Trade*, quoted in Hall, *Theft, Law, and Society*, 28.
43. Hall, *Theft, Law, and Society*, 28.
44. Ibid., 22.
45. Ibid., 27–28.
46. Ibid., 18.
47. Ibid., 10.
48. Ibid., 31.
49. Thomas Bradshaw, *A Social History of England* (London: W. B. Clive, 1918).
50. 23 Ed. 111.
51. Caleb Foote, "Vagrancy Type Law and Its Administration," *University of Pennsylvania Law Review*, 104 (1956): 615.
52. 25 Ed. III, c. 2.
53. 12 R. II.
54. William J. Chambliss, "A Sociological Analysis of the Law of Vagrancy," *Social Problems*, 12 (Summer 1964): 67–77.
55. Quoted in Margaret Gay Davies, *The Enforcement of English Apprenticeship* (Cambridge, Mass.: Harvard University Press, 1956), 34.
56. Harold L. Walensky and Charles M. Lebaux, *Industrial Society and Social Welfare* (New York: Free Press, 1965), 58.
57. Chambliss, "A Sociological Analysis of the Law of Vagrancy," 72.
58. 1 Ed. VI, c. 3.
59. Davies, *The Enforcement of English Apprenticeship*, 2.
60. Ibid., 4.
61. Hazel B. Kerper, *Introduction to the Criminal Justice System* (St. Paul, Minn.: West Publishing Co., 1972), 27.

CHAPTER 5

Development of Law in the American State

Introduction: The English Heritage of American Law

When the first English settlers arrived in the New World they brought with them founding charters granted by the English government and a centuries-old tradition of common law. Although the legal system in America today differs in a number of significant ways from contemporary English law, the roots of both systems reach far back into English history. England's transition from a quasi-tribal society to a full-fledged capitalist civilization laid the groundwork for many elements of the legal order that we take for granted today. Key among these were (1) the right of the state to ajudicate disputes between individuals, (2) the right of courts to create legal precedent, (3) the role of the state in providing and promoting a secure environment for economic growth, (4) the validity of using state law to shape the labor market, and (5) the legitimacy of using state law to control the negative consequences of unemployment and poverty when manifested in the form of crime, unrest, and other social problems.

In addition to these specific characteristics, the history of law building in England established another fundamental characteristic of law in the liberal, bourgeois state: the two-class system of law that defined economic elites as essentially free from legal liability for the harms resulting from their pursuit of profit (e.g., poverty, unemployment, dislocations, vagabondage, etc.) while placing the working class under strict legal control for the types of harms its members might have the opportunity to commit (e.g., common theft, interpersonal violence, riot, etc.). The legal system of England evolved in such a way as to criminalize most of the harmful acts *available* to members of the working classes while at the same time placing the emerging class of capitalist elites beyond incrimination for the very real harms that they, *and only they,* could visit upon large numbers of individuals at any one time.

LAW IN THE COLONIAL ERA: 1611–1781

Social Class and Ideology in the Colonies

At the beginning of the seventeenth century English society was characterized by a variety of social classes. Not all of these, however, were transplanted to the new world in equal measure. Particularly underrepresented were the declining feudal aristocracy, the bureaucrats and courtiers of the royal court, and the landless rural poor. The absence of these groups meant that "There was a corresponding absence of the belief system of these strata—the ideologies of waning feudalism, royal absolutism and/or rural traditionalism."[1] While class division among the colonists ranged from wealthy rural landowners to comfortable urban merchants and craftsmen to propertyless and usually penniless indentured servants and laborers, there was by and large a general acceptance among these settlers of a *liberal bourgeois ideology.* This particular way of viewing the world held that humans were rational beings with inherent rights to own, acquire, and manipulate property; enter into voluntary contracts to buy and sell anything they saw fit, including labor; and, where *men* of substance were concerned, participate in a degree of self-governance. According to this view *the ideal form of society would emerge naturally if individuals pursuing their own economic ends were allowed the freedom to enter into whatever voluntary contracts they felt were in accord with these personal goals.* This ideology was an important and recurring theme in the development of law in colonies and later the American state. It served as the basis for the American concept of "rights" and as the ideological justification for a broad spectrum of laws and decisions denying that the powerless were any less "free" to choose the conditions of their existence than the wealthy and powerful.

Criminal Law in the Colonies

The first legal code in the colonies, the "Lawes Divine, Morall and Martiall" of Virginia, sometimes known as Dale's Code, was established in 1611. Where crimes were concerned it was stern and uncompromising. Even seemingly minor crimes such as the theft of food or a boat could be punished by death. As one historian commented, however, such harsh penalties were essentially reflections of the difficulties of the time. The early years of the Virginia colony were referred to as the "starving time," and the harsh laws of this time "speak not so loudly of severity as they do of the importance of the stores [food] and of the boat."[2] After this colony became more firmly established Dale's code was replaced by one which lessened the punishments for more minor offenses.

Generally criminal cases in the colonies were an assortment of common law and moral offenses. In 1641 the Massachusetts Body of Liberties gave that colony its first formal body of laws.[3] A study of court records for colonial Massachusetts found that prosecutions were a mixture of offenses against morals, property, and persons, with offenses against church or morals constituting the largest single category. According to Nelson, between 1760 and 1774 there were 2,784 criminal prosecutions in Superior and General sessions courts in Massachusetts. Of these, 13 percent (355 cases) were for crimes against property such as robbery, breaking and entering, larceny, receiving stolen goods, and counterfeiting. Crimes of violence contributed another 15 percent (419 cases). Together crimes against property and persons constituted only 28 percent of all criminal prosecutions in Massachusetts between 1760 and 1774 while *38 percent* of all criminal prosecutions during that time period (1,074 cases) were for sex-related offenses such as adultery, cohabitation, indecent exposure, lewdness, prostitution, and fornication, with charges of fornication constituting 95 percent of all sex-related cases. Another 13 percent (359 cases) of the criminal prosecutions were for specifically church-related offenses such as missing services, working on Sunday, or blasphemy. The remaining 21 percent (577 cases) were for a broad variety of offenses, with prosecutions for killing the king's deer, various forms of market frauds such as using false weights or selling spoiled foods, and libel among the most common.[4]

The courts of colonial Massachusetts were not alone in their concern with "enforcing puritanical religious and moral standards."[5] Most colonies, particularly during the early colonial period, made little distinction between crime and sin.[6] This concern with "morality," however, does not mean that colonial law was unconcerned with protection of other, less spiritual components of the economic and political order. While "morality" in most Western societies is seen as deriving from some relationship between individuals and a God, it also serves as a blueprint for arranging more earthly matters.

The creation of a stable economic and political environment and the establishment of a moral society were seen by many early colonial leaders as a single task. Laws governing matters of personal moral behavior were enforced not only with a view toward protecting the souls of the colonists but the stability of the social order.

For colonists, fornication was not only an act against the will of God but also one that could add fatherless children to the community's economic burden. It is for this reason that most prosecutions for fornication were initiated against unmarried women who became pregnant and that most penalties required the alleged father to make some provision for the illegitimate child.[7] Where such arrangements could not be made fornicators were often placed in indenture if they appeared to have no means of support readily available such as a family willing to shelter the woman and her child. The law's concern was not simply in stopping the *sin* of fornication but in controlling the negative economic consequences such acts could foster.

Similarly, insolence and disobedience were often treated as serious forms of immorality. This was not a strictly theological concern. In a society that relied heavily on the labor of indentured servants, laws prohibiting disobedience and insolence also protected the economic order by creating a *legal obligation* that servants and slaves remain subservient to their masters. In this case the power of law to enforce what on the surface appears to be strictly a matter of theological concern actually had a significant bearing on the underlying basis of economic order.

The laws governing debtors and creditors in the Massachusetts colony also reveal the close relationship between the enforcement of morality and the maintenance of social order in the colonies. These laws provided creditors with broad latitude in collecting debts while leaving debtors almost totally powerless. For example, if a person failed to meet a mortgage debt on a piece of property, the mortgage holder had the right not only to reclaim the property but also to sue for payment of the mortgage—even if the repossessed property was of equal or greater value than the debt.[8] That is, if a man owed $2,000 on a piece of property, he would often *still* be in debt for $2,000 even after the property was repossessed and even if the mortgage holder had been able to recoup the debt by selling the land to someone else for $2,000. Attempts by debtors to have established laws of insolvency that would permit the discharge of a debt by giving the creditor everything the debtor owned met with repeated failure. First, the legal arrangements that gave nearly all the power to creditors were a forceful implementation of the liberal bourgeois concept of the sanctity of free contract. If the debtor had agreed to undertake the debt, there should be no leeway in the law permitting him or her to avoid its fulfillment. Further, in the minds of many the issue was a moral and not merely a practical or economic one. Debts occurred because people were displaying an immoral concern for the material things of this world instead of giving primary consideration to the state of their souls and preparation for the afterlife. As Cotton Mather, one of the most influential religious and political leaders of the Massachusetts colony, proclaimed, "the grand cause of peoples running into debt" was their unwillingness to "bear the humiliations of a low and mean condition in the world," instead trying to create lives "lived in splendor."[9] Thus, while the Massachusetts debt laws provided great direct benefit to those who were affluent enough to be creditors instead of debtors, the laws themselves were couched in the language of morality. Moreover, it is likely that they were perceived in those terms, even by those whose direct economic self-interest was being served. The language of morality spoke of the duty to honor contracts and the obligation to accept one's place in society.

For the leadership of colonial Massachusetts the appropriate order was one based on rigid Christian morality and a division of society into ranks or stations, with lower ranks willingly accepting the moral superiority of the higher ones and for this reason submitting to their rulership. Morality was accepting this vision; immorality was to violate it.

In addition to these more indirect ways of preserving the established order through the enforcement of religious morality, colonial law also reflected, often more directly, the need of colonial economies for protection and facilitation. In Virginia, for example, where hogs were a more important source of income than sheep, it was a more serious crime to steal hogs than it was to steal sheep.[10] That is, the criminal law in this case was a direct reflection of the economic exigencies of the time. Similarly, in Maryland, which relied heavily on tobacco for its income, it was a capital offense to burglarize a tobacco warehouse.[11] Most other forms of burglary, however, were not punishable by death. Colonial law also reflected the underlying needs of the economy in its use of criminal sanctions to control both the labor force and disruptions of predictable market relations.

Labor Laws. The economic life of the colonies required an available supply of labor at profitable rates, and criminal sanctions were frequently used to insure this supply. The Laws and Liberties of Massachusetts made it a punishable offense for anyone to "spend his time idly or unprofitably." During the early colonial years most colonies faced a shortage of labor, which placed those with labor to sell in an advantageous position. Despite their bourgeois orientation colonial leaders were not above abridging the worker's right of voluntary contract when it came to the price of labor. Massachusetts, for example, lowered by law the wages normally paid to carpenters and general laborers.[12] Free laborers, however, comprised only a small part of the colonial work force, probably no more than 10 percent by the time of the Revolution.[13] A more important source of labor were indentured servants and slaves, and here the criminal law played an important part in insuring economic stability.

Colonial courts enforced the contracts of indentured servants, frequently punishing infractions with additional service. Servants who ran away or were otherwise disobedient to their masters frequently had additional time added to their period of service by the court.[14] This was also the ordinary punishment for indentured females who gave birth to illegitimate children and for indentured servants convicted of noncapital offenses.[15] To punish indentured servants with imprisonment would have been an economic hardship to their masters as well as a general loss to communities facing labor shortages. Extra service, on the other hand, was a boon to both the master and the community, and the criminal courts of the colonies made full use of this option.

As the plantation economies of the southern colonies grew, black slaves began increasingly to replace white indentured servants as the primary source of labor. White slaveowners lived with the ever-present fear of slave rebellion and the economic threat of runaways.[16] The criminal laws of the time spoke loudly of these threats. A 1718 Rhode Island law made it a crime for a slave to be in the house of a free black and provided that both should be whipped.[17] In North Carolina the law prohibited a slave from hunting with a gun on any but his master's land, while another law authorized court-appointed representatives to search slave quarters and confiscate any weapons found.[18] Most southern colonies made it a crime, sometimes punishable by death, to teach a slave to read, and most also legislated strict punishment for anyone who aided a slave in escaping to freedom.

CREATING A CAPITALIST STATE: FROM REVOLUTION TO THE MACHINE AGE, 1781–1865

Bourgeois Revolution and Liberal Government

The American War of Independence resulted largely from conflicts of interest between the colonial bourgeois and powerful economic interests in the British Isles. As historian James Willard Hurst commented, "Men wanted national independence largely for economic reasons, but they said they wanted it because their legal rights were invaded."[19] At the time of the Revolution, the colonial bourgeois consisted to two distinct groups: a middle class of small farmers, artisans, lawyers, and merchants and a wealthy elite comprised of large slaveowners and powerful mercantilists. While members of each group favored independence from England, they did so for somewhat different reasons. The middle class, which consisted mostly of independent farmers, wanted an end to the prerogatives of wealth and power enjoyed by both the American and British elites in the colonies. Specifically, they sought an end to the voting restrictions that limited suffrage to only larger landholders in many states and the feudal remnants in the law that complicated the buying and selling of land, popular control over taxation, and relief from disadvantageous laws of mortgage and foreclosure. By and large members of the colonial middle class were true adherents to the ideology of liberal democracy; they believed in political equality (at least for free, white males), private property, and a legal system that would stimulate free enterprise.

Many of the restrictions opposed by the colonial middle class, particularly limited suffrage and mortgage and foreclosure laws, had been created by the *colonial* governments themselves and not the British Parliament, although British oppression often became the emotional focus of resentment. In contrast, the colonial elite often found themselves in direct conflict with wealthy British interests rather than colonial governments themselves. British manufacturing and mercantile interests had managed to keep the colonies a source of cheap raw materials as well as a ready market for manufactured goods through trade laws that prohibited all but the most inconsequential colonial trade with any country except Britain. This directly inhibited the growth of both mercantile and manufacturing wealth in the colonies. Large slaveowning planters in the southern colonies sought expansion of the slave system into western lands, since this would increase the value of slave offspring and provide a ready outlet for surplus slaves. Concessions to British fur-trading interests, however, kept lands west of the Appalachians closed to expansion.[20] These conflicts of interest between the colonial upper class and the powerful British capitalists and traders, combined with the more egalitarian concerns of the colonial middle class, sparked the American Revolution.

With liberation from England came the need to create an American state to replace the colonial governments. Initially, the free colonies were loosely organized under the Articles of Confederation, which provided for a weak central government with neither the power to tax nor the authority to raise an army. Under the Articles these functions were the exclusive province of the individual states. While this decentralization of power was in accordance with the interests of the middle-class farmers who were by far the largest proportion of the American population at the time, it proved quite unsatisfactory to a variety of more powerful economic interests.

Without the ability to tax, the Confederation would not be able to redeem at face value paper money it had issued and that had been purchased by wealthy colonists at significantly devalued rates during the Revolution, thus depriving them of handsome profits. Slaveholders sought a strong central militia or army that could be used to suppress potential slave revolts. Merchants sought a strong central navy to protect shipping, and bankers and others in the financial community wanted a central government to establish a single, uniform currency to facilitate financial exchange. Industrial interests sought some central power to establish and enforce protective tariffs throughout the colonies.[21]

It was these plantation owners, wealthy merchants, industrialists, and large creditors, unhappy with the economic consequences of decentralized government, who agitated for a constitutional convention. Of the fifty-five delegates to the constitutional convention there was not one small farmer, artisan, or laborer, and certainly no women, slaves, or servants. Rather, the convention consisted of those with a direct financial interest in strengthening the Federal government. Forty of the delegates held substantial quantities of paper money issued by the Continental Congress; fifteen were slaveowners; fourteen held land west of the Appalachians; eleven were either wealthy merchants or manufacturers, and twenty four were mortgage or credit holders.[22]

The original document produced by these interests was concerned almost solely with the protection of private property and the establishment of a government with the power to insure a physical and social environment conducive to free enterprise. Provisions for personal liberties—other than the right to free contract—were added only later as a concession to the more egalitarian interests of the middle-class farmers and artisans. The new constitution also established procedures whereby wealthy citizens could participate in government more directly while limiting the participation of the lesser to representation. Although the new American state lacked a hereditary aristocracy, the constitution established a bicameral (two-house) legislature that mimicked the British Parliament. The Senate (much like the House of Lords) was designed as the more powerful body, with individuals *appointed* for six-year terms by state legislatures. This effectively insured that the Senate would be comprised largely of important—that is, wealthy—citizens from the states, particularly since the state legislatures themselves were comprised largely of affluent farmers and merchants. The House of Representatives (much like the House of Commons) was to be elected every two years, making it a less stable and less powerful body. The president was to be chosen by a body of individuals appointed by state legislatures. As with appointments to the Senate, this helped guarantee that only the most notable citizens—and this usually meant the more wealthy and influential—would participate in presidential selection. To further insure that presidential behavior would coincide with the interests of the upper strata of American society, the Senate (but not the House of Representatives) was given veto power over all presidential appointees.[23]

The Constitutional Congress created a strong central government that spoke the ideology of self-governance but largely insured that direct participation would be limited to the affluent and the powerful at both the state and Federal levels. The interests of others would at all times be filtered through representative bodies that characteristically consisted mostly of the upper middle class and the elite. Government in the new American state would be government by the elite and the bourgeois. Research has shown, for example, that state legislatures during the postrevolutionary period consisted overwhelmingly of elite and upper middle class representatives, with an "accompanying lack of any nearly proportionate direct representation of the lower middle class (small farmers, artisans and shopkeepers), farm tenants, farm labor or industrial labor." Even more notable is the fact that these proportions did not change with later changes in the labor force.[24] While the independent holders of productive wealth became an ever smaller proportion of the population, they remained the largest proportion of law-making bodies.

Legal Ideology and Capitalist Law

The class-based visions of legislators in the American state shaped the types of laws they made. The dominant consciousness among law makers in early America was characteristically bourgeois, that is, it emphasized rationality, voluntary contract, and the right of individuals to acquire, own, use, and sell property for solely personal advantage, unfettered by the cumbersome legal and social traditions of feudalism that had narrowly circumscribed the prerogatives of property ownership.

The legal ideology associated with this bourgeois consciousness emphasized above all else the individual right of *voluntary contract.* That is, the right of persons to enter into any economic or other agreements should be free from all governmental interference or abridgement, with the exception of agreements to commit criminal acts against persons or property. The Constitution itself clearly proclaimed the sanctity of free contract by expressly prohibiting state or Federal government interference in business or labor contracts.[25]

Bourgeois ideology was not an elite theory that opposed the interests of the common man in the new America. Its strength in legitimizing the new government was precisely in its elevation of the common interests to an apparent place of importance in the new social system. However, the real consequences of the new system for the common man are found not in the ideology of that system but in its actions and effects.

Bourgeois *theory* proclaimed that the way to national peace and prosperity was through creating a society where every many was his own producer, where every family lived off its own farm or shop—at least where free whites were concerned. This ideology was clearly attractive to small farmers and businessmen and to all those indentured servants and wage laborers who sought personal independence. The new Americans were interested in "Dynamic rather than static property, property in motion or at risk rather than property secure and at rest."[26] This was no more obvious than in the case of land law.

In keeping with the bourgeois concept that private ownership of land and other property should be unfettered by any obligations other than to use it as one saw fit, legislatures moved swiftly to eliminate vestiges of feudal limitations in land law, substituting in their place the concept of "title," which facilitated easy sale of land. Both the wealthy and the middle class saw advantage in having few restrictions on the buying and selling of land. The creation of a free and open land market made possible wide speculation in land by two groups, the affluent and lawyers, the former because they had the money to speculate and the latter because they could find their way better than others through the complexity of the emerging land law. From 1790 to about 1830, in fact, land speculation was so rampant that notes based on land parcels became a kind of business currency for the wealthy. Most of the land west of the Appalachians went not to small, independent farmers but first to the hands of land speculators and later into the hands of large farm and mining interests. The development of the automatic reaper made the assembling of large parcels of land by the more affluent attractive because they could afford to use the new technology to gain competitive superiority in the grain market.[27] The development of an industrial economy in the northeast similarly accelerated the consolidation of ore-rich western lands owned by large-scale mining interests. In the southwest a freewheeling land market led also to the eventual development of large cattle baronries, not to a society based on small, independent producers.

At the abstract level, the new state spoke the bourgeois ideology of small-scale, independent production. The *legal ideology* of free contract derived from these more abstract propositions, however, led to legal forms and laws that for the most part favored the concentration of wealth.

In the case of *Bronson* v. *Kinzie,* for example, the United States Supreme Court declared unconstitutional an Illinois state law that gave property owners one year to reclaim land lost due to foreclosure. This law had originally been passed to provide some relief to small farmers who found themselves periodically short of cash to meet mortgage payments as the economy went through a series of upswings and downturns. Monied interests argued that such laws (and they had become common in many states) were an unconstitutional infringement on their right of voluntary contract. After all, the farmer had freely contracted for the mortgage on the farm, and if it couldn't be paid, the mortgager—usually a bank—had every right to claim the property for its own. The Supreme Court agreed.[28] This same law also provided that any foreclosed land must be sold at auction for at least two-thirds of its appraised value. This would help insure that the former owner would recoup at least a portion of his equity and would also reduce the incentive for land speculators, who were often closely associated with the banks auctioning off the foreclosed land, to buy cheaply during economic slumps and sell profitably during economic upswings. Such rationale was soundly attacked by the money community. The *New York Journal of Commerce,* for example, condemned the Illinois law, saying that such attempts to use the law to protect small farmers from bankruptcy was indicative of "the hopeless depravity and corruption of the age."[29] The legal ideology of free contract was not necessarily compatible with the legal needs of small entrepreneurs, the supposed beneficiaries of the new American state.

The concept of free contract has always been closely associated with the ideals of free enterprise and competition. Free contract is necessary for healthy competition, and according to the logic of capitalism, competition is necessary for economic growth and well-being. It was during the early years of the Republic that these two ideas—free contract and competition—became legally linked. During the colonial era it was not uncommon for the government to play a direct role in establishing economic arrangements through the "franchise" or "patent." These were grants either by the king, Parliament, or the colonial government of the exclusive right to operate certain businesses or use certain land in specified locales. The concept of the government's right to ordain such monopoly arrangements had not automatically passed from the legal scene with founding of the new American state. In 1824, however, the case of *Gibbons* v. *Ogden* sharply narrowed the government's authority to determine the shape of economic arrangements.

Robert Livingston and Robert Fulton had been given by the state of New York the exclusive right to operate all steamboats plying the waters of that state. Livingston and Fulton had granted Ogden a license to operate two steamboats between New York and New Jersey. Gibbons also operated two boats between New York and New Jersey, but based in New Jersey and not New York, as was the case with Ogden. Ogden sought and won in a New York court an injunction prohibiting Gibbons from operating in New York waters on the argument that he had not been licensed by Livingston and Fulton. Gibbons appealed this injunction and eventually the Supreme Court held that state-granted monopolies were unconstitutional.[30] This decision was important for two reasons: (1) It enshrined the concept of competition as an important value to be protected by law and (2) it extended the government's authority over commerce within the states, making the central, national government the focal point for pressure by the commercial interests.

While government *interference* in business activity was generally opposed during the early years of the new Republic, government *stimulation* of economic productivity was not. The lifeblood of the growing economy was transportation, and the business community generally saw no conflict between the ideology of free enterprise and the use of public monies to develop transportation systems to stimulate the economy. President George Washington supported the building of the Baltimore and Ohio Railroad with Federal funds. The Pennsylvania Railroad was originally built and owned by the state of Pennsylvania. In 1825 the state of New York completed construction of the Erie Canal, connecting New York City with the Great Lakes at a cost of $7 million, and numerous other canals and railroads enjoyed government sponsorship at both the state and national level.[31] The government was also expected to maintain the other necessities of lively commerce: a stable, uniform currency; a civil law system for the peaceful and predictable resolution of business disputes; an effective postal system; and sufficient social peace to allow the conduct of business. Thus began the ambivalent relationship between the American capitalist class and the American government. Government was not to interfere in the workings of free enterprise, but it was to provide all those elements of social organization that made free enterprise possible and profitable. Above all else the government was not to make laws abridging the rights of free contract, a legal orientation that was to have a substantial impact on both labor law and government regulation of business— the basis of our contemporary concepts of white-collar crime. It was during these early years of the Republic that the bourgeois ideology that justified the revolution was transformed into a capitalist legal system that by and large was more advantageous to the emerging capitalist class than it was to the middle-class small farmer or artisan who staunchly defended the bourgeois concept of freedom.

Legal conflicts such as those between small farmers and mortgage institutions or between monopoly and nonmonopoly steamboat interests are sometimes taken as evidence that the American government operates to accommodate a wide plurality of interests to the particular or persistent advantage of no single one. Such an interpretation of the early years of the Republic is, however, unwarranted. Government was the forum for the resolution of conflicts between *property owners,* be they small farmers, steamboat owners, plantation owners, merchants, or industrialists. The legislatures and the courts were forums that debated and determined the shape of American capitalism, not whether America would be capitalist. Slaves, free blacks, women, and propertyless workers were entirely excluded from this debate. The government may have represented the pluralism and divisions among the propertied, but it did not faithfully represent the pluralism of the population as a whole.

Criminal Law in the New American State

Crimes are those acts for which the state will initiate and bear the cost of prosecution. Criminal law is an expression of state policy and a dramatization of state power. With the coming of independence the new American state was faced with the task of constructing a criminal law that expressed its vision of a proper social and political order and effectively demonstrated the state's power to rule. After the revolution a number of changes took place in both criminal law and the practice of criminal justice that began to distinguish it from its colonial predecessors. Most notable were the emerging emphasis upon statutory law, an increase in prosecutions for property offenses coupled with a decrease in prosecutions for moral offenses, a changing view of the criminal, and an increased concern with rehabilitating this newly perceived criminal.

The Rise of Statutory Law. The criminal law of the new American states did not change radically or immediately after the Revolution. The majority of lawyers and jurists were trained in common law principles and steeped in common law traditions. Moreover, after the Revolution there were few law books other than those written in English and reflecting English legal tradition.[32] Yet at the same time, the Revolution had been a break with the old legal order, and this was reflected in a gradual turning away from the concept of common law. The new Americans had fought to end what they had felt were arbitrary and unpredictable legal controls, and while their concern had been largely with English control of the colonial economy, this concern spilled over into the criminal law. The emerging American legal system gradually took away from judges the power to create new crimes and vested that power in legislatures. In the 1821 case of the *United States* v. *Hudson and Goodwin*, for example, two men were charged with libeling both Congress and the president. An appeals court, however, ruled that there was no specific law prohibiting such behavior and that therefore the court had no power to prosecute.[33]

The gradual transformation of criminal law from common to statutory law enabled individuals to know the *limits* of their liability under the law. It also made the criminal law considerably more rigid and less susceptible to the direct pressures of community sentiments. Creating criminal law eventually became, for the most part, the sole province of legislatures. Popular sentiment could only shape criminal law to the extent that such sentiment could be filtered through the apparatus of representative government. This emphasis upon statutory law and its subsequent limitation on the power of popular sentiment came to provide a protection against the stigma of criminality for a multitude of socially harmful acts that emerged in the conduct of free enterprise.

The Rise of Property Crime. From shortly after the Revolution to the early part of the nineteenth century there was a steady rise in the prosecutions for property crimes and a corresponding decline in the number of prosecutions for moral offenses. In Massachusetts, for example, before the Revolution over half of all prosecutions were for offenses against morals, while 13 percent were for property crimes. By 1810, however, theft alone had escalated to 50 percent of all prosecutions, while offenses against morals had declined to barely 0.5 percent.[34]

This radical transformation in the concerns of criminal justice can be attributed to several factors. First, the Revolution had placed elite property owners and entrepreneurs squarely in control of the new government, and their secular concern for the inviolability of property rights was reflected in the operations of the law. Attacks against property in the form of thefts and burglaries were more than disruptions of individual lives; they were attacks upon the very basis of the emerging capitalist social order. Increased criminal prosecutions for property offenses were not just attempts to protect individuals; they were an expression of the dominant class's vision of the appropriate priorities for the new society.

Second, independence from English domination stimulated the growth of manufacturing, and the development of this capitalist industrial sector brought with it a corresponding growth in the urban proletariat. Throughout the nineteenth century the proportion of urbanized wage laborers increased steadily. One consequence of industrial wage labor in capitalist society, however, is the creation of a body of urban poor. The economics of profit insure that at any time a proportion of the labor force will be unemployed. The net result is a body of urban poor consisting of the temporarily unemployed and those who are periodically or chronically unemployed. Some members of this latter group particularly, with little expectation of legitimate access to labor force participation, often develop predatory or vice-related adaptations to the problems of daily survival. Control of these urban criminals becomes a major concern for state law in capitalist society.

The period following the Revolution was characterized by several serious economic depressions that stimulated increased prosecutions for property crime. These increased prosecutions may have resulted from an actual growth in the rate of property offenses due to increased poverty and unemployment. However, they also reflected an increased concern with the ability of the urban poor to destabilize the fledgling social order through crime and to question its legitimacy by dramatizing, by their very existence, the contradiction of poverty amidst profit. By moving forcefully against the property crimes of the urban working class the state helped insure that these crimes would be seen as the result of individual criminality rather than as any indication whatsoever of the emerging social order's inability to provide adequately for all citizens. Unemployment was condemned as "idleness" and poverty equated with vice and crime by the ideologues of the new state, even though the social order made both poverty and idleness inevitable for some.[35]

Theft by the urban poor was not the only taking of property occurring during the economic depressions of the post-Revolutionary era. Banks and mortgage holders claimed the lands of impoverished farmers, and poor urban workers saw access to adequate food and shelter taken away by the economic system's inability to provide work. These types of taking, however, were integral to the political economy and were not criminalized.

Rehabilitation and Changing Perceptions of the Criminal. During the colonial era crime and sin were seen as similar forms of human frailty. Crime, like sin, could strike even the best of people if they relaxed their guard. Because of the predominant use of fines and corporal punishment, however, the criminal was not cut off from the colonial community but remained in it. Indeed, it has been suggested that even the most long-term punishment—the selling into indenture of a convicted thief—may have helped "integrate him more fully into society by reorienting him toward normal social contracts."[36] Like sin, however, crime was serious business, and the colonial penalties were by no means lenient. Historian David Rothman has suggested that the equation of crime with sin made it difficult for early colonial law makers to distinguish between major and minor offenses. All sin was an abomination and had to be punished accordingly.[37] But what was the purpose of this punishment? Its primary purpose was to insure that sin did not go unchecked, for if it did, God's wrath would fall not just on the offender, but upon the community as a whole.[38] A secondary aim was to convince the offender to reform his ways out of pure fear of the same or harsher punishment in the future. There was little thought that punishment could *rehabilitate* the offender, that is, cause some fundamental, internal change that would make the individual want to conform to the social norms.[39] After all, morality was a matter of grace and as such was dependent upon the relationship between a person and God, not on the relationships between people.

With the advent of secular society after the Revolution came a shift in the general understanding of the nature and causes of crime, which led to a corresponding shift in the treatment of criminals. This shift is attributable to several factors. First, increasing prosecution of the urban wage laborers for property crimes made it difficult to view criminals as simply community members gone astray. Criminality was increasingly an obviously class-related phenomenon. This made it easier to see criminals not simply as ordinary individuals who had succumbed to temptations but as individuals with defects that set them apart from the ordinary person, for indeed they were already members of a class set apart. Once criminals were perceived as defective, it was a short step to asking, How could this defect be corrected and the offender rendered normal?

Second, the new Republic was based on an ideology of equality, and its legitimacy required crime control strategies that were ostensibly blind to social class. Early sentencing experiments with urban criminals—such as sentencing them to hard labor "cleaning the streets of the city and repairing the roads," as was the case in post-Revolutionary Pennsylvania—provided all too visible public evidence that the weight of the criminal law was resting squarely on the poor. Such observations were clearly inconsistent with the new state's need for legitimacy.[40]

Third, the emerging capitalist order was seen as a triumph of rationality over the antecedent order with its class privileges and harsh treatment of lesser men. The punishments of the past were increasingly viewed as barbaric and totally inappropriate for a rational society. Such views were stimulated by the writings of men such as Jeremy Bentham and Cesare Becarria, who argued that exceedingly harsh punishments were not only barbaric but irrational, for they drive people "to commit additional crimes to avoid punishment of a single one"[41] and, where they are equally harsh for all offenses, provide no incentive to commit any but the most serious offense.[42]

Fourth, and perhaps most importantly, capitalist society brought with it the view that humans were inherently rational beings seeking to minimize pains and maximize pleasures through free contracts in the marketplace. If humans were thus, then crime was not the consequence of sin but a calculated risk aimed at achieving some desired gain. This new view of crime not as a submission to temptation but as a rational if misguided act coupled with the need for a less barbaric, less visible method of dealing with the growing number of poor, urban offenders, brought about two important changes in public policy regarding criminals. First, criminal law had to be a tool for social engineering, with penalties arranged in such a way as to convince the rational potential offender that the risks of punishment exceeded the possible gains, or failing this, to at least convince the potential offender that greater risk was associated with greater crimes. Second, the aim of penal sanctioning, so far as the specific offender was concerned, had to be to rehabilitate that individual, that is, to remove the defect of character, personality, or reasoning that led to the crime in the first place.[43] These views led directly to the establishment of imprisonment as the primary form of punishment and a reduction in the usage of the death penalty.

Imprisonment was seen as beneficial on three counts. First, it allowed an easy means of varying the severity of punishment according to the crime while being less "barbaric" than public whippings, which could also be varied with the offense. Second, it theoretically provided an environment within which the offender could be isolated from all influences save those deemed "rehabilitative." Third, prisons isolated offenders from public observation, thereby obscuring the class nature of the prison population. This isolation of prisoners from the rest of society helped foster the idea that criminals were truly different from normal people, a substantial change from the way in which most criminals had been viewed in colonial society.

After the Revolution many state governments began limiting the usage of the death penalty, with northern states moving more forcefully in this direction than southern ones. The New Hampshire constitution of 1784 stated that "The true design of all punishments [is] to reform, not to exterminate mankind" and that use of the death penalty for a wide variety of crimes was excessive and "impolitic."[44] In 1794 Pennsylvania limited the usage of the death penalty by distinguishing between *degrees of murder*. Murders that were deliberate or premeditated, committed by the use of poison, or that occurred in connection with crimes of robbery, burglary, arson, or rape were held to be murders in the first degree and punishable by death. All other homicides were held to be murders in the second degree and not punishable by death. This Pennsylvania innovation was gradually adopted by the other states. In 1845 Michigan went so far as to abolish its death penalty.

INDUSTRIAL CAPITALISM AND THE GROWTH OF STATE LAW: 1865–1929

During the period between the Civil War and the Great Depression the United States experienced fundamental economic and political changes. The Civil War tore apart the Federal Union and then reassembled it with the North's industrial economy in a position of clear dominance over the agrarian economy of the South and with the Federal government as the essential source of state power. The ascendancy of the North's industrial economy created a clear field for more rapid industrialization. This subsequent burgeoning of industrial capitalism radically altered the social, economic, and political landscape of American society in a number of ways.

First, the growing need for an industrial labor force stimulated both urbanization and immigration, changing the ethnic and social class makeup of the American population. This had a direct impact on crime problems and crime control. Second, new machines, industrial work, and mass-produced products created the possibility of additional harm to society. This led to a corresponding development of new laws to control or in some cases to legitimize the new harms. Third, the rise of industrial capitalism produced massive concentrations of wealth that ended the possibilities for achieving the ideal bourgeois nation based on a population of self-employed workers. At the same time the development of regulatory law, presumably to keep in check this new power, tended to keep alive the liberal ideology of the now moribund bourgeois society. In short, it was during this period that many of our contemporary perceptions of and responses to the crime problem developed into their mature form.

Urbanization, Immigration, and the Crime Problem

After the Civil War the United States experienced a dramatic surge of industrial growth. Ten years before the Civil War there were approximately 125,000 businesses in the United States engaged in manufacturing. Many of these were not factories in the modern sense but were instead small businesses engaging in hand production rather than machine production of durable goods. Fifty years later, at the turn of the century, the number of manufacturing businesses exceeded 500,000. More importantly, by this time the majority of manufacturing was taking place in large machine-powered factories employing masses of laborers. Between 1848 and 1899 the number of manufacturing workers grew from 957,059 to 5,097,652—a more than fivefold increase. This shift from farming and small-scale hand production to mass, urbanized manufacturing represented a fundamental change in the organization of American society.

A key requirement for this growth of American industry was the expansion of the urbanized work force. Industrial production centralizes both material and labor and is poorly served by the dispersed settlement patterns of an agricultural society. After the Civil War internal migration stimulated by both the closing of the Western frontier and cyclic depressions, a reduction in the urban death rate, and the large-scale immigration of Europeans from the east and Orientals from the west provided the necessary urbanized work force.[45]

In 1860 only 20 percent of the American population lived in urban areas with populations of 2,500 or more. By 1900 the proportion of urbanized Americans had doubled to 40 percent. Because of the substantial growth in the overall size of the American population, however, the *actual* number of people living in cities had increased almost *500 percent*, going from approximately 6.3 million to slightly more than 30 million between 1860 and 1900. By 1920 the urban population reached 51 percent of the entire population. This meant that over 54 million people were now living in cities, almost nine times as many as only sixty years earlier.[46]

The majority of those who swelled the population of American cities after the Civil War entered the industrial labor force. They represented a sizable element of the American population, and one quite different from the individual entrepreneurs imagined by the colonial ideologues who dreamed of creating a new bourgeois society based on free enterprise. The new industrial system needed more than just a labor force, however. As a system designed to produce private wealth through maximization of profit, the capitalist industrial economy needed specifically a proletarian labor force—a large pool of potential workers with nothing to sell but their labor. Workers in this position would have little choice but to accept the wages and working conditions offered by the emerging industrial order. In the last half of the nineteenth century, with declining fortunes of small farms in America driving many rural residents into the cities and successive waves of foreign immigrants seeking alternatives to the poverty and famines of Europe, industrial capitalism had available exactly what was needed, an "apparently inexhaustible reserve of cheap labor for mines, mills and factories."[47] This does not mean, however, that they were gladly absorbed into the mainstream of American society. Those who worked for wages had never been looked upon favorably by either the middle class or the elite of American society. The non-Anglo cultures of these new immigrants, particularly those from southern Europe, Russia, and Poland, when added to this already established prejudice against wage laborers, led to their being perceived as the "dregs" and "social scum" of society. While their labor was needed, they were generally held in low esteem. Moreover, their growing numbers threatened to make the proletariat the numerically dominate segment of society.

The growth of urban, industrial centers populated by a proletarian work force is paralleled by both the emergence of the "crime problem" as an important element of public consciousness and the growth of urban police forces. Cities full of immigrant wage laborers were seen by the established classes as dangerous, disordered, and presumably rife with crime. During the last half of the nineteenth century numerous social commentators spoke of cities in these terms, and newspapers devoted considerable space to dramatizing crime and violence.[48] The threats of labor unrest, riot, and mob attacks by the growing urban proletariat added to the image of the new industrial city as a dangerous environment. As one writer said of Buffalo, New York,

> Rowdies paraded the streets at night, unmolested, and taxpayers became alarmed regarding both life and property.[49]

This nineteenth-century comparison of "taxpayers," that is, the property owners of Buffalo, with "rowdies" is indicative of the fear generated among the solid elite and middle-class citizens by the existence of a propertyless urban mass.

Both the elite and middle class tended to view urban disorder as the result of the "low" quality of the urban proletariat—or the "dangerous classes," as they were called—rather than the consequences of social injustices and economic deprivations that needed remedy. The response was to protect the status quo distribution of wealth, power, and property by focusing attention on the depredations of the propertyless rather than the reasons why so many lived in the brutalizing and dehumanizing conditions that produced crime and social unrest.[50]

There were several ironies in this, however. First, there is little evidence that there was, in fact, any increase in the actual *rates* of crime—the number of crimes per 1,000 or 100,000 persons—in growing urban industrial areas between the Civil War and the turn of the century.[51] Second, the gangs of urban thugs so greatly feared by the middle and upper classes largely preyed upon the poor and propertyless, not the affluent or the wealthy. Third, while labor troubles and poor riots resulted from conflicts between the propertied elite and propertyless workers, neither the popular press nor the more learned publications examined them in terms of the underlying economic issues. The bourgeois consciousness of the nation largely precluded any analysis of the problem as one of class conflict. Instead, the apparent urban decay was more often identified as the result of "contaminating" the once-pure American society with undesirable foreign elements. If crime and disorder resulted from the *kind of people* who made up the working class rather than the kind of social order in which this working class existed, then what was needed was some means of controlling those people, or at least the overabundance of "criminal types" among them. This type of thinking, devoid of any class-based analysis, favored the expansion of urban police forces as a means of maintaining order.

Urbanization has traditionally been seen by social scientists as making an *independent* contribution to increased crime as well as being associated with a variety of other crime-generating factors such as poverty and inequality. *Decreasing social cohesion* is most often identified as the key link between urbanization per se and rising crime rates. City life is seen as atomistic, composed of a great agglomeration of separate individuals who have few meaningful ties to one another. Compared with rural communities cities have often been described as places where individuals are relatively anonymous and less likely to be incorporated into a network of binding social relations that will insure their conformity.[52] This lack of close social ties increases the possibility of deviant behavior by leaving the individual without clear guidelines and by freeing him or her from constant scrutiny by personal acquaintances, friends, and family.[53]

The accuracy of this hypothesis is difficult to assess. It is clear that industrialization and its concomitant urbanization in the United States led to an increased *concern* with crime. However, without adequate pre- and post-urbanization data it is difficult to know whether urbanization brought with it any actual increase in per capita crime. It is even more difficult to assess the effects of urbanization independent of other important factors, particularly social inequality and economic conflict. Two studies, one conducted in 1935 and another conducted in 1962, using largely the same variables, both found that the amount of economic opportunity was much more strongly related to crime rates than was city size. Thus cities that are better able to meet the occupational and economic aspirations of their citizens appear to have lower crime rates, regardless of their size.[54] In another study, sociologist William F. Whyte lived for several years in a supposedly "disorganized" neighborhood of Boston. What Whyte found was that individuals were essentially living not in the city as a whole but in a smaller social community and therefore enjoyed a variety of meaningful personal associations. Lawbreaking, when it occurred, appeared to result more from a lack of sufficient legitimate avenues for economic gain than from personal anonymity or a lack of normative guidelines.[55] Such findings suggest that while the social patterns associated with urban living may be more conducive to crime than those of more closely knit rural communities, urbanization itself in American history has been a less important cause of crime problems than the social inequality and class conflicts upon which the growing industrial cities were based.

New Laws for the Industrial Economy

The transition from an agrarian to an industrial economy brought new forms of harm into the daily life of many Americans. The machines of the industrial age posed unprecedented threats to life and limb; they had, as one historian noted, "a marvelous capacity for smashing the human body."[56] With the coming of the railroads and factory work the number of suits for personal injury grew, and with it also grew the body of laws governing the dangers of the industrial age. These suits were for the most part resolved in ways that protected the developing industrial economy from any *criminal liability* for these harms and often denied or limited financial liability under civil law as well.

Railroads were the preeminent symbol of the emerging industrial age, and like industrialization generally, they left behind a growing number of dead and injured as they roared through the countryside bringing the benefits of progress. Suits against railroads for redress of these damages left their mark on both the laws of negligence and labor law.

Laws of Negligence. Suits seeking redress for damages caused by railroad accidents helped to establish two important doctrines concerning negligence: *contributory negligence* and *last clear chance.* The legal doctrine of "contributory negligence" required that the injured party be free of any fault in connection with the incident for which damages are sought. If the plaintiff contributed in *any* way, no matter how small, to creating the situation that led to his or her injury, under the doctrine of contributory negligence the defendant was not liable for damages. Thus, for example, if a farmer's cow wandered onto a railroad track where it was subsequently struck and killed by a train traveling at an excessive speed, but it could be shown that the farmer had failed to repair the broken fence through which the cow escaped, the railroad would not be liable for damages. By 1850 this doctrine had become widely accepted in American courts.

The contributory negligence doctrine placed most of the responsibility for safe conduct on the injured party by providing that any amount of negligence on the plaintiff's part abrogated all claims for damage. In doing so it served to protect the railroads and other industries from any claim that they had an inherently greater power for causing damage. It is the train and not the cow, in the previous example, that makes the situation a dangerous one, but under the doctrine of contributory negligence, it is the farmer who bears the greater responsibility for adhering to standards of safe conduct. The doctrine of contributory negligence required, in effect, that individuals *adapt* to the dangers of the machine age rather than placing those who profited from these machines under any particular responsibility for insuring safety.

Today in many jurisdictions the doctrine of contributory negligence has been replaced by that of *proportional negligence*: The award of damages will be reduced by the proportion of the plaintiff's contribution to the situation. However, this is a relatively recent legal innovation. During the years of rapid industrial growth the doctrine of contributory negligence was a huge boon to the capitalist industrial sector by insuring that its legal liability for transportation and industrial accidents would be held to a minimum.

The doctrine of *last clear chance* places the liability for damages on the individual who had the "last clear chance" to avoid harm, even if the other party contributed to, or even caused, the dangerous situation. This doctrine was based on the case of *Bavies* v. *Mann* in which the driver of a team of horses was sued for damages for failing to avoid a mule and wagon crossing a road unsafely. Because he had the "last clear chance" to avoid an accident, the driver of the horse team was held to be at fault despite the plaintiff's contributing negligence.[57] On the surface the last clear chance doctrine appears to modify the harshness of the doctrine of contributory negligence, and in suits involving potential dangers wholly under the control of individuals this may be the case. However, where the engines and machinery of industrial society were concerned, this doctrine placed the greater responsibility for safety on the individual victim. This was no more evident than in cases involving steam locomotives. These engines had no ability to stop quickly, particularly before the invention of the air brake, and therefore the "last clear chance" to avoid injury always rested with the individual.[58] As in the case of contributory negligence, the last clear chance doctrine required that individuals adapt their behavior to the dangerous world of machines. This logic was appropriate to the needs of industrialists who sought limits on their legal liability for the consequences of industrialization, but it did little to meet the needs of private individuals and workers to be safe from injury. Technology and progress were given the protection of state law by legal doctrines that questioned only how well individuals adapted to machines, not whether they should be required to bear the full burden of adapting to the new technology in the first place.

Adapting the Laws of Injury to Labor.   During the early years of industrialization the courts tended to protect industries from liability for injuries to their workers. The *fellow-servant rule* and the *assumption of risk* doctrine made it exceedingly difficult, if not impossible, for an injured worker to receive compensation from his or her employer.

Under English common law the *law of agency* held that masters were responsible for the actions of their servants. For instance, if an innkeeper's servant robbed a guest, under the law of agency the innkeeper was liable for making restitution to the victim. Similarly, if a servant offered bad wine to a tavern patron, the tavern owner and not the server was liable for damage to the patron's health.[59] By extension, the law of agency could be interpreted to mean that factory workers could sue their employers if they were injured by the actions of co-workers. This was clearly inhospitable to the needs of a growing industry, and the law of agency was replaced in American courts by the fellow-servant rule. The fellow-servant rule held that workers could not sue their employers if they were injured as the result of action by co-workers, that is, fellow-servants. A worker could sue an employer only if that employer was *directly* responsible for the worker's injury as a result of personal negligence. The case of *Farwell* v. *Boston and Worcester Railroad Corporation,* settled in 1842, served as the basis for applying this doctrine during the years of industrial growth after the Civil War. Farwell, an engineer for the Boston and Worcester Railroad, lost a hand when his train went off the track as the result of a switchman's error. Farwell sued the railroad for compensation. In denying compensation from the railroad the court held that because Farwell's injury resulted from a fellow-servant's action, that is, from the actions of a co-worker, the railroad was in no way responsible for providing Farwell with compensation for either his injury or his inability to work any longer at his trade.[60]

By focusing on the actions of "fellow-servants," this ruling placed all the responsibility for a safe work environment on the worker and provided no incentive for employers to create work environments that would reduce the likelihood of workers injuring one another. Since industrial workers had little money or property, there was little realistic benefit to be gained from suing a fellow-servant for injury. Injured and maimed workers during the last half of the nineteenth century found themselves thrown on the trash pile of human wreckage and could only hope for the uncertain generosity of local charities.

The *Farwell* case also served as the precedent for another doctrince that substantially limited the liability of employers with respect to injuries oc-curing to their employees. This was the *assumption of risk* doctrine. In denying Farwell compensation the court held that he had freely taken the engineer's job and had thereby assumed the ordinary risks of that job, including de-railment. The court further reasoned that the wage paid for any job included an adjustment for the dangers of the job. Thus, since the worker had assumed the risk of the job and had been compensated for taking that risk, the court concluded that no further compensation for injury was warranted. This ruling had far-reaching impact, the most important of which was to limit substan-tially the legal liability of industry for injuries to workers and to insure that industry had little to lose by failing to make the workplace a safe one. It would be many years and many struggles later before workers acquired even minimal rights to a safe workplace and guarantees of minimal compensation for injury.

Labor Law and Liberal Doctrine.   Liberal legal ideology rests on the twin foundations of free contract and the right to private property. The belief that voluntary agreements made by individuals seeking personal gain is the fundamental basis of an ideal social order was given substantial legitimation by legal rulings governing the relationships between workers and employers. During the last half of the nineteenth century the law, through rulings such as the assumption of risk doctrine, repeatedly denied that gross imbalances in the economic power of parties to a contract in any way compromised the "voluntary" nature of that contract. Those who worked in dangerous conditions for low wages were assumed to have *chosen* that employment, and any legal interference violated the workers' right to free contract![61]

Contracts made under duress were involuntary in the eyes of the American legal system, but the ability of a potential employer to withhold livelihood from any worker not willing to accept the wages and working conditions offered was not considered to constitute duress. The labor bargain was treated as a free contract between equals. Liberal ideology served to obscure the fundamental inequality of the bargaining position between a worker with no possibility of livelihood other than being able to sell his or her labor and an employer who can choose from many such individuals. In many instances this ideology was allegedly used to protect workers' rights to free contract while in practice it was being used to limit workers' attempts to gain better wages and working conditions.

In 1886, for example, the Pennsylvania Supreme Court ruled unconstitutional a law requiring all mines and manufacturing companies to pay their employees monthly in *legal tender*, not "other paper." This law was aimed specifically at the practice of paying employees with "chits" which could be spent only at the company-owned stores, guaranteeing that money paid out in wages would return to the company in the form of profit on high-priced, low-quality merchandise at the company store. The court found such a law "utterly unconstitutional and void" not because it violated the employer's right to pay employees as they wished but because it was "subversive" of the rights of workers in its attempt to "prevent persons . . . from making their own contracts."[62] In another case the Illinois Court in 1895 struck down a law limiting women to an eight-hour day and a forty-eight hour week in factories because it limited the right of an individual "to control his or her own time and faculties."[63] Laws such as these had been sought by labor groups as protections against exploitative labor practices, yet they were frequently declared unconstitutional because they supposedly violated the constitutional rights of workers to enter into voluntary contracts. In fact, what these laws threatened was the employer's freedom to dictate the conditions of labor. Yet time and again the liberal ideology of free contract was used in the courts to undercut any attempt at altering the imbalance of power between workers and employers.

Workers were not wholly without legal victories. In 1877 a Wisconsin court ruled for the first time that railroads had a duty to "provide safe and suitable machinery" for its workers.[64] However, where the right of free contract was not held to be violated by legislation aimed at worker protection, the other prong of liberal legal ideology—the right to private property—came into play. In a New York case, for example, the court ruled that a law prohibiting the manufacture of cigars and other tobacco products in tenement houses because of the threat to the health of workers and the public in general was unconstitutional because it deprived the cigarmaker of "his property and some portion of his liberty."[65]

This situation produced substantial conflict between labor and industry. The latter half of the nineteenth century was a period of nearly constant labor strife. This turmoil helped reinforce the belief among middle class and elite Americans that the working class was indeed the "dangerous class" and fueled the demand for increased state investment in insuring social peace through the expansion of urban police forces.

The Era of Regulation

The growth of monopoly capital throughout the last half of the nineteenth century radically altered the economic and political structure of American society. The once relatively powerful petit bourgeois found itself increasingly squeezed between the large capitalist interests on one hand and the "dangerous classes" of urban workers and urban poor on the other. The petit bourgeois sought protection in state law, first through the Granger and Populist movements in the midwest and the west and later in the Progressive movement, which attempted to eliminate political corruption and place governmental controls over big business.[66]

Prior to 1850 corporations were legally prohibited from holding stock in other corporations. This substantially limited the potential size of corporations and reflected the general mistrust of big business and corporate power shared by the agrarian bourgeois and the agrarian elite, who dominated most state legislatures prior to the Civil War.[67] After the Civil War, however, under heavy pressure from railroad and manufacturing interests, state legislatures began to relax prohibitions on corporate stock ownership. In 1888 a landmark New Jersey law formally established the principle that any corporation could own stock in any other corporation. This opened the door to large-scale corporate development, the purchase of controlling interests in small companies by larger, more successful ones, and the creation of both horizontal and vertical monopolies.[68] Small companies began disappearing rapidly. Wealth became increasingly centralized, and those who were not among the corporate elite found themselves losing control over important sectors of their economic and social life.

Railroads were not the only industry where the formation of industrial capital threatened the liberal ideal of bourgeois society. Wherever the growing capitalist industrial economy led to great concentrations of wealth, the middle class saw its power eroded. As the institutions of transportation, finance, insurance, and mass retailing "acquired an unprecedented influence over the affairs of ordinary men," they created "the sense of an evil turn in national development" among the class of professionals, small businessmen, and farmers.[69] At the same time that this middle-class fear of the power of monopoly capital was developing, the growing proletarian labor force was also experiencing the harmful effects of capitalist industrialization in the form of long hours, low wages, unsafe and unsanitary working conditions, and little control over one of the most basic elements of human life—work. However, except for the relatively brief Populist era, the mutual interests of the middle- and working classes in limiting the growth of monopoly capital did not produce any unified movement. By and large the bourgeois retained its suspicion of the "dangerous classes" and continued to support the liberal ideology of free contract and private property, leaving them more ideologically aligned with the capitalist oligarchy than with workers.

Populism and Legislative Regulation. Beginning in the 1870s coalitions of small farmers, miners, and factory workers in many midwest and western states sought to limit the growing power of monopoly capital. These movements were loosely identified under the banner of Populism. A key strategy of the Populist movement was to limit the ability of state legislatures to cater to powerful economic interests by redrafting the state constitution at Populist-initiated constitutional conventions. These Populist constitutions generally contained prohibitions on "special laws" and in some cases empowered the state to regulate specific industries or make laws governing matters such as wages and worker safety. The Illinois constitution of 1870, for example, required that "where a general law can be made applicable, no special law shall be enacted" and expressly prohibited special interest legislation in twenty-three areas, including finance and railroad development. The aim was to neutralize the power of monied interests to buy protective legislation tailored to their particular needs. Other sections of the Illinois constitution set out policies for the regulation of warehouse and grain elevators and directed the legislature to "correct abuses and prevent unjust discrimination" in freight and passenger rates charged by railroads.[70]

A number of other states followed Illinois's lead. In 1873 a revision of the Pennsylvania constitution outlawed, among other things, granting free railroad passes, an important tool in the hands of the railroad lobby.[71] The Nebraska constitution gave the legislature the specific power to establish "maximum rates" for railroad freight charges.[72] Railroads were not the only targets of these Populist constitutions. Monopolistic business in general came under attack. In the state of Washington, for example, the constitution of 1889 specifically prohibited price fixing and combinations and stated combatively that "monopolies and trusts shall never be allowed in this state."[73] In Colorado, where organized mine labor had become a powerful force, the constitution of 1876 directed the legislature to make laws requiring mines to provide proper ventilation and escape shafts and prohibiting child labor in the mines.[74]

Populist constitutions limited the usefulness of state legislatures as sources of protective legislation for the capitalist sector, and in some cases had stirred them to make laws directly threatening capitalist interests. Faced with this erosion in the control over legal evolution, the capitalist sector turned much of its attention away from state legislatures and toward the courts and the Federal government. As previously discussed, during the last quarter of the nineteenth century the courts provided industry relief from laws aimed at improving the position of workers by frequently declaring such laws unconstitutional violations of the rights to free contract and private property. During this time several important court decisions, as well as the establishment of Federal agencies to "regulate" business, were to play an important role in opening the door for the domination of the nation's economy by a relatively small number of massive business corporations.

In 1876 the Supreme Court held in the case of *Munn* v. *Illinois* that the Illinois state legislature had not deprived a warehouse company of its "property" when it required a reduction in the rates that company charged for the use of its facilities. The law in question arose from the Populist constitution of 1870, which directed the Illinois legislature to regulate warehouse and grain elevators. The court held that the warehouse company had not lost physical possession of its property. It was merely subject to the regulation of the "use and enjoyment" of its property, which the court held to be an appropriate exercise of state power.[75] In essence, the Supreme Court had ruled that the right to "property" protected under the 14th Amendment extended only to the physical possession of property, that is, its *use value,* not to the right to profit from the ownership of property, that is, its *exchange value.*[76] This meant that the states were free to limit corporate profit making where legislatures felt that it arose from excessive prices or unfair practices. The Supreme Court, perhaps inadvertently, had opened the door to a limited version of state socialism, to a set of legal principles that would require enterprise to operate to insure common benefit rather than private profit. This door was quickly closed.

The exclusion of "exchange value" from the definition of constitutionally protected property posed serious threats to the growth of monopoly capital. The value of capital rests not in its use by the owner but in its exchange value, that is, in its ability to produce profit for the owner in some future market transaction. A warehouse, for example, is valuable as capital only to the extent that its owner can charge others for its use in the future. Commenting on *Munn* v. *Illinois,* one writer noted that property "is empty as a business asset if the owner is deprived of his liberty to fix a price on the sale of the product of that property."[77]

With Populist state legislatures moving to narrow the growth of industrial capital, big business continued to press for relief at the Federal level. Within a few years the capitalist sector won several important victories. In 1886 the Supreme Court held in the case of *Wabash Railway* v. *Illinois* that states could not regulate commerce whose destination was beyond their boundaries. Such interstate commerce could only be regulated by the Federal government.[78] In the *Minnesota Rate* case of 1890 the Supreme Court reversed its earlier holding in *Munn* v. *Illinois* and extended the 14th Amendment to the protection of exchange value. The court held that the Chicago, Minneapolis, and St. Paul Railroad had in fact suffered a "confiscation" of its property when its rates were set by the state legislature and that such confiscation "is eminently a question for judicial investigation."[79] Together these two cases insured that the regulation of business would occur at the Federal level where there was less suspicion of business and the power of local interests was also substantially less.

Between 1887 and 1914 the Federal government enacted a number of laws regulating the conduct of big business. In 1887 the Interstate Commerce Commission was created. The Sherman Anti-Trust Act of 1890 prohibited any business combination "in restraint of trade." In 1906 the Meat Inspection Act and the Pure Food and Drug Act were passed to regulate the production of foodstuffs, and in the same year the Hepburn Act placed additional regulation on the railroads. In 1914 the Federal Trade Commission was created to enforce regulations prohibiting "restraint of trade."

The conventional view of this growth in Federal regulation of business is that it was an attempt to curb the concentration of wealth and power in the hands of monopolies and oligopolies. It is often claimed that the burst of Federal regulation during the late nineteenth and early twentieth centuries was antagonistic to big business and sought to protect consumers by guaranteeing a competitive marketplace.[80] Yet while there was clearly opposition to such regulation from some quarters of the business community, there was also recognition in others that making the Federal government a "partner" in the development and protection of capitalism was ultimately in the best interests of business.

First and most importantly, *Federal regulation of business protected the interests of private capital from the fundamental threat of socialism.* By the late 1800s there was widespread opposition to the power and practices of big business. This opposition had already manifested itself in the form of Populist constitutions and Populist-oriented state laws, which threatened to coalesce "into some kind of socialist movement which would fundamentally transform the social order."[81] Federal regulation of business extended constitutional protection to the right to profit and legitimized corporate competition by prohibiting "restraint of trade," effectively placing big business beyond the reach of Populist state legislatures. Arguments presented in favor of the Sherman Anti-Trust Act, for example, heavily stressed the dangers of socialism if the Federal government failed to diffuse the growing hostility toward large-scale private enterprise.[82] It also served partially to quiet public demands that something be done about big business by giving the appearance of regulation without actually interfering with the profit-making endeavors of those businesses: Most of the regulations were vaguely worded and only rarely invoked. The Sherman Anti-Trust Act, for example, was notable for its distinct lack of any effective measure to curb the "restraint of trade" that it prohibited.

Second, facing grass-roots opposition, Federal regulation provided big business with a comparatively more predictable and controllable legal framework for conducting profit-making enterprise. No longer would business be subject to a variety of state regulations. Furthermore, it was far easier to influence the formation of regulations at one level—the Federal government— than to attempt to influence each state legislature. For this reason big interstate businesses like the railroads actively worked for transfer of regulation from the state to the Federal level.[83]

Third, Federal regulation provided a protective environment for profit making. A predictable rate of return insured by stable Federal regulation was far more attractive to big business than the uncertainties of a truly competitive marketplace. As John P. Green, president of the Pennsylvania Railroad said of the creation of the Interstate Commerce Commission:

> A large majority of the railroads in the United States would be delighted if a railroad commission or any other power could make rates upon their traffic which would insure them six percent dividends. . . .[84]

Fourth, Federal regulations benefited the interests of big business directly by forcing smaller competitors out of the market. The requirements of the Meat Inspection Act, for example, were strongly supported by large meat-packers, who knew that their smaller competitors could not afford to comply. The effect was to create an oligopolistic meat industry, rather than insure competitive enterprise.[85] The continued growth of massive corporations and the concomitant decline in the number of small businesses from 1900 until the present is testimony to the hospitable nature of government regulation for the formation of monopoly capital.

The Rise of Political Capitalism

The Progressive movement by and large accepted the basic tenets of capitalism and its liberal, bourgeois ideology. Unlike the Populists its key aim was to eliminate the corruption of legislators and government officials by corporate money, not to control capitalist enterprises directly. In the Progressive view, all that was needed to solve the social problems of the nation was to enable the processes of liberal democratic government to operate uncorrupted by the economic influence of big business.[86] Lacking any clear analysis of the political economy, the Progressive movement failed to recognize two key facts. The first was that increased control over the private economy by ever fewer but ever larger corporations would occur as the inevitable result of capitalist competition, even in the absence of government corruption. The second was that as this control increased the government would be increasingly required to place the needs of this more centralized but also more fragile economic system ahead of all other interests, including those dear to the middle class that dominated the Progressive movement.

The rise of government involvement in stabilizing the economy and regulating business between the late 1800s and the early 1900s represented the beginnings of a shift from laissez-faire capitalism to what historian Gabrial Kolko terms *political capitalism*. Political capitalism is characterized by the active intervention of political power to insure "stability, predictability and security" within the private-sector economy.[87] While the power of the state has always been used to some degree to achieve these ends, the era of political capitalism ushered in with the Progressive movement involved a significant increase in the level of *direct* government efforts to facilitate economic order.

Political capitalism seeks stability in several ways. One is by using the power of law to reduce and control extreme forms of competition such as bribery and the destruction of competitors' property, which had been practiced by the nineteenth-century "robber barons." While this approach limits the freedom of business to compete in any way possible, most investors and managers saw this as preferable to an open war of "each against all" in the marketplace. A second approach to achieving stability is to utilize government power to minimize and smooth out fluctuations in the economy by such strategies as increasing or decreasing the money supply, selective tariffs, and government stimulation of key sectors of the economy. The third approach is to utilize both the power and the money of the state to minimize the effects of such things as unemployment, social disruption, increased poverty, and increased crime, which would occur whenever private capital found it more profitable to decrease rather than increase production and investment. Popular demands for relief were thus deflected away from capital and toward the government.

The increased uses of these governmental strategies was not the consequence of corruption of the political process by cynical business leaders. In fact, the need by businesses to corrupt the political process directly was increasingly supplanted by a political economy that *as a system* required the state to satisfy the economic needs of capital to forestall the occurrence or minimize the consequences of economic collapse. The reality of this would become starkly evident with the Great Depression of the 1930s. The government's response to this crisis would establish the capitalist welfare state in America, concretizing our contemporary vision of crime problems and crime control.

The Great Depression and the New Deal

Economists, historians, and political scientists still debate the causes of the Great Depression. Its effects, however, are not in dispute. Fifteen million heads of households were unemployed, and more than twice that number saw a drastic reduction in the real buying power of their incomes. Nearly 40 percent of the American industrial capacity was idled. Thousands upon thousands of small farmers, already in debt due to low prices for farm products during the 1920s, lost their land. The banking system and the financial infrastructure essential to investment lacked credibility.[88] In the face of this massive failure of the economic order many individuals found little legitimacy in the liberal bourgeois assertion that would explain their personal suffering as simply the consequences of their own inadequate efforts to promote their personal economic interests. Many saw clearly that they were the victims of the voluntary decisions of others over whom they had no control, and certainly with whom they did not share equal power.

The colonial visionaries had imagined a society where everyone (i.e., free, white males) would have an "opportunity to own or manage or at least share in the owning or managing of productive property." By the 1920s, however, this type of opportunity had all but vanished for the mass of the American populace. It had been replaced with

> . . . an ersatz [artificial] type of opportunity—to work for other men for ever higher wages and ever rising levels of consumption—and an ersatz type of property—common stock, or claims on profits but no real role in management—which replaced an earlier dream of farm or shop.[89]

With the Great Depression even this vision of opportunity—the industrialized counterpart of bourgeois ideology—was in jeopardy. The task, which fell to the Federal government under Roosevelt and his New Deal associates and supporters, was to preserve capitalism from both its own inability to regain its pre-Depression vitality and the demands for more fundamental changes arising from increasingly vocal segments of unemployed and to erect a new vision of social order on the crumbled foundations of the old bourgeois ideology.

That America was and would remain a capitalist nation was never questioned by the political and economic leaders of the 1930s. However, unlike the bourgeois leadership of early America, the majority of New Deal leaders—most of whom, including Roosevelt, were drawn from the upper and upper–middle-income segments of America—believed that for capitalism to recover from the Depression, grow, and avoid future cycles of boom and bust, the state would have to play a more active role in coordinating and stimulating private enterprise both domestically and internationally.[90] This was not their initial vision. Between 1933 and 1935 the primary aim of New Deal policies was simply to provide an environment that would facilitate business recovery through tax concessions and other economic stimuli. These policies had little effect, however, and the Roosevelt administration came to recognize that more direct measures would be required.[91] The inability of the private sector to recover and on its own provide some measure of relief to the millions of unemployed and impoverished Americans forced a new role on the government.

There were two significant components to this new role. One was the planned stimulation of private enterprise through Federal spending and policies that would make investment once again attractive to the capitalist class. The other was to use Federal money to provide a measure of economic relief and social welfare for the masses of individuals who were unemployed and impoverished as a result of the Depression. In 1935 Congress voted nearly $5 billion for public relief, the single largest government appropriation ever made up to that time. This step represented a significant break with the past, for it was an admission that the private enterprise economy would not or could not, if simply left to its own devices, provide for the general public welfare as the bourgeois forefathers had imagined. By taking on the direct burden of public welfare through such programs as unemployment compensation and Social Security, the Federal government of the New Deal era removed this burden from the private sector. Through its public relief and social welfare programs the Federal government stepped into the breach, compensating for the failure of the private sector.

Whatever the particular motives behind the institution of government-sponsored and -funded welfare programs, their creation had several important benefits for the private owners of the nation's wealth. First, the government made itself the focus of public demands for relief, diverting attention away from the private sector's failure to provide a viable economy. Second, by insuring at least a minimum of economic relief to the unemployed, the homeless, the hungry, and the disheartened, the New Deal welfare programs reduced the possibility that these individuals would coalesce into a powerful movement demanding more radical socialist restructuring of the American economic order. In a sense the Federal government paid industry's bill for the economic disruption and public anger caused by the Depression. "Welfare, by stilling the voice of dissent, and by stimulating more consumption and higher profits, represented a type of government insurance for the existing economy.[92] In its attempts to minimize both public suffering and public outrage, the government emerged as the ultimate protector of the capitalist economy from the consequences of its own inadequacies.

The New Deal, however, cannot be seen as simply a clever and cynical creation of a unified capitalist class seeking to protect its own interests. Rather, the New Deal era provides an excellent example of the types of conflicts that can arise among various segments of the capitalist class and of how the state serves to mediate these conflicts within a legal and ideological framework that rules out any solution that would fundamentally alter the basic rights to private ownership and usage of productive property for personal profit. The conflicts between various segments of business and the government during the New Deal era should not be mistaken as an example of true pluralism in American government. These conflicts occurred between individuals committed to the preservation of a capitalist social order. The debates were not over *whether* capitalism should be preserved but over *how* this would be accomplished. The Unemployed Worker's Councils and other socialist groups pressing for more radical redefinition of the rights and responsibilities of the owners of capital were by and large excluded from direct participation in these struggles.[93] In fact, the Depression era and the policies established to cope with it ultimately served to eliminate socialist and radical labor movements as a legitimate and viable political force in America.[94]

The social welfare policies of the New Deal government were not without their costs and contradictions. Paying for the new array of welfare programs such as Social Security, the Works Progress Administration, and the Federal Housing Authority as well as programs designed to stimulate industrial development such as the TVA (Tennessee Valley Authority) was costly. The Federal Government was caught in a contradiction. The government needed new revenue, but it could not afford to risk heavy taxation of private wealth and corporate profits. Such taxes would minimize rather than increase investment incentives among the capitalist class. The watered-down corporate tax act of 1935 raised barely 5 percent of the $5 billion voted for economic relief that year.[95] The Federal government was forced to turn to taxes on wages (e.g., Social Security Tax, personal income tax) and deficit spending to meet the shortfall. It was in the context of these decisions that what James O'Conner calls the "fiscal crisis of the state" was born.

The policies of the New Deal established the state in the form of the Federal government as both the stimulator and facilitator of private profit and the major provider of social welfare services. As the facilitator of private investment and profit the state must avoid any truly progressive forms of taxation that would lead to a fundamental redistribution of wealth. As the provider of public welfare, however, it is increasingly called upon by the public to provide services for which it has difficulty paying since it cannot sufficiently tap the private wealth of the capitalist class.[96]

SUMMARY: THE NEW DEAL AND THE CONTEMPORARY IDEOLOGY OF CRIME

The Depression and the New Deal era played an important role in shaping modern-day understandings of crime and crime control both because of what it changed and what it did not change in the American political economy. It did not fundamentally change the liberal belief that freedom resides in (1) the right to own property and (2) the right to enter into free contracts to advance one's property interests. Retained also was the ideology that equality under the law overrides and justifies other, more concrete economic inequalities. That is, as long as individuals enjoy equality under the law, the liberal image of a free and just society arising from a system based on free contract is validated. The preservation of these ideas has shaped modern-day conceptions of crime and state law in several ways.

First, the preservation of the right to the private ownership of productive property and the right to compete for the expansion of this property meant that harms resulting from the usage of private property would still remain essentially peripheral to the concerns of criminal law. While increased growth of state involvement in economic activity led to increased *regulation* of business activity, the fundamental right of a relatively few to decide upon the economic fate of many was preserved. The rights of the owners and managers of capital to hire or lay off workers and close plants or move them elsewhere in the United States or to other countries deemed more conducive to profit remained part of the perceived inalienable right to pursue the goal of profit. Moreover, where the harms resulting from corporate activity (e.g., air pollution, employment discrimination, water pollution, antitrust violations, etc.) were regulated by government, these harms were not accorded the same stigma associated with crime, and as we shall see in later chapters, numerous limitations were placed on the state's power to regulate economic activity based on the right of industry to enjoy the free use of its property.

Second, the preservation of the view that all rights and liberties flow from the fundamental right to own property meant that state law could and would be used to suppress individuals such as Socialists and Communists who openly worked for a replacement of private property rights with collective property rights. Since all liberties are viewed as arising from the right to private property, the state has seldom—when the need arose—hesitated to limit the rights to free speech, free press, and free assembly for those who challenged the right to the private ownership of productive property. As political scientist Edward Greenberg notes,

> In fact, from the passage of the Alien and Sedition Acts during the administration of John Adams, up to the present, the Supreme Court has never declared unconstitutional any act of Congress designed to limit the free speech of dissidents.[97]

With respect to crime and crime control this has meant that those who see the crime problem as rooted in the fundamental nature of property relations in America have been more limited in their opportunities to communicate this perspective to the public than have those who are more supportive of the basic soundness of a capitalist social order.

Third, retention of a belief in free contract and equality under the law tended to keep alive the view that if some people were poor, propertyless, ghettoized, or chronically unemployed it was probably due in no small measure to their *individual* failings rather than the consequences of a particular social system. If people view the world through an ideology that emphasizes (1) their right to free contract and (2) the fact that they are equal before the law to pursue the making of free contracts, they will tend to see themselves "as equal in some respect more fundamental than all the respects in which they are unequal."[98] Where equality of opportunity is seen as overriding differences of condition, there is a strong tendency to see those in unfavorable conditions as simply having failed to make the best of their opportunities. This particular view of those who are less equal, in turn, has affected our modern-day image of crime in three important ways.

First, it has tended to reinforce the suspicion that the lowest socioeconomic classes are "dangerous," contributing to an even greater fear of the crimes "they" might commit and consequently to the high priority placed by the law enforcement system on the kinds of common crimes believed to be most often associated with these classes. Second, if both crime and the conditions associated with it, such as poverty, unemployment, and lack of education, are seen as the consequences of individual failings, attempts to treat criminals and prevent crime will be focused on *improving individuals,* not on changing the social order. This focus on the individual characteristics of the criminal and the correction of individual offenders has dominated both crime control policies and criminology in America.

Third, retention of the belief in free contract has caused the justice system to direct substantial emphasis upon the deterrent effect of law and criminal punishments. The concept of free contract as the basis for social order contains within it the belief that individuals act, first and foremost, out of rational self-interest. This belief in the importance of rational calculation as the basis of all human actions implies that we can expect to influence the choices of potential lawbreakers by threatening them with punishment. As we shall see, this concept of human nature has played a significant role in shaping our policies concerning crime control.

In addition to retaining and in some ways strengthening the liberal ideology, the New Deal brought about several significant changes in the actual functions of the government that have influenced our contemporary approach to the crime problem. First, the state was established as the primary institution responsible for maintaining social welfare. With the establishment of programs such as Social Security, unemployment insurance, aid to families with dependent children, aid to the blind and disabled, subsidies to education, health care, and public housing and through a variety of other social service expenditures the Federal government sought to ameliorate some of the more extreme economic and social inequities generated by the private economy. The effect of this was that the bulk of Americans came to view the government as (1) responsible for social problems such as poverty, unemployment, urban decay, and crime and (2) the place to which demands for improvement of such problems should be directed. In many ways the emergent role of the government as social service provider served to blunt public awareness of the role of the private economy in generating these problems. If poverty and crime increase it is commonly seen as the result of the *government's* failure to do something about them. As will be discussed in Chapters 7, 8, and 9, this means that for many Americans the contemporary crime problem is to be blamed on the failure of the justice system to effectively control crime. The role of the private economy in generating the conditions that produce crime has all but disappeared from the public consciousness in America. Increased demands that the state "do something" about social problems has also served to accelerate the "fiscal crisis of the state" by requiring increased expenditures that can only be paid for through deficit spending.

Second, the coming together of (1) an increased involvement by government in the amelioration of social problems and (2) a continued emphasis upon the concept of equality under the law has led to increased demands for equal protection under the law by groups who see themselves as victims of social problems. From the end of World War II until the present nonwhites, women, the poor, and the elderly have appealed to the government through its courts or legislatures for equal protection under the law with some degree of success. The development of laws attempting to guarantee civil rights for nonwhites and insure equal opportunities in housing, occupations, and other areas represents an extension of the narrow economic concept of equality characteristic of early bourgeois liberalism. However, this situation does not represent a fundamental change in the concept of equality as meaning *equality under the law.* The protection of blacks' voting rights does not make black Americans politically equal in a system dominated for several centuries by the entrenched power of affluent whites. The protection or apparent protection of equal employment opportunities for nonwhites and women does not negate the generations of discrimination that have rendered these groups less ready to compete with white males. The provision of legal services to poor defendants does not alter the larger social inequities that lead to the majority of criminal defendants' being poor to begin with. The extension of "equality" since World War II has been essentially an extension to historically disadvantaged minorities of the abstract right to compete in an economic and social system within which they are not equal in any objective sense. Equality under the law and real equality are not the same, although they are presented as such within the liberal ideology.

Third, the New Deal established the state as an active partner of the private enterprise economy. The government, particularly the Federal government, has come to play a major role in regulating the private economy to protect it from its own inherent tendencies toward cycles of boom and bust. However, once established as a regulator of the economy, the possibility for regulatory growth was great. Between the 1930s and the present there has been an enormous proliferation of regulatory law. This body of law has sought both to keep the economy on an even keel and to respond to public demands to limit various forms of harm (e.g., environmental damage; worker injury, illness, and death; consumer injury and consumer fraud) resulting from actions taken by the private sector. This body of regulatory law, what it is and how it developed, is an important part of our modern-day concept of what constitutes "white-collar" crime, as we shall see in subsequent chapters.

The last three chapters have provided an overview of the development of state law in England and America in order to place the contemporary problems of crime in their appropriate historical and political-economic context. As we begin in the next section to explore the contemporary problems of crime in America, it is important to remember that those things we call crime and the way in which we deal with them are the social products of the evolution of liberal-bourgeois political ideology and capitalist political-economy in America. It is the interaction between these two sets of forces, one rooted in ideology and the other in the social structure of modern capitalism, which give shape to both our consciousness of what acts should be considered "criminal" and how those who commit them should be treated.

NOTES

1. Roberta Ash Garner, *Social Movements in America* (New York: Rand McNally, 1977), 20.
2. Wesley Frank Craven, *The Southern Colonies in the Seventeenth Century: 1607–1689* (Baton Rouge: Louisiana State University Press, 1949), 106.
3. Edwin Powers, *Crime and Punishment in Early Massachusetts* (Boston: Beacon Press, 1966), 264–273.
4. William E. Nelson, *The Americanization of Common Law* (Cambridge, Mass.: Harvard University Press, 1975), 37–38.
5. Ibid., 40.
6. David J. Rothman, *The Discovery of the Asylum: Social Order and Disorder in the New Republic* (Boston: Little Brown, 1971), 15.

7. Nelson, *The Americanization of Common Law,* 39.
8. Ibid., 41–43.
9. Cotton Mather, quoted in Ibid., 45.
10. Arthur P. Scott, *Criminal Laws in Colonial Virginia* (Chicago: University of Chicago Press, 1930), 225–227.
11. Lawrence Friedman, *A History of American Law* (New York: Simon and Schuster), 62.
12. *Colonial Laws of Massachusetts, 1660–1672,* vol. 1, 174.
13. Garner, *Social Movements in America,* 31.
14. See for example, Leon de Valinger, Jr., ed., *Court Records of Kent County, Delaware: 1680–1705,* 283–284.
15. Friedman, *A History of American Law,* 63.
16. E. Franklin Frazier, *The Negro in the United States* (New York: MacMillan, 1957), 86–87.
17. Lorenzo J. Greene, *The Negro in Colonial New England: 1620–1776* (New York: Columbia University Press, 1942), 142.
18. John Spencer Bassett, *Slavery and Servitude in the Colony of North Carolina* (Baltimore: John Hopkins University Press, 1896).
19. James Willard Hurst, *The Growth of American Law* (Boston: Little Brown, 1950), 3.
20. Albert Szymanski, *The Capitalist State and the Politics of Class* (Cambridge, Mass.: Winthrop Publishers, 1978), 151.
21. For a detailed discussion see Charles Beard, *An Economic Interpretation of the Constitution of the United States* (New York: MacMillan, 1962), chaps. 2, 3, and 4.
22. Ibid., chap. 5.
23. Szymanski, *The Capitalist State,* 156.
24. Hurst, *Growth of American Law,* 48.
25. U.S. Constitution, sect. 10, Clause 1. See also early Supreme Court interpretations of the constitutional rights to contract in *Fletcher* v. *Peck* (1810), *Dartmouth College* case (1819), and *Charles River Bridge Co.* v. *Warren Bridge Co.* (1837).
26. James Willard Hurst, *Law and the Conditions of Freedom* (Madison: University of Wisconsin Press, 1967).
27. Hurst, *Law and the Conditions of Freedom,* 36.
28. 1 How. 311 (1843).
29. Charles Warren, *The Supreme Court in United States History* (Boston: Little Brown 1926) 2:103.
30. *Gibbons* v. *Ogden,* 9 Wheaton 1 (1824).
31. For a detailed discussion see Carter Goodrich, *Government Promotion of American Canals and Railroads: 1800–1890* (New York: Columbia University Press, 1960).
32. Friedman, *A History of American Law,* 95.
33. *Hudson and Goodwin* v. *United States,* 7 Cranch 32 (1821).
34. William S. Nelson, "Emerging Notions of Modern Criminal Law in the Revolutionary Era," in Richard Quinney, ed., *Criminal Justice in America* (Boston: Little, Brown, 1974), 109.
35. Ibid., 108.
36. Nelson, *"Emerging Notions of Modern Criminal Law,"* 104.
37. Rothman, *The Discovery of the Asylum,* 15.
38. Powers, *Crime and Punishment in Early Massachusetts,* 57.
39. Rothman, *The Discovery of the Asylum,* 17–18.
40. Paul Takagi, "The Walnut Street Jail: A Penal Reform to Centralize the Powers of the State," *Federal Probation* (December 1975): 18–26.

41. Cesare Becarria, *On Crimes and Punishment,* trans. Henry Paolucci (Indianapolis, Ind.: Bobbs-Merrill, 1963), 58.
42. Jeremy Bentham, *The Writings of Jeremy Bentham* (New York: Russell and Russell, 1962).
43. Rothman, *The Discovery of the Asylum,* 80–88.
44. Constitution of the State of New Hampshire, 1784, art. 1, sect. 18.
45. Edgar W. Butler, *The Urban Crises: Problems and Prospects in America* (Santa Monica, Calif.: Goodyear Publications, 1977), 36.
46. See U.S. Bureau of the Census, *1970 Census of Population* (Washington, D.C.: Government Printing Office, 1971), 42; and *Historical Statistics of the United States: Colonial Times to 1957,* Dept. of Commerce (Washington, D.C.: Government Printing Office, 1960).
47. W. S. Woytinsky et al., *Employment and Wages in the United States* (New York: Twentieth Century Fund, 1953).
48. Evelyn Parks, "From Constabulary to Police Society: Implications for Social Control," *Catalyst,* no. 5 (Summer 1970): 79.
49. Mark S. Hubbell, *Our Police and Our City: A Study of the Official History of the Buffalo Police Department* (Buffalo: Bensler and Wesley, 1893), 57–58.
50. See Alan Silver, "The Demands for Order in Civil Society," in David Bordura, ed., *The Police: Six Sociological Essays* (New York: Wiley, 1967) 1–24.
51. Roger Lane, "Urbanization and Criminal Violence in the 19th Century: Massachusetts as a Test Case," in Hugh Graham and Ted Gurr, eds., *The History of Violence in America* (New York: Bantam Books, 1970), 468–484.
52. The pioneering sociologist Georg Simmel, for example, observed that the urban environment "grants to the individual a kind and an amount of personal freedom which has no analogy whatsoever under other conditions." Georg Simmel, *The Sociology of Georg Simmel,* ed. and trans. Kurt Wolff (MacMillan, 1955).
53. Walter Reckless, *The Crime Problem* (New York: Appleton-Century-Crofts, 1973), 5.
54. William F. Ogburn, "Factors in the Variation of Crime Among Cities," *Journal of the American Statistical Association,* 30 (March 1935): 12–34; Karl Schuessler, "Components of Variation in City Crime Rates," *Social Problems,* 9 (Spring 1962): 314–323.
55. William F. Whyte, *Street Corner Society* (Chicago: University of Illinois Press, 1955).
56. Friedman, *A History of American Law,* 409.
57. *Bavies* v. *Mann,* 10 M&W 546 (1842).
58. Friedman, *A History of American Law,* 389.
59. 1 Blackstone Commentaries, 438.
60. *Farwell* v. *Boston and Worcester Railroad,* 45 Mass. (4 Metc.) 49 (1842).
61. John R. Commons, *Legal Foundations of Capitalism* (1924; reprint, Madison: University of Wisconsin Press, 1957), 57.
62. *Godcharles* v. *Wigeman* 113 Pa. St., 6 Atl. 354 (1886).
63. *Ritchie* v. *People,* 155 Ill. 98, 40 N.E., 454 (1895).
64. *Wedgwood* v. *Chicago and Northwestern Railroad Co.,* 41 Wis. 478 (1877).
65. *Matter of Jacobs,* 98 N.Y. 98 (1885).
66. Grant McConnell, *Private Power in American Democracy* (New York: Vintage Books, 1966), 38–40.
67. Hurst, *Law and the Conditions of Freedom,* 47.
68. See William R. Compton, "Early History of Stock Ownership in Corporations," *George Washington Law Review,* 9 (1940): 125.

69. McConnell, *Private Power,* 31.
70. Illinois Constitution of 1870, art. IV, sect. 22.
71. Friedman, *A History of American Law,* 306.
72. Nebraska Constitution of 1875, art. XI, sect. 4.
73. Washington Constitution of 1889, art. XII, sect. 22.
74. Colorado Constitution of 1876, art. XVI, sect. 2.
75. *Munn* v. *Illinois,* 94 U.S. 113 (1876).
76. Commons, *Legal Foundations of Capitalism,* 14.
77. *Ibid.,* p. 15.
78. *Wabash Railway* v. *Illinois,* 118 U.S. 557 (1886).
79. *Chicago, Minneapolis and St. Paul Railroad* v. *Minnesota,* 134 U.S. 418 (1890).
80. Gilbert Geis, *White Collar Crime* (New York: Free Press, 1977).
81. Frank Pearce, *The Crimes of the Powerful* (London: Pluto Press, 1976), 86.
82. Richard Hofstadter, "What Happened to the Anti-Trust Movement?" in *The Paranoid Style in American Politics* (New York: Vintage Books, 1967), 197.
83. See Gabriel Kolko, *Railroads and Regulation: 1877–1916* (Princeton, N.J.: Princeton University Press, 1965), 144–151.
84. Quoted in ibid., 35.
85. Pearce, *Crimes of the Powerful,* 87–88.
86. McConnell, *Private Power,* 42.
87. Gabriel Kolko, *The Triumph of Conservatism* (New York: Free Press, 1963), 2–3.
88. For a general description of the Depression and its consequences see Lester V. Chandler, *America's Greatest Depression, 1929–1941* (New York: Harper & Row, 1970).
89. Paul K. Conklin, *The New Deal* (Arlington Heights, Ill.: AHM Publishing Co., 1975), 53.
90. Arthur Schlesinger, *Politics of Upheaval,* vol. 3 of *Age of Roosevelt* (New York: Houghton Mifflin, 1960) provides a good overview of this new direction in government policy.
91. Raymond Moley, *The First New Deal* (New York: Harcourt Brace Jovanovich, 1966).
92. Conklin, *The New Deal,* 55
93. Piven and Cloward, 44–49.
94. Richard O. Boyer and Herbert M. Morias, *Labor's Untold Story* (New York: Marzani and Munsell, 1965), 329–365.
95. Conklin, *The New Deal,* 63.
96. James O'Connor, *The Fiscal Crisis of the State* (New York: St. Martin's Press, 1973).
97. Edward S. Greenberg, *The American Political System* (Cambridge, Mass.: Winthrop Publishers, 1980), 357.
98. C. B. Macpherson, *The Political Theory of Possessive Individualism* (New York: Oxford University Press, 1962), 272.

PART III

State Law and the Institutions of Justice

CHAPTER 6

The Legal Bases of Crime and Justice in America

Introduction

The preceding section examined the relationship between forms of social organization and systems of social control, making particular reference to the evolution of state law in England and America. This section will look more closely at the specific institutions of law and justice in America, particularly as they exist today.

This chapter examines the philosophical and ideological bases of contemporary American law, focusing on the definition and control of crime. As we saw in the preceding section, the ultimate basis for our modern-day understanding of the crime problem is the replacement of communal forms of social control by state law as the primary mechanism for defining wrongdoing and punishing wrongdoers. The historical evolution of state law, however, is intimately related to the interplay between demands that the state operate to protect and facilitate the economic order on which it is based and the often contradictory need for the state to maintain legitimacy in the eyes of its citizens. This contradiction is particularly intense in capitalist societies such as the United States where the economic order is privately owned and controlled by a relatively small proportion of the population. Acts by the state designed to facilitate and protect the interest of those who derive the greatest economic and political benefit from the existing political economy threaten to reveal the state as primarily the protector of the interests of a small minority of the population rather than the majority.

Under these conditions the need for forms of law that enhance state legitimacy is great. The legitimacy of the American legal system derives largely from the liberal bourgeois ideology, and particularly its emphasis upon the concept of *equality under the law*. In this chapter we will examine how the liberal ideology manifests itself in specific concepts and principles that serve to legitimate the practice of crime control through law in America.

THREE KINDS OF LAW

Law in America can be divided into three general categories: criminal law, civil law, and regulatory or administrative law. This division classifies possible forms of harm into distinct categories according to the kinds of efforts the state will make to control them. In many ways this division is the direct consequence of a capitalist political economy. The legislative and judicial decisions that have determined what kinds of harms will be controlled through criminal law and what kinds will be handled either as civil or regulatory matters is the product of a political state that has historically been dominated by the world view of that relatively small proportion of Americans who own, control, and/or manage the private economy.

Each of the three categories of law mentioned—criminal, civil, and regulatory—can be further subdivided into substantive and procedural laws. *Substantive laws* designate specific acts or omissions, or specific classes of acts or omissions, as legitimate targets for legal intervention. *Procedural laws* specify how this legal intervention can take place. Laws prohibiting the possession of marijuana, for instance, are substantive laws while those that specify when and under what conditions police may search individuals, their residences, or their automobiles for marijuana are procedural laws. Similarly, laws that define the legal limits of cotton dust in a factory are substantive while those that specify the official steps that must be followed by an employee requesting investigation of the air quality at his or her place of work are procedural. Procedural laws essentially constitute limitations on the power of the state. It is through the maintenance and expansion of procedural laws that state legitimacy, and in particular the promise of equality under the law, has been maintained.

The general categories of criminal, civil, and regulatory law each encompass both substantive and procedural laws unique to their particular focus. There is, however, some degree of overlap. Individuals charged with assault under the criminal law, for instance, may also be sued by their victims for damages under civil law. Similarly, certain actions by businesses that are held to be "in restraint of trade" may be handled solely within the confines of a regulatory agency *or* turned over to the United States Department of Justice for prosecution as a criminal offense. In addition, certain procedural guarantees such as those in the Fourteenth Amendment to the Constitution, which state that individuals cannot be deprived of liberty or property without "due process of law," serve as overarching principles that can be applied to procedures undertaken in any area of law. Despite the various areas of overlap, however, criminal, civil, and regulatory law remain relatively distinct types of law, each with its own characteristics and functions.

Criminal Law

Crimes are acts or omissions deemed to be (1) wrong, (2) threats to society as a whole, and (3) punishable by the state. *Substantive criminal laws* designate specific acts or omissions as crimes while *laws of criminal procedure* delimit the legally appropriate methods for capturing, prosecuting, and punishing those charged with crimes.

Acts are defined as crimes not simply because they cause injury to specific individuals but because they are viewed as threatening the general social order, that is, as victimizing society as a whole. *Society as a whole*, however, does not exist as a tangible thing; it is a concept. Instead, the *state* is defined as representing this intangible "society as a whole," and it is the legal mechanisms of the state and not "society as a whole" that determines what specific behaviors represent general threats to social order. The view that the state is nothing more than the legal manifestation of the will of the people is the very heart of the liberal democracy's claim to legitimacy.

As the legal embodiment of society, the state pursues and prosecutes criminal offenders in its own name. The cost of crime control and criminal prosecution is in effect socialized. Court actions taken under criminal law list the state as the plaintiff (the alleged injured party), for example, *The State of Wisconsin* v. *Smith*. Furthermore, under criminal law the convicted offender generally makes satisfaction not directly to the person harmed but to the state by participating in some correctional or rehabilitation program or by paying a fine to the state, for where crime is concerned it is society as represented by the state and not the individual that is defined as the principal victim.

Civil Law

The term "civil law" encompasses an enormous body of substantive and procedural rules for determining the legal duties of each member of society to others and for litigating claimed violations of those duties. This term includes tort law, the law of corporations, contract law, and a variety of laws governing other aspects of business, property, family and interpersonal relations.

Of particular relevance to the study of crime is the law of *torts*. Torts are acts that cause injury to the financial, physical, emotional, or psychological well-being of some individual. Nearly all forms of injury other than those resulting from contract violations can be litigated under the law of torts. Tort law provides that

> If a person, without legal defense or justification harms or interferes with the legally recognized interests of others as the result of conduct falling below recognized social standards, such a person will be held liable.[1]

Nearly all crimes could also be litigated as torts since criminal acts, like torts, interfere with the "legally recognized interests of others" and are "below recognized social standards." Indeed, until the emergence of English common law and the eyre system many acts now defined as crimes under Anglo-American law were handled as torts, that is, as personal suits for damages. Today, victims seldom sue their criminals for redress of damages, although such suits would be legally possible under the law of torts.

The primary difference between tort law and criminal law is that under

the law of torts the state is not actively concerned with capturing and punishing offenders. Tort law provides a person claiming injury a legal framework
within which to seek redress, but such legal actions under tort law occur
only when the injured party initiates a suit for damages. Because torts are
not socialized, that is, they are defined as harms to individuals rather than
society, the state neither initiates nor prosecutes torts as it does crimes. Legal
actions under tort law (as well as most other civil actions) list the person(s)
claiming injury, rather than the state as the plaintiff (e.g., *Franklin* v. *Smith*).
In further contrast to criminal law, any reparation assessed under tort law is
usually paid to the plaintiff rather than the state.

Tort law tends to be more general in character than criminal law. Rather
than prohibiting *specific* acts, the law of torts identifies broad categories of
conduct as below acceptable standards and therefore as a basis for suit. These
general categories are interference with personal rights, interference with
property rights, and acts of negligence resulting in harm. Under tort law
interference with personal rights covers such things as assault and battery,
false imprisonment, defamation, malicious prosecution, violations of rights
to due process, interference with rights of privacy, and infliction of mental
distress. Violations of property rights under tort law encompass trespass to
land, trespass to other property, fraud, and certain business rights. Tort law
recognizes suits for negligence in those instances where injury results from
actions that a person of ordinary prudence would have recognized as potentially harmful to others.[2]

The real distinction between criminal acts and civil wrongs under tort
law is not the actual amount of injury caused but the legal definition of who
is the primary victim. For instance, the failure to maintain adequate safety
standards at a building site may lead to the death of several workmen. In
the absence of any law specifically defining the lack of safety as criminal,
however, these deaths remain only harms to individuals, not threats to the
social order. In contrast, the theft of a television that causes an actual loss
of $100 is a criminal offense, not because the loss is great but because the
victim has been defined as "society as a whole" and not simply as the owner
of the television. The kinds of harms a state chooses to socialize and the
kinds it does not socialize are an important expression of social policy and
that state's vision of the ideal social order.

Suits under tort law, as well as litigation under other areas of civil law,
lack the social stigma of criminal prosecutions. This plays an important role
in shaping our consciousness of what constitutes the "dangerous classes" in
society. Those acts normally defined as crimes under Anglo-American law
can be committed by almost everyone in society, although their return is so
limited that the affluent and the elite have little reason to engage in them.
As one social critic said, the law in its wisdom prohibits both the rich man
and the poor man from stealing bread. Most forms of injury that can result
from callous or questionable business practices or from the conduct of professions and politics are defined under American law as civil wrongs. These
wrongs, whose injury often exceeds the injury caused by conventional crime,

can generally only be perpetrated by those in upper-middle or elite positions— those with access to positions of power and trust. Socially recognized harms in America have been divided into civil and criminal wrongs in a way that generally protects middle-class and elite Americans from being stigmatized as "criminals" for the harms they are most likely to cause. In contrast, nearly all those forms of harm that the working class and the underclass can commit bear the full weight of criminal stigma.

Regulatory Law

Regulatory law is based on legislation granting broad rule-making and rule-enforcing powers to governmental agencies charged with overseeing the conduct of particular sectors of economic life such as business relations, labor relations, communication, transportation, and so forth. Regulatory law consists of both the initial legislation creating these various regulatory bodies and the rules subsequently established by them. Actions taken under regulatory law occur most often not in courts but in the agencies, commissions, and boards established by legislation.

Regulatory law reflects certain characteristics of both civil law and criminal law but is like neither. On their own initiative regulatory agencies may actively investigate and adjudicate violators, just as police agencies and courts seek to enforce criminal law. However, they may also serve as forums for the resolution of disputes between conflicting parties, as do civil courts. These agencies also have at their disposal a number of options for regulating business behavior drawn from both criminal and civil law. Like criminal courts, regulatory agencies may levy a penal sanction in the form of a fine paid to the state, but like civil courts, they may also arrange for the payment of damages to injured parties or order the individual or business to refrain from a particular practice. Finally, regulatory law resembles criminal law in its concern for protecting the overall operation of a larger system rather than simply providing a forum for the resolution of individual disputes. Regulatory law has grown significantly since the New Deal as the state has sought to maintain stability in the private economy while also instituting reforms in response to public opposition to environmental, occupational, and economic damage resulting from actions within the private economy.

PUNISHMENT AND THE JUSTIFICATIONS FOR CRIMINAL LAW

Punishment is in general the imposition of some suffering or deprivation upon an individual or group of individuals in response to some wrongful act. The term "punishment" usually implies a deliberate action taken by a person or group in response to the behavior of another person or group. While we might say that a person who was burned after throwing gasoline onto an open fire was "punished" for having behaved foolishly, this instance lacks the quality of *social interaction* normally associated with punishment. That is, punishment normally involves some relationship between a punisher and the punished.[3]

Punishment *under law* is the imposition of some suffering or deprivation upon an individual or group of individuals by delegated agents of the state in response to some violation of state law. All systems of state law impose deprivations or suffering upon those who violate the law. It is through the imposition of punishment upon lawbreakers that political states dramatize their authority to govern the behavior of individual citizens and demonstrate the limits of acceptable behavior.

Regardless of the motives for which it is undertaken, from the sufferer's point of view the imposition of suffering or deprivation constitutes punishment. The child who looses his or her allowance for failing to come home on time will feel punished whether the parent imposed this penalty simply to make the child suffer for the wrongdoing or as a means of convincing the child to return home on time in the future. Similarly, whether offenders are imprisoned simply so they will "pay their debt to society," or out of a genuine desire to rehabilitate them, they will experience their imprisonment as punishment.

When it appears to occur without justification, punishment tends to be seen as arbitrary and tyrannical. Where law is concerned, such an assessment can be particularly damaging. Modern legal systems claim legitimacy on the premise that they will insure social order, that is, give everyday life a measure of predictability. Where state law imposes suffering or deprivation without justification it violates the very premise of predictability upon which it claims to rest. Under such circumstances state law looses legitimacy, inviting opposition not only from those who actually suffer unjust deprivations but from those who perceive that they might. Under the worst of circumstances, state law perceived as illegitimate by a sufficient mass of people invites rebellion.

State law must justify its imposition of punishments upon citizens. While it can be claimed that law and its associated punishments for violations will insure social order, by itself this claim is too broad to meet the requirements for justification. What is needed is some explanation of *the way in which* the imposition of punishment will in fact create social order. Thus the stated reasons for punishment and the justifications for punishment become one and the same. The primary justifications for punishment under criminal law in America are (1) retribution and (2) deterrence. Two secondary reasons— (1) rehabilitation and (2) incapacitation—are also offered, but as justifications for punishment these are less significant than the first two and are also relatively recent concerns.*

Retribution

Retribution is the imposition of punishment upon convicted lawbreakers for the sole purpose of ensuring "that offenders atone by suffering for their offenses."[4] Retribution is backward-looking; it is concerned only with making

---

*Some may take issue with identification of rehabilitation as a secondary justification for the criminal sanction. However, an examination of criminal justice expenditures is testimony to the secondary nature of rehabilitation.

the offenders "pay" for their crimes by insuring that they suffer in some measure equal to the harm they have done. When punishment is imposed with some future goal in mind, such as convincing the offender to refrain from further wrongdoing or keeping others from committing crimes by dramatizing the risks associated with lawbreaking, its purpose extends beyond simple retribution.[5]

As a justification for the imposition of punishments upon lawbreakers, retribution became relatively unpopular with legal theorists, politicians, and social scientists during the middle decades of the twentieth century. Punishment for its own sake was criticized as "barbaric," "unenlightened," or as one writer put it, "sadly defective in human understanding, not to say human sympathy."[6] The imposition of penal sanctions was justifiable only if it led to some future good, not if its purpose was simply punishing a person for some past offense. In his book *The Crime of Punishment* Karl Menninger reflected this sentiment when he said of retribution

> Actually, it does not remedy anything, and it bypasses completely the real and unsolved problem of how to identify, detect and detain potentially dangerous citizens.[7]

More recently some criminologists and social philosophers have taken issue with these criticisms of punishment for its own sake. They argue that simple retribution is both necessary and morally required by the simple proposition that the wicked should suffer for their misdeeds. It is frequently argued that "justice" requires a balancing of misdeeds with appropriate punishments. Professor van den Haag, for example, claims that

> Justice is done by distributing punishments to offenders according to what is deserved by their offenses as specified by law. . . . Benefits such as the rehabilitation of offenders, the protection of society from them while they are incapacitated, or, even more, the deterrence of others, are welcome, of course. But they are not necessary—and never sufficient—for punishment, and *they are altogether irrelevant to making punishment just.*[8] (emphasis added)

Criminologist Graeme Newman concludes his philosophical and historical examination of punishment with the statement that "There is little grace in punishment. Only justice."[9] Political scientist James Q. Wilson, although concerned to some extent with the future benefits to be derived from punishment, concludes that justice suffers when we fail to recognize that "Wicked people exist" and punish them accordingly.[10] These modern-day observations concerning the just nature of retribution are essentially restatements of the Biblical prescription that

> When one man strikes another and kills him, he shall be put to death. Whoever strikes a beast and kills it shall make restitution, life for life. When one man injures and disfigures his fellow-countryman, it shall be done to him as he has done; fracture for fracture, eye for eye, tooth for tooth; the injury and disfigurement that he has inflicted upon another shall in turn be inflicted upon him.[11]

The rightness of punishing lawbreakers solely for the purpose of making them suffer for their misdeeds is closely linked to the belief in free will. The concept of free will asserts that human decision making is the primary determinant of behavior. Retribution is generally treated in Western legal thought as morally justifiable to the degree that people deliberately choose to behave wickedly. While this view has long been a key source of justification for criminal sanctions in Western law, it has also been a problematic one.

It has long been recognized that the capabilities and experiences allocated to individuals by the conditions of their birth, upbringing, social position, and opportunity have some bearing upon their decision making. There has been a continual need to rectify these observations with the premise that humans are free moral agents.

This problem is an old one. The ancient Greek philosopher Aristotle, in trying to reconcile the polar opposites of free will and determinism, comments that

> You may say that very likely he could not help it, he is just that sort of man. . . he can not stop being unjust or dissolute merely by wishing it. Yet the illness may be voluntary. . . .[12]

This idea—that while they may be exposed to social conditions and experiences that are essentially beyond their control, people retain the ability to choose how they will respond to them—has been an important means of buttressing the doctrine of free will. John Stuart Mill, the influential nineteenth-century English philosopher, supports this view, saying, "We are exactly as capable of making our own character, if we will, as others are of making it for us."[13]

The most serious challenge to the doctrine of free will came with the rise of determinist views of human nature associated with the positivist revolution in social sciences. The acceptability of retribution as a deliberate aim of criminal law declined during the mid–twentieth century in proportion to the increasing acceptability of other explanations of human behavior that deemphasized the importance of free will. For example, in the 1959 edition of their textbook criminologists Harry Barnes and Negley Teeters write

> If a criminal does what he must do in light of his background and his hereditary equipment, it is obviously both futile and unjust to punish him as if he could go straight and had deliberately chosen to do otherwise. . . . This consideration entirely destroys whatever logic there was to social revenge as a basis for punishment.[14]

Their message was clear; retribution is unjust because human behavior is the result of biological and social forces beyond individual control. Furthermore, a concern with retribution was inconsistent with the aim of applying the tools of behavioral science to the control and reduction of deviant behavior. In this vein, another writer argued that

> The retributive approach is too subjective and emotional to solve problems that have their roots in social conditions and the consequent impact on individual

personality. Such an approach can only obstruct the job of evolving techniques for social control utilizing what we now know about the forces that control human behavior.[15]

During the 1940s, 1950s and 1960s there was a general optimism that the social sciences were on the verge of producing a genuine solution to the crime problem. By the 1970s, however, this optimism began to wane as crime rates grew despite the substantial amounts of money that had been spent for "scientific" crime control and rehabilitation. In part, the resurgence of support for retribution reflects a frustration with the apparent failure of sociological and psychological theories of human behavior to produce any acceptable, effective strategies for reducing or even slowing the growth in the rate of crime. This failure has led some, including political scientist James Q. Wilson, to conclude that what may be "interesting and legitimate" for social scientists to study is not particularly useful when it comes to "doing something" about crime by way of public policy. This decline in the attractiveness of behavioral science as a guide to crime control has led to the conclusion in some quarters that at least where public policy is concerned, individual choice should still be viewed as the final determinant of individual behavior. Thus van den Haag says

> Causation of one's choice of behavior does not deprive it of its character as free choice or relieve the actor of responsibility for it—unless the causation is compulsion, internal or external. . . . Unless these distinctions are made, the point most relevant to legal judgments—the difference between the person who could have done otherwise and the person who could not—is obscured.[16]

This return to free will as the explanation for human behavior has brought with it the reassertion that punishment for its own sake is indeed moral.

As a legitimate aim of criminal law, retribution is also supported on the basis of its usefulness in maintaining social order. This perceived usefulness derives from the belief that humans possess an inherent desire to exact revenge for harms done to them. The legal scholar Gerald Gardner said, for example, "The desire to hurt the thing that hurt you is as old as mankind itself and can be shown to have existed throughout the history of punishment."[17] While this desire for revenge may be natural, it also can be disruptive to social order—or so it is argued—because revenge can be taken by "anyone who feels injured and wishes to retaliate."[18] Legal retribution helps avoid the social disorder that would result if individuals extracted personal vengence as they saw fit by providing a controlled and orderly opportunity for the expression of this natural desire for revenge. According to this view, retribution is an appropriate and necessary component of penal sanctions because it provides a means of satisfying the desire for revenge while at the same time avoiding the socially disruptive consequences of personal vengence that, if given free rein, might often exceed the initial harm done or in its fury even fall upon those actually innocent of wrongdoing. Whatever loftier aims or future goals may be sought through the punishment of offenders, consideration must be given, it is felt, to the basic desire to see those who cause harm suffer in return.

A Comment on Retribution. The argument that retribution is both a moral imperative of "justice" and a necessary mechanism for the orderly expression of the desire for vengence is felt by many to be a persuasive justification for punishing criminals. However, as an *explanation* of the specific nature of penal sanctions in various state societies or a specific response to trouble in nonstate societies, it suffers from several inadequacies.

First, not all human societies have been equally concerned with insuring that wrongdoers suffer for their offenses. As we saw in Chapter 3, many simple societies are far more concerned that the victim receive some compensation or restitution for the harm done than that punishment be inflicted for its own sake. What is felt to constitute "justice" can vary from seeing that victims are compensated for the harms suffered to seeing that wrongdoers suffer for their offenses. In other words, different societies imagine justice differently. It is a mistake to assume that because punishment for its own sake is part of the definition of justice in modern Western societies that it reflects some universal understanding of justice.

Second, while all societies respond to wrongdoers, their reasons for inflicting punishment, how it is imposed, and the amount imposed for various offenses differs substantially. To say that humans have an inherent desire to revenge the harms they suffer does not explain these differences and may in fact serve to obscure the very real differences in the way societies resolve trouble. Humans do appear to have some desire to resolve trouble, that is, to restore order to their lives if it has been disrupted by the behavior of others. However, what individuals will understand as an appropriate resolution to trouble is conditioned by the structural arrangements and the cultural beliefs of their society, for it is these factors that define what constitutes order in the first place.

Third, and most importantly, even if humans do wish to see those who harm them atone for this harm in some way, there is a huge gap between saying that people have a desire to make offenders pay for their crimes and concluding that *state-imposed* punishments fulfill this desire *or are even designed to do so.* The gap between human needs and state-designed options for resolving the trouble that can emerge under the American system of criminal justice is demonstrated by one victim of a purse snatching, who said:

> I didn't want Earl [the accused purse snatcher] to go to jail; I didn't even want him fined. But I wanted something. . . . I was willing to make a deal. I would drop charges if Earl would agree to talk with me. I was sure I could wring a confession out of him. . . . I finally figured out what I want. Whatever happens, I want Earl to say "I'm sorry." It won't happen in court—nobody wins at 100 Center St.—but maybe in the hall, on the elevator or by the hot dog stand.[19]

While state-imposed punishments may be justified as a means of meeting the human desire for revenge, their primary purpose is to meet the state's need to be the final arbiter of trouble. The political mechanisms of the state determine what the victim needs to be satisfied and in doing so may ignore or overlook forms of satisfaction, other than retribution, that might be equally or even more satisfying means of resolving trouble from the victim's point of view.

Deterrence

The concept of deterrence is based on the proposition that individuals will refrain from acts that they believe will bring them unpleasant consequences. This hypothesis rests on the belief that humans are rational actors seeking to maximize pleasure and minimize pain; although as a strategy for influencing behavior, deterrence is generally concerned with only the latter half of this formula—the desire to minimize pain. Specifically, this concept asserts that threatening those tempted to break the law with pain in the form of legally imposed punishments should inhibit them from actually breaking the law. That is, the threat of punishment reduces crime because

> Many individuals who are tempted by a particular form of threatened behavior will refrain from committing the offense because the pleasure they might obtain is more than offset by the risk of great unpleasantness communicated by a legal threat.[20]

Unlike retribution, which is concerned only with punishing individuals for past offenses, deterrence is focused on future behavior. It is concerned with what people *will do* rather than with what they *have done*. While a person's past behavior in the form of some criminal offense may be the *occasion* for punishment, from the standpoint of deterrence the *reason* for punishment is the inhibiting effect this punishment will have on future criminal activity. While the concept of deterrence suggests that punishments should keep the person *actually punished* from future wrongdoing (special deterrence), its larger and more important premise is that the threat of punishment, communicated by demonstrating what happens to those lawbreakers who are detected and prosecuted, should inhibit others tempted to break the law from ever doing so (general deterrence).

Because it suggests a way of influencing the behavior of a large number of individuals—those who might be tempted but who have not yet committed some criminal offense—the concept of deterrence is more easily linked to the goal of creating general social order than is retribution. As a justification for the imposition of punishments upon lawbreakers, the concept of deterrence has played a major role in modern legal thought. Indeed, as deterrence theorists Franklin Zimring and Gordon Hawkins observe,

> Belief in the deterrent efficacy of penal sanctions is as old as the criminal law itself. It has informed and does inform political, administrative and judicial policy to so great a degree that deterrence has been described as a "primary and essential postulate" of almost all criminal law systems.[21]

The deterrence hypothesis offers the hope that through the use of criminal sanctions the state can effectively inhibit individuals from committing undesirable acts.

Deterrence Justifies Punishment, but do Punishments Deter?   Do penal sanctions deter crime? This question has been the source of considerable debate among legislators, judges, correctional official and the public in general for the last twenty years. Unfortunately, there is no simple answer to this question, in part because it is the wrong question. Deterrence (if it occurs) results when the state threatens a *particular* punishment for a *particular* crime and does so in a manner that convinces a proportion of those who would have otherwise committed the crime to refrain from doing so. Questions about deterrence can only be answered with respect to the relationship between specific crimes and specific punishments. When considering whether penal sanctions are effective deterrents, it is important to avoid what criminologists Franklin Zimring and Gordon Hawkins labeled "straight-line thinking," that is, the tendency to assume

> If penalties have a deterrent effect in one situation they will have a deterrent effect in all; if some people are deterred by threats, then all will be deterred; if doubling a penalty produces an extra measure of deterrence, then trebling the penalty will do still better.[22]

Rather than asking whether penal sanctions deter crime, a more answerable question is, To what extent does a particular sanction deter a particular crime?

In the last twenty years a number of researchers have sought to determine the deterrent effectiveness of a variety of penal sanctions. This research has produced confusing and often contradictory results. Consider the case of capital punishment.

Studies comparing the murder rates in states that had abolished capital punishment with murder rates in states that had not, in states before and after the abolition of the death penalty, and in various jurisdictions before and after the death penalty was rendered or a person executed all found *no evidence* that capital punishment deters homicide.[23] These studies, all conducted with one exception prior to 1960, laid the foundation for the belief prevalent among criminologists in the 1960s that penal sanctions do not deter criminal behavior. However, all of these studies suffered from one or more serious methodological problems.

Those studies comparing different states generally failed to control for differences between these states regarding such factors as the age, sex, and racial makeup of the population; socioeconomic factors; and cultural backgrounds. All these factors, however, have been shown to have a bearing on the rate of homicide independent of the death penalty. Some studies compared states only on the basis of whether they did or did not permit capital punishment, regardless of whether they actually utilized capital punishment. Deterrence theory, however, would suggest that the effectiveness of a sanction is based upon whether or not it is used rather than upon its mere existence. Studies over time within the same jurisdiction generally failed to examine other changes in either socioeconomic or justice system factors that could also have influenced either the actual or the official murder rate.[24]

In 1975 the economist Isaac Ehrlich, using a far more statistically sophisticated method than had the earlier studies of capital punishment, analyzed the relationship between homicide rates and executions in the United States between the years 1933 and 1969.[25] His analysis demonstrated a significant inverse relationship between homicides and executions (i.e., as executions went down, homicide rates tended to rise). Ehrlich's findings were heralded by some as conclusive proof of the deterrent effectiveness of capital punishment and were submitted by the Solicitor General of the United States to the Supreme Court in the late 1970s to be considered in several cases concerning the constitutionality of the death penalty.

In the same year that Ehrlich's study was reported, another researcher, Peter Passell, using equally sophisticated techniques, found no evidence that capital punishment produced any additional deterrent effect when compared with prison sentences for homicide.[26] Other studies that have reanalyzed Ehrlich's research have shown that his findings are "sensitive to minor technical variations"; that is, slight changes in the data or the assumptions underlying the statistical model Ehrlich used tend to produce very different results.[27] Additionally, when the years 1962–1969 are removed from Ehrlich's study, no deterrent effect is found for the years 1933–1961, indicating that the rise in homicide rates in the 1960s may have been the result of the general rise in crime rather than the consequence of a decline in executions.[28]

These contradictory findings concerning the deterrent effects of capital punishment led a National Science Council Panel that reviewed current deterrence research to conclude, "The results of the analyses on capital punishment provide no useful evidence on the deterrent effect of capital punishment." However, the panel added that

> Our conclusion should not be interpreted as meaning that capital punishment does not have a deterrent effect, but rather that there is currently no evidence for determining whether it does have a deterrent effect.[29]

The deterrent effectiveness of noncapital sanctions is equally uncertain. It has long been held by students of deterrence that increases in the certainty of punishment will produce a greater deterrent effect than will increases in the severity of punishment. That is, potential lawbreakers will be more likely to refrain from crimes where the penalty may be mild but the certainty of punishment high (providing the penalty outweighs the gains from the crime), than from crimes where the potential penalty may be very severe but the chances of actually being punished are slight. Superficially, it appears that deterrence research offers considerable support for this proposition.

Certainty of punishment is generally defined in deterrence research as (1) the probability of arrest and/or (2) if arrested, the probability of being convicted and sentenced. Research using as measures of arrest probability either police clearance rates (the proportion of crimes known to the police that lead to arrest) and/or police expenditures per capita have generally found an inverse relationship between these measures of arrest probability and crime rates.[30] That is, as either the proportion of crimes known to lead to arrest or the amount of police expenditure per capita increase, crime rates tend to decrease. Similarly, studies using as measures of sanction probability the proportion of crimes known or crimes charged that lead to prison sentences have found support for the proposition that increased certainty of punishment leads to a decrease in crime rates.[31]

Studies of the severity of punishment have produced less consistent findings than studies of the certainty of punishment. While several studies have shown that as the lengths of prison sentences for murder increase, murder rates tend to decline, most studies have failed to find similar inverse relationships between sentence severity and other types of crime.[32]

When taken together studies of the deterrent effectiveness of noncapital sanctions would seem to suggest that (1) increases in certainty of punishment produce decreases in crime rates, (2) increases in severity of punishment have less effect on crime rates, and (3) greater marginal deterrence is produced by increases in certainty of punishment than by increases in severity of punishment. However, nearly all the studies from which such conclusions can be drawn suffer serious methodological limitations, and extreme caution must be used when interpreting their findings.

The relationship between changes in criminal penalties and changes in rates of crimes can be explained by a number of factors other than the operation of deterrence. Factors such as the reporting of crimes, the recording of crimes by police, justice system capacity, and incapacitation of offenders all play a part in shaping the relationship between crime rates and sanction levels, although they have little relationship to the deterrence process per se.

A Final Note on Deterrence   The deliberate imposition of suffering upon a person by the state involves more than such practical issues as, "Will this penalty deter other potential offenders?" Whether we recognize it or not, the deliberate choice to cause another human being to suffer is also a moral issue. Unfortunately, the pragmatic concern with controlling crime has led many deterrence researchers as well as many in the criminal justice system to overlook the moral issues involved. From an ethical standpoint, the imposition of penalties upon individuals because we believe that those penalties will deter others from crime comes dangerously close to saying that ends (in this case deterring crime) justifies the means (making some individuals suffer). In a sense the ideology of deterrence accepts the proposition that the state can use the suffering of individuals as a means to its own ends.

It is quite likely that the concept of deterrence leads us to accept longer prison sentences than we would find appropriate if we asked only how much suffering constitutes an appropriate punishment for a given crime. To the extent that a proportion of any particular punishment is imposed solely for the anticipated deterrent effect, the individual is made to suffer not for the act committed but simply as a means of reducing crime. Even if penalties are effective deterrents to crime, at what point does punishing some for the sake of what *others* might do compromise the basic human right not to be a mere tool in the hands of the state?

A second problem with the contemporary concern with deterrence is that it suggests that the sole explanation for crime is found in the process of individual decision making. The deterrence hypothesis views all crime as a matter of choice, as if individuals were free to choose at all times whether to be burglars or executives. Yet the human experience leading to participation in crime is far more complex than such a simplistic vision of humans suggests. Humans are not simply rational calculators of gains and losses, weighing possible outcomes of each and every contemplated action. They also act out of spontaneity, habit, learned predispositions, passions, and thoughtlessness— none of which are particularly rational. The application of a capitalist vision of human nature—that is, that humans are rational competitors for scarce resources—so predominates the deterrence hypothesis that it obscures the fact that participation in crime involves forces well beyond the narrow confines of individual decision making.

A third and very grave consequence of the deterrence ideology is that as it is actually implemented within the American justice system, it is called into play far more often to justify harsh punishments for those who commit common crimes than for those who commit offenses in pursuit of corporate profits or political power. We wave the banner of deterrence to justify years of imprisonment for the armed robber or the house burglar; we are less quick to use this logic when deciding on the penalties for those who cause injury, illness, or loss of money to workers, consumers, and everyone who must live with the consequences of such things as air and water pollution. Thus the practical application of the concept of deterrence serves to justify harsh penalties for one class of criminals—those who are most often poor and nonwhite—while maintaining the impression that forms of harm other than common crime are not grave enough to warrant serious efforts at deterrence.

THE LEGAL BASIS OF CRIME

Crime is defined by state law. That is, in a *formal, legal* sense, a crime occurs only when someone's actions meet the state's criteria for crime. The definition of crime in America reflects the interplay between political-economic forces, as discussed in the preceding chapter, and such ideological forces as the belief in free will, free contract, and the deterrent power of penal threats. As these forces are translated into concrete definitions of crime they take on their own life and character and raise the possibility of new problems and contradictions within the state.

The necessary elements of crime under American law are (1) an overt act, (2) legal prohibition of the act, (3) intent or *mens rea*, and (4) capacity. Absence of any one of these requirements renders behavior noncriminal, although in some instances, notably behavior attributed to mental illness, the state may intervene through mechanisms other than criminal law.

Crime Requires an Overt Act

The legal definition of crime in America requires, first of all, that an overt act be committed. In principle individuals cannot be held criminally liable for *intending* to break the law or for *talking about* breaking the law if they never act upon their intentions or words. The establishment of this principle in Anglo-American law represented an important check upon the arbitrary uses of state power. This check on state power was originally an important part of the struggle to replace government by nobility with government by economic elites, and it has remained a basic tenet of liberal, Western law.

The practice of limiting criminal prosecution to "overt acts," while consistent with political ideology in America, has never been completely followed. For instance, one important implication of requiring that crime involve an overt act is that individuals should not be held criminally liable for a *state of being*. Yet at various times individuals have been subject to police powers for "being" something rather than "doing" something. Arrests of individuals for vagrancy or being "suspicious persons" are prime examples.

By alleging that certain *types* of people pose potential public threats, laws against vagrancy and suspicious persons give police broad discretionary powers to determine what "overt" acts (e.g., arriving in town without income or a place to live, being permanently homeless, dressing strangely, habitually hanging out on some street corner, etc.) are indications of being this type of person. In effect, it is not the quality of the person's action but the quality of their being that authorizes police intervention. While such laws have long been favored by police departments as important tools for the "prevention" of crime and the removal of "undesirable types" from cities, they have more recently come under limitations. In 1972 the Supreme Court held that

> A presumption that people who might walk or loaf or loiter or stroll or frequent houses where liquor is sold, or who are supported by their wives or who look suspicious to the police are to become future criminals is too precarious for a rule of law.[33]

Vagrancy laws and laws regarding suspicious persons are good examples of the kinds of contradictions that can arise between the state's need to control crime and its need to preserve legitimacy. These laws may very well facilitate social control efforts by the justice system, but at the same time they can violate the "rule of law," as the Court noted. Because the rule of law is one of the basic premises upon which the legitimacy of the liberal state rests, the state at times may be required to undercut efforts at social control to preserve legitimacy.

Conspiracy.   Another attempt to circumvent the limitations of requiring that overt acts be committed before police powers can be invoked is the law of *conspiracy.* The laws of conspiracy allow the state to use its police powers in certain situations where an actual harm has not been committed but where intervention is deemed desirable. The instances where "conspiracy" substitutes for an overt harmful act are (1) planning a crime with others, (2) hiring others to commit a crime, or (3) urging or inciting others (as in the case of riot) to commit crime.

When conspiracy laws are invoked in the first two instances (and this is relatively rare) it is most often in connection with prosecutions involving such things as organized crime, racketeering, or homicides for hire. In one such instance an informant notified Federal authorities that he had been hired by a Texas multimillionaire to kill a Federal judge. The informant cooperated in the investigation and claimed he presented his co-conspirator with a posed picture of the bullet-riddled body of the judge to prove he had carried out the contracted murder. While the murder never actually occurred, the multimillionaire was charged with conspiracy to commit murder.[34] What was charged was not the *act* of murder but the *act of planning* to have a murder committed.

Conspiracy and the Repression of Dissent. The third form of conspiracy, "urging or inciting others" to commit crime, has played a particular role in the repression of dissent in America. According to the Constitution individuals have the right of free speech and public assembly. Furthermore, the First Amendment has generally been held to *permit* public and private expression of sentiments favoring such things as a change in the form of government or economic organization. This is consistent with the liberal ideology of individual liberties. However, there are two important exclusions to this: (1) speech that urges others to violate the law and (2) speech that poses a "clear and present danger" to life or property. These two concepts allow for such broad interpretation that they facilitate the use of the law of conspiracy to repress what have been judged to be politically undesirable or dangerous organizations and individuals.

Conspiracy prosecutions aimed at limiting the public expression of opinion and ideology have mostly focused on the leaders of the political Left. It has been noted,

> There is no conviction of a right-wing speaker that has been upheld by the United States Supreme Court. On the other hand, left-wing speakers . . . have been convicted of abstract advocacy of ideas, and on review these convictions have been affirmed by the high court.[35]

During the first third of this century labor leaders were frequently prosecuted for conspiracy to violate various Federal laws governing the production of goods and services. In 1917, for example, the U.S. government indicted leaders of the I.W.W. (a socialist labor movement) with conspiracy to violate the Food and Fuel Control Act on the basis that strikes would disrupt the supply of food and fuel to the army. The "overt acts" used to prove these conspiracy charges were mostly "official statements, policy declarations, newspaper articles and personal expressions of opinion" made by I.W.W. leaders.[36] None of these statements of opinion expressly urged the violation of the Food and Fuel Control Act. They did urge, however, that workers unite and organize to demand an equal share in the control and rewards of production—a viewpoint clearly threatening to the capitalist economy.

Similarly, in the aftermath of the antiwar demonstrations that occurred in Chicago during the 1968 Democratic Convention, seven antiwar movement leaders were indicted for conspiracy to incite riot. The "overt acts" with which they were charged generally involved speaking to groups of people, although no evidence was presented to establish that any of the defendants had urged anyone to violate the law.[37] They were prosecuted for urging that antiwar protestors gather in Chicago during the Democratic National Convention to protest the war as a means of influencing the Democratic party to nominate an antiwar candidate. According to the Kerner Commission, which studied the subsequent disturbance, the presence of these war resisters led to a "police riot." This naked use of police power to suppress the legitimate and legal expression of public antiwar sentiment was one of those embarrassing events that tend to delegitimize a liberal government's claim that it is democratic. The use of conspiracy laws to prosecute leaders of the antiwar movement as criminal rioters, however, served to establish in the minds of many the idea that the Chicago police were behaving lawfully and in accordance with the principles of democracy in curbing the "illegal" behavior of demonstrators.

Crime Requires Legal Prohibition

Before an act can be treated as a crime under American law that act must be *specifically* prohibited. The concept of a "rule of law" as it has been defined within the American system of justice requires that laws (1) be sufficiently specific as to "give a person of ordinary intelligence fair notice that his contemplated conduct is forbidden by the statute"[38] and (2) reduce the possibility of arbitrary and erratic arrests and convictions by clearly indicating what overt acts justify legal intervention.[39] Where individuals can be arrested on vaguely worded statutes they cannot know beforehand whether their actions might be illegal, and police will have wide discretion in determining what is crime.

Governance by highly specific laws is seen by most legal scholars as the primary achievement of modern (i.e., Western, capitalist) legal systems. This "progressive reduction of the arbitrary element of positive law" is generally held as one of the primary tasks of an effective legal system.[40] Within capitalist societies individuals rather than groups are defined as the primary units of action. Capitalist law therefore requires that individuals be given the maximum legal protection to conduct their lives as they see fit. That is, individuals should enjoy what some legal scholars have called the right to maximum individual self-assertion. Only where this individual self-assertion leads to direct violation of specific laws should the state have the right to intervene. This emphasis on legal specificity, while it provides one type of personal liberty, is not without its costs.

First, an emphasis upon legal specificity separates moral obligations from legal ones. As general standards of behavior, moral obligations are necessarily vague; for example, "Thou shalt not steal." Additional interpretation must be applied to determine when a particular act has violated a particular moral standard; for example, what behaviors constitute "stealing"? No legal system can specifically enumerate every possible violation of a general moral standard. As a result, where the law emphasizes specificity a proportion of moral violations will always fall beyond the law's reach. Furthermore, where particular interest groups have played an important role in determining what specific behaviors violate the general moral premise upon which a law is based, moral violations common to members of this group will generally not be defined as crimes. In America, for instance, we find

> Wide areas of legal but immoral sharp practices in business, labor and politics, often severely damaging to society but generally subtle enough to keep just beyond effective range of society's formidable but *fixed* legal gun positions.[41] (emphasis added)

Second, legal specificity reduces the power of community and social groups to influence and control the behavior of their members. According to a "rule of law," others have no right to interfere in our lives unless our behaviors violate some specific legal prohibition, and then this interference normally can be undertaken only by designated agents of state law (e.g., police, courts, correctional agencies, etc.). Because the state specifies both when and how intervention can occur, state law becomes the overriding guideline for behavior.

It is sometimes argued that increased reliance on the formal institutions of state law for social control occurs as the result of a "breakdown" or at least a reduction in the importance of other institutions of social control such as the family, the community, and the church. For example, James S. Campbell, general counsel to the National Commission on the Causes and Prevention of Violence says,

> When a society becomes highly complex, mobile and pluralistic; the beneficiary, yet also the victim of extremely rapid technological change; and when at the same time and partly as a result of these factors, the influence of traditional stabilizing institutions such as family, church and community wanes, then that society of necessity becomes increasingly dependent upon highly structured, formalistic systems of law and government to maintain order.[42]

While this perspective is superficially accurate it fails to take into account the facts that (1) the state itself plays a major role in stimulating technological growth through its support of the private economy's search for ever-newer methods of profitable production and (2) the emergence and growth of state law is an important stimulus to the decline of all other forms of social control. The existence and promulgation of supposedly uniform standards of behavior to which all citizens must conform tends to weaken other forms of social control. The reason is that nonstate forms of social control arise out of the needs and world view of specific communities and groups of people. Of necessity these will vary from one group to another. The uniformity of behavior required by state law weakens the possibility for variations in what will and will not be tolerated by smaller collectivities and thus reduces their viability as mechanisms for the social control of behavior.

Third, legal specificity helps promote a cultural emphasis upon self-oriented rather than altruistic behavior. As criminologist Harold Pepinsky observed,

> If I know that the limits of my duties towards others in my society as specified by law, it can readily be inferred that these limits will define the extent of my identification with those others.[43]

Where individuals identify their obligations toward others as legal and specific rather than moral and general, it becomes difficult to motivate people to engage in altruistic acts that may benefit others or society as a whole. Thus in America pleas for voluntary wage and price restraints as a means of reducing inflation or voluntary reductions in individual consumption to conserve natural resources tend to be relatively ineffective partly because individuals do not identify themselves as being morally responsible for what happens to "the rest of society." As long as people obey the letter of the law, under a "rule of law" they are meeting their obligations as citizens.

Crime Requires Intent: Sometimes

The criminal law is concerned primarily, but not exclusively, with intentional acts. In most instances, before an individual can be convicted of committing a crime, the state must prove that the person "had in mind" causing harm or violating the law. This concern with intentionality is closely related to the emphasis of liberal ideology upon the willfulness of behavior (free contract) and rationality (the mind as the locus of control). The term *mens rea,* which is often used to refer to the concept of criminal intent, means literally "things in the mind." The legal interpretation of criminal intent, however, is not limited to the narrow requirement that individuals specifically intend those harms that actually occur.

Individuals can be held criminally liable for harms that they did not specifically intend as long as it can be shown that there was some intent to cause harm. If Smith strikes Jones, and Jones falls, hits his head on the floor, and dies, Smith can be charged with homicide even though he had no intention of killing Jones. The occurrence of a harm greater than the one intended does not absolve an individual from criminal liability for the unintended greater harm, although the lack of specific intent may lead to a lesser charge, for instance, manslaughter rather than first degree murder.

Individuals can also be held criminally liable for harms resulting from wrongful acts even if there is no intent to cause any actual harm. If one man fires a rifle at another honestly intending only to frighten him but because of poor aim actually kills him, he can be charged with the crime of murder despite the claim that he never intended to harm the victim. This principle was clearly described in *State* v. *Blue,* decided in 1898. In this case the court held that, "The criminal intent . . . need not necessarily be to do the very act forbidden by law, but it must at least be to do a wrong thing."[44]

Criminal charges can also be placed against individuals who fail to follow reasonable standards of safe conduct, even if their intention was to perform a good rather than a wrongful act. That is, individuals can be held criminally liable for the unintended consequences of acts that a reasonable person could foresee would very likely result in harm. Consider the case of the man who in 1882, representing himself as a physician, ordered a female patient to be kept wrapped in kerosene-soaked flannel. The patient subsequently died of burns caused by this treatment, and the man was charged with homicide even though his intention was to cure rather than kill. In the case the judge instructed the jury that "it is not necessary to show an evil intent . . . if by gross negligence he caused the death, he is guilty of culpable homicide." The jury found the man guilty of manslaughter although the defense argued that he had "an honest purpose and intended to cure the disease."[45]

In addition to these various legal interpretations of criminal intent, there are also certain laws that specifically exclude any requirement of criminal intent. Traffic laws are a prime example. Where traffic violations are concerned the act alone (e.g., speeding, running a red light, making an illegal turn, etc.) is sufficient for conviction. The driver's intention is immaterial. Such laws are referred to as laws of *strict liability.* In some jurisdictions certain violations of traffic laws that result in death can lead to charges of homicide by vehicle. In such cases conviction for the traffic offense constitutes an absolute proof of guilt for the charge of homicide by vehicle regardless of the driver's intent.[46]

Another form of strict liability law is that governing *felony murder.* Many jurisdictions provide that if a death should result from the commission of a felony, the person committing the felony may be charged with the crime of murder, even if the death was not foreseeable. If a merchant, for instance, sets fire to his store in order to collect insurance, he would normally be liable only for charges of arson or unlawful burning and insurance fraud, none of which is a capital offense. However, if unknown to the merchant two employees were in the store at the time of the fire and were subsequently killed, the merchant could be charged with the capital offense of felony murder despite the fact that he sincerely believed no one was inside the building. Other areas of strict liability under criminal law are bigamy and statutory rape.[47] In both cases the act is sufficient for conviction in many jurisdictions.

The concept of intent plays a much less important role in tort actions under civil law than it does in cases of alleged criminal violations. The essence of a tort is the allegation that some act or omission on the part of the defendant was the cause of unjustifiable harm to the plaintiff. It is generally not necessary to prove that the harm was intended but only that it could have been avoided if the defendant had behaved in a more socially responsible manner. However, in some areas of civil law, such as employment discrimination based on age, proof that the discriminatory effect was intended entitles the plaintiff to "treble damages," that is, three times the amount actually lost.[48] This is done not so much to compensate the victim as to serve as a punishment and a deterrent for the discriminatory behavior. Such measures tend to blur somewhat the distinction between civil and criminal charges, although even where intentional harm is proven in a civil suit, the defendant avoids the stigma of having been convicted of a criminal offense despite the amount of harm caused.

Crime Requires Capacity

Our legal definition of crime reflects, among other things, the belief that humans possess free will. That is, we believe that humans are capable of freely choosing between right and wrong courses of action. However, the law also recognizes certain conditions that reduce an individual's capability to choose freely between right and wrong actions. Individuals who cannot control their behavior or who cannot fully understand the difference between right and wrong are seen as less responsible for the consequences of their actions than individuals who are believed to enjoy the full benefit of free will.

Before individuals can be convicted of criminal wrongdoing under American law they must have the "capacity," that is, the ability to (1) control their actions and (2) understand the meaning of their actions. While "capacity" is generally recognized as a requirement for defining harmful behavior as *criminal,* under law the presence or absence of capacity is not easily ascertained. Our legal system recognizes three *general* conditions that can reduce an individual's capacity to commit a crime: (1) duress, (2) being under the "age of reason," and (3) insanity. What constitutes specific indicators of these conditions, however, varies with time and place and remains a perennial source of debate and conflict.

Duress.   By law, persons forced to commit crimes "against their will" because of some threat to their own well-being are not held fully responsible for those crimes. Under these conditions it is felt that a person's ability to freely choose between alternative courses of action is reduced and consequently so is their responsibility for the choice made.

At what point a threat is of sufficient gravity to constitute a genuine reduction of free will, however, is not always clear. Traditionally, the courts have defined "duress" as a relatively immediate threat to one's *physical* well-being. The threat of financial or social loss is not usually considered a sufficient defense against a charge of criminal conduct. Even where physical threat is alleged, however, the adequacy of "duress" as a defense is not always self-evident. In the celebrated trial of kidnapped newspaper heiress Patty Hearst on charges of bank robbery, the defense argued that fear of her Symbionese Liberation Army captors left her with no alternative other than to participate in the bank robbery. The prosecution, on the other hand, was successful in convincing the jury that she did in fact have realistic alternatives to participating in the robbery and was therefore criminally liable.[49]

Capacity and the Age of Reason. It is a long-standing belief in Anglo-American culture that the ability to differentiate between right and wrong is developmental. That is, people are not born with an understanding of the difference between right and wrong but develop this understanding during childhood.

Within Western culture this belief was first formalized as a theological doctrine. Under Catholicism, the dominant theology of medieval England, a child was held to be incapable of committing sin until he or she reached the "age of reason," which was defined as seven years of age. This doctrine was later applied to crime as well as sin and was incorporated into English common law. Under English law it was held that children under the age of seven were incapable of committing crime because, not knowing the difference between right and wrong, they were incapable of having a "guilty mind."[50] Today, many jurisdictions in the United States under common law still recognize seven as the minimum age of criminal liability.[51] Children under the minimum age of criminal liability cannot be punished under law for acts that would be criminal if committed by an adult, no matter how grave the offense.

Age and the Idea of Delinquency. While a child under the age of seven could not be punished for a crime under early English law, a child beyond that age could be held as legally responsible for the commission of a crime as any adult and could be punished accordingly. However, if a child between the ages of seven and fourteen was accused of a crime before that child could actually be punished as a criminal offender, it was required under English common law that the prosecution prove the child knew that he or she was doing wrong.[52] This common law doctrine was carried over into early American law. In general the punishment of children between the ages of seven and fourteen as criminal was *possible* as long as *mens rea* could be demonstrated.

By the mid-1800s industrialization and the accompanying emergence of an impoverished, urbanized, and largely immigrant work force in America presented the society with a new problem: a growing number of young lawbreakers. While these young people could be prosecuted as criminals, there emerged in certain sectors of the society a feeling that this was an inadequate response to the problem. What was needed was a new definition of the relationship between age and criminal liability. The pressure for such redefinition stemmed from three interrelated factors.

First, a society based upon an industrial economy requires a longer period of preparation before young people can assume adult roles. For some reformers, punishing young people for crimes as if they were adults when in fact they could neither undertake the other responsibilities of adulthood nor fully enjoy its benefits appeared to be both inconsistent and unjust. Some type of *reduced liability* was felt to be more consistent with the reality of a lengthened transition to adulthood.

Second, young people represented a potential but undeveloped source of industrial labor. An effective transition from agricultural to industrial economy required that this potential labor force be trained in both the skills and the *attitudes* appropriate to industrial work. Simply punishing large numbers of wayward youths as criminals would do little to render them useful adults. Some type of *reformation,* rather than punishment, was required.

Third, the growing number of youthful criminals represented an unprecedented threat to the security of property. In many early industrial towns gangs of impoverished youths depended on theft and other forms of crime as a means of survival. It was felt that punishment after the fact would do little to reduce the movement of young people into lives of crime. Thus *prevention* came to be seen as equally or more important than punishment.

These factors led to a redefinition of the age of criminal liability and a system of justice for juveniles that in theory emphasized reformation and prevention rather than punishment. While noble claims of "saving" the children were often used to justify these reforms, they were designed primarily with a view to children as potential workers. As Nan Berger comments,

> Some of the more far-sighted [reformers] saw the need to give children education which would enable them to man more efficiently the machines of the developing industries of the future. Some also saw the need for protecting property against destitute children who were forced into crime in order to exist at all. The employing classes—the owners of the new mills who were also the property owning classes—saw only one aspect of children's lives: their ability to work in the mills and make profit for the masters.[53]

With the passage in 1899 of the "Act to Regulate the Treatment and Control of Neglected Dependent and Delinquent Children" in Illinois, the concept of partial responsibility for criminal acts based on age was given statutory recognition. Prior to this there had been private attempts to reform wayward youth, such as the House of Refuge movement begun in New York in 1825, as well as public experiments with reform schools and alternatives to incarceration, such as probation. These programs, however, did not challenge the legal status of the young offender as a *criminal.* The Illinois act "invented" a new legal category, that of juvenile delinquent, by transforming the common law doctrine of an age of *possible* responsibility into an age of *partial* responsibility. Under this law children below the age of sixteen could no longer be convicted of criminal offenses, even if they were capable of having a "guilty mind." On the other hand, the lack of a "guilty mind" no longer absolved young people from legal intervention, as it had under the earlier common law doctrine. Young offenders were defined as neither wholly responsible nor wholly guiltless for criminal acts but rather partially responsible. The state could intervene in their lives but could not bring to bear the full weight of criminal sanctions.

The concept of partial responsibility is based not on the inability of juveniles to understand the difference between right and wrong but upon their inability to understand the consequences of illegal actions for their own future lives. The Illinois act was concerned with protecting juveniles from a life of crime by providing a mechanism for early intervention that would direct delinquent youth toward law-abiding lives without imposing upon them the stigma of "criminal." Young lawbreakers would be treated under the law

. . . not as a criminal, or legally charged with crime, but as a ward of the state, to receive practically the care, custody and discipline that are accorded the neglected and dependent child, and which . . . shall approximate nearly as may be that which should be given by its parent.[54]

In practice, this "care" often took the form of placement in harsh, prisonlike reform or "industrial" schools or minimal supervision by overworked and understaffed probation officers.

Both in philosophy and wording the Illinois act served as the basic model for juvenile delinquency legislation in the United States. Within ten years after its passage ten states had passed similar statutes, and by 1912 twenty-two states had established juvenile courts. By 1925 only two states had failed to establish separate courts for juveniles.[55]

The innovation of separate justice for juveniles limited their liability for punishment under criminal law. However, since it was based on the philosophy that the court should protect young people from lives of crime, it increased the *overall* legal liability of young people by making them responsible under the law for acts that would not be criminal if committed by adults. A child could be the target of legal control for acts ranging from habitual truancy to disobedience at home in addition to ordinary criminal offenses.

Today, all states provide some official legal recognition of the status of "juvenile" by specifying a minimum age below which a child is liable only to the juvenile court and cannot be prosecuted for a criminal offense in an adult court. This minimum age ranges from fourteen to twenty-one, depending upon the state, with eighteen being the most common dividing line between adult and juvenile.[56] The relationship between age and criminal responsibility,[57] however, remains problematic. Many states have attempted to distinguish between young people who can be "saved" from a life of crime by the intervention of the juvenile court and those who appear already committed to a criminal identity by establishing a "gray area" within which a child may or may not be prosecuted as an adult. In some states with a minimum age of criminal liability of sixteen, a child between fourteen and sixteen who is charged with a felony offense *may*, upon the decision of a juvenile court judge, be sent to adult court for trial as a legal adult. Furthermore, any child over the age of fourteen charged with a capital offense is automatically considered a legal adult.[57] Juvenile law has never successfully reconciled the goals of saving children from lives of crime and of protecting society from the crimes of children.

Capacity and Insanity. A third condition that is recognized by law as reducing a person's capacity to commit a criminal offense is that of insanity. Because the *mind* is viewed as the locus of responsibility for criminal acts, persons whose minds do not function normally are defined as not fully responsible for their behavior. However, arriving at a definition of insanity—when is a mind not functioning normally?—has been a source of considerable debate within the legal system.

In American courts the normalcy of a person's mental functioning may be measured by one of four tests, depending upon the jurisdiction. These are the M'Naughten rule, the irresistible impulse test, the Durham rule, and the Model Penal Code rule.

The M'Naughten rule, first adopted as a test for insanity in 1843 in England, is concerned solely with a person's ability to distinguish between right and wrong. M'Naughten was charged with murdering the secretary to the prime minister of England. He presented a defense of insanity based on the fact that he suffered from delusions. The court found in M'Naughten's favor and ruled that

> . . . the party accused was labouring under such defect of reason, from disease of the mind, as not to know the nature and quality of the act he was doing; or if he did know it, that he did not know it was wrong.[58]

The M'Naughten rule is the basic test of insanity in approximately thirty of the fifty state jurisdictions in America. In most of these jurisdictions it is the only test of insanity. However, in eighteen states it is combined with the "irresistible impulse" rule, which recognizes that there are certain forms of "mental disease" that do not impair the ability to distinguish between right and wrong but that do reduce the ability to control one's behavior. Under the "irresistible impulse" rule, defendants who suffer from "mental disease" cannot be held criminally accountable if it can be shown that this disease rendered them incapable of controlling their actions, even though they may have known that these actions were wrong.[59]

The M'Naughten rule treats the "mind" solely as the center for rational decision making. According to this view "mental disease" constitutes a defense against charges of criminal conduct where it causes a "defect of reason," that is, it reduces a person's *cognitive* ability to distinguish between right and wrong. In 1954, David Bazelon, a Federal court judge ruling in the case of *Durham v. United States,* expanded the legal concept of "the mind" to incorporate emotional as well as rational functions. Judge Bazelon was of the opinion that "Man is an integrated personality and that reason, which is only one element in that personality, is not the sole determinant of behavior." Based on this expanded view of human behavior, he ruled, "an accused is not criminally responsible if his unlawful act was the *product* of mental disease or mental defect"[60] (emphasis added). This rule required only that a defense of insanity show some link between mental disease and the alleged criminal act. It did not require that some "defect of reason" be shown or that the accused acted on the basis of some irresistible impulse.

The Durham rule, formulated during an era of rapidly expanding concern with "mental health," allowed a broad miscellany of mental and emotional disorders to be admitted as a defense against criminal charges. Persons who could present psychiatric evidence that they suffered from "character defect," "transient stress disorder," "psychopathic personality," or any one of the hundreds of mental disorders listed in the American Psychological Association's catalogue of mental health problems could potentially construct a defense of insanity if they could show a link between the mental disorder and the alleged criminal act. It has also been observed that in some cases the Durham rule encouraged defenses of insanity based on circular reasoning. As one criminologist observed,

> . . . the criminal act itself can be, and has been, used as evidence of the "mental sickness" which is alleged to have caused it, and which, it is argued, should excuse the offender.[61]

This type of reasoning is particularly common in cases involving notably grotesque or bizarre crimes. In such cases it is often difficult to understand how a "normal" person could commit such acts and therefore the act itself is felt to be an indication of insanity.

Although adopted in some state and Federal courts, the Durham rule did not replace the M'Naughten rule as the most common test of insanity in American courts. Its broad view of defensible mental illness is often criticized as being even less adequate to the need for legal precision than the M'Naughten rule. In recent years some courts have adopted the test of insanity proposed by the American Law Institute in its Model Penal Code. The Model Penal Code rule holds that a person is not criminally accountable for a wrongful act if

> . . . at the time of such conduct as a result of mental disease or defect he lacks substantial capacity to either appreciate the criminality of his conduct or to conform his conduct to the requirement of law.[62]

This rule does not place as much emphasis on humans as purely rational beings as does the M'Naughten rule. Under the Model Penal Code test people must be able to "appreciate" the criminality of their behavior rather than "know" the difference between right and wrong. Yet in comparison with the Durham rule, it defines more narrowly the relationship between mental disease and reduced capacity. The Model Penal Code test requires that the mental disease have some impact upon the ability to "appreciate" the wrongfulness of an act rather than simply being related to the production of that act in some unspecified way.

A Final Note on Capacity. As limitations on a person's liability under criminal law, duress and insanity bring into focus important aspects of the concept of capacity. They also receive considerable public notariety when someone charged with a spectacular crime such as shooting President Reagan, killing singer John Lennon, or committing the Son of Sam mass murders in New York pleads not guilty by reason of insanity. However, in the *everyday* administration of justice neither is particularly prevalent or important. To begin, a relatively small proportion of criminal justice activity involves cases of homicide. Moreover, estimates indicate that annually the insanity defense is used in only about 100 cases. When compared with an average of 17,000 arrests for homicide each year, this means insanity pleas occur in less than one tenth of one percent of all homicides resulting in an arrest.[63]

Age is the only limitation upon capacity that plays a significant role in the everyday operations of justice. The existence of a separate system of justice for juveniles, coupled with the fact that nearly half of all those arrested for burglary, larceny, and auto theft (these categories account for approximately 80 percent of all arrests) are under the age of eighteen, means that the justice system in America funnels a substantial number of persons charged with crime into a special system of adjudication because of an assumed reduced capacity due to age.[64]

CONCLUSION: LEGITIMACY AND THE RULE OF LAW

The promise of a *rule of law* is central to claims of political legitimacy by the liberal democratic state. The express function of a rule of law is to restrain the state from arbitrary and capricious intervention in the lives of its citizens. Where criminal law is concerned this means that, among other things, the state should proceed against suspected criminal offenders only in a legally prescribed and predictable manner that is in accordance with the constitution or other founding documents of that state.

Since the United States emerged as a separate nation the various appellate courts frequently have been asked to determine whether existing rules of criminal procedure are constitutional or whether they have been violated in the process of some particular case. The various decisions rendered in these cases has contributed substantially to the constant revision and refinement of the meaning of the "rule of law."

Procedural law has been a source of almost constant conflict. These conflicts reflect a basic tension in the American legal system resulting from the opposition of two sets of forces. On the one hand is the state's need to preserve its legitimacy by maintaining a rule of law and the desire of private citizens to be free from arbitrary intervention in their lives by the state. These forces favor a strict rule of law. On the other is the state's need to meet citizen demands for the repression of crime and its own need to repress individuals and ideas threatening to the state or the underlying economic organization it is designed to protect. These forces favor a relatively free hand in the enforcement of law.

The role of the criminal law apparatus is complex, as the opposition of these two sets of forces demonstrate. The overt control of the poor and the near-poor through the extensive criminalization of nearly all forms of harm such individuals can possibly commit is but one function of criminal law in capitalist society, and it may not be the most important one. It is certainly not a function of criminal law unique to capitalist societies; socialist societies also find themselves required to control the predatory behaviors of some individuals. The more important function of criminal law in capitalist society is its role in dramatizing the state's commitment to the "rule of law." In doing this, criminal law provides a continual demonstration of the legitimacy of the capitalist state and the liberal ideology upon which it is based. This may be the most important function of criminal law in capitalist society, for by preserving the legitimacy of liberal ideology, the legal system protects the underlying capitalist mode of production. It does this by insuring that *individual rights* will be the focus of attention; by emphasizing that questions of justice are questions whether *the law* acted justly, not whether the underlying social order itself is just; and by promulgating the idea that a capitalist social order leads to a just and predictable state. This is not a consciously intended role of criminal law in capitalist society but one that over time has become increasingly important.

NOTES

1. Harold J. Lusk, Charles M. Hewitt, John P. Donnell, and A. James Barnes, *Business Law: Principles and Cases* (Homewood, Ill.: Richard D. Irwin, 1978), 49.
2. Ibid., 51–68.
3. Graeme Newman, *The Punishment Response* (New York: Lippincott, 1978), 9.
4. Nigel Walker, *Sentencing in a Rational Society* (New York: Basic Books, 1971), 5.
5. Ernest Van den Haag, *Punishing Criminals: Concerning a Very Old & Painful Question* (New York: Basic Books, 1975), 10–11.
6. Henry Weihofen, "Retribution Is Obsolete," in *Responsibility,* C. Truedrick, ed. (New York: Atherton Press, 1960), 119–120.
7. Karl Menninger, *The Crime of Punishment* (New York: Viking Press, 1966), 108.
8. Van den Haag, *Punishing Criminals,* 18.
9. Newman, *The Punishment Response,* 287.
10. James Q. Wilson, *Thinking About Crime* (New York: Basic Books, 1975), 209.
11. Leviticus 25:17–22.
12. Quoted in Ernest Van den Haag, *Punishing Criminals: Concerning a Very Old & Painful Question,* 107.
13. John Stuart Mill, *Systems of Logic,* book VI, chap. II, sect. 3 (New York: Harper Bros., 1874).
14. Harry E. Barnes and Negley K. Teeters, *New Horizons in Criminology* (Englewood Cliffs, N.J.: Prentice-Hall, 1959), 817–818.
15. Weihofen, "Retribution Is Obsolete."
16. Van den Haag, *Punishing Criminals,* 109.
17. Gerald Gardiner, "The Purposes of Criminal Punishment," *Modern Law Review,* 21 (1958): 119.
18. Van den Haag, *Punishing Criminals,* 18.
19. Deborah Larnet, "Doin' the New York Hustle: The Real Footwork Begins After You Catch the Thief." *Mother Jones,* 3, no. 9 (November 1978), 23–29.
20. Franklin E. Zimring and Gordon Hawkins, *Deterrence* (Chicago: University of Chicago Press, 1975), 75.
21. Ibid., 1.
22. Ibid., 19.
23. These studies include D. R. Campion, "Does the Death Penalty Protect State Police?" in H. Bedau, ed., *The Death Penalty in America* (Garden City, N.Y., 1969), originally presented to the Joint Committee on Capital Punishment and Corporal Punishment and Lotteries, Canadian Parliament, 1955; R. Dann, *The Deterrent Effect of Capital Punishment,* Friends Social Service Series, Bulletin 29 (Philadelphia: Committee on Philanthropic Labor, 1935); W. F. Graves, "The Deterrent Effects of

Capital Punishment in America," in Bedau, *The Death Penalty in America*; Leonard
Savitz, "A Study in Capital Punishment," *Journal of Criminal Law, Criminology and
Police Science*, 49, no. 4 (1958): 338–341; Thorsten Sellin, *The Death Penalty* (Phila-
delphia: American Law Institute, 1959); Nigel Walker, *Sentencing in a Rational Society*
(London: Penguin Press, 1969), 60–61.

24. For a detailed discussion of the methodological inadequacies of early studies of
the death penalty see Panel on Research on Deterrent and Incapacitative Effects,
Deterrence and Incapacitation: Estimating the Effects of Criminal Sanctions on Crime Rates
(Washington, D.C.: National Academy of Sciences, 1978), 59–62.

25. Isaac Ehrlich, "The Deterrent Effect of Capital Punishment: A Question of Life
and Death," *The American Economic Review*, 65, no. 3 (1975) 397–417.

26. Peter Passell, "The Deterrent Effect of the Death Penalty: A Statistical Test,"
Stanford Law Review, 28, no. 1 (1975): 61–80.

27. Panel on Research on Deterrent and Incapacitative Effects, p. 61; see also P.
Passell and J. B. Taylor, "The Deterrent Effect of Capital Punishment: Another
View," Discussion Paper 74–7509, Columbia University, Department of Eco-
nomics; and William J. Bowers and G. L. Pierce, "The Illusion of Deterrence in
Isaac Ehrlich's Research on Capital Punishment," *Yale Law Review*, 85, no. 2 (1975):
187–208.

28. Lawrence R. Klein, Brian Forst, and Victor Filatov, "The Deterrent Effect of
Capital Punishment: An Assessment of the Estimates," in *Deterrence and Incapaci-
tation: Estimating the Effects of Criminal Sanction on Crime Rates*, Panel on Research on
Deterrence and Incapacitative Effects, 336–360.

29. Panel on Research on Deterrence and Incapacitative Effects, 62.

30. See for example James Q. Wilson and B. Boland, "Crime," chap. 4 in W. Gorham
and N. Glaser, eds., *The Urban Predicament* (Washington, D.C.: The Urban Institute,
1976); C. H. Logan, "Arrest Rates and Deterrence," *Social Science Quarterly*, 56, no.
3 (1975): 376–389; L. Phillips and H. Votey, Jr., "An Economic Analysis of the
Deterrent Effects of Law Enforcement on Criminal Activities," *Journal of Criminal
Law, Criminology and Police Science*, 63, no. 3, 1972, 336–342; L. McPheters and W.
B. Stronge, "Law Enforcement Expenditures and Urban Crime," *National Tax
Journal*, 27, no. 4 (1974): 633–644.

31. See for example J. B. Gibbs, "Crime, Punishment and Deterrence," *Southwestern
Social Science Quarterly*, 48, no. 4 (1968): 515–530; Charles Tittle, "Crime Rates and
Legal Sanctions," *Social Problems*, 16, no. 4 (1969): 409–423; G. Antunes and A. L.
Hunt, "The Deterrent Impact of Criminal Sanctions: Some Implications for Crim-
inal Policy," *Journal of Urban Law*, 51, no. 2 (1973): 145–161; Isaac Ehrlich, "Par-
ticipation in Illegitimate Activities," *Journal of Political Economy*, 81, no. 3: 521–565.

32. Daniel Nagin, "General Deterrence: A Review of the Empirical Evidence" in
Panel on Research on Deterrence and Incapacitative Effects, 111.

33. *Papachristore et al.* v. *City of Jacksonville*, 405 V.S. 170, 92 S. Ct., 839 (1972).

34. *New York Times*, 1 August, 1977, 48.

35. Alexander B. Smith and Harriet Pollock, *Crime and Justice in Mass Society* (New York:
Xerox, 1972), 65.

36. William Preston, Jr., *Aliens and Dissenters* (New York: Harper & Row, 1966), 120.

37. Judy Claver and John Spitzed, ed., *The Conspiracy Trial* (Indianapolis: Bobbs-Merrill,
1970), 603.

38. *United States* v. *Harris*, 347 U.S. 612–617, 74 S. Ct. 808–812.

39. *Thornhill* v. *Alabama*, 310 U.S. 88, 60 S. Ct. 736; *Herndon* v. *Lowry*, 301 U.S. 242,
57 S. Ct. 732.

40. Philip Selznick, "The Sociology of Law," in *International Encyclopedia of the Social Sciences,* David Sells, ed. (New York: MacMillan and Free Press, 1968), 52.
41. Frank Gibney, "What's An Operator?" in John M. Johnson and Jack D. Douglas eds., *Crime at the Top* (New York: Lippincott, 1978), 11.
42. James S. Campbell, "The Rule of Law," in *Law and Order Reconsidered* (New York: Bantam Books, 1970), 5.
43. Harold E. Pepinsky, *Crime and Conflict* (New York: Academic Press, 1976), 86.
44. 53 p. 978 (1898).
45. *Commonwealth* v. *Pierce,* 138 Mass. 165 (1884).
46. R. J. Michalowski, "Violence in the Road: the Crime of Vehicular Homicide," *Journal of Research in Crime and Delinquency,* 12, no. 1: 34.
47. Despite the Appeals Court ruling in *People* v. *Hernandez,* 393, p. 673, 674, 677 (1964), most courts do not admit evidence concerning a statutory rape defendant's lack of intent to commit rape based on a sincere belief that his partner was of age.
48. Age Discrimination Act of 1967; see Lusk et al., *Business Law,* 369.
49. *New York Times,* 20 March 1976, 1–2.
50. Nan Berger, "The Child, the Law and the State" in *The Rights of Children* (New York: Praeger, 1971), 161.
51. Task Force on Juvenile Justice and Delinquency Prevention, *Report to the National Advisory Committee on Criminal Justice Standards and Goals* (Washington, D.C.: Government Printing Office, 1976), 297.
52. Task Force on Juvenile Delinquency, *Juvenile Delinquency and Youth Crime,* report to the President's Commission on Law Enforcement and the Administration of Justice (Washington, D.C.: Government Printing Office, 1967), 2.
53. Berger, "The Child, the Law, and the State," 154.
54. Chicago Bar Association, report to Illinois State Legislature, 1899.
55. Task Force on Juvenile Delinquency, *Juvenile Delinquency and Youth Crime,* 2.
56. Barry Krisberg and James Austin, *Children of Ishmael* (Palo Alto, Calif.: Mayfield Publishing Co., 1978), 65.
57. See for example General Statute N.C. 7A–557 art. 49.
58. M'Naughten's Case, 8 Eng. Rep. 719.
59. U.S. Senate Report on S1762 (Washington, D.C.: Government Printing Office, 1983), 224.
60. *Durham* v. *United States,* 214F 2d 862, 871 (1954).
61. Gwynn Nettler, *Explaining Crime* (New York: McGraw-Hill, 1974), 27.
62. American Law Institute, *Model Penal Code* (Philadelphia: American Law Institute, 1962), sect. 4.01.
63. Barbara Ann Stolz, "The Federal Insanity Defense: Tangible Versus Symbolic Politics." Paper presented at the American Society of Criminology meeting, November 1983.
64. Federal Bureau of Investigation, *Crime in the United States—1978* (Washington, D.C.: Government Printing Office, 1979), 171.

CHAPTER 7

Policing the Crime Problem

CRIMINAL JUSTICE AND THE LIVING LAW

The preceding two chapters examined the historical development and ideological underpinnings of law in American society. This chapter, which examines the police, and the following two, which examine the courts and correctional agencies, respectively, explore the actual implementation of criminal law by the contemporary justice system. It is the *implementation* of law that transforms written rules of conduct into *social realities.*

The way people respond to behavior determines the everyday meaning of that behavior. Following this logic sociologist Howard Becker has argued, "Deviance is *not* a quality of the act the person commits, but rather a consequence of the application by others of rules and sanctions to an 'offender.'"[1] In essence Becker is saying that we come to know certain behaviors as "deviant" because we observe or are told that they are treated (or should be treated) as such. Crime is simply those forms of behavior *defined* as offenses against the state. Extending Becker's logic we might therefore agree with sociologist Clayton Hartgen that ". . . the criminal character of behavior is the product of an interpretation of an individual's conduct made by some person or persons in a position to make this designation."[2] Some criminologists have criticized this particular view of crime as too relativistic and too likely to produce a kind of moral ambivalence that in the name of scientific detachment would make it impossible to become an active participant in the struggle for a more just society. For example, criminologist Richard Quinney says that such social constructionist approaches to the definition of crime ". . . fail to provide a yardstick for judging whether one reality has more good in it than another. Social relativism . . . prevents a critical understanding of the social world."[3]

Yet whether or not certain behaviors "ought" to be seen as unacceptable it is *how they are treated* that determines their *actual* meaning in everyday life. To understand the meaning of crime at a given point in time in a particular society we must study how those delegated to enforce the law actually apply or fail to apply rules and sanctions to members of the society.

While we may recognize, as do social constructionists, that the *social reality* of crime is not inherent in certain behaviors but in the responses to those behaviors, this does not mean that we must enter a state of moral paralysis that prohibits us from constructing a vision of a better set of human affairs. Indeed, the recognition that "crime" is a definition applied to certain types of behavior should free us for further moral inquiry. If crime and deviance are human definitions applied to behavior, then humans can create new definitions of unacceptable behavior and discard old ones.

As it is actually experienced in society, law is not what legislators have written or appellate courts have ruled; it is what law enforcers enforce. In 1897 the eminent jurist Oliver Wendell Holmes observed much the same thing when he wrote that the law is "nothing more pretentious" than "prophecies of what the courts will do in fact."[4] He urged that legal scholars study the law in action, or the "living law" as he termed it, not simply the law as it is written. While the written law plays an important role in defining the boundaries of law enforcement, it is the law in action that gives law sociological meaning in everyday life.

The law in action involves more than the behavior of courts. It involves any actions taken with reference to the enforcement or nonenforcement of the criminal law. This includes actions by all those individuals exercising delegated state power in the enforcement of law—police officers, clerks of courts, judges, prison guards, probation officers, and so forth—and also in some instances the actions of private citizens. Defining an event as "important enough" to report to the police, for example, is also part of defining someone's behavior as criminal.

Depending upon what actions law enforcers take, those whose behavior could be construed as criminal may or may not become actual criminal offenders under the law. In this sense the justice system determines who are society's criminals by bringing the penal response to bear on a select proportion of those who *might be* criminalized.

The actions of law enforcers determine not only what behaviors will be treated as crimes but also the relative importance of various forms of criminality. The priorities according to which police departments allocate resources, judges assign sentences, prosecutors determine to drop or try cases, and parole boards decide to release or retain prisoners all contribute to shaping the everyday reality of crime. The fact that regulatory violators are more likely to be fined than given active jail sentences than are individuals convicted of conventional property crimes such as burglary or larceny contributes to the social reality that white-collar criminals are not "real" criminals while burglars and shoplifters are the true crime problem.

The criminal justice system does not simply *respond* to the crime problem. It plays an active role in defining what is the crime problem. When we study the justice system we are not merely studying the technical apparatus for capturing, convicting, and punishing criminals. We are studying the primary mechanism for creating public consciousness about the nature of crime.

HISTORICAL DEVELOPMENT OF POLICING

The Emergence of Police

Policing is the use of state power by delegated authorities for the purposes of law enforcement and the maintenance of order. Law enforcement requires the identification or apprehension of suspected lawbreakers so that some *future* action may be taken. The *maintenance of order* involves providing short-term solutions to immediate problems by returning a disturbed situation (e.g., family argument, riot, traffic jam, etc.) to normal or aiding persons in distress (e.g., helping a lost child, taking home the inebriate, giving directions to travelers, etc.).

Policing is unique to state societies. In the kinds of nonstate societies discussed in Chapter 3, rules and customs are enforced and order maintained by ordinary individuals in the process of conducting their daily lives, not by designated representatives of state power. In these types of nonstate societies an individual may on occasion behave in a policelike fashion, perhaps by acting as the intermediary designated to collect compensation from an offending clan or by engaging in an act of self-help or blood revenge against an offender.[5] However, such individuals are not acting as representatives of some central authority, nor are they specialists in law enforcement and order maintenance.[6]

As a specialized occupational role policing can only develop in societies with a relatively complex division of labor and a comparatively high degree of centralized power. Richard Schwartz and James C. Miller have studied how order was maintained and disputes resolved in fifty-one societies representing differing levels of societal complexity. Eighteen of these societies had police, which the authors defined as a "specialized armed force available for norm enforcement." These societies were generally "economically advanced enough to use money," tended to have a substantial degree of occupational specialization and also tended to have full-time governmental officials. In other words, these societies had reached that degree of division of labor and centralization of power associated with state-level societies. Less complex societies tended to rely on private intermediaries for the resolution of difficulties.[7]

Policing has taken four basic forms: (1) military power, (2) court officers, (3) community watchkeepers, and (4) professional police. In most ancient and early medieval cities the policing function, if performed at all, was generally handled by a component of the military. In these early cities the relationship between policing and political power was unmistakable and obvious. The ancient cities of Rome and Constantinople, as well as later medieval cities such as Florence, Venice, Paris, Geneva, and London, also contained a variety of courts for resolving various forms of dispute. In medieval cities there could generally be found royal courts, which represented the temporal power of the state; ecclesiastical courts, which handled church-related matters such as patrimony and inheritance; and private courts such as the courts of "law merchants," which handled private disputes arising from commerce.[8] For the most part, however, these courts had little to do with the everyday maintenance of order and the prosecution of criminal offenders. In both England and France such matters were generally handled at a more local level through courts of the manor, hundred courts, and county courts. With the decline of feudalism and the twin growth of mercantile capitalism and state power, courts representing central government came to play a more significant role in policing the everyday problems of ordinary citizens, as we saw in Chapter 4.

From approximately 1300 to around 1650 courts were the primary mechanism for law enforcement. In England after the creation of the eyre, courts began hearing a growing volume of "common pleas" and played an important role in creating the common law through their development of a body of legal precedents.[9] During this period, however, the task of bringing suspected offenders before the court remained largely a private matter unless the offense was specifically against the crown, such as poaching the king's deer or treason. Individual victims of violence, theft, or fraud were required to bring suit against their suspected offenders to activate the law-enforcement powers of the state. There were no public police to seek out and capture the alleged common offender, although certain individuals would hire themselves out for this purpose.

While courts may be effective for enforcing the law regarding those charged with violations, they are not effective tools for maintaining order. Courts have little facility for responding to immediate problems, nor can they effectively *prevent* crimes or disorder. Courts can only act after the fact.

The gradual transition from a feudal mode of production to a capitalist one slowly eroded the ability of communities to maintain order as an ongoing part of daily life. The increased geographic mobility made possible by the separation of labor from the land created a new problem for community life— the constant coming and going of strangers. The elimination of feudal bonds of mutual responsibility between serfs and their lords also created a growing class of wage laborers who threatened civil order during times of scarce employment through riots and uprising.[10] The transition to capitalism also brought about a more subtle erosion of community solidarity as individuals became competitors with one another for scarce resources in a money economy rather than individual producers of subsistence. Order became less and less of a natural by-product of daily life.

At the beginning of the sixteenth century cities and towns in both England and the American colonies began to rely on watchmen and constables to maintain order. Though courts remained the primary institutions for law enforcement, reliance on watchmen and constables gradually transformed the maintenance of order into a specialized function as community solidarity began to decline.

The earliest law enforcement officers in the American colonies were constables. Constables were not professional police. They were ordinary citizens who were elected or drafted to serve a term as constable. Rather than initiating law enforcement, their duties for the most part required that they help complaining citizens in their efforts to bring alleged offenders before the court.[11] The task of constable was generally considered an onerous one. Given the highly moralistic nature of colonial law constables were required to devote much of their effort to enforcing laws governing swearing, drinking, working on the sabbath, attending church services, and sexual conduct.[12] This meant that

> Because he had to keep such a close watch over his neighbor's morals, and frequently had to have a hand in their chastisement, the constable was not destined to be a popular figure in the community. . . .[13]

The task of constable also involved other unattractive duties such as collecting taxes, levying fines, and whipping the convicted. In addition, assaults on constables as they tried to enforce these laws were not an uncommon occurrence.[14] As a result, many of the more affluent members of colonial society sought to avoid serving as constables either by paying a small fine or hiring others to serve in their place.[15]

Constables generally enforced the law during the *day*. In most colonial towns and cities order was maintained during the night by a "watch." The watch consisted of one or more citizens charged with insuring the general welfare during the night by keeping an eye out for fires, disbanding the rowdy, reporting time and weather, and occasionally helping travelers or strangers. Like the job of constable, serving as watchman was considered an unpleasant or disruptive task, and many hired others to serve in their place.[16]

While not professional law-enforcement officers themselves, we can find the seeds of professional policing in these early colonial constables and watchmen. They represented the first step in separating the task of maintaining order from the normal run of everyday life and placing it in the hands of individuals specifically and exclusively charged with the responsibility of enforcing legal rules of social conduct.

Policing the Dangerous Classes

The transition to industrial capitalism brought with it a corresponding intensification of social class divisions, the growth of large cities, and an increasing population of rootless and unemployed citizens. These forces, first in England and later in the United States, led to the metamorphosis of the constabulary and night watch into a system of professional policing. The first signs of this transformation began to appear in England in the early part of the 1700s as city life grew more wretched for the poor and unemployed and more threatening for the established citizenry. In a pamphlet dedicated to the mayor of London in 1730, the author Daniel Defoe wrote,

> The Citizens . . . are oppressed by Rapin and Violence; Hell seems to have let loose Troops of human D——ls upon them; and such Mischiefs are done within the Bounds of your Government . . . which, if suffered to go on will call for Armies, not Magistrates, to suppress.[17]

The concern with increasing crime, however, was only symptomatic of a greater anxiety created by the emergence of a class of impoverished urbanites. As sociologist Allen Silver wrote,

> In the London and Paris of the late eighteenth and early nineteenth centurys people often saw themselves as threatened by . . . the rapidly multiplying poor of cities whose size had no precedent in Western History. It was much more than a question of annoyance, indignation, or personal insecurity; the social order itself was threatened by an entity whose characteristic name reflects the fears of the time—the "dangerous classes."[18]

In England and later in the United States the threat of social upheaval caused by these "dangerous classes" led to calls for a more highly organized, professional, and centrally controlled police force.[19] The need was presented not just as one of controlling crime but preventing civil society from collapse.

In 1829 the English Parliament passed the Metropolitan Police Act, which established the first modern, professional police force. The Metropolitan Police were to be a force of full-time salaried police officers whose activities would be controlled by a central administration directly responsible to the government.[20] The purpose of the Metropolitan Police was to *prevent* crime by patrolling the streets. This represented an entirely new concept of law enforcement. The police were expected to both enforce the law by identifying and capturing offenders and to maintain order by preventing crimes from occurring. Crime prevention would result from both the deterrent effect of police presence and the effective removal of "criminals" from free society, it was thought. This theory mandated that police be far more active in initiating enforcement activities than had heretofore been the case.[21]

The creation of a preventive police force tended to shift the responsibility for crime away from the society and onto the newly created professional police. If cities were crime-ridden, it was not because the social order generated a class of impoverished and brutalized citizens but because the police had *failed* to prevent crime. This transition of responsibility to a professional police force effectively masked the role of the emerging capitalist economy in creating the conditions for crime and urban disorder.

By the early 1800s a similar process was taking place in the United States. The emergence of an urban proletariat consisting largely of those who were poor, unemployed, homeless, or ethnically different from the dominant Anglo culture led to an increased fear of disorder and crime stemming from the "dangerous classes."[22] This fear prompted calls for more effective methods of policing these threats to civil society. Between 1834 and 1866 most major American cities established full-time police departments patterned largely after the London Metropolitan police. The first of these was in Boston, which established a department in 1834. This was followed by the creation of police departments in New York in 1845, New Orleans in 1853, and in San Francisco, Kansas City, St. Louis, Buffalo, and Cleveland over the next thirteen years.

Historical evidence indicates that it was fear of civil disorder rather than fear of crime that was largely responsible for the emergence of professional police in the United States. Boston's experience supports this line of reasoning.

Beginning in the summer of 1825 Boston was periodically racked by "riots and tumultuous assemblies" among the poor and unemployed laborers of the city. In response to these upheavals Boston established a night watch in 1834 to see that all "disturbances and disorders in the night shall be prevented and suppressed." Apprehending ordinary criminals and thieves, however, was not part of their charge. This effort to prevent disorder among the poor failed, however, and between 1834 and 1837 Boston suffered three major riots. While conventional wisdom suggests that police forces come into existence to fight common crime, historical data indicate that in Boston there was no noticeable growth in the rate of serious crimes during the years that gave rise to its police force.[23] This supports historian Roger Lane's conclusion that it was fear of mass action by the "dangerous classes" more than fear of crimes such as robbery and assault that prompted Boston to replace its night watch with a full-time police force in 1837.[24]

Between their initial appearance in the 1830s and the turn of the century, the size and scope of urban police forces in the United States grew substantially. While the relationship between the development of full-time police and urban unrest is generally recognized by historians and criminologists, the relationship between the growth of industrial capital and the emergence of professional police is more often overlooked.

The poor and unemployed "dregs" of nineteenth-century urban America were direct products of the transition to industrial capitalism. By separating formerly agrarian workers from access to the means of survival the industrial economy created a proletariat with nothing to sell but their labor power. Since there were usually more sellers than buyers of labor power, wages could be kept low. The combination of periodic widespread unemployment and low wages, however, created a restive labor force in most urban, industrial areas. Many of the disorders and "riots" of the nineteenth century were in fact worker strikes and other protests by the poor and the unemployed against the conditions of their existence. The "dangerous classes" were by and large not some demented rabble seeking to destroy social order for the sake of destruction but ordinary human beings attempting to find an escape from their oppression and poverty.

Because efforts to improve the conditions of labor were a direct threat to industrial profits, they were met with resistance. In one study sociologists Sidney Harring and Lorraine McMullin detailed the close relationship between labor strife and the growth of the police force in Buffalo, New York, between 1872 and 1900.[25] Their analysis showed that while the Buffalo police force nearly tripled in size during that time, there was no comparable growth in either population or rates of crime. There was, however, a considerable increase in labor troubles during those years and a corresponding concern by the police that they be able to control and discourage strikes. The authors write,

> Crime frequently got much less mention in police reports than labor problems did. Furthermore, the force was organized to more effectively deal with strikes at the expense of effectively controlling crime. Emphasis was on the platoon

system with a strong reserve for occasions "when a number of officers are immediately needed." . . . (Annual Report of the Buffalo Police Dept., 1893)[26]

According to Harring and McMullin, this concern about labor unrest did not originate with the police themselves but with the city government of Buffalo, which at the time was controlled largely by major employers or persons closely allied with them.[27] This pattern of using the newly expanding urban police forces to combat worker organizations was not unique to Buffalo. In Chicago during the late 1800s, for example, the police force was used to break up labor meetings, jail labor organizers indiscriminately, and attack picket lines as if the police "were a private force in the service of employers."[28] There was little concern whether such acts were in accordance with the law, as evidenced by the Illinois state attorney for Chicago's telling the police to "Make the raids first and look up the law afterwards."[29]

There is some evidence that the growth of cities did increase opportunities for crime, leading to a slightly greater frequency of crimes against property, although rates of violent crime appear to have remained relatively constant during this period.[30] There is little evidence, however, that the growth of crime in any way corresponded to the growth in police forces. Rather, what the historical record appears to indicate is that the creation and expansion of urban police forces during the last two-thirds of the nineteenth century was a response to the class conflicts and social disruptions that accompanied the transition to industrial capitalism in America.

Police and the Positive Prevention of Crime

Early police forces were created not only to control criminals but also to *prevent* crime. This orientation began with the night watches of the 1830s and 1840s, and as these watches evolved into professional, full-time police forces, the emphasis upon preventive policing was largely one of prevention through deterrence. It was assumed that the visible presence of police in the community and the threat of arrest or injury they posed for potential criminals and other "undesirables" would deter them from committing crimes or causing trouble. To enforce this threat early police forces relied extensively on the use of violence.[31] In the early 1900s, however, the concept of crime prevention through policing was expanded beyond the idea of simple deterrence. In the United States the period between 1900 and 1925 was characterized by a variety of movements seeking social reform. This time period came to be known as the Progressive Era. The Progressive Movement was largely a middle-class political effort to eliminate waste and corruption from government while leaving the basic structure of American capitalism unchanged. As middle-class professionals and small business owners, the Progressives found themselves threatened by the growing power of industrial capital on the one hand and an expanding urban proletariat composed increasingly of foreign immigrants on the other.

In the eyes of many Progressives big business had corrupted fundamental liberal democratic principles through bribes and favors aimed at securing beneficial legislation and other government favors. While not necessarily in sympathy with labor unions and their struggle against industry, Progressives still found the obvious use of police forces to crush labor organization a violation of the ideal of equality under the law. At the same time riots, rising crime rates, vice, poverty, and intemperance among the proletariat seemed to portend the destruction of society. In response, the Progressives sought to reform government so that it would provide the "equality under the law" promised by the ideals of capitalist democracy and insure stability in a society disquieted by social class tensions.[32]

The Progressive Movement had a substantial impact upon policing. Through its efforts the concept of crime prevention was extended to include the use of the police for social engineering as well as deterrence. Police should not only restrain crime by posing threats to potential criminals but should also actively work with other community agencies in *positive* efforts to steer individuals, particularly the young, away from lives of crime. In 1931 the Wickersham Commission, a presidential commission comprised of mostly Progressive lawyers, police reformers, and scholars, urged the police to work with other community agencies to "reach youthful delinquents before they become hardened repeaters." This emphasis reflected the growing influence of social science theories stressing the developmental rather than fixed nature of human personalities and human behavior. In this vein the Wickersham Commission concluded that the police could be effective in steering troubled youths from lives of crime because "the young are plastic . . . and can usually be influenced to go along in productive paths if taken in hand early enough."[33] From this line of thinking arose the modern-day emphasis upon building positive police–youth relations and positive police–community relations in general as a means of crime prevention.

THE ORGANIZATION OF POLICING IN AMERICA

The Size and Scope of Policing

Currently, the number of local, state, and Federal police agencies exceeds 40,000, and together these agencies spend an annual budget in excess of *$37 billion*. This is nearly equivalent to the total amount of money authorized in the 1982 Federal budget for education, housing, urban development, and environmental protection combined.[34]

In addition to public policing there exists an enormous private police industry in the United States dominated by such multimillion-dollar corporations as Pinkerton's, Burns, and Walter Kidde and Co. detective agencies. Estimates indicate that by 1980 the private police business in the United States employed over 400,000 private guards and detectives and constituted a *$7-billion-a-year* industry.[35] From this vantage point crime certainly does pay, at least for the private police industry.

In comparison with most nations of Western Europe, public policing in America is highly decentralized. Nearly every governmental unit in the United States has a police force of some kind. Most cities have their own police departments. In all but a few metropolitan areas where the city encompasses an entire county, there is usually a county police department or a sheriff's department as well. In some metropolitan areas there is both a county police force, which handles regular police functions such as traffic and crime control outside the city limits, and a sheriff's department, which performs specialized functions such as running the county and/or city jail, transporting prisoners to state prisons, serving warrants and other official notices, and transporting persons committed to mental institutions.

In addition to city and county police, there are usually a variety of state-level police agencies. These include state police or highway patrol, state bureaus of investigation, and specialized agencies such as alcohol, tobacco, and firearms control agencies. When we add to this the police departments of small towns and rural areas, we find that even a small state can have several hundred individual police agencies and large states several times that amount.

In the future there may be a slight decrease in the total number of *local* police agencies if consolidated city–county police forces such as those in Dade County, Florida, and Nassau and Suffolk counties on Long Island become more prevalent. As urban centers sprawl, particularly in Sun Belt states, they cover increasingly larger sections of their counties, thereby creating pressures for consolidated police forces. However, there are also countervailing pressures as various citizens' groups in these areas seek to avoid annexation into cities or consolidation of their services with those of the city.

Federal Policing

At the Federal level, there are a variety of agencies with police powers. The most visible is of course the Federal Bureau of Investigation—the FBI. Begun in 1908 as an enforcement agency for the Department of Justice, the FBI (originally named the Bureau of Investigation) is a relative newcomer to Federal policing.

The Founding Fathers intended the new government to provide a stable economic environment for the growth and expansion of private wealth. This meant among other things insuring that taxes and tariffs on imported goods were paid, thereby protecting domestic producers against competition from less costly foreign goods; providing a stable currency; and generating sufficient revenue to maintain the armed forces necessary to deal with domestic insurrection (particularly among slaves) or foreign interference. For the first one hundred years of the nation's history, nearly all Federal policing took place under the Department of the Treasury and was concerned primarily with problems of revenue.

The first Federal police agency was the Revenue Cutter Service established under the Department of the Treasury in 1790. Its primary purpose was to prevent smuggling, thereby insuring that taxes and tariffs were paid on foreign goods. The Customs Service was added to the Treasury Department in 1799, and by the early 1800s Treasury agents were being used to regulate, inspect, and audit the minting and printing of money. In 1868 the Bureau of Internal Revenue (today known as the Internal Revenue Service) received authority to field its own agents to investigate and arrest tax violators.

By the late 1800s the growth of industrial capital was threatened by widespread labor agitation. In addition, the cultural hegemony of the white, Anglo-Saxon bourgeois was being eroded by the massive influx of foreign labor needed to maintain industrial growth. These problems led to a significant growth in Federal policing. The Bureau of Investigation was established in 1908 to aid in the enforcement of the Sherman Anti-Trust Act. This meant primarily slowing or halting the forces of unionization, since these worker combines were held to be "in restraint of trade." While ostensibly an anti-monopoly law, the first criminal prosecution under the Sherman Act had been against Eugene Debs and the International Workers of the World (IWW) for their part in the strike against Pullman in Chicago in 1894. Following this "antitrust" tradition the newly formed Bureau of Investigation played an important part in Attorney General Mitchell Palmer's firestorm of union-busting, which has been described as "the most flagrant case of official law-lessness in American history."[36]

During its first twenty-five years the Bureau of Investigation used its agents extensively to investigate, raid, and infiltrate unions.[37] The majority of Federal antiunion prosecutions by the Justice Department relied heavily on the investigative work of the Bureau of Investigation.[38]

From 1900 to 1930 the United States was swept by strong nativist sentiments against immigrants and the offspring of the foreign-born. These sentiments manifested themselves in the Harrison Narcotics Act of 1914 and the Volstead (Prohibition) Act of 1920. These laws were largely aimed at controlling the perceived threats to domestic tranquility posed by immigrant populations. The Harrison Act, which prohibited the importation of opium, originally grew out of anti-Chinese sentiment on the West Coast.[39] The Temperance Movement had been a part of the American scene since colonial days. It succeeded in having Prohibition established in the 1920s largely because the evils of drink had become associated with the squalor, crime, and decay thrust upon large segments of the Mediterranean and eastern European immigrant populations found in most eastern and Great Lakes cities at that time.[40] These Federal laws required Federal enforcement and contributed substantially to the growth of both the FBI and the Intelligence Unit of the IRS, which was particularly active in efforts to enforce prohibition.

The scope and extent of Federal law enforcement has grown steadily since the turn of the century. This growth reflects important changes in the structure of the American political economy. In the late 1800s the American economic system began a transition from *industrial capital* to *monopoly capital*. Under industrial capital production and distribution is managed by a large number of relatively small, localized industries and businesses owned by individual entrepreneurs or small groups of local investors. Monopoly capital is characterized by comparatively few large, transnational corporations owned by a widely disparate group of individual stockholders and institutional investors. At the turn of the century, for example, there were literally several hundred manufacturers of automobiles, every city had its own or perhaps several breweries, newspapers were locally owned, and book publishers numbered in the thousands. Today there remain only four American automobile manufacturers, nearly all beer is produced under the auspices of four major companies, newspapers most often belong to large national or international chains, and most major publishers are now subsidiaries of multinational corporations like Xerox, IBM, Time, and CBS. This change from local production to a small number of large-scale national or international conglomerates has taken place in nearly every industry.[41] As this shift occurred, monopoly capital increasingly required and depended upon national-level law enforcement to provide a predictable and secure environment for corporations dealing in a variety of states. Fostering the distinction between crimes *by* business versus crimes against business, the FBI, which is the most policelike Federal law-enforcement agency, has largely limited its activities to the investigation of crimes *against* business or the political order. Unions, radicals, bank robberies, hijacking of interstate commerce, embezzlement, and the like normally fall under the jurisdiction of the FBI. By contrast, antiunion practices by corporations, interstate commerce violations, banking irregularities, the marketing of questionable or contaminated foodstuffs, and other similar crimes by business are more often handled by administrative agencies such as the Department of Labor, the Interstate Commerce Commission, or the Securities and Exchange Commission than by the FBI. Since these agencies lack the policelike characteristics associated with the Federal Bureau of Investigation, the offenses by business that they handle avoid the stigma of "real" crime.

Federal Government and Local Policing

In 1965 the Law Enforcement Assistance Act created the Office of Law Enforcement Assistance under the Department of Justice.[42] This signaled an important shift in the relationship of the Federal government to local crime control. Until 1965 the Federal government had played a limited role in the control of conventional crime at the city and county levels through various professional and technical training programs offered by the FBI and through the compilation of national crime statistics from local data.[43] The Office of Law Enforcement Assistance was given a much broader role in providing Federal services to local police.[44] The creation of a special Federal agency for this purpose indicated that the problem of crime was becoming nationalized, that is, transformed from an issue of primarily local concern and local expenditure to one that seemed to need the involvement of Federal policy makers and Federal expenditures to be controlled.

The emergence of crime as a national concern, and particularly its emergence as a political issue, began in the mid-1960s. During the presidential campaign of 1964 Senator Barry Goldwater and Alabama Governor George

Wallace, both extreme conservatives, raised the specter of the breakdown in "law and order," accusing then-president Lyndon B. Johnson of being "soft on crime." Goldwater said, for example,

> The growing menace in our country tonight, to personal safety, to life, to limb and to property, in homes, in churches, in the playgrounds and places of business, particularly in our great cities, is the mounting concern of every thoughtful citizen in the United States. Security from domestic violence, no less than from foreign is the most elementary and fundamental purpose of any government, and a government that cannot fulfill this purpose is one that cannot long command the loyalty of its citizens.[45]

The real concern of conservatives such as Goldwater and Wallace, however, was not simply with crime but with larger social changes threatening to conservative interests, particularly the growing militancy of the civil rights movement and the emergence of a youth culture that began to question the materialist values of the society. As Malcolm Feely and Austin Sarat observe in their study of Federal crime control policy, conservatives sought to mobilize public hostility against

> . . . all those elements of contemporary culture which seemed to threaten the values of hard-working, upstanding middle-class Americans. Crime and the rhetoric of law and order were symbols of that threat.[46]

Restoring "law and order" became a political code phrase not simply for controlling crime but for repressing forms of social change that threatened both established interests and established values. It is interesting to note that in 1964, the year crime first became a national political issue, a national opinion survey found that crime did not rank particularly high among those things Americans feared. War, illness, a lowered standard of living, unemployment, lack of opportunities for children, unhappy family life, and dependency or loneliness in old age were mentioned far more frequently. Less than 5 percent ranked crime as a significant personal fear.[47] Thus the emergence of "law and order" as a significant political issue may have been as important in stimulating public fear of crime as any actual increases in crime rates.

With crime established as a significant political issue, after reelection in 1964 Lyndon Johnson established the Office of Law Enforcement Assistance to help finance with Federal dollars local efforts at improving law-enforcement efficiency. He also created a presidential commission to study the problem of crime and recommend policies to combat this newly discovered national menace. In 1967, partly based on the recommendations of this commission, President Johnson proposed the Safe Streets and Crime Control Act. However, between the time of the commission's creation and the passage of this bill, the social climate of the country took a violent turn.

By the mid-1960s the stark contradiction of grinding poverty amid increasing affluence and continuing patterns of racial discrimination and police brutality sparked a period of intense urban disorder. In New York, Los Angeles, Buffalo, Newark, Detroit, and a number of other American cities, the frustrations and unmet expectations of ghetto life erupted into widespread uprisings characterized by burning, looting, and attacks on firemen and police. At the same time, civil rights groups around the country, particularly in the south, were confronting and challenging long-established patterns of racial discrimination and political oppression. These confrontations frequently led to violent overreactions by state and local police authorities. Campus radicalism and the Vietnam era antiwar movement further supported the sense that traditional methods of social control were inadequate to handling these new threats to social stability.

By 1968, when Congress finally voted on the Safe Streets and Crime Control Act rioting in Watts had taken thirty-six lives, in Newark twenty-three, and in Detroit forty-three; most other major cities had experienced riot-related death and injury; the official crime rate had risen by 48 percent between 1965 and 1968; and both Martin Luther King and Robert Kennedy had been assassinated. Amid public and political demands for "law and order" the Safe Streets Act was passed, establishing the Law Enforcement Assistance Administration (LEAA) to replace the Office of Law Enforcement Assistance.[48] The newly created Law Enforcement Assistance Administration was to be a crime control "superagency" provided with a budget of several billion dollars annually that would support local justice agencies through education, research, training, and improved equipment. In the words of Congress, the need for this agency was mandated by the fact that the "high incidence of crime in the United States threatens the peace, security and general welfare of the Nation and its citizens."[49]

In addition to the presidential commission whose recommendations led to the Safe Streets and Crime Control Act, several other governmental commissions were impaneled in the late 1960s specifically to identify the causes of urban disorders and to recommend policies that would prevent such occurrences in the future. Their findings generally showed that some conflict with the justice system was most often the spark that ignited ghetto riots, with incidents of police brutality or excessive force most frequently the immediate factor. In addition it was becoming clear that police overreaction to civil rights and antiwar demonstrators was increasing rather than decreasing the tensions. In short,

> The police were not only incapable of containing the violence and disaffection of the sixties, but were actually contributing to it and accelerating the decline of the legitimacy of the American government.[50]

This led to a two-pronged strategy to reestablish the "domestic tranquility" promised by the constitution. As described by the Center for Research on Criminal Justice in their volume, *The Iron Fist and the Velvet Glove*, this strategy contained a "hard side" and a "soft side." The hard-side strategy emphasized improved police capabilities to handle both crime and domestic disturbance through the use of sophisticated technology in the areas of weapons, communications, and surveillance and through more advanced techniques of po-

police work.[51] The soft-side strategy emphasized the development of improved police–community relations through the use of more minority and college-educated police, the creation of cooperative citizen–police action programs, and the establishment of community-based team-policing.[52]

LEAA became the implementation arm of this two-pronged strategy, dispensing funds for both "hard" and "soft" programs. During its first four years of operation—1969 to 1973—approximately 45 percent of LEAA's total budget of $3.5 billion went to the police and another 13 percent to programs involving both the police and other justice system agencies. The bulk of LEAA funds for policing, however, have been devoted to the "hard" rather than the "soft" side. In 1973 LEAA granted approximately $225 million in assistance. Of this, 70.6 percent was for crime control through deterrence and apprehension of criminals. The remaining 29.4 percent went for crime prevention and community relations programs.[53] LEAA monies spent on research have shown a similar bias toward the "hard" end of the spectrum.[54]

By the mid-1970s LEAA became the focus of substantial criticism. Conservatives complained that the large expenditures of Federal funds for crime control had produced little in the way of tangible results. More liberal-minded critics argued that far too much LEAA money was spent for hardware and too little for basic research into the causes and prevention of crime.[55] The bulk of LEAA expenditure in the police area—and this constitutes the largest concentration of LEAA funds—has been for operational hardware such as vehicles, helicopters, and weapons and sophisticated crime control technology in the form of computers, surveillance devices, night scopes, and extended information retrieval networks. A large proportion of LEAA money earmarked for research actually was spent not on basic research but on funding various innovative crime control or community relations programs run by police departments. These complaints, coupled with a decline in urban disorders and the increasing inability of the Federal government to support costly programs without massive budget deficits, led to the eventual demise of LEAA as a superfund crime control agency in 1979.

THE FUNCTIONS AND BEHAVIOR OF POLICE

The Functions of Policing

Police, particularly local police departments, perform a number of different functions, some of them more obvious than others. The key functions of police in American society are (1) dramatizing state power, (2) legitimizing state power, (3) maintaining order, (4) controlling crime, and (5) labeling criminality. At times these various functions are complementary, and at other times they place conflicting demands upon police.

Dramatizing State Power. Police dramatize the power of the state. For most people police provide their most common source of contact with state authority. Whenever we receive a traffic ticket, call on the police to perform some service, are directed in traffic, are questioned as suspects or witnesses, or merely buy a ticket to the policeman's ball, we interact with a representative of state power.

This dramatization of power takes two forms, symbolic and real. The police officers' uniform, badge, and weapons are symbols of state power. They represent that portion of state power delegated to police. This ever-present image of the authority of the state over our lives helps us take for granted that the state *should* exercise this power.

In addition to symbolic displays, the dramatization of state power also takes a more tangible form. As police officers actually exercise the power delegated to them, they reveal that power to us. When we allow ourselves to be directed in traffic by someone wearing a police uniform or allow a stranger into our home because we are shown a police badge, we experience firsthand the real power of the state to command our lives. When we read or hear about someone's being arrested by the police, or perhaps injured or killed by the police in the process of arrest, we are presented with the very real and extraordinary power—including the exclusive right to use deadly force—delegated to police by the political state. Like the symbolic displays of state power, these authoritative actions by police occur with such frequency that we come to take them and the power they represent for granted.

Legitimizing State Power.   Police not only dramatize the power of the state, they also serve to legitimize that power in several ways. First, by controlling or appearing to control crime, police represent the power of the state to be a benevolent force used to preserve social peace and protect citizens from harm. In addition to controlling crime, the unquestioned power of the police is frequently used to deal with a variety of other problems of daily life. Sociologist Egon Bittner contends that the common practice of "calling the cops" to deal with such things as domestic disputes, rowdy teenagers, neglected children, or even the undesirable behavior of maids has developed precisely because police can employ their nonnegotiable authority to *force* a resolution to the situation.[56] This nonnegotiable authority can be seen in the following examples of police activity:

> In a downtown residential hotel, patrolmen found two ambulance attendants trying to persuade a man, who according to all accounts was desperately ill, to go to the hospital. After some talk, they helped the attendants in carrying the protesting patient to the ambulance and sent them off.
>
> In the apartment of a quarreling couple, patrolmen were told by the wife, whose nose was bleeding, that the husband stole her purse containing the money she earned. The patrolmen told the man they would "take him in" whereupon he returned the purse and they left.
>
> In a tenement, patrolmen were met by a public health nurse who took them through an abysmally deteriorated apartment inhabited by four young children in the care of an elderly woman. The babysitter resisted the nurse's earlier

attempts to remove the children. The patrolmen packed the children in the squad car and took them to juvenile hall, over the continuing protests of the elderly woman.[57]

Both by responding to crime and helping individuals deal with other problems police tend to legitimize the view that the centralization of power in a political state that can then authorize its use by representatives such as police ultimately provides greater security for everyone.

Maintaining Order.   In modern societies police are expected to maintain order; that is, insure that disruptions to normal patterns of interaction are brought under control. Maintaining order often requires that police do something about or "put a stop to" some immediate problem situation.[58] This need to provide immediate solutions to trouble of one sort or another distinguishes police from other elements of the justice system. Courts and correctional agencies are seldom involved in immediate problem situations. They normally act only after the troublesome event, such as a crime, has long since ended.[59]

The expectation that police *do something now* has several important implications for police behavior. First, it increases the likelihood that police will be involved in a variety of problem situations that are only slightly related, or not related at all, to matters of law. As the agency charged with handling disturbances to normal patterns of social order police are called upon to find lost children, block off areas where there might be some immediate hazard such as a gas-main leak or downed power lines, aid the injured, speed women in labor to the hospital, and offer assistance in a multitude of other situations unrelated to the enforcement of the law. One study of calls for police services found that only 20 percent of incoming calls were related to traditional criminal matters.[60] A similar study in another city found that only 10.3 percent of the calls coming into the police department concerned crimes other than those arising from interpersonal disputes.[61]

Second, the need to respond to an immediate problem situation increases the likelihood that police will rely on extra-legal remedies in situations that involve the possible violation of law. Confronted with a person drunkenly staggering through heavy traffic a police officer may choose to simply see that the person arrives home safely by driving him there rather than resorting to the legal remedy of arrest. By doing so, the police officer is fulfilling the order maintenance aspect of his or her job. This ability of police to perform at least part of their job through the use of extra-legal remedies gives them greater discretion than most other justice system personnel.[62] It also can create conflicts between the order maintenance and the crime control aspects of policing.

Controlling Crime.   The control of crime is the most dramatic and obvious function of policing. To most people crime control means investigating crimes and apprehending criminals. In actuality these activities comprise only a small portion of what police do. It is estimated that the actual amount of time police officers spend on traditional crime control activities varies between about 20 and 30 percent of their time on the job.[63] However, the crime control function of modern police extends well beyond those activities related to conducting investigations and making arrests related to specific crimes.

As previously discussed, the crime control function of modern police is as much to act as a deterrent to potential lawbreakers as to identify and bring to justice actual offenders. To fulfill this function police need not arrest all lawbreakers, or even a majority of them. They simply need to provide an active, ongoing demonstration that crime does not pay. It is the *presence* of police in society that constitutes their primary crime control function because along with this presence exists the *possibility* that a criminal act can result in arrest and punishment. While police departments undertake a variety of policies and practices to increase the rate of arrests, there is little expectation that these will lead to the arrest of most or even a majority of lawbreakers.

While deterrence is the aim, many police doubt that even the most effective police strategies can dramatically or even noticeably reduce crime. Arguing for a "realist" position on crime control, James Q. Wilson writes,

> I do not believe that, were we to have taken a correct view and as a consequence adopted the most feasible policies, crime would have been eliminated, or even dramatically reduced.[64]

Thus to a certain degree Wilson feels that Americans must "get used to" relatively high rates of crime. In an article entitled "Getting Used to Mugging" sociologist Andrew Hacker writes with equal pessimism that, given that high crime rates in America persist even though an exceptionally large proportion of our population is engaged in policing, there is little reason to expect that adding still more police will reduce crime—at least not without expanding police presence to the level of a police state.[65] This pessimism about crime control possibilities pervades the police establishment itself, as evidenced by the fact that a decline in the *rate of increase* in crime is often heralded as an achievement.[66]

Labeling Criminality. As the first officials to respond to crime situations, police play an important role in determining the effective limits of the law and deciding who will and will not be labeled as criminal. In the normal course of police activity, however, the task of labeling criminality is highly selective. Police departments generally exercise jurisdiction only over those crimes most likely to lead to the arrest of working class citizens, particularly those who are poor and nonwhite. Local police departments focus on common crimes involving interpersonal violence; robbery, burglary, and larceny; and public order offenses such as intoxication, disorderly conduct, prostitution, and narcotic violations. As we shall see in Chapter 9 this tends to produce a body of arrested and convicted offenders who are more often poor, undereducated, unemployed and nonwhite than the population at large.

The kinds of crimes most likely to be committed by middle-class or elite citizens such as fraud, price fixing, stock manipulations, false advertising, and deceptive marketing practices are generally beyond the jurisdiction of local police. Where they are involved in the investigation of such crimes it is generally focused on small businessmen or local "operators," not on large corporations. As a result those who are held up to the community as its criminals are almost exclusively working-class offenders despite the fact that the amount of financial loss and injury resulting from crimes in corporations, smaller businesses, and private professionals far exceeds that resulting from the kinds of common crimes that consume the bulk of police attention.[67] This kind of selectivity in law enforcement does not arise from police decisions. It is built into the American legal system, which for the most part protects the more powerful and affluent from the stigma of being handled by local police when they use their power or affluence to break the law.

Police–Citizen Encounters

The majority of encounters between police and citizens are initiated by the citizen. In a study of four police departments sociologist Richard Lundman found that slightly more than two-thirds of the encounters observed were initiated by citizens. While 39 percent of these citizen-initiated encounters were related to law enforcement, 44 percent occurred as the result of citizen requests for services or maintenance of order, including dealing with noisy neighbors, barking dogs, and unruly teenagers.[68] As these figures suggest, the majority of police time spent in contact with citizens is not related to dealing with criminal matters. Of all police citizen encounters observed by Lundman, whether initiated by the citizen or by the police, only 29 percent were related to traditional law enforcement activities. While we normally think of police as investigating crimes, interrogating suspects, and capturing fleeing criminals, these activities constitute less than one-third of the contacts between police and the public.[69]

Despite the fact that the majority of their contacts with citizens do not involve dangerous or criminal situations, police tend to respond to most citizen contacts as posing a potential threat. One of the reasons for this is that as criminologist Johnathan Rubenstein observes,

> Even when he stops people for a traffic violation or some other minor matter, he cannot know whether the person he is approaching will treat the moment casually; he does not know whether he might be stumbling into a situation that is explosive for reasons he cannot anticipate.[70]

This sense of suspicion with which police tend to approach citizen contacts derives from several sources.

First, except for calls for aid, police–citizen encounters usually involve, if only in a minimal way, a demonstration of police authority to intervene in the lives of individuals.[71] When a police officer stops a citizen to ask even the most routine question the situation is characterized by a great imbalance of power. The citizen knows that a refusal to respond or attempt to avoid the officer can bring with it a more serious application of police power than merely being stopped and questioned. Additionally, citizens do not necessarily know why they are being stopped, and the initial moment of contact is usually accompanied by some anxiety. While this imbalance of power favors the police officer, it does not produce a sense of certainty or ease on his or her part. Knowing that the person stopped may react with hostility or resentment to the unilateral power of the officer to initiate a contact tends to make patrolmen wary and suspicious until matters prove otherwise, even where the contact does not involve a criminal matter.[72] Even contacts initiated by citizens seeking help contain an element of threat to police. If the police will not or cannot help the person with their problem the citizen may react angrily or disrespectfully, thus escalating the contact into a confrontation.

Second, police are trained to be suspicious. Being on the constant lookout for possible trouble is part of what sociologist Jerome Skolnick calls the policeman's "working personality." One article offering guidelines for police while in the field quoted by Skolnick states quite clearly, "Be suspicious. This is a healthy police attitude. . . ."[73] In addition, because their work periodically brings them into contact with those who have broken the law or who have something to hide sociologist Arthur Neiderhoffer suggests police may have a tendency to become cynical about people in general. He quotes one officer as saying: "I am convinced we are turning into a nation of thieves. I have sadly concluded that nine out of ten people are dishonest."[74] This type of cynicism on the part of police can contribute to making almost any police–citizen contract, regardless of who initiates it, a basis for police suspicion.

Third, police work is occasionally dangerous. While the rate of death or injury on the job is less for police than for many mining and industrial jobs, police work with a sense of personal fear. While few will be shot or knifed, most will be involved in fights at some point in their careers. This sense of danger requires that police be constantly on the lookout for potential or "symbolic" assailants. This can be anyone the officer does not know or has reason to be suspicious of.[75] Since this includes the majority of police–citizen contacts, officers "stand ready to take charge of encounters" to protect themselves.[76] This is particularly the case in situations where someone is stopped in connection with a violent crime, as the following example of a street interrogation of a man in the area of a reported shooting shows:

> The man was ordered to stop. He complied and asked, "What's the trouble officer?" Instead of answering, the officer asked a series of questions concerning the citizen's identity, residence etc. The citizen answered the questions and then reached for his wallet to support his statements. He was ordered not to reach for his wallet. Instead, he was searched for concealed weapons. When none was found he was allowed to produce his wallet and enclosed identification.[77]

Police–citizen encounters are also often equally anxiety-provoking for citizens. Police represent the extraordinary power of the state to intervene in people's lives. This sense of being confronted by power is heightened by the almost always guarded and frequently authoritarian demeanor of the police officer as he or she attempts to take charge of the encounter. When confronted by a police officer, as in the case above, or even for less serious matters, many people are aware that a wrong move or a wrong answer might lead to arrest, injury, or possibly even death. While the probability of these things occurring is relatively small, the very possibility that they might happen is usually sufficient to make people uneasy in police–citizen encounters, particularly those initiated by the police.

Police–citizen encounters often arouse citizen hostility toward police, particularly when people have been questioned in connection with a crime. When confronting someone they think might be guilty of a crime and feeling a need to protect themselves, police will often behave toward the suspect *as if* they are guilty until the situation proves otherwise. For the innocent citizen, however, being treated as a "criminal" is often demeaning and a source of anger. This is particularly true when citizens are not subsequently given any explanation for why they were stopped. In the case above, the citizen's asking "What's the trouble?" received no response. One study of citizen complaints to police departments found that the majority were not complaints about the patrolman's behavior itself but about the failure to give them any adequate explanation for the action.[78]

Police and citizens are locked in an ambivalent relationship. In the absence of any other forms of community social control or protection most citizens support the presence of police in their community. As Johnathan Rubenstein notes,

> Even in communities where there is an intense conflict between police and citizens, there is little resistance to the notion that there ought to be people patrolling the streets, licensed to regulate public traffic and even forcibly to restrict and restrain people.[79]

At the same time police pose a threat to average citizens simply by virtue of the power they have to intervene in their lives. The police, on the other hand, find themselves committed to protecting a public many of whom are wary or even hostile toward them. Moreover, the suspicion and the cynicism that often results from their training and work experience leaves many police feeling that they are protecting a populace made up of a disproportionate number of lawbreakers and other untrustworthy types.

The tension between police and public exists in large part because police are enforcing state laws through the exercise of state power. On a day-to-day basis the community has little control over either the rules police enforce or the police organization itself. In many areas, but particularly in low-income neighborhoods and urban ghettos the police are often accepted as a necessary but alien force, one that can harm as well as protect.

Arrest Situations

About one-third of all police–citizen encounters are related to actual or suspected criminal offenses. The majority of these—Lundman estimates about 90 percent—are initiated by citizens wishing to report or provide information about a crime.[80] While situations not initially involving a criminal offense, such as traffic violations, telling a group of youth to vacate a corner hangout, or responding to a complaint about a noisy party, might lead to an arrest if the citizens involved behave uncooperatively or hostilely, the typical arrest situation involves a confrontation between police and someone they either suspect is guilty of a crime or have observed violating the law.

Whether or not the confrontation between police and suspects actually results in an arrest, however, depends upon a variety of factors. Of particular importance in arrest situations are the nature of the offense, the way the suspect behaves toward the police, and the preference of the complainant. Arrest situations are thus seldom clear-cut. Police enjoy considerable discretion regarding whether or not to invoke their power to arrest, and it is often the nature of the interaction between the police and the suspect that will determine whether an arrest will actually occur.

Offense Seriousness. Studies of police behavior indicate that if police happen to observe someone in the process of committing a major felony offense such as rape, robbery, burglary, or auto theft, or if they respond to a call for help related to a serious felony while the offender is still present, more likely than not an arrest will result. As one researcher noted, if police respond to a reported felony and the suspect is present, "the officer's decision has already been made. Almost without exception the alleged felony violator is arrested."[81] Instances such as these, however, are relatively uncommon. Where most serious crimes are concerned police tend to arrive after the offender has left.

> Some of the more common felonies, such as burglary and auto theft, generally involve stealth and occur when the victim is absent; by the time the crime is discovered the offender has departed. Other felonies such as robbery and rape have a hit-and-run character, such that the police can rarely be notified in time to make an arrest. . . .[82]

Moreover, few such crimes occur in ways that might actually be observed by police, making possible an on-the-scene arrest. Thus the majority of serious crimes do not lead to an arrest—in 1982 only 18.6 percent of serious felony offenses resulted in an arrest.[83] It also means that most arrest situations involve confrontations between police and people suspected of minor violations of law.

The majority of police contacts with suspects—and these contacts usually involve minor offenses—do not result in arrest. Donald Black and Albert Reiss report that in the three cities they studied only 14 percent of police contacts with suspects ended in an arrest. In the remaining 86 percent of the cases the person was judged to be either innocent or, if not innocent of any offense, not deserving to be arrested.[84] The large proportion of police–suspect contacts that do not result in arrest underscores the substantial discretion of police.

Suspect Behavior. Where the alleged offense is not a serious one, the behavior of the suspect plays an important role in shaping the police response. Studies have indicated that the likelihood of arrest increases with the degree of disrespect toward the police shown by the suspect.[85] This appears to be particularly true where juveniles are concerned. One study found that while approximately 26 percent of those juveniles who were antagonistic to police were arrested, only 6.5 percent of those who behaved in a "civil" fashion were taken into custody.[86] One curious characteristic of police–juvenile encounters, however, was that those who behaved "very deferentially" toward police were more likely to be arrested than those who were merely civil. The reason for this may be that overly polite and deferential behavior tends to create suspicion that the person is tryng to hide something.[87]

Complainant Preference.   How police will handle a particular situation is influenced by the preference of the complainant. Complainants may want the police to make an official report of the crime and may demand that the alleged offender, if known or present, be arrested. On the other hand, complainants may request a less formal handling of the situation such as making the offender return a stolen piece of property or simply "putting a scare" into him or her.

Several studies have indicated that if a preference is expressed by the complainant police are inclined to follow it in the majority of cases. Complainants more often than not ask for formal action; the seriousness of the offense appears to have little bearing on this pattern. Donald Black reports that in 78 percent of the felony situations observed where the complainant expressed a preference it was for formal actions, and in 75 percent of the misdemeanor situations a similar preference was stated. Police, however, were more inclined to act in accordance with the complainant's preference in felony situations than misdemeanor ones, complying with the request for formal action in 84 percent of the felony situations but only 64 percent of those involving misdemeanor crimes.[88] This may reflect in part the general tendency of police to take formal action where the situation involves a serious crime. Another study drew a similar conclusion concerning the importance of complainant preference:

> In those encounters where it was possible to determine citizen preference, it was clear that when complainants preferred arrest, the probability of arrest was significantly greater than when complainants preferred an informal disposition.[89]

Since citizens appear to ask for formal dispositions more often than more lenient actions by police, arrest situations where a complainant is present are generally more likely to result in an arrest than those where the only participants are the police and a suspect.[90]

Police Force and Police Brutality

The use of force is central to the enforcement of law by police in state societies. The threat of possible physical harm often underlies the ability of police to obtain citizen compliance with their requests or commands, particularly if the individual is guilty of, or suspected of, having committed a crime.

Police in the United States, as in all other state societies, are authorized to use force against citizens where deemed necessary to enforce the law or to protect life and property. In America police are generally permitted to use nonlethal force (i.e., anything short of firearms) whenever it is required to (1) make an arrest, (2) restrain an individual who is a threat to himself or others, or (3) for self-defense. The use of lethal force in most jurisdictions is presumably limited to situations where the suspect is armed, believed to be armed, or poses a significant threat to the physical security of the officer(s) or others. These are the theoretical limits of police force.

In practice these official limitations on the use of both lethal and nonlethal force are not always followed. The term "police brutality" is generally used to refer to such extralegal application of police force. For example, in 1982 20 percent of all persons killed by police in New York City were unarmed. Additionally, excessive force against suspects while they are being taken into custody, beatings and other physical abuse *after* suspects have been physically restrained, and the use of physical force against individuals who are never arrested for a crime are not uncommon police practices.

The problem of unnecessary and/or excessive police force is not a new one. In 1903 a former police commissioner of New York City wrote,

> For three years there has been through the courts and the streets a dreary procession of citizens with broken heads and bruised bodies against few of whom was violence needed to effect an arrest. Many of them had done nothing to deserve an arrest.[91]

It is estimated that the actual frequency of excessive force by police has declined since the heyday of the "third degree."[92] However, it remains a persistent source of conflict between the police and the public and, as previously mentioned, the most common immediate cause of urban riots.

When are police likely to use excessive force? Situations most likely to result in police brutality are those involving (1) disrespect to police authority or people who the police define as "assholes," (2) injury or death to police, or (3) political conflict.

Disrespect for Authority. The situation most likely to produce police violence is one where the citizen shows some form of disrespect for the authority of the police. In the eyes of police this disrespect may manifest itself in several ways. First, anyone who physically resists police attempts at arrest or detainment presents a serious challenge not only to the physical safety of the police but also to their authority to arrest and detain. While police in this situation must often use force to effect the arrest or detention of a suspect, there is always the possibility that the level of police violence will extend well beyond what is needed to accomplish this. As one police officer said,

> It is true that sometimes we have to beat people up. It comes down to this. When I have a choice of whether I'm going to punch somebody in the nose or wait for them to punch me, I hit him. . . . What's more, if some guy takes a swing at me, I'm not going to let it drop when I hit him back. I've got to teach him a lesson. People have got to learn that they can't hit cops. Three weeks ago I

arrested some guy and he tried to hit me over the head with a chair. We beat the living hell out of him. . . .[93]

Second, in the eyes of some police disrespect need not involve physical resistance. It can merely involve questioning police authority or behaving in a manner that the patrolman finds insolent or sarcastic. One boy described an interaction of this sort as follows:

> One day we were standing on the corner about three blocks from school and this juvenile officer comes up. He says, "Hey, you boys! Come here." So everybody else walked over there. But this one stud made like he didn't hear him. So the cop say, "Hey punk! Come here!" So the stud sorta look up like he hear him and start walking over real slow. So the cop walk over there and grab him by the collar and throw him down and put the handcuffs on him, saying, "When I call you next time, come see what I want."[94]

According to Donald Black "when a man refuses to submit totally to an officer's authority" he invites violence. This may be true even when the citizen is objecting to an illegal exercise of authority.

> In one case a man protested when an officer appropriated $11 from his wallet during a street search: "Since when do you look for a gun or a knife in an man's wallet?" For this he was severely beaten and required four stitches to close a wound on his head.[95]

The importance of disrespect in provoking police violence is highlighted by the fact that much physical force against suspects occurs after the individual is taken into custody. That is, once a resisting or insolent citizen is physically subdued some police take the opportunity to "teach him some respect for the law." During a seven-week period spent observing police behavior in Boston, Chicago, and Washington, D.C., a research team observed excessive police violence against forty-four citizens. Only half these citizens were actually taken into custody, meaning that in the remaining cases police felt that the force used had served its purpose—a purpose obviously not associated with effecting an arrest. Additionally, in fifteen of the twenty-two arrest situations violence continued after the person was in custody, and in thirteen of them after the suspect was at the police precinct station.[96]

Dealing with "Assholes." John Van Maanen argues that some individuals are viewed by police as legitimate targets of violence because they are what the police term "assholes." Assholes may or may not invite police violence by questioning police authority. More importantly, according to one officer, "assholes don't listen to reason." Van Maanen reports of interaction where the label is applied because of disrespect:

> Policeman to motorist stopped for speeding: "May I see your driver's license please?" Motorist: "Why the hell are you picking on me and not somewhere else looking for real criminals?" Policeman: "Cause you're an asshole, that's why . . . but I didn't know that until you opened your mouth."[97]

Disrespect is not always required to earn the label, however, as this situation reported by sociologist Albert Reiss demonstrates:

They [two officers] were told to investigate two drunks in a cemetery. On arriving they found two white men "sleeping one off." Without questioning the men, the older policeman began to search one of them, ripping his shirt and hitting him in the groin with a nightstick. The younger policeman, as he searched the second, ripped away the seat of his trousers, exposing his buttocks. The policemen then prodded the men toward the cemetery and forced them to climb the fence, laughing at the plight of the drunk with the exposed buttocks. As the drunks went over the fence, one policeman shouted, "I ought to run you fuckers in!" The other remarked to the observer, "Those assholes won't be back; a bunch of shitty winos."[98]

The importance of the concept of "asshole" in these cases is that it provides the police involved with a conceptual framework to devalue the person, to see him or her as something less than fully human. As an "asshole" rather than a human being the citizen does not deserve and has no right to expect to be treated kindly or even civilly, and violence is then more easily justified in the mind of the officer involved.

Injury to Police. When a police officer is injured, and more significantly, if an officer is killed in the line of duty, the potential for police violence increases. There are two reasons for this. First, serious injury or death to a police officer increases the sense of danger and threat that is part of the daily life of police. Immediately after such an incident police tend to become more cautious and more likely to resort to force in potentially threatening situations than they might otherwise. As one officer reported,

The rightful worry about our own safety leads to a belief that any kind of physical response—or sometimes even an angry word—is cause for a crack across the head or a few punches. I've seen an old drunk being creamed for having taken a harmless swing.[99]

A second possible consequence of a police death is increased police violence as a form of revenge against those who are either believed to have been involved or who are merely residents of the area where the killing occurred. This is particularly true if the killing occurred in low-income or nonwhite areas of the city. In November 1980, for instance, a white patrolman was found shot to death near his patrol car near a black housing project in the Algiers section of New Orleans. The police began what amounted to a rampage through the black district, searching for the slayer. A number of individuals were accosted by police, questioned, and beaten. Ultimately four residents—three black men and one white man—were killed by police during this investigation. Seven officers were indicted by a Federal grand jury for violating the civil rights of citizens, although they were not charged with the killings themselves. Evidence provided to the grand jury included information that

. . . the officers handcuffed or tied persons in their custody to a chair, struck them over the head with a large book, struck them in their chests with their fists and bagged them, that is, placed a bag over their heads and sealed it at the bottom to cut off the person's air supply. . . . persons were held for long hours and in many instances were locked in a cell. Some of these people were held for as long as 12 to 16 hours and were threatened and beaten, and taken to a "secluded area" where they were beaten, assaulted and . . . threatened with firearms.[100]

The indictments were eventually overturned by a U.S. District Court judge. The kind of brutal treatment arising out of the Algiers cop killing are indicative of the extreme tensions that exist just below the surface for police who find themselves required to patrol and control areas where they know they are targets for the hostility and frustrations of victims of social injustice. The violent retaliation by the police for a cop killing serves as a warning to the community that any attack upon an officer will be met with massive police violence. Recent history also tends to confirm that violent police retaliation for a cop killing will not generally result in homicide convictions for the officers involved.

Police Violence and Political Repression.   Since the beginning of the industrial era in the United States police have served as the first line of defense against those who use mass political action to challenge either the power of the state or the larger economic order. As previously discussed, police have been used extensively in the past to break up and destroy radical labor movements. In more recent years police violence has been utilized on numerous occasions against those protesting social and economic injustice or the actions of the government.

During the 1960s numerous civil rights marches, demonstrations, and sit-ins met with extreme violence on the part of police and/or National Guardsmen called in to supplement police power. In most of these instances those demonstrating had not committed any serious violation of law. Yet the police sometimes argued that they were "provoked" into a violent response by the demonstrators through insults and jeers. Like one-on-one instances of police violence, these situations of "provocation" result in excessive use of force not because life or property are threatened but because police authority has been challenged.

Police violence against groups of citizens—and this occurs most often in the context of some type of demonstration—may constitute a police attack or a police riot, depending upon its extent. Rodney Stark defines these situations as follows:

> An event is a police riot when roving bands of policemen set upon non-provocative persons and/or property in an excessively violent manner. When only one small group of policemen sets upon citizens and/or property in a single location it may be useful to call this a police attack.

Stark goes on to say that a nonprovocative person is anyone "who represents no significant threat to life, physical safety, or property."[101] While individuals may anger police by behaving disrespectfully, expressing political opinions contrary to their own or appearing to lead life-styles disapproved by the police, there is no legal basis to express this anger through the use of violence.

During the 1960s there were a number of police riots against civil rights and antiwar demonstrators. Perhaps the most dramatic of these was the week-long rampage of the Chicago police in response to the various civil rights and antiwar groups that converged on that city during the 1968 Democratic convention. Some of the demonstrators had angered police with insults and obscene epithets, and in several instances sticks and rocks had been thrown at the police. The police response was

> . . . unrestrained and indiscriminate . . . violence on many occasions, particularly at night . . . [made] all the more shocking by the fact that it was often inflicted upon persons who had broken no law, disobeyed no order, made no threat.[102]

Nearly all of the groups demonstrating in Chicago were protesting United States involvement in the war in Vietnam. In addition, some of the demonstrators were "hippie" types. These groups represented both political ideologies and life-styles objectionable to police. As one police officer commented after participating in a violent attack on "hippie-type" antiwar demonstrators at Grand Central Station in New York City in 1968:

> Here's a bunch of animals who call themselves the next leaders of the country. . . . I almost had to vomit. . . . It's like dealing with any queer pervert, mother raper, or any of those other bedbugs we've got crawling around the Village. As a normal human being, you feel like knocking every one of their teeth out. It's a normal reaction.[103]

To this officer, and many others who participated in police riots during the 1960s, those who through their appearance or life-style challenge the values of hard work, clean living, and sobriety, or who openly challenge government policy such as the use of American military power to crush socialist revolutions in third-world countries, are "queer perverts" and "bedbugs" who deserve to be physically abused. The significance of this is not that police may strongly object to unconventional life-styles or political protest but that when they act upon their objections with violence, they bring to bear the political power of the state to stall or crush legitimate forms of opposition to the political and economic status quo.

By definition, any group that seeks major changes in the status quo or objects strongly to government policies will be viewed as "radical" or "extremist." Police stand ready to protect the social order from those who would seek to change it through methods outside of the normal political processes that are safely dominated by vested interests. While their opposition to those who take their politics into the street may arise from personal belief in the values being attacked or questioned, as an institution the police can generally be expected to use their power—often in extreme ways—to protect the interests of the dominant classes against individuals or groups who threaten those interests.

CONCLUSION: DIRTY WORK AND STATE LEGITIMACY

"The policeman's lot is not a happy one"—so the saying goes. And indeed the policeman's lot in America is not enviable. This is primarily because police work is "dirty work." The maintenance of law and order and the preservation of social peace through the exercise of *state power* is made necessary by the conflicts and contradictions of capitalism in America. However, those who are called upon to perform these tasks on a day-to-day basis—the police—find the work they are called upon to do often both socially stigmatized and fraught with contradictions.

The Social Stigma of Dirty Work

Police are socially stigmatized much the same way as are garbage men. It matters not that garbage men are an important link in maintaining public health in modern societies. Because they handle the physical refuse of our society, their work is regarded as tainted and they are held in low esteem by the remainder of the society. Like garbage men police also handle refuse, only it is the social refuse, the "social junk" capitalism most often creates out of the poor and the oppressed.[104]

Law enforcement in America requires that police spend a large part of their time in intimate contact with the less attractive aspects of life in contemporary America: public drunks, drug addicts, the homeless, the mentally ill, the violent, prostitutes, those whose family problems spill into the public arena, and those who have resorted to crime to maintain the precarious survival imposed by urban poverty. Most of this contact also takes place in the "less desirable" sections of cities and towns. The affluent generally have access to private resources for handling most of their social, interpersonal, and family problems. They are also less frequently the victims of common crimes. Thus much police work concerns the poor or near-poor.

Just as garbage men keep us from personally having to deal with the less attractive by-products of our physical existence, police insulate much of the society from having to personally confront the less attractive by-products of life in America, particularly urban America. We do not want to think about the broken hopes and dreams, the personal frustrations and the anger generated by a political economy that cannot provide meaningful places for all its people. This is particularly true if the system that is disadvantageous to others helps us. When disappointment, frustration, and anger reveal themselves through family violence, theft, robbery, drug addiction, and riot we count on police to control the situation and protect society. Yet because of its nature many find police work tainted. It offends the aesthetic sensibilities of many middle- and upper-class Americans, who then tend to shun police socially and look down upon them professionally.

The Legal Contradiction of Police Work

The "dirty" nature of police work places those who do it in the contradictory position of often feeling required to behave in ways not legally permitted by the very system whose laws they are trying to enforce. Moreover, when police engage in illegal searches to obtain evidence against lawbreakers or beat someone to "teach them respect" for the law or violently disperse a crowd of political demonstrators, they often feel—and not necessarily incorrectly—that they are doing just what the state and most of its citizens wish them to do.

Only when excessively brutal or discriminatory police tactics become *public* and stir open controversy does the state respond. State legitimacy rests on the ideology of fair and equal treatment under a legal system dispassionately enforced by professional police. When police behavior appears to contradict this image the state must respond to protect its legitimacy. Court decisions are made, commissions formed, police practices strongly criticized, and reform legislation passed in response to the threat to state legitimacy. For example, nearly every commission report arising out of the civil disorder of the 1960s urged changes in police practices toward the poor, the nonwhite, and the dissident to restore "respect for the rule of law"—that is, to restore legitimacy to the legal order of capitalist society.

All of this tends to leave police feeling bitter and alienated. Were they not going about society's business? Were they not doing what was expected of them? Why are they being condemned now? This confusion arises from their ambiguous status as "dirty workers" expected to do the unattractive and perhaps even officially illegal but expected also to keep the remainder of society from having to confront the reality of what they do. To many middle- and upper-class Americans, it is not so much brutality against the poor that is offensive; it is having to know about it.

NOTES

1. Howard Becker, *Outsiders* (New York: Free Press, 1973), 9.
2. Clayton A. Hartgen, *Crime and Criminalization* (New York: Praeger, 1978), 6.
3. Richard Quinney, *Criminology*, 2d. ed. (Boston: Little, Brown, 1979), 15.
4. Oliver Wendell Holmes, "The Path of Law," *Harvard Law Review*, no. 10 (1897): 457.
5. E. Adamson Hoebel, *The Law of Primitive Man* (New York: Atheneum, 1973), 25.
6. There is substantial disagreement among anthropologists as to when "law" can be said to exist. Some, such as Stanley Diamond and Marvin Harris, treat law as the unique property of state societies, while others, such as E. Adamson Hoebel and Leonard Pospisil, hold that law exist whenever there is a degree of "institutionalized social control." However, the fundamental differences in the social organization of control that exist between state and nonstate societies are so vast that they must be considered, at best, qualitatively different forms of law, not merely analogs of one another.
7. Richard Schwartz and James C. Miller, "Legal Evolution and Societal Complexity," *American Journal of Sociology*, 70 (September 1964): 159–169.
8. Michael E. Tigar and Madeleine R. Levy, *Law and the Rise of Capitalism* (New York: Monthly Review Press, 1977), chap. 2, 8–52.
9. S. Francis Milsom, *The Historical Foundations of English Common Law* (London: Butterworths, 1969), 15.
10. Margaret Davies, The Enforcement of English Apprenticeship (Cambridge, Mass.: Harvard University Press, 1956), 34.
11. Evelyn L. Parks, "From Constabulary to Police Society: Implications for Social Control," *Catalyst*, no. 5 (Summer 1970): 77–78.

12. William E. Nelson, "Emerging Notions of Modern Criminal Law in the Revolutionary Era: An Historical Perspective," *New York University Law Review,* 42 (May 1967), 450–482.

13. Edwin Powers, *Crime and Justice in Early Massachusetts* (Boston: Beacon Press, 1966), 428–429.

14. Henry B. Parkes, "Morals and Law Enforcement in Colonial New England," *The New England Quarterly,* V (1932): 448.

15. Carl Bridenbaugh, *Cities in the Wilderness: The First Century of Urban Life in America* (New York: Knopf, 1955), 65.

16. Parks, "From Constabulary to Police Society," 78.

17. Quoted in Allan Silver, "The Demand for Order in Civil Society: A Review of Some Themes in the History of Urban Crime, Police and Riot" in *The Police: Six Sociological Essays,* D. J. Bordua, ed. (New York: Wiley, 1967), 1.

18. Ibid., 4.

19. See Thomas A. Critchley, *A History of Police in England and Wales* (Montclair, N.J.: Patterson Smith, 1972); and Roger Lane, *Policing the City* (Cambridge, Mass.: Harvard University Press, 1967).

20. See Patrick Colquhoun's *A Treatise on the Police of the Metropolis* (London: Joseph Mawman, 1806), which served as the basic model for the Metropolitan Police Act.

21. Parks, "From Constabulary to Police Society," 84.

22. See Henry Mayhew's *London Labour and the London Poor* (1851 reprint, London: Spring Books, 1950); and Charles Loring Brace's *The Dangerous Classes of New York and Twenty Years' Work Among Them* (1872; reprint, New York: Wynkoop and Hallenbeck, 1972) for descriptions of the life of the urban proletariat in England and the United States contemporaneous with the development of urban police.

23. Roger Lane, "Urbanization and Criminal Violence in the 19th Century: Massachusetts as a Test Case" in Hugh Gram and Ted Gurr, eds., *The History of Violence in America* (New York: Bantam Books, 1970), 472.

24. Roger Lane, *Policing the City-Boston, 1822–1885.* (Cambridge, Mass.: Harvard University Press, 1967), 26.

25. Sidney L. Harring and Lorraine M. McMullin, "The Buffalo Police 1872–1900: Labor Unrest, Political Power and the Creation of the Police Institution," *Crime and Social Justice,* no. 4 (Fall–Winter 1975): 5–14.

26. Ibid., 11.

27. Ibid., 8–9.

28. Henry David, *The Haymarket Affair.* Quoted in Richard O. Boyer and Herbert M. Morias, *Labor's Untold Story* (New York: Cameron Associates, 1955), 91.

29. Boyer and Morias, *Labor's Untold Story,* 97.

30. Louise Shelly, *Crime and Modernization* (Carbondale: Southern Illinois University Press, 1981).

31. Center for Research on Criminal Justice, *The Iron Fist and the Velvet Glove* (Berkeley, Calif.: Center for Research on Criminal Justice, 1977), 28–30.

32. Grant McConnell, *Private Power and American Democracy* (New York: Knopf, 1966). See pp. 31–42 for a capsule summary of the development and character of the "progressive" era.

33. National Commission on Law Observance and Enforcement (Wickersham Commission), vol. 13, *The Police* (Washington, D.C.: Government Printing Office, 1931), 114.

34. Office of Management and Budget, *Budget of the United States Government, Fiscal Year, 1983* (Washington, D.C.: Government Printing Office, 1982), 9–5. Figures on

criminal justice expenditures were taken from U.S. Department of Justice, *Expenditure and Employment Data for the Criminal Justice System, 1978* (Washington, D.C.: Government Printing Office, 1981), adjusted for inflation to 1982 levels.

35. James S. Kaklik and Sorrel Wildhorn estimate in their RAND Corporation study *The Private Police Industry: Findings and Recommendations, Vol. 1* (Washington, D.C.: Government Printing Office, 1972), 10 that private security constituted a $3.3 billion industry in 1969 and employed nearly 300,000 persons. In *The Private Police Industry: Its Nature and Extent, Vol. II* (Washington, D.C.: Government Printing Office, 1972), 4 these authors project an annual growth rate of between 10 and 15 percent for the private police industry. Using even their most conservative estimate this would yield current figures of over 400,000 private police and an industry budget in excess of $7 billion.

36. Boyer and Morais, *Labor's Untold Story*, 214.

37. William Preston, Jr., *Aliens and Dissenters: Federal Suppression of Radicals, 1903–1933* (New York: Harper Torchbooks, 1963), 119.

38. Ibid., 127.

39. See John Helmer, *Drug Use and Minority Oppression* (New York: Seabury Press, 1975); Patricia A. Morgan, "The Legislation of Drug Law: Economic Crises and Social Control," paper presented at the American Society of Criminology meeting, August 1976; and David Musto, *The American Disease: Origins of Narcotic Control* (New Haven: Yale University Press, 1973) for detailed analyses of the relationship between working class immigration and the criminalization of drug usage.

40. Joseph R. Gusfield, *Symbolic Crusade: Status Politics and the American Temperance Movement* (Urbana: University of Illinois Press, 1963).

41. Paul A. Baran and Paul M. Sweezy, *Monopoly Capital* (New York: Monthly Review Press, 1966), 63.

42. Law Enforcement Assistance Act of 1965, Pub. L. No. 89–197, 79 Stat. 828.

43. Herman Goldstein, *Policing a Free Society* (Cambridge, Mass.: Ballinger Publishing Co., 1977), 33.

44. 42 U.S.C. 3701 (1973).

45. Quoted in Malcolm Feeley and Austin D. Sarat, *The Policy Dilemma: Federal Crime Policy and the Law Enforcement Assistance Administration* (Minneapolis: University of Minnesota Press, 1980), 37.

46. Ibid., 35.

47. Gallup Poll surveys on what Americans fear. Reported in William Watts, "Americans' Hopes and Fears: The Future Can Fend for Itself," *Psychology Today*, 15, no. 9 (1981): 36–48.

48. Title I, Omnibus Crime Control and Safe Streets Act of 1968, 82 Stat. 197 et. seq. (1968).

49. See Goldstein, *Policing a Free Society*, pp. 322–325 for a discussion of the justifications underlying the creation of LEAA; also Feely and Sarat, *The Policy Dilemma*.

50. Center for Research on Criminal Justice, *The Iron Fist and the Velvet Glove*, p. 30.

51. Ibid., chap. 3, 31–52.

52. Ibid., chap. 4, 53–80.

53. U.S. Department of Justice, *Fifth Annual Report of LEAA, Fiscal Year 1973* (Washington, D.C.: Government Printing Office, 1975), 18.

54. Ibid., 100.

55. Goldstein, *Policing a Free State*, 324.

56. Egon Bittner, *The Functions of the Police in Modern Society* (Washington, D.C.: National Institute of Mental Health, 1970), 45–47.

57. Ibid., 38–40.

58. James Q. Wilson, *Varieties of Police Behavior* (Cambridge, Mass.: Harvard University Press, 1968), 16–17.
59. Bittner, *Functions of the Police in Modern Society.*
60. Elaine Cumming, Ian Cumming, and Laura Edell, "Policeman as Philosopher, Guide and Friend," *Social Problems,* 12 (1965): 285. See also Thomas Bercal, "Calls for Police Assistance," *American Behavioral Scientist,* 13 (1970): 682; and Albert J. Reiss, Jr., *The Police and the Public* (New Haven: Yale University Press, 1971), 75 for similar estimates of the nature of police calls for service.
61. Goldstein, *Policing a Free State,* 94–95.
62. Kenneth Culp Davis, *Discretionary Justice: A Preliminary Inquiry* (Urbana: University of Illinois Press, 1971).
63. See Joseph Livermore, "Policing," *Minnesota Law Review,* 55 (1971): 651–665 for a description of routine police duties and the time absorbed by each.
64. James Q. Wilson, *Thinking About Crime* (New York: Basic Books, 1975), 198.
65. Andrew Hacker, "Getting Used to Mugging," *New York Review of Books,* 1970. Reprinted in Henry Etkowitz, ed., *Is America Possible?* (New York: West Publishing Co., 1974).
66. See for example, U.S. Dept. of Justice, *Crime in the United States, 1977* (Washington, D.C.: Government Printing Office, 1978), 35.
67. Chamber of Commerce of the United States, *A Handbook on White Collar Crime,* (Washington, D.C.: Government Printing Office, 1974), 6.
68. Richard J. Lundmann, "Police Patrol Work: A Comparative Perspective," in Richard J. Lundmann, ed., *Police Behavior* (New York: Oxford University Press, 1980), 61.
69. Ibid., 55.
70. Johnathan Rubenstein, *City Police* (New York: Farrar, Straus and Giroux, 1973), 270.
71. Bittner, *Functions of the Police in Modern Society,* 46.
72. Rubenstein, *City Police,* 269.
73. Quoted in Jerome Skolnick, *Justice Without Trial* (New York: Wiley, 1966).
74. Arthur Niederhoffer, *Behind the Shield* (New York: Doubleday and Co., 1966).
75. Skolnick, *Justice Without Trial,* 43–70.
76. Lundman, Police Patrol Work, 66.
77. Mary Glenn Wiley and Terry Hudik, "Police-Citizen Encounters: A Field-Test of Exchange Theory," *Social Problems,* 22 (1974): 121.
78. James R. Hudson, "Police-Citizen Encounters That Lead to Citizen Complaints," *Social Problems,* 18 (1970): 179–193.
79. Rubenstein, *City Police,* 267.
80. Lundmann, *Police Patrol Work,* 61.
81. Ibid., 106.
82. Donald Black, "The Production of Crime Rates," *American Sociological Review,* 35 (1970): 736.
83. Federal Bureau of Investigation, Crime in the United States, 1982 (Washington, D.C.: Government Printing Office, 1983), 157–159.
84. Donald J. Black and Albert J. Reiss, Jr., "Patterns of Behavior in Police and Citizen Transactions," *Studies in Crime and Law Enforcement in Major Metropolitan Areas,* vol. 2, sect. 1. Report of a research study submitted to the President's Commission on Law Enforcement and the Administration of Justice (Washington, D.C.: Government Printing Office, 1967), 78.
85. Donald J. Black and Albert J. Reiss, Jr., "Police Control of Juveniles," *American*

Sociological Review, 35 (1970): 63–77; Irving Piliavin and Scott Briar, "Police Encounters with Juveniles," *American Journal of Sociology,* 69 (1964): 206–214; Richard J. Lundman, "Routing Police Arrest Practices: A Commonwealth Perspective," *Social Problems* (1974): 127–141.

86. Calculated from Richard J. Lundmann, Richard E. Sykes, and John P. Clark, "Police Control of Juveniles: A Replication," *Journal of Research in Crime and Delinquency,* 15 (1978): 89.
87. Ibid., 88.
88. Black, *The Production of Crime Rates,* 740.
89. Lundmann, *Police Patrol Work,* 81.
90. Ibid., 82.
91. Quoted in Albert J. Reiss, Jr., "Police Brutality—Answers to Key Questions," *Transaction,* 5 (1968); reprinted in Arthur Niederhoffer and Abraham S. Blumberg, eds., *The Ambivalent Force: Perspectives on the Police* (Hinsdale, Ill.: Dryden, 1976), 333.
92. David Burnham, "Police Violence: A Changing Pattern," in Niederhoffer and Blumberg, *The Ambivalent Force,* 188.
93. Donald J. Black, *The Manners and Customs of Police* (New York: Academic Press, 1980) 22.
94. Ibid., 24.
95. Ibid., 32.
96. Reiss, "Police Brutality," 336.
97. John Van Maanen, "The Asshole," in Peter K. Manning and John Van Maanen, eds., *Policing: A View from the Streets* (Pacific Palisades, Calif.: Goodyear Publishing Co., 1978), 228.
98. Reiss, "Police Brutality," 336.
99. Burnham, "Police Violence," 188.
100. *New York Times,* 10 July 1981, 1.
101. Rodney Stark, *Police Riots* (Belmont, Calif.: Wadsworth Publishing Co., 1972), 17.
102. Daniel Walker, *Rights in Conflict: Report Submitted to the National Commission on the Causes and Prevention of Violence* (New York: Bantam Books, 1968), 1.
103. Stark, *Police Riots,* 110.
104. Stephen Spitzer, "Toward a Marxian Theory of Deviance," *Social Problems,* 22 (1975): 645–646.

CHAPTER 8

Courts: Judging the Wrongdoer

The criminalization process is a journey from the status of ordinary citizen to the special status of officially labeled criminal. There are a number of stages along the way, and at each decisions are made and actions taken the cumulative effect of which determines whether or not an individual will arrive at the final stage: conviction for a criminal offense.

INITIAL APPEARANCE

The criminalization process begins with arrest. However, it is an initial appearance before a magistrate or judge that begins the process of validating that arrest. The Sixth Amendment to the Constitution provides that individuals cannot be held as criminal suspects for an indefinite period of time without benefit of court review. In the case of *Mallory* v. *United States* the Supreme Court ruled that a criminal suspect must be presented before an officer of the court as soon as possible after arrest.[1] In practice this usually means presentation by the next working session of the relevant court. Many cities maintain twenty-four-hour magistrates or police courts so that the requirement of an initial appearance soon after arrest can be met.

Except in cases of traffic offenses and minor violations where the magistrate is authorized to conduct a summary trial and assess a fine or some other penalty, an initial appearance is nonadjudicatory. At this point the prosecutor would not yet have prepared a case and the arrestee in many instances would not yet have a defense attorney. The primary purpose of the initial hearing is to arrange for bail or some other form of pretrial release and to ascertain that the arrest meets minimum standards of acceptability. At the first appearance, the date for a preliminary hearing, an arraignment, or a trial (depending on how the case will be handled) may be set.

PRELIMINARY HEARING

A preliminary hearing is a more exacting pretrial scrutiny of a case than an initial appearance. The purpose of a preliminary hearing is to determine "probable cause" and in some cases to set bail. This means demonstrating to the court that there is sufficient evidence to reasonably conclude that (1) a crime has been committed and (2) the person arrested or identified as a suspect *may be* guilty of that offense. A finding of probable cause is not a determination of guilt. It is rather a determination that the weight of evidence is at least sufficient to warrant further proceedings.

Preliminary hearings are not held in all cases. In some instances the initial appearance serves the judicial-review and bail-setting functions of a preliminary hearing. Particularly, in cases involving minor offenses, there is often no distinction between preliminary hearing and initial appearance. In both felony and misdemeanor cases defendants frequently waive their right to a preliminary hearing. Overworked public defenders are often reluctant to have already crowded schedules of trial and plea-negotiation meetings further burdened by preliminary hearings and often tend to downplay their importance to the defendant. In some cases defendants themselves feel that a preliminary hearing will not benefit them or that it will do little to expedite the case and so of their own volition waive the preliminary hearing. It is also likely that a proportion of criminal defendants do not fully or even partially understand the functions of a preliminary hearing. It is simply another appearance in court, and one that they can avoid simply by saying so. Generally, however, the more serious the case the more likely it is that a preliminary hearing will be held.

BAIL, BOND, AND PRETRIAL RELEASE

Bail is the practice of releasing criminal suspects from custody in exchange for a sum of money that then acts as a guarantee that the suspect will return for trial. Should the defendant not return at the specified time, the bail money is forfeited to the court. In theory the amount of bail should be sufficient to insure that the defendant will return rather than forfeit. If the individual does appear in court, the bail money is returned.

The practice of bail is an old one that may very well have arisen from the early medieval device of offering hostages as surety that treaty conditions between formerly warring lords would be met. By the twelfth century bail as a device for releasing untried prisoners was common practice in England and was officially recognized and regulated by law in the 1275 Statute of Westminster.[2]

The Eighth Amendment to the Constitution states, "Excessive bail shall not be required." This has been interpreted by the courts to mean that defendants, at least in noncapital cases, have a constitutional *right* to bail. In the 1951 case of *Stack* v. *Boyle* the Supreme Court held that

> . . . federal law has unequivocally provided that a person arrested for a noncapital offense *shall* be admitted to bail. This traditional right to freedom before conviction permits the unhampered preparation of a defense, and serves to prevent the infliction of punishment prior to conviction.[3]

While most legal scholars agree with this interpretation of the Constitution, the right to pretrial freedom has periodically come under attack because of the supposedly large number of crimes committed by defendants while on bail. During the late 1960s as part of the Nixon administration's "war on crime" several bills were introduced in Congress that aimed to limit pretrial freedom for "dangerous" offenders. These bills authorized *preventive detention*, that is, the denial of bail to defendants deemed dangerous or likely to commit further crimes while free on bail. With the exception of a bill authorizing preventive detention in the District of Columbia, these laws met with sufficient opposition to prevent their passage.

The attempts to establish preventive detention laws led to several projects aimed at ascertaining the *actual* amount of crime committed by defendants on bail. Two studies in 1971 found that contrary to popular impressions, only about 5 percent of accused felons were involved in another major offense while on bail.[4] These findings, along with the constitutional questions raised by proposals to allow judges to deny bail on their estimation that the offender was "dangerous" led to a decline of interest in establishing preventive detention as a part of the normal justice process. In more recent years, however, there has been a resurgence of political interest in preventive detention, particularly among conservative politicians.

The Justice Department under the Reagan administration endorsed a policy of "allowing judges to consider the safety of the community" when setting bail. In effect this policy would permit judges to set unattainable bail amounts for offenders judges deemed threats to the community, even when a lesser amount would be sufficient to insure the suspect's return for trial. Claiming that a "startling amount of crime" is committed by persons on release while awaiting trial, Chief Justice of the Supreme Court Warren Burger also endorsed changes in bail laws that would prevent crimes by "dangerous" defendants.[5] If established, preventive detention laws would give substantial discretion to judges in determining who is and who is not a "dangerous" offender. They would also violate the constitutional guarantees of pretrial freedom and a presumption of innocence. However, the conservative political climate of the early 1980s may enable such legislation to succeed where it failed in the late 1960s.

While the "right" to bail has been generally supported by the courts the question of "excessive" bail has proven more problematic. Few criminal defendants can raise the actual amount of money necessary to make bail. One study estimated that fully 79 percent of criminal defendants in New York City whose bail was set at $500 could not raise this amount. Those who cannot raise the full amount of their bail must either remain in custody until their trial date or seek the services of a bail bondsman. For a fee, usually 10 percent of the bail amount, bondsmen take on a defendant's bail responsibility. Depending upon the jurisdiction the bondsman may either be required to post with the court the actual amount of the defendant's bail or some portion thereof or simply to sign a statement making the bondsman liable for the bail amount should the defendant fail to appear for trial.

The bondsman's fee is a cost that only the poor must pay for their pretrial freedom. While those with sufficient resources to make their own bail can reclaim their money upon returning for trial, those who must use the bondsman's services do not recoup the money posted for freedom. Using a bondsman's services would cost a defendant $250 if bail were set at $2,500. Given that over three-quarters of criminal defendants are incapable of raising even $500, the majority of criminal defendants in all but the most minor cases must utilize a bondsman's services. That is, they must *pay* for their pretrial freedom or remain in jail until trial unless they qualify for one of the more recent nonmoney pretrial release programs. Thus the bail system requires the poor to pay a fine for merely being arrested, regardless of the outcome of ajudication. The case may be dismissed or the defendant acquitted, and yet a penalty will have already been extracted in the form of bond money. The justice system punishes the poor merely for being poor as well as for having violated the law. Money bail, although obviously inequitable, is not a deliberate or conscious attempt to harass the poor. It is, however, an excellent example of the consequences of applying the ideology of equality under the law to individuals in a society based upon inequality.

Bondsmen themselves constitute a curious adjunct to the justice system. Within walking distance of the courtrooms in any major city are the offices of bail bondsmen. Often they are located in deteriorating buildings, converted garages, or other similarly unattractive surroundings. One study of bail in major American cities described the typical bondsman's office as

> . . . furnished with chairs that appear to be refugees from a deserted bus terminal. A single file cabinet or whiskey cartons are used for storage. On top of an isolated desk is located a row of telephones, obscured by a mountainous collection of phone books from various cities. The floor is rugless and carpeted only with a bed of cigarette butts and ashes.[6]

The bondsman is a justice system soldier of fortune, making a living by selling freedom to poor defendants. As the Supreme Court noted in 1912, the bondsman's "interest to produce the body of the principal in court is impersonal and wholly pecuniary."[7]

The most unfortunate criminal defendants are those who can neither post their own bail nor acquire the services of a bondsman either because they cannot afford even a small proportion of their bail or because their case is of a type bondsmen are reluctant to handle. Petty theft, public intoxication, disorderly conduct, and some drug offenses are generally unattractive to bondsmen because the fee is small or the clients highly unreliable. Those who can acquire neither bail nor bond must face the prospect of awaiting their trial in custody, in essence serving a sentence before being convicted. Not only are these defendants deprived of their freedom before trial, they also stand a greater likelihood of being convicted when they do come to trial and of being sentenced to prison if convicted than do those at liberty before trial. One study in Philadelphia found that 25 percent of those who made bail were acquitted at the trial stage compared with 16 percent of those who awaited their trials in custody.[8] Another study in New York found a 31 percent acquittal rate for those free on bail compared with a 20 percent acquittal rate for those unable to make bail.[9] These findings refer only to acquittal at the *trial stage* and as such obscure the importance of bail status upon other possible actions. Those who are incarcerated pending trial have a greater incentive to plead guilty to expedite their case than do those free on bail and tend to do so proportionally more often.[10] Furthermore, those free on bail can mount a more effective opposition to the charges against them and therefore are more likely to succeed in having charges dropped. The importance of bail status on pretrial actions was shown by the Philadelphia bail study, which found that acquittal rates *at trial* were 25 percent and 16 percent respectively for the bailed versus the jailed suspect, but when all those cases that never reached the trial stage were included, this difference in acquittal rates jumped to 58 percent for those making bail versus 18 percent for those in pretrial detention, a net increase of 31 percent in the rate of acquittal for the bailed over the jailed.[11]

Bail status appears to be similarly related to sentencing. One study found that while 64 percent of those who remained in custody until the time of sentencing received jail terms, only 17 percent of those free on bond were subsequently incarcerated. Another found the bail status of defendants to be the most important variable contributing to sentence variation in twenty-five out of twenty-seven offenses.[12] Yet another study, this one on sentencing recommendations, found that recommendations to the court for nonprison sentences were followed in 90 percent of the cases where the defendant was free on bail, while only 68 percent of the nonprison recommendations were followed for those defendants awaiting sentencing in jail.[13]

Bail status does not effect case outcome in isolation from other factors, and this complicates the assessment of bail. Those too poor to make bail or bond generally are also unable to retain their own attorneys. Some researchers have suggested that the quality and type of legal representation is more closely associated with the likelihood of conviction and incarceration than is bail status.[14] While there is merit to this argument, it does not obviate the fundamental fact that requiring unequal individuals to submit to a justice system predicated upon equal treatment produces injustice.

The inequities of the bail system have not gone unnoticed, and in recent years there have been a number of attempts at reform. Such reform, it must be understood, is an attempt to minimize the negative consequences of an inadequate system, not to fundamentally alter that system. The most influential reform of recent years has been the emergence of release-on-recognizance (ROR) programs. In 1961 the Manhattan Bail Project sponsored by the Vera Institute of Justice demonstrated that with proper screening a large number of defendants could be released on nothing more than their promise to return for trial with no increase in the rate of failure to appear.[15] The success of this project stimulated the development of ROR programs in many cities, and they have now become relatively commonplace. These programs tend to maintain forfeiture rates that are on the average about half that of bail bondsmen, although for both types of release the rate of "no shows" is low. A comparison of forfeiture rates for bondsmen with those for release-on-recognizance in four major cities shows an average forfeiture rate of 9.2

percent for bondsmen and 4.1 percent for ROR programs.[16] Some of this difference, however, is not based on the inherent effectiveness of ROR programs but on the fact that these programs tend to skim off the more reliable clients, leaving bondsmen to handle some of those who do not qualify for ROR. By allowing thousands of defendants to be released without posting bond, pretrial release programs have weakened the bail bond industry by beating them out of some of the better clients available—those least likely to "skip" before trial.[17]

The National Advisory Commission on Criminal Justice Standards and Goals recommended in 1973 that all release of defendants prior to trial should be made in accordance with pretrial screening programs and that "Participation by private bail bond agencies in the pretrial release process should be eliminated."[18] This has not yet happened, however, and pretrial release remains a mixture of bail, bond, and release-on-recognizance programs.

Diversion constitutes another avenue for pretrial release. Unlike release-on-recognizance programs that are aimed at providing the defendant with liberty *until* trial, diversion programs offer defendants a cessation or suspension of further criminal proceedings in exchange for some action on the part of the defendant, usually participation in a designated rehabilitation program or a promise to make restitution.[19] In one sense diversion occurs whenever an agent of the justice system chooses a nonjudicial course of action in the handling of a suspect or defendant. The police officer who takes the drunk or juvenile runaway home instead of to the police station is engaging in diversion, as is the judge who agrees to dismiss a case if the defendant agrees to make restitution to the victim. Although this type of diversion has always been one of the consequences of discretion within the justice system, it has tended to be informal and relatively hidden from public view. In the last decade, however, there has emerged a trend toward institutionalizing and formalizing the process of diverting defendants away from the justice system.

Diversion programs fall into two general categories: those that divert the defendant to some program within the justice system and those that funnel him or her into some program outside the justice system. Dismissal of a driving-while-intoxicated charge in return for the defendant's participation in a driver improvement program run by the state highway patrol or dropping charges of petty theft in return for restitution to the victim to be monitored by a court officer are examples of diversion within the system itself. Cessation of assault proceedings in return for a defendant's agreement to participate in a program through a local community mental health center or taking a public inebriate to an alcohol rehabilitation center or shelter rather than to the local drunk tank are forms of diversion outside the criminal justice process.

Many arguments have been put forth favoring diversion, including minimizing the stigma of conviction[20] and allowing individuals to receive needed rehabilitative services instead of unneeded punishment.[21] The most influential reason, however, is that diversion reduces both the case load and cost of criminal justice when compared with prosecution and sentencing. As government budget deficits have grown, there has been increased demand for thrift on the part of state and Federal governments.[22] Diversion programs have the unique advantage of appealing to both the rehabilitative goals of liberals and the fiscal goals of conservatives.[23] This unlikely union of interests has provided considerable support for the expansion of diversion programs.

THE DECISION TO PROSECUTE

Next to arrest, the decision to prosecute is probably the most important one made on the route to conviction. Once an arrest has been made, an initial appearance and/or preliminary hearing concluded, and the defendant's bail status determined, the public prosecutor must decide whether the case will actually be ajudicated.

If the prosecutor does decide to proceed with the case, the defendant will in all likelihood be convicted. Approximately 90 to 95 percent of all criminal cases actually brought before trial courts result in conviction.[24] Thus the decision to prosecute is crucial. It should be recognized, however, that the high rate of conviction obtained by prosecutors reflects the fact that prosecutors generally only take to court those cases that they feel they can win at trial or for which they can obtain a guilty plea.

In 1976 there were 7,547 prosecutorial agencies in the United States, and the majority of these were municipal district attorney's offices.[25] The local prosecutor or district attorney is usually an attorney elected to office in partisan or nonpartisan municipal elections.

Public prosecutors perform a number of functions. However, the most important is deciding whether or not formal charges will be filed against a criminal suspect. Prosecutors enjoy substantial discretion in making this decision, and within the limits of the law they can choose to prosecute or not prosecute with little pressure from either the police or the courts.[26] When making the decision to prosecute or to *nol pros* (i.e., drop) a case, prosecutors weigh several sets of factors. The first and most important set of considerations are those that bear upon the likelihood of winning the case.[27] The sufficiency of legally admissible evidence, the availability and credibility of witnesses, the apparent competence of the defense attorney, and the criminal record and character of the defendant all influence the likelihood of conviction and are weighed by the prosecutor in making a decision to prosecute.[28]

Winning the maximum number of cases is important to public prosecutors for a variety of reasons. A high win–loss record improves the prosecutor's position for plea bargaining by convincing defendants that they stand little chance of winning in court and therefore would be better off accepting conviction on a lesser charge. It is also an important measure of the prosecutor's performance and is absolutely necessary if the prosecutor seeks reelection or hopes to run for higher political office. Successful performance as a prosecutor can also serve as a springboard into a lucrative private practice. As one researcher noted, prosecutors are acutely aware of their personal "batting averages."[29]

Winning cases is also seen as necessary if the justice system is to maintain its credibility. As one judge noted, "Too many acquittals are bound to call into question respect for law and the validity of the process of the courts."[30] Since there are never the funds to prosecute even the majority of cases, district attorneys tend to select the "best" cases, that is, those they can most likely win. To do otherwise would violate the organizational pressure for efficiency.[31]

While winning cases is perhaps the primary concern of prosecutors, a number of other criteria also influence the decision to prosecute. Prosecutors are generally sensitive to the impact of both the crime and of prosecution of victims. Facts such as the seriousness of the crime and the amount of harm done to the victim enter into the decision to prosecute, with more serious offenses and those aggravated by physical harm being more likely to result in a decision to prosecute. In some cases, such as rape, incest, and other family crimes where prosecution might prove stressful to the victim, prosecutors may choose not to prosecute.[32] Prosecutors are also influenced by what they think would constitute justice for the accused. Prosecutors are more likely to drop cases where they feel the severity of the probable punishment is too harsh in light of the crime or the nature of the defendant.[33] Prosecutors also weigh rehabilitative considerations when deciding whether or not to prosecute. Most often it is the district attorney who determines or at least formally agrees that a particular suspect would benefit more from entrance into some diversion program than from criminal prosecution. These decisions of course reflect the prosecutor's personal understanding of who is and who is not a likely candidate for rehabilitation.

The prosecutor's decision-making authority extends beyond the decision to file formal charges. The prosecutor selects the specific charge to be lodged against the defendant. Selecting this charge is more than the technical exercise of matching the accused's conduct with the appropriate criminal statute. The criminal law prohibits general categories of behavior such as assault, gambling, theft, and so forth. However, it cannot specify each and every exact set of circumstances that fit these general categories. The prosecutor must decide, for example, if four youths found in possession of a stolen automobile should be charged with grand theft of an auto (a felony crime) or operation without owner's consent (usually a misdemeanor). Similarly, it is the prosecutor who must determine if the defendant found with two ounces of marijuana should be charged with "possession with intent to sell," since the law clearly states that possession of any amount over one ounce constitutes presumed intention to sell, or whether a charge of "simple possession" would be more appropriate. In most states there is a significant difference in the maximum possible penalty for these two offenses, and the determination of the defendant's liability rests with the prosecutor.

In selecting specific charges the prosecutor is generally influenced not only by the behavior in question but also by the likelihood of conviction or negotiation of a guilty plea. In some instances prosecutors will select the maximum possible charge to allow more room for bargaining at a later point.

In others, particularly where the prosecutor feels that a court trial is likely, the most easily proven charges will be selected, even though the overall case involved more serious offenses.[34] For instance, a defendant caught fleeing from the scene of a burglary might be charged with possession of stolen property or perhaps possession of burglary tools if there are no witnesses to establish that the suspect was actually ever in the burglarized building.

ARRAIGNMENT

Once specified charges have been selected by the prosecutor, the defendant is arraigned. At this point the defendant is given formal notice of the charges and asked to enter a plea; either guilty, not guilty, or if the court accepts, *nolo contendere*—that is, no contest. In many jurisdictions, where a capital offense is alleged the only permissible plea is *not guilty*. By the time of arraignment, the prosecutor, defendant, and defense counsel will most likely have already arrived at a negotiated plea of *guilty*, and the arraignment actually serves as an adjudicatory hearing. This is particularly true in the case of misdemeanor offenses. It is estimated that approximately 95 percent of all convictions in these cases result from a guilty plea at arraignment.[35] Since misdemeanors constitute the majority of criminal offenses charged, arraignment is usually the final stage in the process toward criminalization for the majority who end up in trouble with the law.[36]

When a plea of *not guilty* is entered, the defendant will be asked to indicate a choice of trial by jury or trial before a judge. The majority of defendants who plead not guilty ask for trial before judge rather than a jury.[37] If the offense is minor and the defendant chooses trial by judge, the trial may be conducted in conjunction with the arraignment proceedings. In other cases a future trial date is set.

THE NEGOTIATED PLEA

The guilty plea is the cornerstone of criminal prosecution in the United States. Approximately 90 percent of all defendants formally charged with the commission of a crime plead guilty, thereby all but insuring their own conviction.[38] Trial by a jury of one's peers is the idealized route to justice espoused by the liberal democracy of America; the guilty plea is the reality. The high percentage of guilty pleas entered in American courts does not stem from some overwhelming sense of remorse on the part of criminal defendants but from a variety of personal and organizational pressures on the defendants.

Guilty pleas are most often the consequence of a process of negotiation between the prosecutor, defense counsel, defendant, and sometimes the presiding judge. This process of negotiation is essentially extra-legal; it is not provided for under statutory law and only recently has the role of plea bargaining in the justice process been recognized under case law. As an informal adjunct to the justice process, plea bargaining is relatively hidden from scrutiny. Negotiations take place in private and are seldom made public. For this reason it is difficult to know the actual extent of plea negotiation, although research has indicated that the majority of all guilty pleas are the result of some negotiation between the prosecution and defense.[39]

In the process of plea negotiation, the defendant bargains away the opportunity to be acquitted at trial in return for one or more considerations, usually involving either a reduction of charges or a more lenient sentence. Negotiations for reduced charges most often involve such things as (1) pleading guilty to a lesser offense included in the charges (for instance, assault instead of robbery), (2) pleading guilty to one or several offenses in return for dropping additional charges (for example, pleading guilty to one count of burglary when charged with five offenses), and (3) pleading guilty to a related misdemeanor in return for dropping some felony charge (for instance, trading a plea for possession of burglary tools in return for dropping a burglary charge).

Bargained pleas may also involve sentencing considerations. Defendants may agree to plead guilty in return for the prosecutor's promise to recommend probation or some other less-than-maximum sentence or for the promise of concurrent rather than consecutive sentences on multiple charges.[40] In some instances judges are privy to sentencing negotiations before a guilty plea is entered and may even take an active role in convincing the defendant that a guilty plea will result in a more lenient sentence. Even when courts do not take an overt role in pressuring defendants to plead guilty in return for sentencing leniency, there is evidence that judges tend to "punish" those who put the court to the trouble and expense of a trial by assigning heavier penalties.[41] This leads to what has been called the "tacit bargain." Knowing the negative consequences of asking for a trial, the defendant offers to plead guilty without ever having been actually promised sentencing leniency in return for a guilty plea.[42]

Given the variety of pressures on criminal defendants, it is apparent why many would choose to plead guilty rather than face trial. What remains to be explained is why prosecutors and judges, supposedly charged with the enforcement of the law, would allow and in fact even urge defendants whom presumably they believe to be guilty of more serious offenses to plead guilty to lesser ones.

The primary reason offered to explain the prosecutor's active role in seeking bargained pleas is that the organizational demands upon the prosecutor's office make it impossible to try even a significant minority of the cases it must handle. Abraham Blumberg, a lawyer and a sociologist who conducted one of the first in-depth studies of the prosecutorial process, concluded that the personnel and resources of the prosecutor's office simply cannot support the "impossible burden" of going through the elaborate court procedures required to try every case.[43] Like any organization, the court, of which the prosecutor's office is a part, seeks efficiency. In the justice system efficiency is measured by the number of cases processed. Thus to meet the demands of organizational efficiency, the prosecutor must seek to expedite the disposition of cases and to do so within the resources available. Plea bargaining makes possible a steady flow of cases through the system.

In addition to the search for organizational efficiency, there are a number of other pressures upon prosecutors that favor plea bargaining as the basic mechanism for disposing cases. A high ratio of wins to losses is the essential measure of a prosecutor's performance. It is therefore more advantageous to accept a guilty plea to lesser charges, which constitutes a guaranteed score in the win column, rather than risk a possible loss if the defendant is brought to trial on more serious offenses. Still, the prosecutor's motivation in accepting a guilty plea to a lesser offense is not necessarily always consciously self-serving. Prosecutors recognize that certain charges are often difficult to prove. For example, given the frequent lack of witnesses or physical evidence, rape is often a difficult charge to prove at trial. Rather than risk acquittal, prosecutors are sometimes willing to accept a charge of aggravated or simple assault as a means of insuring that at least some penalty will be extracted for the crime.

Prosecutors also share organizationally defined exchange relations with other members of the justice system.[44] Particularly where promises of lenient sentencing are concerned, a prosecutor's bargaining power depends upon positive working relationships with trial judges. To the extent that the trial judges have made it clear that they do not want their court calendar cluttered with a large number of criminal trials, the prosecutor may experience additional pressure to bargain for guilty pleas. The prosecutor is similarly involved in role reciprocity with defense attorneys, who must be relied upon to convince their clients to plead guilty. Because they have an ongoing relationship that extends beyond any single case, prosecutors and defense attorneys will sometimes bargain several cases together as a package, with each accepting less than the desired deal in some cases in return for better deals in others.

Guilty pleas are not necessarily entered because the defendant is alert to the possibility of obtaining a deal. Defense attorneys play a critical role in getting defendants to accept bargained pleas. Blumberg found that in over half the cases studied it was the *defense counsel* who first suggested that the defendant plead guilty.[45] Indeed, Blumberg suggests that one of the most serious shocks experienced by many first-time criminal defendants was that their attorney was not unswervingly committed to fighting for their innocence but instead appeared to have an independent interest in bringing the case to a swift conclusion.

Privately retained attorneys and public defenders differ somewhat in their readiness to encourage clients to plead guilty. A study of criminal defendants conducted for the National Institute of Law Enforcement and Criminal Justice found that only 30 percent of those represented by public defenders said that their attorney was more interested in obtaining justice than in "getting the case over with quickly." This compares with 64 percent of those with private counsel who felt that their attorney was more interested in justice than speed.[46] There are two types of public defenders: those who work for public defenders or legal aid office supported by state funds and those who are local, private attorneys assigned indigent cases on a rotation basis and receive a flat fee out of local revenues for each case handled. For both, however, there is substantial pressure to select speedy handling over a strong commitment to the client's interests.

Public defenders offices are characteristically underfunded, understaffed, and overworked, reflecting the token concern that exists for insuring equality under the law for the poor. Few public defenders have sufficient time to prepare a trial-ready defense for the majority of their clients, and in many cases they meet their clients for the first time in court, just prior to arraignment. Like prosecutors, public defenders offices must meet organizational demands that they process a large volume of cases, and these demands supersede the loftier goal of insuring justice for the indigent. In addition, most public defenders are either relatively young and inexperienced attorneys, or those who have been unsuccessful in private practice. In either case the indigent defendant does not have the benefit of skilled and experienced counsel. Those public defenders who do come to their task imbued with a commitment to justice and an unwillingness to plead the majority of their clients guilty will often find such zeal leads to their being reprimanded for cluttering the courts with unnecessary trials.[47] Furthermore, if the public defender hopes to establish a successful private practice in the community after leaving the defender's office, there is little to be gained by alienating the local legal fraternity through an unwillingness to cooperate with established plea-bargaining practices.

The private attorney assigned to serve indigent clients on a rotation basis is under slightly different pressures. To the private attorney, who is an independent entrepreneur, time is money. Since the defense of indigent criminal defendants is by no means lucrative, few private attorneys feel they can devote much time to such cases, whatever their personal feelings about equal justice. In addition, since few private attorneys specialize in criminal cases, the majority serving on rotation will be relatively unfamiliar with criminal practice and often willing to follow the lead of the prosecutor to expedite the case.

The pressures upon public defenders to bring cases to a swift conclusion mean that *poor defendants are more likely to be convicted than those who can afford private counsel.* Attorneys who serve the indigent are more anxious to plead their clients guilty than privately retained counsel. Blumberg found that privately retained attorneys recommended a guilty plea to their clients at the initial meeting in 35 percent of the cases studied, while 49 percent of the public defenders and 60 percent of the assigned attorneys suggested at the initial interview that their clients plead guilty.[48] Another study found that in Little Rock, Arkansas, private attorneys entered guilty pleas for 41 percent of their clients, while those representing the indigent did so in 64 percent of their cases.[49] The tendency of appointed counsel to dispose of cases quickly through guilty pleas, coupled to some extent with their limited experience in criminal cases, also results in lower rates of dismissal for poor clients. A report by

Dallin Oaks and Warren Lehman revealed that while privately retained attorneys obtained dismissal of charges for 29 percent of their clients, lawyers for the poor did so in only 16 percent of their cases.[50]

The practice of plea bargaining has been strongly criticized by some in recent years as a danger to the rights of defendants and to the security of society. Underlying the bargained plea is the assumption that failure to plead guilty could lead to harsher consequences such as a more severe sentence or conviction on more serious charges. As the National Advisory Commission of Criminal Justice Standards and Goals observed,

> An innocent defendant might be persuaded that the harsher sentence he must face if he is unable to prove his innocence at trial means that it is to his best interests to plead guilty despite his innocence. If these persons have a realistic chance of being acquitted at trial, a plea negotiation system that encourages them to forfeit their right to trial endangers their right to an accurate and fair determination of guilt.[51]

Plea bargaining is also criticized because it allows defendants to plead guilty to crimes less serious than they have actually committed. To provide an incentive for the defendant to plead guilty the prosecutor must offer something in return, and this is often the opportunity to avoid conviction for the most serious offense actually committed. This, it is argued, reduces if not destroys the deterrent effect of the law and breeds a general disrespect for the justice system.

In recent years the Supreme Court has been asked to consider the constitutionality of plea bargaining. The Court has held that to be constitutional a guilty plea must be made knowledgeably and voluntarily by the defendant.[52] In 1970 the Court went one step further toward legally institutionalizing plea bargaining by ruling in the case of *Brady* v. *United States* that the promise of leniency in return for a guilty plea did not compromise the "voluntariness" of a plea, even though there is an implicit threat of more severe punishment for failure to plead guilty.[53] One year later the Court took the final step in validating plea bargaining by ruling in *Santobello* v. *New York* that if a guilty plea is based upon some promise by the prosecutor, that promise must be kept or the defendant given an opportunity to change the plea.[54] While the Court has recognized the dangers inherent in a system of negotiated justice, it has also agreed that the negotiated plea is an unavoidable part of the contemporary justice process. Thus the direction of the Court as well as of several crime commissions has been to formalize and bring out into the open the plea-bargaining process in the hopes that this will reduce the possibility of due process violations. Only the National Advisory Commission on Standards and Goals has taken a different approach. The committee recommended in 1973 that

> As soon as possible, but in no event later than 1978, negotiations between prosecutors and defendants—either personally or through their attorneys—concerning concessions to be made in return for guilty pleas should be abolished.[55]

Since that recommendation, however, there has been little effective movement toward the abolition of plea bargaining, although some states have passed laws prohibiting plea bargaining for specific crimes. The volume of criminal offenses brought to or generated by the justice system, as well as the tendency for organizational efficiency to supersede the concerns of justice, combine to make the elimination of plea bargaining unlikely. Beyond these factors, however, is the more salient one that *justice is not the primary business of the justice system.* Maintenance of social order is its primary task, and if order can be maintained expeditiously and economically through practices such as plea bargaining, there will be little real pressure on the justice system to change its operations. Only if the inherent contradictions in bargain justice threaten the overall legitimacy of the justice system will there emerge the impetus *and the financial resources for change.*

TRIAL

Trial is the most dramatic, best known, and least important part of the justice process. Popular dramas such as "Perry Mason" and "Judd for the Defense" have engrained in the minds of most Americans an idealized image of the trial as a central part of the justice process. Rather than being central to the justice process, however, trials are more like a centerpiece on a dining table— interesting to look at but not an important part of the meal.

Trials, as previously discussed, occur in only about 10 percent of all criminal cases, and only about half of these occur before a jury; the remainder take place before a judge only. It is an essential part of American legal ideology that an adversary trial before a jury of peers constitutes the best way to ascertain the truth of a criminal suspect's innocence or guilt. Critics of the adversary system suggest that in the trial process, however, neither the defense nor the prosecution are concerned with *truth.* Each side at trial is primarily, if not solely, concerned with *winning,* not just for the defendant's or the state's sake, but because the adversary system establishes winning cases as the primary measure of an attorney's competence. Thus the prosecutor and defense counsel have a personal stake in the outcome of a trial, which compromises the virtue of trial as a truth-finding exercise.

SENTENCING

Once convicted, criminal defendants must face the imposition of a sentence. The transformation of an individual from the status of ordinary citizen to that of criminal grants to the state the legal authority to inflict imprisonment or some other punishment upon the offender.

The most significant decision a judge must make is whether or not to sentence the offender to some form of custody—that is, imprisonment—or to return him or her to the community via a suspended sentence, probation, or some other community-based sentencing alternative. If a judge decides upon imprisonment, the next question that must be addressed is the length of sentence. Here statutes may specify maximum sentence, minimum sentence, or both, placing some limitations on judicial discretion, although within the statutory range judges are usually free to specify the sentence. There are two significant exceptions to this.

First, in some jurisdictions certain offenses carry *mandatory* sentences. If a conviction results the sentence is automatic, eliminating any judicial decision making. The other case is that of the indeterminate sentence. In this case the offender is simply sentenced to the correctional authority for either (1) a period of time within a range set by legislatively established minimum and maximum sentences or (2) for a wholly unspecified amount of time. In either instance it is the correctional authority in conjunction with a parole board that decides the actual amount of time served. The only decision made by the sentencing judge is whether offenders will be sent to prison, not how long they will stay there. Popular during the late 1950s and 1960s, the indeterminate sentence has been substantially limited or eliminated in many jurisdictions today.

Sentencing judges enjoy substantial discretion, although within the limits set by the statutes governing specific offenses. Criminal sentencing in the United States is far from uniform. Studies of judicial sentencing practices have repeatedly shown that there is significant variability in the types of sentences handed down for similar cases both within jurisdictions and between different jurisdictions.[56]

Discriminatory Sentencing

There has been considerable debate in recent years over whether the justice system discriminates against poor and nonwhite offenders by giving them harsher sentences than their more affluent, white counterparts. Sentencing discrimination can only be understood, however, if we recognize that it takes two very different forms, *legislative discrimination* and *judicial discrimination*.

The most important form of discrimination takes place at the legislative level. American law assigns penalties to various categories of harm in such a way that *those crimes more likely to be committed by the poor almost always carry harsher penalties than those more likely to be committed by the affluent.*

The statutory distinctions between civil, regulatory, and criminal law are such that those who come before courts charged with committing those forms of harm defined as crimes are most often poor and are also disproportionately nonwhite. Such things as industrial safety violations that lead to worker illness, injury, or death; violations of environmental regulations producing decreased health and increased illness among large segments of the population; or violations of rules governing consumer safety will most often be treated as civil or regulatory matters. Consequently, those responsible will seldom appear in criminal courts facing the possibility of criminal sanctions such as imprisonment. Moreover, in many instances these offenses will be treated as corporate violations, and while the business may be assessed a fine, the particular individuals involved will themselves not be charged with or punished for wrongdoing. As a result, the majority of those receiving criminal sanctions in the United States will come disproportionately from the poorer segments of society.

This type of discrimination is often difficult to recognize because it is *institutionalized* rather than personal. We cannot identify this or that judge who, out of personal malice or general mistrust of poor or black defendants, chooses to give them harsher sentences than other defendants. Rather, we are faced with a type of sentencing discrimination that is integral to the organization and ideology of American society. No judge need be particularly hostile to poor defendants for the poor to serve longer and more frequent sentences when they cause someone harm or financial loss than will the corporate violator causing equal or greater injury or loss. That is a form of discrimination built into the legal system. Sentencing judges in criminal cases seldom have anything but poor and/or nonwhite defendants before them.

In addition to the fact that the legal system tends to direct middle- and upper-class wrongdoers away from criminal prosecution, there is some evidence that suggests that nonpoor defendants charged with "white-collar" criminal offenses tend to fare better when sentenced than the poor who appear in court for common crimes. One study of sentences in the Southern District of New York found that only 36 percent of those convicted for white-collar offenses that could have led to a prison term were actually sentenced to serve time. By contrast, 53 percent of those convicted for *nonviolent* common crimes received prison sentences.[57]

This is only part of the story, however. When sentenced to prison, common criminals tend to receive longer sentences and spend more time in prison than white-collar offenders. For example, a Federal Bureau of Prison report, shows that on the average embezzlers are sentenced to 21 months in prison and serve approximately 13 months, while those convicted of common theft are given an average sentence of 32.8 months and serve approximately 18.7 months.[58] This means that the average sentence is 40 percent longer for common theft even though the amount stolen is usually substantially less than that involved in embezzlement!

When people think of sentencing discrimination they usually think about it in terms of equal justice, that is, whether or not offenders charged with similar offenses and who have similar prior records receive equal treatment by the courts. This logic, of course, takes for granted the legitimacy of differential sentencing for different classes of crimes and in doing so ignores the most fundamental source of sentencing discrimination in American justice—the division of sentences along class lines, harsh sentences for the common crimes of the poor, and lighter sentences and penalties for the harms committed by the middle class and elite offenders. But even where similar offenses are compared, evidence suggests that poor and nonwhite defendants receive the more afflictive punishments.

In addition to being found guilty more often, indigent defendants are less likely to be recommended for probation and less likely to receive probation when recommended than are more affluent offenders with private counsel. An analysis of Federal sentencing data has shown that 27 percent of indigent defendants with *no prior record* were not recommended for probation, while only 16 percent of the nonindigent defendants failed to receive a probation recommendation.[59] Furthermore, where there is no recommendation for probation judges are substantially more likely to sentence indigent offenders to prison than those who have sufficient resources to be represented by private counsel. The Vera Institute of Justice Sentencing Project found that fully 95 percent of indigent offenders who did not receive a probation recommendation were sentenced to prison while only 54 percent of the nonindigent who failed to receive a probation recommendation were given active sentences. The project also showed that 32 percent of those too poor to obtain pretrial freedom had their probation recommendations rejected by the sentencing judge compared with only 10 percent of those free on bail or bond. In addition, recommendations for prison sentence "were followed in 95 percent of the custody cases, but in only 66 percent of the non-custody cases."[60] It has also been shown that attorneys for the indigent are less likely to insure that ajudication and sentencing will occur before a lenient judge than are private attorneys. This means that indigent offenders appear statistically more often before severe judges and as a result more often receive prison sentences instead of probation.[61]

It has been argued that most of these forms of sentencing discrimination can be explained as the indirect effects of poverty upon criminal defendants rather than the result of discriminatory attitudes on the part of sentencing judges. The poor, it is said, simply cannot afford the kind of legal representation that helps reduce the likelihood of avoiding conviction, or if convicted, of avoiding a prison sentence.

Several studies that have controlled for relevant legal variables such as the nature of counsel have shown little sentencing discrimination on the basis of income.[62] The problem with these findings is that once indigency with respect to obtaining defense counsel is eliminated as a variable, there is little variation in the income levels of defendants remaining to be compared against sentences. That is, defendants with public attorneys tend to be poor and those with private counsel tend to be slightly better than poor. Even where the nature of counsel is not used as a control variable, studies of sentencing practices can only compare the differences in treatment of the poor and near-poor. In one study of 10,488 criminal convictions in three southeastern states sociologists Theodore Chirocos and Gordon Waldo found little evidence of any relationship between socioeconomic status and severity of sentence as measured by length of prison terms. However, only 3.4 percent of their sample had incomes that would qualify them as affluent.[63] The simple fact is that the majority of defendants brought to court for common crimes are of relatively low socioeconomic status, with unemployed or underemployed unskilled laborers constituting the majority of common law offenders. It is therefore relatively meaningless to ask whether social class influences sentencing for common crimes when essentially only one class appears in court charged with these crimes, just as it is pointless to ask whether poor defendants receive harsher sentences for "white-collar" crimes than more affluent offenders. While the poor do fare somewhat worse as the result of inadequate legal counsel, the bulk of social class discrimination in the justice process occurs long before sentencing.

Race and Sentencing

Blacks constitute a larger proportion of those in prison than would be expected given either their proportion of the general population or the proportion of those arrested. Blacks constitute about 25 percent of all people arrested annually but nearly 40 percent of those in prisons and jails.[64] Whether this overrepresentation of black Americans behind bars is evidence of racial discrimination in sentencing has been the focus of much debate and research over the years.

The overall implications of this research, however, has been equivocal. Older studies and studies in southern states have generally shown that for capital offenses blacks are more likely to receive the death penalty and are also more likely to receive longer sentences than their white counterparts. These studies have also tended to show that the severity of sentence is strongly influenced by the nature of the victim–offender relationship. One study examining homicides in the state of North Carolina between 1930 and 1940 showed that the harshest sentences were given to blacks convicted of killing whites and the most lenient to whites who killed blacks. Whites who killed whites and blacks who killed blacks ranked second and third respectively regarding severity of sentence.[65] Another study by sociologist Harold Garfinkle in 1949 reconfirmed these findings.[66] A 1958 study of sentencing in Texas showed that blacks tended to receive longer prison sentences than whites for all crimes except burglary.[67] More recently, a 1973 study of eleven southern states found that in cases of rape the death penalty was imposed more frequently on blacks than whites, most often on blacks who raped whites, and almost never in cases where whites raped blacks.[68]

The most frequent criticism leveled at those studies that found clear indication of racial differences in sentencing has been that these studies failed to control for significant legal and social history variables such as nature of the original charge, pretrial status, and prior record.[69] Where these variables have been controlled, the findings of racial discrimination in sentencing have generally been either weaker than earlier studies or nonexistent. For example, a study of 662 homicides occurring in Cleveland between 1947 and 1954 found that blacks were convicted of first-degree murder more often than whites charged with this crime and thus more often received the harshest sentences for those convicted of homicide. However, this difference in sentencing outcomes was explained by the researchers as the result of a higher proportion of blacks being charged with "felony murder" (wrongful death resulting from the commission of another crime), which is easier to prove at trial than other forms of first-degree murder.[70] A review of twenty sentencing studies by John Hagan concluded that none of those focusing on noncapital crimes showed any evidence of sentencing disparity by race and that all those that showed sentencing disparity in capital cases were conducted in the south.[71] A study of Federal sentencing practices reported that race was significantly related to sentencing only for the crime of counterfeiting.[72]

Other studies have found mixed evidence of racial variations in sentencing. A study of 2,583 offenders sentenced in Florida between 1969 and 1970 found that black offenders with no prior record received longer sentences than whites without prior records for every crime except auto theft, but for those offenders with prior records, whites received longer sentences in seven of the ten categories studied, with longer sentences being given to blacks only for the crimes of rape, aggravated assault, and unarmed robbery. When race was combined with socioeconomic status, it was found that low-status blacks received significantly longer sentences for the four violent crimes of murder, rape, robbery, and assault than low-status whites, although no racial difference in sentencing appeared for the nonpoor.[73] An extensive study of sentencing in California found patterns that were similarly mixed. While blacks received probation less frequently than whites, and when given prison sentences were sentenced for longer periods than whites, the bulk of this difference disappeared when prior record was controlled. Only in the case of blacks convicted in rural jurisdictions did the pattern of more frequent prison sentences remain after controlling for prior record.[74]

Blacks tend to receive more and longer prison sentences than white offenders, whether male or female. According to recent research, however, much of this differential can be explained as the effect of intervening legal variables such as the specific offense charged, prior record, type of counsel, and bail status. Does this mean that sentencing courts discriminates against blacks or that sentencing in America is race-blind? The answer to this question depends upon whether we accept the standard definition of "discrimination" and whether we limit our examination to the narrow issues of selecting sentence or place the sentencing process in its larger legal and social context.

According to liberal ideology "discrimination" occurs when equals are treated unequally. Given this view racially discriminatory sentencing occurs only when two offenders, one white and one black, with similar prior records and convicted of similar offenses are given different sentences. However, when we limit our assessment of justice and equality to such narrow comparisons, we are forced to overlook the more complex social processes culminating in criminal sentences.

As previously discussed, the poor and the near-poor face a greater likelihood of arrest and conviction than the more affluent. The proportion of blacks among the poor and near-poor grossly exceeds their proportion of the population. Thus blacks face a proportionally greater likelihood of arrest and conviction than whites and are consequently more likely than whites to have a prior record. As a result black offenders will more often appear to sentencing judges as "dangerous to society" or "career criminals" than whites and consequently will be given longer sentences. In the final analysis blacks receive harsher sentences than whites not because individual judges engage in overt discrimination (although probably some do) but because the American social system places the poor (who are disproportionately nonwhite) at greater risk with respect to the legal variables that influence sentencing.

CONCLUSION

The judicial system in America is charged with the dual task of adjudicating the civil, regulatory, and criminal litigation brought before it and through its appellate function insuring that the liberal ideals of equality under the law are sufficently met to preserve the legitimacy of the state. It is probably safe to say that many who work in the court system, particularly judges, genuinely believe in the ideals of equal justice. However, for many equal justice means simply insuring that similar charges against similar defendants receive similar consideration. The more complex social processes that place poor and non-white Americans at greater risk under the law often go unrecognized. Those judges who do understand that achieving equality under the law in a society based upon a variety of fundamental inequalities is unattainable can do little to alter that reality. Moreover, the court system, particularly criminal courts, find themselves administering assembly-line justice in response to caseloads that dramatically exceed their budgets and staff. Pressures for expedient disposal of cases increases the likelihood of transgressions of the narrow liberal ideal of equal justice and renders consideration of the broader issues involved beyond reach.

In the next chapter we will examine the kinds of punishments and correctional programs imposed upon those convicted in criminal courts.

NOTES

1. *Mallory* v. *United States*, 354 U.S. 455 (1957).
2. Daniel J. Freed and Patricia M. Wald, *Bail in the United States*, working paper for the National Conference on Bail and Criminal Justice (Washington, D.C.: Government Printing Office, 1964), 1.
3. *Stack* v. *Boyle*, 342 U.S. 1–4 (1951).
4. J. Locke et al., *Compilation and Use of Criminal Court Data in Relations to Pre-Trial Release of Defendants: Pilot Study*. National Bureau of Technical Assistance: Note 535 (1970); "Preventative Detention: An Empirical Analysis," *Harvard Civil Rights and Civil Liberties Review*, 6 (1971): 300.
5. *New York Times*, 11 February 1981, 1; *New York Times*, 25 February 1981, 28.
6. Paul B. Wice, *Freedom for Sale* (Lexington, Mass.: Lexington Books, 1974), 5.
7. *Leary* v. *U.S.*, 224 U.S. 567, 595 (1912).
8. Caleb Foote et al., "Compelling Appearance in Court: Administration of Bail in Philadelphia," *University of Pennsylvania Law Review*, 102 (June 1954): 1031–1079.
9. J. W. Roberts and J. I. Palermo, "A Study of the Administration of Bail in New York," *University of Pennsylvania Law Review*, 106 (March 1958): 727.
10. U.S. Department of Justice, National Institute of Law Enforcement and Criminal Justice, *The Bronx Sentencing Project of the Vera Institute of Justice* (Washington, D.C.: Government Printing Office, 1972), vi.

11. Foote, "Compelling Appearance in Court," 1065.
12. Anne Rankin, "The Effects of Pre-Trial Detention," *New York University Law Review*, 39 (1964); C. Engle, "Criminal Justice in the City: A Study of Sentence Severity and Variation in the Philadelphia Court System" (unpublished Ph.D. diss., Temple University, 1971).
13. U.S. Department of Justice, *The Bronx Sentencing Project*, 8.
14. Ibid., 20–21.
15. Charles Ares et al., "The Manhattan Bail Projects: An Interim Report on the Use of Pre-Trial Parole," *New York University Law Review*, 37 (1963): 67–95.
16. Wice, *Freedom for Sale*, 143.
17. Ibid., 141.
18. National Advisory Commission on Criminal Justice Standards and Goals, *The Courts* (Washington, D.C.: Government Printing Office, 1977), 83.
19. Ibid., 17.
20. Ibid., 33.
21. See Nicholas Kittrie, *The Right to be Different: Deviance and Enforced Therapy* (Baltimore: Johns Hopkins University Press, 1971) for a discussion of the expansion of legal controls over deviant forms of behavior.
22. James O'Connor, *The Fiscal Crisis of the State* (New York: St. Martin's Press, 1973).
23. Andrew Scull, *Decarceration* (Englewood Cliffs, N.J.: Prentice-Hall, 1977), 139.
24. Abraham S. Blumberg, *Criminal Justice* (Chicago: Quadrangle Books, 1967), 28–29.
25. U.S. Department of Justice, *National Survey of Court Organization* (Washington, D.C.: Government Printing Office, 1973), 4.
26. David Neubaur, *Criminal Justice in Middle America* (Morristown, N.J.: General Learning Press, 1974).
27. Blumberg, *Criminal Justice*, 59; Neubaur, *Criminal Justice in Middle America*, 45–51.
28. See Newman F. Baker, "The Prosecutor-Initiation of Prosecution," *Journal of Criminal Law, Criminology, and Police Science*, 23, no. 5: 770–796; Kenneth Culp Davis, "Discretion Exercised by Montana County Attorneys in Criminal Prosecutions," *Montana Law Review*, 28, no. 1: 41–93; John Kaplan, "The Prosecutorial Discretion—A Comment," *Northwestern Law Review*, 60, no. 2 (May–June 1965): 174–193; and Richard Mills, "The Prosecutor: Charging and Bargaining," *University of Illinois Law Forum*, 1966, no. 3 (Fall 1966): 511–522.
29. Kaplan, "The Prosecutorial Discretion," 186.
30. Aubry M. Cates, "Can We Ignore Laws?" *Alabama Law Review*, 14, no. 1 (Fall 1961): 1–10.
31. Frank Miller, *Prosecution—The Decision to Charge a Suspect with a Crime* (Boston: Little, Brown, 1969).
32. Charles D. Breitel, "Controls in Criminal Law Enforcement," *The University of Chicago Law Review*, 27, no. 3 (Spring 1960): 427–435.
33. Ibid., 430–431.
34. Peat, Marwick, Mitchell, and Co., "Prosecutorial Discretion in the Duplicative Statutes Setting," *University of Colorado Law Review*, vol. 42, no. 2: 455–466.
35. Tully L. McRea and Donald M. Gottfredson, *A Guide to Improved Handling of Misdemeanant Offenders* (Washington, D.C.: Government Printing Office, 1974), 9.
36. United States Department of Justice, *Crime in the United States, 1978.* (Washington, D.C.: U.S. Government Printing Office, 1979). In 1978, for example, Part I Index Offenses constituted only 22.2 percent of all arrests. The majority of other arrests (though not all) were for misdemeanor violations. The crimes of vandalism, minor assault, driving under the influence, intoxication, disorderly conduct, and miscellaneous misdemeanors constituted 56 percent of all arrests that year.

37. McCrea and Gottfredson, *Improved Handling of Misdemeanant Offenders*, p. 11.
38. Standards and Goals, *The Courts*, 1977, 42.
39. Dominick R. Vetri, "Guilty Plea Bargaining: Compromise by Prosecutors to Secure Guilty Pleas," *University of Pennsylvania Law Review*, 112 (1064): 896–908.
40. Donald J. Newman, "Pleading Guilty for Considerations: A Study of Bargain Justice," *Journal of Criminal Law, Criminology and Police Science*, no. 46 (1956): 787.
41. A. Keith Bottomley, *Decisions in the Penal Processes* (London: Martin Robinson, 1973): 120–122. See also P. W. Greenwood and S. Wildhorn, *Prosecution of Adult Felony Defendants* in Los Angeles County (Santa Monica, Calif.: RAM, 1973).
42. Arnold Enker, "Perspectives on Plea Bargaining," President's Commission on Law Enforcement and the Administration of Justice, *Task Force Report: The Courts* (Washington, D.C.: Government Printing Office, 1967).
43. Blumberg, *Criminal Justice*, 59.
44. George F. Cole, "The Decision to Prosecute," *Law and Society Review* 3 (1970): 331.
45. Blumberg, *Criminal Justice*, 92–93.
46. Johnathan D. Casper, *Criminal Courts: The Defendant's Perspective* (Washington, D.C.: Government Printing Office, 1967).
47. Standards and Goals, 1977, *The Courts*, 250, 334.
48. Abraham Blumberg, "Lawyers with Convictions," in Blumberg, ed., *Law and Order: The Scales of American Justice* (New York: Aldine-Transaction, 1970), 62–65.
49. R. Gitelman, "The Relative Performance of Appointed and Retained Counsel in Arkansas Felony Cases," *Arkansas Law Review*, 24 (1971): 442.
50. Dallin Oaks and Warren Lehman, "Lawyers for the Poor," in Blumberg, *Law and Order*, 95; see also, Gregg Barak, "In Defense of the Rich: The Emergence of the Public Defender," *Crime and Social Justice*, 3 (1975): pp. 2–14.
51. Standards and Goals, *The Courts*, 1977, 44.
52. *Boykin* v. *Alabama*, 395 U.S., 238 (1969).
53. *Brady* v. *U.S.*, 387 U.S. 742 (1970).
54. *Santobello* v. *New York*, 404 U.S. 259 (1971).
55. Standards and Goals, *The Courts*, 1977, 46.
56. See L. Paul Sutton, *Federal Criminal Sentencing* (Washington, D.C.: Government Printing Office, 1978a), 2–13 for a review of studies in sentencing variation.
57. Ibid., 13.
58. Federal Bureau of Prisons, *Statistical Report for Fiscal Year, 1973* (Washington, D.C.: Government Printing Office, 1974).
59. Stuart Nagel, "The Tipped Scales of American Justice," in Blumberg, *Law and Order*, 39.
60. U.S. Department of Justice, *The Bronx Sentencing Project*, vii.
61. Stanton R. Wettick, "A Study of the Assignment of Judges to Criminal Cases in Allegheny Country: The Poor Fare Worse," *Duquesne Law Review*, 51 (1970).
62. L. Paul Sutton, *Variations in Federal Criminal Sentences: A Statistical Assessment at the National Level* (Washington, D.C.: Government Printing Office, 1978b); J. Hogarth, *Sentencing as a Human Process* (Toronto: University of Toronto Press, 1971); John Hagan, "Extra-Legal Attributes and Criminal Sentencing: An Assessment of a Sociological Viewpoint," *Law and Society*, 8 (1974): 357–383.
63. Theodore Chiricos and Gordon P. Waldo, "Socioeconomic Status and Criminal Sentencing: An Empirical Assessment of a Conflict Proposition," *American Sociological Review*, 40 (1975): 753–772.
64. U.S. Department of Justice, *Survey of Inmates of State Correctional Facilities, 1974* (Washington: D.C.: Government Printing Office, 1976), 24–25.
65. Guy Johnson, "The Negro and Crime," *The Annals*, 277 (1941): 94–104.

66. Harold Garfinkle, "Research on Inter- and Intra-racial Homicides," *Social Forces*, 27 (1949).
67. Henry Bullock, "Significance of the Racial Factor in the Length of Prison Sentences," *Journal of Criminal Law, Criminology, and Police Science*, 52 (1941): 93–104.
68. Marvin Wolfgang and Mark Riedl, "Race, Judicial Discretion, and the Death Penalty," *The Annals*, 119 (1973).
69. L. Paul Sutton, *Federal Criminal Sentencing*, 13.
70. Robert G. Bensing and Oliver Schroeder, *Homicide in an Urban Community* (Springfield, Ill.: Charles C. Thomas, 1960).
71. Hagan, "Extra-Legal Attributes and Criminal Sentencing."
72. Sutton, *Variations in Federal Criminal Sentences*, 29.
73. Theodore Chiricos et al., "Race, Crime and Sentence Length," Paper presented at the American Sociological Association Annual Meeting, New Orleans, 1972.
74. Carl E. Pope, *Sentencing of California Offenders* (Washington, D.C.: Government Printing Office, 1975), 11–21.

CHAPTER 9

Punishment and Penal Discipline in America

PUNISHMENT AND SOCIAL STRUCTURE

It is commonly said that the purpose of punishment is to "protect society." What is less frequently articulated is that the purpose of punishment is to protect a particular form of society, that is, the form of society that has established the penal system in question. To understand the usage of penal sanctions in contemporary America, we must examine the relationship between these sanctions and the protection of the capitalist social order. Since criminal punishments in capitalist societies are applied most frequently to the laboring classes of that society, the types of punishments utilized will be shaped by (1) the form of labor, (2) the relative value of labor, and (3) the conditions of the laboring classes.

Punishment and the Form of Labor

The nature of the basic productive activities of a given society will determine the forms of punishment appropriate to that society. During the feudal era the basic productive activity was agricultural in nature, and the relations of production were such that serfs—the basic laboring class—were tied to a form of involuntary servitude by the feudal bond. This affected the possibility of punishment in several ways.

First, the form of production required a decentralized form of punishment. Population distribution in agrarian societies is highly decentralized. Where there is no concentration of populations there is no concentration of offenders. Thus any form of punishment such as imprisonment that holds offenders in a centralized penal institution is inappropriate to the nature of agricultural societies.

Second, by virtue of the feudal bond the laboring class was already in a condition of involuntary servitude. Therefore those forms of punishment involving forced labor such as slavery, indenture, or imprisonment would be redundant. That is, they would place the offender in a situation generally not much worse than that he or she was in prior to the crime both with respect to the conditions of life and the exploitation of his or her labor power.

Because imprisonment or involuntary servitude were inappropriate penal sanctions during the feudal era, feudal societies were limited to corporal punishments, banishments, fines, and death as their basic response to crime. Two of these, banishment and execution, meant a loss of the potential labor of the offender. Their attractiveness therefore depended on the relative value of labor during any particular historical period. By contrast, fines and corporal punishment were more generally attractive and hence were used extensively as the primary forms of punishment in feudal society.

As the form and mode of production began to change during the late feudal era, setting the stage for the emergence of early mercantile capitalism, so did the appropriate forms of punishment. With the gradual transition from an almost wholly agrarian form of production to one that mixed agriculture with the guild-based production of mercantile goods came a shift in population distribution. As guild work in villages and towns attracted larger numbers of serfs seeking freedom from feudal bondage, the concentration of both people and criminal offenders increased. Additionally, since the emerging form of commodity production could make use of concentrated labor, centralized forms of punishment became more consistent with societal organization. It was during this period extending from about 1300 to 1700 in England that we find the emergence and growth of the workhouse, the forerunner of the modern prison, as a common form of punishment.[1]

As the form of production changed from guild labor to the rudimentary industrial factory another change occurred that made imprisonment more attractive as a form of punishment. Prior to industrialization the bulk of work was relatively unsupervised. Serfs, while bonded to the manor, generally performed their daily duties free from the ever-present vigilance of some overseer. While guild labor involved a degree of supervision, guilds were not strictly divided into workers and overseers. By contrast the emerging factory involved just such a division of labor.

The emergence of factory work as the dominant form of labor required the creation of new methods of directing the activities of workers. A central component of factory work in capitalist society is that the nature of the work tasks, when they will be performed, and the speed at which they are expected to be performed are determined by those who own or manage the factory, not by the labor force. The labor force must be disciplined into accepting these externally determined conditions of work and must be supervised during the work process to insure that work is done in the appropriate fashion. Thus as industrial capitalism grew the concept of *discipline* emerged as a central tool in the control of labor. Prisons are disciplined environments and hence are highly consistent with the factory form of production in capitalist societies. It is this consistency, as criminologist Dario Melossi argues, that is the primary reason for the persistence of prisons as the basic form of punishment in capitalist societies.[2] Melossi's conclusion suggests that imprisonment would also constitute a favored form of punishment in noncapitalist industrial societies to the extent that they also adhere to the notion of labor force discipline within the industrial sector.

Punishment and the Value of Labor

Taken together, the criminal offenders in any society represent a proportion of that society's labor force. The kinds of punishments that will be imposed upon this segment of the labor force will be influenced by its value. Where labor is relatively scarce, thereby increasing the relative value of any unit of labor, punishments such as execution or banishment that constitute a total loss of the offender's labor have generally been avoided or at least used only sparingly. However, in situations where the supply of labor has been excessive punishments that meant lost labor have been used more frequently.

During the tribal and early feudal periods in England, for example, both the death penalty and banishment were reserved for the most serious offenses. This was largely a reflection of the value of labor in a wholly agrarian society. With the emergence of more efficient farming techniques in the fifteenth century the value of agrarian labor declined.[3] At the same time the emerging system of commodity production had not reached a stage of development that would allow it to absorb the emerging labor surplus. Additional dislocations of labor resulting from the enclosure movements further depressed the value of labor. Under these conditions, which reached crisis proportions by the middle of the eighteenth century, capital punishment and transportation emerged as frequent penal sanctions for relatively minor as well as serious offenses.

With the total replacement of feudalism by the wage labor system, the value of labor changed again. While substantial unemployment remained in nineteenth-century England, labor power that could be extracted at less than the going wage constituted a potential source of profit or at least a nearly cost-free form of punishment. Under these conditions, placing offenders in prisons where they could be put to profit-making labor emerged as a viable penal alternative. In England entire prison populations were farmed out as laborers to the highest bidder or to private managers who "requested the smallest subsidy for overhead and feeding of the prisoners."[4] For the first half of the nineteenth century prisons in the United States likewise were operated as profit-making or at least as nearly self-supporting endeavors. In some states prisons were leased to private interests while in others the prison labor force was contracted to the highest bidder. In a few states prison labor was managed directly by the states.[5] A study of twelve American prisons showed that in 1851 while only four of the states showed a profit from prison labor, a total of eight managed to recoup at least 75 percent of the cost of imprisoning convicts. For the twelve states combined, the total earnings generated by prisoners was over 90 percent of the total expenses incurred in operating the prisons.[6] As the 1800s progressed the use of prison labor for profit-making activities declined. The primary reason for this decline was that as prison labor grew it began to compete with private enterprise, initiating a strong antiprison labor movement. Numerous states passed laws regulating the sale or transportation of prison-made goods. In 1888 the state of New York passed the Yates Law prohibiting the sale of prison-made goods on the open market in New York. This legislation, which became the model for many other states, brought profitable prison labor to an end.[7]

The value of labor is not the sole determinant of what form of punishment is favored. Penal sanctions must also be consistent with the ideology and current social climate of any society. For example, modern liberal states cannot easily return to the widespread use of capital punishment for anything other than serious crimes. To do so would violate the ideology of social equality and humanitarianism so crucial to the legitimacy of these states. At the same time the usages of punishment in contemporary society is not wholly unaffected by the relative value of labor.

It has long been suggested that the frequency of imprisonment is significantly influenced by the rate of unemployment.[8] That is, when unemployment is low, labor is in short supply and imprisonment will be utilized less frequently. By comparison, when unemployment is high and labor overabundant, imprisonment will be utilized more liberally. Several tests of this hypothesis found a significant relationship between rates of imprisonment and rates of unemployment. This relationship remained *after controlling for changes in rates of crime* associated with changes in rates of employment.[9] These findings suggest several possible conclusions. It is possible, for instance, that the decreased value of labor during periods of high unemployment leads to an increased willingness to waste additional portions of the labor force through imprisonment. There is also some evidence that increases in unemployment lead to public fear that crime *will rise*, resulting in pressure on the courts to increase the rate of punishment as a way for forestalling the anticipated danger. Another possibility is that during periods of high unemployment offenders appear to be poorer risks for probation or other community-based forms of treatment since there is little expectation that they can obtain gainful employment. While at this point the exact dynamics of the relationship remain unclear, current research does offer a degree of empirical confirmation of the relationship between punishment and the value of labor.

Punishment and the Conditions of the Laboring Class

In 1933 social theorist Georg Rusche introduced the concept of "less eligibility" to describe the relationship between social structure and forms of punishment. The concept of "less eligibility" is based upon the fact that, in Rusche's words, criminal punishment is reserved largely for those "whose class background, poverty, neglected education, or demoralization drove them to crime." Rusche carefully points out that he is not arguing that poverty is the sole or the direct cause of crime, noting that "not everybody necessarily becomes a criminal even under the heaviest social pressure" and that the "range of possibilities extends from law-abiding people in a wretched environment to confirmed criminals in a bourgeois milieu." He adds, however, that we generally expect a very high degree of resistance to the temptations of crime by those with the least reason to resist:

> At any rate, an extremely high capacity for resistance is expected of the lower

strata, of whom large masses are regularly deprived of their livelihood . . . and the spiritually and physically weakest [who] are thrown into the path of crime.

Regardless of the specific causes of crime in any individual case, the fact that the system of criminal punishments is designed to maintain a high level of resistance to crime among those who least benefit from the social structure influences the types of punishments that will be used. To serve as a deterrent to crime among the least affluent, penal sanctions "must appear even worse than the strata's present living conditions."[10] This is the principle of less eligibility.

Rusche's concept of less eligibility is particularly useful in understanding changes in prison conditions. According to the principle of less eligibility we could expect the quality of prison life to improve as general improvements in the quality of life result in some advance in the living conditions of the poorest segments of society. The maintenance of gratuitously harsh punishments can threaten a state's legitimacy. At the same time, too great a reduction in harshness can weaken the deterrent effectiveness of the punishment. Thus prison conditions will tend to float at a level just below the quality of life among the poorest members of society.

Rusche points out that the principle of less eligibility is not the only factor that can influence punishments in modern liberal states. Harsh prison conditions will periodically spark reform movements seeking to humanize the experience of punishment. To the extent that the preservation of legitimacy requires it, states will respond to such reform movements. However, as Rusche points out, where "penal reforms are demanded by public opinion and carried out" they will eventually be "undermined by a more subtle deterioration of prison conditions."[11]

The principle of less eligibility is reflected in contemporary arguments that we must stop making prisons "too comfortable"—"country clubs" for the convicted. Behind this statement is the awareness that prisons must threaten to impose a quality of life worse than that already experienced by those from the poorest segments of society who will be their basic clientele.

PENAL SANCTIONS IN CONTEMPORARY AMERICA

Imprisonment, fines, and various forms of involuntary supervision and therapy constitute the primary forms of penal sanctions used in America today. While by far the most controversial form of punishment, execution is by comparison extremely rare. Its infrequency notwithstanding, as the ultimate sanction the state can impose, capital punishment deserves some consideration before the more common forms of contemporary penal sanctions are examined.

Capital Punishment

Execution of convicted offenders has been a penal option since colonial times. Unlike England, which prescribed capital punishment for a broad variety of both major and minor crimes during the seventeenth and eighteenth centuries, capital punishment in the American colonies was generally prescribed only for the most serious offenses. This is partly because the American colonies were settled largely by liberal bourgeois seeking a degree of freedom from what they felt to be the tyranny of the English monarchy. One element of this liberal ideology was a belief in a "rational" system of punishments consistent with utilitarian principles. These utilitarian principles emphasized that the severity of punishment should be proportional to the severity of the crime as a way of providing the rational offender with an incentive to commit less serious rather than more serious offenses.

Another reason for the relatively parsimonious usage of capital punishment in the colonies was the scarcity of labor. The New World provided boundless land and other resources but little in the way of indigenous labor that could be used to exploit these resources. Attempts to entice native American Indians into wage labor or to use them as slaves met with little success. Thus punishments such as indenture—which provided a source of free labor power—or corporal punishment—which did not lead to a loss of the offender's labor—were favored over execution for minor offenses during the early colonial period. While much attention has been given to the fact that early Massachusetts colony laws permitted the execution of disobedient children, there is little evidence that this punishment was ever actually invoked.[12]

With the coming of independence the new American states retained capital punishment as a penal option but generally limited it to serious offenses such as murder, rape, arson, and in some cases trespass (a forerunner of modern-day burglary). Even where slaves were concerned the death penalty was used sparingly since slaves represented valuable capital investments. Where state law did prescribe the death penalty for slaves, provisions to reimburse the slave's owner for his loss were usually included.[13]

While the death penalty has been largely used against common criminal offenders, an important footnote to its usage in America is the fact that from the end of the Civil War until the beginning of World War I a minimum of twenty to thirty prominent labor organizers were executed under criminal law. In many of these cases evidence indicates that the criminal charges that led to the execution of labor organizers were false.[14]

Between 1930, when the Federal government first began compiling crime statistics, and 1980 there were 3,862 executions in the United States. All but three of these occurred prior to 1967, when an "informal moratorium on executions began as states reexamined the entire issue of capital punishment."[15] Of those executed between 1930 and 1980, 54 percent were black and 99 percent were males.[16]

During the 1970s and early 1980s capital punishment has gone through several stages of legal metamorphosis. In 1972 in the case of *Furman* v. *Georgia* the Supreme Court ruled that the death penalty was applied so arbitrarily as to constitute "cruel and unusual punishment" and was therefore unconstitutional.[17] The effect was to lift the death sentence from approximately 600 offenders who had accumulated on death row since the start of the informal capital punishment moratorium in 1967.

The Supreme Court did not rule in *Furman* v. *Georgia* that the death penalty per se constituted cruel and unusual punishment, only that its arbitrary usage was unconstitutional. Subsequent to the *Furman* decision many states began revising their death penalty statutes to minimize or eliminate arbitrary applications of capital punishment. The bulk of these revisions fell into two categories: (1) statutes making death a mandatory punishment for specific crimes and (2) statutes allowing for a degree of *directed discretion* in the application of the death penalty. In 1976 Supreme Court rulings in two cases, *Roberts* v. *Louisiana* and *Woodson* v. *North Carolina,* overturned the practice of mandatory death sentences. The court expressed concern over the constitutionality of capital punishment statutes that deprived offenders of the opportunity to have mitigating circumstances taken into consideration prior to sentencing.[18] In 1978 the Supreme court further held in the case of *Lockett* v. *Ohio* that sentencing authorities must be free to consider *all* mitigating circumstances in deciding whether or not to impose the death sentence.[19]

Incarceration

Incarceration is the placement of a criminal offender under some form of secure custody. As a reflection of the multiple jurisdictions that characterize the American legal system incarceration in the United States takes three forms. Offenders may be incarcerated in Federal prisons as the result of convictions for Federal offenses or in either state prisons or local (usually either city or county) jails. In most states incarceration in state prisons is reserved for those convicted of felony offenses while jailing is used for violations of local laws or misdemeanor convictions under state laws. A few states, however, also utilize incarceration in state prisons for certain misdemeanor offenses.

The functions of incarceration are generally considered to be threefold. First, the threat of incarceration is thought to serve as a deterrent to potential criminal offenders. Second, it is presumed that the experience of being incarcerated will decrease the likelihood of the offender's committing future crimes once released either by providing opportunities for rehabilitation or simply by convincing the offender that crime does not pay. Third, it is increasingly argued that incarceration can contribute to a reduction in crime by simply removing a portion of the "criminal element" from society for a time.

Of these three purposes—deterrence, rehabilitation and incapacitation—it is rehabilitation that has served as the primary justification for imprisonment—at least until very recently. The concept of rehabilitation through imprisonment has taken two forms. The initial model of prison rehabilitation presented work as the primary agent of rehabilitation. Utilizing this concept of rehabilitation early American prisons served largely as institutions for the exploitation of convict labor. By the late 1800s the work-as-rehabilitation model began to lose support for a variety of reasons. The use of cheap convict labor to produce goods that could be sold on the free market was opposed both by free-market capitalists and free workers. Additionally, the potential for corruption, collusion, and misuse of public funds to aid private entrepreneurs who sold materials to prison industries or contracted prison labor reached scandalous proportions. One investigation by the Prison Commission of New York State in 1876 revealed a widespread pattern of swindles, fraud, overcharges, false entries, and questionable accounting procedures. Thus prison labor had become a financial burden rather than a financial boon to the states. Others questioned the rehabilitative potential of prison labor charging that the simple experience of working long hours for low wages offered little promise of reforming convicted criminals.[20]

As the promise of rehabilitation through prison labor lost legitimacy a new model of imprisonment emerged. This new model emphasized a more individualized and psychological approach to rehabilitation. By the 1920s this new approach, particularly through its association with the Progressive Movement, had coalesced into what has come to be known as the New Penology. The New Penology emphasized the careful classification of prisoners into offense and personality types, resulting in "individualized" treatment based on the presumed therapeutic needs of the various classes of prisoners. This approach was stimulated and shaped by the growth of the academic sciences of human behavior, particularly psychology. Implicit in this new science of "treating" offenders was the idea that crime resulted from some form of personal psychological or emotional defect that presumably could be cured in much the same way as a disease is cured. Many of those associated with the New Penology recognized the criminogenic effects of poverty, poor living conditions, unemployment, and lack of education.[21] However, the treatment strategies they promoted sought not to change these conditions but rather took the opposite approach of trying to change the individual offender. The responsibility for criminality was placed upon the offender for his or her failure, because of personal defects, to resist what the New Penologists recognized to be the very real pressures toward criminal alternatives associated with an economically and socially impoverished life and not upon the social arrangements that subjected individuals to those pressures.

With the emergence of the New Penology prisons appeared to shift toward a "therapeutic" model of confinement. A key component of this therapeutic model was the introduction of indeterminate sentences. Under an indeterminate sentence the offender's release would be determined not by a fixed sentence length but by parole boards presumably acting upon information provided by prison personnel concerning the offender's progress toward "rehabilitation." Advocates of indeterminate sentencing argued that this process would involve the offender in his or her own process of rehabilitation by offering the incentive of early release for the rehabilitated. It would also provide a mechanism for insuring that the more incorrigible offenders remained incarcerated for the maximum length of time.

By the early 1970s the therapeutic model of imprisonment and the indeterminate sentence were under increasing attack. Advocates of prisoner rights challenged the indeterminate sentence on three points. First, it was argued that there was little proof of any therapeutic benefit resulting from indeterminate sentences. Rates of recidivism, that is, return to crime after release from prison, remained high. It was estimated that at least 50 percent of released offenders eventually were returned to prison for the commission of another serious offense.[22] Furthermore, after nearly fifty years of research the correctional establishment was still unable to effectively predict who would and who would not become a recidivist.[23] The implication of this, it has been argued, is that those engaging in "rehabilitation" and the determination of prisoner release have no real idea of what constitutes rehabilitation, thus calling into question the entire logic of therapeutic imprisonment.

Second, it was argued that indeterminate sentences led to more rather than less punishment, and since an offender's time in prison was determined not by the gravity of the offense by his or her progress toward "rehabilitation," it made possible wholesale departure from any form of equal punishment under the law. One study found that the adoption of the "rehabilitative ideal" in California prisons led to a significant increase in sentence length and the number of persons incarcerated at any one time.

> From 1959 to 1969 the median time served has risen from twenty-four to thirty-six months, the longest in the country. Second, the number of persons incarcerated per 100,000 has continued to rise, from 65 in 1944 to 145 in 1965. . . . During a period when the treatment ideal was maximized, when vocational training programs, group and individual therapy programs, milieu therapy, and many other rehabilitative experiments were introduced, *more than twice as many persons served twice as much time.*[24] (emphasis added)

The increase in sentence length and perhaps more importantly, the uncertainty of when release would come, appears to have done little to improve prisoner rehabilitation. While the rehabilitative theory underlying indeterminate sentences may be understood by those who devised and implemented such programs, it is not necessarily understood or experienced by inmates as anything other than official arbitrariness. As one female inmate complained:

> The total waste of time spent while here and the constant mental torture of never really knowing how long you'll be here. The indeterminate sentence structure gives you no peace of mind and absolutely nothing to work for.

> The total futility of this time is the most maddening thing to bear. You realize nothing but frustration from the beginning to the end of your confinement. This situation is compounded by the "never knowing" system of the indeterminate sentencing law.[25]

Third, opponents of the indeterminate sentence such as the American Friends Service Committee, argued that enforced therapy, even if effective, was a fundamental violation of an individual's rights and a powerful potential tool for racial, social class, and political repression. Because the criteria for release are "individualized" and essentially vague under a therapeutic model, there exists the very real potential that discriminatory and repressive criteria such as the race, political ideology, and life-style of offenders can play an important role in determining how long an offender will remain in prison.[26]

Challenges to therapeutic imprisonment and its related dependency upon indeterminate sentencing were first initiated by liberal and progressive groups seeking to humanize imprisonment or to focus public attention on the essentially discriminatory nature of the *entire structure of penal sanctioning.* Those seeking a humanization of imprisonment felt that replacement of indeterminate sentences with fixed sentences would actually result in offenders spending less time in prison once lengthy sentences could no longer be justified as "therapeutic." This perspective was fortified by a growing body of research findings that tended to contradict the claims made for the rehabilitative effect of various prison programs. An extensive review of the rehabilitation research literature by Douglas Lipton, Robert Martinson, and Judith Wilkes published in 1975 concluded that there was little valid evidence to support the rehabilitation claims made for various prison programs designed to reform criminal offenders.[27]

Evidence of the lack of therapeutic effectiveness was viewed by more radical, progressive opponents of therapeutic sentencing as proof that the promise of "rehabilitation" represented an attempt to legitimize an essentially repressive system of social control aimed at restraining working class and nonwhite lawbreakers while permitting extensive social harm by the owners and representatives of capital. As criminologists David Greenberg and Drew Humphries wrote,

> Seen in this light, rehabilitation was not merely a laudable goal that scientific research had failed thus far to achieve, but something more insidious—an ideology that explained crime in highly individualistic terms and legitimated the expansion of administrative powers used in practice to discriminate against disadvantaged groups and to achieve covert organizational goals (such as alleviating court backlogs and repressing political opposition).[28]

These early opponents to the treatment model of imprisonment were later joined by far more conservative opponents to therapeutic sentencing who sought its end for substantively different reasons. Alongside liberal and radical criticisms of indeterminate sentencing emerged proponents of a "justice model" of punishment. The central component of this justice model is that punishment should represent "just deserts" for the crime committed, rather than a vehicle for individualized rehabilitation. As its base the justice model is simply a restatement of the liberal principles of equality under the law; that is, similar actions should receive similar treatment. As observed by the authors of *Doing Justice,* the report of the Committee for the Study of Incarceration, an influential advocate of the justice model of punishment, this model "emphasizes justice, not mercy" and is not concerned with "considerations such as generosity and charity, compassion and love."[29]

The "justice model" of punishment has never been taken, or intended to be taken, to its logical conclusion by its proponents. By focusing solely on the punishments given to those convicted of common crimes the justice model completely sidesteps any consideration of the form of injustice imbedded in a legal system that assigns harsher penalties to those types of harm more likely to lead to the arrest and conviction of poor and nonwhite offenders than those types more commonly committed by middle- and upper-class wrongdoers in the pursuit of private profit.

The justice model of sentencing found considerable support among conservative and neo-conservative speakers, writers, and politicians. It offered an alternative to the heavily criticized and increasingly costly treatment model of imprisonment without requiring any major, overall consideration of our system of penal sanctions. As such, the justice model became a powerful justification for conservative fixed-sentencing proposals. Contrary to the liberal expectations concerning fixed sentencing that sought to replace indeterminate sentences with relatively *short* but fixed sentences, the conservative proposals tended to set sentences at or near their existing maximums while removing the possibility of early release based on progress toward rehabilitation. The net effect of the justice model proposition is to institutionalize for *all offenders* the lengthy sentences formally given to some under the ruberic of rehabilitation. The concept of "justice" within the justice model of punishment is limited strictly to the liberal ideology of treating offenders equally. It gives little consideration to the kind of treatment to which they are being "equally" subjected.

Regardless of the degree to which it meets the expectations placed upon it to either rehabilitate offenders or to do justice, incarceration remains the cornerstone of criminal punishment in America. This is true even though at any given time the number of convicted offenders actually in prisons or jails is a relatively small percentage of the total number of offenders under some form of sentence. In 1976, for example, there were approximately 1.8 million persons under some form of criminal sentence. Of these, only 30 percent were either incarcerated at the time or on parole after having been incarcerated. The remaining 70 percent were on probation or under some other sentence not involving incarceration.[30]

Overall, probation is utilized more frequently than incarceration as a punishment for crime, particularly where first-time offenders and property offenders are concerned. However, it is the threat of incarceration upon which the sanction of probation rests. Failure to abide by the conditions of probation can result in probation revocation and placement in a prison or jail. Thus incarceration remains the fundamental penal threat in America.

WHO GETS INCARCERATED

On December 31, 1983, there were 438,830 persons incarcerated in state or Federal penitentiaries. Of these, 93 percent were in state prisons serving sentences for violation of state-level criminal laws.[31] An additional estimated 212,282 persons were incarcerated in local city or country jails, bringing the total incarcerated population to well over a half million people on the last day of 1983.[32] Not all those in local jails, however, were serving sentences.

About 42 percent of the jail population, an estimated 89,158 persons, were in jail awaiting trial.[33] Thus about 562,000 persons were actually incarcerated under penal sentence at the end of 1983.

These figures represent only the incarcerated population on a single day in a specific year. They do not give any indication of how many Americans actually spend time behind bars for committing crimes. With an average of 150,000 new admissions to prison per year for the last twenty years, and with approximately 50 percent of these being first-time admissions to prisons, we can estimate that between 1963 and 1983 roughly one and a half million Americans spent some time in state or Federal prisons. Since local jails generally only hold individuals under sentences of one year or less, and their subsequent rate of turnover is considerably higher, it is reasonable to estimate that on an annual basis over the last twenty years, an additional one million persons served some time in local jails. This means that over the last twenty years approximately two and one half million people, about 1 percent of the current American population, spent some time behind bars, not counting those who were jailed awaiting either trial or sentencing.

Who are these people? In both prisons and jails they are almost exclusively people from the poorest segments of the working class. A detailed census of prison inmates showed that less than 10 percent of those incarcerated in state prisons were employed in professional or managerial positions at the time of their arrest. By comparison 31 percent were unemployed and another 7 percent were working only part time. The majority of the employed remainder were working at unskilled labor or blue-collar craft jobs when arrested. Sixty percent had incomes of under $6,000 and 42 percent were earning less than $4,000. Sixty-one percent had not completed high school.[34]

In addition to these economic and employment characteristics, prisoners tend to be proportionally more often male (97 percent) and black (47 percent) than the general population.[35] The average age of prison and jail inmates is older than would be expected given that a large proportion of those arrested for common crimes are under eighteen. Generally, less than 40 percent of prison and jail inmates are under the age of twenty-five.[36] There are two primary reasons for this. First, probation tends to be utilized more frequently for first-time offenders and for those convicted of property crimes not involving violence. In both cases younger offenders predominate, skewing prison admissions away from young offenders and toward older ones. Second, many young offenders are ajudicated in juvenile courts and if incarcerated are placed in juvenile institutions rather than state or Federal prisons. Annually, juvenile facilities hold a total population of around 45,000 adolescents on any given day.[37] Not all of these are confined for having committed criminal offenses. Some are held for involvement in juvenile status offenses such as truancy, running away, and incorrigibility, although in recent years many states have drastically limited the utilization of confinement for juveniles not involved in adult crimes. If we add those in juvenile facilities to the prison population, the proportion of incarcerated persons younger than twenty-five years of age rises to 50 percent. In general, the demographic,

Figure 9.1 Comparison of Selected Characteristics of Prison Inmates with the General Population

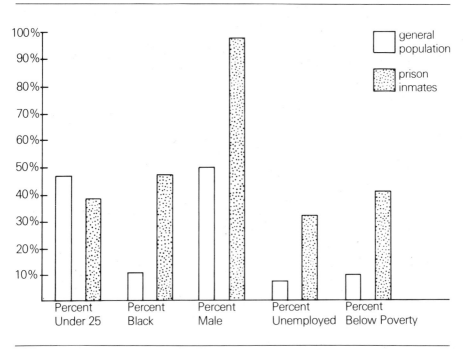

Sources: U.S. Department of Justice, *Survey of Inmates of State Correctional Facilities* (Washington, D.C.: Government Printing Office, 1976); U.S. Department of Commerce, *Statistical Abstract of the United States, 1974* (Washington, D.C.: Government Printing Office, 1974).

employment, and income characteristics of jail inmates parallels those of people in state prisons.[38]

In many instances the characteristics of the prison and jail population contrasts sharply with those of the general public, as Figure 9.1 shows. While males constitute only 49 percent of the general population they make up 97 percent of those in prison. Although the unemployment rate was approximately 5.5 percent for the general population during the early 1970s, about 31 percent of those imprisoned in 1974 had been without work at the time of arrest. Similarly, while 10 percent of the general population tends to have incomes below the official government poverty level, over 40 percent of those imprisoned come from this most destitute segment of the American public. As dramatic as they are, these figures tend to underestimate the relationship between incarceration and socioeconomic status. Many of those prisoners listed as employed at the time of arrest were working at marginal, low-income jobs rather than better-paying blue-collar or clerical positions. Furthermore, while around 40 percent of those in prison come from the *official* poverty class, many more could realistically be considered among the poor, particularly considering that the amount of money necessary to live what the Federal government defines as a decent, no-frills existence is slightly more than twice the official poverty level figure.[39] In 1974 slightly over 85 percent of all prisoners came from the lowest half of the income scale and 50 percent came from the lowest quarter.

Another important characteristic of the prison population in America is that the proportion of black inmates far exceeds the proportion of blacks in the general population. While blacks represented only 11 percent of the general population in 1978 they constituted 47 percent of the inmates in state and Federal prisons that year. The proportion of black inmates in American prisons is even more dramatic if we consider that incarceration is limited largely to males. While black males constituted 5.4 percent of the U.S. population, they were nearly 46 percent of the prison population in 1980. That is, black males were *8.5 times* more prevalent in prisons than they were in the society generally. Moreover, the *rate* of black imprisonment has been rising in recent years. Between 1973 and 1979 the rate of incarceration for whites rose from 46.3 to 65.1 per 100,000, an increase of 40 percent. During that same period black imprisonment rates increased by 48 percent, from an already high 368 per 100,000 to 544.1 per 100,000.[40]

The black proportion of prison inmates is just slightly less than double the black proportion of those arrested, indicating that once arrested blacks face a significantly greater likelihood of being incarcerated than their white counterparts. The majority of current research on the subject tends to show that when significant legal variables such as the nature of the crime, the prior record of the offender, and aggravating circumstances are controlled, the sentences given to black offenders are only slightly, if at all, more severe than those given white offenders with similar records, although there are some notable variations to this pattern by jurisdiction.[41] Thus racial discrimination in sentencing appears to be of limited utility in explaining the disproportionate presence of blacks in prison. Part of the reason for the high black prison population is that blacks tend to be arrested and convicted proportionally more often than whites for those crimes that carry heavier penalties, that is, murder, rape, and robbery.[42] Of equal if not greater importance in creating a disproportionately black prison population is the fact that under indeterminate sentences, once in prison black offenders on the average are held longer than their white counterparts convicted of similar crimes.[43] This slower rate of turnover for black prisoners inflates the proportion of blacks in prison on any given day.

However, the disproportionate representation of blacks both in prison and among the arrested appears less closely tied to racial factors per se when economic variables are taken into account. While according to U.S. census figures, black Americans may constitute only 11 percent of the population, approximately 34 percent of all those living in families below the official poverty level in 1972 were black and about 20 percent of those living in families with incomes under $7,000—at a time when the median income was over $10,000—were likewise black.[44] Furthermore, the black unemployment rate is overall about twice that of whites, and among teenagers the black unemployment rate is two and one half times greater than that of whites.[45] Thus the higher proportion of blacks among those arrested and incarcerated is largely related to their greater representation among those impoverished segments of the society most likely to be prosecuted and punished for wrong-doing, rather than their racial identity itself.

Doin' Time

At the best of times prisons are not pleasant places, and at the worst they can be places of fear, deprivation, and dehumanization. As one prisoner re-lates,

> I arrived at this Branch of the Illinois State Prison system on Thursday afternoon. . . . When I looked around at the place where I was to spend the next thirty-nine months of my life, a feeling of fear went sweeping through me.[46]

Part of this fear is a basic gut-level terror. Prisons can be and often are violent places, as one Soledad prisoner discovered upon arriving there:

> The first day I got to Soledad I was walking from the fish tank [holding pen for new inmates] to the mess hall and this guy comes running down the hall past me, yelling, with a knife sticking out of his back. Man, I was petrified. I thought, what the fuck kind of place is this?[47]

While this first-day experience is not the norm, new inmates learn early on that the fear of violence with which free citizens live is magnified many times over for the inmate.

The potential for physical injury is not the only threat the new inmate faces. Perhaps equally terrifying is the threat to one's personal identity and sense of self that comes after being separated from the normal world on which that identity was based. Sociologist and former prison inmate John Irwin writes,

> These experiences—arrest, trial, conviction—threaten the structure of his [the prisoner's] personal life in two separate ways. First, the disjointed experience of being suddenly extracted from a relatively orderly and familiar routine and cast into a completely unfamiliar and seemingly chaotic one where the ordering of events is completely out of his control has a shattering impact upon his per-sonality structure. One's identity, one's personality system, one's coherent think-ing about himself depend upon a relatively familiar, continuous and predictable stream of events. In the Kafkaesque world of booking room, the jail cell, the interrogation room and the visiting room, the boundaries of the self collapse.[48]

The effect of these events leading to imprisonment are even more true for the offender once he or she reaches prison. Prison, as convict Alfred Hassler wrote in 1954, is "fashioned on totalitarian lines" that serve to destroy the human identity of the inmate. He says:

> The prisoner has no rights, but only privileges which may be taken away at the whim of the authorities. In every way the prison authorities can contrive he is

deprived of his individuality. He stands in line to get the same drab clothes every other convict wears, which are handed out to him with a minimum of regard for size and condition. . . . his letters are read, his belongings pawed through every day or so, his movements regulated through the day by bells and whistles and observed by night by flashlight-carrying guards who periodically peek through the "judas-window" of his cell door. That some convicts still manage to evade this all-seeing observation long enough for the final contemptuous gesture of suicide must stand as a tribute to the indomitable ingenuity of man.[49]

While some modern prisons are structured in a dormitory- rather than cell-like fashion, and nighttime checks are often not the norm in these prisons, many of the other practices Hassler describes are still part of contemporary prison life. Mail is censored and prisoners' comings and goings, including when to eat, when to shower, when to lie on one's bunk, when to write letters, and when to see family and friends are determined by prison authorities, not the individual. In many medium and minimum security prisons today prisoners can "earn" the right to wear their own clothes. The fact that prisoners must *earn* the right to express their personal identity through clothing—something that most free citizens take for granted, is indicative of the prison's power to dominate.

This totalitarian power to dominate is also expressed through overt acts to dehumanize the individual. Even the prisoner's most private activities are subject to scrutiny and sometimes punishment, as these two inmate descriptions attest:

> The institutional rules are so broad that they encompass everything from not wearing socks (no show for two weeks) to masturbation (10 days in the hole).[50]
>
> These men would ask who needed to use the washroom. If you raised your hand, the men would have you form a line in the hall—and then make you do five hundred knee-bends or one hundred, depending on how you had to use the washroom. A piss was only a hundred knee-bends, but to take a shit was worth five hundred.[51]

It is sometimes tempting to dismiss such humiliations as simply the warped practices of sadistic prison guards. However, to do so is to overlook a larger and more critical issue. The relations of production in capitalist society tends to transform workers from human beings into a means to an end—that end being profit. People in a sense become objects; they are dehumanized. Where they are valuable objects they are treated well, but they are objects nonetheless. Those people who have little or no value regarding the relations of production lose much of their claim to be treated humanely. Since the majority of prisoners come from the poorest segment of the working class—that which is least valuable to the relations of production—and since they are of little value as workers while in prison, they are doubly dehumanized. It is from this larger social context of dehumanization that prison humiliations arise as an exaggerated or twisted reflection of the more general patterns in society.

Prisons exaggerate and exacerbate other characteristics of American society. Two of the most notable are sexual subjugation and racial conflict.

Relations between men and women in Western culture are characterized by an imbalance of power both economically and socially. This means that sexual relations between men and women can become an arena for the symbolic expression of male dominance and female submission. Certainly many American males view sexual relations as "scoring," that is, achieving a kind of conquest over the female. In its extreme form this ideology is expressed in rape, the ultimate form of sexual subjugation. This aspect of sexual relations outside the prison walls becomes magnified among the imprisoned. Rape becomes a mechanism not simply—and not necessarily at all—for achieving sexual gratification but for subjugating others. New inmates may find that they must fight to keep from being raped and that if they are unsuccessful they are seen as second-class citizens within the prison, or as the prisoners call them, "pussys."[52] Rape may also be used as subjugation and punishment in the female prison, as one inmate describes:

Ruby's first blow caught me on the side of my head. As soon as she hit me, a scream went up from the others, "Kill the stool pigeon bitch." All eight of them fell on me at once. Somebody set fire to my skirt. . . . I fell and they kicked me repeatedly in the left eye. They kicked my breasts and jumped up and down on me. Then somebody pulled off my panties, thrust them into my mouth as a gag, and I was raped.[53]

This use of forced sex in prison is not simply the consequence of sexual deprivation. As Herman and Julia Schwendinger note, whatever form it takes, "rape is mediated by socially acquired attitudes," and the use of rape within prison is but a magnification of the element of dominance that surrounds sexual relations in American society generally.[54]

The racial tensions that exist in American society generally are similarly magnified in the American prisons. As Jean Genet wrote,

Racism is scattered, diffused throughout the whole of America, grim, underhanded, hypocritical, arrogant. There is one place . . . that it reaches its cruelest pitch, intensifying every second, preying on body and soul; it is in this place that racism becomes a kind of concentrate of racism: in the American prisons. . . .[55]

There are several reasons for this. First, the bitterness and frustration of imprisonment itself finds a ready outlet in racial hostility and race-related violence. Racial prejudices learned by both blacks and whites in free society can become magnified in prison as individuals and groups struggle for scare resources, and perhaps even more importantly, to maintain some sense of personal identity in an environment whose very structure tends to weaken or destroy identity. For whites the maintenance of race superiority over blacks becomes the last avenue for expressing dominance. In Soledad prison, for example, as George Jackson relates,

> The blacks had to sit in the rear of the TV room on hard, armless, backless benches while the Mexican and whites sat up front on cushioned chairs and benches with backrests! Now, check this, if one of those punks was in his cell or the shower, no one could sit in his seat and certainly no black dare sit there. I'm serious![56]

The expression of dominance through racial discrimination reflects the behavior of humans stripped of all other avenues of dominance but who remain products of a society that tends to link personal worth with superiority over others.

Second, the racial mix in American prisons itself tends to breed racial conflict because it varies from the norm in free society. Blacks find themselves a statistically larger proportion of prison populations than in free society, and this becomes an avenue for power seldom experienced on the outside. By contrast, whites used to their numerical superiority must confront a weakened numerical position in prison. As one white inmate said,

> A new inmate upon entering the institution discovers probably for the first time in his life that the Negro is "king." "Might makes right" can be no more meaningful than behind these walls as the Negros outnumber whites by about 75% to 25%. . . . The Negros within these walls . . . stick together like a "pack of wolves." Their number and size alone is threat enough to both the white inmates and the white officers alike, but this is magnified more so by their "johnny on the spot" willingness to "help out a brother." . . .[57]

With their superiority threatened by the prevalence of blacks, white inmates may respond by attempting to rigidify the lines of racial segregation. The effect is to create a climate of racial conflict that can eventually absorb all inmates:

> Before I came to the penitentiary 16 months ago I had no real racial prejudices. Upon being exposed to strong racism from both blacks and whites I realized that it was part of the adaptation process. Racial factors enter into everything from seating at meals to sporting events.[58]

To the extent that prison inmates exist in a racially polarized environment, the prison experience can serve to escalate and magnify the racist tendencies of the society at large.

While prisons are places where humiliation, violence, rape, and racism exist in abundance, they are not wholly devoid of the human will to resist. Between the mid-1960s and the mid-1970s prisoners in a number of states joined together to form political organizations and prisoner unions in a collective struggle to achieve a humane environment and an end to the dehumanizing practices of the prison system. There is perhaps no better statement of the goals of this effort than the Folsom Prisoners Manifesto (see box). Among the demands made by the Folsom prisoners were

1. Legal representation at parole hearings
2. Adequate medical care and an end to the dispensing of medicine by untrained personnel

3. An end to the punishment of prisoners, usually by placing in solitary confinement, for those "who practice the constitutional right of peaceful dissent" regarding prison practices
4. An end to the tear gassing of prisoners while in their cells
5. The right to be paid a regular wage scale for their work and the right to use portions of this wage to support their families on the outside[59]

The effect of the prisoner's movement was not ultimately a liberalization of prisons. Instead it provided the fuel for a full-scale return of the custody perspective to the control of American prisons. "Many top administrators

THE FOLSOM PRISONERS MANIFESTO OF DEMANDS AND ANTI-OPPRESSION PLATFORM

We the Imprisoned Men of Folsom Prison Seek an End to the Injustice Suffered by All Prisoners, Regardless of Race, Creed, or Color

The preparation and content of this document has been constructed under the unified efforts of all races and social segments of this prison.

We the inmates of Folsom Prison totally and unlimitedly support the California state wide prison strike on November 3, 1970, under the united effort for designated change in administrative prison practice and legislative policy. . . .

We the men of Folsom Prison have been committed to the State Correctional Authorities by the people of this society for the purpose of correcting what has been deemed as social errors in behavior, errors which have classified us as socially unacceptable until re-programmed with new values and a more thorough understanding of our roles and responsibilities as members of the outside community. The structure and conditions of the Folsom Prison program have been engraved on the pages of this manifesto of demands with the blood, sweat, and tears of the inmates of this prison.

The program which we are committed to under the ridiculous title of rehabilitation is likened to the ancient stupidity of pouring water on the drowning man, in as much as our program administrators respond to our hostilities with their own.

In our efforts to comprehend on a feeling level an existence contrary to violence, we are confronted by our captors with violence. In our effort to comprehend society's code of ethics concerning what is fair and just, we are victimized by exploitation and the denial of the celebrated due process of law.

In our peaceful efforts to assemble in dissent as provided under the nation's United States Constitution, we are in turn murdered, brutalized, and framed on various criminal charges because we seek the rights and privileges of *all American people.*

In our efforts to keep abreast of the outside world, through all categories of news media, we are systematically restricted and punished by isolation when we insist on our human rights to the wisdom of awareness.

Source: Reprinted from *If They Come in the Morning* by Angela Y. Davis, copyright 1971 by the Third Press, Joseph Okpaku Publishing Co., New York, pp. 57, 63.

who had been straddling the fence for years, juggling custody and treatment forces, leaped over to the custody side" in response to the threat of a unified prisoner's movement.[60] Prisoner organizations were disbanded and in some states made illegal and prison movement leaders were punished and often segregated from other inmates.[61] According to prison expert John Irwin the consequence was that

> The administrators stopped the development of alternative group structures that could have prevented the rise of hoodlum gangs involved in rackets, formed on racial lines, and engaged in extreme forms of prisoner-to-prisoner violence.

As it turned out, repression of the prisoner's movement undercut the position of the "most respected and resourceful" prisoners and eliminated those organizations that had the potential to bring together the different racial and ethnic groups in the prisons. Irwin continues:

> If permitted to develop, this incipient movement might have been the basis for a new prisoner social order. It would have been more formal and it would have been bothersome to the administration, because, in order for it to succeed, it would have had to have some real power. However, in its intense and vengeful retaliation, the administrations stopped this development, and violent cliques and gangs emerged as the dominant force in many prisons.[62]

The voice of prison radicalism had been stilled for the time being. This can be attributed not only to the repressive policies of prison administrations but also to the withdrawal of public support for prisoners. The conservative political climate that began to emerge in the mid-1970s and continues into the 1980s has rendered prisoner rights an unfashionable cause. With the reemergence of a highly punitive attitude toward those who are convicted of common crimes, those in prison have little chance of achieving a humanization—however limited the humanization of prisons must inevitably be—of the prison world.

GETTING OUT OF PRISON

There are two basic ways of achieving release from prison: unconditional release and conditional release. *Unconditional release* occurs when an offender who has completed an assigned sentence, usually with some time off for "good behavior," is returned to the community free of any further responsibilities to the penal system. This type of release, sometimes referred to as "maxing out," fits the traditional image of the offender who has "paid his debt to society."

Conditional release involves release of an offender from prison prior to expiration of the full sentence assigned on the condition that he or she remain under the supervision of the penal system for a time while in the community. Parole is the most common form of conditional release. It is distinguished by the fact that the prisoner's release date is determined not strictly by the legislatively or judicially established sentence but by the discretion of a parole board. The prisoner is released to the community on the condition that he or she accept supervision by a parole officer and follow certain other rules for a period of time, including finding and maintaining employment, avoiding future criminal involvement, not associating with other known offenders, paying court costs, and keeping a regular schedule of contact with a parole officer. Failure to meet the conditions of parole can result in a parole revocation and the return of the offender to prison to serve out the remainder of the original sentence. Revocation can result either from the offender's involvement in some new crime or violation of some other parole condition. Violations of the latter sort are frequently referred to as "technical violations" of parole.

Conditional release constitutes the most common type of release from prison. In 1978, for example, 84 percent of the 166,132 persons released from state or Federal penitentiaries were given some form of conditional release.[63] This pattern has existed for some time. Conditional release first became popular in the late nineteenth century as the prison labor system became increasingly unable to pay for the costs of imprisonment. Conditional releases served the symbolic function of allowing lengthy sentences for common crimes to remain "on the books" while freeing the state and Federal governments from actually having to support prisoners for the full term of those sentences.

On December 31, 1979—the day the parole census was taken—there were 186,349 people on conditional release under parole supervision. This represented about 60 percent of those in prison on that same day, bringing the total number of people under some form of state or Federal correctional supervision to a little over a half million at the end of 1979. If we add to the stock parole population the number of persons released from parole that year we find that 275,000 offenders had been on parole at some time during 1979.[64] In recent years the number of persons on parole has been growing, and growing faster than the number of persons in prison. This is due largely to the fact that increases in the crime rate and in the frequency of sentencings to prison rather than to probation have led to prison overcrowding and subsequent pressures on correctional systems to release offenders from prison early.[65]

The basic theory underlying the supervision of conditionally released prisoners in the community is that this supervision will help the offender become reintegrated into normal life, thereby reducing the likelihood of a return to crime. The degree to which this theory is vindicated by the actual performance of supervised parolees is difficult to assess. Since the majority of those released from incarceration are released to some form of community supervision there is little against which to compare the effectiveness of parole supervision. More importantly, the selection of persons for release to supervision, particularly in the case of parole, is not random. Those who serve the full term of their sentences in prison generally do so because they have been judged poor risks for early release on parole. Furthermore, compared with those receiving early release, individuals who serve their entire sentence in prison have had a more lengthy exposure to the criminogenic experiences of prison life and also often feel more hostile toward the justice system for having denied them parole.[66] These factors combine to make the recidivism rate for paroled prisoners generally less than that for those given unconditional releases.[67] It is therefore difficult to say for certain whether or not the actual experience of parole supervision decreases the likelihood of a return to crime or not.

COMMUNITY CORRECTIONS

Even as the era of indeterminate sentencing and "rehabilitation behind walls" was in full swing, criticisms were being raised. Criticisms of imprisonment took several forms. Some argued that the goal of rehabilitation was fundamentally contradictory to the basic reality of imprisonment. In this vein pioneering criminologist Harry Elmer Barnes wrote in 1965 that

> The prisons operate primarily as an agency for suppressing human freedom, whatever their other rationalized aims and purposes. . . . the human animal does not suffer caging gladly, even at the hands of the most genial and sympathetic keepers or trainers. His dominant motive, as every student of prison life and every prison official knows all too well, is to get out of his cage.

Barnes went on to point out that all prison programs aimed at rehabilitation had little chance of success because they inevitably operated in a climate of hostility between "caged animals that want to get out and a prison staff which is consecrated to seeing to it that they do not realize this ceaseless and overpowering ambition."[68]

Others attacked the ideology of rehabilitation behind bars as politically and racially repressive. Still others pointed to the high cost of imprisonment relative to its rehabilitative success.[69] These various criticisms fueled a search for alternatives to incarceration by those still committed to the idea of rehabilitation but who had come to view imprisonment as an inappropriate means to this goal. These alternatives generally involved some form of rehabilitation program that allowed the offender to either remain in the community or return to it sooner than would normally be the case under the established indeterminate sentencing model. Taken together these programs have come to be termed *community corrections.*

Technically, probation and parole are forms of community correction in that their aim is to provide rehabilitative services to offenders in the community. However, to these older forms of community correction have been added a variety of newer alternatives to traditional patterns of release from incarceration. Some of these, such as work release and study release programs, are seen as routes to the early return of incarcerated offenders to the community.

Work release and study release programs allow qualified incarcerated offenders to leave prisons or jails during the day to either work at jobs in the community or to attend classes at local educational facilities. Supporters of these programs argue that they serve as a "bridge" between the offender and the community. This bridging of the gap between the prison experience and the outside world both enables the offender to maintain positive ties within the community and to develop job skills and work experience. These will presumably serve as a route to gainful employment and subsequently to a reduction in the likelihood of a return to crime once the offender is released from prison altogether.[70] Additionally, the continuation of ties to the community, even while under prison sentence, are thought to ease the problems of reintegration into the community after release.

Studies of work release programs, in particular, have generally shown this alternative to traditional incarceration to be effective as a rehabilitative tool, with offenders maintaining employment and avoiding a return to crime more often than inmates who have not had the benefit of such programs.[71] While these findings are generally optimistic they are clouded by the fact that assignment to work or study release programs is not random. Usually only "selected" inmates are allowed on release programs. Common criteria for selection into release programs, such as having no prior record or at least no record of convictions for violent crimes and no history of drug abuse or alcoholism, means that these programs often start with offenders who are most likely to make a successful adjustment to release. Thus claims that release programs are successful must be interpreted cautiously.

Another important factor contributing to the growth of work release programs is their ability to defray the costs of imprisonment. Not only do they often lead to an early release of the offender from confinement, but they also provide the offender with a source of income, a portion of which is usually given to the prison to pay for the inmate's living costs.[72] At a time when both prison populations and the costs of supporting them is rising, work release programs become increasingly attractive. By the mid-1970s the majority of state prison systems had implemented some form of work release for offenders. For similar reasons work release programs have found considerable favor with local governments seeking ways of holding down the costs of maintaining jails for misdemeanants.

Another alternative to traditional patterns of release from prison that has developed in recent years is the halfway house. This alternative should perhaps be called a *halfway-out* house since its clientele are those moving from prison to the community. The halfway house usually consists of a community residential facility serving a limited number of prisoners on conditional release. These facilities are frequently located in low-income or depressed neighborhoods. One of the most persistent problems faced by halfway house supporters is the resistance—often backed by substantial political clout—by residents in more stable or affluent neighborhoods to the location near them of facilities that would house "criminals." Halfway houses for recently released prisoners are sometimes financed and run by correctional departments under state governments, but in many cases they are either sponsored by nonprofit foundation grants or are run on a for-profit basis by corporations contracting their services to the state government.

While residents are supervised by the halfway house staff and must observe a variety of conduct rules governing their behavior both in the house (e.g., no drugs or alcohol, no women in the house, no gambling, etc.) and in the community (e.g., staying out of bars, actively seeking or maintaining employment, avoiding other known offenders, etc.) the facility is generally open. That is, house residents can come and go as they choose, subject to curfew rules, and they can establish and maintain ties to family and friends in the community. The theory behind "halfway-out" houses is to provide the recently released offender with a semisheltered environment that can offer support and counseling services during the difficult initial transition from the prison to the community.[73]

In addition to community-based programs for incarcerated or recently released offenders there has emerged in the last fifteen years a number of community corrections programs aimed at keeping convicted offenders out of prison altogether. As previously discussed, probation is the prototype community corrections program. Alongside probation there exists today a number of programs that are either diversionary in nature or, unlike probation, do not rest directly upon the threat of imprisonment although they are imposed after conviction.

Diversion programs, crime prevention programs, and alternative community-based treatment programs for convicted offenders are not always easily distinguishable. In recent years some cities have begun experimenting with community treatment centers aimed at providing educations, counseling, and recreational services to a variety of both convicted and "potential" offenders. In 1971, for example, the Gulf Coast Trades Center was opened to serve the city of Houston, Texas. The center provided services aimed at improving the educational and occupational skills of those between fourteen and eighteen who had either dropped out of school, had a history of school problems, or had been convicted of minor crimes.[74] This type of multiclient community center has become a common strategy for expanding both diversion and community rehabilitation programs for the already-convicted. Community treatment centers enable courts to direct both the convicted and the accused to a single program to receive rehabilitative services.

In some cases community treatment centers serve an even broader purpose than providing out-client diversion or correctional programs. The "integrated" community treatment center, which some view as the most hopeful alternative to traditional incarceration, can serve as a detention facility for those awaiting trial, a treatment facility for the diverted or convicted, an adjustment center for those just released or about-to-be released from prison, an evaluation center for those awaiting sentencing, and a counseling center for problem or troubled youth who have not yet been convicted of crimes.[75] This type of multipurpose correctional facility has the advantage of reducing duplication and its corresponding costs in the overall correctional system. It also provides for centralization of records and information about community residents with either a presumed potential or an actual record of law violation. As such it can be a powerful tool for integrating and expanding social control over those working-class members who may be inclined to seek criminal alternatives, as well as a relatively inexpensive means compared with adjudication and/or imprisonment for dealing with those who have broken the law or are thought to have broken the law.

CONCLUSION: CORRECTIONS AND THE FISCAL CRISIS OF THE STATE

The political state in capitalist society must serve two contradictory functions: the facilitation of private accumulation of capital and the legitimation of its own existence and the economic base upon which it rests. Facilitating capital accumulation is accomplished in two broad ways. First, the state must maintain institutions and policies conducive to the economic growth of the private sector.[76] Second, in the eyes of the general public the political state in capitalist society must insure the legitimacy of both the economy of private ownership and the state's own actions to facilitate that private economy. To do this the state promises to protect individual freedoms and the right of people to be equal before the law. These promises, however, contribute to state legitimacy only if the state behaves in ways consistent with these ideals. The maintenance of legitimacy also requires that the state temper the negative consequences arising from private ownership of the means of production— including poverty, economic and political inequality, and high rates of crime—through various social welfare and crime control programs.

Attempts to facilitate legitimacy, however, can contradict attempts to facilitate capital accumulation. For example, the potential for political unrest inherent in high rates of poverty, unemployment, and inequality are minimized through the institution of various social welfare programs designed to alleviate at least the severest forms of impoverishment. Maintaining these programs, however, drains a certain portion of government revenue away from its efforts to facilitate capital accumulation in the private sector.

Corrections are currently caught between rising crime rates and the fiscal crisis of the political state. Rising crime rates have produced a substantial increase in the prison population. From 1970 to 1979 the FBI Crime Index total increased by 38.6 percent, and this was matched by a 36.9 percent increase in the number of persons arrested.[77] Other things being equal, an increased number of arrests will lead to an increase in the number of persons in prison or under some other form of correctional supervision. Increases in rates of crime can also stimulate increased public demands for more punishment of criminals, adding to the rise of prison populations.

The failure of liberal correctional reforms during the 1960s and 1970s to produce noticeably lower rates of recidivism has generated a general disillusionment with the goal of rehabilitation. This disillusionment is in turn heightened by rising crime rates. These three factors—rising crime rates, increased public demand for social order, and a sense of failure of the liberal, rehabilitative mission of prisons—have generated public, political, and academic support for a return to punishment and deterrence as the primary function of corrections. They have also generated an increase in the absolute number of prisoners. Between 1971 and 1984 the stock prison population rose from 177,113 to 438,830—an increase of 248 percent. This increase in the number of prisoners between 1971 and 1984 was more than double the increase in the number of persons arrested between those years. The current trend toward ever larger numbers of prisoners is occurring, however, in the context of a fiscal crisis of the state.

The inability of the private sector to provide for continued economic growth and full employment has led to increased demands that the state provide the necessary stimulus for private capital to achieve these goals. The primary mechanism for stimulating the private economy is the transference of large amounts of capital from the public sector to the private in the form of tax concessions, waiver or lax enforcement of regulatory laws, loan guarantees, and price supports to insure profits and stimulate private investment. This was precisely the general policy of the Reagan administration to boost the American economy out of stagnation.

This transference of capital to the private sector to stimulate growth and stabilize the economy is consistent with the state's function of facilitating private accumulation. However, it also weakens the legitimation function, for the state must draw on the same body of public funds to minimize the potentially dangerous consequences of unemployment, poverty, and crime. Like many other social welfare and crime control agencies correctional agencies are caught in this squeeze.

Demands for fiscal responsibility on the part of government in recent years usually resulted in decreased monies for social welfare and crime control activities to pay for increased subsidies to the private sector. In the criminal justice arena this has meant the demise of the Law Enforcement Assistance Administration and its multimillion dollar annual conduit to state governments to help them pay for the costs of policing and imprisonment. It has also meant an increased reluctance on the part of the individual state governments to enter into costly new prison building programs.

The net effect of these forces has been an increased tendency toward prison overcrowding. One possible response to this growing problem of overcrowding is increased usage of early release and community-based corrections programs such as those described above. Another alternative would be to build more prisons. And still another would be simply to let prison conditions deteriorate as the result of overcrowding. Each of these possible alternatives, however, poses problems arising from the current contradictions of the capitalist welfare state.

More extensive use of early release and community corrections programs contradicts growing public demands, stimulated by conservative politicians, for increased—not decreased—use of imprisonment. Public demands for more imprisonment are based not on a simple desire among the general population to see prisoners suffer but rather upon their legitimate desire to be free from the growing fear of crime that pervades the society. Political responses to the failures of both social welfare and rehabilitative programs of the 1960s and

1970s have sought to direct public demands toward punishing criminals rather than more substantial alterations in the basic factors underlying high rates of crime. State failure to respond to these public demands for protection from crime could pose serious threats to state legitimacy. Thus the current demand for more punishment acts as a constraint on the possibility of alleviating prison overcrowding through decreased use of imprisonment as a penalty.

The second alternative, building more prisons, contradicts the current demands upon the government to stimulate private investment and private accumulation. It is interesting to note, for example, that in a 1981 speech to the International Association of Chiefs of Police, President Reagan emphasized the need to utilize prisons more extensively for criminals but failed to offer any indication that Federal funds would be forthcoming to help build the facilities needed to house these prisoners.[78] Individual state governments thus find themselves facing their own fiscal crises. Federal policies aimed at reducing Federal expenditures in the areas of social welfare and crime control place an increased financial burden on the individual states, forcing them to apportion less money among a greater variety of expenditures. This makes new prison construction even more burdensome than in earlier years, particularly in the face of citizen opposition to tax increases during a time of economic uncertainty.

The last alternative is simply to let prisons become increasingly overcrowded. Here, however, the state comes into contradiction with itself. Prison overcrowding makes even more inhumane an already dehumanizing system. It also leads to such things as prison riots, which call public attention to the conditions inside prisons. This, however, is not simply a problem of public attitude. If it were, it might be possible to convince the public that however inhuman, prison conditions are no worse than offenders deserve. However, prison overcrowding also poses a legal problem with respect to the government's own ideology concerning human rights. As of 1978, seventeen states were under court order to relieve prison overcrowding and thirteen more were involved in similar suits.[79] In essence these rulings and suits represented challenges to the state to live up to its ideology of avoiding cruel and unusual punishment. To the extent that the state openly condones extreme forms of cruelty in its punishments, it fails to follow its own rules, thereby compromising its legitimacy.

There are two possible routes of escape from the problem posed by increased prisoner populations during a time of fiscal crisis within the state. The first is to redefine the concept of "cruel and unusual punishment" to allow for increased levels of overcrowding. To some extent this strategy is reflected in a 1981 Supreme Court ruling that housing two prisoners in cells designed for one does not constitute "cruel and unusual punishment" because prisoners have no constitutional right to a "comfortable" stay in prison.[80] While the court may attempt to mandate a redefinition of what constitutes cruelty, these legal manueverings will do little to reduce the likelihood of prison disruptions and riots. The definition of "cruelty" in the minds of prisoners will remain the same, as will their responses.

The second possibility is to redefine the "dangerous" criminal in a way that increases public tolerance of community corrections programs. Since public fear of crime is largely fear of violent crime, there will likely be attempts to redefine the nonviolent property offender as not-so-dangerous. This dichotomization of the offender population into the dangerous violent offender and the not-so-dangerous property offender would facilitate the increased incarceration of the former and increased utilization of community corrections for the latter. This is the most likely direction that corrections will take in the near future. Imprisonment will be utilized more frequently and for longer periods of time for those convicted of violent crimes, particularly murder, rape, and robbery. To some extent this would help demonstrate to the public that the state is serious about providing protection from criminals. At the same time increased use of community corrections for the redefined property offender would ease prison overcrowding somewhat. This in turn would minimize the need for new prison expenditures and also reduce the potential threats to state legitimacy posed by riots and other public demonstrations of deteriorating prison conditions.

NOTES

1. See David Fraser, *The Evolution of the British Welfare State* (New York: Macmillan, 1973), 34–50 for a discussion of the role of the English workhouse).
2. Dario Melossi, "George Rusche and Otto Kirchheimer: Punishment and Social Structure," *Crime and Social Justice,* no. 9 (1978). See also Michel Foucault, *Discipline and Punish* (New York: Vintage Books, 1979).
3. Fernand Braudel, *Capitalism and Material Life: 1400–1800* (New York: Harper Colophon Books, 1975), 66–113.
4. George Rusche and Otto Kirchheimer, *Punishment and Social Structure* (New York: Russell and Russell, 1939), 110.
5. B. Mckilvey, *American Prisons* (Montclair, N.J.: Patterson Smith, 1968), 92–95.
6. Martin B. Miller, "At Hard Labor: Rediscovering the 19th Century Prison," in Tony Platt and Paul Takagi, eds., *Punishment and Penal Discipline* (Berkeley, Calif.: Crime and Social Justice Associates, 1980), 83.
7. Ibid., 84.
8. Thorsten Sellin, *Research Memorandum on Crime in the Depression* (New York: Social Science Research Council, 1937); Leon T. Stern, "The Effects of the Depression on Prison Committments and Sentences," *Journal of Criminal Law, Criminology, and Police Science,* 31 (1940): 696–711.
9. Ivan Jankovic, "Social Class and Criminal Sentencing," *Crime and Social Justice,* no. 10 (1978); David F. Greenberg, "The Dynamics of Oscillatory Punishment Processes," *Journal of Criminal Law and Criminology,* no. 68, 1977:643–651; Harvey Brenner, *Mental Illness and the Economy* (Cambridge, Mass.: Harvard University Press, 1973); Steven Box and Chris Hale, "Economic Crisis and the Rising Prisoner Population in England and Wales," *Crime and Social Justice,* no. 17 (1982); William H. Robinson et al., "Prison Populations and Costs: Projections to 1980" (Washington, D.C.: Congressional Research Service, 1974).
10. George Rusche, "Labor Market and Penal Sanction," in Platt and Takagi, 11.
11. Ibid., 12.
12. Hugo A. Bedau, "The Death Penalty in America," in James A. McCafferty, ed., *Capital Punishment* (New York: Atherton, 1972) 11.

13. W. O. Black, *The History of Slavery and the Slave Trade* (Columbus, Ohio: H. Miller, 1862), 214.
14. See Richard O. Boyer and Robert M. Morias, *Labor's Untold Story* (New York: Marzani and Munsell, 1965) for detailed descriptions of false chargings and executions of U.S. labor leaders from 1870 to 1946.
15. U.S. Department of Justice, *Capital Punishment—1980* (Washington, D.C.: Government Printing Office, 1980), 1.
16. Ibid., p. 9.
17. *Furman* v. *Georgia*, 408 U.S. 238 (1972).
18. *Roberts* v. *Louisiana*, 96 S. Ct. 3001 (1976); *Woodson* v. *North Carolina*, 96 S. Ct. 2979 (1976).
19. *Lockett* v. *Ohio*, 434 U.S. 889 (1977).
20. State of New York Prison Commission, *Investigation of State Prisons and Report Thereon* (Albany, 1876), 16: see also E. C. Wines and Theodore W. Dwight, *Report on the Prisons and Reformatories of the United States and Canada* (Albany: Prison Association of New York, 1876).
21. As late as 1966, for example, Karl Menninger in his popular book *The Crime of Punishment* (New York: Viking Press, 1966) concludes after lengthy discussion of the importance of social conditions on the production of criminal behavior that what is needed are new ways of treating criminal *persons.*
22. Jessica Mitford, *Kind and Usual Punishment* (New York: Vintage, 1974), 243; Michael Hindelang, "A Learning Theory Analysis of the Correctional Process," *Issues in Criminology*, 5, no. 1 (Winter 1970): 43.
23. David L. Greenberg and Drew Humphries, "The Cooptation of Fixed Sentencing Reform," *Crime and Delinquency*, April 1980, pp. 206–207; also Stephen Pfohl, "Deciding on Dangerousness" in Platt and Takagi, *Punishment and Penal Discipline*, 113–128.
24. American Friends Service Committee, *The Struggle for Justice* (New York: Hill and Wang, 1971), 91.
25. Quoted in David A. Ward and Gene G. Kassenbaum, *Women's Prison* (Chicago: Aldine).
26. American Friends Service Committee, *The Struggle for Justice*, 100–123.
27. Douglas Lipton, Robert Martinson, and Judith Wilks, *The Effectiveness of Correctional Treatment: A Survey of Treatment Evaluation Studies* (New York: Praeger, 1975).
28. Greenberg and Humphries, "The Cooptation of Fixed Sentencing Reform," 369.
29. Andrew von Hirsch, *Doing Justice: The Choice of Punishments* (New York: Hill and Wang, 1976), xxxix–xl.
30. U.S. Department of Justice, *State and Local Probation and Parole Systems* (Washington, D.C.: Government Printing Office, 1978), 1.
31. U.S. Department of Justice, *Prisoners in 1983*, Bureau of Justice Statistics Bulletin, April 1984.
32. Estimated from U.S. Department of Justice, *Profile of Jail Inmates: 1978* (Washington, D.C.: Government Printing Office, 1980) and rate of growth in arrests between 1978 and 1982 as reported by the Federal Bureau of Investigation, *Crime in the United States*, 1978 and 1982.
33. Ibid., 3. Update to 1983. as per note 32.
34. U.S. Department of Justice, *Survey of Inmates of State Correctional Facilities: 1974 Advance Report* (Washington, D.C.: Government Printing Office, 1976), 24, 25, and 27.
35. U.S. Department of Justice, *Prisoners: 1979* (Washington, D.C.: Government Printing Office, 1980), 13, 14, 18, 19.
36. U.S. Department of Justice, *Survey of Inmates*, 24.

37. U.S. Department of Justice, *Children in Custody: Advance Report on the 1979 Census of Public Juvenile Facilities* (Washington, D.C.: Government Printing Office, 1980), 3.

38. See Department of Justice, *Profile of Jail Inmates.*

39. U.S. Department of Labor, "Changes in the Spendable Earnings and Real Earnings for 1978," in *Employment and Earnings*, March 1978, 9–18.

40. Scott Christianson, *Our Black Prisoners* (Albany, N.Y.: Center on Minorities and Criminal Justice, 1980), 4.

41. John Hagen, "Extra-Legal Attributes and Criminal Sentencing," *Law and Society Review*, no. 8 (1974).

42. Scott Christianson and Richard Dehais, *The Black Incarceration Rate in the United States* (Albany, N.Y.: Center on Minorities and Criminal Justice, 1980), 10–19.

43. Leo Carroll and Margaret Mondrick, "Racial Bias in the Decision to Grant Parole," *Law and Society Review*, 11, no. 1 (1976).

44. U.S. Department of Commerce, *The Social and Economic Status of the Black Population in the United States, 1972* (Washington, D.C.: Government Printing Office, 1973), 19, 28.

45. Ibid., 38–39.

46. Wilbur Harmon quoted in Dae Chang and Warren B. Armstrong, eds., *The Prison: Voices from the Inside* (Cambridge, Mass.: Schenkman Publishing Co., 1972), 145.

47. Interview with prisoner quoted in John Irwin, *The Felon* (Englewood Cliffs, N.J.: Prentice-Hall, 1970), 69.

48. Ibid., 39.

49. Alfred Hassler, *Diary of a Self-Made Convict* (Chicago: Henry Regnery Co., 1954), 178.

50. From Chang and Warren, *The Prison*, 157.

51. Ibid., 161.

52. Alan J. Davis, "Sexual Assaults in the Philadelphia Prison System and Sheriff's Vans," *Transaction*, December 1968, 15–16.

53. Dorothy West, "I Was Afraid to Shut My Eyes," *The Saturday Evening Post*, 241 (July 1968): 23; reprinted in David M. Petersen and Marcello Truzzi, eds., *Criminal Life: Views from the Inside* (Englewood Cliffs, N.J.: Prentice-Hall, 1972), 157.

54. Julia Schwendinger and Herman Schwendinger, "Rape, Sexual Inequality, and Levels of Violence," *Crime and Social Justice*, 16 (1982): 18.

55. Jean Genet, Introduction to George Jackson, *Soledad Brother* (New York: Bantam Books, 1970), 4.

56. Ibid., 162–163.

57. Chang and Armstrong, *The Prison*, 206–207.

58. Ibid., 193.

59. The Folsom Prisoners Manifesto of Demands and Anti-Oppression Platform, reprinted in Angela Y. Davis, *If They Come in the Morning: Voices of Resistance* (New York: The Third Press, 1971), 57–63.

60. John Irwin, *Prisons in Turmoil* (Boston: Little, Brown, 1980), 139.

61. Ibid., 140–150.

62. Ibid., 152.

63. U.S. Department of Justice, *Prisoners: 1979*, 26.

64. U.S. Department of Justice, *Parole: 1979*, 5.

65. Lawrence J. Travis and Sandra Evans, "The Fiscal Squeeze: Off with Their Heads." Paper presented at the American Society of Criminology meeting, Washington, D.C., November 1981.

66. U.S. Department of Justice, *Parole: 1979*, 8.

67. Ibid., 9.

68. Harry Elmer Barnes, "The Contemporary Prison: A Menace to Rehabilitation and the Repression of Crime," *Key Issues in Criminology*, 2 (1965): 13–14.

69. Andrew Scull, *Decarceration* (Englewood Cliffs, N.J.: Prentice-Hall, 1977) discusses the role of fiscal considerations in stimulating the movement toward community corrections.

70. Ronald Goldfarb and Linda R. Singer, "Work Release," in *After Conviction*, Goldfarb and Singer, eds., (New York: Simon and Schuster, 1973), 527–552.

71. Richard K. Brautigam, "Work-Release—A Case Study and Comment," *The Prison Journal*, 52, no. 2 (1972): 20–35; Robert Jeffery and Steven Woolpert, "Work Furlough as an Alternative to Incarceration," *Journal of Criminal Law and Criminology*, 65, no. 3 (1974): 404–415; Minnesota Department of Corrections, *Work Release in Minnesota, 1970* (St. Paul, 1971).

72. Alvin Rudoff and T. C. Esseltyn, *Jail Inmates at Work* (Sacramento: California Department of Rehabilitation, 1971); Virginia McArthur et al., *Cost Analysis of the District of Columbia Work Release Program* (Washington, D.C.: District of Columbia Department of Corrections, 1970); Elmer Johnson, "Work Release: Conflicting Goals within a Promising Innovation," *Canadian Journal of Corrections*, 12, no. 1 (January 1970): 67–77.

73. P. F. Cromwell, Jr., "Halfway House and Offender Reintegration," in Killinger and Cromwell, eds., *From Corrections to the Community* (St. Paul, Minn.: West Publishing Co., 1978).

74. Robert C. Trojanowicz et al., *Community Based Crime Prevention* (Pacific Palisades, Calif.: Goodyear Publishing Co., 1975), 30.

75. Harry E. Allen et al., *Crime and Punishment* (New York: Free Press, 1981), 47.

76. Michael E. Tigar and Madeleine R. Levy, *Law and the Rise of Capitalism* (New York: Monthly Review Press, 1977).

77. Federal Bureau of Investigation, *Crime in the United States* (Washington, D.C.: Government Printing Office, 1980), 40, 190.

78. *New York Times*, "Reagan Outlines Reforms in Laws to Combat Crime," 29 September 1981), 1, A18, A19.

79. CONtact, Inc., *Corrections Compendium* (Lincoln, Neb.: CONtact, Inc., 1979), 2–5.

80. *Bell et al.* v. *Wolfish et al.*, 441 U.S. 520–599.

PART IV

Patterns of Crime and Social Injury in America

CHAPTER 10

Common Crime: How We Know What We Think We Know

CRIME AND SOCIAL POSITION

This chapter begins our inquiry into patterns of crime in contemporary America by examining the nature and sources of data about crime. Until the late 1960s conventional crimes such as murder, rape, robbery, burglary, and larceny, crimes most often associated with the "dangerous classes," tended to dominate criminological discussions about crime patterns. Since that time, however, there has been a growing awareness that upperworld crimes, that is, crimes in businesses, professions, and politics, are an equally significant part of the overall crime picture in America.[1] The following chapters will examine both conventional crimes and upperworld crimes, both those offenses normally associated with poverty and powerlessness and those intimately connected with affluence and authority.

When considering conventional and upperworld types of crime it is tempting to see the *types of people* who commit them as the primary difference between them. For instance, when Edwin Sutherland first used the term "white-collar crimes" to direct criminological attention to business-related offenses he defined them as "violations by persons in the upper socioeconomic class."[2] While it is true that in general those arrested for conventional types of crime tend to be significantly less affluent than those involved in upperworld crime, this fact does not explain the differences between these types of crime.

The key distinction between conventional and upperworld types of crime is the *social position* required for their commission. The term "social position" does not refer to an individual's level of income or wealth, although certainly some social positions are associated with affluence and others with poverty. Social positions are not "places" in the society. A social position is one side of a reciprocal relationship, and it is defined by the rights and obligations an individual has relative to the other participants in that relationship.[3] When we speak of social positions such as parent, employee, or citizen, we are actually referring to the socially defined, reciprocal relationships between parent and child, employee and employer, and citizen and state. Each of these relationships refers to a set of reciprocal (although not necessarily equal) rights and obligations that the participants to the relationship have relative to one another. It is the rights and obligations associated with the social positions we hold that determine (1) our possible courses for both correct and incorrect actions and (2) whether the specific actions we take will be considered acceptable or deviant, law-abiding or criminal.

In state societies the citizen–state relationship defines certain rights and obligations as common to all citizens. For instance, in America all citizens are obligated to accept the limitations on their action inherent in the state definition of property. Specifically, we can only use and dispose of property that "belongs" to us or has been authorized by its "owner" for our usage. Any use of property outside these limitations will be considered a crime. On the other hand, certain citizens also occupy special positions in social institutions that give them rights and obligations that extend beyond those available to all citizens. A banker, for instance, has a *legal* right, not shared by your neighbor, to make certain inquiries into your finances before granting you a loan. Conversely, the banker has a legal obligation, not shared by your neighbor, to refrain from using his or her knowledge of your finances for direct personal profit. Similarly, a high-level corporate executive has the right of access to corporate information that the average citizen does not and a corresponding obligation to avoid utilizing this "insider" information for personal financial advantage. In these cases occupants of "uncommon" positions have special opportunities to commit crime or cause injury not available to the average citizen.

In this and following chapters we will refer to crimes that are violations of the general obligations of the citizen–state relationship as *common crimes*. Those that are violations of the special obligations inherent in positions within economic and political institutions will be termed *crimes of capital*. Chapters 10, 11, and 12 will utilize this distinction in contrasting the crimes of the powerless with the crimes of the powerful. Before that, however, it is important to examine how we have come to know what we think we know about patterns of crime in America.

CRIME STATISTICS AS CULTURE WORK

In the early 1800s statistical pioneers such as Andre-Michel Guerry and Lambert Quetelet first began analyzing state-published crime data as a means of understanding the "moral" condition of society.[4] Since that time our consciousness of crime has increasingly come to be shaped by *general and abstract* statistical data rather than personal knowledge. In the days of small, integrated agrarian communities knowledge about crime was specific. Most people knew the details of the various types of crime and trouble that occurred in their community. With industrialization and the emergence of mass society, this type of specific knowledge was less feasible. Specific knowledge was gradually supplanted by aggregate data about *crime in general* as the primary force shaping people's understanding of the nature and extent of crime.

The term *culture work* refers to activity that serves to create or maintain widely accepted perceptions of the nature of reality. Insofar as our understanding of crime is shaped by the institutional mechanisms for gathering and disseminating crime data, those institutional mechanisms play an important role in shaping what we perceive to be the "reality" of crime. In this sense producing and distributing crime data is culture work.

Crime statistics are created by compiling information concerning specific instances of wrongdoing into general categories of data. These categories can be formulated according to a number of dimensions, including (1) types of crimes, (2) the geographical regions or political units in which they occurred, or (3) the characteristics of offenders and victims. The kinds of information chosen for inclusion in crime statistics will illuminate certain "facts" about crime and, conversely, obscure others.

The production and distribution of crime data in America reflects the distinction between common crimes and crimes of capital. Only those institutions charged with controlling common crimes actively produce and publicly disseminate data about the offenses under their jurisdiction. Every three months, with public press conferences and considerable fanfare, the FBI and local police departments release their current statistics on murder, rape, robbery, assault, burglary, larceny, auto theft, and arson. There is no comparable release of statistics on consumer frauds, injuries, and deaths due to violations of worker safety regulations, illegal stock manipulations, price-fixing arrangements, or corporate kickbacks. Neither the agencies that handle them nor the press treat aggregate data about corporate violations as a media event. Furthermore, information about upperworld crime often is not centralized in a fashion similar to data on common crime. Thus it is frequently more difficult for those interested in data about higher-class crime to locate such information.

This selective generation and dissemination of data on social harms in America serves to shape our awareness of crime in such a way that the category "crime" in American culture generally includes only those harms most often committed by the poorer segments of American society. Excluded from our consciousness of "crime" are all those harms more often committed by middle-class and elite Americans in pursuit of profit.

Data on common crime in America can be grouped into two broad categories: *official statistics* and *unofficial statistics*. Official statistics are generated by those institutions charged with the actual enforcement of the law. Data such as crimes known to the police, crimes cleared by arrest, persons prosecuted, and prisoner characteristics are all official statistics. Unofficial statistics consist of data about crime and criminals gathered outside the normal operations of the justice system. Victimization studies that ask individuals to report what crimes they have been victims of and self-reporting studies that ask individuals to indicate what crimes they have committed are examples of unofficial statistics.

Official statistics, particularly police statistics gathered and disseminated by the FBI, are the most prevalent form of crime data in America. It is also these figures that receive the greatest media attention. Like the production of crime statistics by the justice system, the dissemination of crime data through the media is also "culture work." To the extent that both the electronic and print media devote more time and space to official police statistics about common crime than any other source of crime data, they play a major role in creating and maintaining the image of crime in America as primarily a working class phenomenon.

The image of crime as a working class phenomenon is advantageous to the major corporations and businesses in America, for it diverts attention from *their* misdeeds. Contrary to popular ideology, the media are not wholly independent of the world of big business. Most of America's newspapers, television, and radio stations are owned by large corporations and furthermore depend upon business for the advertising revenues that constitute the bulk of their income.[5] For this reason it has been suggested by some that corporate elites may actively pressure media either directly or indirectly to promote news about common crime and periodically to generate the impression that the society is in the midst of a crime wave.[6] A more likely scenario, however, is that while corporate elites do not necessarily *promote* news about common crime, they can actively *discourage* the reporting of corporate crimes and other information detrimental to their interests. Reporter David Halberstam's extensive history of the American news industry details a number of instances where the content of news was specifically manipulated in accordance with the wishes of various elites.[7] By downplaying news about corporate and political crimes, the media creates a general impression that these events are relatively rare and/or insignificant in comparison with offenses more commonly linked to working class lawbreakers.

Another factor effecting the role of the media in shaping our consciousness about crime is that the media is largely reactive. For the most part, it responds to stories brought to it from outside sources. While there has been an increase in "investigative journalism" in recent years, the bulk of crime reporting is determined by what information comes to the media in the form of press releases or other information relayed to it by the justice system. Information and data about common crimes are provided freely and often in substantial detail to the media by local police and the FBI. No similar service is provided by those institutions regulating corporate crime.[8] Stories about corporate wrongdoing, even if not actively suppressed by interested elites having influence on the media, can generally only be developed by costly and time-consuming investigative reporting and therefore can only be done infrequently.

Budgetary and manpower limitations on investigative reporting insure that the media will primarily report information given to it by other sources. As long as only the criminal justice system regularly provides news items for the media, media presentation of crime will be heavily skewed toward common crimes.

In addition to focusing most heavily on common crimes the news media tends also to give greater emphasis to certain kinds of crimes. Violent crimes such as murder, rape, and robbery generally receive more attention than property crimes because they are more dramatic and more closely linked to a sense of personal threat. This tends to obscure the fact that the bulk of crime in America consists of property crime, not crimes of violence.[9] Besides leading most people to believe they are more vulnerable to crimes of violence than they actually are, the media emphasis upon crimes of violence tends to divert attention from the role that fundamental socioeconomic inequities play in making property crime rather than violence the most common form of lawbreaking in America.

How crime statistics are presented is also part of culture work. The FBI Uniform Crime Reports, for example, regularly includes "Crime Clocks." The Crime Clock presented in Figure 10.1 shows that there is one forcible rape every seven minutes. Using the same data by which the Crime Clock is calculated we can also conclude that for the average American female the odds *against* being the victim of a rape were 1,493 to 1 in 1979.[10] Similarly, "one robbery every sixty-eight seconds" means that the odds against being a robbery victim are 472 to 1.[11] While neither way is "more correct," these two forms of presenting the same data have substantially different implications. Crime Clocks convey a sense of greater frequency and immediate threat than do odds against victimization. By and large the FBI has tended to use forms that maximize the sense of threat and growth in crime as opposed to those which minimize these perceptions.

OFFICIAL STATISTICS: POLICE DATA AND THE UNIFORM CRIME REPORTS

The first steps toward the production of national crime statistics in the United States began in 1930. In that year the International Association of Chiefs of Police began a voluntary program of national crime data collection. In that same year Congress directed the FBI to serve as a national clearinghouse for gathering these statistics and to compile annual reports on the amount of crime in the nation, a task it has done every year since.

The FBI Uniform Crime Reports are compiled from data that are reported monthly to the FBI by state and local law-enforcement agencies. Although reporting is voluntary at the Federal level, in recent years many states have passed laws making participation by law-enforcement agencies in those states mandatory.[12] Although not every law enforcement agency in the United States participates in the Uniform Crime Reports program, the FBI estimated that by 1978 the participating agencies encompassed about 99 percent of all persons living in large metropolitan areas, about 96 percent of those in other cities, and about 94 percent of those living in rural areas.[13]

Reporting agencies transmit a variety of information about crimes to the FBI. This includes data concerning the number and types of weapons used, the amount of money or goods stolen, and whether an arrest was made. Data concerning the age, race, and sex of victims and offenders are also provided

Figure 10.1

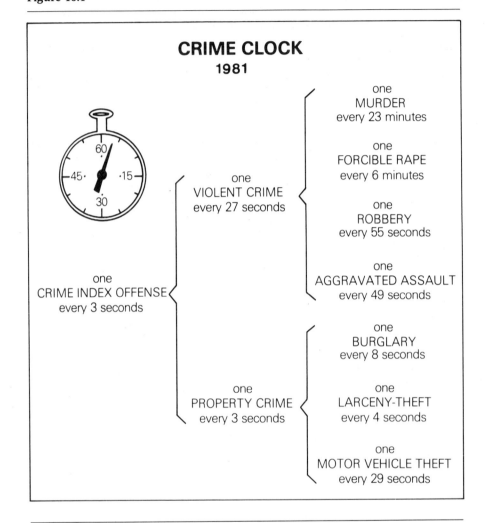

The crime clock should be viewed with care. Being the most aggregate representation of UCR data, it is designed to convey the annual reported crime experience by showing the relative frequency of occurrence of the Index Offenses. This mode of display should not be taken to imply a regularity in the commission of the Part I Offenses; rather, it represents the annual ratio of crime to fixed time intervals.

Source: Federal Bureau of Investigation, *Crime in the United States, 1979* (Washington, D.C.: Government Printing Office, 1980), 5.

to the FBI. The Uniform Crime Reports program does not gather data concerning the social class characteristics of either victims or suspected offenders.

Counting Crime

The task of counting crime is not as straightforward as it might seem. Yet how crime is counted determines what crime data tell us and do not tell us. The term "crime" is a legal label applied to some form of human behavior. Unfortunately, human behavior often fails to fit neatly into legal categories. Often considerable interpretation is required to decide just what kind of crime has occurred. In an attempt to standardize how such interpretations about what to count are made, the FBI provides guidelines to police departments participating in the Uniform Crime Reports. Of particular importance is the way in which multiple offenses and multiple victims are counted where various crimes are concerned.

1. *From a legal standpoint a single criminal event may involve more than one type of offense.* If two youths break into a home and hold the owner at knifepoint while loading stereo equipment and silver into the owner's car, which they then use for escape after knocking the owner unconscious, a number of legally distinct crimes have occurred. At a minimum this single event involves the crimes of breaking and entering (burglary), armed robbery, larceny, assault, and auto theft. According to FBI guidelines, where several different crimes are encompassed by a single event, only the most serious crime is counted, which in the case above would be that of armed robbery. Whether or not an event involving different types of crimes leads to the recording of one or more than one crime depends upon the nature of the most serious crime committed and whether or not this offense involved more than one victim.

2. *A single criminal event may involve more than one victim.* Where there are multiple victims the FBI distinguishes between the crimes of murder, rape, and assault, which it directs departments to record on the basis of *one crime per victim*, and larceny and robbery, which it indicates should be recorded on the basis of *one crime per event*. If a man loses his temper and stabs five patrons at a bar, this event would be recorded as five separate assaults. If that same man used his knife to rob the five patrons of their wallets, according to the FBI this event would constitute a *single* armed robbery. The crimes of burglary and auto theft, like those of murder, rape, and assault, are generally counted on the basis of one crime per unit victimized. Where auto theft is concerned, the rule is fairly clear-cut. Each vehicle stolen constitutes one crime of theft. Where burglary is concerned, the distinctions are a bit more complicated but generally follow the rule of one crime recorded for each unit victimized, with the exception of burglaries of multiple units reflecting single ownership, such as several rooms in a hotel or several buildings on a single piece of property—a house and garage, for instance. In these cases only one burglary would be recorded by police.[14]

In the case of an event that involved both multiple victims and several legally different crimes the task would be first to identify the most serious event—assault, armed robbery, and so forth—and then determine if this particular event is counted on a one per victim or a one per event basis. If someone breaks into a house, robs two victims of their money at knifepoint, and then steals their car to escape, this would be recorded as a single case of armed robbery. However, if that same person broke into the house, killed the inhabitants and then stole the car to escape, this would be recorded as two homicides. The decision to count robberies and larcenies on a per event basis and things such as murder, assault, and rape on a per victim basis is somewhat arbitrary. As long as the guidelines are followed, however, they provide a certain amount of internal consistency in the rates of crime for various offenses, although they introduce a certain lack of comparability between rates of crime calculated on a per event basis and those calculated on a per victim basis.

One other consequence of this counting procedure should be noted. The pattern of recording each victimization as a separate crime for murder, rape, and assault insures that crime rates for these offenses always reflect the maximum number of possible victims. Since the counting procedures for larceny and robbery can include more than one individual victim per event, the rates for these crimes will always be lower than if they were counted on the basis of individual victims rather than events.

In compiling the Uniform Crime Reports the FBI divides crimes into *Part I crimes* and *Part II crimes*. (see Table 10.1.) Part I crimes are those considered to be serious felony offenses and include murder, voluntary manslaughter, rape, robbery, assault, burglary, larceny-theft, motor-vehicle theft, and arson. All other offenses, whether felony or misdemeanor, are classified as Part II offenses.

Table 10.1 **Crimes Reported by the FBI**

Part I Crimes	*Part II Crimes*
Murder	Other assaults
Forcible rape	Forgery and counterfeiting
Robbery	Fraud
Aggravated assault	Embezzlement
Burglary	Stolen property; buying, receiving, etc.
Larceny-theft	Vandalism
Motor-vehicle theft	Weapons, carrying, possessing
Arson	Prostitution and vice
	Sex offenses (except rape and prostitution)
	Drug abuse violations
	Gambling
	Offenses against family and children
	Driving under influence
	Liquor laws
	Drunkenness
	Disorderly conduct
	Vagrancy
	All other offenses (except traffic)
	Curfew and loitering law violations

The Part I crimes, also known as the Crime Index Offenses, are used by the FBI to calculate crime rates. A *crime rate* is a measure of the amount of crime occurring per a given unit of population. The FBI calculates crime rates on the basis of the number of crimes for every 100,000 people. In 1979, for example, the FBI reports that there was an estimated 466,881 robberies in the United States.[15] It also estimated the population of the United States to be 220,226,886 during that year. The rate for robbery was then calculated as follows:

$$\frac{466,881}{220,226,886} = .00212 \times 100,000 = 212.1 \text{ per } 100,000$$

These rates are calculated for each of the eight Index Offenses as well as for all the Index Offenses combined and for violent crimes and property crimes. (See Table 10.2.)

By balancing the amount of crime against the population, crime *rates* attempt to provide an assessment of how widespread are certain crimes or crime in general. By contrast, the numerical totals for various crimes measure only how many crimes occur but do not provide any information about the relative frequency of criminal victimization within the population. Furthermore, numerical totals do not provide an accurate basis on which to compare differences in the amount of crime either over time or between places. In 1970, for example, there were 349,860 robberies reported in the United States. By 1979 the number of reported robberies had increased to 466,880. Using these raw totals it would appear that robbery had increased by *33 percent* between 1970 and 1979. However, during those years the population had grown from approximately 203 million to 220 million, yielding a robbery rate of 172.1 per 100,000 in 1970 and 212.1 per 100,000 in 1979, an increase of 23 percent.[16] This latter figure, because it is adjusted for changes in population size, provides a more accurate assessment of increase in robbery between 1970 and 1979. Similarly, only if crime totals are converted to crime rates can we

Table 10.2 **Number and Rate of Index Offenses Reported by the FBI for 1982**

Type of Offense	Number of Offenses	Rate per 100,000
Murder and nonnegligent manslaughter	21,010	9.1
Forcible rape	77,760	33.6
Robbery	536,890	231.9
Aggravated assault	650,040	280.8
Total Violent	1,285,710	555.3
Burglary	3,415,500	1,475.2
Larceny	7,107,700	3,069.8
Motor-vehicle theft	1,048,300	452.8
Total Property	11,571,500	4,997.8

Source: Federal Bureau of Investigation, *Crime in the United States, 1982* (Washington, D.C.: Government Printing Office, 1983), 40.

compare victimization frequencies between cities, towns, or other areas with varying populations.

While calculated rates provide a standardized way of measuring the frequency of crimes, they are based on the assumption that all individuals in the population are equally likely to be the victim of the crime considered. This assumption is inaccurate and leads to crime rates that overestimate the likelihood of victimization for some and underestimate its likelihood for others. In 1978, for example, black males were *7 times more likely* to be the victim of an armed robbery committed by a stranger than were white females and *2.4 times more likely* than white males.[17] There are likewise differences in rates of victimization by age and income for various Index Offenses.[18]

A similar problem is posed by multiple victimizations. Some individuals, such as those living in a neighborhood that has high rates of drug addiction and its attendant crimes, are situated so that their personal rate of victimization is very high, while other people may be wholly isolated from the risk of victimization by living in exclusive suburban communities complete with security forces, checkpoint entrances, and patrolled perimeters. Multiple victimization may contribute substantially to inflating the *apparent average* rate of victimization for the population as a whole.[19]

The variability of risk for different categories of individuals and patterns of multiple victimization can create a general fear of crime that for many individuals exceeds the actual likelihood of becoming a crime victim. Poor Americans and black Americans, for example, tend more often to be the victims of violent crimes such as murder, rape, and robbery. However, when crime rates are calculated their higher rates of victimization are diffused throughout the population, often creating a sense of high crime risk among white, affluent Americans as well. By overestimating the probability of victimization for most Americans, crime rates tend to maintain high levels of general fear of conventional crime that in turn diverts attention from the crimes by the more powerful in the context of business, the professions, and politics.

How Reliable are Police Statistics?

The reliability of police-generated statistics about crime has been questioned ever since they were first used to analyze patterns of crime. The central problem effecting the reliability of police statistics is the existence of what has been called "the dark number." This "dark number" represents the unknown difference between the number of crimes *recorded* by the police and the number of crimes *actually occurring* in the society. Today, warnings against interpreting police crime statistics as a true measure of crime are commonplace in criminology texts. For example, we are told

> Using official statistics on crime to measure incidence of criminality is a questionable practice.[20]

> These statistics ("crimes known to the police") are an inadequate measure of the true crime rate.[21]

> Crime statistics are the most unreliable and questionable social facts.[22]

Despite these criticisms, official police statistics are held by many criminologists to be the best source of information about crime among those available; that is, they are "probably the best way out of a bad situation."[23] Or, as another criminologist said, "although these statistics do not represent the total volume of crimes, they are the best source of statistics on crime."[24] This acceptance of official police statistics is based on the recognition that most other sources of crime data are liable to provide an even *more* inaccurate picture of the crime rate than police statistics.

The journey from criminal event to criminal statistic is long and labyrinthian. Every step leading to a crime statistic provides certain opportunities for a crime not to appear as final statistics. Not all crimes known to the police lead to an arrest; in fact, many do not. Thus arrest statistics would presumably provide less accurate data concerning rates of crime than would statistics on crimes known to the police. Similarly, since only a small proportion of those arrested are ever incarcerated, prisoner statistics would be a less reliable measure of crime rates than would arrest statistics.

In 1931 Thorsten Sellin summarized this tendency in the proposition that *the value of a statistic for purposes of estimating crime rates decreases as the distance from the crime itself in terms of procedure increases.*[25] This dictum has become the central defense in the use of police statistics on "crimes known" as the basic measure of crime in America.

In recent years there has been an attempt to narrow the distance between criminal events and criminal statistics through the usage of victimization surveys. These surveys ask representative samples of the American population to indicate what crimes they have experienced during a specific period of time. From these survey responses it is possible to estimate the rates of victimization among the general public.[26] While this procedure reduces the number of institutional steps between criminal events and criminal statistics, it also introduces its own possible sources of error such as failure of victims to remember certain events or to remember them inaccurately.[27]

Official statistics on crimes known to the police are subject to a number of sources of possible error. These sources of error fall into two groups, technical sources of error and political sources of error. Technical sources of error arise as the result of problems inherent in the process of gathering crime data. Political sources of error result from deliberate decisions to manipulate crime data to meet certain ends, such as inflating crime rates to justify larger budget requests for crime control or deflating them to demonstrate that last year's appropriations were well spent.

There are five key points in the process leading to police statistics on crimes known at which errors, some technical and some political, can arise. These are the five Rs of recognition, reporting, responding, recording and reclassification.

Problems of Recognition.   Not all events in violation of the law are recognized by someone as a crime. Individuals may attribute the consequences of a criminal act to some other source. For instance, someone may think his or her wallet was lost when in fact it had been stolen. Conversely, some individuals may think a crime has occurred although the presumed criminal consequence was due to some other cause—a wallet presumed stolen may in fact have been lost. In this latter case, police investigation may provide some check on the accuracy of the individual's claim. However, there is no way of identifying those circumstances that are never recognized by anyone as a crime.

Problems in Reporting.   The most significant contribution to the "dark number" of crime statistics is the large number of crimes that individuals recognize but do not report to the police. The National Crime Survey conducted for the Department of Justice by the Bureau of the Census estimates that only 44 percent of all crimes against persons or property were reported to the police in 1978.[28] As Table 10.3 shows, rates of reporting vary substantially according to the type of crime. Reporting tends to be highest for crimes of violence such as rape and robbery and for property crimes where insurance claims may be involved such as burglary and auto theft. Other forms of theft are reported at a lower rate. However, even in cases where the rate of reporting is relatively high, seldom does it reach much beyond 50 percent.[29]

Victimization surveys have also sought to identify the reasons why victims *do not* report crimes to the police. The findings indicate that the most common reason for failure to report a crime was the feeling that police could not do anything about it. In 1976, 29.7 percent of all those who failed to report a violent crime and 35.7 percent of those who failed to report a property crime gave this as their reason. The next most commonly mentioned reason was the feeling that the incident was not important enough to call the police. In 1976 this reason accounted for 25.9 percent of the nonreports in cases of violent crime and 29.7 percent of the nonreports for property crimes. Together these two factors accounted for approximately 60 percent of all unreported crime identified by the 1976 victimization survey. Other common reasons given for nonreporting were that the police would not want to be bothered or that it was too inconvenient or time-consuming to report. In the case of interpersonal crimes such as assault, rape, and robbery two other reasons were given: the incident was a personal matter or the victim feared reprisal.[30]

If rates of reporting were *consistent across time and place* for various crimes, while it might lead to underestimates of the amount of crime, accurate comparisons of differences in crime rates between places or over time would be possible. Unfortunately, they are not consistent. Rates of reporting differ from one jurisdiction to another and also vary from year to year. From 1976 to 1977, for instance, the rate of reporting rape increased by 5.7 percent, from 52.7 percent to 58.4 percent.[31] Consider the consequences of this change if the *actual* number of rapes had remained the same. If there were, for sake of argument, 150,000 rapes in each year, *the increase in reporting alone* would lead to crime statistics showing 8,550 *more* rapes in 1977 than 1976, even though there had been no change in the actual number of rapes. If a rate of rape was calculated for each year for a population of approximately 112 million women, the increased *reporting* of rape would appear as a rise in the rate of rape from 70.6 per 100,000 in 1976 to 78.2 in 1977—an increase of nearly 11

Table 10.3 **Personal, Household, and Commercial Crimes: Percent of Victimizations Reported to the Police by Type of Crime in 1976**

Type of Crime	Percent
Crimes of violence	48.8
Rape	52.7
Robbery	53.3
Robbery with injury	62.9
From serious assault	66.2
From minor assault	59.9
Robbery without injury	48.6
Assault	47.5
Aggravated assault	58.4
With injury	62.0
Attempted assault with weapon	56.5
Simple assault	40.6
With injury	45.7
Attempted assault without weapon	38.8
Crimes of theft	26.6
Personal larceny without contact	26.3
Personal larceny with contact	36.2
Household crimes	38.3
Burglary	48.1
Forcible entry	70.1
Unlawful entry without force	38.8
Attempted forcible entry	33.1
Household larceny	27.0
Completed larceny[1]	27.1
Less than $50	15.0
$50 or more	52.5
Attempted larceny	26.5
Motor-vehicle theft	69.5
Completed theft	88.6
Attempted theft	38.9
Commercial Crimes	74.6
Burglary	72.5
Robbery	86.6

[1]Includes data, not shown separately, on larcenies for which the value of loss was not ascertained.

Source: U.S. Department of Justice, *Criminal Victimization in the United States, 1976* (Washington, D.C.: Government Printing Office, 1976), 82, Table 92.

percent. If according to the Uniform Crime Reports the rate of rape increased by 11 percent from one year to the next, this would be reported by the FBI and the news media as a significant increase in that particular crime when in fact no change had occurred at all. Annual fluctuations in rates of reporting occur for most crimes and require caution when assessing FBI announcements that crimes have increased or decreased from one year to the next. Similar variations in rates of reporting also exist from police jurisdiction to jurisdiction, making any judgment based solely on official police statistics that one city has a lower or higher crime rate than another difficult to assess.

While errors in police statistics caused by the nonreporting of crimes is generally technical in nature, police departments can to some extent also influence the likelihood that individuals will report crimes to them. Departments that develop a reputation among the poor or the nonwhite as not being particularly responsive to their calls for police services may depress the rate of reporting crimes among these groups. Conversely, a department that establishes a program to increase minority-group reporting or creates a special program such as an all-women rape response squad may increase crime reporting and therefore the apparent rate of crime in that city. This places many police departments in a dilemma. Those things that would improve police–public relations and hence arrest rates due to increased public willingness to provide information may also increase reporting. This apparent rise in rates of crime could then be taken as a measure of police department *failure* to control crime. It is reasonable to assume that at least some police administrators are aware of this dilemma and take it into consideration when evaluating programs that may increase the rate of crime reporting. Increased reporting and its attendant increase in the crime rate may be a useful tactic to demonstrate the need for increased funding for a police department. It may also be disastrous for the police chief already under heavy criticism for being ineffective in controlling crime.

Problems in Responding.   Not all crimes reported to the police become crime statistics. In some cases the police department may not respond to the citizen report. One study indicated that only 77 percent of the calls for service coming into a police department actually led to a response.[32] To the extent that this rate of response fluctuates from year to year and between departments, it can introduce inaccuracies in the comparison of crime rates similar to those resulting from nonreporting by citizens. While victimization studies have provided some information on rates of citizen nonreporting, we have little in the way of similar data concerning police nonresponse. One local victimization study, however, did find that on the average the rate of crime indicated by official police statistics was 8 percent lower than what would be predicted from the number of respondents who indicated they *had reported* crimes to the police.[33]

Recording and Reclassification.   The process of actually recording crimes occurs at three levels. First, there is an initial determination by the responding officers whether a crime occurred and if so, what crime. Second, the report by the investigating officers must be recorded by either the central police administration or in some cases first by a precinct captain and then by the central administration. Finally, before a crime enters the national FBI crime reports it must be transmitted to the FBI and recorded at that level. At each of these stages, there exists opportunities for both technical and politically induced errors.

Technical errors in recording the reported crime may arise simply from incorrect assessments on the part of the responding officers. Reports of crimes that actually occurred may be held "unfounded" by the police and never enter into the body of crime statistics. When investigating officers acknowledge a crime as having occurred, they may at times affix a legal label to the event that does not best indicate what actually happened. A rape or an attempted rape may be defined as an assault, an attempted burglary as vandalism, a planned and paid-for arson as malicious mischief, or an argument over money as an attempted robbery. Such misjudgments may result from inaccurate or inadequate information provided to an investigating officer or from the officer's own inclination to mistrust the complainant.

The dismissal of certain complaints as unfounded may also reflect more systematic bias on the part of police. Assessments that poor or minority complainants are more often "cranks" or unreliable come easily in a society where racial and social class bias is an established component of the culture.

Inaccuracies in recording crimes may also reflect *systematic policies* on the part of the police administration. Crime statistics are important tools in the measurement of police performance. Increases or decreases in crime rates and rates of arrest are the central measures of a department's effectiveness and as such provide significant temptation for manipulation.

Crime statistics can be manipulated in several ways to meet a department's political ends. First, the department may establish policies favorable to the department's goals, governing how investigating officers should classify certain offenses. Investigating officers may be instructed to downgrade certain offenses, such as recording a breaking and entering where little or nothing of value was taken as malicious destruction of property or classifying attempted rapes or rapes not involving injury to the victim as assaults. Not all policies are necessarily aimed at reducing the apparent rate of serious crimes. A department seeking to increase its funding or obtain money for a particular crime prevention program may manipulate crime data upward to demonstrate the need for additional manpower or equipment. Burglary statistics may be inflated by describing any theft from a van or camper involving forced entry as a burglary rather than a larceny from vehicle. Similarly, if a department decides it needs additional funding for a "war" on violent crime, it may for example require that all purse snatchings be recorded as assaults rather than larcenies.

Second, once investigating officers have classified an offense, it is recorded and possibly reclassified at the departmental level. Here similar manipulations can occur. One study found that in 1950 the New York City police department recorded about half the number of property crimes as had been reported to insurance agencies.[34] This apparently reflected an official policy of deflating crime statistics. As one New York officer at that time commented,

> The unwritten law was that you were supposed to make things look good. . . .
> I know captains who actually lost their commands because they turned in honest reports.[35]

A similar pattern of underrecording known crimes was found to still exist in

New York City in 1966.[36] In another study Donald Black found that overall only 72 percent of suspected felonies and 53 percent of suspected misdemeanors were recorded by police departments of Boston, Chicago, and Washington, D.C.[37] In addition to indicating that the crime rate is lower than it in fact is, underrecording known crimes improves a police department's record regarding the proportion of known crimes cleared by arrest. According to political scientist David Seidman police in Washington, D.C., "tend not to even record crime they believe they have little or no chance of solving."[38]

In addition to the overt manipulation of statistics to advance organizational interests, the process of recording or reclassifying crime reports makes possible numerous technical errors. The mere logistics of recording investigating officers' reports, compiling these records into monthly crime statistics, and transferring these statistics to the FBI introduces opportunities for clerical errors. Furthermore, because police departments do not always share the same classification procedures, aggregating statistics from individual departments into national figures can lead to noncomparable offenses being placed in similar categories.

NOTES

1. John Conklin, *Illegal But Not Criminal* (Englewood Cliffs, N. J.: Prentice Hall, 1977), 32.
2. Edwin Sutherland, *White Collar Crime* (New York: Holt, Rinehart and Winston, 1949), 9.
3. See Fredrick L. Bates, "A Conceptual Analysis of Group Structure," *Social Forces*, 36, no. 2 (December 1957), 104–105; Paul Bohannan, *Social Anthropology* (New York: Holt, Rinehart and Winston, 1963), 17; and Peter M. Blau, *Exchange and Power in Social Life* (New York: Wiley, 1967), 104–105 for descriptions of the reciprocal nature of role relationships.
4. See George Vold, *Theoretical Criminology* (New York: Oxford University Press, 1958), 162–165; also Michel Foucault, *The Order of Things* (New York: Vintage Books, 1973), chapter 5, "Classifying," 125–165.
5. David L. Sallach, "Class Domination and Ideological Hegemony," *Sociological Quarterly*, 15 (Winter 1974): 38–50.
6. Harvey Molotch and Marylyn Lester, "News as Purposive Behavior: On the Strategic Use of Routine Events, Accidents and Scandals," *American Sociological Review*, 39 (February 1974): 101–112.
7. David Halberstam, *The Powers That Be* (New York: Dell Books, 1979).
8. The Administrative Office of the Courts annually reports a variety of information on legal actions involving business wrongdoing—see *Report of the Director: Administrative Office of the Courts* (Washington, D.C.: Government Printing Office, 1978). This includes only those incidents that result in actual litigation. This document also is not given wide circulation.
9. Federal Bureau of Investigation, *Crime in the United States, 1979* (Washington, D.C.: Government Printing Office, 1980), 37.
10. The FBI estimate of 67 rapes per 100,000 women (FBI, *Crime in the United States, 1979*, 14) yields a risk ratio of 1,492.5 to 1.

11. The FBI estimate of 212.1 robberies per 100,000 persons (Ibid.) yields a risk ratio of 471.5 to 1.
12. Ibid., 1.
13. Ibid., 3.
14. Federal Bureau of Investigation, "Uniform Crime Reporting," in Simon Dinitz and Walter C. Reckless, eds., *Critical Issues in the Study of Crime: A Book of Readings* (Boston: Little, Brown, 1968), 63–82.
15. FBI, *Crime in the United States*, 16.
16. Calculated from data on crime trends 1970 to 1979, presented in Ibid., 41.
17. U.S. Department of Justice, *Criminal Victimization in the United States: 1973–1978 Trends.* (Washington, D.C.: Government Printing Office, 1980), 4.
18. U.S. Department of Justice, *Criminal Victimization in the United States, 1976* (Washington, D.C.: Government Printing Office, 1976), 31, 36; U.S. Department of Justice, 1973–1978 Trends, 5.
19. Albert J. Reiss, Jr., "Victim Proneness in Repeat Victimization by Type of Crime," in Albert J. Reiss and Stephen Fienberg, eds., *Indicators of Crime and Criminal Justice: Quantitative Studies* (Washington, D.C.: U.S. Department of Justice, Government Printing Office, 1980), 41–53.
20. Richard Quinney, *Criminology*, 2d. ed. (Boston: Little, Brown, 1979), 63.
21. Edwin Sutherland and Donald Cressey, *Criminology*, 9th ed. (New York: Lippincott, 1974), 25.
22. Donald C. Gibbons, *Society, Crime and Criminal Careers.* (Englewood Cliffs, N.J.: Prentice-Hall, 1973), 100.
23. Sue Titus Reid, *Crime and Criminology* (Hinsdale, Ill.: Dryden, 1976), 48.
24. Sutherland and Cressey, *Criminology*, 25.
25. Thorsten Sellen, "The Basis of a Crime Index," *Journal of Criminal Law and Criminology*, 22 (September 1931): 346.
26. Albert D. Biderman, "Surveys of Population Samples for Estimating Crime Incidence," *Annals of the American Academy of Political and Social Science*, 374 (November 1967): 16–33.
27. Stephen E. Fienberg, "Victimization and the National Crime Survey: Problems of Design and Analysis," in Reiss and Fienberg, *Indicators of Crime and Criminal Justice*, 36.
28. U.S. Department of Justice, 1980, p. 22.
29. Ibid., p. 22, Table 15; U.S. Department of Justice 1976, p. 82, Table 92.
30. U.S. Department of Justice, *Criminal Victimization: 1973–1978 Trends*, 86, Table 101.
31. U.S. Department of Justice, *Criminal Victimization in the United States, 1976*: 24.
32. Thomas Bercal, "Calls for police assistance," *American Behavioral Scientist*, 13 (1970): 682.
33. Raymond J. Michalowski and John G. Hayes, *Citizen Victimization and Satisfaction with Police Services* (Charlotte, N.C.: City Office of Budget and Evaluation, 1976).
34. Daniel Bell, *The End of Ideology* (New York: Free Press, 1960).
35. Quoted in Fred J. Cook, "There's Always a Crime Wave," in Donald R. Cressey, ed., *Crime and Criminal Justice* (Chicago: Quadrangle Books, 1971), 27.
36. Marvin E. Wolfgang, *Crimes of Violence: Report to the President's Commission on Law Enforcement and the Administration of Justice* (Washington, D.C.: Government Printing Office, 1967), 33.
37. Donald J. Black, "Production of Crime Rates," *American Sociological Review*, 35 (1970), 746.
38. David Seidman, in "Street Crime; Who's Winning?" *Time*, 23 October 1972, 55.

CHAPTER 11

Crimes of the Powerless: Offenses Against Persons, Property, and Public Order

Introduction

This chapter examines the patterns of common crime in America today. *Common crimes are acts punishable under criminal law that can be committed by almost anyone regardless of social position.* This does not mean that all individuals have either identical opportunities or motives to commit common crimes. It means that common crimes are those offenses that constitute a violation of one or more of the obligations common to all individuals under state jurisdiction.

Common crime can be subdivided into three general categories: (1) interpersonal crimes of violence, (2) crimes for profit, and (3) public order crimes. Each category is somewhat differently related to society and the state. Interpersonal violence and crimes for profit clearly cause harm to their victims. Similarly, while public order crimes such as prostitution, drug abuse, and gambling are sometimes termed "victimless" crimes, they often have negative consequences for the consumer or provider of the illicit service.[1] However, the specific harm crimes cause individuals is not the key determinant of the state's response to these behaviors. It is the particular impact that acts have upon either the power of the state or the political economy in general that is the fundamental determinant of whether or not they will be defined as crimes by the state.

Acts of interpersonal violence are threats to the political state on two accounts. First, they challenge indirectly the state's exclusive political right to authorize violence. Second, they bring into question the validity of the state's promise that it will insure social peace for its citizens. From the social contract writers of the eighteenth century to the present, the promise that the state will insure social peace has been the most basic argument offered for the legitimacy of state power over the lives of individuals.[2]

Violations of property rights as they are defined in a particular society threaten both the basic economic order and the distribution of power that arises from it and will therefore be criminalized. It is not the *amount* of harm such acts cause individual citizens that lies at the root of their criminalization; it is their impact upon the established distribution of property and power. Acts that cause individuals serious harm will often go uncriminalized as long as they are in accordance with the established rules of property while acts in violation of those rules, even where less direct harm is caused, will usually be the target of state control. Thus, in America, for example, it is not a crime for a mortgage-holding bank to evict a family from a home on which they have been unable to make payments. It is a crime, however, for a homeless family to move into an empty house owned by the bank.

The kinds of behaviors that become public order crimes do not usually pose *direct* threats to either the state or the political economy. The enforcement of traffic laws, for instance, represents essentially technical mechanisms for maintaining orderly and safe patterns of travel rather than direct attempts to insure state legitimacy or protect economic interests, although in the long run they contribute to both. Other public order laws such as those prohibiting prostitution, drug abuse, and gambling have a more complex relationship to the political economy and state legitimacy. Some arose as an attempt to enforce certain general concepts of morality that were consistent both with needs of a capitalist economy and the value system of certain social groups. Others, particularly in the case of drug usage, were related to the control of specific minorities because they were perceived as threats to either economic stability or Anglo-Saxon cultural dominance.

Common crimes represent a selective criminalization of certain harmful behaviors in accordance with some consciousness of right and wrong as it has been reflected within the political state. What that consciousness is and how it has been reflected through the political state will in turn be a product of the underlying economic and political dynamics of the society. As we saw in earlier chapters, in America these are the dynamics of a capitalist mode of production and a liberal democratic state.

A Caution

The following discussion of violent crime, property crime, and public order crimes utilizes both official police statistics and those derived from unofficial procedures such as victimization and self-reporting studies. Utilizing both sources of data in combination provides the best opportunity for understanding the extent of common crime in America. However, it is only the best among a variety of bad alternatives. Thus the data presented should be seen as only an *approximation* of the extent of common crime in America, not an exact description of it.

INTERPERSONAL CRIMES OF VIOLENCE
The Nature of Violence

Human violence comes in many forms. Violence can be as limited as one individual's striking another or as sweeping as the death and destruction caused by war. In the broadest sense *human violence is any act, event, or condition resulting from human behavior that causes death, injury, or some other damage to the physical or psychological well-being of one or more individuals.* When Americans think of violence, particularly criminal violence, the image that most often occurs is of some evil-minded person who intends, and probably enjoys, bringing harm to others. Western legal thought and practice has so closely linked crime to intent or *mens rea* that it is often difficult for us to conceptualize forms of violence other than those such as murder, rape, or assault that we feel are linked to some form of guilty intent. More importantly, the focus on specific intent to do violence makes it difficult to recognize the gravity of other forms of violence less obviously linked to "evil" intentions.

In general we can distinguish several distinct varieties of human violence: interpersonal violence, organized violence, systemic violence, and state violence. The first two fit the Western conception of criminal violence and are the focus of this chapter. The latter two, which pose equal if not graver threats to human well-being, will be discussed in the following chapters. Before discussing common criminal violence in America it is useful to look at the differences between the various forms of human violence.

Interpersonal violence consists of acts of violence arising from face-to-face interactions. This form of violence is seldom preplanned. It most often occurs in the context of a deteriorating set of interactions and is usually reactive or expressive rather than calculatingly instrumental.[3] The argument or dispute that leads to a fistfight, a knifing, or a shooting is the archetypal case of interpersonal violence. Most violence associated with the commission of other common crimes is also situational. Injuries or deaths resulting from crimes such as burglaries, robberies, or rapes result most commonly from a hostile escalation of the initial confrontation rather than from a preexisting intention to cause physical harm to someone.

Interpersonal violence is the most basic, although far from the most extensive, form of human violence. It is the only form of violence that can be found with few exceptions in every form of human society from the least to the most complex. Because it is the most basic form of violence, interpersonal violence is often mistaken for the most significant form of human violence, although in terms of the amount of harm caused it is in fact the least significant form.

Organized violence is characterized by preplanned acts of violence committed by one or more individuals acting on their own initiative to resolve a problem, achieve a goal, or make a public statement. Unlike interpersonal violence, organized violence is characteristically instrumental, that is, a means to an end rather than a purely personal expression of hostility toward a particular individual. Individuals involved in organized violence can be seen as acting on their own initiative insofar as their activities are not directly part of or connected to some established and legitimate institutional arrangement. Organized violence ranges from gang warfare to terrorism. In most, although not all, instances the target of organized violence is relatively impersonal and in some cases symbolic. An attack by one street gang upon another generally arises out of a conflict between the gangs as entities themselves struggling for dominance over particular "turf" rather than personal disputes between specific individuals.[4] Likewise the assassination of former Italian premier Aldo Moro by the Red Brigade represented an attack on a *symbol* of established economic and political power rather than an interpersonally motivated act of violence.[5] Gangland killings arising from disputes over territory or related to struggles for power within crime syndicates represent another type of organized violence, as do conflicts between various unofficial partisan groups such as attacks on antinuclear demonstrators by nuclear power construction workers.

Systemic violence refers to the violent outcomes of established institutional arrangements. It is generally not intentional but is instead the by-product of institutional arrangements that *are* intentional. In the United States, for example, economic and social inequality means that poorer Americans live in generally less safe, less healthy environments than the more affluent and consequently are more frequently the victims of both accidents and disease, resulting in lowered life expectancy.[6] While no one may specifically intend that poor Americans die younger than the more affluent, the political-economic system that grants less life to the poor than the affluent *is intended.* However, because the connection between the intention and the violent consequence is a distant and complex one it is possible to support existing economic arrangements without ever recognizing their long-term consequences.

State violence encompasses all forms of politically authorized violence. Interpersonal violence and organized violence are in most instances illegitimate; that is, they are usually at least officially prohibited by political authority. Systemic violence, while seldom illegal, is seldom specifically authorized. State violence, on the other hand, has the formal and official sanction of the state and in many instances is seen as a positive attribute within the society rather than a negative one.[7]

State violence arises from the police and military powers of governments. The authority of police to physically subdue criminal suspects, forcefully disband illegal, unruly, or otherwise offensive gatherings, and forcefully act against illegitimate violence are all varieties of state violence. Foreign military activity as well as the domestic repression of dissidents or revolutionaries through police or military action are also forms of state violence. As previously discussed, political states reserve to themselves the sole right to determine when violence is legitimate. The fact that state violence is "legal" within any given political context, however, should not tempt us to overlook the fact that it is nonetheless violence.

The Consequences of Violence

In terms of the amount of death and misery caused, systemic violence and state violence together have far outstripped interpersonal and organized violence over the broad sweep of human history. However, because the reality of systemic violence is hidden from our view by a complex causal chain of events and because state violence is perceived as both legitimate and necessary, most people see violent crime as the major source of violence in America. This awareness of violent crime and the fear it brings has substantial consequences for the way people lead their lives. National Crime Panel surveys in thirteen American cities found that 46 percent of the respondents felt unsafe being out in their neighborhoods alone at night, and 49 percent had altered their activities in the last few years from fear of crime.[8] In the early 1980s there emerged a substantial increase in the ownership of handguns kept for personal protection.[9] (This in itself is likely to produce an increase in the amount of death and injury due to gunshot wounds.) Real or perceived increases in the risk of falling victim to a violent crime exert other destructive effects on social life. Individuals tend to become more suspicious and fearful of strangers. This type of paralyzing fear, criminologist John Conklin suggests, can lead to a breakdown or a weakening of community solidarity, making organized community responses to an increase in criminal violence difficult.[10] Increases in criminal violence also have a disastrous impact on race relations. While most violence occurs between individuals of similar racial and social class backgrounds, a few widely reported interracial crimes can "drive a wedge between disadvantaged blacks and other minorities who provide a disproportionate share of the prison population and middle-class whites who in fear set themselves up in enclaves."[11] The identification of blacks and minorities in the minds of white Americans as the primary source of criminal violence tends to weaken political support for programs and legislation aimed at improving the conditions of oppressed minorities.

High rates of criminal violence also exert an impact upon political processes in general. Since the 1960s fighting crime has been an important theme in most presidential campaigns and a part of presidential policy after election. This focus on conventional forms of criminal violence, while to some degree a response to public fear, can also serve both to generate additional fear by giving crime prominence and diverting public attention from other concerns. In the early 1980s, for instance, the Federal government, citing increased public fear of crime, increased funding for the control of common crime, and decreased it for the anti-white-collar crime program initiated under the Carter administration.[12]

Murder

Murder is probably the most dramatic and most feared of all violent crimes. It is one of the few crimes whose consequences can never be undone. The Uniform Crime Reports defines murder as "the willful killing of one human being by another" and lists such offenses under the category of "Murder and Nonnegligent Manslaughter." Because victimization surveys are out of the question where murder is concerned, homicide data are primarily limited to police statistics. Such data, however, are more accurate for homicide than any other offense. All known deaths require the issuance of a death certificate indicating cause of death. While it is likely that some "missing" individuals are probably the victims of murder and some killings are mistakenly identified by coroners or medical examiners as due to accident or natural causes, the official scrutiny given all deaths makes homicide one of the more difficult crimes to conceal.[13] Furthermore, homicide figures are less prone to errors based on nonreporting than any other crime.

Extent of Homicide. In 1982 the FBI recorded 21,012 homicides. This constituted a rate of approximately 9.1 homicides per 100,000 persons.[14] While murder is the most serious of violent interpersonal crimes it is also the least common. In 1982 homicide accounted for 1.6 percent of all serious violent crimes listed by the FBI and slightly less than 0.2 percent of all serious personal and property crimes combined.[15]

America's homicide rate is among the highest in the world, and it is *the* highest among the industrialized nations of the Western world. In 1983 the United Nations listed the United States as having the seventh highest rate of violent death (excluding traffic deaths) in the world. All those nations with higher rates of violent death were less developed or Third World countries in Africa, Latin America, and South America. Furthermore, according to the UN the rate of violent death in America was more than double that of any other developed country.[16]

Trends. As the population of the country has grown, so has the number of murders, as might be expected. More disturbing is the fact that the *rate* of homicide has also shown a steady growth since the 1960s. Between 1968 and 1982 the homicide rate rose from 6.9 to 9.0 per 100,000, an increase of 30 percent.[17] This steady growth in murder, while grim, does not mean that the United States is more violent now than it has ever been or that we are experiencing an unprecedented breakdown of respect for law, as politicians sometimes claim. Despite periodic fluctuations, the rate of homicide in America has remained relatively constant between 1933, when national crime statistics were first gathered, and the 1980s. The current growth in murder rates represents an increase over the rates of the late 1940s and 1950s, which themselves had represented a substantial *decrease* in homicide compared with the 1930s.[18] The lower rates in the 1940s and 1950s to some extent reflect shifts in the age and sex structure of the American population due to lowered birth rates during the Depression and the reduction in the resident male population during World War II. The climb back to murder rates similar to those of the 1930s may represent not so much a decline of law and order but a return to demographic, economic, and social conditions more similar to those of the 1930s.

Ecological and Geographic Distribution. Homicide rates vary by city size and region. In 1982 metropolitan areas (cities with populations of 250,000 or more) recorded an overall homicide rate of 10 per 100,000. By comparison, rural areas and other cities had murder rates of 6.6 and 5.9 per 100,000 respectively.[19]

Murder rates have been consistently higher in the southern states than any other region of the country. In 1982 the southern states contained 34 percent of the nation's population but accounted for 45 percent of the murders.

While the northeastern and north central states had homicide rates of 7.4 and 6.5 respectively, the southern states recorded 12.1 murders per 100,000. Next were the western states, with a rate of 9.0 murders per 100,000.[20]

In 1967 criminologists Marvin Wolfgang and Franco Ferracutti proposed that the higher rates of violent crime in the south were the result of a "subculture of violence," that is, a social climate where violence is a more accepted form of problem resolution and where individuals are consequently more prepared to resort to violence in difficult social situations.[21] In 1971 another criminologist utilized what he termed an "index of southernness" to lend support to the subculture of violence thesis by showing that the more heavily states had been influenced by migration from the south, the higher were their rates of violence.[22] The subculture of violence hypothesis is more descriptive than explanatory in a sociological sense, however. It is focused primarily upon the social-psychological consequences of living in a "subculture of violence" and how this would lead to more frequent violent behavior than upon *why* such a subculture arose in the first place.

If we place the higher rates of southern violence in a historic context, the existence of a "subculture of violence" in the south begins to make sense. Based upon a slave mode of production, survival of the early southern economy necessitated the frequent and often gratuitous use of violence against slaves to forestall rebellion, resistance, and escape. This participation in, and condoning of, violence by the socially and economically dominant slave-owners had the effect of *legitimizing violence* as an appropriate form of response to difficulty, for in all historical periods the dominant cultural ideas tend to be the ideas of the dominant classes. Once widespread violence is established within a culture as a legitimate form of problem resolution it is difficult to contain it within the specific context that provided its initial justification— in this case slavery—and so violence in itself becomes widespread.

Compared with the industrializing north the south was also relatively poor before the Civil War and desperately so afterward. Poverty of itself does not necessarily generate violence. However, where it is the product of inequality and exploitation the potential for violence is increased. The exploitation of southern production by the north after the Civil War and the efforts of the southern establishment to reassert the dominance over the labor force it lost with the demise of slavery generated a brutally competitive and repressive social and economic environment that was not tempered by the ethnic and labor solidarity more common in northern areas. Within this context violence continued to reign as a favored tool of the powerful, continuing its legitimation.[23] Furthermore, competition for scarce resources and jobs intensified racial divisions within the working class, providing a basis for white working class support of violence against blacks. Lastly, the relative poverty of the south in comparison with the industrial north has contributed to creating a social environment where the ability and readiness to resort to violence serves as a substitute mark of manly virtue where the other primary mark of male accomplishment in America—economic success—is (or at least until recently, has been) difficult to achieve.

Circumstances.   Most murders result from disagreements between persons who know one another over what is often described as relatively trivial matters, although they were apparently not trivial to those involved.[24] In 1982 the FBI indicated that approximately 40 percent of all murders resulted from arguments of one sort or another.[25] Probably at least half the 36 percent of homicides for which the motive is unknown or unspecified also arise from similar circumstances. Quarrels over money, infidelity, family relations, and a variety of other concerns are the most common *immediate* causes of fatal arguments. However, the social relationships culminating in murder are often characterized by longstanding patterns of tension, hostility, or argument. In many instances the immediate disagreements serve only as the final focus for the release of preexisting hostility, such as the wife long angered by her husband's gambling who stabs him in an argument over whether or not she is spending too much money on food.

Where murder is but the final act in a deteriorating set of social interactions, the victim as well as the murderer often contributes to the escalation of hostility that eventually leads to a killing. Not only may victims contribute to growing hostility but in some instances may precipitate their own deaths by initiating open violence. One study found that approximately 25 percent of homicide victims in Philadelphia instigated their own death by starting a fight or being the first to show a deadly weapon such as a gun or knife.[26]

Not all homicides result from personal arguments. Some (approximately 18 percent in 1982) occur in connection with other crimes. About half of these are connected with robberies, while the remainder are associated with narcotics offenses, sex crimes, and other felonies.[27] These *felony murders* are almost always classed as first-degree murder although in most instances the offender did not plan to commit murder but only to effect some other crime and then either panicked, overreacted to a resisting victim, or was swept up in the momentum of the crime.

Guns and Homicide.   Firearms are the most common murder weapon in the United States. In 1982 *45 percent* of all homicides were committed with a handgun, while rifles and shotguns contributed another 6 percent and 9 percent, respectively.[28] The debate over the relationship between gun ownership and murder has been a long and heated one. The pro-gun bumper sticker that reads "Guns don't kill people. People kill people," perhaps best summarizes the viewpoint of those who oppose any restrictions on personal ownership of firearms. The pro-gun lobby, particularly the National Rifle Association, represents not just individual citizens interested in personal gun ownership but also the gun industry, whose annual earnings of approximately *$2 billion* represent a strong incentive to maintain and expand private gun ownership.

While it may be true that it is people who pull the trigger, there is evidence that the greater the availability of guns the greater the number of gun-related murders and accidental deaths.[29] The south, which has the highest rate of homicide, also has the highest rate of gun ownership, while the northeast has the lowest rate of gun ownership and the lowest rate of murder.[30] The high rate of gun ownership in the South is, of course, not the sole explanation of its high murder rate. The greater acceptance of and preparation for violence in the south is part of the reason for the high rate of gun ownership to begin with. However, firearms are very efficient implements of violence, and their presence in any situation of personal hostility or crime increases the likelihood of death or serious injury.

Murder is an assault resulting in death. Proportionately more individuals survive assaults by knives, clubs, fists, and feet than survive gunshot wounds. If we combine FBI figures for homicide and aggravated assault, we find that assaults with firearms are *five times* more likely to result in death than assaults with any other weapon.[31] For this reason, as one longitudinal study of the relationship between homicide rates and gun ownership in Detroit found, there is a significant relationship between increased gun ownership and increased homicide rates.[32]

In recent years increased public fear of violent crime has stimulated a new round of gun buying as individuals seek some sense of personal security. This new infusion of guns may very likely produce higher rates of both accidental and criminal gun deaths. Furthermore, a proportion of for-protection handguns are stolen in burglaries every year and find their way onto the black market that is a primary source of weapons for those seeking guns for criminal purposes.

While the personal ownership of guns for protection is to some degree a reflection of the cultural emphasis in America upon self-reliance, it is also a response to the very real conditions of aloneness faced by most Americans, particularly city dwellers. The industrial development of America has made this a nation of largely urban transients who view one another with a fearful or competitive eye and who live with little sense of community or solidarity with those around them.[33] We have become, in the words of sociologist Vance Packard, "a nation of strangers." When we are surrounded by strangers, nearly everyone poses a potential threat. As we walk down the street or go to sleep in our houses or apartments, we have little confidence that strangers or even our neighbors will come to our defense, if needed. Police are a distant and uncertain source of protection from potential harm. Guns, with substantial help from gun sellers, have come to be seen by many Americans as the only effective antidote for the fear bred of aloneness. While a gun on the nightstand or in the purse may help reduce fear of personal crime in the short run, it is a bitter pill, for the very act of owning a gun to feel safe from others underscores the essential alienation and aloneness that has become part of life in America.

Assault

Aggravated Assault. Aggravated assault is "an unlawful attack by one person upon another for the purpose of inflicting severe or aggravated bodily injury." By definition, it is a felony offense. A charge of aggravated assault does not require that injury actually has occurred. Any use of a weapon that "could and probably would result in serious personal injury" is considered aggravated assault, as well as attacks either with or without weapons that do result in actual injury.[34] Assaults that involve neither serious injury nor the use of a deadly weapon are generally misdemeanor offenses and are classed by the FBI as "simple assaults."

Extent of Assault. In 1982 the FBI recorded 650,042 aggravated assaults, a rate of 280 assaults per 100,000.[35] According to the Department of Justice, however, only 50 to 55 percent of aggravated assaults are reported to the police.[36] Taking the highest figure of 55 percent this means that in 1982 there were nearly 1.1 million aggravated assaults. This higher figure represents a rate of approximately 507 aggravated assaults per 100,000, or 1 for every 200 persons. If we add to this the fact that there are approximately one and a half times as many simple assaults (assaults not involving attempt to inflict serious injury) as aggravated assaults, we can estimate that in 1982 there were approximately 2.75 million assaults in the United States, or a rate of 1 assault for every 80 persons.[37] In short, violence is a not uncommon feature of interpersonal relationships in America.

Patterns and Trends. Aggravated assault and homicide are closely related crimes. From a behavior standpoint, aggravated assault may be considered either an unsuccessful murder attempt or a highly successful attempt to inflict personal injury. In either case the circumstances surrounding these two crimes are similar, as are the general patterns and trends for these offenses.

Like homicide, aggravated assault rates tend to be higher in urban areas, decreasing with declines in city size and population density. One difference in the geographical patterns for these two crimes, however, is that the western rather than the southern states generally record the highest rates of assault. In 1982 the western states recorded a rate of 331 aggravated assaults known to the police for every 100,000 inhabitants, while the southern rate was 323. Northeastern and north central states reported substantially lower rates of 257 and 206 per 100,000, respectively.[38]

While both offenses increased somewhat during the 1970s, the rate of aggravated assault, at least as indicated by official statistics, has increased more rapidly than the rate of homicide. According to the FBI, between 1973 and 1982 the rate of homicide decreased by .03 percent while aggravated assault increased 40 percent.[39] How much of this increase is due to vagaries of police statistics and perhaps improvements in emergency medical services that can transform a potential murder into an assault by insuring victim survival is difficult to ascertain. However, given the fact that there has been something of a decline in rates of reporting both aggravated and simple assaults between 1975 and 1979, it appears that the FBI statistics may represent a real growth in the frequency of assault.[40] This would tend to lend support to the hypothesis that when economic conditions deteriorate, violence, particularly family violence, tends to increase as individuals vent the frustrations caused by the anonymous economic order on the only targets available—the people in their lives.[41]

Rape

Forcible Rape. Rape is legally defined as sexual intercourse with a woman achieved "forcibly and against her will." Assaults or other attempts to force women into sexual submission are also classified as forcible rapes by the FBI.[42] Forcible rape should not be confused with *statutory rape*, which refers to sexual intercourse—or sometimes just the presumption of sexual intercourse—between consenting partners when one is under a legally specified age of sexual consent. Charges of statutory rape are generally brought not by the underage partner to the sexual act but by a parent or some other person exercising authority over the underage partner. Some states limit statutory rape to underage females, while others leave open the possibility of charging females with statutory rape of underage males, although in practice such charges are relatively rare.

Extent of Rape. In 1982 the FBI reported a total of 77,763 rapes in the United States. This constituted a rate of 33.6 rapes per 100,000.[43] Victimization studies indicate that approximately 45 to 50 percent of all rapes go unreported, although this figure is probably an underestimate.[44] Rape is a psychologically traumatic, highly personal, and socially stigmatizing event. These factors often make it difficult for rape victims to report to the police and may very well also inhibit rape victims from responding candidly to a victimization survey. Victimization studies do indicate, however, that the frequency of rape is *at a minimum* nearly double that indicated by official police records.

Rape: Contradictions and Myths. Rape is a violent crime. The sexual component of this violence, however, has tended to obscure the contradiction surrounding our legal response to rape and has served as the basis for the generation of a variety of rape myths.

Rape is a crime against an oppressed group—women. Historically, the development of Western civilization was accompanied by the subjugation of women into second-class roles. The ownership of land and later capital, political participation, and until recent years participation in all but the more menial aspects of labor in industrial society have been generally denied to women either by law or custom.[45] The contradiction posed by rape laws is that although political states seldom go to great lengths to protect second-class citizens, rape has been traditionally treated as one of the most serious offenses in Western societies. This appears to be contradiction only if we assume that the gravity of punishment for rape reflects a concern for protecting women. In fact, the severity of rape law arises from, rather than contradicts, the secondary status of women in society.

Within Western culture a young woman's virginity and her adult sexuality have traditionally not been her own possessions but rather the property of the males in her life. Generally, women have not been allowed to offer their virginity or adult sexuality to whom they please, when they please. Traditionally, sexual intercourse became legitimate for a young woman only when ownership of the woman and her sexuality was symbolically and legally passed from her father to her husband. It is interesting to note that in the traditional wedding ceremony the father "gives away" his daughter to the husband-to-be, symbolizing her role as a possession of the parent and later of her husband. While the so-called "sexual liberation" of the 1960s may have brought about some changes in these attitudes, in general female sexuality is still largely circumscribed by male "rights." More significantly, these ideas played a central role in the historical formation of Western rape laws. As criminologist Carol Smart noted,

> The severe penalty for rape . . . was a punishment for the defilement of another man's property rather than a form of protection for women or a recognition of women's rights over their own bodies.[46]

It is for this reason that at one time *rape victims* as well as rapists were often punished and that rape victims must still face significant social stigma as "soiled goods" rather than being treated as the genuine *victims* of a violent act. We find further confirmation of the relationship between rape and the role of women as sexual possessions in the cultural myths surrounding rape.

In a 1974 article Herman and Julia Schwendinger discuss three common rape myths: the "impossibility of rape" myth, the "asking for it" myth, and the "uncontrollable passions" myth. To these can be added a fourth myth— the "irresistible urge" myth. Each of these focus on the sexual component of rape and doing so tend to place the blame for rape on women.

The "impossibility of rape" myth is best summed up in the locker-room joke that "There is no such thing as rape because a woman with her skirt up can run faster than a man with his pants down." The implication is that any woman who is the victim of rape must have willingly submitted to her rapist, shifting the blame from him to her. In practical terms, as the Schwendingers point out, such thinking has led to rape laws that frequently require women to forcefully resist a potential rapist before she can legitimately claim she was raped.[47] Such legislation places a woman's obligation to protect her "sexual goods" when confronted by an armed or physically stronger attacker above her right to protect her life or avoid injury by submitting to sexual assault.

The "uncontrollable passions" myth presents rape as the "natural" consequence of imbalances in the ratio of males to females.

> If women outpopulate men, then allegedly rape will increase because sexual frustrations among men are intensified by a scarcity of women. Conversely, if men outpopulate women, then allegedly women are forced to act more provocative sexually in order to effectively compete for sexual partners. The increased provocation, it is claimed, will increase the likelihood of rape.[48]

In the first instance—an overabundance of men—this viewpoint assumes that rape is a biologically instigated and therefore legitimate response to sexual frustration among men. This tends to ignore the fact that there exists a multiplicity of human responses to sexual frustration other than rape and that most of these responses, with the possible exception of masturbation, are socially learned. In addition, this aspect of the "uncontrollable passions" myth tends to reinforce the sexist viewpoint that sexual frustration is a problem only for males. The second instance—an overabundance of females— argues that if females are sexually provocative in the competition for male attention, it is a reasonable expectation that men will resort to rape. This view is closely linked to the "asking for it" and "irresistible urges" myths.

The "asking for it" myth holds that if a woman excites a man, be it either a stranger or someone she knows, by dressing, talking, or acting "provocatively," she is to blame if he resorts to rape to gratify his sexual desires. The "irresistible urge" myth is a variation of this view that argues that if a woman refuses to engage in intercourse with a man after she has allowed him enough physical intimacy—kissing, holding, petting, and so forth—to become "turned on," the man cannot be blamed for resorting to rape to satisfy his sexual urges. In both cases it is the woman's behavior *prior to rape,* rather than the male's *response* to her behavior, that is condemned. The male is absolved of responsibility for the act because of the presumption that once sexually stimulated males *must* be satisfied.

All these rape myths overemphasize the sexual component of rape and ignore the fact that rape is a hostile act aimed at subjugating and humiliating women rather than just a clumsy attempt to achieve physical intimacy. Rape is not a simple biological response to sexual frustration. A study of 646 rapes in Philadelphia found that 71 percent of all rapes were planned acts, not spur-of-the-moment responses to sexual provocativeness or rejection. Furthermore, 27 percent of the rapes studied involved specific acts of sexual humiliation such as requiring the victim to perform fellatio, submit to anal intercourse, or undergo repeated acts of intercourse.[49] Even without these forms of aggravated humiliation, rape is a degrading experience. It is an act aimed at dramatizing dominance by forcing the victim to surrender to the humiliation of unwanted sexual intercourse. The power-domination aspect of rape is most obvious in male prisons, where rape is frequently used to establish lines of dominance within the prison power structure. New inmates are frequently challenged to either "fight or fuck," and those who cannot defend themselves against rape become "girls" or "pussys" to the prison community.[50] In essence, they enter a second-class citizenship with respect to power within the prison community analogous to the second-class citizenship of women in the outside world. Prison rape victims can only protect themselves from future acts of exploitation by providing sexual or other services to dominant males in the prison community who then act as their protectors, in much the same way as males—the dominant sex in free society—"protect" their women. In either case, the "protection" is needed because the individual occupies a second-class role.

Heterosexual rape is no less an act of dominance and subjugation than are prison rapes. However, because it involves a man and a woman rather than two men, forcible rape is frequently misperceived as an unfortunate variant of *normal sexual processes,* that is, "the expression of uncontrollable desire or some kind of compulsive response to overwhelming attraction." It is instead, as feminist Germain Greer wrote, an act that expresses hatred for, rather than an attraction to, women.[51]

The popular misperception of rape as a sexual act rather than a violent crime aimed at dramatizing dominance over women is a reflection of the fact that dominance over women is a normal component of traditional sex-role relations in America. Because women occupy subordinate roles generally, the power-domination aspect of rape is easily overlooked in favor of sexual explanations of why men rape. If men and women occupied truly equal social roles, rape would be less common since males would not learn early in life that an important component of "manhood" is exerting power over women, and it would be more starkly obvious that rape is an attempt to dominate, not some twisted expression of attraction.

Violent Crimes: Offenders and Victims

The violent crimes of murder, assault, and rape are committed proportionally more often by young males than any other demographic group. Additionally, black males are substantially overrepresented among those arrested for these crimes. In 1982 males constituted 88 percent of those arrested for murder, rape, or assault. Of all persons arrested for these crimes, 40 percent were black.[52] (See Table 11.1.) Whether the higher proportion of black males arrested for these crimes is a reflection of greater involvement in violent crimes or the consequence of selective law-enforcement practices has been a point of substantial controversy, as previously discussed. This controversy can never be settled absolutely, for as long as a proportion of violent crimes do not result in arrest, there is always the possibility that arrest patterns are discriminatory. However, because they frequently occur between people who know one another, murder, aggravated assault, and forcible rape have the highest clearance rates of any Index Offenses. In 1982 the clearance rates for murder, aggravated assault, and rape were 74, 60, and 51 percent, respectively.[53] Given these relatively high rates of clearance, it is likely that not all the overrepresentation of black males can be explained as a consequence of biased arrest patterns, although one study that compared race of offenders as identified by victims with official police arrest figures found police figures to overestimate the involvement of blacks by about 10 percent for assault.[54]

While the race and sex of criminal offenders is compiled and presented by the FBI annually, there is little information provided by official records concerning the social class of violent offenders. The majority of the information available is based on investigations of criminal violence in specific cities. By and large these studies indicate that murder, rape, and assault are more prevalent among, although not exclusively limited to, lower-income groups and more impoverished areas of cities. Wolfgang's study of homicide in Philadelphia found that approximately 90 percent of the homicide offenders

Table 11.1 Percentage Distribution of Persons Arrested for Index Offenses in 1979 by Race and Age

Offense	All Persons Arrested				Persons Under 18 Arrested			
	White	Black	All Others	Total	White	Black	All Others	Total
Murder	49.4	47.7	2.9	100.0	51.5	44.1	4.4	100.0
Rape	50.2	47.7	2.1	100.0	43.2	54.5	2.3	100.0
Assault	60.9	37.0	2.1	100.0	63.4	34.6	2.0	100.0
Robbery	41.0	56.9	2.1	100.0	35.0	62.5	2.5	100.0
Burglary	69.5	28.7	1.8	100.0	72.1	25.9	2.0	100.0
Larceny	67.2	30.0	2.8	100.0	70.0	27.5	2.5	100.0
Motor-Vehicle Theft	70.0	27.2	2.8	100.0	75.0	21.7	3.3	100.0
Arson	78.9	19.2	1.9	100.0	83.8	14.3	1.9	100.0

Source: Federal Bureau of Investigation, *Crime in the United States, 1979* (Washington, D.C.: Government Printing Office, 1980), 200–201.

studied came from the lowest occupational categories.[55] Two other studies, one in Atlanta and another in Houston, found rates of violence to be greatest in areas that scored high on indices of poverty. In Atlanta census tracts that had the highest percentages of persons below the poverty level, persons living in overcrowded domiciles, and persons without high school education also tended to have the highest rates of homicide.[56] The Houston study found a similar relationship between rates of interpersonal violence and the poverty, density, and proportion of blacks in the city's census tracts. This relationship, however, was not perfectly linear, with the rates of violence falling steadily as measures of social status increased. Instead it was found that

> Rather than continuing to decline as wealth and status rise, the personal crime rate falls rapidly as values on these indicators increase beyond the lowest levels but then stabilize within *narrow limits* across the middle and upper income ranges.[57] (emphasis added)

In other words, while some interpersonal violence is likely to occur among all socioeconomic groups, the bulk of interpersonal violence appears to be a product not of some natural propensity for violence in human relationships but of the conditions of life at the bottom of the wealth and income scale.

Interpersonal crimes of violence tend to be intraracial and intraclass in nature. That is, the victim and the offender are most likely to be of both the same race and the same social class. Of 10,799 whites murdered in 1982, for instance, 89 percent were killed by other whites. The figures show an even stronger intraracial pattern for blacks. In 1982, 95 percent of all black murder victims had been killed by someone of the same race.[58] The crimes of rape and assault tend to show similar intraracial patterns. In cases of interpersonal violence victims and offenders also tend to come from similar economic backgrounds. This reflects the fact that violent crimes frequently occur between people who either know or reside near one another, both factors that increase the likelihood that the victim and offender will be of the same social status.

The intraracial and intraclass nature of personal violence means that nonwhites and the poor run the highest proportional risk of becoming victims of violent crime. The racial and social class biases imbedded in the dominant American consciousness, however, tend to make us more aware of nonwhites and the poor as perpetrators of violence than as *victims of violence.* That is, while our popular stereotype of the violent offender is often of someone from a lower-income neighborhood who is probably black, we are less likely to envision someone with those same characteristics when we think about victims of violence. Yet it is just those characteristics which increase the likelihood of being the victim of a violent crime.

In 1982 42.2 percent of all homicide victims were black; yet black Americans constitute only 11 percent of the total population. This means the black rate of victimization is four times greater than the black proportion of the population. For crimes of rape and assault, victimization surveys indicate that blacks and the poorest income groups face the greatest risk. In 1978, for instance, the risk of being the victim of rape was *two and one half* times greater for black women than white women. Blacks also reported a 43 percent higher rate of victimization by aggravated assault than whites that same year.[59]

The poor, both white and black, are generally more likely to be the victims of violence than other income groups. In 1978 those with incomes under $3,000 were more than twice as likely to be the victims of rape than any other income group. Rates of assault victimizations similarly trend downward as income increases, with the rate for those in the under-$3,000 income bracket being one-third higher than that for any other income category.[60]

Poverty brings with it many disabilities. One of the worst may be the greater likelihood of being either the victim or the perpetrator of common crimes of violence. Poverty of itself does not necessarily produce violence, as indicated by lower rates of violent crime among rural poor as compared with urban poor. However, poverty that results from the systematic exploitation and oppression of the unemployed and underemployed in American cities tends to weaken both individual sense of self-worth and sense of community among the poorer segments of the urban working class. It is the loss of these important insulators against futility and frustration that contributes to the relatively high rates of violence among the urban poor in America.

COMMON CRIMES FOR PROFIT

Financial gain is the primary motive for most serious forms of common crime, just as it is the motive for corporate and white-collar crime. Lacking the institutional resources and positions of trust available to corporate managers and other business professionals, poorer offenders are limited to relatively crude forms of acquisition through illegal advantage. Because they require little or no capital, robbery, burglary, larceny, and auto theft are the modal forms of serious crime among the working class.

According to the FBI, 90 percent of all Index Offenses in 1982 were property crimes. However, the FBI lists robbery with violent crimes, not with property offenses. The aim of robbery, unlike most murders, assaults, and rapes, is the acquisition of someone's property, although "force or the threat of force" is the means used. Because the basic motive underlying robbery is economic gain rather than the expression of hostile emotions, it is sociologically and psychologically more similar to property crimes that it is to other crimes of violence even though it results in injury about one-third of the time.[61] If we consider robbery as a property crime, in 1982 crimes for gain constituted *95 percent* of all serious crime reported to police.

Robbery

Robbery is taking or attempting to take something of value from someone by the use or threat of force or by putting the person in fear. Robbery involves face-to-face confrontation, and in this regard it differs from the other Index Offenses against property.

The term "robbery" actually encompasses several distinct types of crime, which vary by the nature of the threat and the type of victim. Where the offender displays or leads the victim to believe he or she has a deadly weapon, the offense is generally referred to as *armed robbery*. If the offender uses or threatens to use only personal weapons (i.e., fists and feet, which is the case in about 40 percent of robberies), the offense is termed *strong arm robbery*. This distinction often has a bearing on the severity of the sentence given for the crime, and in recent years a number of states have established particularly stringent penalties for armed robbery committed with a gun.

About 60 percent of all robberies are committed against individuals in their capacity as private citizens. Another 27 percent are robberies of business establishments such as retail stores, gas stations, convenience stores, and bars.[62] When people talk of "crime in the streets," they generally mean robbery. Nearly half of all robberies are in fact victimizations of private citizens outside their home. In 1982 the FBI reported approximately 289,919 street robberies in the United States, although since personal robbery is reported slightly more than half the time, the actual number was probably closer to 450,000, or approximately one robbery for every 500 persons that year.[63]

High rates of robbery have probably more than any other offense influenced the way people live. Between the years of 1965 and 1974 the National Opinion Research Center found that the proportion of people who feared walking in their own neighborhood alone at night had increased by one-third.[64] As many social commentators have indicated, this type of fear can have a paralyzing effect on the social life of a city. As the fear of strangers grows, people become increasingly alienated from one another. This creates a downward spiral. Fear produces alienation; alienation reduces the possibility for collective action; and as collective action declines and social life becomes more atomized, individuals become even more vulnerable to street crime, leading to still more fear and alienation.

Burglary

Burglary is the unlawful entry into any building or other structure to commit theft or some other felony. Burglary can take one of three forms: unlawful entry without force, forced entry, and attempted forced entry. Forced entry is most common, characterizing 73 percent of all reported burglaries in 1982.[65]

Burglary is the second most common serious crime, constituting 28 percent of all serious crime recorded by the FBI in 1982. While police statistics indicated that approximately 3,415,500 burglaries were committed that year, the actual number was probably slightly less than double this due to a rate of reporting for burglary, which tends to fluctuate between 45 and 50 percent.[66]

Most jurisdictions divide the crime of burglary into four offense categories: burglary of an inhabited dwelling at night, burglary of an inhabited dwelling during the day, burglary of an uninhabited building at night, and burglary of an uninhabited building during the day. Penalties tend to be highest for burglaries of inhabited dwellings at night and lowest for burglaries of uninhabited dwellings during the day. Residential burglaries outnumber burglaries of other buildings by about two to one. In 1982, for example, 66 percent of all reported burglaries were residential.[67]

Larceny

Larceny is the unlawful taking of the possessions of another. This category, as used by the FBI Uniform Crime Reports, includes shoplifting, pocket picking, purse snatching, thefts of parts or other objects from motor vehicles (but not theft of the vehicles themselves), bicycle thefts, and thefts of other objects that do not involve force, fraud, or some type of unlawful entry. (See Figure 11.1.)

Larceny is by far the most common Index Offense. In 1982 larceny accounted for *55 percent* of all Index Offenses reported by the FBI! The high degree of media and justice system attention given to crimes of violence or more dramatic crimes for gain such as robbery and burglary tend to obscure the fact that the bulk of property crime is committed without personal force or unlawful entry. Larceny is also the least frequently reported of all Index Offenses, with most types being reported slightly less than 30 percent of the time. Two deviations from this pattern are purse snatching and household larcenies, which are reported in about 50 percent of the cases.[68] However, these more frequently reported forms of theft account for less than 20 percent of all larcenies. Considering the relatively low rate of reporting for larceny compared with other property crimes, larceny probably accounts for close to 70 percent of all serious crimes in the United States.

Motor-Vehicle Theft

Motor-vehicle theft is simply a specific form of larceny—unlawfully taking or attempting to take a motor vehicle. Many jurisdictions distinguish between *grand theft of a motor vehicle* and *operation without owner's consent.* The former generally applies to the theft of a motor vehicle with the intent of either keeping it for one's personal use or selling it for gain. The latter is reserved for "joyriding" or other unlawful use of someone else's motor vehicle where there is no apparent intention of keeping the vehicle or converting it for profit. Grand theft of a motor vehicle is normally charged as a felony, while joyriding is most often a misdemeanor.

Automobiles represent both significant possessions for most Americans as well as important tools for the conduct of commerce and industry. The economic and symbolic importance of motor vehicles is reflected in the fact that they are stolen with some frequency and that a special category of legal prohibition has been created to protect this particular form of property.

According to the FBI, in 1982 slightly over one million automobiles were stolen. Because motor vehicles are almost always insured against theft, successful motor-vehicle thefts (as compared with attempted thefts) are reported just slightly less than 90 percent of the time.[69]

Figure 11.1. LARCENY ANALYSIS 1982

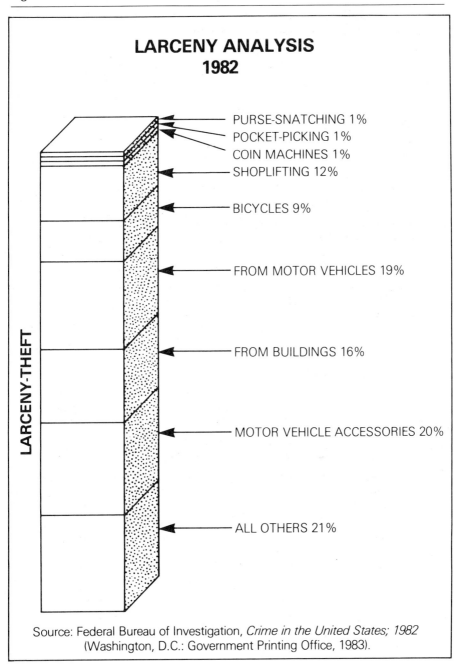

**LARCENY ANALYSIS
1982**

LARCENY-THEFT

PURSE-SNATCHING 1%
POCKET-PICKING 1%
COIN MACHINES 1%
SHOPLIFTING 12%

BICYCLES 9%

FROM MOTOR VEHICLES 19%

FROM BUILDINGS 16%

MOTOR VEHICLE ACCESSORIES 20%

ALL OTHERS 21%

Source: Federal Bureau of Investigation, *Crime in the United States; 1982*
(Washington, D.C.: Government Printing Office, 1983).

Source: Federal Bureau of Investigation, *Crime in the United States: 1982* (Washington, D.C.: Government Printing Office, 1983).

Arson

Arson is the willful or malicious burning of any building, vehicle, or other property. In 1978 this offense was added to the Crime Index by an act of Congress after several years of substantial lobbying.

In 1982 the Uniform Crime Reports listed 106,510 arsons in the United States. These offenses were estimated to represent a loss of close to $1 billion, with the bulk of this loss resulting from the destruction of business or industrial property.[70] Because the FBI excludes from its compilations all fires of suspicious origins that cannot be clearly established as arson, the actual number of willful burnings is probably considerably higher, particularly in the case of professional arsons. The two most common motives for arson are personal revenge and insurance fraud. Arson for fraud has become one of the fastest growing crimes of recent years. While arson is a common crime— that is, its commission is not dependent upon the ownership or management of capital, or on a position of trust—many arson frauds are connected with the world of capital and capital accumulation.

Patterns of Victimization

The vast majority of serious crime in the United States is property crime. According to National Crime Survey data serious property crime constitutes nearly 97 percent of all serious criminal victimizations if we include robbery as a crime for profit.[71] These offenses tend to victimize black and poor more often than white and affluent Americans. For robbery and burglary the black rate of victimization is higher than the white rate for all income categories, and for both races the rate of victimization tends to decrease as income increases. The one exception to this pattern is the rate of burglary victimizations among the highest income group—incomes over $25,000. For both whites and blacks in this category the burglary victimization rate is higher than for middle-income categories, although the highest rate of burglary victimizations is reported by blacks with annual incomes under $3,000.

The distribution of victimizations by household larceny tends to show a somewhat different pattern. For this crime the rate of victimization tends to increase with income, and among the three lowest income groups the white rate of victimization exceeds the black rate. For the three highest income categories this pattern reverses itself, with the black rate exceeding the white. The black rate of victimization by motor-vehicle theft exceeds that for whites in all income categories, and for both races the frequency of victimization tends to increase with income.

Overall, blacks and the poor tend to be the most frequent victims of the more serious and personally disruptive property crimes. Robbery involves personal fear and sometimes injury. Burglary, while it does not involve direct confrontation with the offender, is a violation of secure space and tends to generate both a sense of violation and a reduced sense of personal security within the home. It is these offenses that weigh most heavily upon blacks and those in the lower-income categories.

Table 11.2 Victimization Rates Per 1,000 Persons by Race, Income, and Type of Offense for 1975

Annual Income	Robbery		Burglary		Larceny		Vehicle Theft	
	White	Black	White	Black	White	Black	White	Black
Less than $3,000	9.7	16.6	99.1	145.4	103.3	96.2	10.5	11.7
$3,000–$7,499	7.1	16.6	91.7	125.9	118.0	99.4	16.1	17.9
$7,500–$9,999	6.0	14.3	81.7	132.0	133.0	120.2	19.3	44.4
$10,000–$14,999	5.2	9.9	78.7	128.2	129.2	145.0	19.9	40.1
$15,000–$24,999	4.2	11.1	84.4	109.4	138.0	153.7	21.8	38.8
$25,000 or more	4.0	6.3	107.0	130.3	130.9	133.9	21.7	96.2

Source: U.S. Department of Justice, *Criminal Victimization in the United States, 1975: A National Crime Survey Report* (Washington, D.C.: Government Printing Office, 1977), 26, 31, 32.

AGE, COMMON CRIME, AND THE IDEA OF DELINQUENCY

The problem of common crime in America is largely one of property offenses, and property offenses are primarily committed by the young, at least judging by arrest figures. In 1982, depending on the specific offense, those under twenty-one accounted for between one-half and two-thirds of all people arrested for property crime. Moreover, between one-third and one-half of all those arrested for property crime were under eighteen. By comparison less than 20 percent of persons arrested for violent crimes were under 18.[72]

While property offenses constitute the most common form of felony arrests for all ages, they represent nearly *all* arrests of juveniles for serious crime. In 1982 90 percent of youth under eighteen who were arrested were taken into custody on suspicion of a property crime. That same year property offenses accounted for 76 percent of adult arrests.[73]

Given the significant relationship between youth and common violations against property, it is not surprising that significant energy has been devoted by both the justice system and the field of criminology to the problem of "juvenile delinquency." The recognition of crimes by young people as a significant social problem and the corresponding invention of the idea of "juvenile delinquency" were the consequences of two correlates of industrialization in America: urbanization and immigration. With the emergence of a growing and largely impoverished working class in the middle 1800s there began to appear youth gangs in many major American cities. As the offspring of generally underpaid and often unemployed segments of the working class, gang members certainly experienced significant motivation to turn to theft and other property crimes and apparently did so to some extent. However, the assumption that these gangs were *fundamentally* criminal in nature may have resulted as much from the fact that these gangs were made up of the children of what were viewed as the "dangerous classes" by more affluent Americans as it did from the actual behavior of these gangs. After studying over 1,000 gangs in Chicago in the 1920s sociologist Fredrick Thrasher concluded that while members might periodically engage in some crime, the gangs were essentially noncriminal associations that devoted substantial amounts of energy to companionship and noncriminal forms of recreation.[74]

In 1899 the state of Illinois passed the first juvenile delinquency law, creating a new category of offender: one who by virtue of age was held to be only partially responsible for his or her wrongdoing. According to this law those under eighteen should not receive the full weight of criminal punishment but instead should receive from the court "the care, custody and discipline" that would "approximate as nearly as may be that which should be given by its parent."[75] Within twelve years of the Illinois law twenty-two states had passed similar legislation and by 1925 all but two states had delinquency statutes.

On the surface the development of "juvenile delinquent" as a special legal status appears to have been a well-meaning attempt to "save" young people from lives of crime.[76] In practice, however, because they were receiving "care" and "rehabilitation" instead of punishment, juvenile offenders often spent lengthy periods of time in some form of custody. These therapeutic sentences often exceeded the maximum amount of time an adult could be incarcerated for the same offense. Moreover, since the bulk of those defined by the courts as juvenile delinquents came from the working class, the "rehabilitation" given was largely oriented toward preparing them to become industrious wage laborers rather than developing their intellectual capabilities.[77]

Explaining Delinquency

The belief that delinquency was largely confined to youth from the lower classes was reflected in a wide range of sociological theories that sought to explain this phenomenon. A variety of theories have been proposed and tested to explain juvenile delinquency and youth crime. The most influential of the early sociological theories were those of (1) differential association, (2) anomie and structural blockage, (3) delinquent subcultures, (4) delinquency and opportunity, and (5) lower-class culture as a criminal milieu. Each of these approaches either implicitly or explicitly saw characteristics presumed to be unique to the lower classes as the primary motivating force behind delinquency and by extension behind crime in general.

Sutherland's theory of differential association proposed that deviant behavior was *learned* behavior, that this learning took place primarily in the context of face-to-face personal interactions, and that it involved essentially the same process by which normal behavior was learned. In effect, Sutherland suggested that the delinquent was basically a *normal individual* who had learned deviant skills and values. When first proposed in 1939 this theory diverged significantly from the dominant scientific thought of the time, which tended to view delinquents and criminals as individuals whose biology or personality structure was in some way fundamentally abnormal. As an explanation for delinquency, Sutherland's approach also included the idea that lower-class communities, which he called "disorganized communities," contained a higher proportion of "deviant patterns of behavior" to be learned and greater opportunities for young people to learn them.[78]

The idea that the material and psychological frustrations of poverty are a basic cause of youthful deviance has also played a significant role in criminological theory. At the same time that Sutherland was developing his theory of differential association, sociologist Robert Merton elaborated the theory of "anomie" as an explanation for deviant behavior. As it related to delinquency, the key component of Merton's theory was the notion of structural blockage. According to this concept, while nearly all individuals in American society accept the basic goals of success and material gain, the social structure does not provide all individuals with equal access to legitimate means for obtaining these goals. That is, some individuals are blocked from attaining their goals legitimately. A proportion of these will seek "innovative" (i.e., deviant) ways to attain the socially approved goals. Thus, according to Merton, some proportion of lower-class youth, finding themselves without legitimate means to obtain the things they want, will turn to property crimes as an innovative alternative.[79]

Merton's approach is largely limited to explaining "instrumental" delinquency, that is, delinquency aimed at achieving a concrete and usually material goal. Clearly, the bulk of serious juvenile crime is property crime and could conceivably be explained by the idea of "blockage." However, there is also a proportion of deliquency that is more "expressive" in nature; that is, acts whose satisfaction arises simply in doing them. There is evidence, for instance, that juveniles will sometimes steal things they could afford to buy.[80] That is, even though they have legitimate means at their disposal, they choose a deviant route to their goal. Young people also account for a large proportion of vandalism.[81] While some of this vandalism is actually connected with other crimes for profit, such as tearing out plumbing in vacant houses to sell it, much of it is purely expressive.[82] The theories of delinquent subcultures, delinquency and opportunity, and lower-class culture as a criminogenic environment better explain expressive forms of delinquency.

Cohen's theory of delinquent subcultures posited that working class youth in general find themselves unable to meet the kinds of middle-class standards of acceptability by which they are judged both in schools and in the wider society. Those who feel this most intensely rebel by rejecting these standards and coming together to create a youth subculture that emphasizes values that invert those of the adult world. Within this deviant youth subculture vandalism becomes a way of symbolizing rejection of the adult world of property rights; truancy, a rejection of adult authority; short-run hedonism, a denial of the validity of delayed gratification; and fighting, a rejection of the adult emphasis on peaceful resolution of disputes.[83]

The theory of delinquent opportunity set forth by Richard Cloward and Lloyd Ohlin was in some way a combination of the differential association, anomie, and subculture theories. The theory of delinquent opportunity held that while lack of access to legitimate means to standard success goals did create a strong motivation toward delinquency, it did not necessarily produce a uniform response. The available opportunities to act on these motivations, Cloward and Ohlin argued, must also be considered when attempting to understand patterns of delinquency. Where the opportunity to obtain desired goals by illegitimate means is available, youth who feel blocked from legitimate pathways will form criminal gangs. On the other hand, if such opportunities are absent, the subsequent frustration will result in youth gangs that are primarily expressive and violent in nature. Cloward and Ohlin also suggested that not all individuals have equal access to membership in delinquent subcultures. For various reasons some individuals may find themselves rejected by both the legitimate world and the world of deviant youth groups. These individuals, it was proposed, are most likely to turn to drug addiction as a final escape.[84]

Miller's assessment of lower-class culture as a generating milieu, for delinquency explained delinquent behavior not as product of the frustrations of working class life, but as the natural outgrowth of the values of lower-class culture. The prevalence of values such as freedom from restraint, "excitement," "toughness," and the ability to outwit others were offered as explanations for lower-class delinquency.[85] However, Miller's approach tended to overlook the fact that many of these things were equally valued by other social classes in America, although they were symbolized differently. For the affluent "smartness" is getting a "good deal" on a new car or an appliance, not a clever street hustle. Similarly, the belief in the value of "toughness" is held by many who are not lower class. However, it is symbolized not by personal, physical toughness but by the belief that America must be strong and ready to use force in the world of international politics. A more fruitful line of analysis would be to inquire as to how different classes come to symbolize similar values differently.

While we can find some useful ideas in each of these social theories of delinquency causation, they tend to presume, as did most biological and psychological theories before them, that crime is by and large the product of the "dangerous classes." Starting from this proposition they then seek to find the characteristic qualities or experiences of these classes that would explain their criminality. (The one exception to this is Sutherland, who attempted to support his theory of differential association by showing how it could be utilized to explain deviance among the "white-collar" classes.[86] However, when treating common crime, Sutherland did emphasize the disorganized nature of lower-class communities as uniquely suited to the transmission of deviant learning.) A key problem posed by the underlying assumption of these theories is that delinquency is not confined to the lower class.

Social Class and Delinquency

Self-reporting studies that ask juveniles to indicate what offenses they have committed have consistently shown that nearly all young people engage in *some* law violation before they become adults.[87] There has, however, been considerable controversy surrounding the implications of this finding.[88] The contrast between self-reporting studies that showed little social class difference in the proportion of young people who engage in delinquent acts, and official police figures showing a significantly higher rate of arrest for lower-class youth, have been interpreted by some as evidence for social class bias in the justice system.[89] If most young people, regardless of social class, break the law but it is largely those from poorer classes who are arrested, then it would appear that the law is selectively targeting the poor for legal control.

Others have countered this interpretation with the argument that studies showing no relationship between social class and delinquency have tended to ask young people primarily about minor offenses like truancy, shoplifting, and underage drinking while excluding serious ones like robbery and burglary, or have failed to adequately distinguish such things as "fighting," which many young males have done, and "assault with a deadly weapon," which is a less common offense.[90] When these factors are taken into account, it is argued, a clear relationship between social class and youth crime emerges.

Moreover, since serious offenders and frequent offenders are more likely to be arrested, this, and not bias in the justice system, would explain the higher proportion of lower-class youth among those arrested.[91]

Recent studies using national youth samples and more sophisticated questionnaires have tended to confirm both interpretations. That is, there appears to be no significant difference between lower-class, working class, and middle-class youth when it comes to self-reported involvement in property crimes (excluding robbery); drug offenses (either selling or using); status crimes such as truancy, runaway, and underage drinking; or public disorder crimes such as carrying a concealed weapon, drunkenness, hitchhiking, and so forth.[92] However, lower-class youth report a significantly greater involvement in the interpersonal crimes of sexual assault, other assaults, and robbery. Additionally, lower-class youth appear disproportionately among those reporting a high frequency of offenses. It should be noted, however, that high-frequency offenders accounted for less than 5 percent of the juveniles surveyed in each of the three social classes.[93]

The implications of these findings depend upon the question one seeks to answer. Certainly they could be taken as evidence, as some have done, that the view of the lower classes as the "dangerous" ones is indeed valid. After all, lower-class juveniles appear to be more often involved in violent crimes than other classes, and they account for the largest proportion of high-frequency delinquents. On the other hand, there do not appear to be significant differences between social classes where other offenses are involved. Particularly important is the lack of a significant difference between classes where property crime is concerned. Violent crimes may be more serious in their consequences, but property crime represents the bulk of crime in America. From this standpoint juveniles in all social classes are a part of the basic crime problem in America, and theories are needed that do not address the problem of delinquency as the lower-class phenomenon alone.

Nils Christie has offered one such theory. He has argued that the key factor underlying delinquency is the segregation of youth into a separate group within society as a consequence of industrialization. As industrialization advances, young people play fewer meaningful roles in the society and find the age of full participation delayed well beyond the age of physical maturity due to the need for an increasingly, lengthy education. In addition, industrialization separates the home place from the work place, reducing the integration of young people into the daily round of family life. In a sense young people are set adrift, free to create their own society and their own social rules. It is this freedom that provides the fertile seedbed for much youthful lawbreaking. Christie says,

> An integrated person is . . . beautifully tied into a web of social relations. An unexpected move results in a magnitude of subtle counter-moves. Deviant behavior is not necessarily seen as deviance or called deviance, but is kept under control through daily interaction with a number of other persons who are of great importance for the socially integrated person.

In industrial societies, however, youth are not fully integrated in this way. They are a segregated category, and as Christie notes,

Segregation means lack of integration. . . . It means being isolated from the mainstream of society. The category is thereby less influenced by that society. And potential for control is highly reduced.[94]

Thus industrialization may produce the conditions for high rates of juvenile deviation. The fact that the bulk of this deviation is in the direction of property offenses, however, reflects other characteristics of industrial society.

Industrial society is characterized by wage labor and an emphasis upon commodities—that is, what can be purchased with wages—as the primary endpoint of work. This characteristic is especially strong in capitalist societies, particularly contemporary ones, that tend to stimulate high levels of material desire both as a means of insuring continual market growth and as a mechanism for redirecting worker concerns away from seeking control over the nature and form of their labor.[95] Given the central role of commodities in the consciousness of capitalist societies, it is predictable that most violations of law will focus on these.

GENDER AND COMMON CRIME

Female participation in crime has always been a small fraction of male involvement, at least as indicated by arrest statistics. In 1960, for example, women accounted for slightly under 11 percent of all those arrested.[96] In more recent years, however, there has been considerable discussion of the growth in female participation in crime. Freda Adler, for example, points out that between 1960 and 1972 female arrest rates for robbery increased by 277 percent as compared with an increase of 169 percent for men. She goes on to say that

> Except for parity in the categories of murder and aggravated assault the picture of female arrest rates rising several times faster than male arrest rates is a consistent one for all offenses.[97]

Nearly all of this growth resulted from increased female participation in property crime.[98] The implications and causes of this change in statistical patterns of female arrests is the subject of some controversy. Some have taken the increase in female arrest rates as a clear indication that recent changes in the sex-role identity and the sex-role status of women resulting from the women's movement and other social changes are being reflected by an increased participation of women in formerly "masculine" crimes. Others have questioned the reliability of arrest statistics as accurate indicators of female participation in crime, particularly in light of recent changes in investigating and recording crime. For instance, the increased representation of females among Index property offenders may reflect in part the fact that as inflation increases the value of property, certain thefts that were once misdemeanors may now be classified as felonies. Author Laura Rans, for example, points out that while females went from 10.7 percent of *all arrests* in 1960 to 15.7 in 1975—an increase of only 47 percent—the female proportion of Index Offense arrests nearly *doubled*, rising from 15.9 percent to 29.4 percent.[99]

One change that is apparent is that when they violate the law, women appear to be increasingly likely to commit property crimes. In 1960 women were arrested four times as often for property crimes as for violent crimes. By 1977 this ratio had increased to almost nine property crime arrests for every arrest of a female for interpersonal violence.[100] While women may be more psychologically prepared to participate in formerly "masculine" property crimes as a result of sex-role changes, an equally important factor is the deteriorating economic position of women, particularly since lower-class women—those most likely to commit conventional property crimes—have been generally less influenced by the women's movement than middle- and upper-class women. While the number of women in the labor force has increased substantially since the 1950s, the majority of these women remain concentrated in the lowest-paying jobs. Furthermore, the income gap between men and women has tended to increase rather than decrease in recent years. Between 1955 and 1974, for example, the income gap between men and women rose from $1,911 to $3,433. In addition, the number of households headed by women has been rising steadily since the 1960s, as has the proportion of single and divorced women who must support themselves in a market economy where the average female salary is less than 60 percent of the average male salary.[101] These factors mean that there is an increasingly larger proportion of women under the kind of economic stress and receiving the low rate of legitimate return that makes crime attractive. This may contribute as much to the increase in female property crime arrests as any developing sense among women that they are the criminal equals of men, although the latter would make a criminal alternative more likely under conditions of economic stress.

PUBLIC ORDER OFFENSES

In terms of the volume of cases handled, public order offenses represent the predominant form of law violation in America and as such place a larger burden on the resources of the criminal justice system than any other form of law violation. Public order offenses include public intoxication; disorderly conduct; gambling; the possession, sale, and use of narcotics, hallucinogens and other controlled substances; prostitution; homosexual solicitation, liquor law violations, and traffic violations. These offenses are classified by the FBI as less serious (Part II) offenses. Most public order offenses are either misdemeanor violations or what are termed "lesser felonies," and unlike serious felonies, they are adjudicated in lower courts.

Extent of Public Order Enforcement

In 1982 slightly over 12 million Americans were arrested. Of these, only 21 percent—about 2.5 million people—were arrested for Index Offenses. The remainder were taken into custody for a variety of misdemeanor and minor felony violations, and the vast majority of these arrests were for public order violations. Crimes such as minor assaults, forgery, fraud, embezzlement, receiving stolen property, vandalism, weapons offenses, and juvenile offenses constituted just slightly over 19 percent of the arrests for non–Index Offenses. The remaining 81 percent—over *7.5 million arrests*—were for public order crimes.[102] Because public order crimes do not normally involve complaining victims, these 7.5 million arrests are only those public order offenses identified by police and as such represent just a small proportion of the total amount of drunkenness, prostitution, drug use, driving under the influence, and sex offenses that occur.

The alcohol-related offenses of drunkenness, disorderly conduct, liquor law violations, and driving under the influence are the most common reasons for arrest. These offenses accounted for 36 percent of all arrests in 1982 and just under 50 percent of all arrests for non–Index Offenses.[103]

Drug abuse violations are the second most common type of public order arrest. In 1982 there were slightly over a half million arrests for drug abuse. Seventy percent of these were for possession or sale of marijuana. It is difficult to estimate the true extent of both drug law violations and alcohol-related offenses for two reasons. First, most violations are clandestine and do not result in arrest. Secondly, arrests of juveniles for both these and other offenses are often recorded only as acts of "juvenile delinquency." While only 30 percent of recorded arrests for drug law violations involved persons under eighteen, there is evidence that drug use, particularly marijuana, is widespread among youth. In 1982 there were an estimated 121,200 arrests for prostitution and 41,200 arrests for gambling.[104] Most cities experience periodic "cleanups" of prostitution and gambling, but for the most part these enterprises enjoy a relatively high degree of tolerance by law-enforcement officials. Gambling operations enjoy a peaceful coexistence with law enforcement in most cities.

The enforcement of laws prohibiting gambling and prostitution is largely symbolic. There is no commitment or intention within law enforcement or the larger operations of the state to eliminate these activities. Both prostitution and gambling provide sources of hidden income for police and other justice system officials in many large urban centers through payoffs made to avoid arrest or prosecution. Moreover, these illegal services represent important safety valves for the release of working-class frustrations. At the same time, legitimizing these activities would run counter to several basic themes of the world view central to maintaining work force discipline. Sufficient arrests are made annually to provide the impression of opposition to these illegal enterprises but generally too few to disrupt business-as-usual.

Why Public Order Crimes

Most people take for granted that one function of law is to insure order. When we observe such things as traffic enforcement, it is relatively easy to see what type of "order" is being maintained. Many other offenses that fall into the public order category are less clear.

Public order offenses for the most part constitute a selective enforcement of certain images of personal moral conduct against working class members who violate them. This selective enforcement takes three forms. First, some acts that violate these moral precepts become public order crimes only when committed *publicly*. In particular, laws prohibiting drunkenness and prostitution are generally only enforced when violations occur in public or quasi-public situations. The poor are arrested for drunkenness more often than the affluent not because they drink more often but because they do it more often in public places. As sociologist Arthur Stinchcombe noted, the homeless alcoholic runs a high risk of arrest not for being drunk but for being homeless.[105] Middle- and upper-class Americans who are frequently drunk at parties, while weekending at their summer place, or vacationing at private resorts do not run a similar risk.

A similar distinction is made with respect to prostitution. Prostitutes can be roughly divided into two groups, street prostitutes or "working girls," and call girls. Street prostitutes generally serve working class customers while the call girl's clientele are more often middle-class businessmen, professionals, and other financially well-off men.[106] Because her clientele can pay less, the "working girl" must often turn many "tricks" per night and to do so must aggressively play the streets, constantly looking for new "johns." Consequently, "working girls" are subject to frequent arrests and roundups.[107] Meanwhile, the call girl services her more affluent customers in the privacy of apartments or comfortable hotel rooms, free from the threat of arrest.

Second, laws prohibiting public order offenses are most often enforced against working class consumers of illegal services, or low-level providers of these services, but seldom against those whose capital provides the foundation for illicit trade. Narcotics users and street-level pushers are those most commonly arrested for drug law violations. Those who provide the capital for purchasing large quantities of narcotics for distribution, as well as the ships, planes, and international connections that make this distribution possible, are seldom subject to arrest.[108] The same is true of gambling. While working class numbers runners and small bookies are periodically subject to arrest, those who control the legitimate and illegitimate forms of capital that underwrite a national gambling network seldom feel the weight of the law.

Third, some public order offenses entered into the law as part of an attempt to (1) promote and enforce standards of moral conduct conducive to maintaining discipline in the labor force and (2) control minority members of the working class.

Laws against drunkenness and drug abuse, for instance, also protect the consciousness appropriate to capitalism. The use of alcohol or other drugs to alter mental and/or emotional processes directly opposes the emphasis upon the sobriety, rationality, and hard work that was an important part of the world view through which the capitalist class sought to create an effective industrial labor force during the early days of machine capitalism. The relationship of drug use to maintaining labor force discipline is reflected in the types of drugs prohibited. Where the purpose of drug use is to enable a person to function within the labor force or to cope with the problems and frustrations of being marginal to the mainstream of social production, as in the case of many housewives, drugs are generally legally available via prescription. Valium, Librium, and other mood-altering drugs are a common part of contemporary life in America. Valium is the single most commonly prescribed drug in the nation.

If you need a pill to face the day as a worker or housewife or to get to sleep at night so you can face the next day, it is readily and legally available. In many ways these drugs serve to anesthetize people from considering and perhaps changing the objective conditions of their lives that produce their feelings of anxiety or depression. On the other hand, drugs used for recreational purposes, that is, for the sole purpose of altering consciousness independent of any instrumental aim like going to work or facing the kids, is generally prohibited.

The history of drug law enforcement has also been closely tied to control of minority groups. The passage of antiopium laws in the 1870s—the first narcotics control laws in the United States—was a direct attack on the Chinese working class that constituted a significant proportion of the West Coast and western labor force at that time. Much of the agitation for these anti-Chinese laws came from members of the white working class who saw the Chinese willingness to work for lower wages as a threat to their own standard of living. While this dual labor market had not posed an obvious problem in the mid-1800s, with the onset of economic depression in the 1870s anti-Chinese agitation grew. This agitation and the antiopium laws were generally supported by the capitalist class at the time since they served to create a division between the white and Oriental segments of the working class, insuring that the solidarity necessary for viable opposition to the capitalist class could not emerge.[109] The prohibition of cocaine in 1914 and marijuana in 1937 were similarly linked to antiminority sentiments. Cocaine was popularly linked to violence and sexual assaults by blacks and marijuana was denigrated as the drug of Mexicans.[110] In all three cases the drug was prohibited not because of concrete evidence of their detrimental effects but because of their association with specific minority groups.

The nature of the class conflict surrounding drug prohibitions is a complex one. In part it has reflected conflicts between white and nonwhite segments of the working class as white working class groups have sought to protect their market position against successive waves of minority immigrants. While there has frequently been white working class support for these prohibitions, it must be remembered that the conditions of working class conflict are themselves by-products of capitalist relations of production, which places the working class in competition with itself. Moreover, conflict within the working class has the beneficial effect of limiting unified opposition to the capitalist class. Additionally, drug use has generally been viewed as a detriment to labor productivity (at least until recent years) and has generally been viewed by the elite as a threat to the capitalist values of hard work, sobriety, and perseverance.

The prohibition of working class forms of gambling is another attempt to protect the Protestant ethic world view that hard labor is the appropriate route to success by branding as immoral and illegal working class attempts to short-circuit the hard work route to gain what might be considered "windfall" profits. Gambling offers the promise of maximum returns for minimal effort. In one sense it epitomizes capitalist consciousness. However, once again morality is selectively defined. Gambling within the boundaries of the capitalist economy is defined as both legitimate and desirable behavior. The entrepreneur who gambles that a new product will succeed or the person who invests heavily in a stock he or she thinks is about to undergo significant growth, if successful, are seen as shrewd participants in the competition for material advantage. By contrast, the worker who plays the numbers or places illegal bets on horses or sports events, is engaging in an illegal form of economic speculation. This is true even though the shrewd horse player or sports bettor may be as rational and know as much about the probability of success as the entrepreneur or investor.

A necessary requirement of a capitalist economy is the existence of a labor force with no routes to gain other than selling their labor to industry. While it seldom lifts individuals out of wage labor status, gambling challenges the ideology that selling labor power is the only route to material gain. It is for this reason that working class forms of gambling remain illegal, while risk taking within the structure of capitalist economy is held to be of great merit.

CONCLUSION

Common crimes are offenses that either can be committed by persons with no capital other than their labor power or that provide illegal services to primarily working class clientele. Because of the class-based nature of law and law enforcement in the United States, those offenses under the jurisdiction of the criminal justice system are almost exclusively common crimes. Crimes that require capital or positions of trust are unavailable to working class members. Since the perpetrators of these latter offenses are usually from managerial, professional, or capitalist strata and these offenses most often serve the interests of capital, they are handled in ways that avoid the stigma associated with crime.

Crimes of interpersonal violence and crimes against property are committed most frequently by members of the working class, particularly those from the most impoverished segments of that class. While this fact has been used to buttress the image of the poor and near-poor as the "dangerous classes," much less recognition has been given to the fact that persons from the lowest segments of the working class are almost most often the victims of conventional violent and property crimes.

Only if we recognize the class-based nature of American society does the division of crime and law enforcement into two categories with substantially different penalties unrelated to the seriousness of the harms caused begin to make sense. Public fear of conventional crimes against persons and property is most frequently used to explain the greater attention in terms of law enforcement and stringent penalties given these offenses. While it is true that conventional crimes are a genuine source of fear for most Americans, this does not explain why many of the crimes of business that are equally damaging to life, health, and economic well-being are handled in a fundamentally different manner than conventional crimes. Nor does it explain the inconsistent enforcement of public order crimes that by and large permits to the middle and upper classes behaviors that it prohibits the working class.

One purpose of law is to maintain order on a day-to-day basis. In a capitalist society this means primarily enforcing limits on the fundamentally antisocial motivations generated by a social system that endorses acquisitiveness through gaining advantage over others and maintaining a set of moral precepts advantageous to the interests of capital in having a tractable labor force. The former task is a particularly difficult one because in a society that is based upon gain through exploitation, there is little fundamental moral difference between those forms of exploitation that are permitted and those that are prescribed. In addition to maintaining social peace on a day-to-day basis, law is also central to the maintenance of the existing form of social order in state society. Thus criminal law in America and the patterns of its enforcement can only emerge in ways that do not threaten the interests of capital accumulation, for it is upon this foundation that the social order is built. The following chapter examines the way in which the contradiction between maintaining social peace and maximizing the accumulation of capital results in a broad variety of crimes and social harms that, while serious in their consequences, avoid the stigma and the repression applied to those forms of social disruption available to those without capital.

NOTES

1. Edwin Schur, *Crimes Without Victims* (Englewood Cliffs, N.J.: Prentice-Hall, 1965).
2. See George Vold, *Theoretical Criminology* (New York: Oxford University Press, 1958), 14–18 for a discussion of the impact of social contract ideology on criminological theory.
3. See Marshall B. Clinard and Richard Quinney, *Criminal Behavior Systems* (New York: Holt, Rinehart and Winston, 1973) for an expanded typology of criminal behavior.
4. Lewis Yablonski, *The Violent Gang* (New York: MacMillan, 1962).
5. *New York Times,* 10 May 1981, 1.
6. Robert L. Eichhorn and Edward G. Ludwig; "Poverty and Health," in *Poverty in the Affluent Society,* Hanna H. Meissner, ed. (New York: Harper & Row, 1973).
7. See Monica Blumenthal et al, *Justifying Violence: Attitudes of American Men* (Ann Arbor, Mich.: Institute for Social Research, 1972) for discussion of positive acceptance of state violence.
8. Michael Hindelang, et al., eds., *Source Book of Criminal Justice Statistics, 1976* (Washington, D.C.: Government Printing Office, 1977), 310.
9. *Esquire Magazine,* "The Case For Guns," August 1981.

10. John E. Conklin, *The Impact of Crime* (New York: MacMillan, 1975), 58.
11. John Herbers, "The Bid for the Law and Order Vote," *The New York Times,* 22 October 1972.
12. *Charlotte Observer,* "Reagan Seeks War on Violent Crime," 14 March 1981.
13. Trudy Hensen, "Some Sources of Error in the Medicolegal Production of Mortality Statistics." Paper presented at the Annual Meeting of the Southern Regional Demographic Group, October 1980.
14. Federal Bureau of Investigation, *Crime in the United States: 1982* (Washington, D.C.: U.S. Government Printing Office, 1983), 6.
15. Ibid., 43.
16. United Nations, *Demographic Yearbook* (New York: United Nations Publishing Services, 1983), 405–411.
17. Federal Bureau of Investigation, *Crime in the United States: 1977* (Washington, D.C.: Government Printing Office, 1978), 37; and Federal Bureau of Investigation, *Crime in the United States: 1982,* 7.
18. Graeme Newman, *Understanding Violence* (New York: Lippincott, 1979), 67.
19. Federal Bureau of Investigation, *Crime in the United States: 1982,* 43.
20. Ibid., 40–41.
21. Marving Wolfgang and Franco Ferracuti, *The Subculture of Violence* (London: Tavistock, 1967).
22. Robert D. Gastil, "Homicide and a Regional Culture of Violence," *American Sociological Review,* 36 (June 1971): 412–427.
23. Michael Myerson, *Nothing Could Be Finer* (New York: International Publishers, 1979), 190–197.
24. National Commission on the Causes and Prevention of Violence, *To Establish Justice, To Insure Domestic Tranquility* (Washington, D.C.: Government Printing Office, 1969), 25–26.
25. Federal Bureau of Investigation, *Crime in the United States: 1982,* 12.
26. Lynn A. Curtis, "Victim Precipitation and Violent Crime," *Social Problems,* 21 (April 1976), 594–605.
27. Federal Bureau of Investigation, *Crime in the United States: 1982,* 12.
28. Ibid., 10.
29. Joseph C. Fisher, "Homicide in Detroit: The Role of Firearms," *Criminology,* no. 14 (November 1976), 387–400.
30. George D. Newton and Franklin E. Zimring, *Firearms and Violence in American Life.* Report to the National Commission on the Causes and Prevention of Violence (Washington, D.C.: Government Printing Office, 1969), 9–10.
31. Federal Bureau of Investigation, *Crime in the United States: 1982,* 10, 20.
32. Fisher, "Homicide In Detroit," 397.
33. Bertram Gross, *Friendly Fascism* (New York: M. Evans and Co., 1980), 107.
34. Federal Bureau of Investigation, *Crime in the United States: 1979* (Washington, D.C.: U.S. Government Printing Office, 1980), 19.
35. Federal Bureau of Investigation, *Crime in the United States: 1982,* 20.
36. U.S. Department of Justice, *Criminal Victimization in the United States: 1976* (Washington, D.C.: Government Printing Office, 1976), 6.
37. Ibid., 24.
38. Federal Bureau of Investigation, *Crime in the United States: 1982,* 44–46.
39. Ibid., 43.
40. U.S. Department of Justice, *Criminal Victimization in the United States: 1973–1978 Trends* (Washington, D.C.: Government Printing Office, 1980), 6.
41. See Richard J. Gelles, *The Violent Home* (Beverly Hills, Calif.: Sage, 1972); and

Suzanne K. Steinmetz, *The Cycle of Violence: Assertive, Aggressive and Abusive Family Interaction* (New York: Praeger, 1977).

42. Federal Bureau of Investigation, *Crime in the United States: 1979*, 8.
43. Federal Bureau of Investigation, *Crime in the United States: 1982*, 45.
44. U.S. Department of Justice, *Criminal Victimization: 1973–1978 Trends*, 82.
45. Leo Kanowitz, *Women and the Law: The Unfinished Revolution* (Albuquerque: University of New Mexico Press, 1968).
46. Carol Smart, *Women, Crime and Criminology* (London: Routledge and Kegan Paul, 1976), 78.
47. Herman Schwendinger and Julia Schwendinger, "Rape Myths in Legal, Theoretical and Everday Practice," *Crime and Social Justice* (Spring–Summer 1974): 19.
48. Ibid., 21.
49. Menachim Amir, "Forcible Rape," *Federal Probation*, 31, no. 1 (1967): 52.
50. Alan J. Davis, "Sexual Assaults in the Philadelphia Prison Systems," in *The Sexual Scene*, John H. Gagnon and William Simon, eds. (Chicago: Aldine Press, 1970), 107–124; see also Anthony M. Sacco, *Rape in Prison* (Springfield, Ill.: Charles C Thomas, 1975).
51. Germain Greer, *The Female Eunuch* (St. Albans: Paladin Press, 1970), 251.
52. Federal Bureau of Investigation, *Crime in the United States: 1982*, 172, 184.
53. Ibid., 157.
54. Michael J. Hindelang, "Race and Involvement in Crime," *American Sociological Review*, 43, no. 1 (1981): 104.
55. Marvin E. Wolfgang, "Victim-Precipitated Criminal Homicide," *Journal of Criminal Law, Criminology, and Police Science*, 48, no. 1 (1957): 1–11.
56. Robert S. Munford et al., "Homicide Trends in Atlanta," *Criminology*, 14, no. 2 (1979): 213–232.
57. Kenneth R. Mladenka and Kim Quaile Hill, "Examination of the Etiology of Urban Crime." *Criminology*, 13, no. 4 (February 1976), 503.
58. Federal Bureau of Investigation, *Crime in the United States: 1982*, 9.
59. U.S. Department of Justice, *Criminal Victimization: 1973–1978 Trends*, 11.
60. Ibid., 5.
61. Federal Bureau of Investigation, *Crime in the United States: 1982*, 40.
62. Federal Bureau of Investigation, *Crime in the United States: 1978* (Washington, D.C.: Government Printing Office, 1979), 19.
63. Federal Bureau of Investigation, *Crime in the United States: 1982*, 17.
64. U.S. Department of Justice, *Criminal Victimization: 1976*, 16–17.
65. Federal Bureau of Investigation, *Crime in the United States: 1982*, 24.
66. Ibid., 38; U.S. Department of Justice, *Criminal Victimization: 1975*, 82.
67. Federal Bureau of Investigation, *Crime in the United States: 1982*, 24.
68. U.S. Department of Justice, *Criminal Victimization: 1976*, 82.
69. U.S. Department of Justice, *Crime in the United States: 1982*, 32.
70. Federal Bureau of Investigation, *Crime in the United States: 1982*, 36.
71. Based on U.S. Department of Justice, *Criminal Victimization, 1976 and 1980*; lower estimates of reporting for property offenses.
72. Federal Bureau of Investigation, *Crime in the United States: 1982*, 190.
73. Ibid., 194.
74. Frederick M. Thrasher, *The Gang* (Chicago: University of Chicago Press, 1927). See also Clifford R. Shaw, Henry D. McKay, and James F. McDonald, *Brothers in Crime* (Chicago: University of Chicago Press, 1938); and Clifford Shaw, *The Jack Roller* (Chicago: University of Chicago Press, 1930) for discussions of the relationship between youth and crimes for profit in the early 1900s.

75. Illinois Bar Association, "Report to the Illinois State Legislature" (Chicago: Illinois Bar Association, 1899).
76. Anthony Platt, *The Child Savers* (Chicago: University of Chicago Press, 1969).
77. Barry Krisberg and James T. Austin, *The Children of Ishmael* (Palo Alto, Calif.: Mayfield Publishing Co., 1978), 17.
78. See Edwin Sutherland and Donald Cressey, *Principles of Criminology*, 10th ed. (Philadelphia: J.B. Lippincott, 1978), 80–84.
79. Robert Merton, "Social Structure and Anomie," *American Sociological Review* 3 (October 1938): 672–682.
80. See Paul C. Friday and Jerald Hage, "Youth Crime in Postindustrial Societies," *Criminology*, 14, no. 3 (1976), 363–364; and Paul C. Friday, "Research on Youth Crime in Sweden," *Scandinavian Studies*, no. 46 (1974), 20–30 for a discussion of utilitarian and symbolic role of commodities within youth culture.
81. Federal Bureau of Investigation, *Crime in the United States: 1981*, 195.
82. John M. Martin, *Juvenile Vandalism* (Springfield, Ill.: Charles C Thomas, 1961); Herman D. Stein and John M. Martin, " 'Swastika Offenders': Variations in Etiology, Behavior and Psycho-social Characteristics," *Social Problems*, no. 10 (1962), 56–70.
83. Albert Cohen, *Delinquent Boys: The Culture of the Gang* (New York: The Free Press, 1955).
84. Richard Cloward and Lloyd E. Ohlin, *Delinquency and Opportunity* (New York: Free Press, 1960).
85. Walter B. Miller, "Lower class culture as a generating milieu of gang delinquency," *Journal of Social Issues*, 14, no. 3 (1958): 5–19.
86. See Donald Cressy, "Preface" to Edwin Sutherland, *White Collar Crime* (New York: Holt, Rinehart and Winston, 1964 ed.).
87. See for example, James S. Wallerstein and Clement Wyle, "Our Law-Abiding Lawbreakers," *Probation*, 25 (1947): 107–112; Austin Porterfield, *Youth in Trouble* (Fort Worth, Texas: Leo Postisham Foundation, 1946); James F. Short, Jr., and Ivan F. Nye, "The Extent of Unrecorded Delinquency; Tentative Conclusions," *Journal of Criminal Law, Criminology, and Police Science*, no. 49 (1958): 296–302; Robert A. Dentler and Lawrence J. Monroe, "Social Correlates of Early Adolescent Theft," *American Sociological Review*, no. 26 (1961) 733–743; Maynard L. Erickson and LaMar T. Empey, *The Journal of Criminal Law, Criminology, and Police Science*, no. 54, 456–469; Ronald L. Akers, "Socio-Economic Status and Delinquent Behavior: A Retest," *Journal of Research in Crime and Delinquency*, no. 1 (1964) 38–46; Harwin L. Voss, "Socio-Economic Status and Reported Delinquent Behavior," *Social Problems*, no. 13, 314–324; Travis Hirschi, *The Causes of Delinquency* (Berkeley, Calif.: University of California Press, 1969).
88. See John Braithwaite, "The Myth of Social Class and Criminality Reconsidered," *American Sociological Review*, 46, no. 1 (1981): 36–57, for an extensive review of studies indicating higher rates of law violation among lower income as compared to more affluent groups.
89. See for example, Charles R. Tittle, Wayne J. Villemez, and Douglas A. Smith, "The Myth of Social Class and Criminality: An Empirical Assessment of the Empirical Evidence," *American Sociological Review* 43 (October 1978): 651; Richard Quinney, *The Social Reality of the Crime* (Boston: Little Brown, 1970), 129–130; Dennis Chapman, *Sociology and the Stereotype of the Criminal* (London: Tavistock, 1968), 4; Leroy Gould, "Who defines Delinquency: a comparison of self-reported and officially reported indices of delinquency for three racial groups," *Social Problems* 16 (1969): 325–336; Travis Hirschi, *Causes of Delinquency* (Berkeley: Uni-

versity of California Press, 1969); William Chambliss and Richard Nagasawa, "On the Validity of Official Statistics: a comparative study of white, black and Japanese high school boys," *Journal of Research in Crime and Delinquency* 6 (1969): 71–77.

90. Studies such as John P. Clark and Eugene P. Wenniger, "Socio-economic class and area as correlates of illegal behavior among juveniles," *American Sociological Review*, no. 27, 1962, pp. 826–834; Albert J. Reiss and Albert L. Rhodes, "The distribution of juvenile delinquency in the social class structure," *American Sociological Review*, no. 26, 1961, pp. 720–732; Martin Gold, "Undetected delinquent behavior," *Journal of Research in Crime and Delinquency*, no. 3, 1966, pp. 27–46; and LaMart T. Empey, "Delinquency theory and recent research," *Journal of Research in Crime and Delinquency*, no. 4, 1967, pp. 28–42, suggest that delinquency may be somewhat more extensive among lower-income youth as compared to middle and upper income categories.

91. Gary F. Jensen and Dean Rojeck, *Juvenile Delinquency* (Lexington, Mass.: D.C. Heath, 1980), 70–71.

92. Delbert S. Elliot and David Huizinga, "Social class and delinquent behavior in a national youth panel," *Criminology* 21, no. 2 (May 1983): 149–177.

93. Ibid, 169.

94. Nils Christie, "Youth as a crime-generating phenomena," *New Perspectives in Criminology* (1975) 1–10.

95. See Stuart Ewen, *Captains of Consciousness* (New York: McGraw-Hill, 1977) for an excellent discussion of the relationship between commodity orientations and redirecting worker dissatisfactions.

96. Federal Bureau of Investigation, *Crime in the United States: 1972* (Washington, D.C.: Government Printing Office, 1973), 124.

97. Freda Adler, *Sisters in Crime* (Prospect Heights; IL: Waveland Press, 1975, reprinted 1985), 16.

98. Federal Bureau of Investigation, *Crime in the United States, 1975* (Washington, D.C.: Government Printing Office, 1976), 183.

99. Laurel Rans, "Women's Crime: Much Ado About . . .," *Federal Probation* 32, no.1 (March 1978): 41.

100. Ibid., 48.

101. *The Spokeswomen,* 15 December 1976, 3.

102. Federal Bureau of Investigation, *Crime in the United States: 1982,* 167.

103. Diana R. Gordon and Mae Churchill, "Triple I will be tracking us," *The Nation* (April 28, 1984): 497.

104. Federal Bureau of Investigation, *Crime in the United States: 1982,* 167.

105. Arthur L. Stinchcombe, "Institutions of Privacy in the Determination of Police Administrative Practice." *American Journal of Sociology,* 69 (September 1963), 150–158.

106. Jack D. Douglas and Frances C. Waksler, *The Sociology of Deviance* (Boston: Little, Brown, 1982), 327.

107. Christian and Richard Milner, *Black Players: The Secret World of Black Pimps* (Boston: Little, Brown, 1972).

108. Henrik Kruger, *The Great Heroin Coup* (Boston: South End Press, 1980).

109. John Helmer, *Drugs and Minority Oppression* (New York: Seabury Press, 1975), 18–33.

110. Ibid., 55–79.

CHAPTER 12

Crimes of Capital-Part I: Corporate Offenses

INTRODUCTION

What Are Crimes of Capital?

The previous chapter on common crime examined those offenses against persons, property, and public order that can be committed by people independent of any particular position within the relations of production. This chapter examines the other side of the coin—the crimes of capital.

Crimes of capital are socially injurious acts that arise from the ownership or management of capital or from occupancy of positions of trust in institutions designed to facilitate the accumulation of capital. Like common crimes, the crimes of capital can take a number of specific forms. These are (1) corporate crime, (2) occupational crime, (3) organized crime, and (4) political crime. Each category has distinct characteristics and reflects the opportunities for wrongdoing associated with particular positions in the political economy. The various crimes of capital in any society will also share certain characteristics based on the mode of production in that society. That is, the patterns of ownership and usage of capital in a given society will be fundamental in shaping the types of harm that can arise from the usage of this capital. Thus, for example, we could expect to find some differences in the crimes of capital characteristic of a free-market economy such as found in the United States and those more common in a centrally planned economy such as that in the Soviet Union.

The term "crimes of capital" is not limited to acts specifically prohibited under criminal law. As we shall see, it also includes acts prohibited under regulatory law, and some acts that are not even presently under the control of law. This extension of the concept of crime beyond the boundaries of what is now seen as criminal represents one side of a continuing debate in criminology.

The Debate Over What Constitutes Crime

Criminology has traditionally focused most of its attention on the kinds of common crimes believed to be associated with the poor and the powerless. When these crimes are studied criminal law provides a handy, preexisting

314

and unambiguous starting point for inquiry. The criminal law is a less useful guideline when attempting to study wrongdoing by the powerful.

The law embodies the interests and perceptions of an appropriate social order held by those with the political power to shape the law. In capitalist society those who own or manage capital have historically enjoyed a greater ability to shape the law in comparison with other social groups. Moreover, regardless of social position, many individuals will tend to take for granted the preexisting order into which they are socialized, including its distribution of power and its definitions of right and wrong. For these reasons social injuries that result from the behavior of those actively involved in the process of capital accumulation are less likely to be either recognized or criminalized. This does not, however, change the fact of their existence or their consequences.

If the study of crime is limited to those acts defined as "criminal" by law, certain types of social injury become "off limits" to inquiry. In effect, the study of crime becomes defined by the legal order instead of constituting an independent, scientific investigation of the definition and control of harm in the society.

There have been periodic attempts to grapple with the problems posed by limiting criminology to the study of acts defined as criminal by law. These attempts have generally produced substantial controversy. In particular, the works of Thorsten Sellin, Edwin Sutherland, and the "radical" criminologists have occasioned debates over the appropriate boundaries of criminological inquiry.

In 1938 Thorsten Sellin criticized the tendency of criminologists to limit their investigations to "the categories set up by the criminal law" because these categories did not "arise intrinsically from the nature of the subject matter" but instead depended upon "the character and interests of those groups in the population which influence legislation."[1] In an attempt to move criminology beyond the limitations of criminal law, Sellin proposed that all forms of "abnormal conduct," that is, behavior in violation of the social rules established within any group, be added to the subject matter of criminology.[2]

In a somewhat different vein Edwin Sutherland challenged the traditional focus on conventional crimes of the poor by introducing the concept of "white-collar crime" in his 1939 presidential address to the American Sociological Association. Sutherland's initial argument was that violations of the *criminal law* by businessmen and other white-collar workers in the course of their occupations should be treated no less as crimes than the conventional crimes of the lower classes.[3] By the publication of his book *White Collar Crime* in 1945, Sutherland expanded his definition of criminality to include all acts proscribed by law as "socially harmful" and for which there existed a legally prescribed penalty, regardless of whether these acts were prohibited under criminal or regulatory law.[4] For the most part Sutherland did not argue that criminology should examine socially harmful acts whether or not they were punishable under law but rather that criminology should examine *all* behaviors punishable by law rather than only conventional crimes. Yet despite his concern with keeping the focus of criminology within the boundaries of legal categories, Sutherland himself includes a discussion of socially harmful but *technically legal* contract violations in *White Collar Crime*.[5]

While criticizing the tendency of criminology to focus only on those conventional harms defined as crime by law, both Sellin and Sutherland proposed alternatives that sidestepped several fundamental issues. Sutherland recognized that most regulatory laws were designed to facilitate the interests of business in having a regularized and predictable environment for profit-making activity.[6] Yet he did not espouse critical examination of the formulation of those laws or their selective prohibition of only certain forms of social injury. Instead, he remained committed to the idea that the law should be used to define the boundaries of criminological inquiry. Sellin more clearly addressed the issue of law as the manifestation of the interests of the powerful, and therefore thought it inadequate as the basis for deciding the scope of *sociological* criminology. However, by emphasizing the study of "abnormal conduct," Sellin made the same error with respect to "conduct norms" that Sutherland made with respect to the law. Criminological investigation limited to the study of *violations* of established group norms provides little information concerning why those particular norms exist or how they relate to both the objective and perceived conditions of life among the groups who hold them. Yet it is the analysis of why and how some behaviors are selected as "wrong" and others as acceptable that provides us with the best data for understanding the relationship between social structures and social control.

Sellin's concept of "conduct norms" provided an important theoretical orientation for the study of *deviance* within sociology. Sutherland in turn can be credited with initiating criminological interest in "white-collar crime," which did represent a significant addition to the field's earlier, almost exclusive concern with common crime. However, their works notwithstanding, between 1940 and 1970 the majority of criminological analyses centered on the crimes of the powerless.

In 1970 Herman and Julia Schwendinger offered a list of "human rights" the abrogation of which they argued should be defined as crime and studied by criminologists irrespective of their inclusion or exclusion from a state definition of crime. These are

> ... the fundamental prerequisites for well-being, including food, shelter, clothing, medical services, challenging work and recreational experiences, as well as security from predatory individuals or repressive and imperialistic social elites.[7]

The concept of human rights, variously construed but generally following the Schwendinger's argument, has served as the basic guideline for criminological inquiry within what has come to be known as "radical" criminology. Thus radical criminologists argue that social conditions such as racism, sexism, exploitation of labor, ageism, and imperialism can be an appropriate focus for criminological analysis, no less than conventional murders, rapes, and robberies.[8]

Attempts such as those initiated by Sutherland, Sellin, and the radical criminologists to expand criminology beyond the boundaries of criminal law have been criticized by some as "unscientific," as Paul Tappan argued in

1947, because they invite the "subjective value judgements of the investigator."[9] More recently it has been argued that criminologists are "in no position to expand [their] domain" and that those who seek to include in their analyses acts not specifically criminal under law "infuse the phenomenon with their own moral agendas."[10]

This argument for limiting criminological inquiry to the specifications of the law overlooks the fact that the law itself reflects a set of subjectively held values, and limiting investigation within its boundaries reflects a no more inherently "scientific" choice than expanding inquiry beyond the law. As the Schwendingers observe,

> No scholar involved in the controversy about the definitions of crime has been able to avoid direct or indirect use of moral standards in the solution to this problem. . . . In light of this, the claim that moral judgements have no place in the formulation of the definitions of crime is without foundation.[11]

Right and wrong are moral concepts. The criminal law is essentially a politically enforced definition of right and wrong. Therefore, neither those who support a criminology that goes beyond the law's definition of right and wrong nor those who wish to keep it within these limits are making morally neutral choices. Any moral choice, even those about "scientific" data, will reflect the individual's values. As Karl Helibroner noted,

> The position of the social researcher differs sharply from that of the observer of the natural world. The latter . . . is not morally imbedded in the field he scrutinizes. By contrast the social investigator is inextricably bound up with the objects of his scrutiny . . . bringing with him feelings of animus or defensiveness to the phenomenon he observes.[12]

When determining the subject matter for social inquiry the important question is not whether the selection does or does not reflect the values of the researcher at some level, but rather whether the choices made provide a useful and scientifically adequate basis for developing an understanding of the phenomenon being studied. Limiting inquiry to those acts specified as criminal by law may be an adequate basis if one is interested only in *how* (but not why) the criminal justice system operates. However, if the concern is to arrive at a broader understanding of the relationship between law and social order, the way in which the law is selective in its criminalization of social injuries must also be included in what is to be studied. We cannot examine this selectivity unless we compare those things that are illegal with similar forms of social injury that are not.

The following discussion of crimes of capital will include acts prohibited under criminal or regulatory law and *analogous forms of social injury* not specifically prohibited. The concept of "analogous" social injuries refers to legally permissible acts or sets of conditions whose consequences are similar to those of illegal acts. Here, the examination of crimes of capital will focus on acts or conditions that arise in connection with the process of capital accumulation and that, regardless of whether or not they are prohibited by law, result in one of the following:

1. Violent or untimely death
2. Illness or disease
3. Deprivation of adequate food, clothing, shelter, or medical care
4. Reduction or elimination of the opportunity for individuals to participate effectively in the political decision-making processes that affect their lives

Capital, Capital Accumulation, and Crime

The crimes of capital in America arise from the particular forms of social relations associated with the processes of *capital accumulation, concentration,* and *centralization.* Certain of these forms are not unique to capitalist societies, nor are the possibilities for social injury inherent in them. Certainly some of the social injuries that will be discussed here, such as environmental damage, worker injury and death, and political repression, can arise in societies with centrally planned economies as well. However, differences between market and planned economies in the process of capital accumulation will produce both different opportunities for crimes of capital and different responses to them. To understand crimes of capital in America requires an examination of the particular dynamics of capital accumulation that emerge when capital is privately owned and the process of accumulation is managed largely for private rather than public interests.

In the broadest sense of the term, capital is something of value that is in the process of being exchanged for something of greater value. Value can take two forms: *use-value* and *exchange value.* Use value is based on the ability of an object to *directly* meet some need. Exchange value resides in the ability of an object to enable someone to acquire the use-value of other objects through trade.[13] If a weaver produces a blanket to keep himself warm at night, the value of that blanket to the weaver resides only in its ability to provide warmth, that is, its use-value. Should the weaver decide to trade his blanket for fuel, however, the value of the blanket for the weaver transforms from use-value to exchange value. At this point,

> His commodity possesses for himself no immediate use-value. Otherwise, he would not bring it to the market. It has use-value for others; but for himself its only direct use-value is . . . [as] a means of exchange.[14]

He no longer "values" the blanket for its ability to keep him warm but for its ability to enable him to acquire fuel.

For trade to develop beyond the level of simple barter, such as the direct exchange of blankets for firewood, it is necessary for those involved in trade to be able to reckon the value of different commodities in terms of some third commodity that is recognized as an equivalent measure of value. This equivalent measure of value is *money.* Whatever form it takes—beads, salt, cattle, coins, paper, and so forth—money serves as a symbolic representation to the value of commodities expressed in units of measure *that can be applied to all commodities.*[15] Money expands the possibilities for trade by freeing individuals from the need to find others willing to enter into the exact reciprocal exchange they have in mind. Our weaver, if he is to acquire firewood, must find an owner of firewood willing to exchange some for a blanket. If none of the owners of firewood has need of a blanket, the weaver must do without firewood. However, if blue beads serve as a recognized equivalent of value in the weaver's society, he can then exchange his blanket for some quantity of blue beads with someone who wants a blanket, and then exchange the blue beads for firewood. Because it serves as a *universal equivalent* of value within a society, money makes it possible for individuals to purchase *any* of the commodities available in the society.[16] In addition to broadening the possibilities for exchange, the existence of money brings other changes to society.

First, money makes possible exchange *for its own sake.* When individuals trade commodities directly, the primary reason for the exchange is generally because there is a reciprocal desire to acquire the use-value of the objects being exchanged. The woodseller wants the warmth of a blanket and the weaver wants the warmth of wood. Where money is the medium of exchange, however, individuals may engage in trade simply to acquire money.

When the weaver sells a blanket to acquire enough money to buy firewood, he is *selling in order to buy.* However, when a trader buys blankets for five blue beads apiece in order to sell them for seven blue beads apiece in another village, he is *buying in order to sell.* At this point trade becomes a specialized activity in itself, independent of the use-value of the objects traded. It is also at this point that capital comes into existence. When money as the representation of value is set upon a cycle of exchange with the intention of acquiring more money, it becomes capital.

Second, money makes possible the realization of profit through exchange. Where individuals exchange commodities directly it is not possible for one person to acquire more value than the other because the "value" of the commodities exchanged is determined solely by that for which they are traded. Without reducing the values of blankets and firewood to some third measure—money—it is not possible to say that the weaver received more or less value for his blanket than the woodseller received for the amount of firewood traded for the blanket. However, if a trader can buy blankets for fewer blue beads apiece in one town than he sells them for in another, the trader has acquired *surplus-value.* That is, he has acquired more value, in the form of money, through the act of trade than he had to begin with.

Third, by enabling the realization of profit, money makes possible the accumulation of value. Through repeated acts of buying in order to sell, the trader can acquire an ever-growing amount of money—the measure of value. Insofar as this accumulated value represents the opportunity to acquire even more value, we can say that the trader is engaged in the *accumulation of capital.*[17]

Trade, whether selling in order to buy or buying in order to sell, is based upon the exchange of value—usually represented by money. But what is the basis of value? The basis of nearly all value in human societies is labor power. Beyond the level of hunters and gatherers, objects *as they occur spontaneously in nature* have little use-value for human societies in the absence of labor power to impart value to these objects. As Marx observed, all objects of value that cannot be used exactly as they occur in nature ". . . owe their existence to a special productive activity, exercised with a definite aim, an activity that appropriates particular nature-given materials to particular human wants."[18] For instance, iron ore, coal, and limestone, which are the essential elements of steel production, are of little value in the absence of the labor power necessary to extract them from the earth, build smelting furnaces, and transport them to the furnaces where additional labor power can turn them into steel.

The production of value through labor is a social act. Value is imparted to objects when individuals acting in concerted effort apply their labor to create things of value. This is particularly true of industrialized societies where the production of most commodities, whether it is food, bedding, or baseball bats, requires the coordinated effort of hundreds or even thousands of people.

What becomes of the value produced by the social act of labor? In all societies, whatever the mode of production, a portion of the value produced by labor is either consumed directly by labor and its dependents or returned to them to continue life. No society, however repressive, can endure if it fails to effectively reproduce its labor force, for that is the source of all value. However, once the minimum requirements for the reproduction of the labor force are met, in all but the most unfortunate of primitive societies there usually exists a degree of surplus arising from the social act of labor. The way in which, and to whom, this surplus is distributed is determined by the mode of production of the society.

In primitive, egalitarian societies surplus is usually either distributed equally or retained collectively as a hoard against future lean years. In slave societies the owners appropriate to themselves the entire product of the slaves, returning to the slaves only sufficient food and shelter to maintain life. Under a feudal mode of production the lords acquired the bulk of the social surplus by taking the products of the unpaid labor that serfs were required to render as part of their feudal obligation. In slave and feudal societies "the possessing class take for themselves the social surplus product."[19]

The same is true under capitalism, but the mechanism is different. In capitalist society the value produced by the social act of labor is controlled by neither the social body as a whole nor by that portion of it that labors. It is controlled by that portion of the society that has acquired sufficient capital to buy value-producing labor. This private appropriation of social production is made possible by the *extraction of surplus value through wage labor.* Surplus value is extracted when the value produced by labor is less than the value returned to labor in the form of wages and other benefits. The essence of *capitalist* production is the purchase of labor power for wages less than the value that will be produced by this labor. By expending labor power the worker creates new value. Then,

> At a certain moment he will have produced new value exactly equivalent to what he receives in wages. If he were to stop working at that moment, he would not have produced any surplus value. But the employer does not mean this to happen. He does not want to do a favor, he wants to do business.[20]

The essence of doing business is buying in order to sell. The employer buys labor just like any other commodity with the intention of selling it—or in this case its products—for more than the cost of purchase. For this to happen the laborer must work longer than is needed to simply reproduce the value equivalent to his or her wages. The laborer must provide the employer with a certain amount of free labor, free insofar as the employer will appropriate to himself the value produced by this labor as profit rather than paying it back to labor in the form of wages or benefits.

This profit can be utilized in one of two ways. It can be used by owners or managers of capital to finance private consumption of use-value in the form of various commodities, or it can be transformed into capital by applying it to finance further profit-generating activities.[21] Normally profit is divided between both of these uses. In most American industries there is a degree of separation between the ownership of capital and the management of capital. Those who manage the day-to-day operations of most American industries may be stockholders in those industries, but they are not "owners" in the same sense as early industrial capitalists. Instead, they are hired to manage the capital of the industry in ways that will insure that it generates continued profit for the various owners of that capital.[22] In this capacity high-level managers of capital decide upon the allocation of profit between corporate reinvestment, stock dividends, and usage of profit for consumption. A portion of profit is used to finance internal consumption in the form of lavish office suites, services, and other perquisites for high-level managerial employees or private consumption through high salaries paid to upper-level management. Another portion is allocated to corporate investments, and the remainder is paid to stockholders in the form of dividends.[23] That portion that stockholders receive as dividends may in turn be used to finance the private consumption of commodities such as cars, houses, summer homes, jewelry, or art works, or it may be used by these private individuals as capital to be invested in the hopes of generating still more profit.

It is sometimes argued that the emergence of a professional managerial class with control over decisions such as the allocation of capital between stockholders' dividends and reinvestment represents a *fundamental* change in the nature of capitalism and renders any analysis based upon a distinction between workers and owners of capital outmoded.[24] However, a change in the *types of people* who manage the daily operations of capitalist industries does not alter the basic function of those industries.

In the words of a former president of DuPont Corporation, a corporate manager is simply a "symphony conductor under whose hand a hundred or so highly specialized and yet very different skills become a single effort of great effectiveness."[25] This effectiveness is measured in capitalist society today, as it has always been, by the ability to generate profit. As analysts Paul Baran and Paul Sweezy conclude in their study of industries in the monopoly sector, which is comprised of those industries with the greatest "separation" between capital and management, "The giant corporation of today is an engine for maximizing profits and accumulating capital to at least as great an extent as the individual enterprise of an earlier period."[26]

The extraction of surplus-value from labor creates a fundamentally hostile relationship between labor and capital. Capital, or more correctly those who manage its interests, seek to increase the gap between the total amount of value produced by labor and the proportion of that value which must be returned to labor in the form of wages and benefits. The two primary mechanisms for accomplishing this task are (1) holding wages to the minimum that must be paid in order to buy the needed quality and quantity of labor and (2) the replacement of labor with machines that will increase the total amount of value produced by that labor which remains employed.[27] By contrast, labor seeks to continue to be employed and to retain for itself the largest possible proportion of the value it produces. Disputes between employees and employers over wages, benefits, or the elimination of labor through various forms of automated production are essentially disputes over the distribution between employer and employees of the value produced by labor.

The centrally planned economies of socialist countries also engage in a degree of extraction of surplus-value; that is, not all value produced by labor is returned to labor in the form of wages. Portions are retained for reinvestment or expansion, and portions are utilized to support state social service or military expenditures. Theoretically, in socialist societies the value produced by labor is ultimately returned to the population in the form of either expanded economic growth or state services. In practice, however, conflicts can arise between portions of the labor force and the state managers of the nation's capital, as has obviously been the case in Poland. There is, however, one significant difference between such conflicts and those that occur between labor and capital in capitalist societies.

State managers of capital in socialist societies are ideologically and to some extent legally expected to manage capital specifically for the general social good. Conflicts arise over whether they are in fact doing so and over what particular policies will achieve socialist goals. In capitalist societies there is no corresponding ideological or legal obligation. As economist Milton Friedman argued, in a market economy corporations have no obligation except to "make as much money as possible" for their stockholders.[28] While there are periodic discussions of "corporate responsibility" to the society in general, and both corporations and private individuals frequently make "philanthropic" contributions, these are not formal or legal obligations under capitalism. The primary thrust of capitalism remains the extraction of surplus-value to benefit private economic interests.

The pressure to extract surplus-value continually and to increase "productivity," that is, to increase the gap between the value produced by labor and the value paid out in wages derives from the competitive nature of capitalism. Under feudalism lords and serfs were limited in their freedom by the feudal bond, although the reciprocal obligations of this bond did provide a measure of security for each. With the rise of capitalism and the end of feudalism both labor and capital were "free" to seek greater gain. They were also free to fail more utterly. Just as laborers were forced to compete with one another for wages, capitalists were forced to compete to retain their capital.

The emergence of capitalism created a climate of uncertainty for capital wherein the only guarantee of economic survival was the continued accumulation of capital. The underlying threat of capitalism for the capitalist has always been bankruptcy or takeover by more efficient and/or more affluent competitors. As one spokesman for the Reagan administration said, "Capitalism without failure is like Christianity without hell."[29] The primary thrust of capitalist competition is the desire to accumulate ever larger portions of capital as the only possible protection against other competitors.

The pressure toward capital accumulation produces continual *centralization* and *concentration* of capital. The evolution of capitalism has been characterized by the defeat of less efficient competitors by more efficient ones and the acquisition of the capital of the former by the latter. This process results in a continual growth in the average size of industries and a continual reduction in their total number.

> A large number of small enterprises are beaten in the competitive struggle by a small number of big enterprises which command an increasing share of capital, labour, funds and production in entire branches of industry. A few large enterprises centralize means of production and a number of employees such as were not to be found previously except in dozens or even hundreds of factories added together.[30]

The centralization of capital means that factories and other facilities become larger and fewer. It also means that difficulty in any single enterprise effects ever larger numbers of people.

The *concentration* of capital means that fewer and fewer private individuals control, and decide the disposition of, ever larger amounts of capital. In 1880 37 percent of the American population were entrepreneurs of one sort or another; that is, they earned their living through the control of capital rather than working for wages. By 1965 they had dropped to 12.4 percent.[31] In more recent years the process of corporate acquisition and merger has produced an even greater concentration of capital.[32] The ownership of capital in America has always been, and remains today, highly concentrated in relatively few hands.

Since World War II there has been little change in the distribution of wealth.

> It has been constant in every year studied, at roughly five year intervals since 1945. The richest 1 percent own a quarter, and the top half of one percent a fifth, of the combined market worth *of everything owned by every American.*[33] (emphasis added)

It is estimated that the 520,000 Americans who in 1979 were known to be millionaires—less than 0.5 percent of the total population—own about 80 percent of all corporate stock and 90 percent of all tax-exempt state and local bonds.[34] Moreover, within this group of super-rich Americans there is a tiny group of ultra-rich, about 55,400 persons (one-twentieth of 1 percent of the total population), who own 20 percent of *all* corporate stock, 66 percent of *all* state and local bonds, and 40 percent of *all* other bonds and notes.[35] These figures probably underestimate the concentration of wealth and capital in America since the wealthy are protected from public scrutiny of their finances and because the actual ownership of wealth is often obscured by the complexities of trusts, foundations, and nested holding companies.

The processes of extraction of surplus-value, competitively stimulated accumulation of capital, centralization of capital, and concentration of capital have a direct bearing on the nature, likelihood, and consequences of crimes of capital. The need to accumulate capital through extraction of surplus-value shapes the basic relationship between labor and capital and influences the responses of industry in areas such as worker safety and labor practices. The need to accumulate through profit maximization also bear upon industry responses in the areas of consumer safety and environmental protection.

CORPORATE CRIME
The Nature of Corporate Crime

Corporate crimes are actions that are either prohibited by law or that knowingly lead to social injury, taken by official representatives of legitimate businesses to facilitate capital accumulation within those businesses. Specifically, these acts seek to facilitate capital accumulation through profit maximization in illegal or socially injurious ways by either (1) reducing the costs of production or (2) increasing illegally the price and/or the volume of the goods or services marketed. Production costs can be illegally reduced by such actions as failing to make costly changes in known hazardous products, avoiding expenses associated with protecting worker safety or meeting environmental protection requirements, or illegally repressing the organization of labor into effective unions. Price and volume maximization is facilitated through such actions as obtaining monopoly positions in the marketplace, fraudulent or questionable advertising, bribes for favorable contracts offered to governmental or other purchasing agents, or price fixing.

While corporate crimes are ultimately related to the pressures for capital accumulation it is important to recognize the complexity of the process whereby the goal of capital accumulation is translated into a variety of organizational subgoals. As one analyst of corporate wrongdoing noted,

> The central organization cannot leave each of these groups at large to realize "profit" as it sees best. Rather, the farther and farther down the operations ladder one moves, the more the "profit goal" has to be translated into subgoals—targets and objectives for the shop, the department, the plant, the division, the subsidiary. It is these subgoals that define the task environment of the people actually engaged in production at such a plant, not some abstract "corporate profit."[36]

To this must be added, however, that a primary criterion for evaluating how effectively any subsegment of a corporate organization meets its goals is the degree to which it does so with maximum economic efficiency, that is, the degree to which it contributes to the overall profitability of the organization.

A corporate research and design department, for instance, may be charged with the subgoal of developing a new product to eventually be produced and marketed by other organizational components of the corporation. The process of research and design involves not creating the *best* product possible but creating one that can be produced with minimum expense and marketed with maximum effect. Thus, for example, the costs of producing a totally safe product will be balanced against the potential additional expense of including safety features in the design. Similarly, to meet its goals of maximizing sales a marketing department must frequently balance totally truthful advertising against the kind of advertising that will attract the largest numbers of customers.

As Figure 12.1 shows, the *means* to achieve an organizational goal at one level become the *goals* of other organizational subunits, which in turn generate demands on still other units. At each point, subunits can select legal or illegal means to achieve those goals. Pressures to select illegal or questionable alternatives arise from two interrelated sources: (1) the need for organizational survival and (2) pressures for profit maximization.

One characteristic of corporate crime is that the participants in the illegal or socially injurious acts do so not for *direct* personal gain but to facilitate the organization's *legitimate* goal of maximizing profit. While these individuals may be rewarded by promotions or bonuses for facilitating the organization's goals, this reward comes to them indirectly rather than as a direct result of the illegal act, as would be the case when an employee engaged in embezzlement or theft of company property. Corporate crimes are also characterized by the fact that they take place within legitimate business operations. That is, the company or institution has as its primary goal the *legitimate* acquisition of capital, although illegality may play a part in furthering that goal. Thus corporate crime within legitimate businesses can be distinguished from the criminal acts committed by businesses established for the sole purpose of perpetrating some illegality such as a stock swindle or land fraud.

Corporate crime represents the most widespread and costly form of crime in America. Illegal and socially injurious acts within the corporate world touch every American in their various roles as workers, consumers, and citizens.

Crimes Against Worker Safety

Work-related accidents and diseases represent the single greatest cause of disability and untimely death in America. On the average the number of work-related deaths is annually about *6 times* the number of deaths due to homicide and more than twice the number resulting from motor-vehicle accidents.[37] Even the most conservative estimates of work-related injuries indicate that these occur annually about *4 times* as often as assaults. More liberal estimates place the likelihood of on-the-job injuries at *10 times* that for assault.[38] Considering that slightly less than half of the American population is employed during any year, the *rate* of death and injury per 100,000 persons is substantially higher than the rate of death or injury due to conventional

Figure 12.1 Corporate Crime: Organizational Means and Goals

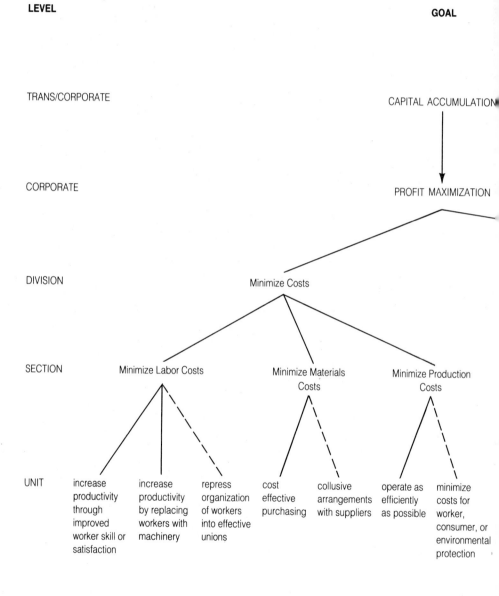

LEVEL   GOAL

TRANS/CORPORATE   CAPITAL ACCUMULATION

CORPORATE   PROFIT MAXIMIZATION

DIVISION   Minimize Costs

SECTION   Minimize Labor Costs   Minimize Materials   Minimize Production
                                                 Costs   Costs

UNIT   increase   increase   repress   cost   collusive   operate as   minimize
        productivity productivity organization effective   arrangements efficiently   costs for
        through   by replacing of workers   purchasing with suppliers as possible worker,
        improved   workers with into effective   consumer, or
        worker skill or machinery   unions   environmental
        satisfaction   protection

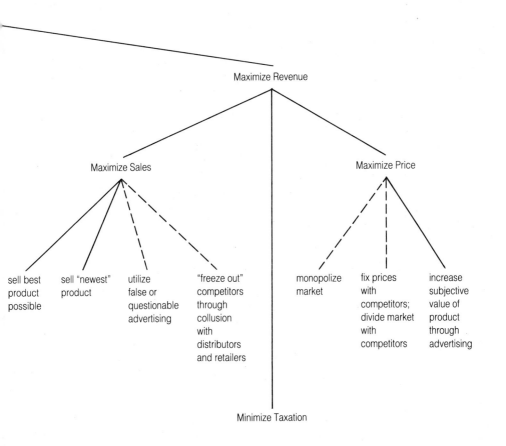

illegal and/or potentially illegal alternatives

legal alternatives

Maximize Revenue

Maximize Sales

Maximize Price

sell best product possible

sell "newest" product

utilize false or questionable advertising

"freeze out" competitors through collusion with distributors and retailers

monopolize market

fix prices with competitors; divide market with competitors

increase subjective value of product through advertising

Minimize Taxation

crime. In 1978 there were nine murders for every 100,000 persons in the United States, while job-related deaths claimed approximately 115 out of every 100,000 workers. Using conservative estimates about 2,200 out of every 100,000 workers are injured annually, while assault rates remain below 275 per 100,000.[39] In addition, about 390 out of every 100,000 workers are afflicted with job-related disabling diseases annually.[40]

Work is hazardous, and certainly not all of the death, injury, and disease it produces is currently preventable. However, the high rates of work-related human suffering in America are not wholly attributable to the inherent hazards of work. Much of this human waste arises from a general disregard on the part of capital for the health and safety of the American worker. Both historically and contemporarily American industry has sought to protect profit margins by *minimizing* the costs of providing for worker safety. Gains that have been made by labor in this area have generally occurred during times of either labor shortage or severe social upheaval. As health researcher Daniel Berman writes,

> When labor is extremely scarce (as in times of war), employers worry about preserving the labor they control by making work more attractive. During times of severe social unrest, workers demand better conditions. In both cases, business tries to jump ahead of workers and create institutions which define the problems of health and safety in non-threatening ways and take the sting out of worker unrest.[41]

In the early twentieth century labor agitation coupled with labor shortages during World War I led to the establishment of an *industry-controlled* system for handling the problems of worker compensation and occupational safety. The primary thrust of this compensation–safety system was to minimize the costs to industry of worker death and injury and to co-opt worker demands for less hazardous working conditions. The key strategies for accomplishing these goals were (1) focusing on *compensation to injured workers* rather than the development and installation of devices to improve the safety of *all* workers, (2) holding compensation to minimal levels, (3) limiting employer liability to on-the-job injuries, and (4) creating a system of company medicine and related medical research to serve as the primary source of information on work-related hazards.

Compensation versus Safety.   From its beginning the system of employee compensation and worker safety has been heavily skewed toward compensation. There are two reasons for this. First, compensating individual workers for injuries is generally less expensive than instituting general measures to reduce injuries. Expenditures to maintain industrial machinery in safe operating order, for example, can be impediments to profits during lean times. As one steel industry executive said,

> Both maintenance levels and costs must follow operational levels . . . when we are in periods of high production and we are making money we can spend it. The converse is also true. When production levels are down and we are not

making money, we cannot spend it. . . . to do otherwise would be contrary to financial reality.[42]

In other words, if several workers die due to faulty machinery, as happened at this particular executive's plant, paying for compensation via insurance is preferable to incurring the profit-eroding costs of insuring general safety.

Second, worker compensation is provided through private liability insurance carriers. In 1974 these insurance companies earned $45 billion in net premiums from employee compensation programs, and controlled $78 billion worth of assets through such programs.[43] The lucrative nature of the compensation system for the insurance industry has created strong incentives for the insurance industry to use its substantial political influence in the form of campaign contributions, control over the ability of states to borrow money, and at times outright bribery to keep compensation–safety legislation tilted toward expanding compensation rather than insuring safety.[44]

In 1960, 60 percent of all private expenditures in the compensation–safety system went for compensation. By 1972 this figure had risen to 66 percent.[45] This division of expenditures reflects rational corporate accommodations to "financial reality," that is, the reality that payments to injured workers or to the families of those killed on the job interfere less with profit margins than would preventive measures designed to reduce hazards for all workers.

Minimizing Compensation Costs. The attractiveness of compensation rather than prevention is enhanced greatly by the fact that the compensation apparatus has managed to hold payments to affected workers or their families at relatively low levels. Berman's analysis of the compensation system revealed that between 1940 and 1972 industry has been able to hold the cost of compensation to little more than 1 percent of total payroll costs. Whether paid in a lump sum such as the $15,000 maximum for worker death in Mississippi or in weekly payments such as the $205 allotted families of dead workers in Illinois, average compensation payments for workers killed on the job amount to barely 10 percent of the total lost wages and benefits.[46]

Limiting Employer Liability. While the amount of on-the-job death and injury is substantial, it is significantly less than the effects of occupational diseases. While on-the-job accidents account for between 14,000 and 20,000 deaths annually, over 100,000 workers die each year due to occupationally related diseases such as black lung, brown lung, lead poisoning, asbestosis, and exposure to a variety of other hazardous substances. In addition, around 400,000 workers a year contract some nonfatal occupational disease.[47]

Given these high numbers, it is understandable that the traditional position of industry has been that occupational diseases should not be compensated. This position remained the cornerstone of the compensation–safety system until the late 1960s. In 1969 after many years of struggle West Virginia coal miners obtained a black lung compensation bill from their state. In that same year Congress approved the Coal Mine Health and Safety Act. In 1970

Congress passed what is probably the most controversial piece of worker safety regulation in America—the Occupational Safety and Health Act. This act required employers to provide workplaces free of recognized hazards that "are causing or are likely to cause" death or serious physical harm.[48] The bill also created the Occupational Safety and Health Administration (OSHA) to enforce this standard.

As with many regulatory reforms, the OSHA bill was a response to serious political pressure from the working class.[49] Like most political compromises of this sort, however, the OSHA act represented only a partial victory for workers. While the law accepted the rights of workers to safe working conditions, the mechanisms established to secure this right were inadequate. The staff and budget of OSHA has always been small relative to the scope of its task. This means that the number of workplaces inspected annually encompass only a small fraction of the American work force. In 1975 only 14 percent of American workers were covered by OSHA inspections, and at a projected rate of 20,000 inspections a year, it will take approximately fifty years from OSHA's inception in 1971 for all industries to be inspected.[50] In addition, enforcement practices provide little incentive for swift industry compliance with safety regulations. On the average, penalties proposed by OSHA for violations revealed by inspection amount to barely $25 per offense, and industry appeals often lead to a reduction or waiving of proposed penalties.[51] Furthermore, the legal complexity and cost of appeal procedures make it relatively impossible for most workers or worker organizations to challenge industry appeals of OSHA rulings and fines.

Despite the limited impact of OSHA, its very existence is a threat to industry goals of profit maximization. OSHA's presence threatens to increase workers' consciousness that they have a *right* to be protected from work-related hazards. This challenges the long-established ideology of industry that workers are fortunate to have an opportunity to work at all and that the hazards of work are simply part of the cost of earning a living. Industry opposition to OSHA has been loud and nearly unanimous. The promise to limit the impact of OSHA through budget cuts and the reduction of its authority was an important source of industry support for the Reagan candidacy for president. In keeping with this promise one of the first acts of the Reagan administration was to order an OSHA slowdown in imposing new cotton dust standards upon the textile industry.

Controlling Medical Knowledge. A key strategy in limiting the costs of worker compensation has been control over the practice of industrial medicine and health research. This control is exercised in three ways. First, in most states injured workers are required to seek treatment for work-related problems from *company* doctors or else pay for treatment out of their own pockets. As company employees or contractors, the role of these physicians is generally to minimize the severity of any work-related injury or disease, particularly since it is their testimony that will be utilized to determine the level of compensation if there is a claim. According to Dr. William Shepard, former head of the Council on Occupational Health of the American Medical Association, the role of company physician is

". . . strictly ancillary to the main purpose of business: production at a profit. His value depends upon his willingness and ability to work with others to achieve that main purpose."[52]

The process of helping industries produce at a profit sometimes involves the practice of concealing from workers the truth about their condition. For example, the Johns-Manville Company for thirty years maintained a policy, enforced by their company physicians, of not notifying workers that they were developing asbestosis—a disease caused by breathing asbestos fibers that is untreatable and often fatal. (See the accompanying box.) As the medical director of one Johns-Manville plant wrote regarding the discovery of asbestosis in seven employees,

They have not been told of this diagnosis, for it is felt that as long as the man feels well, is happy at home and at work, and his physical condition remains good, nothing should be said. . . . it is felt that he should not be told of his condition so that he can live and work in peace and *the Company can benefit by his many years of experience.*[53] (emphasis added)

A similar case of asbestosis coverup occurred at a Pittsburgh-Corning plant in Tyler, Texas, where a number of long-term employees were neither informed of the health hazards of their jobs, although it was known to company medical officers, nor of their own developing lung deterioration.[54]

Second, by financing institutes for setting safety standards, various industries have managed to control the development of standards and the flow of information concerning industrial hazards. In 1972, for example, the private sector spent over $26 million to set industrial safety standards compared with $3 million spent by OSHA.[55] As a result nearly all of the standards adopted by OSHA were taken directly from private organizations representing corporate rather than worker interests. It is characteristic of these organizations to establish standards that are aimed at improving *worker conduct* around hazardous machinery rather than standards aimed at reducing the hazards or to require less effective but also less costly safety precautions such as individual respirators rather than improved ventilation systems in industries involving, say, asbestos or cotton production.

Third, by selectively allocating money for medical research, industry and insurance have retarded the development of knowledge concerning the hazards of work. Where research has been funded it is often with the express interests of providing information to challenge independent findings damaging to industry interests. In 1956, for example, the Asbestos Textile Institute financed a cancer research project to "procure information which would contradict current derogatory literature," in the words of the institute. This "derogatory literature" consisted of independent medical research demonstrating a strong connection between asbestos and cancer, something that the industry already had known for twenty years.[56] There is also evidence of industry attempts to suppress research that could render objectionable findings, as was the case with research into the hazardous effects of cotton dust on textile workers in North Carolina.[57] In another instance, at a February 4, 1971, meeting of the Asbestos Institute, Dr. Selikoff, a medical researcher who had clearly demonstrated the carcinogenic (cancer-producing) effects of asbestos, was described as a "dangerous man," and plans were made to utilize the American Medical Association to put pressure on Mount Sinai Hospital in New York where Selikoff worked to curb Selikoff's research.[58]

The Reality of Workplace Crime. Using Sutherland's proposition that crime is any violation of law for which a penalty can be imposed by the state, we can consider crimes against worker's safety to be *real* crimes. Moreover, these

---

"THE DUST HAS ATE US UP"

"I was a bag feeder for about six months," he said. "It was my job to empty the amosite out of the burlap sacks and into the feeding machines. I fed about seventy hundred-pound bags of asbestos on every eight-hour shift I worked. Trouble was, the asbestos wouldn't just pour out. It was packed in so tight we had to dig it out with our bare hands."

I asked Barron if he had ever worn a respirator when he was a bag feeder, and he shook his head. He had never worn one until August of 1971, he said, when the company suddenly made it mandatory for the entire work force to wear respirators. "Some of us were issued respirators a few years ago, but it was voluntary if we wanted to wear them, and since no one told us until last August that asbestos was dangerous to work with, we didn't," he said. "All of us in the maintenance crew are wearing 'em now, though. Except for Van Horne, who keeps saying that asbestos won't hurt you. He also claims that none of our medical problems are caused by asbestos. . . .

"I'll be sixty-six years old in May," Spencer said. "And I swear I'm just about the onliest one I know that's left alive from that McGregor plant. Except for my son, of course, and he's already got trouble with his lungs. I've had trouble with mine for years. I finally had to quit the Tyler plant in 1968. They disabled me. Just couldn't hardly breathe no more. Now I'm out of breath all the time. Can't do nothing. Can't walk any distance at all. When I quit, they started giving me some retirement payments—eighteen dollars a month. . . .

"I've been going to these local doctors for my lungs for years," he said. "I spit up an awful lot and I'm always out of breath, and I've got a funny-sounding cough. I guess I've been to just about every last doctor in that Medical and Surgical Clinic. All of 'em have told me I had something wrong on my X-rays. Some of 'em have told me I got emphysema, and some of 'em say it's asthma, and at one time they even thought I had cancer, but not one of 'em ever said it was on account of asbestos. Well, they're a bunch of quacks. I know what I got now. I got what Ed Land got. I got what Harold's got. And all the others. I got that dust disease. That dust has ate us up."

Source: Paul Brodeur, *Expendable Americans* (New York: Viking, 1974), 86–87. Reprinted by permission of the Sterling Lord Agency, Inc. Copyright © 1974 by Paul Brodeur.

offenses are not mere technical violations of law; they are acts that can and do result in the loss of life, injury, and impaired health. For instance, in March 1976 an explosion in the Scotia Coal Company mine under Big Black Mountain in Kentucky claimed twenty-six lives. In the several years prior to this disaster, the company had been cited for 652 safety violations, at least sixty of which were for failures to maintain adequate ventilation and methane gas measurement procedures—failures that ultimately caused the deadly mine explosion.[59] While it is relatively easy to identify the relationship between safety violations and large-scale workplace disasters like this, it is more difficult to know the ultimate effect of violations of regulations aimed at reducing worker exposure to carcinogens and other toxic substances. Since only a portion of workers victimized by regulatory violations will contract occupational diseases, and in many cases the effects of exposure do not manifest themselves for years, it is far more difficult to prove conclusively the cause–effect relationship between violation and injury in any particular instance. What we do know is that a proportion of workers exposed to unsafe levels of toxic substances such as asbestos fiber, beryllium, PVC, diatomaceous earth, PCB, lead, radiation, and many of the 250,000 chemicals used in American industry will contract diseases resulting from that exposure.

In the four years between 1971 and 1975, OSHA conducted 206,163 workplace inspections and identified 724,582 violations of workplace safety regulations. These inspections covered about 10 percent of all workplaces in America and about 14 percent of all workers.[60] If violations of workplace safety are roughly proportional to the number of workers, this means that the actual number of violations during the four-year period was around 5.2 million, or about 1.3 million a year. This compares with less than 1 million violent crimes in 1974. Not all violations of worker safety regulations result in actual injury to workers, but neither do all violent Index Offenses since nearly half are robberies, the majority of which do not result in injury to victims. More significant is the fact that while Index Offenses of violence are counted on the basis of one offense *per victim,* regulatory violations of worker safety can and often do encompass *many* actual or potential victims.

When considering a rate of workplace safety violations that is in the neighborhood of 1.3 million a year, it is important to recognize that these are violations of standards a large proportion of which were adopted by OSHA directly from *industry-established* guidelines. While OSHA has been frequently characterized by industry representatives as an overzealous bureaucratic agency enforcing unreasonable safety standards on industrial capital, the fact is that a substantial proportion of the estimated 1.3 million safety violations annually represents the unwillingness of industry to comply even with its own relatively lax estimates of what constitutes a safe workplace.

Despite the scale of death, injury, and disease caused by outright violations of worker safety regulations, public demands for governmental action in this area are far below those related to common crimes. There are three key reasons. First, since the emergence of "free labor," an important part of Western consciousness has been the belief that capital has little obligation to labor other than to pay an agreed-upon wage and, conversely, labor has little right to make demands upon capital that would interfere with the search for profit. This way of thinking has been promoted by many of the great and little thinkers of the Western world for the last 400 years and remains integral to American ideology concerning the relationship between workers and employers. Second, much of the truth about the health hazards of work is hidden from workers. As health researcher Dr. Thomas Mancuso testified before a 1974 Department of Labor hearing on the dangers of polyvinyl chloride: "Invariably, whenever a new occupational cancer is discovered, it is played down for fear of alarming the workers and the general public."[61] It is highly doubtful that many workers would remain casual about the health hazards in their places of work if they were given full and factual information about the dangers to their health these hazards pose.

Third, and perhaps most importantly, a large part of the work force recognizes that they must choose between working in a hazardous environment or having no income at all. As one Texas legislator commented on the investigations into the effects of asbestos on workers at the Pittsburgh-Corning plant in Tyler, Texas; "I think we are all willing to have a little bit of crud in our lungs and a full stomach rather than a whole lot of clean air and nothing to eat."[62] After identification of extensive violations of safety regulations by OSHA, the Tyler plant was indeed closed down, idling hundreds of workers. In recent years a number of industries have sought to circumvent this problem by relocating plants in countries where they not only can hire cheaper labor but can also avoid the costs of insuring worker safety and health.[63] That is, rather than cease violations against worker health and safety, they have sought to locate new and less powerful victims.

Crimes Against Consumer Safety

It is estimated that roughly thirty-six million consumer product–related injuries requiring medical attention occur annually in the United States.[64] Since this estimate is based on surveys of hospital emergency room records it excludes many injuries that are either untreated or treated by private physicians. Moreover, it provides little information concerning the extent of continuing medical problems resulting from the initial injury.

Many consumer product–related injuries result from either genuine accidents, that is, an unforeseeable set of circumstances or consumer errors. However, many do not. While it is not reasonable to expect that all products can be designed and manufactured to be completely hazard free, many of the product-related deaths and injuries that occur each year are the direct consequence of either (1) *industry failure to adequately test products for potentially hazardous design or manufacturing defects* or (2) *failure or unwarranted delay in correcting known product hazards*. Both cases represent corporate decisions to minimize production costs and maximize profits at the expense of the health and safety of consumers.

It is difficult to know the extent of product-related death and injury resulting from culpable industry decisions for two reasons. First, the Consumer Product Safety Commission (CPSC), the primary agency responsible for regulating industry behavior in the area of consumer safety, is charged with reducing product hazards, not with determining responsibility for the hazards. This orientation is mandated by the legal requirement that CPSC "minimize the regulatory burden imposed on industry" through "decreased use of restrictive regulatory techniques such as mandatory bans and standards."[65] As a result CPSC relies largely on the establishment of *voluntary* safety standards within industry. Specifically,

> The Commission believes that by encouraging the development and use of voluntary safety standards, the level of product safety in the marketplace can be increased with a relatively small expenditure of Commission resources, particularly when compared to the resources necessary to issue mandatory safety standards for consumer protection.[66]

This means that when product hazards are identified the commission's primary goal is to convince the relevant industries to voluntarily establish corrective standards, not to investigate the decision-making process that led to the marketing of the dangerous products to begin with. It also means that only a small proportion of cases involving hazardous products will ever be formal violations of law since CPSC avoids establishing mandatory regulations where possible.

Even with its stated commitment to avoid formal regulation where possible CPSC issued regulatory judgments against 589 companies during the fiscal year 1980. Of these, 456 were for violations of existing mandatory standards, while the remainder were for products that posed "substantial hazards" but for which no mandatory standard existed at that time. In most cases the commission's judgment required either recalling or retrofitting the hazardous product. In addition, CPSC sought civil penalties against fifteen companies and cease and desist orders against six others in 1980.[67]

The second factor limiting knowledge of corporate culpability in product-related injury and death is that the degree of industry foreknowledge of hazards inherent in certain products is often hidden in internal documents or obscured through falsified test reports. Revelation of this information often depends either upon civil or criminal litigation through which such documents can be subpoenaed as part of "discovery" or the willingness of industry "insiders" to come forth with documentation. Since relatively little product-safety litigation is initiated by CPSC, and since most corporate overseers and managers are well paid for their loyalty, it is likely that considerable questionable industry behavior in the marketing of products known to contain potential safety hazards is never revealed. However, in recent years several dramatic cases in the auto industry have provided an inside look at the kind of decision making that places profit ahead of consumer safety.

Ford Motor Company—A Corporate Killer? On August 10, 1978, three Indiana teenagers, Judy, Lynn, and Donna Ulrich, were burned to death when the gas tank of the 1973 Ford Pinto in which they were riding erupted in flames after the car was struck from the rear. A year and a half later the Ford Motor Company went on trial to face three counts of reckless homicide arising from this accident, the first time an American corporation had been charged with *criminal* homicide. The prosecution's claim that Ford was criminally liable for the death of the three girls under Indiana's reckless homicide law was based on evidence from internal Ford Company memos that showed that the corporation had known for years of the design defect that increased the likelihood of gas tanks in Ford Pintos erupting in rear-end collisions but had deliberately decided against implementing any corrective measures.[68]

This was not the first time Ford's knowledge of the inherent hazard in Pinto gas tanks had figured in litigation. In 1978 eighteen-year-old Richard Grimshaw of Santa Ana, California, won a settlement of $127.8 million against Ford Motor Company in connection with an accident in which Grimshaw was severely burned over 90 percent of his body when his Pinto burst into flames after a low-speed rear-end collision. One hundred and twenty-five million dollars of Grimshaw's settlement was awarded for *punitive* damages based on the court's belief that Ford had full knowledge of the dangers inherent in the Pinto fuel system but had failed to take any action. This inaction on Ford's part was not based on some morbid desire to cause injury and death but upon rational calculation aimed at profit maximization. Specifically, testimony and evidence in Grimshaw's case established that Ford

1. Had shortened its development and planning schedule by nineteen months to bring the Pinto to market ahead of European and Japanese subcompacts
2. Had knowledge of crash tests that showed the tendency of Pinto gas tanks to erupt in rear-end collisions
3. Had rejected for cost-economy reasons a $10-per-car modification that would have substantially reduced gas tank vulnerability to damage
4. Had accepted the logic of a cost-benefit analysis, which showed that since Ford could save $20 million by delaying life-saving improvements for two years but would lose no more than $200,000 per case in suits arising from gas tank explosions, the delay was cost-effective and therefore appropriate[69] (See Table 12.1.)

This evidence was sufficient to convince the court in Grimshaw's civil suit against Ford that the company was guilty not only of error but of malfeasance.

Ford faired much better against the criminal charges in Indiana, where much of the critical evidence in the Grimshaw case was ruled inadmissible. Specifically, internal memos indicating Ford's knowledge of the gas tank problem, rejection of safety improvements, and the cost comparison of potential lives lost versus corporate savings through delayed implementation of safety procedures were never allowed to be presented by the prosecution. Crash test data that indicated the vulnerability of Pinto gas tanks were also ruled inadmissible by the trial judge on the grounds that these data were based on tests of 1969 Pintos while the one involved in the crash was a 1973 Pinto—despite the fact that there were no significant differences between the 1969 and 1973 models in the design or installation of Pinto tanks.[70] Based on this gutting of the prosecution's evidence, Ford was acquitted.

Table 12.1 **A Cost-Benefit Analysis of Human Life—A Better Idea from Ford?**

Benefits and Costs Relating to Fuel Leakage
Associated with the Static Rollover
Test Portion of FMVSS 208

Benefits

Savings: 180 burn deaths, 180 serious burn injuries, 2,100 burned vehicles.
Unit Cost: $200,000 per death, $67,000 per injury, $700 per vehicle.
Total Benefit: 180 × ($200,000) + 180 × ($67,000) + 2,100 × ($700) = $49.5
million.

Costs

Sales: 11 million cars, 1.5 million light trucks.
Unit Cost: $11 per car, $11 per truck.
Total Cost: 11,000,000 × ($11) + 1,500,000 × ($11) = $137 million.

Source: E. S. Grush and C. S. Saunby, "Fatalities Associated with Crash Induced Fuel Leakage
and Fires," Inter-office Memorandum, Ford Motor Company (1973), 6.

Was this a case of blind justice? Doris Cubbernuss and Beti Thompson,
two researchers who observed the trial, are doubtful. They point out that
Ford had arranged to hire as co-counsel a local attorney in the county where
the case was tried who had been a former law partner of the trial judge. To
trial observers this strategy appeared to pay off.

> The warm smiles from the judge to the defense team were so overt that the
> news media sought fit to report them. . . . The attitude of the bench toward the
> prosecution team was markedly different. Although in the beginning the judge
> attempted to maintain some semblance of objectivity, as the trial progressed his
> ruling more and more reflected the wishes of the Ford team. The situation
> deteriorated to the extent that in the final days of the trial the prosecution was
> not allowed to argue against Ford's objections.[71]

In addition to its positive relationship with the trial judge, the Ford defense
team enjoyed another and perhaps more significant advantage. While the
prosecutor was allocated a total of $20,000 to prepare and try his case against
Ford, Ford spent a reputed $1 million on its defense.[72]

These two cases are only the most dramatic ones to arise so far from
the vulnerability of Pinto gas tanks in rear-end collisions. It is estimated that
in all probability at least one hundred people have been killed and many
more injured in fires resulting from low-speed collisions involving Pintos.[73]
Furthermore, the Pinto case may represent only part of a larger pattern of
sacrificing public safety to meet the demands of capital accumulation by that
company.

More recently the National Highway Traffic Safety Administration has
estimated that 70 people have been killed and over 1,000 injured when the
automatic transmissions on Ford-built vehicles slipped unexpectedly from
park into reverse. Most of the injuries and deaths have resulted when drivers
who had stepped out of their cars momentarily to perform such commonplace

tasks as loading groceries or letting out passengers walked behind their vehicles just as the transmission slipped into reverse. Like the case of the Pinto
gas tank, there is evidence that Ford has been aware of the design flaw
responsible for the unpredictable behavior of its automatic transmissions for
some time—in this case, since the early 1960s. Furthermore, internal company
documents dated as early as 1972 indicate that Ford rejected design improvements that would alleviate the problem.[74]

Unsafe in any Boardroom. Ford is not the only automobile manufacturer to have
its reluctance to incur the cost of rectifying known safety hazards in its
vehicles revealed to the public. In the late 1960s the Chevrolet division of
General Motors became the center of controversy as the result of a rash of
one-car accidents resulting from the failure of the rear suspension systems
on its subcompact Corvair. Both Chevrolet executives and high-ranking officials in General Motors were apparently aware of this defect early in the
car's production but rejected suggestions to incur the costs of rectifying the
problem.[75]

Decisions of this sort are not limited to the automobile industry. In 1980
a civil penalty of $175,000 was assessed against the Bassett Furniture In-
dustries for concealing a design defect in cribs that posed a strangulation
hazard to infants. In that same year, the Advance Machine Company, Inc.,
was assessed a civil penalty of $500,000 for failure to report a defect in
machinery it manufactured that posed a substantial threat of injury to users.
In a similar case the Pittway Corporation was fined $100,000 for concealing
information that supported claims that its smoke detectors posed substantial
health hazards to consumers.[76]

Corporate-level decisions to conceal product hazard information and also
to delay or avoid taking corrective action are not the product of a few antisocial
malefactors in American business. They are *business as usual* insofar as business
within the environment of a capitalist economy requires profit maximization.
The general attitude of American industry toward consumer safety has been
a relatively casual one. Indeed, many industries view the government regulation of product safety as an unwarranted interference in free enterprise and
have opposed government efforts in this area as another example of "overregulation." As a former Ford executive testified, then head of the Ford Motor
Company Henry Ford III told him, "The safety stuff is all a bunch of politics.
It's going to go away. . . . We are going to handle it in Detroit."[77]

American industry is in the business of producing profit, not protecting
the public. Where these two goals do not conflict, all other things being equal,
most corporate decision makers would prefer to produce safe products not
only because it is good business but because most would prefer not to market
hazardous goods. However, profit and safety often become contradictory
goals. Once products have been designed, the tooling built, and units placed
on the market, changes become costly and also require a public admission of
error. At this point the health and well-being of the public frequently becomes
secondary to protecting capital investments. As long as the exigencies of
capital accumulation take priority in industry over protecting the safety of

the public, corporate overseers and managers will find themselves making the kinds of decisions that minimize the cost of product flaws by obscuring information and delaying changes, as Ford and GM officials did in the cases just discussed.

Dumping: A World Crime. The recall or banning of a product as unsafe can represent serious financial loss to any company. Similarly, the failure to gain approval to market products that research reveals to be hazardous can be a serious financial disappointment. Faced with these kinds of adverse decisions many American industries have sought to "dump" hazardous products onto foreign markets where consumer protection laws are lax or nonexistent.

One such case involves the Dalkon Shield, an intrauterine contraceptive device. Within a few months after introducing the Dalkon Shield in 1971, the A. H. Robbins Company, which developed and marketed the device, began receiving numerous complaints of complications resulting from its usage. These included serious uterine infections, blood poisoning, tubal pregnancies, pregnancies ending in spontaneous abortions, and penetrations of the uterine wall by the Shield. By 1974 the Dalkon Shield was responsible for seventeen deaths, 200,000 cases of serious uterine infections, and numerous hysterectomies. As early as 1972, however, faced with an increasing volume of consumer complaints, executives of A. H. Robbins realized that the possibility of sales growth in the United States was unlikely. In response the company began to look for foreign markets.

With government help lent by the Agency for International Development's (AID) Office of Population, Robbins found these markets. The Robbins Company offered to sell the Office of Population several million units of "this fine product" in bulk packages, *unsterilized*, for distribution in Third World countries. The Office of Population accepted, even though distribution of nonsterile intrauterine devices is prohibited in the United States and there were serious questions about the ability of rural paramedics to properly insert the device (this had been one of the difficulties with the Shield experienced by physicians in the United States).

The risk to Third World women was justified by both A. H. Robbins and the Office of Population by the assertion that since Third World birthrates were so high that any contraceptive device was better than none. In short, Robbins's executives had promoted worldwide distribution of back inventory of a product it knew posed a serious health threat to users and that it also knew would eventually be prohibited in the American market. By 1974, when the Food and Drug Administration began hearings on the Dalkon Shield, the dump was nearly completed and A. H. Robbins eventually withdrew its Shield from the market.[78]

The Dalkon Shield is just one of the many unsafe products that have been and are being dumped by American industry on foreign markets. Among these are

1. An organic mercury fungicide prohibited in the American market that caused the death of 400 Iraquis and the hospitalization of 5,000 others after being dumped

2. A chemical pesticide—leptophos—never accepted for use in the United States by the Environmental Protection Agency but distributed to over thirty other countries where it has caused the death of both farmers and livestock
3. Several million units of children's sleepwear treated with the cancer-causing fire retardant, Tris, which were distributed to foreign markets after being banned from sale in the United States by Consumer Product Safety Commission
4. Nearly a half million baby pacifiers removed from the American market by CPSC after a number of choking deaths were attributed to their design that have now been dumped worldwide[79]

In another case similar to that of the Dalkon Shield, AID enabled the Upjohn Company to distribute the injectionable contraceptive drug Depo-Prova to foreign markets despite the fact that it was prohibited from sale in the United States since research revealed that it caused breast cancer in laboratory test animals.

Dumping is an attempt to recoup the financial loss threatened by government regulations against marketing demonstrably dangerous products in the United States. In most cases there is little doubt that the hazards inherent in the products are clearly known to the companies, which nevertheless seek to minimize the losses due to unsold inventory. While various government agencies such as EPA, FDA and CPSC are charged by law to remove clearly dangerous products from the American market, the United States government is under no similar injunction to protect citizens of other countries, particularly those in the Third World. Quite the contrary through its support of such organizations as AID and the World Import-Export Bank the government has actively aided American corporations in finding foreign markets for dangerous products. Dumping, as one writer observed, is *exporting*, and

> . . . although banned and hazardous products represent only about one percent of our total trade, every percent seems to count when we are running a trade deficit of over $25 billion a year.[80]

While the Carter administration established a committee to study the problem of dumping, no action was ever taken. The Reagan administration, with its strong commitment to freeing enterprise from government restriction, likewise took no action to reduce dumping.

Environmental Crime.

While concern for environmental quality is by no means new, over the last twenty years there has been a growing public awareness of our ultimate dependency upon the physical environment for our survival as a species. This awareness includes a recognition on the part of many of the vulnerability of the environment and the people who live in it (not to mention the other creatures) to the polluting effects of industrial and human wastes. In response to this increasing public concern, since the late 1960s Congress has passed a variety of reformist legislation aimed at reducing environmental pollution. Most significant were the National Environmental Policy Act of 1969, which created the Environmental Protection Agency (EPA) to establish and enforce Federal environmental regulations, and the Federal Water Pollution Control

Act Amendments of 1972, which extended Federal jurisdiction over domestic waterways and lakes and established penalties of as much as $50,000 per day for water pollution violations.[81]

The importance of environmental regulation and the gravity of violations of these regulations is substantial. Cancer researchers estimate that between 70 to 90 percent of all cancer is environmentally induced, the majority of these resulting from the release of industrial wastes into the air and water.[82] In addition, pollution represents an enormous financial burden upon American society. EPA estimated that in 1977 alone industrial air pollution cost Americans *$23 billion* in the form of illness, time lost from work, damage to buildings and clothing, and other losses such as declines in the fishing and timber industries due to "acid rain."[83] The cost of air pollution alone was more than *five times* the estimated loss from common crimes in 1977.[84]

Despite its greater demonstrable costs in both dollars and damaged human health, environmental pollution does not evoke the same nearly unanimous public demand for protection as does common crime. Part of the reason for this is that the effects of pollution are seldom immediately obvious. There are occasional environmental disasters such as the smog inversion in New York City in 1973, which took 400 lives.[85] For the most part, however, the effects of pollution are subtle and cumulative. Individuals may become sick, feel nauseated, or develop cancer, but this is generally perceived as a failure of their own body, not the consequences of living in a polluted environment. Additionally, because the pollution of air and water leading to illness and other costs is most often the cumulative result of the actions of a multiplicity of industries, some at great distances from the affected city or region, it is difficult to identify a guilty party. The lack of an easily identifiable cause–effect relationship between polluting and its consequences for human lives often produces a sense of resignation among those who live with unsafe water and air.

Another factor accounting for the relative tolerance of industrial pollution is that for the first half of the twentieth century industry was successful in avoiding any legal responsibility for controlling its effluent. The costs of controlling pollution have always been seen by industry as a threat to capital accumulation and an infringement upon the right to free enterprise. Until the late 1960s American courts have generally agreed with this assessment. In 1931, for example, the New York State Supreme Court ruled that smoke from the 50 coke ovens operated by the Donner-Hanna Coke Plant in Buffalo was only a "petty annoyance" and that air pollution was "indispensable to progress." In 1955, in another suit against Donner-Hanna, which now operated 250 coke ovens in Buffalo, the same court ruled that requiring the company to comply with a city smoke ordinance would constitute an unconstitutional infringement upon the company's right to private property.[86] In essence, the court ruled that Donner-Hanna had a legally protected right to damage *public property*—in this case the air of Buffalo—in its search for *private profit*. As one legal scholar noted, until fairly recently the courts have "tended to overprotect the right to own and use private property and failed to recognize the ecological consequences of pollution."[87]

The passage of Federal environmental legislation in the late 1960s and early 1970s represented not so much a victory for environmentalists as an inability of the government to delay any longer in responding to the storm of controversy that had surrounded the unchecked despoliation of air and water quality by industry for the last fifty years.

The passage of Federal environmental legislation was a significant threat to the interests of industrial capital in four ways. First, it provided access to Federal courts for plaintiffs in pollution cases. Heretofore, industry's liability had for the most part been limited to civil suits for "creating a nuisance" that were heard in state courts—courts over which industry often enjoyed greater political leverage and that therefore ruled most often on behalf of industry.[88] Second, the new Federal remedies included cease and desist orders, injunctions, and in some cases criminal penalties for pollution where previously most state courts had allowed only money damages to successful plaintiffs in pollution suits and generally did not limit or require changes in the activities of the involved corporations.[89] Third, it established environmental protection as a matter of national policy, thereby granting a degree of legitimacy to the long-standing claims of environmental advocates that there should be a reevaluation of the wisdom of progress-at-any-cost. Fourth, and perhaps most importantly, environmental legislation established a regulatory structure to oversee environmental pollution. This meant among other things a growth in quasi-independent research into the hazards of industrial pollution. It also meant that industry would have to contend with government-initiated actions to control pollution as well as actions by private citizens or public interest groups.

Some industries responded to the growing demand for pollution control with forthright willingness to improve environmental quality. Many others, however, responding more directly to the demands for capital accumulation, sought to avoid or delay regulation. The Reserve Mining Company of Silver Bay exemplifies one industry's response to the problem of environmental regulation.

Reserve Mining—Polluter or Regulatory Victim? Beginning in 1956, Reserve Mining Company, a subsidiary of ARMCO and Republic Steel, began dumping waste generated by a new process for extracting iron from taconite ore into Lake Superior at its Silver Bay plant located about fifty miles from the city of Duluth, Minnesota. By the mid 1960s, Reserve was dumping *67,000 tons* of waste tailings into the lake *daily*, creating a green stain covering over twenty square miles of Lake Superior. In 1969, the state of Minnesota, concerned about the effect of Reserve's effluent upon the quality of drinking water in Lake Superior unsuccessfully sought an injunction against further dumping.

In 1972 the Minnesota Pollution Control Agency verified that Reserve's dumping included not only iron ore waste, but millions of tons of asbestos— a known cancer-causing agent. These findings led EPA and the state of Minnesota to initiate a combined legal action to stop Reserve's dumping.

In August 1973, the Justice Department, representing EPA, brought suit in Federal District Court to acquire an injunction against Reserve's waste dumping after the company refused to voluntarily alter its practices. The hearing was to last over nine months. The government brought forth considerable evidence establishing the similarity between the asbestosform particles in the Duluth drinking water and those dumped into the lake by Reserve, as well as grim testimony concerning the carcinogenic effects of asbestos. At one point in the proceedings Dr. Harold L. Stewart, former chief of pathology at the United State's Public Health Service's National Cancer Center, testified concerning the effects of asbestos on Duluth residents:

> This is a captive population. They not only ingest the water, it's virtually a food additive. Everything that's cooked is cooked in asbestosform materials. All the sheets and the pillowcases and the clothes are laundered in the asbestos water. . . . It's a carcinogen introduced through the domestic water supply into the homes of people.

Dr. Stewart went on to say that anyone permitting such pollution "must realize that he's condemning people to exposure to a carcinogen that may take their lives and probably will."

For its part, Reserve denied that the asbestos found in the Duluth drinking water could be conclusively proven to have come from its Silver Bay plant or that there was any real health hazard. Reserve also tried economic blackmail, indicating that if forced to stop its dumping it would close down the Silver Bay plant, throwing its over 3,000 employees out of work and seriously depressing the economy of the region.

On April 2, 1974, Edward M. Furness, president of Reserve Mining Company, admitted that the company had withheld evidence that Reserve had developed but rejected plans for on-land waste disposal as early as 1970. Specifically, Furness admitted that "he had given a key Reserve witness authority to testify that such plans did not exist," thereby strengthening the company's argument that no alternatives to dumping waste in Lake Superior existed.

On April 20, 1974, after Reserve refused to alter its dumping practices the Federal District Court judge ruled,

> Faced with the defendant's intransigence, even in light of the public health problem, the Court must order an immediate curtailment of the discharge.
>
> THEREFORE, IT IS ORDERED
>
> 1) That the discharge from the Reserve Mining Company into Lake Superior be enjoined as of 12:01 A.M., April 21, 1974.

Was this a victory for public health? Not quite. On April 22, 1974, Reserve won from a three-judge panel convened in a motel in Springfield, Missouri, a stay of the District Court order pending Reserve's appeal before the U.S. Circuit Court of Appeals. Sixteen days later William J. DeLancy, president of Republic Steel, Reserve's parent company, told stockholders that 1974 would be a profitable year if the Silver Bay plant was allowed to operate and that the companies involved were "convinced that no health hazard exists." It was a good year for Republic Steel and Reserve. On June 4th, 1974, the U.S. Court of Appeals ruled that because in its opinion whether or not Reserve's dumping would result in "detrimental health effects" was as yet unknown, the District Court had overstepped its authority in resolving these uncertainties "in favor of health safety." The appellate court therefore granted Reserve a five-year delay of the order to cease discharging wastes into Lake Superior. The court added, "The pollution of Lake Superior must cease *as quickly as feasible* under the circumstances." In other words, it must cease on a timetable determined by Reserve Mining Company rather than one reflecting the health safety needs of the citizens of Duluth.[90]

The Reserve Mining Company case is by no means unique. However, it is illustrative of several of the basic problems of regulating environmental pollution. First, it is difficult to prove conclusively that pollutants, once emitted into the air or water, came from a particular source. In a similar case, the General Electric Company was able to deny for years that it was responsible for the carcinogen PCB used in the manufacture of electric transformers and found in concentration in the Hudson River near one of its plants.[91] Second, because they represent the backbone of the American economy, industries can hold the economic life of cities or entire regions hostage against imposition of mandatory cleanup orders. This logic has repeatedly been influential in convincing courts to allow companies to undertake pollution control at their own pace. Third, because the effects of pollution are often delayed and diffuse, it is difficult to prove the health threat posed by industrial pollution. In addition, with the constant introduction of new manufacturing procedures with new by-products and the introduction of over 1,500 new chemicals a year into the air, food, and water supply, it is difficult to know either their long-term health effects or the potential dangers they pose when combined with other chemicals found in the environment. Fourth, the legal procedures surrounding environmental regulation allow a company to continue polluting until a final judgment is reached. That is, doubt about health hazards is resolved in favor of companies as an extension of the "innocent until proven guilty" standard. This provides industry with substantial incentive to contest proposed regulations through the courts over many years. During that time they can continue to enjoy the benefits of cheap waste disposal even if they know that in the end changes will be required.

All the legal and scientific ambiguities surrounding pollution regulation make it possible for corporate managers responsible for pollution to see themselves as victims of "overregulation" rather than perpetrators of serious health and economic damage to Americans. In the end Reserve's activities, for example, were judged by the court to be perfectly legal, even though admittedly dangerous. With a judgment in its favor, the entire process against Reserve can be easily defined by the company as harassment by environmentalists rather than a legitimate effort to protect human life or health. This case also underscores one of the most disastrous contradictions of American society. To enjoy the "good life" of material affluence so heavily promoted by advertising as the route to human happiness, many Americans must submit to a shortening of that life due to environmental pollution.

Restraint of Trade

A basic justification frequently offered in support of a capitalist mode of production is that competition among producers and sellers in a free enterprise economy will lead to (1) higher quality products, (2) lower prices, and (3) consumer control over the economy based on the ability of people to "vote with their dollars" for the corporations that best meet their needs. This rationale, however, is purely theoretical and ignores one of the central, objective contradictions of capitalism: Competition leads to the concentration of wealth in relatively few corporations controlling the majority of the market, not a marketplace divided relatively equally among a large number of actively competing small companies.

The reality of this contradiction became starkly apparent to many Americans in the last half of the nineteenth century when giant monopolies and trusts emerged in such areas as rail transportation, steel, and oil. In an effort to preserve the legitimacy of capitalist ideology and to co-opt public demands for relief from the high prices and unfair practices of corporate giants, Congress enacted the Sherman Anti-Trust Act in 1890. This law declared, "Every contract, combination in the form of trust or otherwise, or conspiracy in restraint of trade or commerce among the several states, or with foreign countries, is declared to be illegal."[92] In 1914 the passage of the Clayton Act and the Federal Trade Commission Act expanded Federal jurisdiction to unfair market practices other than monopolization. The FTC act of 1914 states quite simply, "Unfair methods of competition in commerce, and unfair or deceptive acts or practices in commerce, are declared unlawful."[93] The Federal Trade Commission was empowered to investigate and prosecute all restraints of trade for the claimed purpose of preserving marketplace competition and protecting consumers from unfair or unscrupulous business practices. In general, these "restraints of trade" take one of four forms: (1) mergers or combinations designed to achieve monopoly positions in the marketplace, (2) arrangements between companies to fix prices at predetermined, noncompetitive levels, (3) discriminatory pricing practices providing lower prices to favored customers and higher prices to others, and (4) bribes, kickbacks, or other gratuities designed to insure favorable contracts from organizational purchasers.

Overall, the FTC has for two reasons had little effect upon the increasing concentration of wealth in fewer and fewer corporations and the corresponding decline in competition. First, there has never been a genuine commitment on the part of government to enforce competition in the American economy. This is evidenced in part by the fact that the Sherman Anti-Trust Act made it only a misdemeanor offense to engage in a restraint of trade, and this offense was not upgraded to a felony until 1972. This means that in effect, between 1890 and 1972 restraints of trade costing America millions of dollars annually were placed in the same penal category as thefts of value less than $50! Second, centralization and concentration of capital in the form of ever larger corporations is a basic element of the dynamics of capitalism. Without requiring fundamental alterations in the American economic system, the FTC, even if it aggressively sought to protect competition could at best only present minor obstacles to the concentration of capital.

Monopolization of the American marketplace, with its ability to facilitate other trade restraints such as price fixing, price discrimination, and bribery, represents a substantial economic burden to the average American and one that far outweighs the financial costs of common crime.

Monopolization. While the number of individual corporations in America remains large, the economy is increasingly divided into two sectors: a competitive sector of small businesses struggling with one another for relatively small shares of the total market and a monopoly sector consisting of a relatively small number of corporations that divide between them the bulk of the market. In 1940, for example, the top 500 American corporations, approximately *0.5 percent* of all corporations, controlled 40 percent of all industrial assets. By 1970 the top 500 were in control of 70 percent of all assets. In addition, by 1977 the top 100 companies—barely 0.10 percent of all corporations—earned 71 percent of all profits.[94] In short, American industry is characterized by *oligopoly*.

Oligopoly in industry is defined as a situation where a relatively small number of sellers control a large share of the market. Once this situation is achieved, the companies involved can generate additional profits simply through market dominance, much the same as can a single-firm monopoly.

> The fewer the firms, everything else being equal, the easier it is to collaborate and so align price and production policies at least to travel a goodly way, or nearly all the way, toward monopoly.[95]

This type of near-monopoly control is enjoyed by the largest corporations in a number of key industrial areas. In petroleum the "seven sister" oil companies control nearly 70 percent of all of the world's oil reserves, with the big four alone controlling over half of all oil production.[96] In the areas of computers, heavy electrical equipment, drugs, aircraft, aircraft engines, automobiles, copper, rubber, tobacco, metal containers, photographic supplies, drugs, cereals, and chemicals *four or fewer companies* control at least 70 percent of the market, and in some of these cases, such as helicopters, aircraft engines, and heavy electrical equipment as few as one or two firms control nearly the entire market.[97] In some areas, distribution is also substantially monopolized. Over half of the retail food market, for instance, is controlled by as few as four food chains in many American cities.[98]

The additional profits enjoyed by virtue of marketplace domination constitute a surcharge paid by consumers as the result of the lack of true competition. One study estimated that oligopolization of the marketplace cost Americans 6 percent in income annually.[99] At current income levels this means that an average family of four loses about $1,200 annually due to the monopolization of various markets by a few large firms, well above the average annual family loss due to common crime.[100] Similarly, a 1972 Federal Trade Commission study concluded that the domination of the market by a few small companies in one hundred different industry areas cost Americans approximately $15 billion a year in direct product costs alone. Table 12.2 lists the percentage gain and dollar overcharges resulting from oligopolistic concentration in some of the one hundred industries studied by FTC. While these overcharges represent *illegal* earnings by oligopolists, seldom is action taken by FTC, and there is little effective action that *can* be taken.

The forces of capitalism lead to ever larger shares of the market for industries in the monopoly sector, while industries in the competitive sector continue to decline.[101] However, the bulk of FTC regulation tends to fall most heavily upon the competitive rather than the monopoly sector. One study found that over a twenty-three-year period only 5.6 percent of all cease and desist orders issued by the Federal Trade Commission were issued against the 500 largest corporations representing 66 percent of all manufacturing and mining output over those years.[102] While not all of these cases involved restraint-of-trade issues, this finding reflects FTC's inability or unwillingness to concentrate on its central task, protecting competition from oligopolization by big businesses.

Price Fixing. Additional profits from oligopolistic control of the marketplace do not come automatically. They result, in part, from the ability of the largest corporations to lower production costs by buying raw materials in larger quantities and through other economies of large-scale production. That is, at least to a point, bigness may be more economically efficient. However, the existence of only a few corporations in the market area also increases the possibility of collusive price arrangements. Once the number of competitors is whittled down to a few survivors they generally find it is more profitable to collaborate than to compete.

Price fixing can take two forms: tacit price fixing and overt price fixing. Tacit price fixing occurs when the limited number of controlling corporations in a market follow the lead of one of their "competitors" in price increases. It is quite common to hear, "G.M. announced today that it would increase the price of its automobiles by an average of $160 per model. Ford and Chrysler are expected to follow suit" or "Bethlehem Steel today announced a $3-dollar-per-ton increase in the cost of steel. Similar increases are expected from Republic and U.S. Steel." Where there are few competitors, prices can be kept at noncompetitive levels for similar commodities without any overt, conspiratorial actions. In fact, Americans have generally come to take it for granted that most companies will charge relatively the same for goods of similar quality. This lack of price competition among companies holding large shares of the market contributes to higher overall costs for commodities in America.

Overt price fixing occurs when representatives of supposedly competing industries agree beforehand, often in clandestine meetings or through subtle communications, to engage in collusive practices. The three most common forms of collusion are (1) setting prices at predetermined, similar levels, (2) dividing the market into "regions," with each firm agreeing to stay out

Table 12.2 How Oligopolies Cost You Money

Federal Trade Commission Estimates of Monopoly Profit Margins in 25 Selected Manufacturing Industries

Rank	SIC	Industry	(1) FTC Adjusted Monopoly Margin (As Percent of Sales)	(2) Value of Shipments (Sales in $ Billions)	(1) × (2) Monopoly Overcharge ($ Millions)
1.	3711	Motor Vehicles..	9.11%	$27.3	$2,486.7
2.	2911	Petroleum Refining	6.19	20.3	1,256.2
3.	3312	Blast Furnaces & Steel Mills	6.40	19.6	1,255.7
4.	3714	Motor Vehicle Parts & Accessories....	6.36	11.6	739.3
5.	2011	Meat Packing Plants.........	3.10	15.6	483.9
6.	3861	Photographic Equipment & Supplies	11.01	3.7	403.5
7.	2834	Pharmaceutical Preparations ..	8.04	4.7	377.6
8.	2818	Industrial Organic Chemicals, nec	5.46	6.4	348.2
9.	2711	Newspapers.....	5.67	5.8	315.1
10.	2111	Cigarettes	9.36	3.0	284.9
11.	2819	Industrial Inorganic Chemicals, nec	6.42	4.2	272.7
12.	2026	Fluid Milk	3.28	7.8	256.7
13.	3522	Farm Machinery	5.84	4.3	251.1
14.	2036	Soft Drinks, Bottled & Canned	7.31	3.2	247.8
15.	2042	Prepared Feeds for Animals & Fowls.........	4.20	4.8	201.5
16.	2082	Malt Liquors	6.76	2.9	198.0
17.	2051	Bread, Cake & Related Products......	3.76	5.1	191.9
18.	2821	Plastic Materials & Resins......	5.23	3.5	181.7
19.	3273	Ready-Mixed Concrete......	6.59	2.7	176.9
20.	2841	Soaps & Other Detergents	6.79	2.6	176.1

Table 12.2 (continued)

*Federal Trade Commission Estimates of Monopoly Profit Margins in 25
Selected Manufacturing Industries*

Rank	SIC	Industry	(1) FTC Adjusted Monopoly Margin (As Percent of Sales)	(2) Value of Shipments (Sales in $ Billions)	(1) × (2) Monopoly Overcharge ($ Millions)
21.	2751	Commercial Printing, Except Lithographic ..	5.22	3.3	169.9
22.	2211	Weaving Mills, Cotton........	5.10	3.3	169.7
23.	3731	Ship Building & Repairing	6.39	2.5	160.9
24.	2844	Toilet Preparations ..	6.17	2.5	155.2
25.	3011	Tires & Inner Tubes.........	5.57	2.7	152.3

Source: Food Price Investigation, *Hearings before the Subcommittee on Monopolies and Commercial Law of the Committee on the Judiciary, House of Representatives, June 27, 28, July, 11, 12, 16, 17, and 19, 1973* (Washington, D.C.: Government Printing Office, 1973), 680.

of the others' territory, and (3) agreeing to take turns submitting the winning "competitive" bid for contracts, often from governmental agencies.

In 1961 the business world was shocked when seven defendants were sentenced to thirty-day jail terms in what the trial judge described as "the most serious violations of the anti-trust laws since the time of their passage at the turn of the century."[103] This case involved a long-standing conspiracy among manufacturers of heavy electrical equipment to fix prices, engage in noncompetitive bidding, and divide the market into "reasonable" shares.

> If company A, for instance, had under competitive conditions secured 20 percent of the available business, then an agreement might be reached that it would be given an opportunity to submit the lowest bid on 20 percent of new contracts.[104]

This arrangement, referred to by the defendants as "stabilizing prices," was estimated to have cost consumers of electricity approximately $2 billion a year.[105]

In a similar case in 1981 it was revealed that paving contractors in North and South Carolina had arranged to take turns submitting "low bids" on highway paving contracts offered by both states for over twenty-five years. The estimated costs of this scheme to taxpayers in both states ran into the hundreds of millions of dollars. While several paving company executives were fined, the state of North Carolina backed down from its initial plan to punish the conspirators by barring the offending companies from bidding on state road contracts for one year because of the "economic hardship" this would cause.[106]

It is difficult to know the extent of collusive price or market-share arrangements. However, cases such as the electrical conspiracy and the road paving conspiracy suggest that such arrangements are not one-time deals but instead reflected established practices in these industries.

In his pioneering study of white-collar crime, Sutherland found that between 1890 and 1945 the seventy large corporations he examined had been guilty of 307 separate incidents of restraint of trade, an average of 4.4 per company. In addition, he found that the rate of such judgments was increasing rapidly. For example, between 1940 and 1945, there were 102 restraint of trade decisions, compared with only 59 for the five previous years, and 27 for the five years before that.[107]

Sutherland studied only 70 of the 200 largest corporations at a time when many industries had not yet reached their current levels of oligopoly. Moreover, during the early years covered by the study, government enforcement against restraints of trade was particularly lax. For these reasons his findings substantially underestimated the actual rate of restraint of trade violations by American business. Even so, the rate of violation reported by Sutherland indicated that restraints of trade are not occasional violations but a regular part of business as usual in the struggle for capital accumulation.

More recently Marshall Clinard examined the records of 582 large American corporations. Over the two-year period studied (1975 to 1976) Clinard found that fifty-six manufacturing companies and nine nonmanufacturing ones had been charged with antitrust violations. This represented 11.2 percent of all companies surveyed.[108] If we keep in mind that this figure represents only those violations *identified* and *investigated* by the Federal Trade Commission, an agency whose budget and manpower is a mere fraction of that devoted to control of common crime, it appears that the actual rate of antitrust violation is probably quite high. In addition, the types of violations handled by the Federal Trade Commission represent only those overt forms of trade restraint. Other forms that result from the structure of oligopolistic markets rather than deliberate corporate actions are beyond the energies and the power of FTC. As Clinard indicates,

> In its attempt to maintain competitive markets . . . the government . . . has relied on its ability to prove conscious and covert collusion on the part of the firms involved. With the increasing concentration of the American economy and the growth of oligopolies . . . these tactics and other conventional enforcement strategies have often proved ineffectual against such phenomena as parallel pricing decisions by firms in concentrated industries.[109]

Enforcement of antitrust laws is inherently contradictory. It represents an attempt to enforce free-market competition upon an economic system whose basic mechanisms in the form of capital accumulation leads to increasing domination of markets by ever smaller numbers of industries. This contradiction is further compounded by the irony that in its opposition to government attempts at regulation the corporate sector generally argues that such regulation represents unwarranted government interference in the free market. While both monopoly and competitive sector businesses frequently utilize free-market ideology to secure a degree of freedom from government control, this freedom is sought so that it can be used to obtain noncompetitive positions of market domination.

Bribes, Kickbacks, and Other Questionable Practices

In the 1870s, John D. Rockefeller, Sr., was able to build a monopoly in oil by securing lower rail freight rates than his competitors, largely by offering kickbacks and rebates to railroad contractors.[110] This particular way of securing a competitive edge has remained a part of American business.

In 1975, for instance, it was revealed in Senate subcommittee hearings that the Lockheed Corporation had established worldwide "channels of intrigue" to seek out high-placed officials in foreign governments who could be bribed to help Lockheed secure favorable contracts from those governments. The scandal reached as high as the prime minister of Japan, who was removed from office and jailed for corruption due to a $2.7-million bribe he was believed to have accepted from Lockheed to insure the purchase of their jets by All-Nippon Airways.[111] Closer to home, in 1977 widespread corruption within the Government Services Administration, the central purchasing agent for the Federal government, was uncovered by the Government Accounting Office. In addition to waste and mismanagement, investigations revealed a pattern of bribes, favors, and kickbacks offered to government purchasing agents by various contractors and suppliers to secure advantageous contracts that frequently led the Federal government to pay higher prices for goods than would be paid by the average consumer in any store. In other cases, purchasing agents paid contractors for work that was never done or failed to supervise the quality of the work.[112] While these revelations were presented in the media largely as another example of government incompetence, what they reveal more starkly is the apparently common pattern of businesses that serve the government utilizing bribes and gratuities to corrupt government functionaries to guarantee excess profit margins.

In addition to outright bribes, some American businesses utilize a variety of other questionable and often illegal practices to secure market dominance. In 1980, for example, FTC ruled that Hartz Mountain Corporation, a maker of pet supplies, had engaged in illegal practices to limit the distribution of pet products manufactured by competitors. Specifically, Hartz had used "special rebates, discounts, guaranteed or subsidized products, and other monetary incentives" to convince dealers and distributors to sell *only* their products. Furthermore, Hartz was found to have given false information about competitors—for instance, that they were about to go out of business—to convince distributors to handle only Hartz products.[113] In another case, Eli Lilly and Company, a major drug company and the largest domestic producer of insulin, was found to have engaged in arrangements with slaughterhouses to keep potential competitors from being able to buy the pancreas glands of slaughtered animals (a basic ingredient of insulin production) in an effort to insure continuation of their monopoly position over insulin production.[114]

Actions such as those taken by Hartz and Lilly, as well as other instances of restraint of trade, arise from the inherent contradiction of attempting to enforce standards of "fair play" upon an economic system whose central premise is capital accumulation through *aggressive* competition. It is for this reason that many participants in restraint of trade conspiracies or arrangements do not see their actions as "wrong." Most feel that they are simply taking necessary and justifiable steps to insure competitive success and that government regulation of their practices constitutes unwarranted intervention in "free enterprise." In both the Lockheed and the electrical equipment cases, the key participants denied that they saw anything wrong with their actions, although in both cases they had been careful to hide their activities from public scrutiny.[115] The situation is further complicated by the fact that while FTC and other agencies are empowered to prosecute "unfair" practices the definition of what constitutes "unfairness" is an elusive and shifting one.

False and Questionable Advertising

Advertising is an indispensable part of capital accumulation in contemporary America. It serves to stimulate the high levels of consumer demand for commodities necessary to generate corporate profits. As Jules Henry observed, to keep American industry solvent American citizens must rise to "heroic heights of personal consumption."[116] In addition to stimulating demand, advertising serves another important purpose. By constantly emphasizing the necessity for high levels of personal consumption to achieve "happiness," advertising diffuses labor force demands for improvements in other areas of human life. As Stuart Ewen details in his book *Captains of Consciousness: The Social Roots of Advertising,* during the early part of the twentieth century industrialists were well aware of the utility of advertising in directing the attention of labor toward commodities and away from emerging demands for greater control over the workplace.[117]

The importance of advertising is evidenced by the fact that in 1980 almost *$57 billion* was spent on product advertising in America. This represents more than the total amount of money spent by the Federal government for health care in that year.[118] Much of this expenditure for advertising pays for fraudulent or questionable promotion of products. For instance, in 1980 the Federal Trade Commission ruled that

- There was no truth to the advertising claims made by San-Mar Laboratories that their "Acne Lotion 22" and "Acne Masque" could cure acne or "penetrate the pores of the skin to eliminate bacteria. . . ."
- Montgomery Ward had engaged in false and dangerous advertising by pro-

moting certain woodburning stoves as capable of being safely installed as close as eighteen inches to combustible walls.

- There was no support for the advertising claims made by Hair Extension of Beverly Hills that their "Hair Implant Process" was a safe and effective treatment for baldness.
- Sears and Roebuck engaged in false advertising through its ads, which purported to show that Kenmore Dishwashers would "completely clean dishes, pots and pans without prior rinsing and scraping."[119]

In one case, particularly notable because it involved an ad campaign extending over a period of thirty years, FTC ruled that there was no truth to the claim that Listerine was an effective preventive or treatment for colds.

Ultimately more damaging are the multiplicity of ads that *imply* that wealth, status, respect, love, or sex will come to the user of the advertised product. Nearly all visual ads place the product or its user in lavish settings, and many rely upon subtle or not-so-subtle sexual innuendo to attract customers. Toothpaste ads that promise to "Give your mouth sex appeal," cigarette ads that proclaim "The pleasure is back" or "I'm MORE satisfied," or the ad in which a model breathlessly whispers, "All my men wear English Leather, or they wear nothing at all" play upon basic human needs for love and sexual affiliation to stimulate product sales. Ads also frequently serve to reinforce the capitalist definition of human worth as measured by material possessions. Ads describing Volvo station wagons as "The working car for the leisure class" or Lincoln Continentals as "The final step up" strengthen the image that worth and status are evidenced not by the consequences of what people do but by the nature of their possessions.

The average American receives over 500 advertising messages a day, many of them making fraudulent or questionable claims for products. Whether true or not, these messages constitute a type of propaganda. Regardless of whether people are influenced by the various ads they see and hear to purchase *specific* products, they are constantly being told that commodities are the focus of human life and that whatever the present material conditions of their life, it is inadequate. Constant reinforcement of these ideas, and the consumer debts they generate, keep individuals tied to their positions within the labor force and make it difficult for them to question critically either the purpose of their own existence or the society around them. These ads also tend to generate additional frustration among the poorest segment of Americans with the quality and quantity of their own material possessions, a frustration that in some instances fuels the motivation to commit common crimes to acquire other peoples' property or money.

CONTROLLING CORPORATE CRIME

In recent years much of the writing concerning the control of corporate crime has focused on the legal and technical difficulties of prosecuting corporate illegality. Corporations as "legal persons" enjoy all the rights under the law accorded to other people, but because they are not "real" people they pose special difficulties for legal control.

American criminal law rests heavily upon the idea that *mens rea*—a guilty mind—is an important component of culpability. Because corporations cannot be said to have a "mind," attempts to prosecute corporations for wrongdoing are often forced to focus on the individual executives or managers involved in such things as restraint of trade, price fixing, violations of worker safety, or marketing of known hazardous products to find the "guilty" parties. This poses several problems. First, since most corporate wrongdoing is the *cumulative* result of decisions made by a variety of individuals, it is often difficult to assign responsibility to specific persons. The search for individual defendants, however, often serves to protect the company itself from prosecution.[120] Second, since most wrongdoing is actually performed not by high-ranking corporate officers but by lower-level officials and managers, the corporation itself can often deny responsibility or knowledge. In the heavy electrical equipment case, for instance, the General Electric Corporation had a stated policy prohibiting price fixing, although it was generally understood by the executives who participated in the conspiracy that they were expected by upper management to follow this practice.[121] The ability to deny responsibility for the actions of officials or managers often preserves corporations from having to bear the burden of prosecution or punishment.

The "legal" nature of corporate personhood also poses problems with respect to punishment. Corporations cannot be imprisoned, so punishment is most often limited to fines or other monetary losses. However, since every major corporation is also the source of livelihood for thousands of workers and their families, penalties that would seriously impair the corporation's financial outlook are generally avoided. Guaranteed against penalties that would pose any serious threat to capital accumulation, companies simply see fines as one of the costs of doing business—often well worth the financial gains from illegality. Second, while individuals may be deterred from crime by the threat of social stigma, corporations generally have less fear. Only in cases involving hazardous products is the possibility of social stigma real. However, in these cases the resources of the company can generally be utilized to promote countervailing positive impressions through either advertising or the news media. For example, during the Ford Pinto trials in Indiana there appeared in the local and national press a number of stories portraying the positive aspects of the Ford Motor Company.[122] Similarly, after the product liability scandal involving hundreds of thousands of Firestone 500 radial tires that had been sold with a known design defect, the Firestone company was able to mount a massive ad campaign for their "new" line of radial tires, thereby diffusing consumer concern about the safety of Firestone's products.

Other technical problems are posed by the *complexity* of corporate wrongdoing. Without extensive and expensive laboratory testing it is often difficult to determine the truth or falsehood of many advertising claims. In addition, rules of evidence often prohibit charging parties, whether individuals or the government, from "fishing expeditions" aimed at obtaining a broad variety of corporate documents in an attempt to prove the validity of charges. Frequently, requests for documents during the pretrial period of "discovery" must be limited to documents that are specifically relevant to the case at hand. However, since incriminating evidence is often contained in apparently unrelated internal memos or reports, it is frequently difficult to specify beforehand what information is being sought. Another problem is posed by the protection against "self-incrimination." Just how far a court must go in requiring a corporation to release damning evidence is often at the discretion of the trial or hearing judge.[123] Judges sympathetic to corporations can often stymie prosecution of corporate wrongdoers by limiting the evidence that either must be revealed or that will be allowed to be presented at trial.

NOTES

1. Thorsten Sellin, *Culture, Conflict and Crime* (New York: Social Science Research Council, 1938), 104–105.
2. Ibid., 25–27.
3. Edwin Sutherland, "White-Collar Criminality," *American Sociological Review*, 5 (1940): 1–12.
4. Edwin Sutherland, *White Collar Crime* (New York: Holt, Rinehart and Winston, 1945), 31.
5. Donald Cressey, "Forward" to Edwin Sutherland, *White Collar Crime*, rev. ed. (New York: Holt, Rinehart and Winston, 1961), vii.
6. Edwin Sutherland, "Is 'White-Collar Crime' Crime?" *American Sociological Review*, 10 (1945), 132–139.
7. Herman Schwendinger and Julia Schwendinger, "Defenders of Order or Guardians of Human Rights?" *Issues in Criminology*, 5 (1970): 143.
8. Anthony Platt, "Prospects for a Radical Criminology in the United States," *Crime and Social Justice*, 1 (1974), 3.
9. Paul Tappan, "Who Is the Criminal?" *American Sociological Review*, 12 (1947): 97.
10. Susan P. Shapiro, "The new moral entrepreneurs: Corporate crime crusaders," *Contemporary Sociology*, 12, no. 3 (May 1983): 306.
11. Herman Schwendinger and Julia Schwendinger, "Defenders of Order" 142.
12. Robert L. Heilbroner, *An Inquiry into the Human Prospect* (New York: Norton, 1974), 23.
13. Karl Marx, *Capital*, vol 1 (Moscow: Progress Publishers, 1978) 44–47. Reprint of 1887 English language manuscript.
14. Ibid., 89.
15. Ernest Mandel, *Marxist Economic Theory*, vol. 1 (New York: Monthly Review Press, 1970), 242.
16. Marx, *Capital*, 100–101.
17. For discussions of the process of capital accumulation see Ibid., 543–669; David M. Gordon, "Up and Down the Long Roller Coaster," in *U.S. Capitalism in Crisis* (New York: Union for Radical Political Economics, 1978), 22–25; and Samir Amin, *Accumulation on a World Scale* (New York: Monthly Review Press, 1974).
18. Marx, *Capital*, 50.

19. Mandel, *Marxist Economic Theory*, 132.

20. Ibid., 133.

21. Paul A. Baran and Paul M. Sweezy, *Monopoly Capital* (New York: Monthly Review Press, 1966), 39–40.

22. David Nobel, "The Professional Managerial Class: A Critique," in Pat Walker, ed., *Between Labor and Capital: The Professional Managerial Class* (Boston: South End Press, 1979), 36–38.

23. Baran and Sweezy, *Monopoly Capital*, 16–17.

24. Barbara Ehrenreich and John Ehrenreich, "The Professional Managerial Class" in Walker, *Between Labor and Capital*, 5–45; see also Carl B. Klockars, "The Contemporary Crises of Marxist Criminology," *Criminology*, 16, no. 4: 484–486.

25. Crawford H. Greenwalt, former president of DuPont Corporation, quoted in Baran and Sweezy, Monopoly Capital, p. 48.

26. Ibid., 47.

27. Pierre Jalee, *How Capitalism Works* (New York: Monthly Review Press, 1977), 22–48.

28. Milton Friedman, *Capitalism and Freedom* (Chicago: University of Chicago Press, 1962), 133–134.

29. *The Progressive*, August 1981, 13.

30. Mandel, *Marxist Economic Theory*, 163.

31. Ibid., 164.

32. Federal Trade Commission, Bureau of Economics, *Statistical Report on Mergers and Acquisitions* (Washington, D.C.: Government Printing Office, 1981).

33. Maurice Zeitlan, "Who Owns America? The Same Old Gang," *The Progressive*, June 1978, 15.

34. Bertram Gross, *Friendly Fascism* (New York: M. Evans, 1980), 62.

35. Zeitlan, "Who Owns America?," 16.

36. Christopher Stone, *Where the Law Ends: The Social Control of Corporate Behavior* (New York: Harper & Row, 1975), 43.

37. Work-related deaths from disease are around 100,000 per year, and from injuries around 20,000. *The President's Report on Occupational Health and Safety* (Washington, D.C.: Government Printing Office, 1972), 111; *Accident Facts* (Chicago: National Safety Council, 1975). Homicide deaths, by comparison are annually in the low 20,000s. Federal Bureau of Investigation, *Crime in the United States: 1980* (Washington, D.C.: Government Printing Office, 1981), 41.

38. Estimated worker injuries are annually around 5.5 million according to the U.S. Labor Department, *Daily Labor Report* (Economic Section, October 1974), while assault rates between 1971 and 1980 ranged from 500,000 to 600,000, Ibid., Federal Bureau of Investigation, 41. The National Safety Council, *Accident Facts* annually estimates around 2.3 million work-related injuries using a highly conservative formula since the NSC is an industry-supported organization.

39. Calculated from *President's Report on Occupational Health and Safety*, 1972, 111 and Federal Bureau of Investigation, *Crime in the United States: 1978* (Washington, D.C.: Government Printing Office, 1979); U.S. Department of Labor, *Daily Labor Report*.

40. *President's Report, 1972*.

41. Daniel M. Berman, *Death on the Job* (New York: Monthly Review Press, 1978), ix.

42. *Mother Jones*, August 1980, 57.

43. S. Menshikov, *Millionaires and Managers* (Moscow: Progress Publishers, 1969), 146.

44. William Domhoff, *Who Rules America* (Englewood Cliffs, N.J.: Prentice-Hall, 1967), 53–54.

45. Berman, *Death on the Job,* 237.
46. Ibid., 54.
47. President's Report, 1972, 112.
48. Occupational Safety and Health Act of 1970, 84 Stat. 1590.
49. Patrick G. Donnelly, "The Origins of the Occupational Safety and Health Act of 1970," *Social Problems,* 30, no. 1 (October 1982): 13–25.
50. *New York Times,* 4 March 1976, 12.
51. Nicholas A. Ashford, *Crisis in the Workplace* (Cambridge, Mass.: MIT Press, 1976), 268–269.
52. William P. Shepard, *The Physician in Industry* (New York: Arno Press, 1977), 1.
53. Samuel S. Epstein, "The Asbestos 'Pentagon Papers,' " in Mark Green and Robert Massie Jr., eds., *The Big Business Reader* (New York: Pilgrim Press, 1980), 157.
54. Paul Brodeur, *Expendable Americans* (New York: Viking Press, 1974).
55. Berman, *Death on the Job,* p. 80.
56. Epstein, "The Asbestos 'Pentagon Papers,' " 158.
57. *Charlotte Observer,* 13, March 1982.
58. Epstein, "The Asbestos 'Pentagon Papers,' " 159.
59. Harry M. Caudill, "Unsafe in Any Mine: The Story of Big Black Mountain" in Green and Massie, *The Big Business Reader,* 148.
60. Berman, *Death on the Job,* 34.
61. Quoted in Brodeur, *Expendable Americans,* 254.
62. Quoted in Ibid., 250.
63. Don Stillman, "The Devastating Impact of Plant Relocations," *Working Papers for a New Society,* 42–53.
64. Consumer Product Safety Commission, *Annual Report: 1981* (Washington, D.C.: Government Printing Office, 1981), 1.
65. Ibid., 212.
66. Ibid., 12.
67. Consumer Product Safety Commission, *Annual Report: 1980* (Washington, D.C.: Government Printing Office, 1980), pp. 43–164.
68. Mark Dowie, "Pinto Madness" *Mother Jones,* 1977, pp. 18–32; Ronald C. Kramer, "The Ford Pinto Homicide Prosecution." Paper presented at the Annual Meeting of the American Society of Criminology, 1979.
69. Mark Dowie, "Ford's Unpluggable Leak," *Mother Jones,* May 1978, 52.
70. Doris Cubbernuss and Beti Thompson, "The Philosophical Implications of Conflict Methodology; Theoretical Basis for Researching the Ford Pinto Trial." Unpublished paper, Kalamazoo, Michigan, 1979, 16.
71. Ibid., 11.
72. Ibid., 16–17.
73. While Mark Dowie of *Mother Jones* estimated 500 Pinto fire deaths and Ford claimed that their had been eleven, subsequent research by Randall McCall, *Call Chronical,* 18 September 1977, and by Ronald C. Kramer indicate the actual number closer to one hundred.
74. Karan Branan, "Running in Reverse," *Mother Jones,* June 1980, 41–47.
75. J. Patrick Wright, "How Moral Men Make Immoral Decisions," in Green and Massie, *The Big Business Reader,* 19–35.
76. Consumer Product Safety Commission, 1980, 148; Consumer Product Safety Commission, 1981, 142–143.
77. Mark Dowie, "Ford's Unpluggable Leak," 53.
78. Barbara Ehrenreich, Mark Dowie, and Stephen Minkin, "The Charge: Genocide," *Mother Jones,* November 1979.

79. "The Selling of Depo-Provera," *The Progressive,* December 1979, 45; Mark Dowie, "The Corporate Crime of the Century," *Mother Jones,* November 1979.

80. "Depo-Provera," 46.

81. Federal Water Pollution Control Act Amendments of 1972, 33 U.S.C.A. at 1251–1376 (Supp. 1973); National Environmental Policy Act of 1969.

82. Daniel Spitzer, "Is the Poisoning of Michigan Just the Start?" *Mother Jones,* May 1977, 18–22.

83. Ralph Nader et al., *Taming the Giant Corporation* (New York: Norton, 1976), 18.

84. Federal Bureau of Investigation, *Crime in the United States: 1977* (Washington, D.C.: Government Printing Office, 1978).

85. League of Women Voters, *Facts and Issues,* September 1970, 2.

86. *Bove* v. *Donner-Hana Coke Corp,* 142 Misc. 329, 254 N.Y.S. 403 (Sup. Ct. 1931).

87. Frank E. Maloney, "Judicial Protection of the Environment: A New Role for Common-Law Remedies," *Vanderbilt Law Review,* 25, no. 1 (1972): 148.

88. Comment, "Environmental Law: New Legal Concepts in the Antipollution Fight," *Missouri Law Review,* 36, no. 1, 79–83.

89. See for example *Boomer* v. *Atlantic Cement Co.,* 55 Misc. 2nd. at 1024, 287 N.Y.S. 2nd at 113.

90. Compiled from Brodeur, *Expendable Americans,* 221–245; Epstein, "The Asbestos 'Pentagon Papers,'" 154–165.

91. *New York Times,* 8 February 1977; 9 August 1977.

92. Sherman Anti-Trust Act of 1890, 26 Stat. 209.

93. Federal Trade Commission Act of 1914, 38 Stat. 717.

94. Source: U.S. Bureau of the Census, *Statistical Abstracts of the United States: 1977* (Washington, D.C.: Government Printing Office, 1978), 562.

95. Morris A. Adelman, "Monopoly and Concentration: Comparison in Time and Space," in Richard E. Low, ed., *The Economics of Anti-Trust* (Englewood Cliffs, N.J.: Prentice-Hall, 1968), 48.

96. James Ridgeway, *The Last Play: The Struggle to Monopolize the World's Energy Resources* (New York: Signet Books, 1973), 129.

97. See Edward S. Greenberg, *The American Political System* (Cambridge, Mass.: Winthrop, 1980), 112–122; Douglas F. Dowd, *The Twisted Dream: Capitalist Development in the United States* (Cambridge, Mass.: Winthrop, 1977), 79–83 for data on ologopolistic concentration in the American economy.

98. Hearings before the Subcommittee on Monopolies and Commercial Law, *Food Price Investigation* (Washington, D.C.: Government Printing Office, 1973), 437.

99. H. Barnett, "Wealth, Crime and Capital Accumulation," *Contemporary Crises,* 3, no. 2 (1979): 171–186.

100. Based on estimated mean income of $20,000 for a family of four.

101. Greenberg, *American Political System,* 112.

102. Donna M. Randall, "The Social Control of Big Business." Paper presented at the American Society of Criminology annual meeting, November 1980.

103. Quoted in Gilbert Geis and Robert F. Meir, *White Collar Crime* (New York: Free Press, 1977), 117.

104. Gilbert Geis, "The Heavy Electrical Equipment Antitrust Cases of 1961" in Geis and Meir, *White Collar Crime,* pp. 120–122.

105. Ibid., p. 119.

106. *Charlotte Obeserver,* 8 October 1980.

107. Sutherland, *White Collar Crime,* 21–22, 26.

108. Clinard, *Illegal Corporate Behavior,* 185.

109. Ibid., 183.
110. William H. Allen, *Rockefeller* (New York: Institute for Public Service, 1930), 208–218.
111. Milton S. Gwirtzman, "Is Bribery Defensible?" in John M. Johnson and Jack D. Douglas, eds., *Crime at the Top: Deviance in Business and the Professions* (New York: Lippincott, 1978), 340; Jim Hougan, "The Business of Buying Friends" in Johnson and Douglas, 196–226.
112. Hearing before a Subcommittee of the Committee on Government Operations, House of Representatives, *GSA's Investigative Activities* (Washington, D.C.: Government Printing Office, 1979).
113. Federal Trade Commission, *Federal Trade Commission Decisions* (Washington, D.C.: Government Printing Office, 1981), 283.
114. Ibid., 541.
115. Geis, "Antitrust Cases," 123.
116. Jules Henry, "Advertising as a Philosophical System," in Henry Etzkowitz, ed., *Is America Possible* (New York: West Publishing Co., 1974), 300.
117. Stuart Ewen, *Captains of Consciousness* (New York: McGraw-Hill, 1976), 77–80.
118. *Advertising Age,* January 1981, 5 estimates advertising expenditures to be $57 billion for 1980. The Office of Management and Budget, *Budget of the United States* (Washington, D.C.: Government Printing Office, 1981) shows 1980 Federal health expenditures to be $56.5 billion.
119. *Federal Trade Commission Decisions,* 1981, 236, 265, 361, 406.
120. S. D. Goodwin, "Individual Liability of Agents for Corporate Crimes under the Proposed Federal Criminal Code." *Vanderbilt Law Review,* 31, no. 4, 965–1016.
121. Geis, "Antitrust Cases," 124.
122. Cubernuss and Thompson, "Philosophical Implications of Conflict Methodology," 10.
123. Harvard Law School, "Regulating Corporate Behavior through Criminal Sanctions." *Harvard Law Review,* 92, no. 6 (1979): 1227–1375.

CHAPTER 13

Crimes of Capital-
Part II:Organized Crime
and Political Deviance

INTRODUCTION

The previous chapter introduced the concept of *crimes of capital* and examined those that occur in connection with the process of capital accumulation in legitimate corporate organizations. This chapter examines other crimes and forms of social injury that arise in connection with accumulating or facilitating the accumulation of capital. These are (1) occupational crimes, (2) organized crime, and (3) political crime.

OCCUPATIONAL CRIME

The Nature of Occupational Crime

Occupational crimes are acts that are committed either by (1) individuals misusing the power or trust inherent in occupations or professions to achieve direct personal gain or (2) businesses whose primary purpose is the perpetration of some illegal or fraudulent scheme. Occupational crimes differ from corporate crimes in several ways. First, occupational crimes by employees of corporations are crimes *against* the interests of the corporation rather than crimes committed to further the goals of the company. Acts such as embezzlement, expense account falsification, leaking inside information to competitors or stockbrokers, and employee theft threaten rather than enhance corporate profitability. Second, most occupational crimes, whether embezzlement, false submissions by physicians for Medicaid payments, land swindles, or use of inside information to make a "killing" in the stock market, are committed by individuals for the express purpose of direct personal gain rather than to meet the general performance requirements of some corporate position. Third, most occupational crimes are *criminal* rather than regulatory offenses. This is because these acts threaten rather than serve the interests of big business and because they are committed by individuals for personal gain, making it easier to identify a "guilty" person.

Consumer Frauds

Every year millions of Americans are victimized by consumer frauds. While the actual extent of consumer fraud and the resulting financial loss to people is difficult to determine, one national study concluded that it represented a "serious and pervasive phenomenon that was harmful to a very large number of people." Furthermore, they found that while the loss per fraudulent transaction was most often under $100, the aggregate loss was large. The 1,147 consumer frauds studied, a mere fraction of the total number occurring annually, represented a total loss to consumers of more than $700,000.[1] Frauds connected wtih the sale of merchandise or other things of value generally occur in one of three ways; the paid-for commodity is never delivered, it is of lesser quantity or quality than what was paid for, or the seller refuses to correct defects in the product sold. (See the accompanying box.)

Not all sales frauds involve the purchase of minor items. In some cases, such as land and stock swindles, the loss to the buyer can be substantial. Land swindles are a case in point. Frequently fraudulent developers sell land as potential vacation or retirement homesites that they know cannot be used for residential purposes either because it lacks water—as is frequently the case in Arizona land swindles—or because it lacks access to necessary services. In one case, forty-acre "rancheros" were sold to unsuspecting buyers without informing them that the nearest power and phone lines were six miles away and the closest water was twelve miles away, at a coin-operated pump.[2]

A number of land frauds are less overtly crooked but instead emerge only after it becomes apparent that the developer never intended to make the improvements to the land promised in the initial contract. Often the developer in these cases proceeds very slowly in making improvements until all the property is sold and then after transferring funds to other companies through loans, files or is forced into bankruptcy, leaving the owners with useless property and no legal recourse.

Fraudulent land development provides not only windfall profits for the developer but is often a lucrative source of income for more legitimate enterprises. As one investigator noted, once a landsite was purchased,

> The developer would then obtain a local engineer, real estate agent, and lawyers to do the preparation work and create local influence. With local business in on the action, there was rarely a problem in convincing local authorities to support the subdivision.[3]

Such local support is often indispensable for obtaining the necessary permits to "develop" and sell the land. Perhaps the most significant relationship between land fraud and legitimate enterprise is that between unscrupulous developers and the world of finance. In 1977, a detailed investigation of Arizona land swindles identified what was called the great "paper caper." To assure collecting their profit before the fraud was uncovered, land developers generally sold the mortgages or installment contracts of buyers to banks, private investors, or title companies. In a perfectly legal transaction these investors were then able to reap substantial profits in the form of mortgage

FRAUD VICTIMS TELL THEIR STORIES

- A $22 check accompanied my order for six Bicentennial gold-plated dollars . . . acknowledgement of my order and notice of six-month delay in shipment accompanied another offer for more coins . . . eight months following original order, a court-appointed receiver for the company informed me that the company's funds were exhausted and solicited my order of silver-plated coins ($33 plus a money-back guarantee) as a first step toward ultimate receipt of my set of gold-plated dollars.
- The unusual plants for which I paid $26 were almost dead when they arrived . . . balance of order never received . . . my mail order was prepaid . . . four years later the merchant had not fulfilled the balance of my original order . . . the same ad I responded to still appears in national publications.
- I ordered a radio, stereo, and turntable at a tremendous discount from an incentive program offered through the local educators association . . . mailed a personal check for $267.45 with my order . . . seven months of delays and promises have resulted in no merchandise . . . now there is no phone listing for this "program" organization.
- I have not received my home office storage unit that I ordered by mail six months ago . . . phone calls of inquiry resulted in empty promises of delivery when they caught up with large number of orders received . . . paid special sale price of $395 (reduced from $445) plus $25 shipping charge . . . confirmation received acknowledging payment.
- I purchased an electric clock on sale ($30) because the store was relocating . . . the clock had a one-year guarantee . . . when it stopped running after three days I contacted the new store and was asked to return the clock so it could be sent to the manufacturer for repair . . . six months later I still had no clock . . . during my last conversation with the manager he refused to take action because the clock was purchased on sale . . . he was not responsible for any statements made by the clerk.
- I responded to a telephone solicitation offering brand-name vacuum cleaner bags for a special price prior to an increase . . . I paid in full on delivery . . . when I later opened the package I discovered the bags were of an inferior quality, and were not the brand name offered.

Source: U.S. Department of Justice, *Consumer Fraud: An Empirical Perspective, Summary* (Washington, D.C.: Government Printing Office, 1979), 2.

interests without having any liability to the swindled landholders. As one Arizona real estate agent indicated, "The real fraud was not in land, but in selling contracts. Land simply served as a vehicle for generating paper."[4] Most major land frauds of this sort require a working relationship between illegitimate operators and legitimate capital, and it is naive to assume that the representatives of legitimate capital are wholly unaware of the fraudulent nature of the businesses they aid.

Because it involves tangible property, land fraud often becomes apparent fairly quickly. Frauds involving intangibles such as stocks, bonds, or securities, however, can frequently be maintained for longer periods of time.

For example, the Equity Funding scandle was a stock fraud that lasted for thirteen years—from 1960 until 1973—and ultimately cost millions of investors over a billion dollars. Equity Funding was a combination insurance and mutual-funds investment company of no particular significance at the start of the fraud. However, through a variety of mechanisms, such as listing revenues from fake loans and insurance policies "sold" to nonexistent customers, it was able to create the impression of an up-and-coming fast-growth company that was highly profitable. This attracted thousands of stock investors, who in turn continually increased the value of Equity Fundings stock and attracted still more investors. At its peak, Equity Funding investors held over $300 million of stock and three times that amount in bonds and other securities in a company with *reported* assets of $750 million and a *reported* income in 1972 of $152 million. These assets and income existed only on paper, however, and when the fraud collapsed, the value of Equity Funding stocks and securities plummeted to zero. Investors saw their money evaporate as surely as if they had been the victims of a common theft.

Another type of consumer fraud occurs in the area of repair and warranty work. The Federal Trade Commission estimates that about $12 billion of the $40 billion spent annually for automobile repair goes for unnecessary or undone work.[5] In addition, purchasers of new automobiles are frequently required to pay exhorbitantly high, noncompetitive prices for service and repair work as the result of warranties that require that the car be maintained by a "factory-authorized" dealer.[6] Studies also have found substantial evidence of widespread fraud and overcharging in the repair of homes and home appliances such as televisions, washing machines, and refrigerators.[7]

Both large- and small-scale consumer frauds are a *threat to capital accumulation by legitimate business*. Overtly unscrupulous business practices tend to create a cloud of suspicion around business in general and can often lead to more stringent regulation of legitimate as well as illegitimate enterprise. For this reason, the control and punishment of fraudulent business is often actively supported by corporate capital. It is also for this reason that aggressive law enforcement is generally focused on the small-time operator, not the corporate crimes of legitimate businesses.

Frauds Against Government

State, Federal, and local governments combined represent the single largest purchaser of goods and services in America. Therefore, it is not surprising that government is a major victim of marketplace frauds.

The Government Accounting Office estimates that fraud and abuse of government spending encompasses about 10 percent of the total Federal budget annually.[8] This means that in 1981 the American taxpayer lost approximately *$61 billion* through frauds against the Federal government alone. This dwarfs the estimated $4-to $5-billion loss resulting from common crime. Furthermore, GAO admits that its estimates are probably very conservative and that "no one knows the magnitude of fraud against the government."[9]

The typical impression of fraud against the government presented by the media is that it consists largely of "cheating" by recipients of some social service such as welfare or food stamps. While such cheating undoubtedly exists, the average "take" by individual recipients of fraudulent government benefits is usually small. Studies at both the state and Federal levels indicate that most losses in the area of welfare and food stamp programs result from agency errors rather than fraud.[10] The total loss from welfare due to fraud, waste, and error combined constituted about $475 million in 1977, only 1.2 percent of the total estimated loss due to fraud and abuse of government spending that year.[11]

Benefit recipients represent only one of the groups that enjoy an opportunity to defraud the government. As indicated by a study of fraud and abuse in government three other groups are organizationally better situated to commit fraud and generally undergo less scrutiny than direct recipients of benefits. These are (1) administrators and employees of government benefit programs, (2) third-party providers, that is, persons or agencies who provide services and are paid by the government such as physicians receiving Medicaid or Medicare reimbursements, and (3) auxiliary providers, that is, persons or agencies who provide services to third-party providers such as laboratories that provide blood analyses or other services to physicians who then charge this against Medicaid or Medicare reimbursements.[12]

The largest losses to government due to fraud and abuse by service providers occur in the areas of Medicare and Medicaid, with estimated losses ranging from $5 to $10 billion annually.[13] Much of this loss results from fraudulent activities by third-party and auxiliary providers such as physicians, nursing homes, X-ray laboratories, and other labs. These frauds involve

1. The establishment of "ghost" patients whose bills for medical or nursing care are paid to the third-party provider
2. Overbilling, double-billing, and billing for services not provided to "real" patients
3. Misrepresentation of services provided, that is, billing the government for more costly and more involved services than were actually provided
4. Overutilization of services such as requiring patients to receive continued treatment where unnecessary
5. Tie-ins and interlocking ownerships among clinics, laboratories, and nursing homes
6. "Medicaid mill" abuses such as pingponging—shuttling a patient between two physicians several times to increase the total number of visits billed, or ganging—requiring a patient to see every physician or specialist in a clinic to insure that the patient generates government revenue for each[14]

This kind of widespread abuse and fraud within the medical profession, one of the highest paid and most esteemed occupations in America, offers substantial support for the idea that economic crimes in America are not simply the result of poverty and deprivation but are related to both the opportunities and pressures for illegal gain in a competitive, materialistic society where more may never be enough.

Embezzlement

Embezzlement is the violation by an employee of an economic trust. It usually involves the diversion for personal use of company funds or property by an employee entrusted with handling accounting or cash flow functions in industry or finance. Embezzlement is a relatively modern crime; its growth parallels that of industrial and financial development. With the widespread use of financial instruments such as notes, checks, bonds, securities, and accounts in the nineteenth century there emerged a corresponding demand for special criminal sanctions to deal with those who misused the economic trust of their employer.[15]

In 1982 there were 2,233 arrests for embezzlement reported by the FBI.[16] It is interesting to note that as a crime that generally cannot be committed by working class members since by definition they seldom find themselves in the position of economic trust necessary for embezzlement, this offense is listed by the FBI as a Part II, or "less serious," offense, even though the total dollar loss due to embezzlements generally exceeds that due to common burglaries or thefts. FBI estimates of embezzlement are in all probability highly conservative. Many institutions, particularly financial ones, are reluctant to prosecute embezzlement since revelation of the crime poses a threat to the image of security and responsibility they must present to the public to entice investors and depositors.

A study of convicted embezzlers by Donald Cressy indicates that most initially began their offense by "borrowing" money from the organization for which they work with the intention of repaying it when "things got better." Most found, however, that paying back the "loan" was either impossible or unattractive and that moreover they were required to continue engaging in financial manipulations to keep the evidence of their initial offense hidden.[17]

Employee Theft

Many American workers—one estimate was 50 percent—take things home from their jobs.[18] In most cases this involves minor items such as pencils, pens, hand tools, or materials such as nuts, bolts, wire, and so forth. In addition, employees may act against the interests of their employers by utilizing company equipment or company time for their own projects. While in most cases the value of items taken or time used may be small, the aggregate cost is thought to be substantial. The FBI estimates that employee pilfering amounts to a $15 billion annual loss to industry.[19]

The motivations or justifications for employee theft generally take one of four forms. In some cases, employees view the items taken as a *legitimate* benefit of their job. One study of managers in three chemical plants found that they all had acquired items that they had had made by employees using company materials and company time. Rather than viewing this as theft from the company, the managers felt that utilizing company materials and labor was simply one of the perquisites of holding a managerial position.[20]

Employee theft among blue-collar workers tends to be viewed somewhat differently. Many blue collar workers feel that taking property that clearly belongs to the company is wrong but that taking items of doubtful ownership such as "scrap" materials and "waste" is not.[21] In other cases, employees steal as a form of retaliation against an employer for some act that the employee feels is unnecessarily abusive or humiliating. One study describes a case where, after being lectured on the correct way to mop floors, a cleanup boy in a large store stole several books to "show the manager he was not to be belittled": "Now the books were not made known to the manager, but were shown to friends with a story of how he showed the manager . . ."[22] In another case, an employee explained why she stole from one record store for which she had worked, but not another, by saying that the manager of the store from which she stole ". . . acted like everything was expected of you. Like I worked very hard and never got anything, not even a thank you or something."[23]

By far the most common basis for employee theft is the view on the part of workers that what is stolen represents "wages-in-kind," an attempt by workers to recoup what they feel is the "unpaid value of their labor."[24]

The theft of wages-in-kind by employees is not always opposed by employers. In some instances employers treat employee pilferage as an easier and cheaper way of providing benefits to workers than the formal mechanism of increased salaries.[25] Employers will often tolerate known irregularities as a means of insuring a stable work force. As one worker said,

> If you figure it out, we're making less than $2 an hour. It is hard work, dirty, lots of pressures . . . so how are they going to keep people . . . if they don't let you have this extra?[26]

By permitting employee theft as a form of wages-in-kind, employers can keep the actual rate of pay at a lower level, thus minimizing worker expectations for salary. Since not all employees will steal, and many will steal less than the actual value of the unpaid portion of their labor, the employer comes out ahead.

Professional Deviance

Professional deviance refers to acts by self-employed professionals that are illegal, questionable, or in violation of the trust clients have in them. In recent years, for instance, there has arisen substantial concern over the overquick or unnecessary use of surgery by physicians seeking to maximize their incomes. One study found that the medical necessity of approximately 40 percent of the hysterectomies done in West Coast hospitals was questionable, and in at least 13 percent of the cases there was no evidence to support the need for surgery.[27]

Another area of professional deviance among physicians and pharmacists is the diversion of licit drugs into the illicit market.

Physicians can collect additional fees by attracting "patients" who know they will prescribe drugs with little or no medical justification. In 1977, in

New Hampshire, for example, a single physician was convicted for violating the Controlled Substances Act after being identified as responsible for *60 percent* of all amphetamines legally distributed in that state. He received a suspended sentence.[28] A study of 4,800 physicians in Maryland found that 16 percent of them accounted for 75 percent of all drug prescriptions in that state.[29] Another study of 2,400 physicians and pharmacists conducted under the auspices of the Department of Health, Education, and Welfare in 1977 identified 1,100 pharmacists who appeared to be dispensing drugs with greater frequency and in greater quantity than the allowable parameters. As a result of this particular study, 400 physicians and pharmacists were given administrative sanctions and 55 indicted for drug law violations.[30]

Medical professionals and lawyers can also acquire additional income through such activities as fee splitting, pingponging, and collusion. Fee splitting in the medical and legal professions involves referring a client or patient to another professional who is a "specialist" of one sort or another. An internist might, for example, suggest that his or her patient see a blood specialist, or an attorney might direct his or her client to a psychologist. The referring physician or lawyer would then receive a portion of the "specialist's" fee as a gratuity for making the referral. This practice creates an incentive on the part of physicians and lawyers to direct clients to pay for services that often are not necessary. Another variant of this is to refer patients to all of the various specialists within a medical group to increase the revenue of the business.

Organized Crime
What Is Organized Crime?

For most Americans the term "organized crime" calls forth images of cigar-smoking Mafiosi meeting in inconspicuous restaurants or rural hideaways to arrange the affairs of their illegal enterprises or of "syndicate" thugs shaking down small businessmen for "protection" money. These images generally also imply the existence of networks of criminals organized into local "families" that are in turn interrelated through a national crime syndicate or commission. These images have been created and kept alive largely through the popular press, the news media, movies, and several government commissions established to study organized crime in America. However, the reality of organized crime in America is at the same time both more and less than these popular images suggest.

The term "organized crime" can apply to any form of criminal activity arising from a criminal *organization*. In general, an organization is any set of structured relations characterized by (1) commitment to specific goals, (2) a division of labor related to the accomplishment of these goals, (3) established though usually evolving sets of procedures to obtain these goals, (4) established lines of communication and authority, and (5) some mechanism for recruitment or replacement of members so as to guarantee survival of the organization independently of any of its specific members.[31]

Both criminal and noncriminal organizations break the law as a means of facilitating capital accumulation. The difference is that (1) the specific subgoals of legitimate economic organizations are legal while those of criminal organizations are not and (2) while violation of the law is an auxiliary mechanism to aid goal attainment in legitimate organizations, it is central to goal attainment for the criminal organization. Thus organized crime can be defined as *any structurally coordinated and bureaucratically organized association of individuals that relies almost primarily upon illegal subgoals and means to facilitate the accumulation of capital.*

While there is no doubt that criminal organizations fitting this definition exist in America, two aspects of the popular image of organized crime are particularly open to question. These are (1) the image of ethnic exclusivity and (2) the image of an all-encompassing nationwide syndicate.

Is Organized Crime Ethnic?

Most writings about organized crime in America devote the majority if not all of their attention to the Mafia, which is most often characterized as a secret criminal society composed of Italian or Sicilian Americans engaged primarily in the provision of illegal goods or services such as drugs, gambling, and prostitution and in various forms of racketeering or extortion. The two central problems with this characterization is that first, while there are undoubtedly criminal organizations whose members are largely Italian, there are and have been criminal organizations dominated by other ethnic groups and second, there is little evidence that ethnicity is the primary factor governing membership in criminal organizations.

At various times the distribution of illicit goods and services *in specific locales* has been dominated by Irish, Jewish, Italian, black, or Puerto Rican Americans. Part of this variation has reflected what Daniel Bell described as a pattern of "ethnic succession."[32] That is, as successive waves of immigrants occupied the bottom rung of the social ladder in various urban areas, members of those ethnic groups established criminal organizations to provide illicit goods and services as well as occupations to members of those groups. Bell's concept of ethnic succession, however, tends to give the impression that while not exclusively Italian, organized crime is an exclusively *ethnic* activity. This view, held by many, is prompted in part by the fact that ethnic minorities are both more visible and are generally seen as culturally more exotic than fully assimilated Americans. This may partially explain the predominant focus by the media and popular entertainments on Italian-American–dominated forms of organized crime. Stories about organized crime replete with stereotyped images of ethnic criminals can be more colorful and exciting than ones about average, everyday Americans. Thus, for example, the popular film *The Godfather* can begin with a scene of a festive, Old World–style Italian wedding, cinemagraphically a more appealing beginning than a gathering of average middle-class Americans. Similarly, two popular books about the reputed Mafia summit raided by police in Appalachin, New York, in November 1957 disagreed over how the participants were dressed. One described the men in "immaculate light suits of Italian silk, white on white shirts, and highly polished shoes of soft leather" while the other suggested the basic uniform consisted of "loud Broadway type sports jackets and thin, pointed shoes. . . .[33] In these cases the author(s) relied on existing stereotypes of Italian men to craft a colorful and probably fanciful description of organized criminals.

There is evidence that ethnically dominated criminal organizations exist in America.[34] However, the ethnic nature of these groups is only tangentially related to their operations as organized criminals and is not an explanation for it, as is so frequently implied. The prohibition of various goods and services—public order crimes—is generally aimed at working class Americans. Because a large part of the labor force needed during the early growth of the industrial sector of the American economy was drawn from foreign countries, various groups of ethnic immigrants frequently found themselves closed off from legitimate access to goods and services that had traditionally been a part of their lives. The demand for these goods and services provided a fertile ground for entrepreneurship by other members of these ethnic groups. For instance, the biggest growth period in Italian-American organized crime occurred during the Prohibition years.[35] The reason was not some predisposition to organized crime among Italian-Americans but the fact that prohibition had created a climate for the lucrative distribution of illegal alcohol. Ethnic-organized crime was further fueled by the fact that since members of urbanized ethnic groups frequently found themselves with limited access to legitimate opportunities for financial success, entering the ranks of organized crime served as an alternative opportunity structure for the more ambitious.[36]

The focus on ethnic groups as the source of organized crime in America is a type of "scapegoat" politics. It directs attention and enforcement from the wrongdoing of socially significant Americans involved in organized criminal activity. Some support for this conclusion was provided by sociologist William Chambliss in his study of organized crime activities in the Seattle area. Chambliss found that organized crime in Seattle involved a variety of individuals, many of whom were highly respected members of middle- and upper-class segments of the population in that area.[37] Another consequence of the focus upon ethnicity in organized crime is that as long as organized criminal activity can be associated with various ethnic groups it is possible to view such activity as the result of the corrupt ways of "outsiders," not something endemic to American society.

Is Organized Crime National?

There is substantial controversy surrounding the question whether or not there exists a national organized crime network that oversees and coordinates the operations of criminal organizations in the various parts of the country. In 1951 Senator Estes Kefauver concluded after extensive hearings that

> A nationwide crime syndicate does exist in the United States of America. . . .
> Behind the local mobs which make up the national crime syndicate is a shadowy
> international organization known as the Mafia, so fantastic that most Americans
> find it hard to believe it really exists.[38]

(It should be noted that Senator Kefauver made his discovery in the same social climate that enabled Senator Joseph McCarthy to promote what was ultimately shown to be the patently false notion of a nationwide communist conspiracy.) In 1967 the President's Commission on Law Enforcement and the Administration of Justice agreed with Senator Kefauver. The President's Commission Task Force on Organized Crime went on to identify twenty-four groups or families whose "membership is of exclusively Italian descent" who are in frequent communication with one another and whose "smooth functioning is insured by a national body of overseers."[39] This conclusion was based largely upon testimony taken at the 1966 McClellan subcommittee hearing on illicit drug traffic, and particularly upon the statements of Joseph Valachi, a reputed member of what Valachi called *La Cosa Nostra*.[40] Valachi, who was in prison at the time, provided detailed testimony about the structure of what he claimed was a nationwide criminal syndicate in order "to destroy" his former criminal associates, whom Valachi believed were trying to have him killed. Despite the inconsistencies in Valachi's testimony, his own admitted lack of commitment to truthfulness, and his ulterior motives in testifying, which may have included hopes for pardon or parole, Valachi's testimony was hailed as conclusive proof that organized crime was controlled by a national syndicate.[41] The response to Valachi's testimony is particularly surprising, for until then, as the head of the Department of Justice's Organized Crime Section admitted, there had been "no tangible proof that anything like this actually existed.[42] Why was the testimony of one convicted organized criminal taken as solid evidence of a nationwide crime conspiracy? The primary reason is that his testimony confirmed the belief at that time that organized crime represented a sinister conspiracy of "outsiders" rather than an outgrowth of other, more basic processes in American society.

Aside from the doubtful veracity of Valachi's testimony there are other reasons to question whether a single national organized crime conspiracy exists. Organized crime encompasses a variety of activities such as the sale of illicit goods and services, racketeering, labor union corruption, theft of securities, and other criminal services. As economist Thomas C. Schelling indicated, the existence of a nationwide criminal conspiracy would depend upon the possibility and attractiveness of a single organization achieving a monopoly position over all these activities. Overall, Schelling concluded that while some organized crime activities might lead to monopolies beyond the local level, others are not conducive to this form of organization.[43] Thus, even if there exists a nationwide syndicate to control specific organized crime activities, the likelihood of some national organization overseeing all aspects of organized crime is minimal.

Furthermore, the twenty-four syndicate "families" identified in the President's Commission report cover only sixteen states. Yet as criminologist Gordon Hawkins points out, organized crime activities are found in every city.[44] In 1976 the Task Force on Organized Crime of the National Advisory Committee on Criminal Justice Standards and Goals contradicted the conclusions of earlier government inquiries into organized crime by concluding that while Mafia-type criminal organizations did exist in certain areas, they do not enjoy a monopoly on underworld activities and that "today a variety of groups is engaged in organized criminal activity."[45]

Despite evidence to the contrary, for most Americans as well as for many political spokesmen, organized crime continues to be imagined as a nationwide, ethnically dominated criminal conspiracy. Since an essential component of conservative philosophy and politics is the view that all social problems arise from the existence of "bad people" rather than inherent flaws or contradictions in the social system, we are likely to see a resurgence rather than a waning of the notion of organized crime as largely the province of ethnic or nonwhite criminals.

The Operations of Organized Crime

Criminal organizations attempt to accumulate capital through the use of illegal tactics in a variety of areas. The traditional sources of revenue for organized crime have been the black market distribution of illegal goods and services such as drugs, prostitution, and gambling and economic crimes such as loansharking and racketeering. However, over time the accumulated capital from these enterprises and the pressures for continued capital accumulation have resulted in an expansion of organized crime into many other areas. Takeover of legitimate businesses; provision of illegal services to "legitimate" sectors of the economy such as "laundering" business or corporate money to facilitate tax avoidance or make possible illegal campaign contributions; complex land frauds; planned bankruptcies; and computer manipulations have become commonplace elements of contemporary organized crime. Organized crime has also long played an important role in the corruption of labor unions, an activity that has often proven to be helpful to the interests of corporate capital. Last, but certainly not least, organized crime has engaged in the wide-scale corruption of politics and law enforcement to secure a safe environment for the operation of its illegal enterprises.

Black Market Crimes

Organized crime has long played a central role in the distribution of illegal goods and services. In these areas organized crime has enjoyed a near-monopoly by virtue of the fact that these goods and services are illegal. As legal scholar Herbert Packer noted, laws prohibiting such things as heroin use, gambling, and prostitution serve as a "protective tariff" insulating organized criminals from marketplace competition by legitimate businesses.[46] By exercising monopoly control over illegitimate markets, criminal organizations are able to reap massive profits through exorbitant costs for these goods and services. While no single criminal organization controls the entire national market for any particular illicit service or commodity, various organizations often enjoy a complete or near-monopoly over the black market for particular goods and services in specific cities or geographic regions.[47] Furthermore, since

ds and services being provided are illegal, the clients of organized
ave no recourse to legal protection from fraudulent or unscrupulous
market practices.[48]

Controlled Substances. The manufacture and distribution of alcohol during the
Prohibition era provided a major source of profit for organized crime. With
the repeal of the Volstead Act in 1929, pressures for capital accumulation led
to the investment of this capital in the provision of other illegal drugs, among
other activities. Today organized crime provides the basic capital and equally
importantly, the international connections necessary for the large-scale purchase, transportation, and smuggling of illicit drugs from other countries.
Organized crime's primary involvement is in the heroin trade.[49] This frequently involves not only the importation of heroin but the establishment
of ties with foreign crime syndicates to purchase opium, have it converted
into heroin in clandestine foreign laboratories, and loaded onto ships or planes
bound for the United States.[50] Additionally, there is evidence that organized
crime syndicates, particularly in the southwest, are involved in smuggling
marijuana and cocaine into the United States from Mexico.[51] Besides traffic
in illicit drugs, every year millions of dollars of legally manufactured drugs
"disappear" from the inventory of major drug producers only to reappear on
the streets. As one counselor in a halfway house for juvenile delinquents
said, "Over half the drugs we find on our kids have the name Lilly or Upjohn
written on them, and these kids don't have prescriptions."[52] Just how this
transference takes place has not been clearly documented, but given the
existence of established networks for the distribution of illicit drugs it is not
unlikely that organized crime groups have established affiliations with "insiders" in the drug industry to effect such a transfer from the legal to the
illegal marketplace. Furthermore, as discussed below, infiltration of legitimate
drug companies by organized crime can place syndicate members in positions
advantageous to diverting legal drugs to the street market.

The idea that legal prohibitions against hallucinogens and narcotics provide a protective tariff for organized crime has frequently been used as an
argument for the legalization or decriminalization of these drugs. It is argued
that by creating alternative drug sources organized crime's monopoly over
drug traffic would be broken, reducing the lucrativeness of the black market
trade in drugs. The Organized Crime Task Force disagrees with this assessment, however. They point out that most proposals for "legalization" involve
government clinics that provide maintenance dosages for addicts. Since only
those already addicted would be eligible this "would leave a sizable illegal
market," and furthermore, since maintenance dosages would not provide the
"euphoria" that drug users seek, street-level purchases would remain both
more attractive and "more convenient" for the drug user.[53] On the other hand,
the true legalization of narcotics, that is, making them a commodity like any
other on the legitimate market, might overcome the limitations of such drug
programs. At this point such proposals regarding the legalization of drugs
run up against an important contradiction surrounding the role of drugs—

both licit and illicit—in American society. Drug use is an important social safety valve through which many Americans both poor and affluent insulate or anesthetize themselves from the unpleasant reality of their everyday lives. However, to legalize their usage would be equivalent to both admitting the need for periodic mental and emotional obliteration of the stresses produced by the alienated and often impoverished life experienced by many in capitalist society and a rejection of the ethic of sobriety and industry that drug laws seek to reinforce. To some extent, by providing an illegal market for drugs, organized crime helps insure that many of the most oppressed Americans will turn to self-destruction rather than more radical solutions to their problems.

Gambling. Gambling has traditionally been a mainstay of organized crime revenue. Gambling operations involve both "numbers" betting and betting on sports events such as horse racing, football, basketball, hockey, and prizefighting. Organized crime involvement in gambling takes several forms. The 1967 President's Commission noted that at the time organized crime's primary revenue from gambling operations came not from taking bets itself but from providing loans, often at exceptionally high rates of interest, to individual "bookies."[54] These bookies are themselves not part of any organized crime bureaucracy but rather private entrepreneurs in the underworld economy who utilize loans from organized crime to stay in business, much as legitimate businessmen rely on the legal world of finance capital for operating revenue.

Organized crime syndicates also often provide the network of contacts for "laying off" bets. Laying off is a mechanism whereby bookmakers attempt to protect themselves from losses by placing a proportion of the bets they have taken with some other betting source.

> Thus, if he [the bookmaker] has received a large number of bets on one horse in a given race, he must guard against the possibility of that horse winning. In order to do this, he himself places a portion of his bets on this horse with a lay-off source. If the horse wins, the lay-off source will pay him and in turn he can cover his own losses. These lay-off sources generally consist of syndicate participants who have the necessary capital to cover large amounts of bets of this type.[55]

In many respects the process is similar to "diversification," a mechanism through which legitimate industries attempt to protect themselves from economic downturns in any particular product market.

Organized crime syndicates also operate as financiers and "fixers" for legalized gambling operations. Particularly in Nevada, where gambling was legalized in 1931, organized crime has been involved in both financing gambling operations and stealing from them by placing representatives in key positions within gambling establishments. Currently, organized crime involvement in Nevada entails not only gambling operations themselves, but also hotel and casino development, land speculation, and infiltration of formerly legitimate banks as a way of laundering illegally acquired capital for apparently legal redistribution into the legal gambling industry.[56]

The role of modern organized crime in gambling has largely been that of the finance capitalist. Capital, whether legal or illegal, tends to gravitate toward other capital like magnetized iron filings. Thus gambling has provided one of the more lucrative areas for the interpenetration of illegal and legal capital, to the advantage of both.

Prostitution and Other Sexual Services. Prior to World War I organized crime syndicates derived a substantial proportion of their revenue from financing and in some cases operating brothels and other houses of prostitution. With the passage of the Mann White Slave Act and changes in sexual morals, prostitution became both more difficult and less lucrative and was replaced as a major operation by gambling, bootlegging, and drug smuggling.[57] In recent years there appears to have been a resurgence of organized crime activity in the area of sexual services. Much of this involves relatively small operations seeking to monopolize the massage parlor trade in local areas, using these as fronts for prostitution.[58] In addition, organized crime involvement has been identified in the quasi-legitimate world of pronography and live sex shows. In many large cities this involvement includes establishing relationships with the world of legitimate finance. One investigation of the world of quasi-legal sex-for-sale found that credit card payments made in pornography shops or thinly disguised sex-for-sale operations appeared on the bills of customers as charges to legitimate business such as record stores and restaurants. This enabled customers to utilize credit cards to buy sexual material or services, hide the nature of their expenses from wives or other disapproving parties, and even obtain expense account reimbursement for the sex-related purchase. While the legitimate business was clearly complicit, there was further indication that many of these transformed credit transactions could not have occurred without at least the tacit consent of the major financial institutions handling the credit cards involved.[59]

Economic Crimes

While black market trade has been a traditional source of organized crime revenue there appears to be a current trend for large-scale crime syndicates to turn over the operational aspects of black market trade to smaller local organizations.[60] While remaining the financier and the source for international connections for the marketing of illicit goods and services, large organized crime syndicates focus increasingly on economic crimes as their central operation. Economic crimes involve the utilization of criminal techniques such as intimidation, violence, corruption, and financial manipulation to acquire profit from businesses and finance institutions in the legitimate sector of the economy.

Racketeering. Racketeering is the use of predatory criminal techniques, particularly violence or threat of violence, to extract profits from legitimate businesses. It usually takes the form of either extortion or creation of criminal monopolies, although the two are not always easily separated.

Extortion is the practice of extracting money either in the form of direct cash payments or other considerations from legitimate businesses through the use or threat of violence. The classic and perhaps crudest form of extortion is the "protection racket." In this case the racketeers promise to "protect" businesses from such things as fires, bombings, or death to employees or owners in return for regular cash payments. Most extortion, however, involves not demands for cash but for a variety of other benefits, often aimed at achieving a "monopoly privilege" within a legitimate business such as restaurant supply. Thus, "Instead of taking tribute in cash, a victim signs a contract for the high priced delivery of beer or linen supplies." If organized crime racketeers can pressure the majority of restaurants or bars in an area in this way, "The result looks like monopoly but arose out of extortion. . . criminal firm A destroys competitor B by intimidating customer C, gaining an exclusive right to his (company B's) customers."[61] In some instances, organized crime racketeers achieve criminal monopolies more directly by simply threatening business owners in some area with death, injury, or destruction of their businesses unless they agree to sell their business for a nominal price to the criminal organization seeking monopoly.

Once achieved, criminal monopolies of legitimate business areas can provide a source of substantial revenue. First of all, by enjoying a monopoly position the criminal business can accumulate "unearned" profit through price maximization. In addition, if a criminal business manages to monopolize some market area crucial to the survival of other businesses, it can extract additional profits without directly infiltrating those businesses. The United States Chamber of Commerce's *Deskbook on Organized Crime* notes,

> Organized criminals have an uncanny knack of pinpointing industry lifelines; . . . For example, the lifeline of airfreight truckers—along with many other businesses is reliability of service. Organized racketeers need not secure ownership control of such firms to exploit them. All that is necessary is to hurt service reliability such as through labor trouble or sabotage of equipment.[62]

Once they monopolize flowpoints of goods or services critical to other industries, criminal businesses can demand either higher prices or additional concessions from those industries to expand their revenue and their control of other market areas.

Infiltration of Business and Labor. Not all organized crime involvement in legitimate business or labor is the product of crude forms of racketeering. The most significant source of entry into legitimate businesses for organized crime is through providing loans to businessmen or companies who for one reason or another face difficulty securing them from legitimate financial institutions. The attractiveness of infiltrating legitimate businesses for organized crime is fourfold:

1. Involvement in legitimate businesses provides organized crime members with both social respectability and a means of explaining an affluent life-style without raising potentially embarrassing questions about the source of that affluence.

2. Legitimate enterprises can serve as outlets for investment of capital accumulated through illegal activities and as a means of "laundering" illegally obtained money so that it can be used for other legitimate investments.
3. Legitimate businesses can serve as either fronts for illegal activities or as outlets for illegally acquired goods such as stolen merchandise or securities.
4. Ownership of legitimate businesses enables organized criminals to benefit from the more open channels to political power enjoyed by the legitimate economic community.[63]

The interpenetration of legitimate businesses and illegal capital is a direct outgrowth of the nature of economic organization in advanced capitalist society. The American economic system is divided into a monopoly sector and a competitive sector, as previously discussed. By virtue of their size and net worth, which can be offered as collateral, corporations in the monopoly sector have a greater ability to secure operating or investment capital from legitimate financial institutions than do small businesses operating in the competitive sector. Thus "Far from being imposed, the services of organized crime moneylenders are actively sought, particularly by small businesses with poor credit potential."[64] Organized crime infiltration of business is largely limited to small businesses in the competitive sector of the economy. A study of the business connections of 200 persons with known ties to organized crime in New York state identified a total of 402 infiltrated businesses. Almost all of these were relatively small operations with assets of less than $1,000,000, with the majority being either retail trades (restaurants, clothing stores, service stations, etc.), small manufacturing firms, or local trucking companies.[65] In many cases, business indebtedness to organized crime becomes so great that the business becomes either wholly or partially owned by syndicate members. Once connected to legitimate businesses, organized crime members can utilize those businesses for a variety of ends. These may be aimed either at *exploiting* the business or *enhancing* the business.

Exploitation of businesses connected to organized crime involves using the resources of the business for other than its ostensible purpose. It can occur in a variety of ways. Businesses may be required to provide "cover" for other illegal operations. For instance, one nightclub owner found himself required to hire two syndicate members, one as a club "manager" and the other as a "doorman." He also had to hire on his own two other workers to perform their actual duties, since the two syndicate members merely utilized their positions with the club to conduct business in illegal drugs.[66] In another instance, an "upper echelon person in organized crime" was placed on the payroll of a soft-drink bottling company in New Jersey, ostensibly to check whether the company's products were being favorably displayed in retail grocery outlets. This position provided an ideal cover for racketeering operations against retail grocers.[67] Legitimate businesses can also be utilized to launder illegal money through such tactics as providing fictitious "loans" to organized crime members.[68] These loans then serve as an explanation for the capital used by syndicate members to make other legitimate investments without the Internal Revenue Service's asking embarrassing questions. In some cases the company is required to participate in its own victimization. For instance, a drug company taken over by organized crime was required to hire a convicted narcotics dealer as a "guard" for its warehouse, establishing an ideal precondition for hijacking legal drugs for distribution to the illegal market.[69]

Another important mechanism for exploiting legitimate businesses is through planned bankruptcy. Through a variety of apparently legitimate maneuvers syndicate members can extract all the capital potential from a business it controls and then file, or as is more often the case, be forced into bankruptcy, leaving the company, its investors, and its clients without any legal recourse to recoup their losses. The United States Chamber of Commerce estimated that there are approximately 1,200 such planned bankruptcies annually.[70]

Infiltration of legitimate business is not always detrimental to that business. In many instances legitimate businesses and organized crime enjoy a symbiotic relationship that enhances the profitability of both.

An important part of organized crime activity involves the distribution of stolen merchandise. Some of this derives from hijackings performed by organized crime syndicates themselves, while another portion results from the syndicate's "fencing" stolen goods.[71] These goods are then provided at lower costs to legitimate businesses, who can then sell them at a greater profit margin than legally obtained commodities. Restaurant and nightclub owners, for example, can enjoy greater profits by selling stolen liquor obtained through organized crime syndicates than by selling liquor purchased legally.[72] In another case a portion of 28,000 airline tickets stolen from one travel agency in 1970 showed up in the inventory of other "legitimate" travel agencies.[73] Similarly, in 1971 it was revealed that numerous coin dealers were purchasing for less than their face value silver coins taken in holdups by organized crime members. These could then be melted down into raw silver by the dealers and resold at a substantial profit. The benefit to organized crime was the disposal for a profit of stolen coins that could not easily be placed in circulation without potential risk of detection.[74]

In another case organized crime members utilized small clothing stores and restaurants as a source of revenue from stolen credit cards. The businesses submitted false invoices charged to these cards, and when the banks paid the businesses, the take was split between the business and the providers of the stolen cards.[75]

Labor Corruption. Another important point of contact between organized crime and legitimate business is through the involvement of organized crime in labor unions. The history of labor organization in America has been characterized by a decline in unions demanding radical social change and an increase in unions willing to limit themselves to more "reasonable" demands. Both World War I and World War II brought with them an increase in the power of socialist-oriented labor unions. After each war there was a period of government harassment, arrest, and prosecution of left-leaning labor lead-ers. This repression took the form of the Palmer raids in the 1920s and the period of McCarthyism and the "red scare" after World War II.[76] Part of this process involved the replacement of socialist-oriented union leaders with corrupt officials tied to organized crime. This process has often been supported and in some cases facilitated by industry.[77] Corrupt leaders can be relied upon by business to be more amenable to "sweetheart" contracts and to use the political and economic power of unions for their own ends, rather than for increasing the bargaining power and position of their membership.

Like other forms of business infiltration union power can be utilized either to exploit or enhance legitimate businesses. Exploitation usually occurs through threatening a business with "union trouble" unless it agrees to or-ganized crime demands. In one case, "Stop and Shop" stores in New Jersey were threatened with strikes and work stoppages by the organized crime–dominated Local 464 of the AFL-CIO Amalgamated Meat Cutters Union unless they consented to stock sausages produced by the P. Z. Sausage Com-pany, another organized crime–dominated business.[78] In another case, to get relief from labor troubles that one freight company president described as a "continual nightmare," freight companies operating out of Kennedy Inter-national Airport were required to hire "consultants" who were in fact tied to organized crime. After hiring the "consultants" the labor troubles ceased.[79]

Control over unions is not always utilized to the detriment of businesses. In some instances, corrupt union officials can for a substantial fee provide companies the opportunity to avoid hiring union labor. A New Jersey con-tractor, for example, was able to save $1.3 million on the construction of an apartment complex by paying officials of an organized crime-controlled build-ing trades union $70,000 for the right to operate without union labor.[80] Deals such as this steal from unionized workers the legally established right to collectively bargain for wages and working conditions that union membership is presumably designed to provide. Control over labor unions can also be utilized to obtain other advantages. In 1973, for example, it was revealed that organized crime figures representing the Iowa Beef Processors bribed officials of the already corrupt meatpackers union to avoid labor resistance to the introduction of prepackaged meat into New York City supermarkets, despite the fact that this "innovation" would result in substantial job losses to meat cutters in New York.[81]

Whether utilized to the benefit or detriment of specific businesses, or-ganized crime's involvement in unions always operates to the detriment of workers. The corruption of unions by organized crime deprives workers of leadership that aggressively seeks to protect their interests. More importantly, revelations of organized crime involvement in unions has continually been a powerful ideological weapon to weaken the legitimacy of labor movement in the minds of the American public. Revelations of union corruption are most often used to suggest that unionization itself is undesirable, rather than to show the need for restructuring unions in ways which would make them more representative of worker interests and therefore stronger.

POLITICAL CRIME
Nature and Varieties of Political Crime

Political crime can be broadly defined as *any illegal or socially injurious act committed through the usage or manipulation of political power or designed to facilitate the acquisition or maintenance of political power.* Political crimes are serious offenses. They not only rob citizens of effective political representation, but they also tend to create public disillusionment with government. This disillusionment often leads to a cynical retreat on the part of the average citizen from a concern with political affairs rather than organized efforts to change the political system.

When writing about political crimes many criminologists tend to categorize these offenses according to what *personal* motivations of politicians lead to their commission. For example, Charles McCaghy divides political crimes into those committed to acquire money and those committed to gain or maintain personal political power.[82] Alex Thio suggests a similar categorization, but adds to it crimes that result from the "arrogance of power," that is, from the perception on the part of political office holders that they are above the law.[83] Political crime in America, however, is more complex than the personal malfeasance of corrupt politicians and public office holders. Political crime in America is rooted in the nature of the American *political economy* and involves criminal and socially injurious actions by persons both inside and outside of government committed not only for direct personal gain but also to enhance or preserve political institutions and economic organizations. Table 13.1 presents the various types of political crimes that can be committed to advance the financial or political goals of either individuals or organizations.

Political crimes usually involve a *relationship* between someone who has or is seeking political power and others who hope to acquire some advantage or favor from those in political power. Elements of the private economy, whether large industries, banks and other financial operations, or small businesses, must rely on the various institutions of the political state to facilitate the accumulation of capital. While capitalist economy is characterized by a relatively small class of owners of capital who generally agree upon the *basic* parameters of how society should be organized and who exert the greatest amount of leverage upon the activities of government, there is by no means unanimity among the members of this class regarding *specific* policies and programs.

Influential Americans representing different sectors of the economy may at times find themselves in open conflict over specific governmental actions. For example, agribusiness in conjunction with smaller farmers may favor an extension of food stamp and welfare programs, thereby insuring increased expenditures for their products, while defense industry representatives may strongly support a cutback in social welfare programs so that new weapons purchases by the Federal government can be financed. Owners of capital invested in the construction industry most often favor policies leading to

Table 13.1 Varieties of Political Crime

Beneficiary	By People Holding Political Office or Positions of Delegated Political Power		By People Outside of Government	
	For Economic Gain	For Political Gain	For Economic Gain	For Political Gain
Individuals	accepting bribes or favors; theft of government property or funds; illegal use of campaign funds for personal expenditures; influence peddling	using power of political office to harass or discredit political opponents or critics; seeking or accepting illegal campaign contributions; making deals or doing "favors" in return for campaign contributions; "dirty tricks" political campaigns	bribing law enforcement personnel; offering bribes or favors in return for legislation or regulatory practices favorable to personal businesses	making campaign contribution deals in return for appointed political positions
Private Organizations or Government	lax or nonenforcement of laws regulating businesses or other organizations; legislative favoritism; imperialist policies and actions to potect control over foreign resources, markets, or labor forces	repression of opposition to governmental actions or policy through violations of civil rights; false representation of governmental actions in order to preserve legitimacy; agent provocateurism	offering bribes, favors or illegal campaign contributions in return for directly advantageous legislation, domestic or foreign policy, or avoidance of law enforcement	making campaign contribution deals to have business representatives placed in regulatory or other governmental positions; illegal contributions or other tactics to insure election of candidates who are "in the pocket"

lower mortgage interest rates (such as ceiling on interest rates) as a means of stimulating home building and other construction. At the same time, financial institutions such as banks and mortgage companies are generally more interested in policies that will enable them to maximize interest rates.

Other than stealing government property, most forms of political crimes for personal gain require a relationship between those seeking or holding political office and representatives of capital willing to offer money or other considerations in return for sympathetic treatment by government. Every bribe taken by a politician is offered by someone, just as is every illegal campaign contribution. These types of political crimes arise not simply from personal corruption on the part of politicians. Rather, political corruption is stimulated by competitive pressures within the economy.

Crimes for Personal Financial Gain

The most common political crimes committed by individuals for personal financial gain are (1) accepting or offering bribes, (2) using government funds or services for personal ends, and (3) diverting campaign money to personal use. In addition to these clearly illegal actions, the search for personal financial gain by holders of political offices or positions can also lead to socially injurious actions when such individuals utilize their political power to ingratiate themselves with businesses in the private sector as a means of insuring lucrative positions once they leave public office.

Because law makers and other governmental officials often make decisions that can have substantial economic impact upon both individual members of society and various organizations within it, government represents a fertile ground for bribery. In recent years numerous cases of high office holders accepting bribes for personal gain in return for some action financially beneficial to the person or organization offering the bribe have made national headlines. In 1973, for example, Otto Kerner, former governor of Illinois, was convicted in a bribery scandal involving receipt of stock in an Illinois racetrack.[84] Similarly, former vice-president Spiro T. Agnew was convicted of accepting bribes in return for favoritism in the awarding of state construction contracts while he was governor of Maryland.[85] More recently, in 1980 several U.S. senators and U.S. congressmen were indicted for accepting bribes from FBI agents posing as Arab sheiks seeking various political favors.[86]

In some cases corruption of governmental officials is neither as overt nor as crude as bribery. "Doing favors" for public office holders can also serve the same purpose. Providing free vacations, free services, or giving expensive gifts to politicians or members of their families are common ways of gaining political favor. In these cases the gifts or services are often offered not to secure some specific consideration but rather as an attempt to insure that the office holder will be generally supportive of the interests of the person or organization doing the favor.

In addition to accepting bribes or favors, governmental officials seeking illegitimate sources of personal financial gain can do so by diverting either government money or campaign finances to personal uses. Campaign laws require relatively close accounting for campaign contributions and expenditures. However, campaign money often comes in the form of relatively small and hard-to-trace cash contributions, posing a significant temptation to which some politicians have succumbed. In 1980, for instance, it was reported that Senator Herman Talmadge kept in the pockets of a raincoat approximately $20,000 in cash received from political supporters. This money served as a kind of domestic bank for everyday expenses.[87]

Another source of personal gain occurs in the form of sizable unreported campaign contributions. These most often come from businesses and industries seeking to increase the likelihood that candidates who support their interests will get elected, and most of this money is destined to be used for political rather than personal financial purpose. However, the existence of large cash "slush funds" of essentially "nonexistent" and therefore untraceable campaign money allows some campaign money to be diverted toward personal expenditures. It was estimated, for example, that officials of the Nixon reelection committee had access to several million dollars in *cash* from illegal campaign contributions, some of which was used to finance personal expenditures.[88]

Crimes for Personal Political Benefit

Getting elected is a highly competitive and costly endeavor in America. Individuals seeking election or reelection to public office sometimes succumb to the pressures to utilize illegal or socially harmful methods to increase their advantage in political contests. The major forms of crimes committed for personal political benefit are those which involve (1) illegal or questionable forms of campaign financing, (2) utilization of political power by office holders against opposition parties or candidates, and (3) illegal or questionable "dirty tricks" campaign practices.

The late U.S. Senator Hubert Humphrey called campaign financing the "cesspool of American politics."[89] While campaign fundraising has always involved close and often questionable relationships between wealthy individuals, businesses, and politicians, the advent of the widespread use of television in political campaigning has led to a dramatic escalation of the costs of running political campaigns over the last twenty-five years.[90] This rise in campaign costs has in turn increased the pressure on office seekers to resort to illegal methods of obtaining campaign finances. The most common forms of violation are acquiring illegal and unrecorded campaign contributions, making "deals" for campaign contributions, and using the power of political office to pressure reluctant contributors. The Watergate scandal provided significant examples of each of these. By 1976 150 companies had been convicted of making illegal campaign contributions to Nixon's reelection campaign. These included corporate giants such as ITT, Exxon, Mobil, Lockheed, and Philips Petroleum, as well as smaller enterprises. For the most part these contributions appear to have been made to secure the *general* advantage of insuring that the presidency would be retained by someone whose secretary of state could say, "The Nixon Administration is a business administration. Its mission is to protect American business."[91] In one case, however, the contribution was connected to specific expectations on the part of the contributor. ITT's contributions appear to have been aimed at securing the continued support of the presidency and presidentially controlled agencies such as the FBI and CIA in ITT's attempt to destabilize the democratically elected Marxist government of Salvadore Allende in Chile.[92] In addition, a number of individual contributors were coaxed into making substantial donations to Nixon's campaign in return for the promise of governmental positions, particularly ambassadorships, which would be awarded after the election.[93]

A third means of illegally securing campaign financing used by Nixon's Committee to Reelect the President (CREEP) involved utilizing the power of the presidency to pressure backers into making larger than average contributions. The Nixon administration threatened large milk producers with a decrease in milk-support prices unless they contributed at least $700,000 to the reelection campaign. The pressure apparently worked since the milk producers eventually contributed a total of $739,000 to Nixon's campaign, and the proposed change in milk-support prices was shelved.[94]

It would be a mistake to assume that the kind of corrupt campaign financing practices revealed by Watergate and related investigations were unique to the Nixon campaign. Irregularities in campaign fund raising are a widespread and relatively accepted practice among politicians.[95] Political analysts often argue that corrupt campaign financing practices can be corrected by legislation that would modify but in no way fundamentally alter the American political process. For example, A. James Reichly, tells us in *Fortune* that while Watergate revealed some "grave problems" with the electoral system, we should not feel "disillusion or disenchantment with the system itself." Furthermore,

> The system provides instruments through which many of the flaws that helped produce Watergate can be corrected or brought under control. Democracy has many shortcomings. But at least it always has at hand the means for bringing about its own reform.[96]

Despite this optimism, there has been little interference with the basic links between political power and individual and corporate wealth. If anything, the rise of Political Actions Committees (PACS) has strengthened the link between powerful interests and those seeking elective office.

However, public revelation of the close relationship between office seekers and moneyed interests, as happened with Watergate, threatens the legitimacy of the electoral process, which could in turn lead to demands for fundamental reform. As the Committee for Economic Development observed,

> There is evidence of growing alienation on the part of the American public from their political and governmental institutions. It is imperative that any such tendency be checked and reversed. Adoption of the measures here proposed would . . . strengthen *faith* in our representative democracy.[97] (emphasis added)

A primary function of legislation aimed at reforming campaign financing after the Watergate scandal was to *restore legitimacy* to the electoral process, not to make any meaningful changes in the basic structural arrangements that generated the initial problem. Electoral politics will continue to bring together individuals with the money to finance election campaigns and individuals seeking election. As Greenberg notes, "The wealthy will probably find ways and means to provide financial support to those candidates considered friendly to their interests" regardless of campaign finance laws.[98]

Crimes on Behalf of the Political Economy

The American political economy is a capitalist one. This means the political state must operate in such a way as to protect the basic institution of capitalism, as well as to facilitate the process of capital accumulation by various sectors of the capitalist class. It also means that at the same time, the political ideology of capitalism supports the maintenance of liberal democracy in America with its emphasis upon the values of personal freedom, individual rights, and equality under the law. The task of preserving the economic and political dominance of a relatively small segment of the population through a governmental system that justifies itself by promising to protect individual rights and political equality is one of the most persistent contradictions of liberal democracy in capitalist societies. According to the ideology of the democratic state, the state serves as an impartial forum for the resolution of political disputes, not the special protector of the interests of any particular segment of society, and any social group should be free to seek power in either the economic or political sphere.

If government were to serve strictly as an impartial forum for dispute resolution, however, it would mean that the power of the state could not be used to interfere with the development or growth of organizations or ideologies contrary to the designs of capitalism. As an institution designed to protect the capitalist social order and facilitate the accumulation of capital by a relatively small segment of the society, government cannot act in this "hands-off" fashion, even though the ideology from which it draws its legitimacy says that this is what he must do. This contradiction between facilitating the interests of capital and preserving its own legitimacy places American government in a difficult position. To retard or suppress forms of organization threatening to capitalism, the state must frequently *violate its own laws* concerning civil and political liberties, as well as act in a variety of ways contrary to the spirit of democracy. Preservation of legitimacy, however, requires that these violations either be hidden or justified on the basis of averting some greater danger.

Political Repression and "Communism"

If communism and socialism did not exist, capitalist states would have to invent them or some other similar threat. Since the earliest days of the American labor movement, terms such as "communist" and "socialist" have been used to discredit legitimate opposition to the economic and political injustices arising from a capitalist mode of production.[99] Since that time, a basic part of American political ideology has been a constant reiteration of the dangers of communism and socialism interspersed with examples of the problems or failings of socialist countries. This ideology has been used to justify a variety of illegal repressive tactics by authorized agents of the state against a wide variety of outspoken critics of the government and the economy.

After World War II, in particular, the threat of the "red menace" was used to justify a sweeping attack against domestic "subversives" that was in fact a thinly veiled attempt to weaken the power of organized labor in the United States.[100] The threat of "communism" has served as the basic justification for a broad range of illegal, repressive activities on the part of the FBI and the CIA against dissident Americans. For example, from 1956 to at least 1976, the FBI operated a counterintelligence program (COINTELPRO) that involved surveillance, bugging, wiretapping, burglary, harassment, and public attacks directed at various individuals and groups critical of American policies. The victims of COINTELPRO included black leaders such as Dr. Martin Luther King, Medgar Evers, and Malcolm X; journalists such as David Brinkley, Jimmy Breslin, and Joseph Alsop; and a variety of activist groups including antiwar organizations, civil rights groups, and the women's liberation movement. In testimony before a 1976 Senate committee investigating COINTELPRO activities, James B. Adams, Deputy Associate Director of the FBI, explained that individuals or groups became targets of COINTELPRO because of the *possibility* that they could be infiltrated by Communists. Senator Hart of Michigan summarized the FBI's approach by saying,

> Your theory continues to be that any socially active group of citizens who organize, whether women's libbers or fight the bomb or anything else might be a target for infiltration by the Communist Party and, therefore, you can move in your agents.[101]

Thus, as Senator Hart indicated, the "threat" of communism served to justify twenty years of illegal political repression even though in most cases the FBI had no reason to believe, as James Adams testified, that the groups infiltrated had any *actual* connection with Communists, either at home or abroad.

A comment about the motivations of government agents engaged in repressive activities is in order here. When the FBI or some other government agency infiltrates or attempts to disrupt left-oriented or civil rights groups, its leaders and agents are not necessarily concerned with protecting the interests of the capitalist class. They are primarily concerned with trying to protect American "democracy" from domestic insurrection or external dangers posed by possible communist or socialist influence. Despite their personal view of the situation, however, their repressive actions against individuals or groups seeking to alter the economic and political status quo serves the interests of those who most benefit from the status quo social order.

Varieties of Political Repression

To protect the economic and political arrangements of the status quo social order, the state has engaged in a number of illegal and quasi-legal repressive tactics aimed at retarding social activism. These include illegal surveillance in the form of mail intercept programs, infiltration, and harassment of political groups and their leaders; repression through "legal" mechanisms such as political trials; illegal surveillance; and provocation.

Repression Through Infiltration and Harassment. The COINTELPRO revelations, one of the offshoots of the widespread scrutiny of government activities arising from the Watergate affair, reveals a broad pattern of infiltration and harassment of political groups and their leaders by the FBI. In addition to the Community Party of the United States of America and the Ku Klux Klan, two traditional targets of FBI activity, COINTELPRO focused on a number

---

HOW TO QUIET AN ACTIVIST

The Request

TO: Director, FBI   DATE: 1/30/70
FROM: SAC, St. Louis
SUBJECT: COUNTERINTELLIGENCE PROGRAM
               NEW LEFT
               RACIAL INTELLIGENCE

Enclosed for the Bureau are two Xerox copies of a letter prepared by the St. Louis Division.

Background

Mrs. X[1] is a local New Left figure who is an officer in ACTION, a local Black activist group whose members have engaged in numerous acts of civil disruption and civil disobedience,[2] and a leader in the local branch of the Women's International League for Peace and Freedom, which group is active in draft resistance, anti-war rallies, and New Left activity. Her husband remains aloof from her racial and New Left activities, and is suspicious of her relationship with Negro males in ACTION.

Recently [an informant] advised that Mrs. X complained about her husband's suspicions and was afraid he might severely restrict her activities. On 1/27/70 [an informant] reported that [the husband] had been discreetly inquiring as to whether his wife might be being unfaithful to him by sleeping with Negro males in ACTION.

Recommendation

St. Louis proposes to anonymously send a copy of the enclosed letter in commercial envelope, which would confirm [the husband's] suspicions about his wife. The resulting marital tempest could well result in ACTION losing their

[1] Names were deleted in the documents submitted as evidence to the investigating committee.
[2] The FBI at this time defined a wide variety of *legal* protest activities "civil disruption and disobedience."

of other activist groups. Groups opposing the war in Vietnam, which the FBI chose to label as New Left, and civil rights groups, which the FBI gave the inflammatory name of Black Nationalists, were particular targets of infiltration and harassment. No better description of how the FBI sought to disrupt political groups and damage their leaders can be found than the FBI's own internal communications. "How to Quiet an Activist" details the plans to create marital problems for one white female civil rights and antiwar activist. This particular tactic of creating marital or other personal troubles was used against both significant leaders such as Dr. Martin Luther King and other less prominent individuals who the FBI believed to be "dangerous." As Senator Hart indicated,

> Included in these COINTELPRO activities were anonymous letters, drafted by Bureau offices in the field, sent to headquarters in Washington, approved and then put in the mail, intended to break up marriages, not of Dr. King but of

---

Corresponding Secretary, and the Women's International League for Peace and Freedom losing a valuable leader, thus striking a major blow against both organizations.

Bureau authority is requested to initiate this activity.

* * * * * * * * * *

The Letter

Dear Mr. (blank)
Look man I guess your old lady doesn't get enough at home or she wouldn't be shucking and jiving with our Black Men in ACTION, you dig? Like all she wants to integrate is the bed room, and us Black Sisters ain't gonna take no second best from our men. So lay it on her, man, or get her the hell out of Newstead.

A Soul Sister

* * * * * * * * * *

The Approval

TO:	SAC St. Louis	DATE: 2/17/70
FROM:	Director, FBI	
SUBJECT:	COUNTERINTELLIGENCE PROGRAM	
	NEW LEFT	
	RACIAL INTELLIGENCE	

Provided such action will in no way jeopardize (blank), you are authorized to prepare and anonymously mail the letter as suggested.
In making this mailing, take all steps necessary to protect the Bureau as its source.

* * * * * * * * * *

Source: *Hearings before the Select Committee to Study Governmental Operations with Respect to Intelligence Activities*, vol. 6, Federal Bureau of Investigation (Washington, D.C.: Government Printing Office, 1976), 399–401.

Mary and John Jones because one or the other was thought to be a dissenter, might have dressed strangely or showed up at meetings in company of others who dressed strangely.[102]

The document "The FBI and Black Nationalist Groups," sets forth the basic strategies for disrupting such groups, while "Disrupting the New Left " details strategies used against antiwar activists. It should be noted that while the FBI memoranda emphasizes the *violent and dangerous* nature of the groups being targeted, most of the victims of COINTELPRO, with the exception of the Ku Klux Klan, were *committed to nonviolent strategies for social change* such as peaceful protest and other legitimate varieties of political activity.

Nonviolent civil rights and antiwar groups were treated as threats to the society, but not because they posed a real threat of revolutionary activity. They were attacked by the FBI because they sought to *directly* influence the government by exercising their *constitutional rights* of free speech and public protest. Such action circumvents the normal electoral process, which is dominated by wealthy interests in the society and raises the possibility of democratic action contrary to those interests.

THE FBI AND BLACK NATIONALIST GROUPS

SUBJECT: COUNTERINTELLIGENCE PROGRAM
             BLACK NATIONALIST-HATE GROUPS
             RACIAL INTELLIGENCE

Purpose:

To expand the Counterintelligence Program designed to neutralize militant black nationalist groups from 23 of 41 field divisions so as to cover the great majority of black nationalist activity in this country.

Background:

By letter dated August 25, 1967, 23 field offices were advised of a new Counterintelligence Program designed to neutralize militant black nationalists and prevent violence on their part. Goals of this program are to prevent the coalition of militant black nationalist groups, prevent the rise of a leader who might unify and electrify these violence-prone elements, prevent these militants from gaining respectability and prevent the growth of these groups among America's youth.

Goals:

For maximum effectiveness of the Counterintelligence Program, and to prevent wasted effort, long-range goals are being set.
1. Prevent the *coalition* of militant black nationalist groups. In unity there is strength; a truism that is no less valid for all its triteness. An effective coalition of black nationalist groups might be the first step toward a real "Mau Mau" in America, the beginning of a true black revolution.

In addition to infiltration of activist groups, the FBI at times resorted to outright burglary to gain useful information that could further their plans of harassment. The document, "Justifying Burglary," outlines the bureau's thinking on "black bag" jobs and indicates its commitment to the continued usage of this "invaluable technique" for information gathering.

"Legal" Repression. In addition to covert, illegal repressive activities such as those of COINTELPRO, the state has frequently utilized ostensibly "legal" mechanisms to suppress or retard the development of organizations promoting policies or ideologies threatening to the established economic and political order. This form of repression can take either an active or a passive form.

Passive forms of legal repression involve selective tolerance of illegal repressive activities by individuals or organizations outside of government. For example, in spite of its open commitment to the violent subjugation of blacks, the Ku Klux Klan has enjoyed a remarkable degree of tolerance by law enforcement over the years at all levels of government. During the reconstruction era, the Klan was permitted to burn, rape, and murder with

---

2. Prevent the *rise of a "messiah"* who could unify and electrify the militant black nationalist movement. . . . might have been such a "messiah"; he is the martyr of the movement today. and all aspire to this position. . . . is less of a threat because of his age. could be a very real contender for this position should he abandon his supposed "obedience" to "white, liberal doctrines" (nonviolence) and embrace black nationalism. . . . has the necessary charisma to be a real threat in this way.

3. Prevent *violence* on the part of black nationalist groups. This is of primary importance, and is, of course, a goal of our investigative activity; it should also be a goal of the Counterintelligence Program. Through counterintelligence it should be possible to pinpoint potential troublemakers and neutralize them before they exercise their potential for violence.

4. Prevent militant black nationalist groups and leaders from gaining *respectability*, by discrediting them to three separate segments of the community. The goal of discrediting black nationalists must be handled tactically in three ways. You must discredit these groups and individuals to, first, the responsible Negro community. Second they must be discredited to the white community, both the responsible community and to "liberals" who have vestiges of sympathy for militant black nationalists simply because they are Negroes. Third, these groups must be discredited in the eyes of Negro radicals, the followers of the movement. This last area requires entirely different tactics from the first two. Publicity about violent tendencies and radical statements merely enhances black nationalists to the last group; it adds "respectability" in a different way.

5. A final goal should be to prevent the long-range *growth* of militant black nationalist organizations, especially among youth. Specific tactics to prevent these groups from converting young people must be developed.

Source: Federal Bureau of Investigation Interagency memo, entered as evidence in *Hearings Before the Select Committee to Study Governmental Operations with Respect to Intelligence Activities*, vol. 6, Federal Bureau of Investigation (Washington, D.C.: Government Printing Office, 1976), 389–390.

almost no interference from the official agencies of law.[103] During the 1950s and early 1960s the FBI took a similar half-hearted interest in investigating Klan attacks and killings of civil rights workers. In many cases investigations were conducted cursorily, and in some instances, significant information pointing to criminal involvement by the Klan was not recorded.[104] The violent suppression of worker organizations received similar official tolerance during the early years of the labor movement in the United States. As one author notes, "Governmental officials tolerated . . . private police, private armies and private arsenals with attendant denials of basic political freedoms to millions of workers. . . ."[105] The state has not limited its support for the undemocratic

---

DISRUPTING THE NEW LEFT

SUBJECT: COUNTERINTELLIGENCE PROGRAM
        INTERNAL SECURITY
        DISRUPTION OF THE NEW LEFT

Our Nation is undergoing an era of disruption and violence caused to a large extent by various individuals generally connected with the New Left. Some of these activists urge revolution in America and call for the defeat of the United States in Vietnam. They continually and falsely allege police brutality and do not hesitate to utilize unlawful acts to further their so-called causes. The New Left has on many occasions viciously and scurrilously attacked the Director and the Bureau in an attempt to hamper our investigation of it and to drive us off the college campuses. With this in mind, it is our recommendation that a new Counterintelligence Program be designed to neutralize the New Left and the Key Activists. The Key Activists are those individuals who are the moving forces behind the New Left and on whom we have intensified our investigations.

The purpose of this program is to expose, disrupt and otherwise neutralize the activities of this group and persons connected with it. It is hoped that with this new program their violent and illegal activities may be reduced if not curtailed.

1. Preparation of a leaflet designed to counteract the impression that Students for a Democratic Society (SDS) and other minority groups speak for the majority of students at universities. The leaflet should contain photographs of New Left leadership at the respective university. Naturally, the most obnoxious pictures should be used.
2. The instigating of or the taking advantage of personal conflicts or animosities existing between New Left leaders.
3. The creating of impressions that certain New Left leaders are informants for the Bureau or other law enforcement agencies.
4. The use of articles from student newspapers and/or the "underground press" to show the depravity of New Left leaders and members. In this connection, articles showing advocation of the use of narcotics and free sex are ideal to send to university officials, wealthy donors, members of the legislature and parents of students who are active in New Left matters.
5. Since the use of marijuana and other narcotics is widespread among members of the New Left, you should be alert to opportunities to have them arrested by local authorities on drug charges. Any information concerning the fact

suppression of nonwhites and the working class to simple inaction, however. Both labor and the civil rights movement have been frequent targets of state's judicial and law-enforcement apparatus.

From the earliest days of the labor movement in America, the judicial and police powers of the state have been used to suppress radical labor groups and retard the growth of a strong labor movement generally. One common form of this type of repression has been attempts to break unions by eliminating key leaders through criminal prosecution on false or exaggerated charges. In 1877, in Pennsylvania, for example, ten miners active in establishing a miners' labor union were convicted and executed in connection with

that individuals have marijuana or are engaging in a narcotics party should be immediately furnished to local authorities and they should be encouraged to take action.

6. The drawing up of anonymous letters regarding individuals active for the New Left. These letters should set out their activities and should be sent to their parents, neighbors and the parents' employers. This could have the effect of forcing the parents to take action.

7. Anonymous letters or leaflets describing faculty members and graduate assistants in the various institutions of learning who are active in New Left matters. The activities and associations of the individual should be set out. Anonymous mailings should be made to university officials, members of the state legislature, Board of Regents, and to the press. Such letters should be signed "A Concerned Alumni" or "A Concerned Taxpayer."

8. Whenever New Left groups engage in disruptive activities on college campuses, cooperative press contacts should be encouraged to emphasize that the disruptive elements constitute a minority of the students and do not represent the conviction of the majority. The press should demand an immediate student referendum on the issue in question. Inasmuch as the overwhelming majority of students is not active in New Left matters, it is felt that this technique, used in carefully selected cases, could put an end to lengthy demonstrations and could cause embarrassment to New Left elements.

9. There is a definite hostility among SDS and other New Left groups toward the Socialist Workers Party (SWP), the Young Socialist Alliance (YSA), and the Progressive Labor Party (PLP). This hostility should be exploited wherever possible.

10. The field was previously advised that New Left groups are attempting to open coffeehouses near military bases in order to influence members of the armed forces. Wherever these coffeehouses are, friendly news media should be alerted to them and their purpose. In addition, various drugs, such as marijuana, will probably be utilized by individuals running the coffeehouses or frequenting them. Local law enforcement authorities should be promptly advised whenever you receive an indication that this is being done.

11. Consider the use of cartoons, photographs, and anonymous letters which will have the effect of ridiculing the New Left. Ridicule is one of the most potent weapons which we can use against it.

12. Be alert for opportunities to confuse and disrupt New Left activities by misinformation. For example, when events are planned, notification that the event has been cancelled or postponed could be sent to various individuals.

You are reminded that no counterintelligence action is to be taken without Bureau approval. Insure that this Program is assigned to an Agent with an excellent knowledge of both New Left groups and individuals. It must be approached with imagination and enthusiasm if it is to be successful.

murders attributed to an anarchist labor organization called the "Molly McGuires." There is some question whether the Molly McGuires ever actually existed. What is not in question is that the prosecution was based largely on the testimony of a convicted criminal in the employ of the owner of the mines in which the ten condemned labor activists had been organizing and that there was close collaboration between the prosecutor and the mine

---

JUSTIFYING BURGLARY

SUBJECT: "BLACK BAG" JOBS

The following is set forth in regard to your request concerning what authority we have for "black bag" jobs and for the background of our policy and procedures in such matters.

We do not obtain authorization for "black bag" jobs from outside the Bureau. Such a technique involves trespass and is clearly illegal; therefore, it would be impossible to obtain any legal sanction for it. Despite this, "black bag" jobs have been used because they represent an invaluable technique in combating subversive activities of a clandestine nature aimed directly at undermining and destroying our nation.

The present procedure followed in the use of this technique calls for the Special Agent in Charge of a field office to make his request for the use of the technique to the appropriate Assistant Director. The Special Agent in Charge must completely justify the need for the use of the technique and at the same time assure that it can be safely used without any danger or embarrassment to the Bureau. The facts are incorporated in a memorandum which, in accordance with the Director's instructions, is sent to Mr. Tolson or to the Director for approval. Subsequently this memorandum is filed in the Assistant Director's office under a "Do Not File" procedure.

In the field the Special Agent in Charge prepares an informal memorandum showing that he obtained Bureau authority and this memorandum is filed in his safe until the next inspection by Bureau Inspectors, at which time it is destroyed.

We have used this technique on a highly selective basis, but with wide-range effectiveness, in our operations. We have several cases in the espionage field.

Also through the use of this technique we have on numerous occasions been able to obtain material held highly secret and closely guarded by subversive groups and organizations which consisted of membership lists and mailing lists of those organizations.

This applies even to our investigation of the _____. You may recall that recently through a "black bag" job we obtained the records in the possession of there high-ranking officials of a organization in _____. These records gave us the complete membership and financial information concerning the operation which we have been using most effectively to disrupt the organization and, in fact, to bring about its near disintegration.

Source: Intelligence Activities, *Hearings before the Select Committee to Study Governmental Operations with Respect to Intelligence Activities*, vol. 6, November–December 1975 (Washington, D.C.: Government Printing Office, 1976) 357–358.

owner.[106] In a similar case, four leaders of the Knights of Labor were convicted and executed in 1887 in connection with several deaths resulting from a bomb explosion at a labor rally in Haymarket Square in Chicago. The Knights of Labor at that time were locked in a bitter strike against the McCormack Corporation, a major producer of farm machinery. These men were convicted despite the lack of any evidence that they were personally involved in the bombing. Later, police information revealed that the bomb had been thrown by a hired agent provocateur as a means of creating a situation that would justify prosecution of the leaders of the strike.[107] In 1907 William Haywood, an organizer and labor leader who played an important role in organizing Western miners in Colorado and Idaho, was prosecuted on similarly fraudulent bombing charges. Haywood, however, was acquitted.[108] In 1919 Eugene Debs, head of the International Workers of the World and the most powerful labor leader of the time, was sentenced to ten years in prison for speaking out against the U.S. government's involvement in World War I. While behind bars, Debs was nominated to run for president on the Socialist ticket and received one million votes in the 1920 election.[109]

Such prosecutions of progressive labor leaders are not relegated to the past. In 1981 three activist union leaders were charged with conspiracy to bomb a generating plant at the National Steel and Shipbuilding Company (NASSCO). All three were union officials with strong socialist orientations, and their activism apparently made them a target for infiltration and provocation. The testimony against them was largely provided by an FBI informer who actually initiated the bomb plot.[110]

Judicial repression has also been used extensively against civil rights activists as a means of discrediting and disrupting their movements. Dr. Martin Luther King, for example, was jailed repeatedly on frequently fraudulent or minor charges such as violating parade permit restrictions. In 1976 the Reverend Ben Chavis and nine others who had been active in the struggle for racial equality in North Carolina were imprisoned for the fire-bombing of a store in Wilmington, North Carolina, during a period of race riots in that city. The Wilmington 10 were convicted by an all-white jury on the scantest of evidence and in spite of the fact that all of their activities had been directed toward *ending* the racial conflict in Wilmington.[111] Only after many years of struggle by supporters, including Amnesty International, were they freed from prison. In a similar case three Charlotte civil rights workers, one a poet and one with a doctoral degree in chemistry, were convicted and sentenced to prison in connection with a stable fire that had occurred some three years earlier. Their conviction was based on the frequently contradictory testimony of two convicted armed robbers who were facing possible return to prison for parole violations and who had been promised substantial sums of money and freedom from parole revocation by the prosecution in return for their testimony. In a blatant attempt to put an end to their civil rights work, the three convicted men were given the longest sentences ever rendered in a case of illegal burning in the state, despite the fact that no lives were lost in the fire.[112]

Illegal Surveillance. In recent years it has been revealed that both the FBI and the CIA have engaged in extensive programs of intercepting and reading the mail of private citizens. In just one of four mail projects, the CIA intercepted over 215,000 pieces of mail destined for private citizens.[113] The FBI is known to have done similarly with 130,000 letters.[114] While the ostensible purpose of such activity is to prevent crimes or "revolutionary" violence, the real reason was a relatively naked attempt to compile and update lists of citizens involved in legitimate and legal opposition to government policies.

While the FBI is allowed by law to engage in certain kinds of domestic spying, the conduct of such activity is supposed to be (1) based upon probable cause to believe that the information to be gathered is related to specific crimes that have been or are about to be committed and (2) authorized by judicial warrant. Neither of these limitations was followed in the FBI's Counter Intelligence Program (COINTELPRO). Instead, the FBI read the mail, not of criminals or revolutionaries, but civil rights leaders, antiwar activists, labor leaders, and other critics of the government.[115] The purpose of this invasion of privacy and violation of the laws against unwarranted search was not to prevent crime but to uncover information that could be used to disrupt or discredit legitimate opposition political groups or individuals.

Provocation. Provocation refers to actions undertaken by government agents to stimulate illegal activities by dissident groups. In many cases the aims of provocation are to provide a basis for later "legal" repression through prosecution of individuals for acts initiated by government agents. In other instances the primary aim of provocation is to entice groups into actions that can be used to generate public opposition to their aims.

As an enticement to commit illegal actions, provocation is a form of entrapment. Provocation differs from more common forms of entrapment, such as offers by vice-squad investigators to sell illicit drugs or to buy sexual services, in that it generally involves actual participation in illegal activities by the agent provocateur. In many instances of provocation, the *only illegal action* taken is done by the agent, although it is later blamed on the group or its leaders.

During the 1960s and early 1970s, student activism against the war in Vietnam and black activist opposition to economic and political discrimination were widespread. Equally widespread were actions by government agents and informants aimed at provoking illegal action by antiwar and civil rights activists. In a number of cases the actual illegal act was committed by a government agent to provide an ostensible legitimate reason for immediate forceful police intervention. In others the aim was to get the group to behave in a way that would discredit it in the eyes of the public or would justify later prosecution of group members. The box, "Varieties of Agent Provocation," lists a variety of actions undertaken by agent provocateurs working for Federal or state law-enforcement agencies. As can be seen by this list, in many cases government agents were active in attempting to create situations that would pose serious threats of violent harm to American citizens. This is a curious

Varieties of Agent Provocation

1. One of the people most involved in encouraging the violence that accompanied the Chicago Democratic Party Convention was actually an undercover police officer.
2. A young man who provided a bomb to blow up a Seattle U.S. Post Office was an FBI and city police informer.
3. An FBI informer burned buildings at the University of Alabama.
4. Police agents tried to incite violence at Yale University during the demonstrations of May 1971.
5. The Black Panther Party "Minister of Defense" in Los Angeles, who helped bring about a shootout with the police, was actually a police informer.
6. An informer, who was on the FBI payroll, tried to set up a class to teach students at Hobart University how to make and use bombs.
7. A Chicago police informer provided the false tip that led to the killing of two Panther leaders there.
8. A police informer led an illegal SDS sit-in at an Illinois college and later—claiming he was a Weatherman—helped to hurl the president of the college off the stage.
9. Two men who had led the shutting of a massive gate at Ohio State University and set off a violent confrontation with the police, were officers of the state highway patrol.
10. The false report claiming guns were stored in the Black Muslim Temple in Los Angeles came from a paid police informer, who claims he was instructed to make the report so that the police who employed him would have an excuse to raid the temple.

Source: Paul Jacobs, "Informers: The Enemy Within," *Ramparts,* 12 (August–September 1973), 53–54.

activity for that segment of the state whose ostensible purpose is to "protect" citizens from harm.

In more recent years the specter of government provocation of illegal acts has reappeared, but in slightly different and possibly more sinister form. In November 1979, five labor activists were shot to death and nine more injured in an attack by Ku Klux Klansmen and Nazis in Greensboro, North Carolina. Two of those killed were, respectively, the president and the president-elect of the Amalgamated Textile and Clothing Workers Union local at a Cone Mills plant near Greensboro. They were also members of the Communist Workers Party. While the killings were described as a "shootout" between "extremists" by most newspapers, video tapes of the event made by several local TV stations on the scene show a planned maneuver carried out with militarylike precision by the Klansman and Nazis.

While it is not unimaginable that a coalition of white racists might attack a biracial anti-Klan rally, the role of government agents in this attack is more ominous. One agent on the payroll of the Federal Bureau of Alcohol, Tobacco and Firearms (BATF) had spent the two months prior to the shootings traveling through North Carolina encouraging Klansmen to join the caravan to Greensboro and soliciting money to support the caravan. In an attempt to avoid a direct and possibly violent confrontation, the anti-Klan marchers sought to keep the site of the march secret. However, they did indicate where the parade would form when filing a parade permit with the Greensboro police. A copy of the parade permit was given to an informant working for the Greensboro police, and it was this informant who rode in the lead vehicle that directed the caravan to the site of the eventual killings. Both agents also played key roles in the planning and organization for the Greensboro caravan.[116]

CRIMES OF CAPITAL: CONCLUSION

Crimes of capital are illegal or socially injurious actions committed either in direct connection with the process of legitimate or illegitimate capital accumulation or through the use or misuse of the power inherent in institutions, particularly governmental institutions, designed to facilitate the accumulation of capital. As a generic category of offenses, crimes of capital encompass corporate crimes, white-collar and other occupational offenses, organized crime, and political crimes.

Taken together, the crimes of capital constitute the single greatest source of untimely death, injury, illness, and economic loss faced by American citizens. In addition, many crimes of capital originating with the process of capital accumulation in the United States pose serious threats to the health and well-being of people in other countries. Despite their gravity, crimes of capital receive relatively little attention from law enforcement in contrast to the substantial social control efforts directed toward the common crimes of the working class. The reason most often given for this irony is that "real crimes" such as murder, rape, robbery, and burglary pose more immediate threats to the public and therefore lead to far greater demands for governmental actions.

There is some validity to this explanation. It is true, for example, that the threat of having one's home burglarized is a more immediate and fear-provoking idea than the realization that one may pay higher prices for goods as the result of some corporate offense such as price fixing. There are, however, a number of equally, if not more important, reasons why attempts to control crimes of capital are far less than commensurate with the amount of harm these crimes cause.

First, private accumulation of capital is a basic organizing principle of capitalist society. Insofar as basic profit-making activities are construed as private activities, fairly narrow limits are placed upon the possibilities for public control of the potential for social harm arising from these activities. From a legal standpoint, to the extent that the law has granted the legal right to private ownership of capital, government is limited in the extent to which it can mandate how that capital will be utilized. Thus, for example, it is beyond the power of capitalist law to prohibit actions such as closing a factory or instituting labor-replacing technology, which while privately profitable lead to the displacement of workers. While decades of working class struggle have led to some tempering of the power of private capital through such things as legislation granting collective bargaining rights, and laws governing worker safety, and various other regulatory procedures, the scope of such rules is at all times narrowed by the legal right to private ownership of capital.

From an economic standpoint, legal control of harms arising from the process of the accumulation of capital can only go so far before they create financial difficulties within the economy *as presently constructed.* Regulation aimed at minimizing crimes of capital, particularly in the corporate sector, tend to increase the costs of production. After a certain point these increased costs tend to stifle private investment insofar as they lead to a reduction in profit margins—and profit is the sole basis for stimulating private investment in capitalist societies. Thus the very nature of the present system mandates that economic stability can only be enjoyed at a high cost in crimes of capital.

Second, as it has historically evolved a primary role of the state in capitalist society is to facilitate the private accumulation of capital. This evolution has been shaped by the fact that the capitalist class or those associated with its interests have perennially enjoyed a greater ability to shape the state and its attendant legal institutions than have the working class or representatives of its interests. Thus, in capitalist society the state is not only structurally prohibited from extensive control of crimes of capital, it is also limited by the form that the state takes in capitalist society.

Third, because the economic substructure and the form of the state in capitalist society have led to little actual social control over the crimes of capital, the social definition of crime in America is heavily tilted toward common crimes and away from the crimes of capital. This has particular bearing upon the nature and extent of public demands for law enforcement. The minimal enforcement and relatively light penalties associated with crimes of capital tend to deemphasize the danger they pose. Social psychologists have long known that people tend to learn the meaning of actions in large part from observing how those actions are regarded by others. To the extent that we do not witness corporate and political criminals being treated as "real" criminals, we tend not to think of them as such, and by extension we tend not to think of their crimes as "real" crimes. This then reinforces public responses. Because individuals learn that crimes of capital are "not so serious," they tend not to demand greater protection from them. This in turn keeps enforcement efforts minimal, further establishing the "minor" nature of these crimes.

Fourth, information about the nature and seriousness of crimes of capital is far less widely disseminated than information about working class crime. Because it is oriented toward controlling crimes of the working class, not crimes of capital, the institutions of the state compile and disseminate far more data concerning the former as opposed to the latter. This tends to generate the impression that working class crimes represent the only real source of danger to the health and well-being of Americans.

Fifth, crimes of capital are complex. With the exception of organized crime and political crimes for personal gain, the bulk of the crimes of capital result not from the corrupt intentions of individuals but from the structural dictates of the process of capital accumulation or the contradictary form of the state. In a society that sees individuals as voluntary actors, harmful actions resulting from systemic arrangements rather than individual culpability are not easily understood. The armed robber is far more comprehensible to us as an anti-social actor than is the corporate executive who, simply as part of his job, finds himself engaged in activities to subvert a union or to "stabilize" prices with competitors through price fixing. Additionally, the connection between a given act and the eventual harm is often less direct and less clear in the case of crimes of capital. For example, the relationship between polluting a river and the eventual illness of some individuals is far more difficult to unravel than that between the actions of a mugger and the harm caused to a victim.

All of these factors contribute to the greater attention paid to common crime in America as compared with the crimes of capital. Lesser public concern with crimes of capital, however, in no way lessens the gravity of these offenses. They remain the most deadly, dangerous, and costly crimes in America.

NOTES

1. Jane G. Schubert and Robert E. Krug, *Consumer Fraud: An Empirical Perspective* (Washington: D.C.: Government Printing Office, 1979), xii.
2. Robert P. Snow, "The Golden Fleece: Arizona Land Fraud," in John M. Johnson and Jack D. Douglas, *Crime at the Top: Deviance in Business and the Professions* (New York: Lippincott, 1978), 113–150.
3. Ibid., 137.
4. The Investigative Reporters and Editors (IRE) project assembled in Arizona after the bombing death of reporter Dan Boles, who had been investigating Arizona land fraud. The IRE published a number of articles detailing the involvement of local officials and financial institutions. See in particular *Arizona Republic,* 19 June 1977 and 26 June 1977; *Arizona Daily Star,* 23 March 1977, and 24 March 1977.
5. Gerald F. Seib, "Dallas Ordinance against Car Repair Frauds," in Johnson and Douglas, *Crime at the Top,* 1978, p. 319.
6. William N. Leonard and Marvin G. Weber, "Automakers and Dealers: A Study of Criminogenic Market Forces," *Law and Society Review,* 4, no. 3 (1970), 420.
7. Diane Vaughn and Giovanna Carlo, "The Appliance Repairman: A Study of Victim-Responsiveness and Fraud," *Journal of Research in Crime and Delinquency,* 12 (1975): 153–161.
8. General Accounting Office of Congress (GAO), *Federal Agencies Can and Should do More to Combat Fraud in Government Programs* (Washington, D.C.: Government Printing Office, 1978), 2.
9. Ibid., 5.
10. Andrea G. Lange, *Fraud and Abuse in Government Benefit Programs* (Washington, D.C.: Government Printing Office, 1979), 115.
11. Department of Health, Education and Welfare, *Office of Inspector General Report, April 1, 1977* (Washington, D.C.: Government Printing Office, 1978), 18.
12. Lange, *Fraud and Abuse in Government Benefit Programs,* 17.
13. Ibid., p. 171.

14. Ibid., 176.
15. Allen Z. Gammage and Charles Hemphill, *Basic Criminal Law* (New York: McGraw-Hill, 1974), 232–233.
16. Federal Bureau of Investigation, *Crime in the United States: 1982* (Washington, D.C.: Government Printing Office, 1983), 180.
17. Donald R. Cressey, *Other People's Money* (Glencoe, Ill.: The Free Press, 1953).
18. Mark Lipman, *Stealing* (New York: Harper's Magazine Press, 1973).
19. David L. Altheide et al., "The Social Meanings of Employee Theft," in Johnson and Douglas, *Crime at the Top,* 90.
20. Melville Dalton, *Men Who Manage* (New York: Wiley, 1959).
21. Donald Horning, "Blue Collar Theft: Conceptions of Property Attitudes Towards Pilfering and Work Group Norms in a Modern Industrial Plant," in Erwin O. Smigel and H. Laurence Ross, *Crimes Against Bureaucracy* (New York: Van Nostrand Reinhold, 1970), 52.
22. Altheide et al., "Employee Theft," p. 103.
23. Ibid., 104.
24. Eliot Liebow, *Talley's Corner* (Boston: Little, Brown, 1967), 38–39.
25. Dalton, *Men Who Manage,* 49.
26. Altheide, et al., 1978, p. 98.
27. James C. Doyle, "Unnecessary Hysterectomies," *American Medical Association Journal,* 151 (1973); 360–365; Ivan Illich, *Medical Nemesis* (New York: Bantam Books, 1976), 19–21.
28. Hearing before the Select Committee on Narcotics Abuse and Control, House of Representatives, *Diversion of Licit Drugs to Illegal Markets* (Washington, D.C.: Government Printing Office, 1980), 9.
29. Ibid., 25.
30. Ibid., 83–84.
31. Joseph L. Albini, *The American Mafia: Genesis of a Legend* (New York: Appelton-Century-Crofts, 1971), 37.
32. Daniel Bell, *The End of Ideology* (New York: Free Press, 1962), 141–142.
33. Described in Gordon Hawkins, "God and the Mafia," *The Public Interest,* 14 (1969): 40–51.
34. Francis Ianni, *A Family Business: Kinship and Social Control in Organized Crime* (New York: Russell Sage Foundation, 1972), 89; Albini, *American Mafia,* p. 258.
35. President's Commission on Law Enforcement and Administration of Justice, Task Force Report, *Organized Crime* (Washington, D.C.: Government Printing Office, 1967), 10–11.
36. William F. Whyte, *Street Corner Society* (Chicago: University of Chicago Press, 1955).
37. William J. Chambliss, "The Business of Crime" *Working Papers for New Society,* September 1978, 59–67.
38. Kefauver Committee, 3d Interim Report, S. Rep. No. 307, 82nd Cong., 1st Sess. 150 (1951).
39. President's Commission, 1967, 7.
40. Permanent Subcommittee on Investigations of the Committee on Government Operations, (McClellan Committee), *Organized Crime and Illicit Traffic in Narcotics,* Part I (Washington, D.C.: Government Printing Office, 1963), 6–8.
41. Hawkins, *God and the Mafia,* 26.
42. Quoted in Ibid., 40.
43. Thomas C. Schelling, "Economic Analysis of Organized Crime" in President's Commission, 1967, 114–126.
44. Hawkins, *God and the Mafia,* 28.

45. Committee on Criminal Justice Standards and Goals, 1976, 8.
46. Herbert L. Packer, *The Limits of the Criminal Sanction* (Stanford, Calif.: Stanford University Press, 1968), 351.
47. Schelling, "Economic Analysis of Organized Crime," 121.
48. Packer, *Limits of Criminal Sanction,* 352.
49. Committee on Criminal Justice Standards and Goals, 1976, 238.
50. Sean O'Callighan, *The Drug Traffic* (London: Anthony Blond, 1967).
51. Committee on Criminal Justice Standards and Goals, 1976, pp. 11–12.
52. Personal communication from Dennis Schrantz, counselor at the Relatives juvenile home, Charlotte, North Carolina, November, 1978.
53. Committee on Criminal Justice Standards and Goals, 1976, 66.
54. President's Commission, 1967, 3.
55. Albini, *American Mafia,* 290.
56. Committee on Criminal Justice Standards and Goals, 1976, 14–15.
57. President's Commission, 1967, 4.
58. Committee on Criminal Justice Standards and Goals, 1976, 225.
59. CBS Reports, *Sex for Sale.*
60. *New York Times,* 16 June 1980, 17.
61. Schelling, "Economic Analyses of Organized Crime," 116.
62. Chamber of Commerce of the United States, *Deskbook on Organized Crime* (Washington, D.C.: Government Printing Office, 1969), 11.
63. Jean C. Jester, *An Analysis of Organized Crime's Infiltration of Legitimate Business* (Huntsville, Texas: Institute of Contemporary Corrections and the Behavioral Sciences, 1974), 29.
64. Ibid., 30.
65. Melvin K. Bers, *The Penetration of Legitimate Business by Organized Crime* (Washington, D.C.: Government Printing Office, 1970).
66. *New York Times,* 23 March 1970.
67. *New York Times,* 11 February 1973.
68. Vincent Teresa, *My Life in the Mafia* (New York: Doubleday, 1973) 125.
69. *Wall Street Journal,* 9 September 1966.
70. Jester, *Organized Crime's Infiltration of Legitimate Business,* 19.
71. Teresa, *My Life in the Mafia,* 120.
72. Ibid., 119.
73. *New York Times,* 22 November 1972.
74. *Wall Street Journal,* 17 February 1971.
75. *New York Times,* 21 November 1969.
76. Harvey M. Matusow, *False Witness* (New York: Cameron & Kahn, 1955).
77. Frank Pearce, *Crimes of the Powerful* (London: Pluto Press, 1978).
78. *Wall Street Journal,* 20 February 1969.
79. *Wall Street Journal,* 5 January 1969.
80. *Wall Street Journal,* 27 January 1970.
81. *New York Times,* 18 March 1973.
82. Charles H. McCaghy, *Deviant Behavior: Crime, Conflict and Interest Groups* (New York: Macmillan, 1976), 1–5.
83. Alex Thio, *Deviant Behavior* (Boston: Houghton Mifflin, 1978), 358–362.
84. *New York Times,* 19 February 1973, 16.
85. *Newsweek,* 14 June 1976, 21.
86. *New York Times,* 3 May 1981.
87. *Charlotte Observer,* 16 June 1980; 12 September 1980.
88. *New York Times,* 12 January 1974.

89. Quoted in A. James Reichley, "Getting at the Roots of Watergate," in M. David Ermann and Richard J. Lundman, eds., *Corporate and Governmental Deviance* (New York: Oxford University Press, 1978), 193.
90. *New York Times,* 18 January 1978.
91. Quoted in Richard J. Barnett and Ronald E. Miller, *Global Reach* (New York: Simon and Schuster, 1974).
92. United States Senate, Hearings before the Select Committee to Study Governmental Operations with Respect to Intelligence Activities, vol. 7, *Covert Action* (Washington, D.C.: Government Printing Office, 1975), 159–160.
93. Edward Greenberg, *The American Political System* (Cambridge: Mass.: Winthrop Publishers, 1980), 271.
94. *New York Times,* 17 April 1974.
95. Reichley, "Roots of Watergate," 187.
96. Ibid., 197.
97. *Financing a Better Election* (New York: Committee for Economic Development, 1968), 26.
98. Greenberg, *American Political System,* 272.
99. Richard O. Boyer and Herbert M. Morais, *Labor's Untold Story* (New York: Marzani and Munsell, 1965); Robert L. Friedheim, *The Seattle General Strike* (Seattle: University of Washington Press, 1964).
100. David Caute, *The Great Fear: The Anti-Communist Purge Under Truman and Eisenhower* (New York: Simon and Schuster, 1978).
101. U.S. Congress, Senate Select Committee to Study Governmental Operations with Respect to Intelligence Activities, vol. 6, *Intelligence Activities: Senate Resolution 21* (Washington, D.C.: Government Printing Office, 1976), 74.
102. Senate Select Committee, 1976, vol. 6, 73.
103. Michael Meyerson, *Nothing Could Be Finer* (New York: International Publishers, 1978) provides excellent documentation on this matter. See also James Chafee, *Civil Rights and Civilities* (New York: Oxford University Press, 1980).
104. Senate Select Committee, 1976, vol. 6, 888–947.
105. Alan Wolfe, *Repression: The Seamy Side of Democracy* (New York: McKay and Co., 1973), 549.
106. Boyer and Morais, *Labor's Untold Story,* 43–58.
107. Ibid., 82–104.
108. Ibid., 157–180.
109. Ibid., 140–145.
110. *In These Times,* 18 September 1981.
111. Meyerson, *Nothing Could Be Finer,* 75–82.
112. Raymond J. Michalowski, "The Case of the Charlotte 3," *Crime and Social Justice,* 3 (1975): 36–42.
113. *New York Times,* 29 April 1976.
114. Nelson Blackstock, *Cointelpro: The FBI's Secret War on Political Freedom* (New York: Random House, 1976).
115. See Senate Select Committee, Intelligence Activities: Resolution 21, 348.
116. See Paul C. Bermazon and Sally A. Bermazon, *The Greensboro Massacre* (New York: Cesar Cauce Publishers, 1980).

CHAPTER 14

Conclusion: The Future of Crime and Justice

At this time the future of crime looks good. It is very likely that both common crimes and crimes of capital will continue to flourish. Without fundamental changes in key areas of the existing social system there is little reason to anticipate significant reductions in either type of crime in the near future. There will of course continue to be minor upward and downward fluctuations in the reported rates of common crime. It is reasonable to expect, for instance, that changes in the age structure of the American population will produce some decline in rates of common crime, for it has been suggested that a reduction in the proportion of the American population in the crime-prone years of fourteen to eighteen will result in a decline in common crimes, particularly property offenses, where youthful offenders figure most prominently.[1] Recent declines in burglary and larceny victimizations may be more a reflection of this changing age structure than the consequence of any innovations in crime control implemented in the last decade.[2] These small gains are no reason for optimism, however.

The United States presently has one of the highest rates of crime in the Western world. The rate of homicide in America is *ten times* that of Western Europe.[3] We enjoy a similar leadership in crimes against property.[4] Moreover, our present rate of crime represents a significant increase over earlier years. Between 1960 and 1981 the rate of violent crime rose 360 percent, and the rate of property crime increased by 540 percent.[5]

Even if we were to experience a *substantial* reduction in the present rate of crime, which is not very likely, the picture would remain bleak. A 20 percent decline in the current official rate of crime would still leave the United States with a crime rate four times higher than that of 1960, and we would still be one of the most crime-ridden countries in the developed world. Moreover, these figures refer only to rates of *common* crime. Even more serious is the consequence of continued high levels of law violation and social injury occurring in the contexts of business, politics, and organized crime. The rightward shift of the American political climate in the last decade has produced Federal and state regulatory policies that have reduced rather than increased the possibility of control over corporate and political crimes.[6] The only crime of capital to come under close governmental scrutiny in recent years has been organized crime.[7] Unfortunately, this selective attention to organized crime may serve to divert public concern from other forms of upper-world deviance that are less clearly associated with the popular image of a "criminal element." Crimes and social injuries by those in legitimate businesses and in politics are not easily recognized, and a dimming of the "post-Watergate" spotlight may allow the abuse of economic and political power to become relatively invisible once again.

While there may be a softening of enforcement efforts where crimes of capital are concerned, the same is certainly not true for common crimes. Quite to the contrary; in recent years there have been growing public demands for increased use of imprisonment for common criminals, a substantial increase in both the amount of money and the amount of manpower spent on the control of common crime, and a dramatic increase in the size of our prison population.[8] Because prisons are the end point of "justice" for common criminal offenders, but not for those who commit crimes of capital, the prison population consists predominately of the poor, the undereducated, and the nonwhite. More than ever we have entered an age where, in Jeffrey Reiman's words, "The rich get richer and the poor get prison."[9]

Faced with these facts, the prospects can seem poor for the development of a society where individuals do not live with an ever-present threat of crime and where social control applies *in equal measure* to both the poor *and* the powerful when their actions cause death, injury, or financial loss to others. The failure of our multibillion dollar "war against crime" to yield more than the barest reduction in real rates of crime has led some observers to conclude that the best we can do is recognize the inevitability of high crime rates in modern, industrial society and continue punishing the "wicked" (and this means the poor) in the hopes of achieving at least a modicum of deterrence.[10] At the individual level many Americans have come to assume that personal safety can only be achieved through deadbolt locks, burglar alarm systems, firearms, avoiding "dangerous" places, and in many other ways letting the threat of crime dominate their lives.[11] These responses are understandable adaptations to a world where security of person and property appears to be continually in jeopardy.

Are we doomed to live in fear of common crime and to be continually victimized by crimes of capital? This future is not inevitable or unavoidable. However, any significant improvement requires *fundamental* changes in both the social structure and the value system of American society. The first step is to recognize that for over a century as we have studied crime and sought to develop crime control strategies, for the most part we have been *asking the wrong question.*

A CHANGE OF FOCUS?

As discussed in the first chapter, the predominant question in criminology for over a century has been, "How do individuals become *the kinds of people* who commit crime?" The answer to this question has been sought primarily by "comparing the characteristics and experiences of offenders and non-offenders," that is, by searching for the characteristics of *individuals* that would explain why crime occurs.[12] The answers to the question, "How do people become deviant?" have for the most part led to relatively little improvement in the problem of crime. This is not because the answers are wrong. It is because the question is wrong.

Why is this the wrong question? There are two reasons. First, crime is fundamentally a *social* problem. As we have seen in earlier chapters the way in which a society is organized determines (1) what constitutes the most likely forms of trouble, (2) the frequency with which this trouble will occur, and (3) the nature and operations of the institutions of social control. Attempts aimed at changing *individuals* can only have the most limited effect on the problems of crime in any society. Individual behavior is only the last step in a complex social process that begins with the fundamental elements of social organization: the mode of production, the allocation of political power, and the set of beliefs and ideologies related to them both. It is these factors that largely determine the kinds and numbers of law-abiders and lawbreakers a society will generate, and it is these factors that must be addressed in any attempt to reduce the problem of crime. Trying to correct the problem of crime by focusing on the individual deviant is like trying to eliminate yellow fever by swatting mosquitoes when you should be draining the swamps.

Second, from the level of pragmatic social action, relatively little can be done to predict and control the behavior of *specific* potential lawbreakers. We do not have the ability to predict which individuals will break the law *before* they ever do so. Even if we did, using this knowledge as a justification for incapacitating potential lawbreakers poses serious ethical and legal problems. As Alfred Blumstein correctly observes,

> There is the basic legal objection that in a democracy no individual should be punished by imprisonment for crimes he might commit in the future. Carried to its logical extreme, selective incapacitation might involve prediction at an early age of an individual's potential criminality and incarceration of those judged to be a high risk. Such a procedure would clearly be unacceptable if selective incapacitation were applied to an individual who had not been convicted of a crime.[13]

There are those, including Blumstein, who argue that the ethical and legal problems posed by selective incapacitation are less relevant when this strategy is applied to individuals already convicted of crimes. Yet even where individuals with known offense histories are concerned, our predictive ability is barely over 50 percent.[14] This means that widespread adoption of selective incapacitation strategies is as likely to impose additional sentences on those who do not pose serious future threats as those who do. To argue that legal and ethical constraints on the state's authority to impose penal sanction should apply less to convicted offenders than to noncriminals is to overturn the entire concept of civil liberties. The protection of civil liberties exists precisely to protect the rights of those who come into conflict with the state. Those who do not come into conflict with the state are not in need of protection from abuse of state power.

The institutions of government are the primary tools for planned social change. They are not designed or authorized to seek change by selective treatment of specific individuals. Moreover, these institutions cannot change in any direct sense the way people think and feel. They can do so only indirectly by changing the underlying structural conditions according to which people develop their ways of life and patterns of thought. We cannot reliably predict individual behavior, but we can identify certain conditions that will increase or decrease the *proportion* of law violators within given *social groups*. While there are few places in our own nation or in the world that are crime-free, there are certainly significant variations from one place to another in the frequency and severity of crimes by both the powerful and the powerless. Therefore, the more appropriate question to ask about crime is, *"What kinds of social structures produce the least amount of crime and social injury?"*

The answer to this question is far from clear. This is to be expected, given the relative inattention it has received in this century, particularly within Western industrial nations. However, it is possible to identify certain basic propositions that can help us begin to address the question from a genuinely *social* standpoint.

1. Crime must be defined in a way that evaluates wrongful behaviors on the basis of the *severity of the harm done,* regardless of the class origin of the offense.
2. There must be a fundamental reduction in economic, political, and social inequality.
3. There must be a reduced reliance on legal formalism and an increase in the use of mechanisms for "popular justice."
4. There must be a reduction in the ideologies of materialism and possessive individualism.

Crime Must Be Defined According to Harm Done

There can be no realistic gains in reducing crime as long as the definition of crime and the practice of crime control are organized along class lines. Before there can be genuine improvements in the problem of crime, fundamental changes would need to be made in the existing two-class system of justice in America—a system that devotes substantial enforcement and penal effort to common crimes while treating crimes of capital as relatively insignificant offenses. A change in this pattern is important for several reasons.

First, a legal system that imposes severe penal sanctions on those harmful acts that most often lead to the arrest of relatively poor and powerless members of society while ignoring or treating as relatively minor offenses the grave social injuries committed by substantially wealthier and more powerful people and organizations as they seek to accumulate capital or obtain political power makes a mockery of the concept of justice. In doing so it tends to give those in the poorest segment of society an understandably cynical view of law and justice and to reduce the moral force of law. In the extreme this view provides an easy way for those tempted to commit common crimes to rationalize predatory actions.

Second, the existing system leaves relatively unchecked the most costly and injurious forms of crime. As discussed in the previous two chapters, crimes of capital clearly exceed common crimes in terms of both dollar loss to the populace and threats to life and health. Devoting the bulk of our law-enforcement efforts not to these offenses but to common crimes leaves Americans relatively unprotected from crimes of capital. Moreover, while individuals can take a variety of steps to reduce their personal risk of victimization by common crimes, there is relatively little that can be done on an individual basis to reduce victimization by crimes of capital. *Individuals* can upgrade the locks on their houses, install burglar alarms, avoid "dangerous" areas, and so on, but they cannot improve the basic safety of their workplace, the quality of the air they breathe, the purity of the water they drink, or whether as a result of corporate illegalities they will pay higher prices for the goods they buy. Changes in the level of risk for these kinds of crimes require more collectively organized social action. Thus *the present allocation of justice system energies give citizens the least amount of protection from the harms they can least do something about.*

Third, the disproportionate attention devoted by the justice system to the problem of common crime is a barrier to our assessing crimes according to the harms they cause rather than their social class origins. By continually dramatizing that "criminals" are those who commit common crimes and that these "criminals" are most often poor and nonwhite, the justice system reinforces the ideological perception that it is these offenses and these "kinds" of people who constitute the crime problem.

Not until injuries are judged and punished according to the amount of economic loss caused or the amount of physical harm done can we anticipate any real improvement in the problem of crime or the possibilities for justice. In practical terms this means eliminating from our consciousness and our legal system the class-based distinctions that make it seem reasonable, for instance, that the man who injures someone in a street robbery or a fight deserves to spend time in prison but the executive who permits the injury of workers by failing to install required safety devices does not deserve similar punishment. This is not to argue that they both should be imprisoned, only to suggest that whatever the penal sanction administered, it should be based on the harm done, not the reason for doing it.

Reductions in Inequality

Crime in the broadest sense is stimulated by the inequalities and forms of domination that arise from the division of society into social classes, and any substantial reduction in crime would necessitate reductions in inequality and domination. This applies to both common crimes and crimes of capital, although the relationship between inequality and crime can take a number of different specific forms.

Inequality and Crimes of the Powerful. To say that a society is divided into *social classes* means essentially that it is divided into groups enjoying different degrees of access to the means of survival. It is this differential access that lies at the heart of the ability of some individuals to dominate others, whether directly or through institutions of economic and political power. The major crimes of human history—wars for political or economic gain, slavery, colonialism, imperialism, and the subjugation of people along racial, ethnic, or sexual lines—as well as other contemporary crimes of capital rest fundamentally on the ability of some social classes or groups to exert power over others. This power in turn is derived largely from the ability of some to control or manipulate the access of others to the means of survival and to culturally defined satisfactions and their use of this control to create and maintain a variety of economic, political, and ideological institutions that shape people's lives and thoughts.

Domination is an essential feature of class power, and the only route to reducing crimes of domination is to reduce the power of dominant classes relative to that of other groups. This reduction in turn depends upon the weakening of capitalist class relations that give a relatively small proportion of the American population the power to determine the economic fate of the majority. Not until we at least begin to remove the control of capital from the hands of a relatively few and disperse this control through some form of *economic democracy* can we substantially reduce crimes of capital.[15]

Inequality and Crimes by the Powerless.   Inequality bred of class divisions is also the basis for crimes by those from the poorer and less powerful segments of society. Since the emergence of the capitalist form of class society, it has been repeatedly argued that poverty is an important causal factor in the generation of crime.[16] However, this connection frequently reflects a confusion of poverty with inequality. Poverty is the condition of having little. Inequality is the condition of having less than others, and it is this condition more than poverty itself that serves to stimulate common crime. As we have seen, throughout history there have been many societies and social groups that have been materially poor by contemporary standards, yet their "poverty" was not a fertile seedbed for criminality. Quite to the contrary, many of these societies suffered relatively little crime compared with contemporary industrial nations. Even today we can find societies substantially poorer than our own and pockets of poverty in our own society both of which are comparatively low in crime. It is the objective condition of being unequal, and the subjective consequences of that experience, rather than poverty itself, that serves as a stimulus for crime among the victims of inequality.

Inequality and crime are related in a variety of ways. First of all, *material inequality can stimulate material want simply by increasing the number of things that individuals can desire but do not have.* This is particularly problematic in contemporary capitalist society for several reasons. Capitalism seeks economic growth as its central goal. This requires continual increases in the amount and type of material goods being produced and distributed. This of itself increases the number of opportunities for material want. In essence, the greater the amount and type of material goods, the greater the opportunities and motivations for property crimes. This proposition has generally been confirmed by research showing that the level of property crime in a society is closely associated with the amount of property available in society.[17]

Economic growth in advanced capitalist societies necessitates increasing levels of personal, material consumption to generate profits and capital accumulation.[18] The primary mechanism for stimulation of increased consumption is through product advertising.[19] As it is disseminated throughout the society this advertising message has two consequences: (1) It tends to promote among all members of the society an image of a minimum standard of material luxury and comfort that in fact can be obtained *in toto* by only the most affluent one-third of the society, stimulating personal dissatisfaction and frustration and (2) it tends to link such fundamental human desires as self-esteem, sexual satisfaction, and being loved by the members of one's immediate family to the acquisition and ownership of specific commodities.[20] These messages are transmitted to the average American on the order of 800 times a day.[21] It is reasonable to suspect that this constant reiteration of what they lack may very well increase the sense of deprivation and injustice among those who have the least and provide both a focus and a motivation for criminality among some.

A second major consequence of material inequality is its effect upon social equality and sense of self-worth. *In competitive market societies such as the United States, material inequality tends to erode self-esteem and sense of community among those who find themselves judged less worthy because of their material lacks.* It is abundantly clear that for the most part, in America personal worth is judged by socioeconomic status. This is not to say that there do not exist a variety of nonmaterial routes to self-worth available to the less affluent, the two most significant being family and religion. Nevertheless, generally speaking the higher one's socioeconomic status, the more open are the doors to social approval, self-worth, and opportunity.[22] For those who find these doors closed or barely ajar and who for various reasons also lack access to nonmaterial sources of self-worth, inequality can have several consequences. One is the attempt to improve apparent social worth by personal displays of money or all sorts of items of social value—from cars to clothing, from portable radios to videogame watches—obtained through resort to property crime.

Another consequence of this weakened sense of social worth is the creation of feelings of frustration, hostility, alienation from both self and others, and powerlessness. When turned outward these feelings are often expressed as anger and hostility toward others, and they may serve as the basis for crimes of violence through which people express the impotent fury they feel about their lives. In support of this point, one recent study found that levels of inequality, rather than levels of poverty, was the best predictor of differences in rates of violence among 125 metropolitan areas in the United States.[23]

Third, *inequality tends to increase crime by weakening the social bond.* Humans do not generally attack or steal the property of those with whom they feel a sense of moral community. Moral community refers to that body of people toward whom we feel a sense of obligation and human concern. Inequality tends to narrow people's moral community by creating material and social barriers between different segments of society and by placing individuals in competitive rather than cooperative relations as a result of the struggle to improve *personal* position in a world of inequalities. As individuals, particularly the least well off, come to feel that the deprivations and disappointments in their lives are proof that people in general care little about what happens to them, their sense of shared obligation with those others tends to weaken. This weakening of a felt sense of moral obligation toward others makes committing crimes against them much easier and in fact may be a necessary condition for the commission of most property crimes.

Reduced Reliance on Formal Institutions of Justice

The history of social control strategies demonstrates that *the more bureaucratic, formal, and distant is a form of social control both temporally and socially, the less effective it will be.* The more individuals are integrated into a network of social relations where any inappropriate move, however subtle, is met by a series of proportionate countermoves by others, the more difficult it is for elaborate forms of deviation such as crime to develop.[24] With the emergence of state power, however, direct community controls over deviance are replaced by more abstract legal controls that operate at a distance from the daily unfolding of people's lives. "Justice" becomes something dispensed by the state, not by members of the immediate social community within which one lives. The effect is that individuals and groups within the community tend to have little right or inclination to take an active interest in developing community-based strategies for limiting the emergence of deviant behaviors. Social control is left to the state, which enters the picture only after specific individuals have already developed significant tendencies toward deviance and crime.

Real reductions in rates of crime necessitates a reassertion of community-based social control. It is not possible or necessarily even desirable in today's heterogeneous mass society to return to a system of wholly informal communal justice. Wholly informal justice in heterogeneous societies has the potential of becoming arbitrary and possibly discriminatory. Where it is all-encompassing, as in primitive societies, it tends to significantly limit—although not eliminate—the freedom to be different, and in a rapidly changing world it may be more adaptive to preserve rather than to seek to eliminate variability. However, it is important to explore alternatives that will make the control of deviance and the dispensation of justice more the right and responsibility of communities and neighborhoods than they are today. Reliance on the distant and unreliable institutions of the political state tends to do more to promote the power of the state than to protect the security of its citizens.

Reductions in Materialism and Individualism

From an ideological standpoint *America is a materialist and individualistic society, and these orientations significantly increase the likelihood of crimes by both the powerful and the powerless.* The dominant value system emphasizes that (1) the desire for material acquisition and gain is fundamental to human nature and (2) individuals therefore have an inherent right to compete for unequal shares of the material wealth and to use this wealth for further gain.[25] These values promote what the socialist criminologist Willem Bonger referred to as "egoistic" ways of thinking and behaving.[26] That is, they promote a self-oriented and narcissistic view of the world that places maximization of one's own gains and pleasures well ahead of regard for the conditions and needs of others.

As a form of consciousness, egoistic motivations tend to support and promote the forces for crime mentioned above. Materialism and individualism are fundamental to the maintenance of inequality insofar as they justify a world in which some have much and others little. They also support the conditions needed for domination by emphasizing the *rights of individuals* to utilize their property as they see fit, within some relatively broad limits of honesty and "fair play," over the rights of others to be free from the negative individual and social consequences of those uses of property. The concept of what constitutes "crime" is closely associated with the vision of what constitutes people's "rights." Social harms resulting from "rightful" actions are insulated from criminal stigma. Adherence to the values of materialism and individualism tend to make the acts of economic and political domination that occur when those who own the greatest share of wealth use their property for purposes of profit and accumulation appear "rightful." Thus, for example, we do not question the rights of some to be able to determine if others will or will not have the opportunity to work or whether or not they will earn a wage sufficient to provide a dignified life if they do work.

As we saw in earlier chapters, the liberal ideology of individualism has also served as the guiding principle for the evolution of formal justice in America and the creation of a legal system adapted to the protection and preservation of inequality. Because the law is designed to behave as if all people are *equal individuals* the significant real inequalities that exist between them play little part in determining how justice will be done. The effect of treating unequal people equally is injustice. Lastly, the values of individualism and materialism serve as significant impediments to the exploration of fundamental changes in the American social system that might serve to reduce crime. Widespread popular desires for increasing levels of personal material consumption render it politically impractical to develop public policies that might promote more equality at the cost of less economic growth or that seek to improve the position of the least equal through redistribution strategies that would reduce the upper limits to personal wealth. Socialization into a culture of individualism tends to narrow moral community and make it difficult for Americans to recognize the degree to which improvement in many of the nonmaterial qualities of their own lives depends, in many ways, on improvement in the quality of the lives of others. We cannot be free from the crimes of the poor until there are no poor; we cannot be free from domination by the powerful until we reduce the inequalities that make domination possible; and we cannot live in harmony with others until we begin to limit the competition for material advantage over others that alienates us from one another. To move in the direction of these goals, however, would require that the values of materialism and individualism be relegated to positions of lesser importance in American culture than they presently enjoy.

IS CHANGE POSSIBLE?

Progressives and Socialists who criticize the existing social order in America are often accused of failing to offer solutions to the problems they cite. However, in many cases this accusation is misleading. There is no shortage of both far-reaching and short-range progressive proposals to reduce inequality, limit the domination of the powerful, or establish community-based mechanisms for popular justice.[27] How viable these proposals are is difficult to judge since they are seldom allowed to enter into the forums of either general or specific debate about public policy. Many of them certainly have more promise than a number of those proposals that have been given serious consideration or implemented. However, until they are given equal and honest consideration as possible alternatives it is gratuitous to say that critics of the social order have little to offer in the way of solutions.

What is more to the point is that such proposals are often dismissed as "unrealistic" or "impractical" by those in positions of power and those with significant forums for influencing others. However, these proposals are judged unrealistic not because they promote impossible goals but because implementing them would require significant alterations in the status quo distribution of wealth and power. But then that is the point. They are dismissed not because they would necessarily fail but because if they were to succeed they would result in a social world different from the one in which we now live, and many who enjoy wealth, prominence, or power over others would lose the economic, political, and social advantages that the present set of arrangements now afford them.

Frequently, progressive strategies for change are also judged to be "impractical." It is true that they seldom coincide with the dominant concept of what constitutes a practical way to address the problems at hand. Designs for fundamental social changes are always "impractical" when viewed from the perspective of the dominant consciousness. This is because the dominant consciousness itself is a product of the social order whose change is being sought. However, because a set of facts or conditions are proclaimed to be a practical way to arrange social life does not make them so. Is the following really practical?

- That the law weigh least heavily on those actions that cause the greatest amount of death, injury, illness, and financial loss
- That those with the fewest options in life are punished more severely when they break the law in the ways available to them than those who utilize substantial economic and political advantages to bring harm to others rather than benefit to the society

- That poverty, hunger, illiteracy, and unsafe housing continue to persist in the wealthiest nation in the world
- That a significant portion of the population lives in fear of being victimized by crime
- That the skills and talents of millions go undeveloped or unused because of the color or shape of their skin
- That less than 10 percent of the population have the right to make fundamental economic decisions that effect in very substantial ways the lives of the other 90 percent
- That a proportion of the labor force be unemployed except during times of war

If the social order and its associated consciousness defines these things as acceptable ways of organizing social life, then it is time to begin seeking ways to change that order.

There are no easy answers or pat solutions to the problem of crime. There is no magic formula that will eliminate the problem of crime once and for all, if we can only find it. There are, however, a number of realistic steps that could be identified and taken to begin to effect the kinds of basic changes needed to make genuine inroads into crime. Achieving this goal, however, requires that we first begin to think and talk about crime in new ways that enable us to understand it as fundamentally a problem of social order, not a problem of individual behavior.

Change is possible. When seen from the dominant consciousness it is also an unreasonable goal. However, to paraphrase that former juvenile delinquent George Bernard Shaw:

> Reasonable men and women adapt themselves to the world. Unreasonable men and women seek to change it. Therefore all progress depends upon those who are willing to strive for the unreasonable.

NOTES

1. Gary F. Jensen and Dean Rojek, *Juvenile Delinquency* (Lexington, Mass.: D.C. Heath Co., 1980), 62.
2. Al Paez and Fred Shenck, "Criminal Victimization in the United States." Bureau of Justice Statistics Special Report. (Washington, D.C.: U.S. Department of Justice, 1983).
3. U.S. Bureau of Census, Statistical Abstracts of the United States (Washington, D.C.: Government Printing Office, 1979), 182.
4. Report of the Secretary General, *Crime Prevention and Control*, 32nd Session (New York: United Nations, 1977), 26.
5. Federal Bureau of Investigation, Uniform Crime Reports (Washington, D.C.: Government Printing Office, 1982), 39; U.S. Bureau of the Census, Historical Statistics of the United States (Washington, D.C.: Government Printing Office, 1975), 413.
6. See Fred Ackerman, *Reagonomics: Rhetoric vs. Reality* (Boston: South End Press, 1982), 119–135.

7. *New York Times*, 29 July 1983, I, 1:2.
8. Stephen Gettiinger and Kevin Krajik, "Overcrowded Time: Why Prisons Are Overcrowded and What Can Be Done" (New York: Edna McConnell Clark Foundation, 1982).
9. Jeffrey Reiman, *The Rich Get Richer and the Poor Get Prison.* (New York: Wiley, 1979).
10. James Q. Wilson, *Thinking about Crime.* (New York: Basic Books, 1979); Ernest van den Haag, *Punishing Criminals* (New York: Basic Books, 1975).
11. John Conklin, *The Impact of Crime* (New York: Macmillan Publishing Co., 1975).
12. Judith R. Blau and Peter M. Blau, "The Cost of Inequality: Metropolitan Structure and Violent Crime." *American Sociological Review,* 47 (February 1982): 114.
13. Alfred Blumstein, "Prisons: Population, Capacity and Alternatives," in James Q. Wilson, ed., *Crime and Public Policy* (San Francisco: ICS Press, 1983), 242.
14. Peter Greenwood, *Selective Incapacitation.* The Rand Corporation, R-2815-NIJ, August 1982.
15. Martin Carnoy and Derek Shearer, *Economic Democracy* (White Plains, N.Y.: M. E. Sharpe, Inc., 1980).
16. Ysabel Rennie, "Bread and Danger in the 19th Century," in *The Search for Criminal Man.* (Lexington Mass.: Lexington Books, 1979).
17. Lawrence Cohen and M. Felson, "Social Change and Crime Rate Trends," *American Sociological Review,* 44(1979):588–597; Steven Stack, "Social Structure and Swedish Crime Rates," *Criminology,* 20, no. 4(1982):499–513; Leroy C. Gould, "The Changing Structure of Property Crime in an Affluent Society," *Social Forces,* 48, no. 1 (September 1969).
18. Paul Baran and Paul Sweezy, "The Sales Effort," in *Monopoly Capital* (New York: Monthly Review Press, 1969), 112–141 provides a good analysis of this characteristic of advanced capitalism.
19. Jules Henry, *Culture Against Man* (New York: Random House, 1963).
20. Stuart Ewen, *Captains of Consciousness: Social Roots of the Advertising Industry* (New York: McGraw-Hill, 1978).
21. Michael Real, *Mass Mediated Culture* (Englewood Cliffs, N.J.: Prentice-Hall, 1977), 5.
22. Robert Coles, *The Privileged Ones* (Boston: Little Brown, 1977).
23. Blau and Blau, "The Cost of Inequality," pp. 114–131.
24. Nils Christie, "Youth as a Crime Generating Phenomenon," in Barry Krisber and James Austin, *Children of Ishmael.* (Palo Alto, Calif.: Mayfield, 1975), 221–230.
25. C. B. Macpherson, *The Political Theory of Possessive Individualism.* (New York: Oxford University Press, 1962).
26. Adrian Willem Bonger, *Criminality and Economic Conditions.* (Bloomington: University of Indiana Press, 1969). First published in 1905.
27. It is not possible to list here the many writings on this subject. As a starting point, however, I suggest the interested student see the following. Regarding general issues in political economic change Andre Gorz, *Ecology as Politics* (Boston: South End Press, 1980) provides new windows on how it might be possible to live better with less competition, less material production, less inequality, and less work; Martin Carnoy and Derek Shearer, *Economic Democracy* (White Plains, N.Y.: 1980), provides a point-by-point guide for democratization of both the workplace and the economic order; Harry C. Boyte, *The Backyard Revolution: Understanding the New Citizens Movement* (Philadelphia: Temple University Press, 1980) provides an instructive look at strategies for change at a local level; Hazel Henderson, *The Politics of the Solar Age: Alternatives to Economics* (Garden City, N.Y.: Anchor

Books, 1981) poses an interesting critique of contemporary economic "rationale" and suggests some fruitful new lines of thought; see also Michael Albert and Robin Hahnel, *Socialism Today and Tomorrow* (Boston: South End Press, 1981); Christopher Freman and Marie Jahoda, *World Futures: The Great Debate* (New York: Universe Books, 1978); regarding specific alternatives to traditional forms of state justice in capitalist society see Gill Boehringer et al., " 'Law and Order' for Progressives?" *Crime and Social Justice*, no. 19(1983):2–12; Raymond Michalowski, "Crime Control in the 1980's: A Progressive Agenda," *Crime and Social Justice*, no. 19(1983):13–23; Stuart Hall, "Popular Democratic vs. Authoritarian Populism: Two Ways of Taking Democracy Seriously," in Alan Hunt, ed., *Marxism and Democracy* (London: Lawrence and Wishart, 1980); for an anarchist vision of the future see Larry Tift and Dennis Sullivan, *The Struggle to Be Human* (Cinfuegos Press, 1979); Ian Taylor, *Law and Order: Arguments for Socialism* (London: Macmillan, 1981); Alan Hunt, "Law, Order and Socialism: A Response to Ian Taylor," *Crime and Social Justice,* no. 18(1982):16–22; in that same volume see also Tony Platt, "Crime and Punishment in the United States: Immediate and Long-Term Reforms from a Marxist Perspective," 38–45.

Index

About the Author

Dr. Raymond J. Michalowski is currently Professor of Sociology at the University of North Carolina at Charlotte where he has taught criminology since receiving his Ph.D. degree from Ohio State University in 1973. His research and writings have covered a wide range of topics including vehicular homicide, the social meanings of violent death, the sociology of law, political repression, teaching criminology, progressive alternatives to traditional crime control, the political economy of imprisonment and corporate crime. He is presently investigating the problem of crimes committed by transnational corporations operating in Third World nations.